King George's Army: British Regiments and the Men who Led Them 1793-1815 will contain five volumes, with coverage given to army administration and cavalry regiments (Volume 1), infantry regiments (Volumes 2, 3 and 4), and ordnance (Volume 5). It is the natural extension to the web series of the same name by the same author which existed on *The Napoleon Series* from 2009 until 2019, but greatly expanded to include substantially more biographical information as well as biographies of leading political figures concerned with the administration of the army as well as commanders in chief of all major commands.

Volume 3 covers in great detail the 31st to 60th Regiments of Foot within the army of King George III for the period of the Great War with France; and the men who commanded them. Regimental data provided includes shortform regimental lineages, service locations and dispositions for the era, battle honours won, tables of authorised establishments, demographics of the field officer cohorts and the men, and even sources of recruits from the militia. But the book is essentially concerned with the field officers, the lieutenant colonels and majors who commanded the regiments, and Volume 3 alone contains over 900 mini-biographies of men who exercised such command, including their dates of birth and death, parentage, education, career (including political), awards and honours, and places of residence. Volumes 4 and 5 will extend the coverage to ultimately record over 4,500 biographies across more than 200 regiments.

These biographies will show the regimental system in action, officers routinely transferring between regiments for advancement or opportunity, captains who were also (brevet) colonels, many who retired early, some who stayed the distance to become major generals and beyond. Where it has been possible to accurately ascertain, advancement by purchase, exchange or promotion has also been noted.

Readers with military ancestors will no doubt find much of interest within, and the author hopes that the work will allow readers to break down a few 'brick walls'; either through connecting to the officers recorded, or through an understanding of the movements of the regiments around the world, or from the volunteering patterns of the militia regiments into the regular army.

Encyclopaedic in scope, and aimed to be a lasting source of reference material for the British army that fought the French Revolution and Napoleon between 1793 and 1815, *King George's Army: British Regiments and the Men who Led Them* will hopefully be a necessary addition to every military and family history library for years to come.

Steve Brown edited William Brown's *The Autobiography, or Narrative of a Soldier* and authored *Fit to Command* and *By Fire and Bayonet* with Helion, as well as writing on the 45th Foot and on York's campaign in Flanders. He has also been a keen genealogist for over 40 years and therefore understands the importance of the biographical aspects of his works to those who have, as he does, military ancestors.

I0892760

The King George's Army Series

Volume 1 – Political and Military Administration, Commanders-In-Chief, Household Cavalry, Dragoon Guards, Dragoons and Light Dragoons, Royal Staff Corps, Staff Corps of Cavalry

Volume 2 – British Infantry; Foot Guards, 1st to 30th Regiments of Foot

Volume 3 – British Infantry; 31st to 60th Regiments of Foot

Volume 4 – British Infantry; 61st to 104th Regiments of Foot

Volume 5 – Royal Artillery, Royal Engineers, Royal Waggon Train, Royal Veteran Battalions, Garrison Battalions and Battalions of Reserve

King George's Army

British Regiments and the Men Who Led Them 1793–1815
Volume 3: British Infantry – 31st to 60th Regiments of Foot

Steve Brown

Helion & Company

Helion & Company Limited
Unit 8 Amherst Business Centre
Budbrooke Road
Warwick
CV34 5WE
England
Tel. 01926 499619
Email: info@helion.co.uk
Website: www.helion.co.uk
X (formerly Twitter): @Helionbooks
Facebook: @HelionBooks
Visit our blog at http://blog.helion.co.uk/

Published by Helion & Company 2024
Designed and typeset by Mach 3 Solutions (www.mach3solutions.co.uk)
Cover designed by Paul Hewitt, Battlefield Design (www.battlefield-design.co.uk)

Cover: Attack on the road to Bayonne, by William Heath (Anne S.K. Brown Military Collection)

ISBN 978-1- 804515-41-9

British Library Cataloguing-in-Publication Data.
A catalogue record for this book is available from the British Library.

Contents

Foreword

The literature of Napoleonic scholarship is rich in volumes covering some aspect of the British Army during the period of 1793–1815. My personal library has over 600 books on the topic. They range from memoirs and diaries to uniform books, to regimental histories and histories of virtually every battle and campaign the British Army fought in during those 22 years. But there is a major gap in my collection. There are no books that serve as an encyclopedia of the British Army during that time period. If I need to know something about a particular regiment, I have to search its regimental history and hope I will find it. Until now.

A few years ago, Steve Brown contacted me with an idea for a book that would fill that void. He proposed a book that provide detailed information on each unit, such as names of the unit, uniform colour, facings, badge, and motto; its history from its raising to modern day; and its service history from 1793–1815, with details on its locations in the British Isles, as well as active service throughout the world; and battle honours. It would have the yearly strength of the regiment from 1793 to 1815, with information on the number of subunits (companies and troops), officers (field grade, company, and staff), NCOs, and rank and file. Furthermore, it would also contain statistics about the unit, covering the demographics of the rank and file and the field grade officers (which would answer age-old questions about whether a specific regiment that was identified as being a 'English' regiment, was truly English); and the amount of time the regiment spent on active service. This in itself would be an incredible source, but Steve did not stop there. He would also provide biographical information on the men who commanded the regiments, to include names, dates of birth and death, their education, military service, political careers, awards and honours, and even their places of residence!

I was a bit skeptical at first, thinking that Steve was being over-ambitious. However, he delivered in spades and this book is the first of five volumes! *King George's Army* is one of the most important books on the British Army written in the past 100 years. It is encyclopaedic in scope and will be the reference book that will be turned to by Napoleonic scholars for years to come.

Robert Burnham
Former Editor in Chief,
The Napoleon Series website

Preface

This book exists for two reasons. Firstly, to chronicle the locations and actions of the British Army's most used (and often abused) arm in the period 1793 to 1815 – the infantry regiments, including their demographics, authorised establishments, and battle honours. And secondly, to shine a light on those colonels, lieutenant colonels, majors (and occasionally even captains) who commanded them. From a threadbare and over-committed force in 1793 (only two weak brigades could be found to send to the continent) to Wellington's 'most complete machine for its numbers now existing in Europe'[1] in late 1813, the road to victory (not to mention acceptance by the notoriously fickle British public) was prolonged and paved with fruitless expeditions and bitter experience along the way.

I have chosen to cover the entire period from 1793 until 1815 (and beyond, until 1818 in some cases) as this is the generally accepted range of the 'Revolutionary and Napoleonic Wars'. The combats and stations of the British regiments chronicled will demonstrate that the period was, in reality, the true First World War; European troops fought and died in North America, South America, Egypt, India, Java, Mauritius, the West Indies. In fact, before 1914, the conflict was still referred to as 'The Great War.' The continental view at the time was that Britain would rather spend gold rather than lives to counter the Corsican Ogre; a whiff of accusation that the British Army never truly 'put in' to the same extent as the Austrians, Russians, or Prussians. However, a reading of the service records in this series will show that the British Army was in fact the busiest army in the world in the period. Regiments routinely bounced between distant postings; some units spent 20 years away from home. If there were few regiments on the continent, it was because there were few regiments readily available.

Designed to appeal to military enthusiasts and family historians alike, this series promises to be the most detailed presentation of British regiments and the men who led them committed to print. The regiments and men of King George's Army.

1 John Gurwood, *Selections from the Dispatches and General Orders of Field Marshal the Duke of Wellington* (London: John Murray, 1842), p.767.

Acknowledgements

A work which started in 2009 (even if in different form) has, needless to say, benefitted from the input of many people over a long period of time. The primary credit must go to Bob Burnham, who as the general editor of *The Napoleon Series*, gave me license to create and develop *British Regiments and the Men Who Led Them* in the first place. As Godfather of the work, it seemed only right that I asked him to the write the foreword. I contributed articles to him for eight years before meeting him in person; it was during a spot of whale-watching that he described my regiments series as one of the 'crown jewels' of *The Napoleon Series* and encouraged me to develop it several steps further in book form.

Thanks must also go to an array of like-minded individuals who have offered input or advice over a long period – Zack White, Gareth Glover, Roderick MacArthur, Rory Butcher, Paul Chamberlain, Ron McGuigan, Rory Muir, Ian Soulsby. Kevin Linch and John Grehan. Thanks are also due to the staff at The National Archives at Kew and the Templer Library at The National Army Museum. And of course, my ever patient editors, Robert Griffith and Andrew Bamford, who helped bring this project to reality.

None of this would have been possible without that fateful day when my father took me, aged 10, to see the film *Waterloo*, causing me to eagerly switch my budding model-making activities from Second World War fighters to Imperial Guardsmen and Highlanders; nor without the efforts of my grandmother to write out everything she could remember about our family's ancestry before she left us, setting in motion my own endeavours to research that lineage further, now some 40 years on. I have long since found my military ancestors. I hope that this work allows other people to find theirs.

Steve Brown
Geelong West, Victoria, Australia
July 2024

Introduction

What you hold in your hand is the ultimate outcome of something I started at the beginning of 2009, when having read Tony Broughton's excellent web series on French regiments and the men who commanded them.[1] I contacted series editor Bob Burnham and asked 'do you have any plans to do a like series on British regiments?' And he replied, in his characteristic style, 'Yes. Are you volunteering?' I figured I would give it a shot, and so picked a single battalion regiment about which I knew a little and produced a draft. It was not as easy, or as linear as I had imagined.

Once a British regimental officer reached lieutenant colonel grade at the time, he ought in theory to have exercise substantive command; but even a single battalion regiment, or cavalry regiment might have anything up to four lieutenant colonels, one or two of whom might be general officers; and commanding officers down at field officer grade were often poached for staff duties, leaving the senior major in effective command; and even then, exigencies of campaigning might have put a junior major, or even a senior captain, in effective command. Pinning down a single officer leading the regiment at a given point in time was therefore more difficult task than I heretofore imagined. I realised that it needed to include majors, and senior captains here and there, in the analysis. Early versions were stuttering, with biographies making the subject little more than military cyphers, with promotion dates but not much more, somewhat dry as dust.

Regimental dispositions were based on Cannon's regimental histories, a source that I came to realise as being a bit of a mixed bag – excellent in some periods (particularly for those regiments which served in the Peninsula) – but wholly inadequate in others, with the scantest mention of what regiments actually did or where they served, particularly in the period 1790 to 1800. As time progressed the style and content evolved as more and more reference sources came into play, allowing me to include more useful (and corrected) information, to the point where I was, for the first time, reasonably happy with the results.

By this time, two things had happened: one unexpected, and the other slightly alarming. First was the volume of correspondence received from people looking for further information on, in the minority of cases, the officers featured; or in the majority of cases, any information whatsoever I could proffer on their ancestors who served in these regiments. Sadly, I am not the personnel department of Horse Guards, and my research has been solely focused on field officers. It was clear to me that most people searching for this information were not military history buffs at all. Most were family historians, trying to stitch together possible connexions, clamber over 'brick walls', or have tricky perplexing questions answered. All of the questions received were good ones, and I have provided what I hope are reasonable answers to the 10 most typical questions in the FAQ section at the end of this Introduction. The second, and less satisfying event came when one of my

1 Tony Broughton, 'French Artillery Regiments and the Colonels Who Led Them 1792-1815', 'French Cavalry Regiments and the Colonels Who Led Them 1792-1815', 'French Infantry Regiments and the Colonels Who Led Them 1792-1815', 'French Light Infantry Regiments and the Colonels Who Led Them 1792-1815', 'Auxiliary Regiments in the Service of France and the Colonels who led Them during the period 1804–1815', 'Regiments d'Infanterie Etrangers and the Colonels who led them during the period 1804-1815', *The Napoleon Series*, <https://www.napoleon-series.org/military-information/organization-strategy-tactics/#france>, accessed July 2023.

favourite online resources suddenly dropped out of existence. Websites are wonderful, convenient sources of information, but they are not permanent. Death, illness or change of ownership can banish or bury years of information to a location generally too hard to find, or, at worst, lose it completely. Call me big-headed, but I fancied that what I was providing was worthy of longer-term preservation. And if I was going to take that extra step, then the onus was upon me to satisfy not only the military history cognoscenti, but also all the family historians who were taking a great interest in the work in the first place. Ergo, if I was going to provide biographies (for over 4,500 officers!) I had better put flesh on the bones and evolve them from being the crude outline versions of 2009 into something resembling real people; with dates and places of birth, parentage and relationship connexions, educational institutions attended (where known), dates of entry into the army, known places of residence, dates and places of decease – all on top of the traditional promotion dates and campaigns served.

As to regimental dispositions – a wide variety of sources have been used, varying widely in quality. My main source for the period 1803 to 1815 was the WO 379 series at The National Archives, and WO 17/2782 to /2786, but these are only accurate for units stationed in Great Britain and Scotland, with no detail provided at all for units sailed overseas or stationed in Ireland. Luckily monthly returns for stations such as Ireland and the East Indies came to the rescue in the form of the WO 17 series; not to mention Andrew Bamford's extensive set of online British Army Theatre Returns 1808–1815.[2] Regimental histories have proved, in the main, disappointing in determining troop dispositions, and many (especially in the Richard Cannon series) are riddled with date errors.[3] It was customary at the time for cavalry regiments and infantry battalions to be billeted in numerous dispersed locations within a given area (especially before the creation of permanent barracks) and where such dispersion occurred, the author has chosen only to include the principal locations where two or more troops or companies were located, rather than all locations, which would have doubled the length of the book.

The establishment tables are based upon research data for the years 1802 to 1816 very kindly provided to me by Roderick MacArthur, and material gleaned from the WO 24 series at The National Archives. 'Establishment' was the Horse Guards authorised strength of a unit from which the government calculated the annual cost of upkeep, and against which the regimental colonel could claim. However, regiments rarely met such establishments in reality, especially on campaign. Nonetheless, the figures provide some insight into the rise and fall in troop numbers between 1793 and 1815. Establishments varied every time a unit sailed away from home to somewhere else (home establishments being referred to as 'Guards and Garrisons' to tiptoe around Parliament's dislike of the term 'army'), to either Ireland, Gibraltar, the East Indies, or what were called 'Plantations' (West Indies, North America, or the Cape of Good Hope). Changes in establishment, called 'augmentations' or 'reductions' could happen at any time, usually in response to an external event (such as the Treaty of Amiens in March 1802), meaning that establishments were constantly altering, and must have been a headache for regimental colonels.

For brevity I have generally started biographies from the point that the individual reached field officer rank, usually major. It was from this point that the officer in question might have found himself in command of a regiment. For some selected officers, biographies commence from captain. These biographies show the regimental system in action, officers routinely transferring between regiments for advancement or opportunity, captains who were also (brevet) colonels, many who retired early, some who stayed the distance to

2 Andrew Bamford, 'British Army Theatre Returns: 1808-1815', *The Napoleon Series*, <https://www.napoleon-series.org/military-info/organization/Britain/Strength/Bamford/c_BritishArmyStrengthStudyIntroduction.html>, accessed July to December 2023.

3 See Richard Cannon's works as described in the sources. To be fair, Cannon principally referred to regimental books, many of which were missing or incomplete; he would have been forced to backfill the gaps by guesswork or recollections. The author on the other hand has had access to WO 379 and other series at The National Archives which were prepared by the Quartermaster General and held at Horse Guards, which are believed to be more complete and have been regarded by the author as the main 'source of truth'.

become major generals and beyond. Where it has been possible to accurately ascertain, advancement by purchase, exchange, or promotion (no purchase involved) has been noted. Because this is a regimental study, officers have been ordered according to their regimental (substantive) ranks rather than by brevet (army) ranks, and also according to succession, which determined seniority.

More than a few of the officers biographed in this work had careers which stretched from 1793 all the way to 1815, and indeed there are many whose careers extended well before, or well after, that period. Even to provide a full account of all their exploits under the entry heading 'Service 1793–1815' could easily have tripled the length of this volume, and to avoid this over-run, the author has provided the headline points only, and the reader is encouraged to use the sources referred to for each officer for fuller accounts. A word of warning however: some of the main sources used are maddeningly inconsistent in their coverage of the officer's services. Phillipart's *Royal Military Calendar* for example, a massive work running to five volumes, cheerfully devotes 30, 40 or even 50 pages to officers for whom documentation was available to John Phillipart at the time (1820), yet consigns other equally worthy officers to the back pages of history with a single paragraph for each, detailing promotion dates and little else.[4] This work provides hopefully a more balanced service summary whenever possible (acknowledging where there was little to be said for officers who had short or uneventful careers!) and the sources at the base of each biography provide references to multiple source works for those seeking more information in their research.

The British Army was not cast in stone, and as such the composition of units in the biographical reach of this work – the first half of the eighteenth century through to the late nineteenth century – was variable, particularly with respect to the higher-numbered units. The 95th Foot, for example, had six permutations during this period, all of them discrete entities with no transference of battle honours or traditions.[5] Attempting to differentiate between all these variants in the biographies was found to be too cumbersome. The best advice the author can offer is to state that the version of a regiment that an officer joined was the variant which existed at the time of the commission.

For those not acquainted with the composition of British infantry regiments of the era, the author hopes this small discourse will help. Infantry regiments contained usually anywhere from one to four battalions (although the 60th Foot eventually expanded to eight), each a standalone organisational and tactical entity with its own command structure, staff and authorised 'establishment' (theoretical composition). The average British infantry battalion varied in strength over the era for a variety of reasons, but generally was built around two building blocks: the company and the squad. Each battalion invariably had 10 companies. The grenadier company, the tallest and strongest men, took post on the right flank; the light company, trained to fight in open order and the best marksmen, took post on the left. The other eight companies (usually referred to as the battalion or centre companies) took post in between. Light infantry and rifle regiments had ten light companies. The centre companies were 'paired' (four pairs) and each pair paraded with the senior company commander by date of commission ('eldest') on the right and the junior ('youngest') on the left of each pair. This determined the ordering of companies in the line. A War Office circular dated 27 May 1803 required that '... in future each Troop and Company throughout the Army shall have an effective Captain, and therefore that the Colonels, First Lieutenant Colonels, and First Majors, in the respective Regiments, shall no longer have Troops or Companies.' The complement of captains therefore increased so that each company or troop had one captain.

The building block of the company was the 'squad of inspection' (usually just shortened to squad) commanded by a corporal. From 1805, a squad generally consisted of 20 men, consisting of a corporal and

4 John Phillipart, *Royal Military Calendar: Army Service and Commission Book Containing the Services and Progress of Promotion of the Generals, Lieutenant Generals, Major Generals, Colonels and Majors of the Army* (London: Egerton, 1820), five volumes. Phillipart owned and edited a journal called *The Military Panorama* from which he extracted a lot of his biographical material; he also only biographed officers who were still on active service at the time of publication, so missed many deceased or retired officers.

5 1760–1763; 1779–1783; 1794–1796; 1803–1816 (the 95th Rifles, became the Rifle Brigade in 1816); 1816–1818; and 1823–1881.

19 privates.[6] Anywhere from two to six squads made up a company, giving a notional company strength of 40 to 120 corporals and privates, and therefore battalion 'rank and file' strengths of 400 to 1,200. A typical company was also split into two platoons, each commanded by a subaltern, with each platoon comprising one to three squads.[7] Half platoons and squads were commanded by serjeants. The number of corporals per company generally matched the number of serjeants, since the corporals were expected to 'step up' to undertake the role of the serjeant in the event of a serjeant being incapacitated or absent.[8] Likewise, in some regiments, one of the men in each squad could be nominated to be a 'chosen man' to take charge if both the corporal and sergeant were absent. Lance-corporals and lance-sergeants were generally privates and corporals acting in the rank above them on a longer-term but still temporary basis.[9] All of the above resulted in the following typical company strengths throughout the era:

Rank **(Battalion R&F Strength)**	**(400)**	**(600)**	**(800)**	**(1,000–1,200)**
Captains	1	1	1	1
Lieutenants	1	1	2	2
Ensigns	1	1	1	1
Colour serjeants	1	1	1	1
Serjeants	2	3	4	5–6
Corporals	2	3	4	5–6
Drummers/fifers/buglers	2	2	2	2
Privates	38	57	76	95–114
Total	**48**	**69**	**91**	**112–134**

Grenadier and light companies did not have ensigns, the reasoning being that their specialised duties required more senior subalterns in charge; in such companies, this post was filled by a lieutenant. The rank of colour serjeant was created in 1813 to give the senior serjeant in each company a step-up in rank and pay, equivalent to company sergeant major in the modern army. Each centre/battalion company had two drummers, whereas the grenadier company had drummers and two fifers, and the light company two buglers.

Despite the sanctity of the regiment in the British military, there was no such thing as a formal regimental headquarters in a multi-battalion line infantry regiment, other than the regimental colonel and whatever clerical assistance he borrowed from the regiment. Headquarters were at the battalion level, and by 1813 comprised the following for a typical line infantry battalion:

6 Roderick MacArthur, 'British Army Establishments During the Napoleonic Wars', *Journal of the Society for Army Historical Research*, Vol. 87, No. 350 (Summer 2009), p.158.

7 Company and platoon were tactical designations, whereas squad was not, being merely an organisational term.

8 Refer to <https://rodwargaming.wordpress.com/miltary-historical-research/organisation/authorised-establishments-of-the-british-army-1802-1815/> for a detailed and graphical explanation of battalion structures.

9 The Guards and some other regiments used a single chevron for a lance-corporal, but the practice was far from universal at the time. 'Corporals may be appointed to act as Lance-Sergeants, and the most approved Private Soldiers as Lance-Corporals, who, if they conduct themselves with propriety, should be promoted on the first vacancies.' *General Regulations and Orders for the Army*, 12 August 1811, p.88.

Rank	
Lieutenant Colonel (CO)	1 or 2
Majors	2
Adjutant	1
Quartermaster	1
Quartermaster serjeant	1
Paymaster	1
Paymaster serjeant	1
Serjeant major	1
Surgeon	1
Assistant surgeons	2
Armourer serjeant	1
Schoolmaster serjeant	1
Drum major	1
Musicians	10
Pioneers	11
Total	**36–37**

The appointment of paymaster serjeants was inconsistent – some battalions had one per company. Musicians for the band, if there was one, were drawn from the company rank and file. Pioneers, skilled artisans to oversee fatigue works, were drawn from the company rank and file – 10 privates commanded by a corporal. The rank of schoolmaster serjeant was created in 1813.

The three regiments of foot guards were, as they are to this day, a law unto themselves as concerns organisation and structure. Each of the foot guard regiments had a colonel, lieutenant colonel and two or three majors. However, each regiment had more companies than regiments of the line, and these companies were not permanently organised into battalions. If required for service, companies would be formed into one or more service battalions of eight companies, each under the command of either a major or the most senior captain. As a result, the allocation of companies to battalions was significantly more fluid than in the line infantry, and this led to the tendency for the foot guards to form ad-hoc service battalions of less than 10 companies in strength when needed.

In 1793 the 1st Foot Guards had 23 captains and one captain lieutenant to command the 24 companies, whereas the Coldstream and the 3rd Foot Guards each had 13 captains and one captain lieutenant to command 16 companies. Upon the outbreak of war that year the service battalions were increased to nine companies each, and extra grenadier and light companies were formed to act independently of their parent regiments in converged flank company battalions. Each of three regiments had a headquarters staff comprising the colonel, one lieutenant colonel, a chaplain, a surgeon, and a solicitor.[10] Each battalion had a similar headquarters structure to line regiments, except that the commanding officer was a major, the two subordinate majors did not exist, and the surgeon was termed the surgeon major in each first battalion. A typical headquarters for a service battalion in the foot guards consisted of the following:

10 The colonels and lieutenant colonels in Foot Guards regiments were invariably general officers.

Rank	
Major	1
Adjutant	1
Surgeon	1
Assistant surgeons	2
Quartermaster	1
Quartermaster serjeant	1
Serjeant major	1
Armourer serjeant	1
Schoolmaster serjeant	1
Drum major	1
Musicians	10
Pioneers	11
Total	**32**

Musicians were drawn from the company rank and file. Pioneers were drawn from the company rank and file – 10 privates commanded by a corporal. The rank of schoolmaster serjeant was created in 1813. There were no paymasters or paymaster serjeants, which reflected the fact that household regiments were under the direct control of the Secretary of State at War rather than the Commander in Chief. The foot guards were paid directly by the Paymaster General.

Foot guard regiments always had a higher establishment than line infantry regiments, and after 1803 these usually ranged between 1,200 and 1,400 men. Company organisation was a complex and ever-changing topic, however in the generality the following company strengths were fairly typical:

Rank (battalion R&F strength)	Pre-1803	Post 1803 (1,200)	(1,400)
Captains	1	1	1
Lieutenants	2	2	2–3
Ensigns	1	1	1
Colour serjeants	–	1	1
Serjeants	4	6	7
Corporals	4	6	7
Drummers / fifers	2	2	2
Privates	71	114	128
TOTAL	**81**	**133**	**146**

Grenadier and light companies did not have ensigns. In such companies, this post was filled by a lieutenant. The rank of colour serjeant was created in 1813 to give the senior serjeant in each company a step-up in rank and pay. Each centre/battalion company had two drummers, whereas the grenadier company also had two fifers, and the light company two buglers only.

The foot guards, unlike the French *Garde Impériale*, recruited in exactly the same manner as the line infantry. The foot guards were not the ultimate goal in a career path for an aspiring soldier. However, the foot guards were very selective about who they took. A recruit had to be taller than average – according to inspection reports, many were the better part of six feet tall (or taller) – a fine physical specimen, and because the foot guards were 'popular' regiments for recruits,[11] the foot guards could afford the luxury of turning away anyone not considered 'up to snuff.' The level of drill, discipline and expected deportment in the foot guards was the highest in the army, and thereby (as proven by Wellington's high opinion of them, and their relatively high rate of being awarded commissions), the NCOs in the foot guard regiments were considered the best in the British army.

The service demographics within the regimental descriptions are based upon data sets contained within inspection reports (WO 27 series, The National Archives) since I thought it would be interesting to analyse the makeup of a national army comprising men from four countries (English, Welsh, Irish, Scots) with a sprinkling of foreigners, with some data being based upon data sets kindly provided by Kevin Linch.[12] Extant inspection reports are far from consistent and comprehensive and somewhat patchy in coverage, although better in the period 1806 to 1815 than the earlier years. Hence, the demographics data presented is likewise far from consistent. Notwithstanding, the author hopes that sufficient data is provided to allow the reader to gain an insight into the composition of each unit, and perhaps provide some insight as to what an Irish ancestor was doing serving in an English home counties regiment, as merely one example.

Formally awarded battle honours are shown in UPPERCASE; the capriciousness of the War Office meant that some regiments did not get honours that were deserved, whilst others received them for being mere spectators. The more than 120 infantry regiments that existed in the period 1793 to 1815 have been distilled down to 19 today, through the exertions of the 1881 Childers Reforms, the 1922 amalgamations, the 1957 and 1966 Defence White Papers, 1990s Options for Change, the 2010 Strategic Defence and Security Review and the 2021 Future Soldier reforms. Every current regiment is the descendant of anywhere from two to seven Napoleonic regiments, and battle honours have been handed down as regiments amalgamated. British infantry regiments were awarded only 31 battle honours before 1793, but 250 in the period covered by this book.[13] Those only familiar with the modern British army will find plenty of information to appreciate the ancestry of current regiments – and why some are Rifles and others are Fusiliers.

The author found himself with an overflow of data that seemed too good to waste – hence the Appendices. Abstract 1 provides a batch of statistics related to the number of officers and men serving in the British army between 1793 and 1815. Abstract 2 provides data on the number of battle honours awarded up to 1793, and those awarded between 1793 and 1815 – a massive uplift. Included is a summary of those units with the most honours awarded.

Here then are the first batch of infantry regiments that comprised the army of King George the Third for the period of the Great War with France; and the men who commanded them. Bookshelves may heave with publications about Wellington and his senior commanders; but it was these men, often forgotten by the collective consciousness, who made the machinery of the British Army run, and it seems only right they should be recognised for their service – in King George's Army.

Frequently Asked Questions

What was the selection process for which officers to include in this work?

For the majors and lieutenant colonels, it was a simple rule: any officer holding either of those substantive ranks in their regiment between the start of 1793 and the end of 1815 was included. Note the word substantive – there were many captains holding the brevet (army) rank of major or lieutenant colonel who were not included – but the line had to be drawn somewhere. The only exceptions the author made were to include officers who did not hold the substantive rank of either major or lieutenant colonel, but clearly exercised an important regimental command role at a major action.

11 This was due to the higher pay and perceived status of the guards.

12 Kevin Barry Linch, *The Recruitment of the British Army 1807–1815* (PhD thesis, University of Leeds School of History, 2001).

13 Refer to the 'Battle Honours Legend' in the front matter of this book.

This topic is muddied somewhat in the Foot Guard regiments, where company commanders held the rank of 'captain and lieutenant colonel', meaning they were regimental captains within the Guards, but ranked equivalent to lieutenant colonels in the rest of the army. For the purpose of this work the author has treated them as captains (and therefore not included them *en masse*) but has cherry-picked the few who held important regimental command roles. The Foot Guards regiments frequently embarked on campaign with the senior captain and lieutenant colonel present commanding the battalion.

One my ancestor was born in county X, so why did he serve in a regiment from county Y?
County titles, introduced in 1782, were still a new concept in the Revolutionary and the Napoleonic Wars, and far from being socially embraced, some titles were awarded on their being the home counties of the regimental colonels, regardless of where the men were actually recruited. And notwithstanding the actual titles, regimental recruiting parties took men wherever they could find them, especially in Ireland, which accounted for roughly one-third of all recruits for the period. The only exception to this lack of county of origin affiliation were generally the Highland regiments, and the Irish regiments such as the 27th or 88th Foot, which tended to be more regionally homogenous.

Why did my soldier ancestor have children born all over the British Isles?
There being no police force at the time, the army doubled as the de facto police force of the nation. Combined with the fact that regiments did not have permanent barracks, most regular regiments at home spent their time criss-crossing the country. Cavalry regiments in particular often found themselves ordered to provincial centres where unrest might be expected – such as in the Luddite Uprisings in 1812. The same rules applied equally to the militia regiments, which were raised for home defence only, and more often ordered to garrison towns when regular regiments recently posted had been ordered overseas.

Why did so many retired officers end up living in France?
The massive reductions in the size of the army after 1815 saw many serving officers placed on half-pay, a kind of suspended animation in which the officer was expected to hold themselves in readiness for a call to the colours anytime, whilst receiving exactly 50 percent of their pay. The requirement that they should drop everything and return to the colours deterred many from sustaining professional alternative careers, and many resigned the army. Even for a field officer, half-pay was insufficient in Britain of the 1830s and 1840s, when Great Britain was probably the most expensive country in the world in which to reside. Many moved to France where a similar quality of life cost much less.

Why were some officers promoted by purchase and some by exchange?
Officer promotion could occur in one of three ways – the first, purchase, meant purchasing a step-up in rank by paying the difference in commission price from current (cheaper) to intended rank (more expensive) in order to advance. The second, seniority, involved rising through the officer list within a regiment (from most junior in the holder's current rank to the most senior) and then being promoted to the first non-purchase vacancy occurring in the rank above. The third, patronage was being appointed to a higher rank by the commander in chief. It will be noticed that quite a number of first commissions or promotions did not involve purchase; non-purchase vacancies were those for which the vacating officer was neither eligible nor able to receive the selling price, usually due to death on service, but occasionally because the seller had been dismissed or cashiered. Vacancies caused by the increase in establishment of a unit were also not subject to purchase.

Purchase obviously permitted wealthy officers to rise swiftly, although they were subject to time-in-rank rules set down by the Duke of York in 1795. Seniority provided a career path for talented but poor officers to rise, albeit often slowly. An officer transferring from one regiment to another at the same rank could do so by exchange, a transaction arranged by the regimental agent, wherein two officers of the same rank just switched places.

What is brevet rank?

The regimental system was of such primacy in the British Army that it held an internalised rank system which operated independently of the army's promotion system. An officer could very likely hold a higher rank in the army than he did in his regiment; this was called brevet rank but did not entitle the holder to additional pay in the regiment, nor additional regimental duties, unless acting in an 'army' role – for example, a garrison commander. Only captains, majors, and lieutenant-colonels were eligible for brevet promotion. An officer could neither sell, exchange nor go on the half-pay of his brevet rank. Seniority in the regiment determined promotion in the regiment, based upon regimental rank, not army (brevet) rank. The big advantage of brevet rank was that it placed an officer on the road to higher rank through progressive promotion in the army, which was determined by army rather than regimental rank. Officers holding higher brevet rank could be promoted to the same substantive rank in another unit over the heads of senior officers of the same substantive rank who did not hold a brevet.

What is stationary rank?

Stationary rank was a state decided upon by Horse Guards; when an officer had had not formally resigned but was considered in a state of being unfit for any further service.

How did officers combine military and political careers?

Officers were very frequently sons of leading families in which, for various motives, a sense of national duty was expected of them as young gentlemen. They were generally of a social class that had the vote and rubbing shoulders professional politicians gave them influence, so politics was an attractive career choice, and it was far easier for an officer to be granted leave for such pursuits than lower ranks. However, many military men were not effective politicians, with many apparently never having spoken in the parliament. The Duke of Wellington was an old-school Tory; Sir John Moore, Sir George Anson, Lord Lyndoch and Sir John Byng were Whigs. Sir Thomas Picton and Sir John Hope held seats whilst considering themselves apolitical. Rowland, Lord Hill was another avowed Tory but never attended parliament in person.[14]

Why were officers so young when receiving their first commission?

Army officers we usually aged between about 13 and 18 upon entering the army, with a median age of around 16 years old. This was comparable with and only slightly older than the young officer candidates who joined the Royal Navy, where the median age was 13 to 14 years old.

Why did some officers start their careers as 'Volunteers'?

Volunteers were young civilians who fancied themselves as officer candidates, who attached themselves to regiments on campaign (without rank or position) with the aim of gaining a commission in said regiment when the first officer vacancy arose. They served alongside 'other ranks' whilst waiting for their opportunity. Their reward was to receive a commission without purchase.

It seems that not many officers were awarded medals. Were they not common then?

In the period 1810 to 1814, general and field officers could receive the Army Gold Medal (AGM) for service at major actions. In October 1813 the Army Gold Cross (AGC) was introduced, for general and field officers who had served at four or more actions, with clasps on the ribbon to denote all the actions. Unsurprisingly, the AGC with the largest number of clasps (nine) was awarded to the Duke of Wellington.

The first medal awarded to all ranks of the British army for a military action was the Waterloo medal, which was awarded in April 1816. Earlier veterans, who had served many years prior to 1810 without

14 The History of Parliament website <https://www.historyofparliamentonline.org/> is particularly useful for tracing the political careers of military men.

award, felt slighted. The Duke of Richmond campaigned to both Parliament and Queen Victoria that junior and non-commissioned officers and private soldiers of the Great War with France deserved the same recognition. The Duke of Wellington was strangely reluctant about the idea – he cared little for ribbons and trinkets[15] – but eventually supported the Duke of Richmond's petition, and with his weight behind it, the queen approved the award. Known throughout the army as the 'Silver Medal' or as the GSM (but more correctly called the Military General Service Medal), the MGSM was approved on 1 June 1847 as a retrospective award for various military actions in the period from 1793 to 1814. Actions awarded were shown by clasps on the ribbon (29 actions were sanctioned) and the medal was never issued without a clasp. The medal was only awarded to surviving claimants who had actively applied for it. Many fewer medals were issued compared with the number of men who served during this period. Claims started rolling in in 1847, and the assessment of claims continued until November 1853. The Office for Military Boards assessed each man's claims by trawling through old muster rolls to determine whether a man was present an action he claimed; by this technique, many thousands of applicants had their initial claim either upgraded or rejected.

Why were some officers serving in foreign armies, such as the Portuguese, or in India?

The Portuguese army was placed under a British commander (Lieutenant General William Carr Beresford) in 1809 and reformed so that it would be able to take its place in a line of battle alongside British troops. Beresford needed officers who understood British military practice, and this paved the way for ambitious young British subalterns and captains to join the Portuguese service. The offer was made more attractive by giving the officer a raise one step in rank without purchase on joining. Between March 1809 and September 1810, 158 British officers accepted commissions in the Portuguese army. British officers ultimately represented 11 percent of all Portuguese colonels, 73 percent of lieutenant colonels and 50 percent of majors.[16]

The East India Company (EIC) had at its disposal the world's largest private army; in 1806 the armies of the three presidencies (Bengal, Bombay and Madras) numbered 24,500 British and 130,000 Indian troops. Officer admission was without purchase and all promotions were by seniority. It made for a slower promotion path than the regular army, but an attractive career option for the sons of officers biographed within this work; many of whom were commencing their careers at a time when the post-Waterloo British army was shrinking, and thus offering fewer vacancies.

A quick final note about names and demographics…

A number of officers in this volume (quite a few, actually) changed their names during their lifetime, either as the requirement of a relative's will in order to gain an inheritance or succession; or adopting a hyphenated 'double-barrel' surname upon marriage (which again, might have been related to the same factors). This made finding a few of them more difficult than I had initially imagined. Also, regarding names, I have used the spelling of an officer's name as found in their signatures in documents such as marriage licenses or wills, rather than the versions used in Army Lists, which were often subject to creative clerical intervention.

For the purposes of sorting, officer's ethnic identities (English, Scots, etc) have been based upon their family background rather than place of birth, for the simple reason that a future officer born into

15 See Hew Strachan, *Wellington's Legacy: The Reform of the British Army, 1830–54* (Manchester: Manchester University Press, 1984), p.19, p.102; Charles Dalton, 'On British War Medals', in *Colburn's United Service Magazine and Naval Military Journal* (London: Hurst & Blackett, 1876), p.458.

16 See Pedro de Avillez, 'British Officers in Portuguese Army Service (1809–1814)', The British Historical Society of Portugal, < https://www.bhsportugal.org/uploads/fotos_artigos/files/13_BRITISHOFFICERSINTHEPORTUGUESEARMY_Rev_2_6_final.pdf>; also Pedro de Brito, 'British Officers in the Portuguese Service 1809–1820', at <https://www.thenapoleonicwars.net/forum/general-discussions/british-officers-in-the-portuguese-service>

a Scots family in say, India, but then raised in Scotland, would qualify as Scots rather than Foreign. This is perhaps a highly objective topic, and some no doubt will disagree with the classifications, but the intent was to build up an overall picture of the backgrounds of the overall commanding officer cohort; given some expectation that the author has got it mostly right, with any luck such misidentifications will ultimately balance each other out.[17]

17 In many instances the official inspections returns in TNA:WO27 series, which required officers to list their ages, dates of first commission and nationalities, came to the rescue; the author went with the nationality to which the officer self-identified.

Glossary

ADC	Aide de camp; a personal aide to a senior officer
Adjutant	Regimental staff officer responsible for administration and discipline
Adjutant General	Staff officer responsible for administration and discipline of a large body of troops, garrison, or expeditionary force
Battalion	In the infantry only; a tactical and administration sub entity of the regiment, typically comprising of 10 companies and commanded by a lieutenant colonel
Brevet rank	A rank conferred on an officer by the army usually one or more steps higher than his current rank within his regiment; usually awarded by overall seniority, but also for gallantry or delivery of victory despatches
Brigade	A tactical grouping of two or more battalions or regiments, usually commanded by a colonel or higher
Brigadier General	An appointment given to (usually) a colonel commanding a brigade
Captain	Commissioned rank superior to a lieutenant but inferior to a major; usually commanding a company or troop
CO	Commanding Officer
Colonel	Commissioned rank superior to a lieutenant colonel but inferior to a major general
Colour Serjeant	(After July 1813) The senior NCO in an infantry company, superior to a serjeant but inferior to a serjeant major; denoted by one chevron surmounted by union colour with crossed swords and crown, generally superior jacket and trimmings, and a crimson sash
Commander in Chief	At the highest level, the superior appointment within the British Army in Great Britain and Ireland only; responsible for organisation, discipline, training and promotions only. Also used to denote a local commander of a significant garrison (for example the West Indies); which was often combined with a military governorship
Commander of the Forces	A local Commander in Chief for a garrison, often with the same meaning as above
Company	In the infantry, an organisational sub entity of the battalion, within which there were typically 10 companies
Cornet	The lowest commissioned rank within the cavalry, inferior to a lieutenant; the modern equivalent being second lieutenant
Corporal	The lowest non-commissioned rank in the line cavalry, inferior to a serjeant, and denoted (after 1802) by two chevrons; considered as part of the regimental rank-and-file in returns and reports
Corps	From 1815 onwards, an all-arms tactical formation comprising several divisions. Also used generally to mean any formed body of troops
CRA	Commander, Royal Artillery within a particular garrison, assignment or expeditionary force

CRE	Commander, Royal Engineers within a particular garrison, assignment or expeditionary force
Division	A tactical grouping of two or more brigades, usually commanded by a major general or higher
District	An administrative military region of Great Britain and Ireland, usually commanded by a lieutenant general
Ensign	The lowest commissioned rank within the infantry, inferior to a lieutenant; the modern equivalent being second lieutenant
EOPS	Engaged on a particular service: an officer detailed to perform a specific task or function outside their regiment
Expeditionary Force	A force organised and intended for a specific overseas campaign
Fencibles	Regular infantry or cavalry regiments enlisted voluntarily to serve for the duration of the war only; not permitted to serve overseas
Field Marshal	The highest commissioned rank, superior to a general; infrequently awarded
Field officer	Class of officers superior to company grade officers but inferior to general officers. Usually major, lieutenant colonel or colonel
Flank companies	In the infantry only: the grenadier company (right flank) and light company (left flank) within a battalion, which could be detached for specific roles
Garrison	Body of troops in a particular station, usually applied to overseas locations
General	The highest general officer rank, superior to a lieutenant general but inferior to a field marshal
GOC	General Officer Commanding
King's Regulations	Orders emanating from Horse Guards concerned mainly with everyday affairs of military life such as discipline, interior economy, uniforms and equipment and communication with authorities
Lieutenant	A commissioned rank, superior to an ensign or cornet but inferior to a captain
Lieutenant General	A general officer rank, superior to a major general but inferior to a general
Lieutenant Colonel	A field officer rank, superior to a major but inferior to a colonel; usually commanded a battalion (infantry) or regiment (cavalry)
Light Infantry	Infantry trained to fight in open (skirmish) order, but capable of adopting standard linear or columnar formations when ordered
Major	Lowest field officer rank, superior to a captain but inferior to a lieutenant colonel
Major General	The lowest general officer rank, superior to a colonel but inferior to a lieutenant general
Militia	Regiments raised by ballot in each county, to serve part-time for a stated period, ready to defend the homeland but forbidden to serve overseas
Musicians	In the infantry, drummers and fifers; in the light infantry, buglers and drummers; in the cavalry, trumpeters and hautbois; all generally conducted by a drum major or trumpet major. Regiments usually also had bands (not shown on authorised establishments) not including the foregoing
NCO	Non-commissioned officer – serjeants and corporals
OC	Officer Commanding
Ordnance	Artillery – the Royal Artillery
Platoon	A sub-entity of the company, a firing or training subdivision, usually 20 to 60 privates
Quartermaster	Regimental staff officer responsible for quartering and provisioning
Quartermaster General	Staff officer responsible for quartering and provisioning of a large body of troops, garrison, or expeditionary force
Rank-and-file	Privates and corporals, who made up the ranks and files when a unit was formed, as opposed to serjeants, drummers and officers who were positioned to the front, side or rear.

Regimental Colonel	General officer responsible for the overall administration of a regiment
Rifles	Regiments armed with rifles, a highly accurate muzzle-loaded firelock
Second Lieutenant	The lowest commissioned rank, only used in some units, notably the 95th Rifles and fusilier regiments, inferior to a lieutenant
Serjeant Major	A non-commissioned rank, superior to a serjeant, and denoted by four chevrons, generally superior jacket and trimmings, crimson sash and a pace stick
Squadron	In the cavalry only; a tactical grouping of two troops, commanded by the senior captain present
Subaltern	A junior officer up to and including the rank of lieutenant
Substantive rank	The permanent rank an officer held within his regiment
Troop	In the cavalry, an organisational sub entity of the regiment, within which there were normally eight to twelve troops

British infantry regiments had one or more battalions (for example 1/23rd meaning 1st Battalion, 23rd Regiment of Foot), but battalions of the same regiment rarely served together and might be in different parts of the world at any given time. Cavalry regiments did not have battalions. Battalions in the Royal Artillery, subdivided into companies, were purely administrative and had no tactical meaning. The tactical unit for the artillery was, confusingly, the brigade.

Biography Legend

Explanation of tables:

Born:	Date and place of birth
Relations:	Parentage and family connections, concentrated primarily on military and/or political connections
Entry to Army:	Date and unit in which the officer held their first commission
Education:	Places of higher education and degrees conferred (if any)
Regimental Field Officer Promotions:	Dates and units in which the officer reached field officer rank (major or higher) in their regiment
Brevets:	Dates at which the officer was promoted by brevet to army rank
Colonelcies:	Date and unit in which the officer was appointed regimental colonel
Early Service:	Service details for the period prior to 1793
Service 1793–1815:	Service details for the period 1793 to 1815
Later Service:	Service details for the period after 1815
Militia Career:	Service details for any militia appointments (usually post army career)
Political Career:	Seats and political appointments held
Creations and Dignities:	Date of receipt of letters issued by the monarch granting an office, right, or title in the peerage and baronetage
Awards and Honours:	Titles and dates of awards and honours received by the officer
Residence:	Known residences of the officer
Died:	Date and place of decease
Sources:	Sources referred to in the research of the officer

As a general rule, birth marriage and death records are much better in the nineteenth century than in the eighteenth, and in nearly all instances it has been possible to locate the dates and places of deaths of these officers, who were after all, people of some stature within the community. However, establishing birth details in the eighteenth century, when record keeping was not as good and the officer's families in question may not have had much social stature of which to speak, has been more problematic. It is for this reason and in order to retain some consistency with birth details across the entire cohort, I have generally resorted to county (or country) and year of birth, but place and exact date of death. There are even lieutenant generals and generals in this book for whom birth details have been virtually impossible to pin down – which may have been a deliberate strategy to deter later biographers from discovering the humbleness of their roots.

I also apologise in advance for the male-centric bias of the recorded family relationships, but in order to save space, I have limited such relationships to those of a military nature, or to eminent individuals, in order to stay on topic; rather than trying to list all spouses, siblings and offspring.

Abbreviations Used

1/ 2/ … 7/ 8/	Numbered battalion of a regiment
AG	Adjutant General
AGC	Army Gold Cross (Peninsula)
AGM	Army Gold Medal (Peninsula)
BNC	Brasenose College, Oxford University
Brevet	Army (rather than regimental) rank
Bt.	Baronet
CB	Companion of the Most Honourable Order of the Bath
CCT	Commander of the Royal and Distinguished Spanish Order of Charles III (Spain)
CD	Commander's Cross of Distinction for Peninsular War (Portugal)
CM	Command Medal for Peninsular War (Portugal)
CKS	Commander of the Royal Order of the Sword (Sweden)
CMJ	Commander of the Military Order of Max Joseph (Bavaria)
co	Companies
CSFM	Commander of the Royal Order of Saint Ferdinand and of Merit (Two Sicilies)
CSH	Commander of the Military Order of Saint Henry (Saxony)
FRS	Fellow of the Royal Society
FRSE	Fellow of the Royal Society of Edinburgh
FSA	Fellow of the Society of Antiquaries of London
GCAN	Grand Cross of the Imperial Order of Saint Alexander Nevsky (Russia)
GCB	Knight Grand Cross of the Most Honourable Order of the Bath
GCH	Knight Grand Cross of the Royal Hanoverian Guelphic Order
GCCT	Knight Grand Cross of the Royal and Distinguished Spanish Order of Charles III (Spain)
GCKS	Grand Cross of the Royal Order of the Sword (Sweden)
GCMG	Knight Grand Cross of the Most Distinguished Order of St Michael and St George
GCMT	Knight Grand Cross of the Military Order of Maria Theresa (Habsburg)
GCOL	Grand Cross of the Austrian Imperial Order of Leopold (Habsburg)
GCSJ	Grand Cross of the Order of Saint Joseph (Tuscany)
GCTS	Knight Grand Cross of the Military Order of the Tower and of the Sword (Portugal)
GCSF	Grand Cross of the Royal and Military Order of Saint Ferdinand (Spain)
GCSFM	Knight Grand Cross of the Royal Order of Saint Ferdinand and of Merit (Two Sicilies)
GCSH	Grand Cross of the Royal and Military Order of Saint Hermenegild (Spain)
GCSJ	Grand Cross of the Illustrious Royal Order of Saint Januarius (Two Sicilies)
GMMG	Grand Master of the Most Distinguished Order of St Michael and St George
HEIC	Honourable East India Company
Ire	Ireland
KAN	Knight of the Imperial Order of Saint Alexander Nevsky (Russia)
KB	Knight Companion of the Most Honourable Order of the Bath
KC	King's Counsel
KCt	Knight of the Order of the Crescent (Ottoman)
KCB	Knight Commander of the Most Honourable Order of the Bath
KCH	Knight Commander of the Royal Hanoverian Guelphic Order
KCMG	Knight Commander of the Most Distinguished Order of St Michael and St George
KCSF	Knight Grand Cross of the Royal and Military Order of Saint Ferdinand (Spain)
KCSH	Knight Grand Cross of the Royal and Military Order of Saint Hermenegild (Spain)
KCTS	Knight Commander of the Military Order of the Tower and of the Sword (Portugal)
KESCSJ	The Equestrian, Secular and Chapterial Knightly Order of Saint Joachim (Holy Roman Empire)
KG	Knight of the Most Noble Order of the Garter
KH	Knight of the Royal Hanoverian Guelphic Order

KHGL	Knight of the House Order of the Golden Lion (Hesse-Kassel)
KKS	Knight of the Royal Order of the Sword (Sweden)
KLS	Knight of the Imperial Order of the Lion and the Sun (Persia)
KMT	Knight of the Military Order of Maria Theresa (Habsburg)
KMWO	Knight of the Military Order of Wilhelm (Netherlands)
KORA	Knight of the Order of the Red Eagle (Prussia)
KOSA	Knight of the Order of the Black Eagle (Prussia)
KOSE	Knight of the Order of the Holy Spirit (France)
KP	Knight of the Most Illustrious Order of Saint Patrick
KSA	Knight of the Order of Saint Anna (Russia)
KSAA	Knight of the Order of Saint Andrew the Apostle the First-Called (Russia)
KSFM	Knight of the Royal Order of Saint Ferdinand and of Merit (Two Sicilies)
KStG	Knight of the Order of Saint George (Russia)
KSGG	Knight of the Pontifical Equestrian Order of Saint Gregory the Great (Russia)
KSH	Knight of the Military Order of Saint Henry (Saxony)
KSI	Knight of the Star of India
KSJ	Knight of the Order of Saint Joseph (Tuscany)
KSW	Knight of the Imperial Order of Saint Prince Vladimir (Russia)
KT	Knight of the Most Ancient and Most Noble Order of the Thistle
KTS	Knight of the Military Order of the Tower and of the Sword (Portugal)
MGSM	Military General Service Medal
MP	Member of Parliament
NGSM	Naval General Service Medal
OSSML	Order of Saints Maurice and Lazarus (Savoy)
PC	Privy Council
POW	Prisoner of War
RA	Royal Artillery
RE	Royal Engineers
REI	Royal Engineers in Ireland
RIA	Royal Irish Artillery
RMA	Royal Military Artificers
RS&M	Royal Sappers and Miners
RSC	Royal Staff Corps
RWT	Royal Waggon Train
Rt Hon.	Right Honourable
spec.	Speculative (but with high degree of probability)
tp	Troops
unk.	Unknown
vice	In the place of
WatM	Waterloo Medal

CLASPS TO AGC, AGM and MGSM

Egt	Egypt 1801
Mai	Maida 4 Jul 1806
Rol	Rolica 17 Aug 1808
Vim	Vimeiro 21 Aug 1808
Sah&Ben	Sahagun 20 Dec 1808 and Benevente 29 Dec 1808
Cor	Corunna 16 Jan 1809
Mart	Martinique 24 Feb 1809

Tal	Talavera 27 Jul 1809
Guad	Guadeloupe 6 Feb 1810
Bus	Busaco 27 Sep 1810
Bar	Barrosa 5 Mar 1811
FdO	Fuentes d'Onoro 5 May 1811
Alb	Albuera 16 May 1811
Jav	Java Aug 1811
CR	Ciudad Rodrigo 19 Jan 1812
Bad	Badajoz 6 Apr 1812
Sal	Salamanca 22 Jul 1812
Det	Fort Detroit Aug 1812
Vit	Vittoria 21 Jun 1813
Pyr	Pyrenees Jul/Aug 1813
SS	San Sebastian 9 Sep 1813
Chat	Chateauguay 26 Oct 1813
Nll	Nivelle 10 Nov 1813
CF	Chrysler's Farm 11 Nov 1813
Niv	Nive Dec 1813
Ort	Orthez 27 Feb 1814
Toul	Toulouse 10 Apr 1814

Terms used on the Establishment Tables

Year: Year, generally from 25 Dec of previous year to 25 Dec of current year

Subunits: Number of companies or troops, +r denotes unit had a recruiting troop or company at home (+2r being two recruiting troops or companies)

Field Off: Number of colonels, lieutenant colonels and majors

Off/ Staff: Number of other officers and regimental staff

Sjt: Number of serjeants, quartermaster serjeants, staff serjeants, drum majors and serjeant majors; includes corporal majors in Household cavalry

Mus: Number of musicians (drummers, buglers, fifers etc)

Corp/Pvts: Total number of corporals and privates

Total: Total authorised unit strength

Years for which the establishment is identical to the prior year are omitted in the interests of brevity.

Demographics figures are taken from regimental Inspection Reports for that year, which generally (but not always) considered English and Welsh soldiers as a single entity for counting purposes.

E = English; W = Welsh; S = Scots; I = Irish; A = North American; F = Foreign

Sources Legend

Abbreviations Used

ALBE	Alphabetical List of Officers of the Bengal Army
ALBO	Alphabetical List of Officers of the Bombay Army
ALMA	Alphabetical List of Officers of the Madras Army
ANCB	Baptismal records on Ancestry
ANCM	Marriage records on Ancestry
ANCD	Burial records on Ancestry
ANCS	Soldier records on Ancestry
ANCW	Wills and probates on Ancestry
ANRE	The Annual Register
ARLI	Army Lists (WO 65 series, TNA)
BEAL	The Bengal Almanack
BGNW	British Generals of the Napoleonic Wars (The Napoleon Series, Ron McGuigan)
BLEM	Blackwood's Edinburgh Magazine
BPBK	Burke's Peerage, Baronetage and Knightage
BRBM	British Battles and Medals (Spink)
BRFM	British Field Marshals (Heathcote)
BUPB	A General and Heraldic Dictionary of the Peerage and Baronetage of the British Empire
CHAL	Peninsula Roll Call (Challis)
COPE	The Complete Peerage of England, Scotland, Ireland, Great Britain, and the United Kingdom Extant, Extinct, or Dormant) (Cokayne)
CRAC	Cracroft's Peerage
DALT	Waterloo Roll Call (Dalton)
DEBA	Debrett's Baronetage
DEPE	Debrett's Peerage
DICB	Dictionary of Canadian Biography
DIIB	Dictionary of Irish Biography
DINB	Dictionary of National Biography
EDAR	Edinburgh Annual Register
EIMC	East India Military Calendar
EMLM	Edinburgh Magazine and Literary Miscellany
FFBI	Former Fellows of the Royal Society of Edinburgh Biographical Index
FMPB	Baptismal records on Find My Past

Abbreviations Used

FMPM	Marriage records on Find My Past
FMPD	Burial records on Find My Past
FMPS	Soldier records on Find My Past
FMPW	Wills and probates on Find My Past
GEMA	Gentleman's Magazine
GENE	Geneanet (website)
GHHC	Genealogical and Heraldic History of the Commoners of Great Britain and Ireland (Burke)
GHHI	Genealogical and Heraldic History of the Landed Gentry of Ireland (Burke)
GHLG	Genealogical and Heraldic Dictionary of the Landed Gentry of Great Britain and Ireland (Burke)
GHPB	Genealogical and Heraldic Dictionary of the Peerage and Baronetage of the British Empire (Burke)
HALL	Biographical Dictionary of British Officers Killed and Wounded, 1808–1814 (Hall)
HOKN	History of Orders and Knighthoods (Nicolas)
HPON	History of Parliament Online (website)
LFBI	Landed Families of Britain and Ireland (website)
MENA	Memorandums and Narratives, Parliamentary, Civil, Military, Naval, and Ecclesiastical
NALI	Navy Lists (Admiralty Office)
ODNB	Oxford Dictionary of National Biography
PBBE	The Peerage and Baronetage of the British Empire as at Present Existing (Lodge)
PBKN	Peerage, Baronetage and Knightage of Great Britain and Ireland (Dod)
PEER	The Peerage (website)
PHIL	Royal Military Calendar (Phillipart)
SCMA	Scots Magazine
UATS	Under A Tropical Sun (website)
UNSM	United Service Magazine / United Service Journal
WEBC	Wellington's Brigade Commanders (Burnham and McGuigan)
WEMR	Wellington's Men Remembered
WEOF	Wellington's Officers (Reid)
WLHB	Who Was Who in Late Hanoverian Britain
WOST	World Statesmen (website)
WPWG	Wellington's Peninsular War Generals and Their Battles (Heathcote)

Battle Honours Legend

Awards shown are limited to units contained within this volume.

Battle Honour	Action, Current Name (Location)	Infantry Regiments Awarded
PONDICHERRY 1793	Siege of Puducherry (India) 10–22 Aug 1793	
LINCELLES	Battle of Linselles (France) 18 Aug 1793	
NIEUPORE	Siege of Nieuwpoort (Belgium) 2–30 Oct 1793	53F
MARTINIQUE 1794	Capture of Martinique (West Indies) 5 Feb–25 Mar 1794	31F 39F 43F 58F
VILLERS EN CAUCHIES	Battle of Villers–en–Cauchies (France) 24 Apr 1794	
BEAUMONT	Battle of Beaumont–en–Cambrésis (France) 26 Apr 1794	
WILLEMS	Battle of Willems (France) 10 May 1794	
TOURNAY	Battle of Tournai (France) 22 May 1794	37F 53F
GLORIOUS 1st of JUNE	Naval battle in Atlantic 1 Jun 1794	
ROHILCUND 1794	Battle of Rohilkhand (India) 26 Oct 1794	
ST LUCIA 1796	Capture of St Lucia (West Indies) 26 Apr–25 May 1796	53F
ST VINCENT 1797	Naval battle in Atlantic 14 Feb 1797	
FISHGUARD	French landing in Wales 23 Feb 1797	
EGMONT OP ZEE	Battle of Egmont–op–Zee (Netherlands) 2 Oct 1799	49F
SERINGAPATAM 1799	Siege and capture of Srirangapatna (India) 5 Apr–4 May 1799	33F
MALTA 1800	Siege and capture of Malta 2 Sep 1798–5 Sep 1800	35F
MANDORA	Battle of Mandora (Egypt) 13 Mar 1801	
MARABOUT	Capture of Fort Marabout (Egypt) 21 Aug 1801	
EGYPT	Campaign in Egypt 8 Mar–26 Aug 1801	40F 42F 44F 50F 54F 58F
COPENHAGEN	Naval assault on Copenhagen 2 Apr 1801	49F
ST LUCIA 1803	Capture of St Lucia (West Indies) 22 Jun 1803	
ALLY GHUR	Siege and battle of Aligarh (India) 1–4 Sep 1803	
DELHI 1803	Battle of Delhi (India) 11 Sep 1803	
ASSAYE	Battle of Assaye (India) 23 Sep 1803	

Battle Honour	Action, Current Name (Location)	Infantry Regiments Awarded
LESWAREE	Battle of Laswari (India) 1 Nov 1803	
SURINAM	Capture of Surinam (South America) 26 Apr–5 May 1804	
DEIG	Battle of Deeg and siege of Deeg Fort (India) 13 Nov–24 Dec 1804	
DOMINICA	Capture of Dominica (West Indies) 22 Feb 1805	46F
CAPE OF GOOD HOPE 1806	Capture of Cape of Good Hope (South Africa) 8 Jan 1806	59F
MAIDA	Battle of Maida (Italy) 4 Jul 1806	35F 58F
MONTE VIDEO	Capture of Monte Video South America) 3 Feb 1807	38F 40F
ROLICA	Battle of Roliça (Portugal) 17 Aug 1808	32F 36F 38F 45F 60F
VIMIERA	Battle of Vimeiro (Portugal) 21 Aug 1808	32F 36F 38F 43F 45F 50F 52F 60F
COCHIN	Suppression of Travancore rebellion (India) 18 Dec 1808–19 Jan 1809	
SAHAGUN	Skirmish at Sahagun (Spain) 21 Dec 1808	
CORUNNA	Battle of Coruña (Spain) 16 Jan 1809	32F 36F 38F 42F 43F 50F 51F 52F 59F
MARTINIQUE 1809	Capture of Martinique 30 Jan–24 Feb 1809	60F
DOURO	Battle of the Douro (Portugal) 12 May 1809	48F
TALAVERA	Battle of Talavera (Spain) 27–28 Jul 1809	31F 40F 45F 48F 53F 60F
GUADELOUPE 1810	Capture of Guadeloupe (West Indies) 28 Jan–4 Feb 1810	
AMBOYNA	Capture of Ambon (Indonesia) 17 Feb 1810	
BOURBON	Capture of Réunion (Indian Ocean) 7–10 Jul 1810	
BANDA	Capture of Banda (Indonesia) 9 Aug 1810	
TERNATE	Capture of Ternate (Indonesia) 28 Aug 1810	
BUSACO	Battle of Buçaco (Portugal) 27 Sep 1810	38F 42F 43F 45F 52F 60F
BARROSA	Battle of Barrosa (Spain) 5 Mar 1811	
FUENTES D'ONOR	Battle of Fuentes de Oñoro (Spain) 3–5 May 1811	42F 43F 45F 51F 52F 60F
ALBUHERA	Battle of Albuera (Spain) 16 May 1811	31F 34F 39F 48F 57F 60F
JAVA	Capture of Java (Indonesia) 4 Aug–16 Sep 1811	59F
ARROYO DOS MOLINOS	Battle of Arroyo dos Molinos (Spain) 28 Oct 1811	34F
TARIFA	Siege of Tarifa (Spain) 19 Dec 1811–5 Jan 1812	47F
CIUDAD RODRIGO	Siege and storm of Ciudad Rodrigo (Spain) 9–19 Jan 1812	43F 45F 52F 60F
BADAJOZ	Siege and storm of Badajoz (Spain) 17 Mar–6 Apr 1812	38F 40F 43F 44F 45F 48F 52F 60F
ALMARAZ	Battle of Almaraz (Spain) 19 May 1812	50F

Battle Honour	Action, Current Name (Location)	Infantry Regiments Awarded
SALAMANCA	Battle of Salamanca (Spain) 22 Jul 1812	32F 36F 38F 40F 42F 43F 44F 45F 48F 51F 52F 53F 58F 60F
DETROIT	Siege of Detroit (United States) 15–16 Aug 1812	41F
QUEENSTOWN	Battle of Queenston Heights (Canada) 13 Oct 1812	41F 49F
MIAMI	Battle of Maumee River (United States) 5 May 1813	41F
VITTORIA	Battle of Vitoria (Spain) 21 Jun 1813	31F 34F 38F 39F 40F 43F 45F 47F 48F 50F 51F 52F 53F 57F 59F 60F
SAN SEBASTIAN	Siege and storm of San Sebastian (Spain) 25 Jul–31 Aug 1813	38F 47F 59F
PYRENEES	Battles in the Pyrenees (Spain) 25 Jul–2 Aug 1813	31F 32F 34F 36F 39F 40F 42F 43F 45F 48F 50F 52F 53F 57F 58F 60F
NIVELLE	Battle of Nivelle (France) 10 Nov 1813	31F 32F 36F 39F 40F 42F 43F 45F 48F 51F 52F 53F 57F 58F 60F
NIVE	Battle of Nive (France) 9–13 Dec 1813	31F 32F 34F 36F 38F 39F 42F 43F 47F 50F 52F 57F 59F 60F
ORTHEZ	Battle of Orthez (France) 27 Feb 1814	31F 32F 34F 36F 39F 40F 42F 45F 48F 50F 51F 52F 58F 60F
TOULOUSE	Battle of Toulouse (France) 10 Apr 1814	36F 40F 42F 43F 45F 48F 52F 53F 60F
PENINSULA	The Peninsular Campaign (Spain, Portugal and France) 17 Aug 1808–14 Apr 1814	30F 31F 32F 34F 36F 37F 38F 39F 40F 42F 43F 44F 45F 47F 48F 50F 51F 52F 53F 57F 58F 59F 60F
NIAGARA	Niagara Campaign (Canada) 5 Jul – 15 Aug 1814	41F
BLADENSBURG	Battle of Bladensburg (United States) 24 Aug 1814	44F
WATERLOO	Battle of Waterloo (Belgium) 18 Jun 1815	32F 33F 40F 42F 44F 51F 52F

Regiments of Foot

31st Regiment of Foot

Secondary Title:	Huntingdonshire
Nicknames:	The Young Buffs
Jacket:	Red
Facings:	Buff

Regimental Lineage, 31st Regiment of Foot

1694: Raised as Richard Atkins's Regiment of Foot
1698: Disbanded
1702: Mar – re-raised for service as Villier's Regiment of Marines
1703: Lutterell's Regiment of Marines
1706: Churchill's Regiment of Marines
1711: Goring's Regiment of Foot
1716: Kerr's Regiment of Foot
1728: Cathcart's Regiment of Foot
1730: Hargrave's Regiment of Foot
1737: Handasyd's Regiment of Foot
1745: Beauclerk's Regiment of Foot
1747: Ranked as 31st Regiment of Foot
1749: Holmes' Regiment of Foot
1751: 31st Regiment of Foot
1756: 2nd Battalion formed
1758: 2nd Battalion became 70th Regiment of Foot
1782: 31st (Huntingdonshire) Regiment of Foot
1804: Aug – 2nd Battalion formed in Chester
1814: Oct – 2nd Battalion disbanded in Portsmouth
1881: 1st Battalion, The East Surrey Regiment (on amalgamation with the 70th (Surrey) Regiment of Foot)
1959: 2nd Battalion, Queen's Royal Surrey Regiment (on amalgamation with the Queen's Royal Regiment (West Surrey))
1966: 1st Battalion (Queen's Surreys), Queen's Regiment (on amalgamation with the Queen's Own Buffs, The Royal Kent Regiment, the Royal Sussex Regiment and the Middlesex Regiment (Duke of Cambridge's Own))
1992: Princess of Wales's Royal Regiment (on amalgamation with the Royal Hampshire Regiment)

Service History, 1st Battalion 31st Regiment of Foot

1793: Ireland – Waterford; Sep – flank companies to Barbados
1794: Feb – flank companies in MARTINIQUE; Apr – St Lucia; Guadeloupe; Point-a-Pitre; Fort Fleur d'Epée; Oct – exterminated at Berville
Jul – home companies in Wexford; to England – Bristol; Aug – to Middelburg and Flushing

1795: Walcheren; Feb – to England; Plymouth; Aug – Nursling; Oct – to West Indies; delayed by storms in channel
1796: Feb – Gosport; Mar – Poole; Southampton; to West Indies; May – St Lucia; Morne Fortunée; Morne Chabot; Vigie; Vieux Forts; Dec – to Barbados
1797: Barbados; Mar – cadre to England; Jul – Gravesend; Aug – Chatham; Sep – Doncaster
1798: Doncaster; Feb – York; August – York and Hilstone camp; Nov – York and Hull
1799: York and Hull; Jul – York and Hilstone camp; Sep – Barham Downs; Deal; to Helder; Alkmaar; Oct – Egmont-op-Zee; Bergen; Nov – to England; Deal; Dec – Canterbury
1800: Canterbury; Feb – Canterbury and Whitstable; Apr – Deal Castle; May – Dover; to Ireland; Jun – Cork; Jul – Quiberon; Isle du Houat; Aug – Ferrol; Oct – Cadiz; Nov – Lisbon
1801: Feb – Minorca; not sent to Egypt due to large number of short-term militia men in battalion
1802: Minorca; May – to England; Oct – Portsmouth; Nov – Portsmouth and Gosport
1803: Portsmouth and Gosport; Jun – Bexhill; Sep – Jersey
1804: Jersey; Nov – Portsmouth; Winchester
1805: Winchester
1806: Jan – Nelson's Funeral; Winchester; Apr – Tilbury Forts; to Sicily; Jul – Messina
1807: Messina; Feb – Melazzo; to Egypt; Mar – Aboukir; Rosetta; Alexandria; Sep – to Sicily
1808: Sicily; Sep – to Malta
1809: Malta
1810: Malta; Aug – to Sicily; Messina
1811: Messina; Apr – six companies in Malta, four companies in Messina; Aug – reunited in Messina
1812: Sicily; Nov – grenadier company to east coast of Spain; Alicante
1813: Sicily; Messina; grenadier company in Alicante; Apr – grenadier company to Sicily; Palermo; Dec – Castro Giovanni
1814: Castro Giovanni; Feb – Messina; Mar – Melazzo; to Italy; Apr – Genoa; Livorno; Sestri Levante; Sturla; May – Corsica; Ajaccio; Bastia; Jun – Sicily; Jul – Messina
1815: Messina; May – Melazzo; Naples; Jul – Genoa
1816: Malta (until 1818)

Service History, 2nd Battalion 31st Regiment of Foot

1804: Aug – formed in Chester
1805: Chester; Oct – Winchester
1806: Winchester; Jun – Gosport
1807: Gosport; Jun – Guernsey; May – to Ireland; Limerick
1808: Limerick; Apr – Dublin; Sep – Fermoy; Monkstown; to England; Falmouth; to Portugal; PENINSULA; Nov – Lisbon; Dec – Castelo Branco
1809: Santarem; Feb – Bucelas; Apr – Sacavém; May – joined army at Thomar; Jul – Oropesa; TALAVERA; Sep – Montijo
1810: Abrantes; Feb – Portalegre; Apr – Alegrete; May – Portalegre; Jul – Thomar; Aug – Sarzedas; Sep – Busaco; Oct – Alhandra; Nov – Chamusca; Dec – Pinheiro
1811: Arripiado; Thomar; Mar – Campo Maior; Apr – Almendralejo; May – ALBUERA; Almendralejo; Jun – Torre de Mouro; into 2nd Provisional Battalion with 2/66th; Jul – Vila Viçosa; Aug – Portalegre; Sep – Aldea del Obispo; Oct – Arroyo dos Molinos; Condisciera; Dec – Merida
1812: Castelo Branco; Feb – Portalegre; Mar – Merida; Apr – Villafranca de los Barros; May – Almendralejo; Jun – Albuera; Jul – Fuente del Maestre; Sep – Plascencia; Oct – Villa Mouriqua; Nov – Martiago; Dec – Ceclavín
1813: Ceclavín; Feb – Galisteo; Apr – Placencia; May – Calzadilla; Jun – VITTORIA; Huarte (Pamplona); Jul – PYRENEES; Roncesvalles; Pamplona; Nov – NIVELLE; Cambo-les-Bains; Dec – NIVE; Saint Jean Vieux Mouguerre
1814: Saint-Pierre-d'Irube; Feb – Loubieng; ORTHEZ; Mar – Aire-sur-l'Adour; Apr – Toulouse; Castenet-Tolosan; May – Portets; Jun – Bordeaux; Blanquefort; Jul – to Ireland; Cork; Middleton; Sep – to Portsmouth; Oct – disbanded in Portsmouth

Establishments, 1st Battalion 31st Regiment of Foot

Year	Subunits	Field Off	Off/ Staff	Sjts	Mus	Corp/ Pvts	Total
Dec 1792	10co	3	32	22	12	330	399
Apr 1793	10co	3	32	42	22	790	889
Jul 1794	12co	3	38	40	26	740	847
Aug 1795	10co+2r	5	53	62	30	1,010	1,160
Dec 1797	10co	5	32	53	22	600	712
Dec 1798	10co	5	38	53	22	600	718
Dec 1799	10co	5	43	53	22	1,000	1,123
Dec 1801	10co	5	47	53	22	1,000	1,127
Jun 1802	10co	5	33	34	22	750	844
May 1803	10co	5	36	34	22	750	847
Dec 1804	10co	5	36	44	22	800	907
May 1805	10co	5	46	54	22	1,000	1,127
Dec 1806	10co	4	46	54	22	1,000	1,126
Aug 1808	10co+r	4	50	62	26	1,008	1,150
Dec 1809	10co+r	4	40	52	26	808	930
Dec 1811	10co+r	4	40	53	26	808	931
Dec 1813	10co+r	4	39	53	22	808	926
Dec 1814	10co+r	4	49	73	22	1,208	1,356
Dec 1815	10co+r	4	49	63	22	1,008	1,146

Establishments, 2nd Battalion 31st Regiment of Foot

Year	Subunits	Field Off	Off/ Staff	Sjts	Mus	Corp/ Pvts	Total
Dec 1804	10co	3	35	23	22	400	483
Dec 1806	10co	3	35	33	22	600	693
Apr 1807	10co	3	36	43	22	800	904
Aug 1808	10co+r	3	40	51	26	808	928
Dec 1810	10co+r	3	39	41	26	608	717
Dec 1811	10co+r	3	39	42	26	608	718
Dec 1812	10co+r	3	40	52	26	808	929
Dec 1813	10co+r	3	39	52	22	808	924

Service Statistics, 31st Regiment of Foot

	Lieutenant Colonels	Majors
Number of officers in period 1793–1815	14	21
Average age on appointment to substantive rank	34.5	31
Average time in rank in regiment (years)	4	4
Total field officers by nationality	14 E / 10 S / 5 I / 1 F	
Demographics of other ranks 1807	2/31st: 60% EW / 33% I / 7% S	
Months of overseas service 1793–1815	1/31st: 160 2/31st: 72	

Significant Militia/Volunteer Intakes

1799: 4th Lancashire, Leicestershire
1805: East Suffolk
1807: County Kilkenny, County Wicklow
1808: South Cork, County Kilkenny, County Leitrim, County Limerick, County Londonderry, County Sligo, County Wexford
1811: Wiltshire
1812: County Antrim
1813: King's County, County Sligo
1814: County Londonderry, County Sligo

Regimental Colonels

1. *James STUART (1792–1793)*
Born: Lanarkshire c.1730
Relations: Son of Archibald Stuart of Torrance and Elizabeth (Myreton)
Entry to Army: Captain in 56th Foot 1 Nov 1755
Regimental Field Officer Promotions: Major in 56th Foot 30 Jun 1760; Lieutenant Colonel in 56th Foot 25 Feb 1762
Brevets: Brevet Colonel (East Indies) Nov 1775; Brigadier General (East Indies) Aug 1776; Major General 19 Oct 1781; Lieutenant General 29 Apr 1802; General 1 Jan 1812
Colonelcies: 31st Foot 8 Feb 1792 (vice Clarke)
Early Service: Served in Louisburg 1758; served at Belle Île 1761; served in West Indies and at Havana 1761; second in command on Coromandel Coast in East Indies May 1776; Commander in Chief of Madras Army Dec 1776 (until suspended) and 11 Jan 1781 to Jul 1783, lost leg at Pollilore
Residence: Lower Grosvenor Street, St George Hanover Square, London
Died: London 2 Feb 1793
A controversial figure; was twice suspended whilst in command at Madras (the second time permanently) and fought a duel with his nemesis Lord Macartney in Hyde Park in 1786
Sources: ANCB; ANCD; ANCW; ARLI; DINB; A Letter to the Honourable the Directors of the East-India Company from Andrew Stuart, Esq

2. *Rt Hon. Henry PHIPPS, 1st Earl of Mulgrave (1793–1831)*
Born: Yorkshire 1755
Relations: Son of Constantine Phipps, 1st Baron Mulgrave and Hon. Lepell (Hervey); brother of Major General Hon. Edmund Phipps
Education: Eton College
Entry to Army: Ensign in 1st Foot Guards 8 Jun 1775 by purchase
Regimental Field Officer Promotions: Major in 85th Foot 30 Aug 1779 by purchase; Captain and Lieutenant Colonel in 1st Foot Guards 6 Jun 1783 by purchase
Brevets: Brevet Colonel 18 Nov 1790; Major General (Toulon) 23 Oct 1793; Major General 3 Oct 1794; Lieutenant General 1 Jan 1801; General 25 Oct 1809
Colonelcies: 31st Foot 8 Feb 1793 (vice Stuart)
Early Service: Served in North America 1776–1778; Served in West Indies 1780–1781
Service 1793–1815: Commanded British forces at Toulon 1793; Military envoy to Austria 1799; Master General of the Ordnance May 1810 to Dec 1818
Political Career: MP (Totnes) 1784–1790; MP (Scarborough) 1790–1794; Foreign Secretary 11 Jan 1805 to 7 Feb 1806; First Lord of the Admiralty Apr 1807 to Apr 1810
Later Service: Governor of Scarborough Castle 1796–1831; Chancellor of the Duchy of Lancaster 1804–1805; Lord Lieutenant of the East Riding of Yorkshire 1807–1824
Creations and Dignities: 3rd Baron Mulgrave of New Ross (Ire) 10 Oct 1792; 1st Baron Mulgrave of Mulgrave (GB) 12 Aug 1794; 1st Earl of Mulgrave 7 Sep 1812
Awards and Honours: PC 6 Jun 1804; Vice Admiral of Yorkshire 1809–1831; GCB 20 May 1820
Residences: Mulgrave Castle, Lythe, Yorkshire; Fulham, Middlesex
Died: Mulgrave Castle 7 Apr 1831
Sources: ARLI; DINB; HPON; MENA

Lieutenant Colonels

3. *William COTTON (1788–1793)*
Born: Cheshire 1745
Relations: Son of Sir Lynch Salusbury Cotton of Combermere, 4th Bt, and Elizabeth Abigail (Cotton); brother of Admiral Rowland Cotton RN; uncle of General Sir Stapleton-Cotton, 6th Bt, 1st Viscount Combermere
Entry to Army: Ensign in 31st Foot 10 Apr 1765 by purchase
Regimental Field Officer Promotions: Major in 31st Foot 2 Sep 1781 (vice Nesbitt) by purchase; Lieutenant Colonel in 31st Foot 25 Feb 1788 (vice French) by purchase
Early Service: Served in American War of Independence
Service 1793–1815: Commanded 31st Foot 1788–1793
Retired: 29 Sep 1793
Died: Unknown
Many references (all unsourced) show this officer as dying in 1781; however the author has not been able to locate any such proof of death, whereas the William son of Lynch Cotton born 1745 was known to be a lieutenant colonel in the army, and only one officer fitted that criteria
Sources: ARLI; <http://www.cracroftspeerage.co.uk/cottonb1677.htm>

4. *Adam HAY (1794–1796)*
Born: Edinburgh c.1755
Relations: Son of Sir James Hay, 4th Bt of Hayston and Smithfield, and Danielle (Campbell); brother of Sir John Hay, 5th Bt

Entry to Army: Ensign in 31st Foot 1 May 1772 by purchase
Regimental Field Officer Promotions: Major in 31st Foot 31 Oct 1793 (vice Green); Lieutenant Colonel 29 Sep 1794 (vice Cotton) by purchase
Brevets: Brevet Major 18 Nov 1790
Service 1793–1815: Commanded 31st Foot in West Indies 1794–1796; wounded at Vigie May 1796
Residence: Edinburgh, Midlothian
Died: Of fever at Barbados 15 Dec 1796
Sources: ANCB; ANCD; ARLI

5. *Hon. Sir William STEWART (1795)*

Born: Wigtownshire 1774
Relations: Son of John Stewart, 7th Earl of Galloway and Anne (Dashwood); brother of Admiral Sir George Thomas Stewart RN, Viscount Garlies, 8th Earl of Galloway; father of Captain Horatio Stewart
Entry to Army: Ensign in 42nd Foot 8 Mar 1786 by purchase
Regimental Field Officer Promotions: Major in 31st Foot 14 Jan 1795; Lieutenant Colonel in 31st Foot 14 Jan 1795; Lieutenant Colonel in 67th Foot 1 Sep 1795; formed Experimental Corps of Riflemen and first Lieutenant Colonel of that corps 25 Aug 1800
Brevets: Brevet Colonel 2 Apr 1801; Brigadier General (Mediterranean) 25 Jun 1806; Major General 25 Apr 1808; Lieutenant General 4 Jun 1813
Colonelcies: Colonel Commandant 2/95th Foot 31 Aug 1809; Colonel Commandant 1/Rifle Brigade 2 Jul 1818 (vice Spencer)
Service 1793–1815: Served in West Indies 1793–1794; served in Flanders 1795; served in San Domingo 1796; badly wounded at Ferrol 1800; served in Copenhagen 1801; served in Walcheren 1809; commanded brigade in Peninsula Jan to Feb 1810; commanded Cadiz garrison Feb to Jul 1810; commanded 2nd Division in Peninsula Jul 1810 to May 1811, wounded at Albuera; commanded 1st Division in Peninsula Nov 1812 to Mar 1813; commanded 2nd Division in Peninsula Mar 1813 to Apr 1814, wounded at Vittoria and Nivelle
Political Career: MP (Saltash) 1795–1796; MP (Wigtownshire) 1796–1802; MP (Wigtownshire Burghs) 1803–1805; MP (Wigtownshire) 1812–1816
Awards and Honours: AGM (Alb Vit Pyr Nlle Niv Ort); KCTS (Portugal) 5 Jan 1814; KCSF (Spain); GCB 2 Jan 1815
Residence: Cumloden, Wigtownshire
Died: Cumloden 7 Jan 1827
Michael Glover wrote of him, 'as a battalion commander, Stewart was surpassed only by Moore; as a general he was a menace.' He was 'Auld Grog Willie' to his men
Sources: ANCB; ANCD; ARLI; DINB; CHAL; HPON; PHIL; WEOF; WO 25/748

6. *Robert ARBUTHNOTT (1795–1796)*

Born: Midlothian c.1753
Relations: Son of Robert Arbuthnott of Kirkbraehead and Elizabeth Isabella (Riddell); father of Admiral Sir Alexander Dundas Young Arbuthnott; kinsman of General Hon. Hugh Arbuthnott
Entry to Army: Ensign in 1st Foot 10 Dec 1771
Regimental Field Officer Promotions: Lieutenant Colonel in 31st Foot 1 Sep 1795 (vice Stewart)
Service 1793–1815: Served in West Indies 1795–1796; wounded at Vigie May 1796
Residence: Kirkbraehead, Midlothian
Died: West Indies 10 Jul 1796
Sources: ANCB; ANCD; ARLI; The First Battalion, formerly 65th (2nd Yorkshire, North Riding) Regiment, from 1756 to 1884

7. *Charles Edward McMURDO (1796–1803)*

Born: Dumfriesshire 1744
Relations: Son of Robert McMurdo of Drungans, salt market rent arranger, and Philadephia (Douglas); brother of Lieutenant John McMurdo, 37th Foot; and Major George Lewis McMurdo, Dumfriesshire Militia; father of Major Charles Alured McMurdo, 10th Light Dragoons
Entry to Army: Ensign in 3rd Foot 10 Dec 1760 by purchase
Field Officer Promotions: Major in 25th Foot 25 Feb 1795; Lieutenant Colonel in 31st Foot 10 Aug 1796 (vice Arbuthnott)
Brevets: Brevet Lieutenant Colonel 31 Mar 1795; Brevet Colonel 29 Apr 1802
Early Service: Brigade Major in Jamaica 1787–1795
Service 1793–1815: Deputy Quartermaster General in Cape of Good Hope 1795
Retired: Retaining rank 24 Mar 1803
Residence: Cumberland Street, Edinburgh, Midlothian
Died: Edinburgh 11 Apr 1826
Sources: ANCD; ARLI; WEOF; WikiTree

8. *William Rickart HEPBURN (1796–1799)*

Born: Kincardineshire 1760
Relations: Son of Lieutenant Colonel Robert Rickart Hepburn of Rickarton MP, and Magdalene (Murray)

Entry to Army: Ensign in 51st Foot 3 Jun 1774
Regimental Field Officer Promotions: Major in 31st Foot 1 Sep 1795; Lieutenant Colonel in 31st Foot 16 Dec 1796; Captain and Lieutenant Colonel in Coldstream Foot Guards 17 Oct 1799 (vice Gower) by exchange
Service 1793–1815: Commanded 31st Foot in West Indies 1796–1797
Retired: 18 Oct 1799
Residences: Rickarton House, near Stonehaven, Kincardineshire; Oxford Street, London
Died: London 13 Jan 1807
Sources: ANCB; ANCD; ANCW; ARLI; SCMA (1807)

9. *John LEVESON-GOWER (1799)*

Born: Berkshire 1774
Relations: Son of Rear Admiral Hon. John Leveson-Gower of Bill Hill and Frances (Boscawen); cousin of Rt Hon. Granville Leveson-Gower, Earl Granville
Education: Harrow School
Entry to Army: Ensign in 2/1st Foot 9 Feb 1791 by purchase
Regimental Field Officer Promotions: Major in New South Wales Corps 21 Feb 1794 (vice Vansittart) by purchase; Lieutenant Colonel in 63rd Foot 8 Jul 1794 (vice Stewart) by purchase; Captain and Lieutenant Colonel in Coldstream Foot Guards 17 Jan 1799 (vice Calvert) by exchange; Lieutenant Colonel in 31st Foot 17 Oct 1799 (vice Hepburn) by exchange; to half-pay of 111th Foot 19 Dec 1799
Brevets: Brevet Lieutenant Colonel 2 Jul 1794; Brevet Colonel 1 Jan 1800; Major General 30 Oct 1805; Lieutenant General 1 Jan 1812
Colonelcies: 10th Garrison Battalion 27 Aug 1803
Early Service: Served in Gibraltar
Service 1793–1815: Served in West Indies 1793–1794; served in Netherlands 1794–1795; served in West Indies 1795–1796; served in Helder 1799; ADC to King George III 1800; second in command at Buenos Aires 1807; did not hold command again
Political Career: MP (Truro) 1796–1802
Residence: Bill Hill, near Wokingham, Berkshire
Died: Bill Hill 14 Sep 1816
Sources: ANCB; ANCD; ANCW; ARLI; HPON; WEOF; WO 25/745

10. *Sir Ronald Craufurd FERGUSON (1799–1801)*

Born: Edinburgh 1773
Relations: Son of William Ferguson of Raith and Jane (Craufurd); son-in-law of General Sir Hector Munro; father of Colonel Robert Munro Ferguson, 79th Foot
Entry to Army: Ensign in 53rd Foot 3 Apr 1790 by purchase
Regimental Field Officer Promotions: Major in 84th Foot 31 May 1794; Lieutenant Colonel in 84th Foot 18 Sep 1794; Lieutenant Colonel in Minorca Regiment 8 Aug 1799; Lieutenant Colonel in 31st Foot 19 Dec 1799; Lieutenant Colonel in Duke of York's Own Banffshire Fencibles 10 Apr 1801; to half-pay of 93rd Foot 1802
Brevets: Brevet Colonel 1 Jan 1800; Brigadier General (home staff) 1804; Major General 25 Apr 1808; Lieutenant General 4 Jun 1813; General 22 Jul 1830
Colonelcies: Sicilian Regiment 25 Jan 1809 (vice Sherbrooke); 79th Foot 24 Mar 1828 (vice Cameron)
Service 1793–1815: Served in Flanders 1793–1794; served at capture of Cape of Good Hope 1795; served in East Indies 1796–1799; served in Ferrol 1800; commanded brigade at capture of Cape of Good Hope 1806; commanded brigade in Peninsula Aug and Sep 1808; second in command in Cadiz May to Oct 1810; commanded division in Netherlands 1814
Political Career: MP (Kirkcaldy) 1806–1830; MP (Nottingham) 1830–1841
Awards and Honours: AGM (Rol Vim); KCB 2 Jan 1815; GCB 13 Sep 1831
Residence: Bolton Row, Piccadilly, London
Died: London 10 Mar 1841
Sources: ARLI; CHAL; HPON; PHIL; WEBC; WEOF; WO 25/745

11. *Hon. Robert MEADE (1801–1808)*

Born: County Down 1772
Relations: Son of John Meade, 1st Earl of Clanwilliam and Theodosia Hawkins (Magill); brother of Lieutenant General Hon. John Meade; and Richard Meade, 2nd Earl of Clanwilliam
Entry to Army: Ensign in 2/1st Foot 7 Nov 1787
Regimental Field Officer Promotions: Major in Ward's Regiment of Foot 30 Oct 1794; Lieutenant Colonel in Macdonell's Regiment 10 Mar 1795; to half-pay 1 Mar 1798; Lieutenant Colonel in 31st Foot 10 Apr 1801
Brevets: Brevet Colonel 29 Apr 1802; Major General (Madeira) 21 Jul 1808; Major General 25 Oct 1809; Lieutenant General 4 Jun 1814; General 10 Jan 1837
Colonelcies: 12th Foot 9 Oct 1823 (vice Hastings)
Service 1793–1815: Served in Flanders 1794–1795; commanded 31st Foot 1803–1808; served in Sicily 1806–1807; lost eye in Egypt 1807; commanded forces in Madeira 1808; acting Governor of Cape Colony 18 Oct 1813 to 7 Jan 1814

Residence: Bryanston Square, Marylebone, London
Died: London 11 Jul 1852
Sources: ANCD; ANCW; ARLI; PHIL; WEOF; WOST; WO 25/747

12. *Henry Pasley BRUCE (1803–1815)*

Born: British East Indies 1776
Relations: Son of Colonel Thomas Bruce, Madras service and Sarah (Meetkerke); brother of Major General Sir Charles Bruce; son-in-law of General Alexander Cuppage RA
Entry to Army: Ensign in 105th Foot 23 Apr 1794 by purchase
Regimental Field Officer Promotions: Major in 9th Foot 12 Jun 1800 (vice Charlton) by purchase; Major in 31st Foot 23 Dec 1800 (vice Marriott) by exchange; Lieutenant Colonel in 31st Foot 24 Mar 1803 (vice McMurdo) by purchase; removed from the regiment as a general officer 1815
Brevets: Brevet Colonel 1 Jan 1812; Major General 4 Jun 1814; Lieutenant General 22 Jul 1830
Service 1793–1815: Served in West Indies 1796; served in Portugal 1797; served in Egypt 1801; commanded 2/31st Foot on raising 1804; commanded 1/31st Foot 1808–1814
Residence: Winchmore Hall, near Enfield, Middlesex
Died: Enfield 30 Oct 1837
Sources: ANCD; ARLI; PHIL; WEOF

13. *William Howe CAMPBELL (1804–1809)*

Born: [spec.] England c.1767
Relations: Reputedly of the Campbells of Corries
Entry to Army: Ensign in 65th Foot 31 May 1784 by purchase
Regimental Field Officer Promotions: Major in 35th Foot 11 Dec 1800 (vice Quin) by purchase; Lieutenant Colonel in 35th Foot 10 Aug 1801 (vice McAlister) by purchase; to half-pay of 35th Foot 25 Oct 1802; Lieutenant Colonel in 31st Foot 28 Aug 1804; Lieutenant Colonel in 15th Portuguese Line 17 Apr 1809
Brevets: Brigadier General in Portuguese army 1 May 1809; Brevet Colonel 25 Jul 1810
Service 1793–1815: Served in West Indies 1794–1795; served in Helder 1799; served in Malta 1800; commanded 2/31st Foot in Peninsular Nov 1808 to Mar 1809; served in Peninsula with Portuguese army Apr 1809 to Jan 1811
Died: Of fever in Turcifal, Portugal 2 Jan 1811
This officer's widow and sole daughter later became keen amateur archaeologists in Inverness and Nairn; his daughter eventually became the leader of the English clique in Ajaccio, Corsica
Sources: ANCW; ARLI; CHAL; HALL; WEOF

14. *Sir Alexander LEITH (1811–1815)*

Born: Aberdeenshire 1774
Relations: Son of Alexander Leith of Freefield and Glenkindie, and Mary Elizabeth (Gordon); father of General Robert William Disney Leith; and Major James Leith, 14th Light Dragoons
Entry to Army: Ensign in 42nd Foot 8 Aug 1792 by purchase
Regimental Field Officer Promotions: Major in 31st Foot 1 Aug 1804; Lieutenant Colonel in 31st Foot 7 Feb 1811; to half pay of 48th Foot 25 May 1815
Brevets: Brevet Colonel 12 Aug 1819; Major General 22 Jul 1830; Lieutenant General 23 Nov 1841; General 20 Jun 1854
Colonelcies: 90th Foot 2 Sep 1841 (vice Keating); 31st Foot 14 Jun 1853 (vice Dacre)
Service 1793–1815: Served in Flanders in 1793; served in West Indies 1796; served in Helder 1799, lost eye at Alkmaar; served in Egypt 1807; commanded 2/31st Foot in Peninsula Apr 1812 to Apr 1814, wounded at Nive
Awards and Honours: AGC (Vit Pyr Nlle Niv Ort); KCB 2 Jan 1815
Residence: Freefield House, near North Rayne, Aberdeenshire
Died: Freefield House 19 Feb 1859
Sources: ANCB; ANCD; ANCW; ARLI; CHAL; PHIL; WEOF

15. *George Guy Carleton L'ESTRANGE (1815–1823)*

Born: King's County 1780
Relations: Son of Henry Peisley L'Estrange of Moystown and Mary (Carleton); brother of Colonel Henry Peisley L'Estrange, King's County Militia; cousin of Captain William Henry L'Estrange, 11th Foot; and Major Edmund L'Estrange, 71st Foot
Education: Rugby College
Entry to Army: Ensign in 6th Foot 1 Apr 1798 by purchase
Field Officer Promotions: Major in 98th Foot 22 May 1804; Major in 31st Foot 21 Apr 1808 (vice Stafford) by exchange; Lieutenant Colonel in 26th Foot 10 Dec 1812 (vice Hogge); Lieutenant Colonel in 31st Foot 8 Jun 1815 (vice Wauchope) by exchange; to half-pay unattached 5 May 1823 (vice Fearon) by exchange
Brevets: Brevet Lieutenant Colonel 30 May 1811; Brevet Colonel 19 Jul 1821; Major General 22 Jul 1830; Lieutenant General 23 Nov 1841
Colonelcies: 95th Foot 12 Jun 1843 (vice Buchan);

61st Foot 29 Mar 1848 (vice Dickson)
Service 1793–1815: Served in Peninsula with 31st Foot Nov 1808 to May 1812; on Deputy Adjutant General staff early 1809; commanded 1/26th Foot Dec 1812 to Jun 1815
Later Service: Commanded 31st Foot at Peterloo massacre 1819; Deputy Adjutant General in Mauritius 1826
Awards and Honours: AGM (Alb); CB 4 Jun 1815
Residences: South Audley Street, Mayfair, London; Moystown, King's County
Died: Nidd Hall, Knaresborough, Yorkshire 26 Aug 1848
Sources: ANCW; ARLI; CHAL; PHIL; WEMR; WEOF

16. *William WAUCHOPE (1815)*

Born: Edinburgh 1780
Relations: Son of Captain Andrew Wauchope of Niddrie and Alicia (Baird); brother of Lieutenant Colonel Andrew Wauchope, 20th Foot; nephew of General Sir David Baird
Entry to Army: Ensign in 93rd Foot 14 Apr 1803
Field Officer Promotions: Major in Meuron's Regiment 14 Jan 1813 (vice Zweifel) by purchase; Lieutenant Colonel in 48th Foot 8 Dec 1813 (vice Brooke) by purchase; to half-pay of 48th Foot 24 Oct 1814; Lieutenant Colonel in 31st Foot 25 May 1815 (vice Leith) by exchange; Lieutenant Colonel in 26th Foot 8 Jun 1815 (vice L'Estrange) by exchange; to half-pay of Watteville's Regiment 23 Oct 1817 (vice Oglander) by exchange
Service 1793–1815: ADC to Thomas Maitland in Ceylon 1809
Residences: Genoa, Liguria, Italy
Died: Genoa Apr 1825
Sources: ANCB; ANCD; ARLI; PHIL; History and Genealogy of the Family of Wauchope of Niddrie-Merschell

Majors

17. *Sir Charles GREEN, 1st Bt (1788–1793)*

Born: Gibraltar 1749
Relations: Son of Captain Christopher Green, 31st Foot, and Britania Maria (Hamilton); brother of Major General Christopher Green, Bengal service; and Lieutenant Nicholas Green, 37th Foot
Education: Royal Military Academy, Woolwich
Entry to Army: Gentleman cadet in RA 1760; Volunteer in 31st Foot; Ensign in 31st Foot 10 Aug 1765
Regimental Field Officer Promotions: Major in 31st Foot 25 Feb 1788 (vice Cotton) by purchase; Lieutenant Colonel in 85th Foot 30 Oct 1793; Lieutenant Colonel in 30th Foot 19 Feb 1794 (vice Maxwell) by exchange
Brevets: Brevet Major 19 Mar 1783; Brevet Colonel 26 Jan 1797; Brigadier General (Leeward Islands) 11 Oct 1798; Brigadier General (Ireland) 1803; Major General 25 Sep 1803; Lieutenant General 25 Oct 1809; General 12 Aug 1819
Colonelcies: York Light Infantry Volunteers 16 Jan 1804; 16th Foot 29 Aug 1808 (vice Bowyer); 37th Foot 17 Feb 1814 (vice Ross)
Early Service: Served in Florida 1766–1771; served in served in West Indies 1771–1773; served in American War of Independence 1776–1778, taken POW at Saratoga
Service 1793–1815: Commanded 30th Foot in Corsica 1794; Lieutenant Governor of Grenada 9 Mar 1797 to 8 Jun 1801; temporary Commander in Chief Windward and Leeward Islands Nov 1803 to Apr 1804; commanded forces in capture of Surinam Apr 1804; Governor of Surinam 9 May 1804 to 15 Apr 1805; commander of Malta garrison May 1807 to May 1808; commanded districts on home staff 1812–1814
Awards and Honours: Knight Bachelor 4 May 1803
Creations and Dignities: 1st Baronet of Milnrow 30 Nov 1805
Residence: Cheltenham, Gloucestershire
Died: Cheltenham 12 Jul 1831
Sources: ARLI; DEBA; GEMA (1831); PHIL; WEOF; WOST

18. *Randolph MARRIOTT (1797–1801)*

Born: Yorkshire 1770
Relations: Son of Randolph Marriott of Avonbank and Elizabeth (Wilson); brother of Lieutenant General Thomas Marriott, Madras service; Commander George Marriott RN; Captain Richard Marriott, Madras service; and Major Charles Marriott, Madras service
Entry to Army: Ensign in Independent Company 20 Mar 1794 by purchase
Regimental Field Officer Promotions: Major in 31st Foot 17 Jan 1797 (vice Hepburne); Major in 9th Foot 27 Jan 1801 (vice Bruce) via exchange; Lieutenant Colonel in 9th Foot 14 Nov 1801 (vice Sandeman) by purchase; to half-pay of 9th Foot 25 Jun 1802; Lieutenant Colonel in 11th Battalion of Reserve 11 Jul 1803; Lieutenant Colonel in 24th Foot 1 Sep 1804 (vice Blake); removed from the regiment as a general officer 1814
Brevets: Brevet Colonel 25 Jul 1810; Major General 4 Jun 1813
Service 1793–1815: Served in West Indies 1796–1797; served in Helder 1799; served in Ferrol 1800;

wounded and POW at sea on way to Cape of Good Hope Jul 1808; released Dec 1808; served in British East Indies 1809–1813
Residences: Avonbank, near Pershore, Worcestershire; Newton House, near Monmouth, Herefordshire
Died: 9 Mar 1821
Sources: ARLI; GHHC; PHIL; WEOF; WO 25/747

19. *George FEARON (1795–1796)*
Born: Cumberland c.1760
Relations: Son of Captain Peter Fearon and Mary (Vandome); uncle of Major Robert Brice Fearon, 31st Foot; and Captain Peter Fearon, 31st Foot
Entry to Army: Ensign in 31st Foot 21 Feb 1776
Regimental Field Officer Promotions: Major in 31st Foot 2 Sep 1795
Brevets: Brevet Lieutenant Colonel 22 Sep 1796
Service 1793–1815: Deputy Quartermaster General in Leeward Islands Sep 1796
Residence: Brigham, Cumberland
Died: Martinique 9 Dec 1796
Sources: ANCB; ANCD; ARLI; Dublin Gazette 1796

20. *John SMITH (1796–1803)*
Born: Yorkshire c.1755
Relations: Father of Lieutenant William Slater Smith, 13th Light Dragoons
Entry to Army: Ensign in 57th Foot 3 Dec 1783
Regimental Field Officer Promotions: Major in 31st Foot 31 Oct 1796 (vice Fearon) by purchase; Lieutenant Colonel in 6th Garrison Battalion 9 Jul 1803; Lieutenant Colonel in 2nd Garrison Battalion 25 Feb 1805
Brevets: Brevet Lieutenant Colonel 29 Apr 1802
Service 1793–1815: Deputy Judge Advocate General in Leeward Islands 22 Sep 1796
Residence: Bray, Berkshire
Died: Bray 31 Oct 1809
Sources: ANCW; ARLI; SCMA (1809)

21. *Merrick SHAWE (1803–1804)*
Born: County Galway 1772
Relations: Natural son of Matthew Shawe of the Lodge and Jane (Fersse); half-brother of Lieutenant Colonel Matthew Shawe, 87th Foot; Lieutenant Henry Shawe, 74th Foot; and Captain Charles Fielding Shawe, 6th Foot
Entry to Army: Ensign in 1st Connaught Fencibles Sep 1787; Ensign in 73rd Foot 15 Nov 1788
Regimental Field Officer Promotions: Major in 31st Foot 24 Mar 1803 (vice Smith) by purchase; Lieutenant Colonel in 3rd Foot 29 Dec 1804 (vice Brownrigg) by purchase; to half-pay of 1st Garrison Battalion 6 Feb 1805; Lieutenant Colonel in 5th Garrison Battalion 11 Aug 1808 (vice Macdonald) by exchange; Lieutenant Colonel in 76th Foot 3 Feb 1809 (vice Symes)
Service 1793–1815: Served in British East Indies 1790–1806; confidential secretary to Richard Wellesley in India; served in Walcheren 1809; commanded 76th Foot 1809–1810; Assistant secretary to the Duke of York 1815
Retired: 17 May 1810
Residences: Kingstown, Dublin
Died: Kingstown 7 Nov 1843
Sources: ANCB; ANCD; ARLI; WEOF; WO 25/748

22. *George Augustus TONYN (1804–1819)*
Born: Buckinghamshire c.1762
Relations: Son of General Patrick George Tonyn and Maria (Willing); nephew of Major John Columbine Tonyn, Madras service; and Captain George Anthony Tonyn RN
Entry to Army: Ensign in 39th Foot 25 Sep 1787 by purchase
Regimental Field Officer Promotions: Major in 31st Foot 2 Aug 1804; to half-pay of 95th Foot 26 Aug 1819 (vice Tovey) by exchange
Brevets: Brevet Lieutenant Colonel 4 Jun 1811
Residence: Ramsgate, Kent
Died: Ramsgate 1 Apr 1832
Sources: ANCW; ARLI; PHIL; UNSM (1832); WEOF

23. *Sir James [KYRLE] MONEY, 1st Bt (1804–1805)*
Born: James Money in County Durham 1775; changed surname to Kyrle Money by Royal License 1809
Relations: Son of Captain William Kyrle Money of Stockton on Tees, 43rd Foot, and Mary (Webster); brother of Captain Rowland Money RN; Rev. Kyrle Ernle Money, Prelector and Prebendary of Hereford Cathedral; and Commander John Money, EIC Navy
Entry to Army: Ensign in 84th Foot 2 Nov 1793
Field Officer Promotions: Major in Armstrong's Recruiting Corps 28 Sep 1804; Major in 31st Foot 28 Sep 1804; to half-pay of 14th Garrison Battalion 4 Apr 1805 (vice Arbuthnot) by exchange; Major in 21st Foot 22 Aug 1805 (vice Tayler) by exchange; to half-pay of Armstrong's Recruiting Corps 9 Jun 1808 (vice Armstong) by exchange
Brevets: Brevet Lieutenant Colonel 4 Jun 1811; Brevet Colonel 27 May 1825; Major General 10 Jan 1837
Creations and Dignities: 1st Baronet of Homme House in Herefordshire, Whetham in Wiltshire and Pitsford in Northamptonshire 30 Jun 1838
Residence: Homme House, Much Marcle,

Herefordshire
Died: Gloucester 26 Jun 1843
Sources: ANCW; ARLI; WEOF; WikiTree

24. *John STAFFORD (1804–1808)*

Born: [spec.] East Indies c.1783
Relations: Son of Lieutenant General Hugh Stafford, Bengal service, and Thomasine (Sullivan); brother of Major Edward Stafford, 31st Foot; father of Major General Boyle Torriano Stafford, Bengal service; and Major General William Joseph Fitzmaurice Stafford, Bengal Staff Corps
Entry to Army: Ensign in 31st Foot 14 Apr 1798 by purchase
Regimental Field Officer Promotions: Major in 31st Foot 29 Dec 1804 by purchase; Major in 98th Foot 21 Apr 1808 by exchange; Major in 63rd Foot 4 Apr 1811 (vice L'Estrange) by exchange; to half-pay of Bourbon Regiment 13 Apr 1815 (vice Briscoe) by exchange
Brevets: Brevet Lieutenant Colonel 4 Jun 1811; Brevet Colonel 27 May 1825; Major General 10 Jan 1837
Residence: Semur-en-Auxois, Côte-d'Or, France
Died: Semur-en-Auxois 2 Feb 1846
Sources: ANCW; ARLI; GHHI; PHIL; WEOF

25. *Hon. Sir Hugh ARBUTHNOTT (1805)*

Born: Angusshire 1780
Relations: Son of John Arbuthnott, 7th Viscount Arbuthnott, and Isabella (Graham); brother of John Arbuthnott, 8th Viscount Arbuthnott; kinsman of Lieutenant Colonel Robert Arbuthnott, 31st Foot
Entry to Army: Ensign in 49th Foot 19 May 1796 by purchase
Regimental Field Officer Promotions: Major in 14th Garrison Battalion 23 Nov 1804 (vice Gordon); to half-pay of 14th Garrison Battalion Feb 1805; Major in 31st Foot 4 Apr 1805 (vice Money) by exchange; Major in 52nd Foot 25 April 1805 (vice Burdett) by exchange; Lieutenant Colonel in 52nd Foot 9 May 1811 (vice Barclay); to half-pay of 52nd Foot 8 Apr 1813
Brevets: Brevet Lieutenant Colonel 2 May 1811; Major General 22 Jul 1830; Lieutenant General 23 Nov 1841; General 20 Jun 1854
Colonelcies: 38th Foot 4 Apr 1843 (vice Nicolls); 79th Foot 14 Mar 1862 (vice Sewell)
Service 1793–1815: Served in Helder 1799; served in Copenhagen 1801; served in British North America 1802–1805; served in Peninsula with 1/52nd Foot Aug 1808 to Jan 1809; again in Peninsula with 1/52nd Jul 1809 to Nov 1810; commanded 1/52nd Foot in Peninsula Aug to Nov 1810; commanded 2/52nd Foot in Peninsula Apr to Jul 1811
Awards and Honours: AGM (Bus); CB 8 Dec 1815; NGSM (Cop 01); MGSM (Cor FDO); KCB 10 Nov 1862
Residence: Piccadilly, London
Died: London 11 Jun 1868
Sources: ANCB; ANCD; ARLI; CHAL; PHIL; WEOF; WO 25/744

26. *Sir Bagenal William BURDETT, 3rd Bt (1805–1806)*

Born: County Carlow 1770
Relations: Son of Sir William Vigors Burdett, 2nd Bt, and Henrietta (O'Brien)
Entry to Army: Ensign in 52nd Foot 1 Apr 1792 by purchase
Regimental Field Officer Promotions: Major in 52nd Foot 14 Aug 1804; Major in 31st Foot 25 Apr 1805 (vice Arbuthnott) by exchange; Major in 8th Garrison Battalion 15 Jan 1806
Retired: 25 Nov 1806
Residence: Cheltenham, Gloucestershire
Died: Cheltenham 12 Dec 1840
Sources: ANCB; ANCD; ANCW; ARLI; WEOF

27. *John Williams WATSON (1806–1810)*

Born: London 1780
Relations: Son of David Watson of Ruislip and Mary (Dixon)
Entry to Army: Ensign in 66th Foot 14 Mar 1800 by purchase
Regimental Field Officer Promotions: Major in 31st Foot 15 Jan 1807; Lieutenant Colonel in Dillon's Regiment 6 Dec 1810 (vice Perponcher) by purchase
Service 1793–1815: Served in West Indies 1801–1802; served in Egypt 1807; served in Peninsula Nov 1808 to Jun 1810, commanded 2/31st at Talavera
Awards and Honours: AGM (Tal)
Residence: Dorking, Surrey
Died: Tarragona, Spain 22 Jan 1814
This officer's death is not recorded in Challis' Index, nor in Hall's Biographical Dictionary of Officers in the Peninsula (non-combat section)
Sources: ANCB; ANCD; ANCW; ARLI; CHAL; WEOF; WO 25/748

28. *Robert Bryce FEARON (1810–1823)*

Born: Québec 1783
Relations: Son of Charles George Fearon and Ann (Phillips); brother of Captain Peter Fearon, 31st Foot / 7th *Caçadores*; nephew of Major George Fearon, 31st Foot

Entry to Army: Ensign in 88th Foot 12 Nov 1794
Regimental Field Officer Promotions: Major in 31st Foot 20 Dec 1810 (vice Watson) by purchase; Lieutenant Colonel unattached 24 Apr 1824; Lieutenant Colonel in 31st Foot 5 May 1828 (vice L'Estrange) by exchange; Lieutenant Colonel in 64th Foot 12 Jan 1826 (vice Battersby) by exchange; Lieutenant Colonel in 6th Foot 1 May 1828 (vice Napier); Lieutenant Colonel in 40th Foot 23 Nov 1838 (vice Powell) by exchange; Lieutenant Colonel in 21st Foot 5 Dec 1843 (vice Walker)
Brevets: Brevet Lieutenant Colonel 12 Aug 1819; Brevet Colonel 10 Jan 1837; Major General 9 Nov 1846
Service 1793–1815: Served in West Indies 1796–1797; served in Helder 1799; served in Ferrol and Cadiz 1800; served in Egypt 1807; served in Italy 1814–1815
Later Service: Deputy Adjutant General in Madras 1829–1842
Awards and Honours: CB 2 Apr 1825
Residence: Plymouth, Devon
Died: Committed suicide at Much Hadham, Hertfordshire 26 Jan 1851
Sources: ANCW; ARLI; PHIL; WEOF; WikiTree

29. *John Stewart HAWKSHAW (1811–1814)*

Born: County Down 1776
Relations: Son of William Hawkshaw of Newry and Eleanora (Johnston); nephew of Captain Thomas Hawkshaw, 5th Foot; and Commander Hugh Hawkshaw RN; brother of Lieutenant Colonel Edward Hawkshaw, 3rd Foot / 7th *Caçadores*
Entry to Army: Ensign in 31st Foot 31 Aug 1793
Regimental Field Officer Promotions: Major in 31st Foot 7 Feb 1811; to half-pay of 31st Foot 1814; Major in 91st Foot 1 Jun 1815 (vice Gregorson) by exchange; to half-pay of 91st Foot 20 Jun 1816
Brevets: Brevet Lieutenant Colonel 12 Aug 1819
Service 1793–1815: Served in Peninsula Jun 1811 to Nov 1813; served in Peninsula Apr 1814
Residence: Blairs Lodge, County Down
Died: Blairs Lodge 10 Feb 1848
Sources: ANCD; ARLI; PHIL; WEOF; <https://atkinsonofcavangarden.wordpress.com/hawkshaw-m-atkinson/>

30. *Michael COAST (1812–1814)*

Born: Kent 1779
Relations: Son of William Stacey Coast of Chartham and Hester (Lade); father of Captain Michael William Lade Coast, Rifle Brigade
Entry to Army: Ensign in 31st Foot 13 Jul 1797
Field Officer Promotions: Major in 31st Foot 31 Dec 1812 (vice L'Estrange) by purchase; to half-pay of 31st Foot 25 Oct 1814; Major in 21st Foot 16 Jun 1815 (vice Pringle) by exchange; to half-pay of 21st Foot 25 Feb 1816
Residence: Walmer, Kent
Died: Walmer May 1830
Sources: ANCB; ARLI; FMPD; PHIL; WEOF

Selected Regimental Histories

Cannon, Richard, *Historical Record of the Thirty-first, or, the Huntingdonshire Regiment of Foot (1702-1850): An Account of the Formation of the Regiment in 1702, and of Its Subsequent Services to 1850* (London: Parker, Furnivall, & Parker, 1850)

Regimental Museum

Queen's & Princess of Wales's Royal Regiment Regimental Museum, Dover Castle, Dover, Kent

---

32nd Regiment of Foot

Secondary Title:	Cornwall
Jacket:	Red
Facings:	White
Motto:	One and all

Regimental Lineage, 32nd Regiment of Foot

1702:	Feb – raised by Colonel Edward Fox as Fox's Regiment of Marines
1713:	Disbanded
1714:	Re-raised as Borr's Regiment of Foot
1723:	Dubourgay's Regiment of Foot
1732:	Paget's Regiment of Foot
1738:	Descury's Regiment of Foot

1740: Huske's Regiment of Foot
1743: Skelton's Regiment of Foot
1745: Douglas's Regiment of Foot
1747: Ranked as 32nd Regiment of Foot
1747: Leighton's Regiment of Foot
1751: 32nd Regiment of Foot
1782: 32nd (Cornwall) Regiment of Foot
1804: Aug – 2nd Battalion formed in Launceston
1814: Oct – 2nd Battalion disbanded in Omagh
1858: 32nd (Cornwall) Regiment of Foot (Light Infantry)
1881: Duke of Cornwall's Light Infantry (on amalgamation with 46th (South Devonshire) Regiment of Foot)
1959: Somerset and Cornwall Light Infantry (on amalgamation with the Somerset Light Infantry)
1968: 1st Battalion, The Light Infantry (on amalgamation with the King's Own Yorkshire Light Infantry, the King's Shropshire Light Infantry and the Durham Light Infantry)
1993: The Light Infantry (reduced to two battalions)
2007: 3rd or 5th Battalion, The Rifles (on amalgamation with 1st Battalion, The Light Infantry, 1st Battalion, Devonshire and Dorset Light Infantry, 1st Battalion Royal Gloucestershire, Berkshire and Wiltshire Light Infantry, and Royal Green Jackets)

Service History, 1st Battalion 32nd Regiment of Foot

1793: Gibraltar; to West Indies; Jun – eight companies in Barbados, two companies in Tobago
1794: Eight companies in Barbados, two companies in Tobago; Feb – men drafted into other regiments, officers and cadre home to England; Jul – Guernsey; Portsmouth
1795: Plymouth; Aug – to Ireland; Cork; Sep – put down mutiny of 105th and 113th Foot; to West Indies, delayed by storms
1796: At sea off Ireland; Feb – to West Indies; May – San Domingo; St Nicolas Mole; Jun – Bombarde
1797: San Domingo; Sep – Bahamas
1798: Bahamas; New Providence
1799: New Providence; Dec – to England
1800: Feb – Liverpool; Mar – Abingdon; Jul – Launceston and Newport; Nov – Bridgewater
1801: Bridgewater; Apr – Bristol; to Ireland; Waterford; May – Dundalk; Jul – Kilkenny
1802: Kilkenny; Apr – Dublin
1803: Dublin; Jul – Dublin uprising; Sep – Enniskillen
1804: Enniskillen; Apr – Longford; Aug – Curragh camp; Oct – Longford
1805: Loughrea; Jun – Bandon; Oct – Kinsale; Charles Fort; ordered on foreign service; did not embark
1806: Charles Fort
1807: Charles Fort; Jul – to England; Deal; to Copenhagen; Nov – Deal; Dec – Portsmouth; ordered on secret expedition but did not embark
1808: Falmouth; Jun – Gibraltar, headquarters to Sicily; Cadiz; Aug – to Portugal; PENINSULA; ROLICA; VIMIERO; Oct – into Spain; Castelo Branco; Ciudad Rodrigo; Nov – Salamanca; Dec – Mayorga; Astorga
1809: Retreat to Corunna; CORUNNA; to England; Feb – Horsham; Jul – Downs; Aug – Portsmouth; Sep – Walcheren; Middelburg; Dec – to England
1810: Horsham; Feb – Hailsham; Aug – Bexhill; grand review at Brighton; Sep – Portsmouth; Oct – Guernsey
1811: Guernsey; Jun – to Portugal; Jul – Lisbon; Aug – Villar de Ciervo; Sep – Espeja; Oct – Cheiras; Dec – Mesquitela

1812:	Marialva; Nave de Haver; Feb – Meada; Mar – Almendralejo; Llerena; Apr – Pedrógão; May – Castelo Branco; Villa del Rey; Jul – Salamanca forts; SALAMANCA; Nava de Arévalo; Aug – Olmedo; Sep – siege of Burgos; Oct – retreat from Burgos; Dueñas; Nov – Barquilla; Dec – Santiago
1813:	Santiago; Feb – Travancinha; May – Malhadas; Jun – Mondragón; Jul – San Estevan; Vittoria; blockade of Pamplona; Aug – PYRENEES; pass of Maya; Nov – NIVELLE; Ustaritz; Dec – NIVE; Villefranque
1814:	Villefranque; Feb – ORTHEZ; Mar – Cazères-sur-l'Adour; Apr – Auch; May – Pavie; Jun – Bordeaux; to Ireland; Jul – Cork; Middleton; Aug – Fermoy; Nov – Cork
1815:	Cork; ordered to North America, countermanded; Apr – Monkstown; to Belgium; May – Ostend; Jun – Brussels; Quatre Bras; WATERLOO; Jul – Paris; Allied Army of Occupation; Dec – Calais; to England; Dover

Service History, 2nd Battalion 32nd Regiment of Foot

1804:	Aug – formed in Launceston
1805:	Launceston
1806:	Launceston
1807:	Launceston; Jun – received colours; Aug – Weeley
1808:	Weeley; May – Tilbury Fort; Dec – Guernsey
1809:	Guernsey; Mar – to Ireland; Monkstown; Fermoy
1810:	Fermoy; Mar – Cork
1811:	Cork; Jul – Omagh
1812:	Omagh
1813:	Omagh
1814:	Cavan; Jun – Omagh; Oct – disbanded in Omagh

Establishments, 1st Battalion 32nd Regiment of Foot

Year	Subunits	Field Off	Off/ Staff	Sjts	Mus	Corp/ Pvts	Total
Dec 1792	10co	3	32	22	12	330	399
Jan 1793	10co	3	32	32	22	600	689
Aug 1795	10co+2r	5	53	62	30	1,010	1,160
Dec 1797	10co	5	38	53	22	600	718
Apr 1801	10co	5	43	53	22	1,000	1,123
Jul 1802	10co	5	33	34	22	750	844
Feb 1805	10co	5	36	44	22	800	907
Jul 1807	10co	4	36	44	22	800	906
Oct 1807	10co	4	46	54	22	1,000	1,126
Dec 1809	10co	4	36	44	22	800	906
Dec 1810	10co	4	46	54	22	1,000	1,126
Dec 1811	10co	4	46	55	22	1,000	1,127
Jul 1814	10co	5	46	55	22	1,000	1,128
Dec 1815	10co	4	46	45	22	800	917

Establishments, 2nd Battalion 32nd Regiment of Foot

Year	Subunits	Field Off	Off/ Staff	Sjts	Mus	Corp/ Pvts	Total
Dec 1804	10co	3	35	23	22	400	483
Oct 1807	10co	3	35	33	22	600	693
Dec 1807	10co	3	35	23	22	400	483
Sep 1808	10co	3	35	23	22	600	683
Dec 1808	10co	3	35	33	22	600	693
Sep 1810	10co	3	35	34	22	600	694
Jun 1811	10co	3	35	24	22	400	484
Dec 1813	10co	3	35	25	22	400	485

Service Statistics, 32nd Regiment of Foot

	Lieutenant Colonels	Majors
Number of officers in period 1793–1815	9	23
Average age on appointment to substantive rank	35	35
Average time in rank in regiment (years)	9	4
Total field officers by nationality	12 E / 8 S / 6 I / 1 W / 1 A / 1 unk.	
Demographics of other ranks 1808	2/32nd: 83% EW / 16% I / 1% F	
Demographics of other ranks 1810	1/32nd: 77% EW / 21% I / 1% S / 1% F	
Months of overseas service 1793–1815	1/32nd: 110 2/32nd: no overseas service	

Significant Militia/Volunteer Intakes

1801:	Cheshire Fencibles, Essex Fencibles
1805:	Lanarkshire
1806:	County Galway, County Kilkenny
1807:	Cornwall, 1st Lancashire, Leicestershire
1808:	North Devon
1813:	Cornwall

Regimental Colonels

31. *Rt Hon. Ralph GORE, 1st Earl of Ross (1781–1802)*

Born: County Fermanagh 1725
Relations: Son of Sir Ralph Gore, 4th Bt and Elizabeth St George (Ashe)
Education: Trinity College, Dublin
Entry to Army: Lieutenant in 33rd Foot 1744 by purchase
Brevets: Brevet Colonel 25 May 1772; Major General 29 Aug 1777; Lieutenant General 20 Nov 1782; General 3 May 1796
Colonelcies: Lieutenant Colonel Commandant of 92nd (later 90th) Foot 17 Jan 1760; 32nd Foot 17 May 1781 (vice W. Amherst)
Early Service: Served in War of the Austrian Succession 1744–1747
Political Career: MP (Ire) 1747–1764
Creations and Dignities: 6th Baronet of Magherabegg 25 Sep 1746; Baron Gore of Manor Gore 30 Jun 1764; Viscount Belleisle 25 Aug 1768; 1st Earl of Ross 4 Jan 1772
Residence: Manor Gore, near Glenswilly, County Donegal
Died: Manor Gore 16 Sep 1802
Sources: ANCB; ARLI; DEPE

32. *James OGILVIE (1802–1813)*

Born: Scotland c.1740
Entry to Army: Ensign in 1st Foot 21 Sep 1756 by purchase
Regimental Field Officer Promotions: Major in 4th Foot 22 Apr 1774 by purchase; Lieutenant Colonel in 4th Foot 4 Jun 1777 by purchase
Brevets: Brevet Colonel 20 Nov 1782; Brigadier General (Nova Scotia) 1787; Major General 12 Oct 1793; Lieutenant General 1 Jan 1798; General 25 Sep 1803
Colonelcies: Colonel Commandant of 2/4th Foot 5 Dec 1799 (vice Pitt); 89th Foot 20 Mar 1801 (vice Ross); 32nd Foot 4 Sep 1802 (vice Earl of Ross)
Early Service: Served in West Indies 1758–1763; served in American War of Independence 1774–1778; taken POW in West Indies 1780
Service 1793–1815: Commanded expedition at capture of St. Pierre and Miquelon 1793; acting Lieutenant Governor of Cape Breton Island 29 Jun 1798 to 21 Jun 1799; interim Commander in Chief Nova Scotia Jun to Sep 1799
Residence: Devonshire Street, Westminster, London
Died: London 14 Feb 1813
Sources: ARLI; DICB; WEOF; WO 25/747; WOST

33. *Alexander CAMPBELL (1813–1832)*

Born: Edinburgh 1751
Relations: Son of Robert Campbell of Finab and Monzie, and Inverawe, and Susanna (Erskine)
Entry to Army: Ensign in 42nd Foot 21 Apr 1769 by purchase
Regimental Field Officer Promotions: Major in 74th Foot 26 Dec 1777; Lieutenant Colonel in 62nd Foot 15 Jan 1782 by purchase; Captain and Lieutenant Colonel in 3rd Foot Guards 5 Jun 1789 (vice Horneck) by exchange; to half-pay of 7th West India Regiment 24 Jul 1802
Brevets: Brevet Colonel 12 Oct 1793; Brigadier General (continent) 1794; Major General 26 Feb 1795; Lieutenant General 29 Apr 1802; General 1 Jan 1812

Colonelcies: 116th Foot Feb 1795; 7th (late 8th) West India Regiment 10 Nov 1796 (vice Lewes); 13th Foot 11 Jul 1804 (vice Ainslie); 32nd Foot 15 Feb 1813 (vice Ogilvie)
Early Service: Served in American War of Independence 1776–1782
Service 1793–1815: Served in Flanders 1793–1794; commanded brigade in Netherlands and Hanover 1794–1795; served in West Indies 1796; served on home staff 1797–1804
Political Career: MP (Anstruther Faster Burghs) 1797–1806; MP (Stirling Burghs) 1807–1818
Residences: Monzie, near Crieff, Perthshire
Died: Monzie 24 Feb 1832
Sources: ANCB; ANCD; ANCW; ARLI; HPON; WEOF

Lieutenant Colonels

34. *John FLETCHER CAMPBELL (1767–1793)*

Born: John Fletcher in Midlothian 1727; assumed additional surname Campbell in 1781
Relations: Son of Andrew Fletcher, Lord Milton, Chief Justice Clerk for Scotland and Keeper of the Signet, and Elizabeth (Kinloch); brother of General Henry Fletcher
Regimental Field Officer Promotions: Major in 32nd Foot 30 Mar 1764; Lieutenant Colonel in 32nd Foot 12 Jun 1767 by purchase; to half-pay of 18th Foot 5 Nov 1793
Brevets: Brevet Colonel 29 Aug 1777; Major General 20 Nov 1782; Lieutenant General 12 Oct 1793 General 1 Jan 1798
Colonelcies: 91st Foot 30 Oct 1793
Early Service: Commanded 32nd Foot 1767–1793
Awards and Honours: FRSE
Residences: Saltoun Hall, Midlothian; Boquhan House, Thornhill, Stirlingshire
Died: Saltoun Hall 10 Dec 1806
Sources: ANCW; ARLI; FMPD; GHLG

35. *Richard NORTHEY-HOPKINS (1793–1810)*

Born: Richard Northey in Wiltshire 1756; assumed additional surname –Hopkins in 1800
Relations: Son of William Northey of Ivey House, MP and Anne (Hopkins); uncle of Colonel Edward Richard Northey-Hopkins, 52nd Foot; and Captain and Lieutenant Colonel William Brook Northey-Hopkins, Coldstream Foot Guards; father of Captain Richard Hopkins Northey, 59th Foot
Entry to Army: Ensign in 30th Foot 1 Sep 1773
Regimental Field Officer Promotions: Major in 32nd Foot 29 Aug 1793; Lieutenant Colonel in 32nd Foot 5 Nov 1793 (vice Campbell) by purchase
Brevets: Brevet Colonel 26 Jan 1797; Major General 25 Sep 1803; Lieutenant General 25 Oct 1809
Service 1793–1815: Commanded 32nd Foot 1793–1803
Retired: 17 May 1810
Residences: Oving House, Oving, Buckinghamshire; Gloucester Place, Marylebone, London
Died: London 26 Apr 1845
Sources: ANCB; ANCD; ARLI; WEOF; A Genealogical and Heraldic History of the Commoners of Great Britain and Ireland

36. *Finch MASON (1795–1796)*

Born: London 1758
Relations: Son of John Mason of Aldenham Lodge and Elizabeth (Finch)
Entry to Army: Ensign in 18th Foot 6 Jan 1780 by purchase
Regimental Field Officer Promotions: Major in 32nd Foot (vice Wrottesley) 1 Sep 1795 by purchase; Lieutenant Colonel in 32nd Foot 1 Sep 1795
Brevets: Brevet Major 16 May 1794
Service 1793–1815: Served in West Indies 1796
Residence: Aldenham Lodge, near Watford, Hertfordshire
Died: St Domingue 1 Jul 1796
Sources: ANCW; ARLI; GHLG

37. *Arthur FORBES (1796–1800)*

Born: Aberdeenshire 1760
Relations: Son of Sir Arthur Forbes, Bt of Craigievar and Margaret (Strachan)
Entry to Army: Lieutenant in 2/71st Foot 29 Oct 1775
Regimental Field Officer Promotions: Major in 6th Foot 1 Sep 1795 (vice Scott); Lieutenant Colonel in 32nd Foot 21 Jul 1796
Brevets: Brevet Major 1 Mar 1794; Brevet Lieutenant Colonel 6 Jul 1796
Service 1793–1815: ADC to General Ralph Abercromby
Retired: 13 Mar 1800
Residence: Alford, Aberdeenshire
Died: Aberdeen 10 Dec 1850
Sources: ANCB; ANCD; ARLI; WEOF

38. *James Alexander STUART (1800–1805)*

Born: Scotland c.1769
Relations: [spec.] Natural son of General James Stuart

Entry to Army: Ensign in 78th Foot 13 Feb 1782 by purchase
Regimental Field Officer Promotions: Major in 83rd Foot 30 Oct 1800 (vice Skerrett) by purchase; Lieutenant Colonel in 32nd Foot 13 Nov 1800 (vice Forbes) by purchase; to half-pay of 20th Foot 6 Jun 1805 (vice Power) by exchange
Brevets: Brevet Major 5 Apr 1796; Brevet Colonel 25 Jul 1810
Residence: Charles Street, Berkeley Square, London
Died: London 1 Mar 1813
Presumed son of General James Stuart (1741–1815), whose entry in DINB notes 'died without issue'; however this officer started his career in the regiment in which his putative father was commanding officer; and shared the same address at time of death
Sources: ARLI; DINB (father); WEOF

39. *Sir Samuel William Venables HINDE (1804–1814)*

Born: Hertfordshire 1769
Relations: Son of Robert Hinde of Hunsdon House and Mary (Ball)
Entry to Army: Ensign in 25th Foot 24 Jan 1788
Regimental Field Officer Promotions: Major in 32nd Foot 5 Nov 1800 (vice Stewart); Lieutenant Colonel in 32nd Foot 1 Aug 1804; removed from the regiment as a general officer Jun 1814
Brevets: Brevet Major 6 Jul 1797; Brevet Lieutenant Colonel 29 Apr 1802; Brevet Colonel 4 Jun 1811; Major General 4 Jun 1814; Lieutenant General 22 Jul 1830
Colonelcies: 98th Foot 22 Jul 1829 (vice Conran); 32nd Foot 28 Feb 1832 (vice Campbell)
Early Service: Served in Gibraltar 1788–1791
Service 1793–1815: Served as a marine 1793–1797; served at Toulon 1793; served in Corsica 1794; served in Helder 1799; commanded 2/32nd Foot 1804–1805; commanded 1/32nd Foot 1805–1812; served in Peninsula Aug 1808 to Jan 1809; served in Walcheren 1809; served in Peninsula Jul 1811 to Jun 1812; commanded brigade in 6th Division in Peninsula Jul 1812 to Dec 1813, severely wounded at Bidassoa Oct 1813
Awards and Honours: AGM (Rol Vim Cor Sal Pyr); GCCT (Spain); KCB 13 Sep 1831
Residences: Hitchin, Hertfordshire
Died: Hitchin 20 Sep 1837
Sources: ANCW; ARLI; CHAL; GEMA (1837); PHIL; WEOF; WO 25/746

40. *Sir Manley POWER (1805–1814)*

Born: Devon 1772
Relations: Son of Captain Thomas Bolton Power of Hill Court, 20th Foot, and Ann (Corney); son-in-law of Colonel Kingsmill Evans, 1st Foot Guards; father of Lieutenant Colonel Manley Power, 85th Foot; and Captain Kingsmill Manley Power, 16th Lancers
Entry to Army: Ensign in 20th Foot 27 Aug 1785
Regimental Field Officer Promotions: Major in 20th Foot 7 Oct 1799 (vice Bainbrigge); Lieutenant Colonel in 20th Foot 20 Jun 1801 (vice Brooke) by purchase; to half-pay of 20th Foot 25 Oct 1802; Lieutenant Colonel in 32nd Foot 6 Jun 1805 (vice Stuart) by exchange; removed from the regiment as a general officer Jul 1814
Brevets: Brevet Colonel 25 Jul 1810; Brigadier General (Portuguese service) 5 Aug 1811; Major General (Portuguese service) 4 Jun 1813; Major General 4 Jun 1813; Lieutenant General 27 May 1825
Early Service: Served in Nova Scotia 1798–1792
Service 1793–1815: Commanded 1/20th Foot in Helder Oct 1799; served in Minorca 1800; served in Egypt 1801; Inspecting Field Officer of Militia Oct 1803; commanded Portuguese infantry brigades in Peninsula Aug 1811 to Apr 1814; temporary commander of 3rd Division in Peninsula Sep to Oct 1811; commanded brigade in British North America Sep 1814 to Jan 1815; commanded brigade in France Jul to Nov 1815; commanded brigade in Army of Occupation in France Nov 1815 to Nov 1818
Later Service: Acting Governor and Commander in Chief in and over the Island of Malta and its Dependencies 12 Oct 1819 to 16 Oct 1819, and 18 Dec 1819 to 6 Dec 1821; and again Feb 1822 to 17 May 1822
Awards and Honours: KTS (Portugal); AGC (Sal Vit Nlle Ort Toul); KCB 2 Jan 1815
Residence: Somerset Place, Bath, Somerset
Died: Bern, Switzerland 7 Jul 1826
Various sources describe Power as being of Irish stock; his ancestry however seemingly centred on Herefordshire and Denbighshire, whilst his wife was from Monmouthshire
Sources: ANCW; ARLI; CHAL; DINB; PHIL; WEBC; WEOF

41. *William Augustus JOHNSON (1810–1814)*

Born: Warwickshire 1777
Relations: Son of Rev. Robert Augustus Johnson of Wistanstow and Anna Rebecca (Craven)
Education: Rugby School
Entry to Army: Ensign in Independent Company 18 Sep 1793 by purchase
Regimental Field Officer Promotions: Major in

32nd Foot 2 Apr 1803 (vice Maxwell) by purchase; Lieutenant Colonel in 32nd Foot 17 May 1810 (vice Hopkins) by purchase; to half-pay of 3rd Ceylon Regiment 18 Aug 1814 (vice Maitland) by exchange
Brevets: Brevet Colonel 12 Aug 1819; Major General 22 Jul 1830; Lieutenant General 23 Nov 1841
Service 1793–1815: Served in Copenhagen 1807; served in Peninsula Aug 1808 to Jan 1809; served in Peninsula Jul 1811 to Aug 1811; commanded 2/32nd Foot 1812–1814; commanded 1/32nd Foot 1814
Political Career: MP (Boston) 1821–1826; MP (Oldham) 1837–1847
Residence: Witham Hall, Witham on the Hill, Lincolnshire
Died: Witham Hall 26 Oct 1863
Sources: ANCW; ARLI; CHAL; HPON; PHIL; WEOF

42. *James MAITLAND (1814–1818)*

Born: Ireland c.1781
Entry to Army: Ensign in 62nd Foot 14 Sep 1797
Regimental Field Officer Promotions: Major in 3rd Ceylon Regiment 4 Sep 1806 (vice Pollock); Lieutenant Colonel in 3rd Ceylon Regiment 30 Nov 1809 (vice Brownrigg); Lieutenant Colonel in 32nd Foot 10 Aug 1814 (vice Johnson) by exchange; to half-pay of 103rd Foot 22 Jul 1819; Lieutenant Colonel in 20th Foot 25 Nov 1821; Lieutenant Colonel in 84th Foot 22 Nov 1821 (vice Daubeny); to half-pay of 4th Foot 25 May 1826 (vice Neynoe) by exchange
Brevets: Brevet Lieutenant Colonel 30 Nov 1809; Brevet Colonel 12 Aug 1819
Service 1793–1815: [spec.] Served at Waterloo 1815
Later Service: Inspecting Field Officer of Militia in Ionian Islands 26 Mar 1818
Residence: Hammersmith, London
Died: Hammersmith 6 Sep 1826
This officer is credited by Siborne with leading the 32nd Foot at Waterloo; however he appears in neither the Waterloo Roll Call, nor the Waterloo Medal Roll
Sources: ANCW; DALT; PHIL; WEOF

Majors

43. *Edward EDWARDS (1787–1793)*

Born: [spec.] Ireland c.1745
Entry to Army: Ensign in 32nd Foot 23 Aug 1761
Regimental Field Officer Promotions: Major in 32nd Foot 20 Jun 1787 (vice Strachan) by purchase; to Captain on half-pay 29 Aug 1793
Brevets: Brevet Major 19 Mar 1783
Early Service: Commanded 32nd Foot in West Indies 1792–1793
Retired: Disappeared from the Army List in 1806
Seems to have been resident in Dublin in the 1790's, hence speculative birthplace
Sources: ARLI

44. *Edward WILLIAMS (1793–1794)*

Born: c.1756
Entry to Army: Ensign in 32nd Foot 17 Jul 1771
Regimental Field Officer Promotions: Major in 32nd Foot 28 Dec 1793 (vice Northey) by purchase
Retired: 28 Apr 1794
Later Service: Commissioner of Hackney Coaches in the City of London
Residence: Upper Berkeley Street, Portman Square, London
Died: London 19 Jan 1814
Sources: ANCW; ARLI; GEMA (1814)

45. *Rt Hon. John WROTTESLEY, 1st Baron Wrottesley (1794–1795)*

Born: Staffordshire 1771
Relations: Son of Major General Sir John Wrottesley, 8th Bt, MP and Hon. Frances (Courtenay); grandson of William, 1st Viscount Courtenay; and John Leveson-Gower, 1st Earl Gower; brother of Lieutenant Colonel Hugh Wrottesley, Madras service; and Commander Edward Wrottesley RN; son-in-law of Charles Bennet, 4th Earl of Tankerville; father of Lieutenant Colonel Hon. Charles Alexander Wrottesley, 16th Lancers
Education: Westminster School; de Pignerolles's Military Academy, Angers
Entry to Army: Ensign in 35th Foot 24 Sep 1787 by purchase
Regimental Field Officer Promotions: Major in 32nd Foot 28 Apr 1794 (vice Williams) by purchase
Service 1793–1815: Served in Flanders 1793–1795
Retired: 1 Sep 1795
Militia Service: Lieutenant Colonel Commandant of West Staffordshire Militia 1809
Political Career: MP (Lichfield) 1799–1806; MP (Staffordshire) 1823–1832); MP (Staffordshire South) 1832–1837
Creations and Dignities: 9th Baronet 3 Apr 1787; 1st Baron Wrottesley of Wrottesley 11 Jul 1838
Residence: Wrottesley Hall, Tettenhall, Staffordshire
Died: Wrottesley Hall 16 Mar 1841
Sources: ANCB; ANCD; ANCW; ARLI; HPON; WEOF

46. *Sir Frederick Philipse ROBINSON (1795–1796)*

Born: New York State 1761
Relations: Son of Colonel Beverley Robinson of Albany County and Susan (Philipse); brother of Lieutenant Colonel Beverley Robinson, Loyal American Regiment; Lieutenant Colonel Morris Robinson, Loyal American Regiment; Lieutenant John Robinson, Loyal American Regiment; and Commissary General of the Forces Sir William Henry Robinson
Entry to Army: Ensign in Loyal American Regiment Feb 1777
Regimental Field Officer Promotions: Major in 127th Foot 1 Sep 1794; Major in 32nd Foot 1 Sep 1795 (vice Wrottesley); Major in 134th Foot 29 Jul 1796 (vice Maxwell) by exchange; to half-pay of 134th Foot; Major in 86th Foot 19 Feb 1807 (vice Torrens); Major in 18th Foot 16 Apr 1807 (vice Ross) by exchange; on half-pay of 91st Foot 30 Apr 1807 (vice Tomlinson) by exchange
Brevets: Brevet Lieutenant Colonel 1 Jan 1800; Brevet Colonel 25 Jul 1810; Brigadier General (home staff) 7 Oct 1812; Major General 4 Jun 1813; Lieutenant General 27 May 1825; General 23 Nov 1841
Colonelcies: 2nd Garrison Battalion 14 Jan 1814 (vice Porter); 59th Foot 1 Dec 1827 (vice Ross); 39th Foot 15 Jun 1840 (vice O'Callaghan)
Early Service: Served in American War of Independence 1779–1781, wounded at Stony Point
Service 1793–1815: Served in West Indies 1794; Inspecting Field Officer of Recruiting Districts May 1796 to 1812; commanded brigade in 5th Division in Peninsula Mar 1813 to Apr 1814; temporary commander of 5th Division Apr 1814; served in British North America 1814–1816; Provisional Lieutenant Governor and Commander of Upper Canada 10 Jun 1815 to 21 Sep 1815
Later Service: Governor of Tobago 13 Nov 1816 to 5 Jul 1826
Awards and Honours: AGM (Vitt SS Niv); KCB 2 Jan 1815; GCB 20 Apr 1838
Residence: Bedford Square, Brighton, Sussex
Died: Brighton 1 Jan 1852
Sources: ANCB; ANCD; ANCW; ARLI; CHAL; DINB; PHIL; WEBC; WEOF; WOST

47. *Robert HEDLEY (1796–1797)*

Born: Northumberland 1767
Relations: Son of John Hedley of Newcastle-Upon-Tyne, alderman, and Deborah (Shafto); brother of Major Shafto John Hedley, Northumberland Militia
Entry to Army: Ensign in 57th Foot 21 Dec 1784 by purchase
Regimental Field Officer Promotions: Major in 32nd Foot 12 Mar 1796 by purchase
Residence: Dalton, Northumberland
Died: St Domingue Jul 1797
Sources: ANCB; ANCW; ARLI

48. *William MAXWELL (1796–1803)*

Born: [spec.] Scotland c.1765
Entry to Army: Lieutenant in 73rd Foot 21 Apr 1783
Regimental Field Officer Promotions: Major in 134th Foot 1794; Major in 32nd Foot 29 Jul 1796 (vice Robinson) by exchange
Brevets: Brevet Lieutenant Colonel 1 Jan 1800
Retired: 2 Apr 1803
Later Service: Paymaster of the Leeds Recruiting District Mar 1810
Died: Unknown
This officer was court-martialled, dismissed and gaoled in Oct 1813 for embezzlement; his fate from that date onwards is understandably obscure
Sources: ARLI; A Collection of the Charges, Opinions, and Sentences of General Courts Martial

49. *James Wentworth MANSERGH (1797–1800)*

Born: County Tipperary c.1755
Relations: Son of Nicholas Mansergh of Grenane and Elizabeth (Lockwood); brother of Captain George Mansergh, 22nd Foot
Entry to Army: Ensign in 32nd Foot 24 Dec 1779 by purchase
Regimental Field Officer Promotions: Major in 32nd Foot 1 Aug 1797 (vice Hedley)
Retired: 11 Sep 1800
Died: Cashel, County Tipperary 3 Apr 1808
Sources: ARLI; WikiTree

50. *Sir William NICOLSON, 9th Bt (1800)*

Born: Lanarkshire 1758
Relations: Son of George Nicolson of Tarviston and Catherine (Edmonstone); father of Rear Admiral Sir Frederick William Erskine Nicolson, 10th Bt
Entry to Army: Lieutenant in 80th Foot 21 Jan 1778; resigned 6 Oct 1789; rejoined as Cornet in 2nd Dragoons 1 May 1794
Regimental Field Officer Promotions: Major in 32nd Foot 16 Sep 1800 (vice Mansergh) by purchase; Major in 72nd Foot 30 Oct 1800 (vice Stewart) by exchange; Lieutenant Colonel in 72nd Foot 1 Jul 1813
Brevets: Brevet Lieutenant Colonel 26 May 1803; Brevet Colonel 1 Jan 1812; Major General 4 Jun 1814

Early Service: Served in American War of Independence; in Austrian service 1792–1794
Service 1793–1815: Served as ADC to General Erskine in Flanders 1794; ADC to General Lake in Ireland 1798; Assistant Adjutant General and Deputy Adjutant General in East Indies 1803–1810
Creations and Dignities: 9th Baronet of Carnock 19 Oct 1808
Residence: Brussels, Belgium
Died: Brussels 5 Aug 1820
Sources: ANCW; ARLI; COPE; WEOF; WO 25/747

51. *Richard STEWART (1800)*

Born: Isle of Bute 1756
Relations: Son of John Stewart of Kingarth and Christina (unk.)
Entry to Army: Ensign in 51st Foot 6 Dec 1775 by purchase
Regimental Field Officer Promotions: Major in 72nd Foot 11 Oct 1798 (vice Robertson); Major in 32nd Foot 11 Sep 1800 (vice Nicholson) by exchange; Lieutenant Colonel in 43rd Foot 5 Nov 1800 (vice Montgomery)
Brevets: Brevet Major 12 Sep 1794; Brevet Lieutenant Colonel 30 Nov 1796; Brevet Colonel 25 Sep 1803; Brigadier General (home staff) 1807; Major General 25 Jul 1810
Early Service: Served in Minorca 1776–1782; served in Gibraltar 1791–1792
Service 1793–1815: Served in Toulon 1793; ADC to Charles Stuart in Corsica 1794; Deputy Adjutant General in Portugal 1796–1798; Adjutant General in Minorca 1798; Adjutant General in Malta 1800; ADC to King George III 25 Sep 1803; deputy commander of reserve in Copenhagen 1807; Adjutant General in Baltic expedition 1808; commanded brigade in Peninsula Aug 1808 to Jun 1809; commanded brigade in 2nd Division in Peninsula Jun 1809 to Aug 1810
Awards and Honours: AGM (Tal)
Died: Fell from a balcony in Lisbon Oct 19 1810
Sources: ANCW; ARLI; CHAL; WEBC; WEOF; WO 25/748

52. *Alleyne Hampden PYE (1804)*

Born: London 1767
Relations: Son of Captain and Lieutenant Colonel Robert Hampden Pye, 1st Foot Guards, and Joel Henrietta (Campbell); son-in-law of Captain Francis Grant-Gordon RN; brother-in-law of General Sir James Willoughby Gordon
Entry to Army: 2nd Lieutenant in 23rd Foot 24 Sep 1787
Regimental Field Officer Promotions: Major in 32nd Foot 1 Aug 1804 (vice Hinde); Major in 54th Foot 23 Nov 1804 (vice Bellew); to Lieutenant Colonel on half-pay of 10th West India Regiment 2 Jan 1806
Brevets: Brevet Lieutenant Colonel; Brevet Colonel 4 Jun 1814; Major General 19 Jul 1821
Service 1793–1815: Deputy Quartermaster General in Canada 2 Jan 1806
Later Service: Acting Superintendent for Belize Settlements 4 Apr 1822 to 15 Jan 1823
Residence: Saint-Omer, Pas-de-Calais, France
Died: Saint-Omer 9 Jan 1833
Sources: ANCB; ANCD; ANCW; ARLI; PHIL; WEOF; WOST

53. *John WOOD (1804–1813)*

Born: Sussex 1771
Relations: Son of John Wood of Chichester and Ann (Driskell)
Entry to Army: Ensign in 53rd Foot 16 Feb 1793
Regimental Field Officer Promotions: Major in 32nd Foot 2 Aug 1804
Brevets: Brevet Lieutenant Colonel 4 Jun 1811
Service 1793–1815: Served in Flanders 1793–1795; served in West Indies 1796–1800; commanded 2/32nd Foot 1804–1807; served in Copenhagen 1807; served in Peninsula Aug 1808 to Jan 1809; served in Peninsula Jul 1811 to Jul 1813; commanded 1/32nd Foot 1813; wounded in Pyrenees 28 Jul 1813
Residence: Chichester, Sussex
Died: Of wounds in the Pyrenees 31 Jul 1813
Sources: ARLI; CHAL; HALL; WEOF; WO 25/748

54. *John HICKS (1804–1826)*

Born: London c.1762
Relations: Son of Charles Hicks and Ann (unk.); brother of Lieutenant Colonel Charles Hicks, 24th Foot
Entry to Army: Ensign in 32nd Foot 22 Feb 1786 by purchase
Regimental Field Officer Promotions: Major in 32nd Foot 3 Aug 1804; Lieutenant Colonel unattached 11 May 1826 (vice Gascoigne) by exchange
Brevets: Brevet Lieutenant Colonel 4 Jun 1811; Brevet Colonel 27 May 1825
Early Service: Served in Gibraltar 1786–1788
Service 1793–1815: Served at Gibraltar 1796; served in St Domingue 1796; served in Bahamas 1797–1800; commanded 2/32nd Foot 1809–1810; served in Peninsula Jul 1811 to Apr 1814; commanded 1/32nd Foot 1813–1815; commanded 32nd Foot at Waterloo 1815
Retired: Retaining rank 11 May 1826
Awards and Honours: AGC (Pyr Nlle Niv Ort); CB 22 Jun 1815; WatM 23 Apr 1816

Residence: Abbey House, Malvern, Worcestershire
Died: Malvern 18 May 1838
Sources: ARLI; WEOF; CHAL; DALT; WEOF; WO 25/746

55. *William SHIPLEY (1804–1806)*

Born: Flintshire 1778
Relations: Son of Rev. William Davies Shipley of St Asaph and Penelope (Yonge); son-in-law of Sir William Watkins Wynn, Bt; brother of Captain Conway Shipley RN; and Captain Robert John Shipley, RE; father of Captain William Shipley-Conwy, 3rd Light Dragoons
Entry to Army: Ensign in Independent Company 22 Jan 1793
Regimental Field Officer Promotions: Major in 6th Foot 19 Oct 1804; Major in 32nd Foot 1 Dec 1804; Lieutenant Colonel in 14th Foot 17 Jun 1806 (vice Bligh) by purchase
Brevets: Brevet Major 25 Sep 1803
Retired: 25 Sep 1807
Political Career: MP (St Mawes) 1807; MP (Flint Boroughs) 1807–1812; MP (St Mawes) 1812–1813
Residence: Bodrhyddan, Flintshire; Majorca, Balearic Islands
Died: Accidentally shot by a servant whilst hunting, Hyeres, France 29 Nov 1820
Shipley lived overseas after 1813 to avoid his creditors
Sources: ANCB; ARLI; GHLG; HPON; WEOF; Pedigrees of Anglesey and Carnarvonshire Families

56. *John BENNET (1806–1815)*

Born: Lancashire 1772
Relations: [spec.] Of the Bennets of Barnston and Wallasey
Entry to Army: Ensign in 32nd Foot 3 Jun 1791 by purchase
Regimental Field Officer Promotions: Major in 32nd Foot 12 Jan 1806 (vice Shipley) by purchase; to half-pay of Dillon's Regiment 11 May 1815 (vice Calvert) by exchange
Brevets: Brevet Lieutenant Colonel 4 Jun 1813
Early Service: Served in Gibraltar 1791
Service 1793–1815: Served in West Indies 1793; served in West Indies 1796–1799; commanded 2/32nd Foot 1814–1815
Retired: Jul 1825
Residence: Duke Street, Liverpool, Lancashire
Died: Liverpool 2 Nov 1825
Sources: ANCB; ANCD; ANCW; ARLI; WEOF; WO 25/744

57. *Henry RICHARDSON (1810–1814)*

Born: Ireland c.1778
Entry to Army: Ensign in North Mayo Militia; Ensign in 13th Foot 29 Jun 1800
Regimental Field Officer Promotions: Major in 32nd Foot 17 May 1810 (vice Johnson) by purchase; to half-pay of 32nd Foot 25 Dec 1814
Brevets: Brevet Lieutenant Colonel 12 Aug 1819
Service 1793–1815: Served in Peninsula Aug 1808 to Jan 1809; served in Walcheren 1809
Residence: Lake Lodge, Wakefield, Yorkshire
Died: Wakefield May 1839
Sources: ARLI; CHAL; FMPD; WEOF

58. *Robert COOTE (1814)*

Born: County Kerry c.1770
Relations: Son of Captain Robert Coote of Kerry and Frances (Meredith)
Entry to Army: Ensign in Belvedere's Regiment 1 Sep 1794
Regimental Field Officer Promotions: Major in 32nd Foot 27 Aug 1813 (vice Wood); to half-pay of 32nd Foot 1814
Brevets: Brevet Major 25 Apr 1808; Brevet Lieutenant Colonel 4 Jun 1814
Service 1793–1815: Served as marine 1795; served in Copenhagen 1807; served in Walcheren 1809; served in Peninsula Aug 1808 to Jan 1809; served in Peninsula Jul 1811 to Apr 1814
Residence: Synnot Place, Dublin
Died: Dublin 23 Oct 1828
Sources: ARLI; CHAL; FMPW; WEMR; WEOF; <https://nickreddan.net/trees/coote.pdf>

59. *Felix CALVERT (1815–1818)*

Born: London 1790
Relations: Son of Nicolson Calvert of Hunsdon, MP and Frances (Pery); grandson of Edmond Sexton, Viscount Pery; distant cousin of General Sir Harry Calvert, Bt; the Calverts of brewery fame
Education: Harrow School
Entry to Army: Lieutenant in 52nd Foot 15 Sep 1808 by purchase
Regimental Field Officer Promotions: Major in 32nd Foot 11 May 1815 (vice Bennet); Lieutenant Colonel in 72nd Foot 5 Nov 1818 (vice Leitch) by purchase; to half-pay of 72nd Foot 5 Nov 1818
Brevets: Brevet Lieutenant Colonel 18 Jun 1815; Brevet Colonel 10 Jan 1837; Major General 9 Nov 1846
Colonelcies: 90th Foot 14 Jun 1853 (vice Leith)
Service 1793–1815: Served in Sweden 1808; served in Peninsula with 52nd Foot Aug 1808 to Jan 1809; served in Walcheren 1809; served on staff in Peninsula Apr 1810 to Aug 1813, ADC to General

Graham; served in North America 1814, served in Waterloo campaign 1815
Awards and Honours: WatM 23 Apr 1816; CB 19 Jul 1838
Residence: Hunsdon, Hertfordshire
Died: London 3 Mar 1857
Sources: ANCW; ARLI; CHAL; GHLG; PHIL; WEOF

Selected Regimental Histories

Swiney, George Clayton, *Historical Records of the 32nd, Cornwall, Light Infantry, Now the 1st Battalion Duke of Cornwall's L. I.: From the Formation of the Regiment in 1702 Down to 1892* (London: Simpkin, Marshall, Hamilton, Kent & Co., 1893)

Regimental Museum

Cornwall Army Museum, The Keep, Bodmin, Cornwall

33rd Regiment of Foot

Secondary Title:	1st Yorkshire West Riding
Nicknames:	The Havercake Lads
Jacket:	Red
Facings:	Red
Motto:	*Virtutis fortuna comes* (fortune accompanies honour)

Regimental Lineage, 33rd Regiment of Foot

1702:	Feb – raised in Gloucestershire by George Hastings, 8th Earl of Huntingdon
1703:	Leigh's Regiment of Foot
1705:	Duncanson's Regiment of Foot
1705:	Wade's Regiment of Foot
1717:	Hawley's Regiment of Foot
1730:	Dalzell's Regiment of Foot
1739:	Johnson's Regiment of Foot
1747:	Ranked as 33rd Regiment of Foot
1751:	33rd Regiment of Foot
1782:	33rd (1st Yorkshire West Riding) Regiment of Foot
1853:	33rd (The Duke of Wellington's) Regiment of Foot
1881:	The Duke of Wellington's (West Riding Regiment) (on amalgamation with 76th Regiment of Foot)
1921:	The Duke of Wellington's Regiment (West Riding)
2006:	3rd Battalion, Royal Yorkshire Regiment (Duke of Wellington's) (on amalgamation with Prince of Wales's Own Regiment of Yorkshire and Green Howards)

Service History, 33rd Regiment of Foot

1793:	Dublin; Nov – flank companies to West Indies
1794:	Dublin; Cork; Jun – to Flanders; Ostend; Roosendaal; Sep – Boxtel; Dec – Tuyl; Geldermalsen
	Mar – Flank companies in Martinique; Apr – St Lucia; May – Guadeloupe; Oct – flank companies wiped out in Guadeloupe
1795:	Line of the River Waal; retreat to Bremen; Apr – Bremen; to England; Jun – Ipswich; Jul – Portsmouth; Sep – Nursling camp; Nov – Portsmouth; to West Indies; did not sail; Lymington
1796:	Lymington; Mar – Poole; Apr – to East Indies; Aug – Cape of Good Hope; to India
1797:	Feb – India; Calcutta; Fort William; Aug – to Manila; Penang; to India; Nov – Fort William
1798:	Fort William; Sep – to Madras; Oct – Fort St George
1799:	Fort St George; Feb – Vellore; Mallavelly [Mallavalli]; May – SERINGAPATAM [Srirangapatna]

1800:	Seringapatam
1801:	Seringapatam; Aug – Vellore
1802:	Vellore
1803:	Vellore and Seringapatam; Sep – Nundyall [Nandyala]; Oct – Didagay [Didaga]; Nov – Vellore
1804:	Vellore; May – Mangalore [Mangaluru]; Jun – Sungymyshire [Sangameshwarapete]; Jul – Vellore
1805:	Vellore; Jun – Gooty; Jul – Bellary [Ballari]; Aug – Palmoor; Hyderabad; Sep – Samptapor; Oct – Alsaya; Nov – Magum [Malegaon]; Dec – Akowlah [Akola]; ordered to march to Mahratta Frontier
1806:	Allundah [Alanda]; Feb – Mirsday; Mar – Taunkly [Takli]; May – Hussain Sagar, camp of the Grand Army at Hyderabad
1807:	Hussain Sagar; Jul – Secunderabad; Aug – Hyderabad
1808–1809:	Hyderabad
1810:	Hyderabad; Apr – Jurchilla Fort; May – Wurrubedudah [Guaribidanur]; Jun – Bangalore; Nov – Seringapatam Jun – flank companies to Mauritius; Nov – Port Louis
1811:	Seringapatam; May – Vellore; Jun – Fort St George; Nov – to England
1812:	At sea; Jul – Gravesend (16 years away!); Aug – Chatham; Oct – Hull
1813:	Hull; Feb – Windsor on King's Duty; Jul – Harwich; to Swedish Pomerania; Aug – Stralsund; Sep – Rostock; Nov – to England; Great Yarmouth; to Holland; Dec – Willemstad
1814:	Merxcem; Mar – Bergen-Op-Zoom; Apr – Antwerp; Dec – Menen
1815:	Menen; Feb – Kortrijk; Mar – Menen; Jun – Quatre Bras; WATERLOO; Jul – Paris; Allied Army of Occupation; Dec – Calais; to England; Hull

Establishments, 33rd Regiment of Foot

Year	Subunits	Field Off	Off/ Staff	Sjts	Mus	Corp/ Pvts	Total
Dec 1792	10co	3	32	22	12	330	399
Jan 1793	10co	3	32	32	22	600	689
Aug 1795	10co+2r	5	53	62	30	1,010	1,160
Dec 1796	10co+2r	5	51	62	30	1,010	1,158
Dec 1798	10co+r	5	46	70	26	1,208	1,355
Dec 1800	10co+r	5	46	78	30	1,216	1,375
Jun 1802	10co+r	5	46	41	30	758	880
Dec 1802	10co+r	5	50	62	30	1,008	1,155
Dec 1803	10co+r	5	50	62	26	1,008	1,151
Dec 1807	10co+r	5	50	52	26	808	941
Dec 1811	10co+r	5	50	63	26	1,008	1,152
Dec 1812	10co	4	36	45	22	800	907
Dec 1813	10co+r	4	39	53	22	808	926
Dec 1815	10co	4	36	35	22	600	697

Service Statistics, 33rd Regiment of Foot

	Lieutenant Colonels	Majors
Number of officers in period 1793–1815	8	17
Average age on appointment to substantive rank	34	34
Average time in rank in regiment (years)	7	3.5
Total field officers by nationality	11 I / 7 E / 4 S	
Demographics of other ranks 1808	62% EW / 25% I / 8% S / 5% F	
Months of overseas service 1793–1815	235	

Significant Militia/Volunteer Intakes

1809: East Middlesex, Northumberland, 3rd West Yorkshire
1811: East Middlesex, 1st West Yorkshire, 3rd West Yorkshire
1812: 1st Lancashire, East Middlesex, 1st West Yorkshire, 3rd West Yorkshire
1813: East Middlesex, Northumberland, Staffordshire, 1st West Yorkshire
1814: 1st Lancashire

Regimental Colonels

60. *Rt Hon. Charles, 1st Marquess CORNWALLIS (1766–1805)*

Born: London 1738
Relations: Eldest son of Charles, 1st Earl Cornwallis and Elizabeth (Townshend); grandson of Charles, 2nd Viscount Townshend; nephew of Frederick Cornwallis, Archbishop of Canterbury; cousin of Major Frederick Cornwallis, 33rd Foot
Education: Eton College; Clare College, Cambridge; Turin Military Academy
Entry to Army: Ensign in 1st Foot Guards 12 Nov 1756 by purchase
Regimental Field Officer Promotions: Captain in 85th Foot 5 Jul 1759; Lieutenant Colonel in 12th Foot 1 May 1761 by purchase
Brevets: Brevet Colonel Aug 1765; Major General 29 Sep 1775; Lieutenant General 29 Aug 1777; General 12 Oct 1793
Colonelcies: 33rd Foot 21 Mar 1766 (vice Griffin)
Early Service: Served in Germany 1759–1761; ADC to King George III 1765–1766; Served in North America 1776–1781, second in command 1778–1779; Commanded forces in southern states 1779–1781; Surrendered at Yorktown 1781; Governor General and Commander in Chief in British East Indies 12 Sep 1786 to 28 Oct 1793
Service 1793–1815: Lord Lieutenant and Commander in Chief Ireland 20 Jun 1798 to 25 May 1801 (vice Pratt); Master General of the Ordnance 23 Feb 1795 to 28 Aug 1801 (vice Lennox); Commander in Chief and Governor General of India 30 Jul to 5 Oct 1805
Political Career: MP (Eye) 1760–62
Creations and Dignities: Viscount Brome 30 Jun 1753; 2nd Earl Cornwallis 23 Jun 1762; 1st Marquess Cornwallis 15 Aug 1792
Awards and Honours: PC 1770; KG 2 Jun 1786
Residences: Old Burlington Street, London; Culford Park, near Bury St Edmunds, Suffolk
Died: Ghazipur, India 5 Oct 1805
Cornwallis served in the American War of Independence despite being opposed to the war. Ironically his surrender at Yorktown in 1781 was the event which effectively ended the conflict
Sources: CADB; DIIB; HPON; MENA; WOST

61. *Rt Hon. Arthur WELLESLEY, Duke of Wellington (1806–1813)*

Born: Dublin 1769
Relations: Son of Garret Wesley, 1st Earl of Mornington and Anne (Hill-Trevor); brother of Richard, 1st Marquess Wellesley; son-in-law of Edward Michael Pakenham, 2nd Baron Longford; brother of William Wellesley-Pole, 3rd Earl of Mornington; brother-in-law of Major General Edward Michael Pakenham
Education: Eton College; Angers Military Academy
Entry to Army: Ensign in 73rd Foot 7 Mar 1787 by purchase
Regimental Field Officer Promotions: Major in 33rd Foot on 30 Apr 1793 (vice Gore) by purchase; Lieutenant Colonel in 33rd Foot 30 Sep 1793 (vice Yorke) by purchase
Brevets: Brevet Colonel 3 May 1796; Brigadier General (India) 17 Jul 1801; Major General 29 Apr 1802; Lieutenant General 25 Apr 1808; General (Spain and Portugal) 31 Jul 1811; Field Marshal 3 Jul 1813
Colonelcies: 33rd Foot 30 Jun 1806 (vice Cornwallis); Royal Horse Guards 1 Jan 1813 (vice Percy)
Service 1793–1815: Served in Flanders 1794–1795; served in India 1797–1804; commanded forces in Mahratta war; commanded brigade in Hanover expedition 1805; commanded brigade in Copenhagen expedition 1807; commanded British forces in Portugal Aug 1808; commanded allied forces in Portugal and later Spain Apr 1809 to Jul 1814; commanded allied forces in Waterloo campaign 1815; Commander in Chief Army of Occupation in France Oct 1815 to Nov 1818
Honorary Foreign Ranks: Marshal General of the Portuguese Army 6 Jul 1809; Captain General of the Spanish Army Aug 1809; Field Marshal of the Hanoverian Army 21 Jun 1813; Field Marshal of the Army of the Netherlands 1815; Field Marshal of the Austrian Army 15 Nov 1818; Field Marshal of the Prussian Army 15 Nov 1818; Field Marshal of the Russian Army 15 Nov 1818
Later Service: Commander in Chief of British Army 22 Jan 1827 to 22 Jan 1828; Commander in Chief of British Army 15 Aug 1842 to 14 Sep 1852

Political Career: MP (Rye) 1806; MP (Mitchell) 1807; MP (Newport) 1807–1809; Chief Secretary for Ireland 19 Apr 1807 to 13 Apr 1809; Prime Minister of the United Kingdom 22 Jan 1828 to 16 Nov 1830; Prime Minister of the United Kingdom 17 Nov 1834 to 9 Dec 1834
Creations and Dignities: Baron Douro 26 Aug 1809; Viscount Wellington 26 Aug 1809; Conde de Vimeiro (Portugal) 18 Oct 1811; Earl of Wellington 18 Feb 1812; Duque de Ciudad Rodrigo (Spain) 30 Jan 1812; Marquess of Wellington 18 Aug 1812; Duque da Vitória (Portugal) 18 Dec 1812; Marquês de Torres Vedras (Portugal) 18 Dec 1812; Marquess Douro 3 May 1814; Duke of Wellington 3 May 1814; Prins van Waterloo (Netherlands) 8 Jul 1815
Awards and Honours: KB 28 Aug 1804; PC 8 Apr 1807; PC (Ire) 28 Apr 1807; KG 4 Mar 1813; AGC (Rol Vim Tal Bus FDO CR Bad Sal Vit Pyr Nlle Niv Ort Toul); GCB 2 Jan 1815; GCH 22 Mar 1816; WatM 23 Apr 1816; FRS 25 Nov 1847; *plus 32 foreign orders, not listed*
Residences: Harley Street, London; Apsley House, London; Stratfield Saye House, Hampshire
Died: Walmer, Kent 14 Sep 1852
'He is neither an agreeable man nor in my eyes an "héros de roman", but he is the most unpretending, perfectly natural and amiable person I ever met with' – Countess Granville, 1819
Sources: ARLI; BRFM; CHAL; DALT; HPON: ODNB; PHIL; WEOF

62. *Sir John Coape SHERBROOKE (1813–1830)*

Born: Nottinghamshire 1764
Relations: Son of William Sherbrooke of Arnold and Sarah (Coape)
Entry to Army: Ensign in 4th Foot 7 Dec 1780 by purchase
Regimental Field Officer Promotions: Major in 33rd Foot 30 Sep 1793 (vice Wesley) by purchase; Lieutenant Colonel in 33rd Foot 24 May 1794; to half-pay of 5th Foot 29 Oct 1802 (vice Gore) by exchange
Brevets: Brevet Colonel 1 Jan 1798; Major General 1 Jan 1805; Lieutenant General 4 Jun 1811; General 27 May 1825
Colonelcies: 4th Garrison Battalion 9 Jul 1803; Sicilian Regiment 5 Feb 1807; 3rd West India Regiment 25 Jan 1809 (vice Oakes); 68th Foot 27 May 1809 (vice Trigge); 33rd Foot 1 Jan 1813 (vice Duke of Wellington)
Early Service: Served in British North America 1785–1786
Service 1793–1815: Served in Flanders 1794–1795; served in India 1797–1800; served in Hanover 1805; Acting Commander in Chief Sicily Sep 1807 to Apr 1808 (vice Moore); commanded brigade and later 1st Division in Peninsula Feb 1809 to Apr 1810; Governor of Nova Scotia 16 Oct 1811 to 27 Jun 1816; Governor General of British North America Jun 1816 to Feb 1818
Awards and Honours: KB 16 Sep 1809; GCB 2 Jan 1815
Residence: Calverton, Nottinghamshire
Died: Calverton 14 Feb 1830
Sources: ARLI; DICB; ODNB; PHIL; WEMR; WEOF; WOST

Lieutenant Colonels

63. *John YORKE (1781–1793)*

Born: Northamptonshire 1745
Relations: Son of Daniel Yorke of Thrapston, attorney, and Penelope (Bletsoe); father of Field Marshal Sir Charles Yorke; father-in-law of Major General William Nepean
Entry to Army: Ensign in 33rd Foot 17 Mar 1761 by purchase
Regimental Field Officer Promotions: Major in 33rd Foot 8 Aug 1776 by purchase; Lieutenant Colonel in 33rd Foot 24 Apr 1781 by purchase
Brevets: Brevet Colonel 12 Mar 1783
Early Service: Served in the American War of Independence 1776–1781; commanded brigade at Yorktown 1781
Service 1793–1815: Deputy Lieutenant Governor of the Tower of London 1794–1820
Retired: 30 Sep 1793
Residence: Clifton, Gloucestershire
Died: Clifton 26 Dec 1825
Sources: ANCW; ARLI; DINB (son); <https://www.thrapstonheritage.org.uk/content/topics/feature-pages-people/daniel-yorke>

64. *Rt Hon. Arthur WELLESLEY, Duke of Wellington (1793–1801)*

See 61.
Lieutenant Colonel in 33rd Foot 30 Sep 1793 (vice Yorke) by purchase

65. *Sir John Coape SHERBROOKE (1794–1802)*

See 62.
Lieutenant Colonel in 33rd Foot 24 May 1794

66. *Arthur GORE (1802–1814)*

Born: County Kilkenny 1773
Relations: Son of John Gore of Kilkenny and Bellamira (Munbee); brother of Vice Admiral Sir

John Gore RN; and Lieutenant Colonel Ralph Gore, York Fusiliers
Entry to Army: Ensign in 73rd Foot 14 Nov 1788 by purchase
Regimental Field Officer Promotions: Major in 40th Foot 15 Jul 1802 (vice Boland); Lieutenant Colonel in 5th Foot 23 Jul 1802 (vice Gooch) by purchase; to half-pay of 5th Foot 25 Sep 1802; Lieutenant Colonel in 33rd Foot 2 Nov 1802 (vice Sherbrooke) by exchange
Brevets: Brevet Colonel 4 Jun 1811; Brigadier General (continent) 1813
Service 1793–1815: Served in British East Indies 1791–1796; served in capture of Ceylon 1796; Judge Advocate in British East Indies 1797; served in British East Indies 1797–1800; served in British East Indies 1803–1811; served in Netherlands 1813–1814
Died: Killed in action at Bergen-op-Zoom 8 Mar 1814
Sources: ANCB; ANCD; ARLI; WEOF; WO 25/745

67. *Walter ELLIOT (1806–1807)*

Born: Selkirkshire 1766
Relations: Son of John Elliot of Borthwickbrae and Margaret (Laing); brother of Lieutenant Colonel William Elliot, Roxburgh and Selkirk Light Dragoons
Entry to Army: Ensign in 33rd Foot 28 May 1784 by purchase
Regimental Field Officer Promotions: Major in 33rd Foot 8 Sep 1796 (vice F. Cornwallis) by purchase; Lieutenant Colonel in 33rd Foot 20 Feb 1806 (vice Wellesley)
Brevets: Brevet Lieutenant Colonel 29 Apr 1802
Service 1793–1815: Served in East Indies 1797–1807
Retired: 6 Aug 1807
Died: Doncaster, Yorkshire 7 Jun 1808
Sources: ARLI; SCMA (1808); WEOF; The History and Description of St. George's Church at Doncaster

68. *John CAMPBELL (1807–1810)*

Born: New York c.1766
Relations: Son of Captain Duncan Campbell, 84th Foot, and Eleanor (Baker); brother of Major Archibald Argyle Campbell, 42nd Foot; brother-in-law of Lieutenant General Sir James Hay
Entry to Army: Ensign in Nova Scotia Volunteers 1792; Ensign in 73rd Foot 23 Jul 1783
Field Officer Promotions: Major in 27th Foot 24 Nov 1802 (vice McMurdo) by purchase; to half-pay of 27th Foot 25 Oct 1802; Major in 33rd Foot 27 Sep 1803 (vice Crawford) by exchange; Lieutenant Colonel in 33rd Foot 6 August 1807 (vice Elliot) by purchase
Early Service: Served in East Indies 1783–1793
Service 1793–1815: Served in East Indies 1793–1802; served in capture of Ceylon 1795; Deputy Adjutant General in Madras 1802–1807; Deputy Paymaster General in Madras 1807–1810; commanded flank battalion in capture of Mauritius 1810
Died: Killed in action in Mauritius 2 Dec 1810
Sources: ANCW; ANCW (brother); ARLI; WEOF; WO 25/744

69. *Francis Ralph WEST (1810–1813)*

Born: County Cork 1771
Relations: Son of Captain Milborne West of Bath, 47th Foot, and Mary (Dore); brother of Captain Thomas Milborne West, 7th Foot; father of Lieutenant Charles Milborne West, Madras service; and Captain Henry West, 80th Foot
Entry to Army: 2nd Lieutenant in 23rd Foot 1786; to half-pay; Ensign in 33rd Foot 14 Dec 1791
Regimental Field Officer Promotions: Major in 33rd Foot 6 Aug 1807 (vice Campbell) by purchase; Lieutenant Colonel in 33rd Foot 3 Dec 1810
Service 1793–1815: Served in East Indies 1799–1811
Retired: 30 Sep 1813
Residence: Henley Upon Thames, Oxfordshire
Died: Henley Upon Thames Sep 1853
Sources: ANCB; ANCD; ANCW; ARLI; WEOF

70. *William George Keith Fullerton-ELPHINSTONE (1813–1821)*

Born: London 1782
Relations: Son of William Fullerton-Elphinstone, director of EIC and Elizabeth (Fullerton); brother of Captain Charles Elphinstone, RN; and Lieutenant Colonel James Drummond Buller-Fullerton-Elphinstone, 3rd Foot Guards; nephew of Admiral George Keith Elphinstone, 1st Viscount Keith
Entry to Army: Ensign in 29th Foot 21 Apr 1804 by purchase
Regimental Field Officer Promotions: Major in 8th West India Regiment 2 May 1811 (vice Willock) by purchase; Major in 6th Dragoon Guards 30 Jan 1812 (vice Davenport) by exchange; Major in 15th Light Dragoons 28 Apr 1812 (vice Dalrymple) by exchange; Lieutenant Colonel in 33rd Foot 30 Sep 1813 (vice West) by purchase; Lieutenant Colonel in 16th Light Dragoons 12 Apr 1821 (vice Pelly) by exchange; to half-pay of 16th Light Dragoons 25 Apr 1822
Brevets: Brevet Colonel 27 May 1825; Major General 10 Jan 1837
Service 1793–1815: Commanded 33rd Foot

in Netherlands 1814; commanded 33rd Foot at Waterloo 1815
Later Service: ADC to King George IV 1825; commanded British garrison at Kabul 1842
Awards and Honours: CB 22 Jul 1815; WatM 23 Apr 1816; KMWO (Netherlands); KSA, 2nd Class (Russia)
Died: Of exhaustion during the retreat from Kabul 23 Apr 1842
'At last, on 23 April 1842, before the final catastrophe, the old general died of dysentery, and his coffin was floated down to Jellalabad, where it was buried. By many he was blamed for incapacity, but it is rather the government of India, which selected him for so important a command in full knowledge of his age, infirmities, and long absence from actual warfare, which deserves the blame' – DINB
Sources: ANCB; ARLI; DALT; DINB; GEMA (1842); PHIL; WEOF

Majors

71. *William GORE (1790–1793)*
Born: Ireland c.1753
Relations: Father of Midshipman William Gore RN
Entry to Army: Ensign in 33rd Foot 2 May 1766 by purchase
Regimental Field Officer Promotions: Major in 33rd Foot 21 Jul 1790 (vice Dansey) by purchase
Early Service: Served in American War of Independence
Retired: 30 Apr 1793
Militia Career: Lieutenant Colonel of Bristol Volunteers 1797–1814
Residence: Clifton, Gloucestershire
Died: Clifton 6 Jul 1814
Sources: ANCW; ARLI; Mathews's Complete Bristol Guide

72. *John SHEE (1794–1802)*
Born: County Mayo c.1768
Relations: Son of Anthony Shee of Castlebar, merchant, and Margery (Bourke); brother of Sir George Shee, 1st Bt, Under Secretary of State for War and the Colonies
Entry to Army: Cornet in 13th Light Dragoons 31 May 1789 by purchase
Regimental Field Officer Promotions: Major in 33rd Foot 1 Dec 1794
Brevets: Brevet Lieutenant Colonel 1 Jan 1800
Service 1793–1815: Served in East Indies 1797–1802; commanded 33rd Foot 1799–1802
Retired: 20 Mar 1802
Militia Career: Lieutenant Colonel in 1st Cinque Port Volunteers 1803
Died: 3 Mar 1804
Sources: ARLI; Regimental Journal of The Duke of Wellington's Regiment, No. 212, Spring 1990

73. *Frederick CORNWALLIS (1794–1796)*
Born: Suffolk 1753
Relations: Son of Rev. William Cornwallis of Chelmondiston and Sarah (Cobbald); distant cousin of Charles, Marquess Cornwallis
Entry to Army: Ensign in 33rd Foot 19 Dec 1768
Regimental Field Officer Promotions: Major in 33rd Foot 24 May 1794 (vice Sherbrooke)
Brevets: Brevet Major 18 Nov 1790; Brevet Lieutenant Colonel 1 Mar 1794
Early Service: Served in American War of Independence
Retired: 8 Sep 1796
Residence: Ipswich, Suffolk
Died: Ipswich May 1811
Sources: ANCB; ANCD; ANCW; ARLI; WEOF

74. *George CRAWFORD (1802–1803)*
Born: County Dublin c.1777
Relations: Son of James Crawford of Auburn and Frances Dorothea (Vernon)
Entry to Army: Captain in 110th Foot 6 Jun 1794
Regimental Field Officer Promotions: Major in 33rd Foot 20 Mar 1802 (vice Shee) by purchase; to half-pay of 27th Foot Sep 1803 (vice Campbell) by exchange; Major in 2nd West India Regiment Jun 1805 (vice Ottley) by exchange
Service 1793–1815: Served in West Indies 1805–1807
Died: Fort Augusta, Jamaica 25 Dec 1807
Sources: ANCW; ARLI; Irish Pedigrees Vol. 2

75. *Dennis QUIN (1806–1808)*
Born: Dublin c.1770
Entry to Army: Ensign in 33rd Foot 30 Apr 1793
Regimental Field Officer Promotions: Major in 33rd Foot 6 Mar 1806
Retired: 19 May 1808
Residence: Kirkby Lonsdale, Lancashire
Died: Kirkby Lonsdale 24 Jan 1820
Sources: ANCD; ANCW; ARLI; WEOF

76. *William LAMBTON (1808–1818)*
Born: Yorkshire 1756
Relations: Son of William Lambton of Crosby Grange and Jane (Snowdon)
Entry to Army: Ensign in Lord Fauconberg's Regiment of Foot 28 Mar 1781
Regimental Field Officer Promotions: Major in

33rd Foot 1 Mar 1808 (vice Quin) by purchase; to half-pay of 33rd Foot 25 Dec 1818
Brevets: Brevet Lieutenant Colonel 4 Jun 1814
Early Service: Barrackmaster at St John's, New Brunswick 1785–1797
Service 1793–1815: Served in East Indies 1798–1815
Later Service: Superintendent of the trigonometrical survey of India 1815–1823
Awards and Honours: FRS; Fellow of the Asiatic Society
Died: Hinganghat, India 26 Jan 1823
Spent most of his time with the 33rd seconded as a surveyor and geographer; he began a triangulation survey in 1800 that was later called the Great Trigonometrical Survey of India
Sources: ANCB; ARLI; DINB; PHIL; WEOF; WO 25/746

77. *James TODD (1810–1813)*

Born: Perthshire 1774
Relations: Son of William Todd of Perth and Elizabeth (Cameron)
Entry to Army: Ensign in 73rd Foot 30 Jan 1790
Regimental Field Officer Promotions: Major in 33rd Foot 3 Dec 1810 (vice West)
Retired: 4 Feb 1813
Residence: Castlebank, Kinnoull, Perthshire
Died: Castlebank 6 Aug 1845
Sources: ARLI; FMPD; WEOF

78. *John Lockington HARTY (1813–1814)*

Born: County Kilkenny 1777
Relations: Son of Timothy Harty of Kilkenny and Mary (Lockington); brother of Lieutenant Colonel Joseph Mark Harty, 33rd Foot; and Sir Robert Way Harty, 1st Bt
Entry to Army: Lieutenant in 110th Foot 8 Jul 1794
Regimental Field Officer Promotions: Major in 33rd Foot 4 Feb 1813 (vice Todd) by purchase
Service 1793–1815: Served in Netherlands 1813–1814
Retired: 7 Jul 1814
Residence: Dublin, County Dublin
Died: Dublin 30 Mar 1854
Sources: ARLI; WEOF; A Genealogical and Heraldic History of the Peerage and Baronetage, the Privy Council, Knightage, and Companionage

79. *Edward PARKINSON (1814–1817)*

Born: Ulster c.1778
Entry to Army: Cornet in 33rd Light Dragoons 17 Feb 1796
Regimental Field Officer Promotions: Major in 33rd Foot 17 Mar 1814; to half-pay of 11th Foot 1 Sep 1817 (vice Crookshank) by exchange
Brevets: Brevet Major 27 Oct 1810; Brevet Lieutenant Colonel 18 Jun 1815; Brevet Colonel 10 Jan 1837; Major General 9 Nov 1846; Lieutenant General 20 Jun 1854
Colonelcies: 93rd Foot 10 Dec 1852 (vice Wemyss)
Service 1793–1815: Served in East Indies; served on staff in Isle de France and Bourbon; served in Holland 1814; served in Waterloo campaign, wounded at Quatre Bras
Awards and Honours: WatM 23 Apr 1816; CB Jul 1831
Residence: Pall Mall, St James's, London
Died: London 14 Jan 1858
Sources: ANCD; ANCW; ARLI; PHIL; WEOF

80. *John GUTHRIE [-DAVIDSON] (1814–1815)*

Born: John Guthrie in Angusshire 1774; added -Davidson surname in 1836
Relations: Son of John Guthrie of Dundee, merchant, and Helen (Yeaman); cousin of Major General James David Greenhill, Madras service
Entry to Army: Ensign in 73rd Foot 1 Dec 1798 by purchase
Regimental Field Officer Promotions: Major in 33rd Foot 7 Jul 1814 (vice Harty) by purchase
Service 1793–1815: Served in East Indies 1799–1812, badly wounded at Seringapatam 1799; served in Netherlands 1813–1814, badly wounded at Bergen-op-Zoom
Retired: 8 Jun 1815
Residence: Ardgaith, Perthshire
Died: Ardgaith 21 May 1853
Sources: ARLI; Annual Military Obituary 1854; <https://guthriegenealogy.blog/1a-a-john-guthrie/>

81. *George Washington COLCLOUGH (1815–1818)*

Born: County Wexford 1783
Relations: Natural son of Sir Vesey Colclough MP and Alicia (Harrington); brother of Anthony Caesar Colclough, Inspector General of British Army medical services; nephew of Captain Caesar Colclough, 7th Royal Veteran Battalion; father of Surgeon Anthony Caesar Fitzroy Colclough, 1st Life Guards; father-in-law of Major Barry Thomas, 9th Foot
Entry to Army: Ensign in 4th West India Regiment 2 Feb 1802
Regimental Field Officer Promotions: Major in 33rd Foot 8 Jun 1815 (vice Guthrie) by purchase

Residence: Sloane Terrace, Knightsbridge, London
Died: London 29 Dec 1818
This officer's wife was rumoured to be a natural daughter of the Duke of Wellington
Sources: ANCB; ANCD; ARLI; WEOF

Selected Regimental Histories

Brereton, John Maurice, Savory, A.C.S., *The History of the Duke of Wellington's Regiment (West Riding) 1702-1992* (Halifax: Duke of Wellington's Regiment (West Riding), 1993)

Regimental Museum

The Duke of Wellington's Regimental Museum, Bankfield House, Halifax, Yorkshire

---

34th Regiment of Foot

Secondary Title:	Cumberland
Nicknames:	The Cumberland Gentlemen
Jacket:	Red
Facings:	Bright yellow
Badge:	A laurel wreath

Regimental Lineage, 34th Regiment of Foot

1702:	Feb – raised in East Anglia by Baron Lucas of Shenfield
1705:	Hamilton's Regiment of Foot
1712:	Chudleigh's Regiment of Foot
1723:	Hayes's Regiment of Foot
1732:	Stephen Cornwallis's Regiment of Foot
1738:	Lord Cavendish's Regiment of Foot
1742:	Cholmondeley's Regiment of Foot
1747:	Ranked as 34th Regiment of Foot
1749:	Conway's Regiment of Foot
1751:	34th Regiment of Foot
1782:	34th (Cumberland) Regiment of Foot
1805:	Apr – 2nd Battalion formed at Ashford
1817:	Apr – 2nd Battalion disbanded in Ireland
1881:	1st Battalion, The Border Regiment (on amalgamation with the 55th (Westmorland) Regiment of Foot)
1959:	The King's Own Royal Border Regiment (on amalgamation with the King's Own Royal Regiment (Lancaster))
2006:	3rd Battalion, Duke of Lancaster's Regiment (King's Lancashire and Border) (on amalgamation with the King's Regiment and the Queen's Lancashire Regiment)

Service History, 1st Battalion 34th Regiment of Foot

1793:	Ireland – Limerick; Oct – flank companies to West Indies
1794:	Limerick; Cork; Aug – battalion companies to Flanders; Flushing; Sep – to England Flank companies in West Indies; Mar – Martinique; Apr – St Lucia; Guadeloupe; Oct – light company taken POW at Berville
1795:	Feb – battalion companies to West Indies; May – St Lucia; Jun – St Vincent
1796:	St Vincent; Jun – New Vigie; Jul – Martinique; accompanied Caribs to Isle Ratan (Honduras); Aug – to England; Oct – Poole
1797:	Poole; recruited back to strength with orphan boys aged 12–16; Mar – York; Jul – Bridlington; Nov – Lincoln
1798:	Lincoln
1799:	Lincoln; Oct – Poole; Dec – Hilsea

1800:	Hilsea; to Cape of Good Hope; May – Cape Town; Sep – Wynberg
1801:	Cape Town; Third Xhosa War
1802:	Cape Town; Oct – to East Indies
1803:	Apr – Madras [Chennai]; Jul – two companies to Ceylon; Aug – Fort St George
1804:	Madras; Jun – Fort St George; Oct – Walajabad, reunited with Ceylon detachment; Dec – detachments at Madras and Vizagapatam [Visakhapatnam]
1805:	Walahjabad; Apr – four companies to Vellore; Jul – Damul; Aug – Peroor; Sep – Bellary [Ballari]; Nov – Vellore companies returned
1806–1807:	Gooty, three companies at Bellary
1808:	Gooty; Aug – Bellary
1809:	Bellary; officers detached to native regiments; Sep – Gooty; Nov – Tope Dall; Dec – Pandoorna [Pandhurna]
1810:	Hoosingabad [Hoshangabad]; May – Jaulnah [Jalna]
1811:	Jaulnah; Apr – Oudgheer [Udgir]; May – Secunderabad
1812–1813:	Secunderabad
1814:	Secunderabad; Jun – Naundygaum; Jul – Paughur; Aug – Seringapatam [Srirangapatna]
1815:	Seringapatam; Aug – Mundiem [Mundiyampakkam]; Sep – Hooscottah; Oct – Vellore
1823:	To England (after 23 years away!)

Service History, 2nd Battalion 34th Regiment of Foot

1805:	Apr – formed at Ashford; Jun – Colchester; Nov – Ramsgate; Dec – Brabourne Lees
1806:	To Hanover; returned to England; Mar – Rye; Apr – Jersey
1807:	Jersey; May – Isle of Wight; Sep – to Ireland; Oct – Cork; Nov – Bandon; Dec – to England
1808:	Spithead; Feb – Steyning; May – Portsmouth; Jun – Jersey
1809:	Jersey; Jul – to Portugal; Lisbon; PENINSULA; Aug – joined field army; Santarem; Guadiana – high number of fever deaths; Dec – Sardoal
1810:	Sardoal; Feb – Portalegre; Jun – Alegrete; Jul – Atalaia; Aug – Sarzedas; Sep – Penacova; Busaco; Oct – Bucelas; Nov – Almeirim
1811:	Almeirim; Feb – Alpiarça; Mar – Campo Maior; Apr – Almendralejo; May – 1st siege of Badajoz; ALBUERA; Jun – Torre de Mouro; Jul – Vila Viçosa; Sep – Portalegre; Oct – Castillejo; ARROYO DOS MOLINOS (Arroyomolinos); Nov – Portalegre; Dec – La Nava de Santiago
1812:	Nave de Haver; Feb – Alburquerque; Mar – Merida; Almandralejo; Apr – Talavera la Real; Badajoz; Fuente del Maestre; May – Almaraz; Villamesias; Jun – Albuera; Jul – Zafra; Aug – Huerta; Sep – Oropesa; Oct – Aranjuez; Nov – El Sahugo; Dec – Casas de Don Gómez
1813:	Casillas de Coria; May – Fuente Robledo; Jun – VITTORIA; Jul – Maya; Aug –PYRENEES; Burguete-Auritz; Oct – Valley of Baztan; Nov – Nivelle; Larressore; Dec – NIVE; Saint-Pierre-d'Irube
1814:	Saint-Pierre-d'Irube; Feb – Parenties; ORTHEZ; Mar – Lavelanet; Apr – Baziège; May – Toulouse; Jun – Blanquefort; Jul – to Ireland; Aug – Templemore; Nov – Dublin
1815:	Dublin; Sep – Tipperary; Dec – Clonmel
1817:	Apr – disbanded in Ireland

Establishments, 1st Battalion 34th Regiment of Foot

Year	Subunits	Field Off	Off/ Staff	Sjts	Mus	Corp/ Pvts	Total
Dec 1792	10co	3	32	22	12	330	399
Jan 1793	10co	3	32	32	22	600	689
Jul 1794	12co	3	38	40	26	740	847
Dec 1795	10co+2r	5	51	62	30	1010	1,158
Dec 1797	10co	5	32	53	22	600	712
Dec 1798	10co	5	38	53	22	600	718

Dec 1799	10co	5	43	53	22	1,000	1,123
Dec 1800	10co+r	5	47	61	26	1,008	1,147
Jun 1802	10co	5	33	34	22	750	844
Dec 1802	10co	5	43	52	22	1,000	1,122
Dec 1803	10co+r	5	50	62	26	1,008	1,151
Dec 1807	10co+r	5	50	72	26	1,208	1,361
Dec 1808	10co+r	5	50	62	26	1,008	1,151
Dec 1809	10co+r	5	50	72	26	1,208	1,361
Dec 1810	10co+r	5	50	62	26	1,008	1,151
Dec 1811	10co+r	5	50	63	26	1,008	1,152
Dec 1813	10co+r	5	49	63	22	1,008	1,147
Dec 1814	10co	5	46	55	22	1,000	1,128

Establishments, 2nd Battalion 34th Regiment of Foot

Year	Subunits	Field Off	Off/ Staff	Sjts	Mus	Corp/ Pvts	Total
Apr 1805	10co	3	35	34	22	600	694
Apr 1807	10co+r	3	39	42	26	608	718
Dec 1808	10co	3	35	34	22	600	694
Jun 1809	10co+r	3	50	62	26	1,008	1,149
Dec 1810	10co+r	3	40	52	26	808	929
Dec 1811	10co+r	3	50	63	26	1,008	1,150
Dec 1813	10co+r	3	49	63	22	1,008	1,145
Aug 1814	10co	4	49	63	22	1,008	1,146

Service Statistics, 34th Regiment of Foot

	Lieutenant Colonels	Majors
Number of officers in period 1793–1815	15	21
Average age on appointment to substantive rank	36	29
Average time in rank in regiment (years)	4	3.5
Total field officers by nationality	23 E / 5 I / 3 S / 1 W	
Demographics of other ranks 1809	2/34th: 89% EW / 8% I / 3% S	
Demographics of other ranks 1810	1/34th: 54% EW / 39% I / 6% S / 1% F	
Demographics of other ranks 1815	1/34th: 56% EW / 37% I / 6% S / 1% F	
Months of overseas service 1793–1815	1/34th: 216 2/34th: 62	

Significant Militia/Volunteer Intakes

1805:	1st East Yorkshire, 3rd West Yorkshire, 1st Lancashire, South Lincolnshire, East Essex, County Tipperary
1807:	1st East Yorkshire
1809:	Cheshire, Herefordshire, 1st Lancashire, West Suffolk, Worcestershire, East Yorkshire, North Yorkshire, 3rd West Yorkshire
1811:	Herefordshire, West Kent, 1st Lancashire
1812:	West Suffolk, East Yorkshire, Denbighshire
1813:	Herefordshire, West Suffolk, East Yorkshire, 3rd West Yorkshire, County Galway
1814:	Somerset, Queen's County

Regimental Colonels

82. *Lord Frederick CAVENDISH (1760–1797)*

Born: Derbyshire 1729
Relations: Son of William Cavendish, 3rd Duke of Devonshire and Catherine (Hoskins); brother of William Cavendish, Marquess of Hartington; and Lord George Augustus Cavendish
Entry to Army: Ensign in 1st Foot Guards 29 Apr 1749 by purchase
Regimental Field Officer Promotions: Lieutenant Colonel in 39th Foot 18 Jun 1755; Captain and Lieutenant Colonel in 1st Foot Guards 1 Jun 1756
Brevets: Brevet Colonel 7 May 1758; Major General 7 Mar 1761; Lieutenant General 30 Apr 1770; General 20 Nov 1782; Field Marshal 30 Jul 1796
Colonelcies: 67th Foot 24 Oct 1758 (vice Wolfe); 34th Foot 30 Oct 1760 (vice Effingham)
Early Service: Lord of the Bedchamber to the Duke of Cumberland 1757–1765
Political Career: MP (Derbyshire) 1751–1754; MP (Derby) 1754–1780
Residence: Twickenham Park, Twickenham, Surrey
Died: Twickenham Park 21 Oct 1803
Sources: ARLI; BRFM; DINB;

83. *Rt Hon. George Ferdinand Fitzroy, 2nd Baron SOUTHAMPTON (1797–1810)*

Born: London 1761
Relations: Son of Lieutenant General Charles FitzRoy, 1st Baron Southampton, MP, and Lady Anne (Warren); brother of General Hon. Charles Fitzroy; and Lieutenant General Hon. William Fitzroy; brother-in-law of Major General Sir William Ponsonby; and Lieutenant Colonel Frederick Keppel, 49th Foot
Education: Eton College
Entry to Army: Ensign in 3rd Foot Guards 29 May 1778 by purchase
Regimental Field Officer Promotions: Major in 51st Foot 25 Apr 1792 (vice Fisher); Captain and Lieutenant Colonel in Coldstream Foot Guards 1 Feb 1793 (vice Pennington) by purchase
Brevets: Brevet Colonel 3 May 1796; Major General 1 Jan 1801; Lieutenant General 25 Apr 1808
Colonelcies: 34th Foot 13 Jul 1797 (vice Cavendish)
Early Service: Served in American War of Independence 1779–1780, wounded at Charleston; served in West Indies 1782–1783
Service 1793–1815: Served in Flanders 1793–1794; Groom of the Bedchamber to the Prince of Wales 1783–1797
Political Career: MP (Bury St Edmunds) 1784–1787
Creations and Dignities: 2nd Baron Southampton 21 Mar 1797
Residence: Fitzroy Farm, Highgate, Middlesex
Died: Highgate 24 Jun 1810
Sources: ANCB; ANCD; ARLI; HPON; WEOF; WO 25/748

84. *Sir Eyre COOTE (1810–1816)*

Born: Queen's County 1759
Relations: Son of Very Rev. Charles Evans Coote, Dean of Kilfenora and Grace (Tilson); nephew of Lieutenant General Sir Eyre Coote, HEIC
Education: Eton College; Trinity College, Dublin
Entry to Army: Ensign in 37th Foot 15 Apr 1774 by purchase
Regimental Field Officer Promotions: Major in 47th Foot 20 Feb 1783 by purchase; Lieutenant Colonel in 70th Foot 31 Mar 1788 by purchase
Brevets: Brevet Colonel 24 Jan 1795; Brigadier General (Ireland) 1796; Major General 1 Jan 1798; Lieutenant General 1 Jan 1805; General 4 Jun 1814
Colonelcies: Colonel Commandant of 2/17th Foot 5 Aug 1799; 89th Foot 4 Sep 1802 (vice Ogilvie); 62nd Foot 26 May 1806 (vice Nugent); 34th Foot 25 Jun 1810 (vice Lord Southampton)
Early Service: Served in American War of Independence 1776–1782; taken POW at Yorktown 1781
Service 1793–1815: Commanded battalion of light infantry in Leeward Islands 1794; ADC to King George III 24 Jan 1795; served at Ostend raid 1798, taken POW; commanded brigade at Helder 1799; commanded brigade in Egypt 1801; commanded various districts in Ireland 1803–1805; Governor and Commander in Chief Jamaica 21 Feb 1806 to 26 Mar 1808 (vice Nugent); second in command at Walcheren 1809
Political Career: MP (Ire) 1790–1800; MP (Queen's County) 1802–1806; MP (Barnstaple) 1812–1818
Awards and Honours: KB 19 May 1802; KCt (Ottoman) 1802; GCB 2 Jan 1815 (expelled 25 Jul 1816)
Retired: Dismissed from the army 18 Apr 1816
Residence: West Park, Damerham, Hampshire
Died: London 10 Dec 1823
The Duke of York heard that Coote had been acquitted of an affair involving him offering to flog some schoolboys, and directed Sir John Abercromby, Sir Henry Fane, and Sir George Cooke to prepare a secret report upon the matter. They reported that Coote was eccentric rather

than mad, and that his conduct had been unworthy of an officer and a gentleman – leading to his dismissal
Sources: *ARLI; DINB; HPON; WEOF; WO 25/744; WOST*

Lieutenant Colonels

85. *Rt Hon. Aubrey Beauclerk, 6th Earl of BURFORD, 6th Duke of St Albans (1789–1794)*
Born: Middlesex 1765
Relations: Son of Aubrey Beauclerk, 5th Duke of St Albans and Catherine (Ponsonby); grandson of Vere Beauclerk, 1st Baron Vere; William Ponsonby, 2nd Earl of Bessborough; and William Cavendish, 3rd Duke of Devonshire; brother of Admiral Lord Amelius Beauclerk RN
Entry to Army: Ensign in 1st Foot Guards 30 Mar 1781 by purchase
Regimental Field Officer Promotions: Major in 34th Foot 27 Feb 1789 (vice Ross) by purchase; Lieutenant Colonel in 34th Foot 11 Nov 1789 (vice Hastings) by purchase
Early Service: Commanded 34th Foot 1789–1794
Retired: 22 Oct 1794
Political Career: MP (Kingston Upon Hull) 1790–1796
Creations and Dignities: 6th Duke of St Albans, 6th Earl of Burford, 6th Baron Heddington and 3rd Baron Vere of Hanworth 9 Feb 1802
Residence: St George Hanover Square, London
Died: London 12 Aug 1815
Sources: *ANCB; ANCD; ARLI; HPON*

86. *Richard Mark DICKENS (1794–1808)*
Born: County Durham 1764
Relations: Son of Dr Samuel Dickens of Elvet, prebendary of Durham Cathedral, and Margaret (Hildesley)
Education: Christ Church, Oxford
Entry to Army: Ensign in 44th Foot 26 Sep 1782
Regimental Field Officer Promotions: Major in 86th Foot 30 Oct 1793; Lieutenant Colonel in 86th Foot 7 Jun 1794; Lieutenant Colonel in 34th Foot 22 Oct 1794 (vice Burford)
Brevets: Brevet Colonel 1 Jan 1800; Major General 30 Oct 1805
Service 1793–1815: Commanded 34th Foot in West Indies 1794–1796; Adjutant General in West Indies 15 Jun 1797; served in East Indies 1803–1808
Residence: Hertford Street, Mayfair, London
Died: Mathura, India 29 Apr 1808
Sources: *ANCB; ANCW; ARLI; WEOF; List of Christian Tombs and Monuments of Archæological or Historical Interest*

87. *Dennett Milton WOODWARD (1795–1796)*
Born: Ireland c.1744
Relations: Brother of Lieutenant Colonel Humphrey Aldridge Woodward, Dublin Yeomanry
Entry to Army: Ensign in 59th Foot 27 Aug 1760 by purchase
Regimental Field Officer Promotions: Major in 59th Foot 12 Nov 1794 (vice Haynes); Lieutenant Colonel in 34th Foot 1 Sep 1795
Brevets: Brevet Major 1 Mar 1794
Early Service: Served in American War of Independence
Retired: 23 Nov 1796
Residence: Bank Villa, Shrewsbury, Shropshire
Died: Shrewsbury 23 Sep 1798
Sources: *ANCD; ANCW; ARLI*

88. *Francis CUNYNGHAME (1796–1799)*
Born: West Lothian 1771
Relations: Son of Sir William Augustus Cunynghame, Bt, and Frances (Myrton)
Entry to Army: Ensign in 76th Foot 20 Mar 1783
Regimental Field Officer Promotions: Major in 34th Foot 1 Sep 1795; Lieutenant Colonel in 34th Foot 23 Nov 1796 (vice Woodward) by purchase; Captain and Lieutenant Colonel in Coldstream Foot Guards 24 Jan 1799 (vice Gascoyne) by exchange
Service 1793–1815: Served in Helder 1799, badly wounded at Alkmaar; Lieutenant Governor of Hull 23 Jun 1801; Lieutenant Governor of Edinburgh Castle 21 Sep 1807
Retired: 10 Jul 1801
Residence: Cloncaird, Ayrshire
Died: Frankville, near Ayr, Ayrshire 19 Sep 1816
'This gallant and meritorious officer, in going forward to direct the fire of some gun-boats against a column of the French, happening to have his hand at his face, a cannon ball carried away the whole of his lower jaw, and shattered his left hand to pieces.' Reading Mercury Monday 28 Oct 1799
Sources: *ANCB; ANCD; ANCW; ARLI; WEOF*

89. *Isaac GASCOYNE (1799–1803)*
Born: Essex 1763
Relations: Son of Bamber Gascoyne of Bifrons, MP and Mary (Green); brother of Bamber Gascoyne MP; and Captain John Gascoyne RN; father of General Ernest Frederick Sackville Gascoyne

Entry to Army: Ensign in 20th Foot 8 Feb 1779 by purchase
Regimental Field Officer Promotions: Captain and Lieutenant Colonel in Coldstream Foot Guards 5 Dec 1792 (vice Morgan) by purchase; Lieutenant Colonel in 34th Foot 24 Jan 1799 (vice Cunynghame) by exchange; Lieutenant Colonel in 16th Foot 12 Mar 1803 (vice Fancourt) by exchange
Brevets: Brevet Colonel 3 May 1796; Major General 29 Apr 1802; Lieutenant General 25 Apr 1808; General 12 Aug 1819
Colonelcies: 7th West India Regiment 10 Oct 1805 (vice Don); 54th Foot 1 Jun 1816 (vice Forbes)
Service 1793–1815: Served in Flanders 1793–1794, wounded in Lincelles; commanded Coldstream Foot Guards in Ireland 1798; commanded 16th Foot 1803–1805
Political Career: MP (Liverpool) 1796–1831
Residence: Roby Hall, near Liverpool, Lancashire; South Audley Street, Hanover Square, London
Died: London 26 Aug 1841
Sources: ANCB; ANCD; ANCW; ARLI; DINB; GHLG; PHIL; WEOF; WO 25/745

90. *St John FANCOURT (1803–1806)*
Born: Northamptonshire 1769
Relations: Son of William Fancourt, curate of Woodford, and Mary (Harrington); father of Charles St John Fancourt, Superintendent of British Honduras; and Captain Joseph Edmund Fancourt RN
Entry to Army: Ensign in 55th Foot 26 Jan 1785 by purchase
Regimental Field Officer Promotions: Major in 17th Foot 7 Aug 1799; Lieutenant Colonel in 69th Foot 15 Jan 1801 (vice Atkinson) by purchase; Lieutenant Colonel in 16th Foot 17 Jul 1801 (vice Wallace) by purchase; Lieutenant Colonel in 34th Foot 12 Mar 1803 (vice Gascoyne) by exchange
Brevets: Brevet Lieutenant Colonel 15 Jan 1801
Early Service: Served in British East Indies 1787–1794
Service 1793–1815: Served in Helder 1799; commanded 16th Foot 1801–1803; served in British East Indies 1804–1806; commandant in Vellore 1806
Died: Killed in sepoy mutiny in Vellore 9 Jul 1806
Sources: ANCB; ARLI; 'An Account of the Mutiny at Vellore, by the lady of St John Fancourt, who was killed there July 9th 1806,' Sydney Gazette, 14th June, 1842

91. *David PARKHILL (1805–1807)*
Born: Yorkshire 1767
Relations: Son of Captain David Parkhill of Halifax, 12th Foot, and Anne (Lees)
Entry to Army: Ensign in 101st Foot 3 Jul 1782
Regimental Field Officer Promotions: Major in 10th Foot 19 Jul 1803 (vice Mellifont); Lieutenant Colonel in 10th Foot 6 Jun 1805 (vice Lloyd) by purchase; Lieutenant Colonel in 34th Foot 17 Dec 1805
Early Service: Served in British East Indies 1783–1785
Service 1793–1815: Served in Gibraltar
Retired: 20 Aug 1807
Residence: St George Hanover Square, London
Died: London 21 Aug 1807
Sources: ANCB; ANCD: ARLI; WEOF

92. *George DODSWORTH (1806–1808)*
Born: Yorkshire 1761
Relations: Son of Rev. George Dodsworth of Scarborough and Dorothy (Bell)
Entry to Army: Ensign in East Yorkshire Militia; Ensign in 34th Foot 4 Oct 1780
Regimental Field Officer Promotions: Major in 34th Foot 23 Nov 1796 (vice Cunynghame) by purchase; Lieutenant Colonel in 34th Foot 10 Jul 1806 (vice Fancourt)
Brevets: Brevet Lieutenant Colonel 29 Apr 1802
Service 1793–1815: Deputy Quartermaster General in West Indies 1 Jan 1799; served at Cape of Good Hope 1800–1802; commanded 1/34th Foot in India 1806; commander of garrison at Poonamalee 1806–1808
Residence: Beverley, Yorkshire
Died: Ballari, Karnataka, India 4 Oct 1808
Sources: ANCB; ANCD; ARLI; WEOF; List of Inscriptions on Tombs Or Monuments in Madras Possessing Historical Or Archaeological Interest

93. *John MAISTER (1807–1817)*
Born: Yorkshire 1778
Relations: Son of Arthur Maister of Kingston-upon-Hull and Esther (Rickaby); brother of Colonel Arthur Maister, East Yorkshire Militia; nephew of Colonel Henry Maister, East Yorkshire Militia; uncle of Major General George Maister RA
Entry to Army: Ensign in in East Yorkshire Militia; Ensign in 54th Foot 13 Nov 1793
Regimental Field Officer Promotions: Major in 20th Foot 20 Jun 1801 (vice Power) by purchase; to half-pay of 20th Foot 25 Oct 1802; Major in 39th Foot 9 Jul 1803 (vice Wilson); Lieutenant Colonel in 34th Foot 20 Aug 1807 (vice Parkhill) by purchase; to half-pay of 34th Foot 25 Jun 1817
Brevets: Brevet Colonel 4 Jun 1814; Major General 19 Jul 1821; Lieutenant General 10 Jan 1837; General 11 Nov 1851

Colonelcies: 2nd West India Regiment 3 Jun 1841 (vice Fuller); 86th Foot 25 Aug 1843 (vice Brooke)
Service 1793–1815: Served in Helder 1799, wounded four times; commanded 2/34th Foot in Peninsula Jul 1809 to Jun 1810
Retired: Commander in Chief Windward and Leeward Islands 14 Sep 1839 to May 1843
Residence: Littlethorpe, near Ripon, Yorkshire
Died: Wells, Somerset 18 May 1852
Sources: ANCB; ANCD; ANCW; ARLI; CHAL; GEMA (1852); WEOF; WO 25/747

94. *William FENWICK (1808–1814)*

Born: Northumberland 1777
Relations: Son of Thomas Fenwick of Earsdon and Anne (Dawson)
Entry to Army: Ensign in 34th Foot 29 Jun 1793 by purchase
Regimental Field Officer Promotions: Major in 34th Foot 15 May 1805; Lieutenant Colonel in 34th Foot 15 Dec 1808 (vice Dickens)
Brevets: Brevet Major 1 Jan 1805
Service 1793–1815: Served in Flanders 1794; served in West Indies 1795–1796; served at Cape of Good Hope 1800–1801; served in East Indies 1802–1807; served in Peninsula Jul 1809 to Jun 1810; commanded 2/34th in Peninsula Jun 1810 to Oct 1813, lost right leg at thigh and POW at Maya; released Sep 1813; Governor of Pendennis Castle 1813–1832
Retired: 27 Jan 1814
Residence: Pendennis Castle, Falmouth, Cornwall
Died: Pendennis Castle 7 Jul 1832
Sources: ANCB; ANCD; ARLI; CHAL; HALL; WEOF; WO 25/745

95. *Sir Thomas BRADFORD (1809)*

Born: Yorkshire 1777
Relations: Son of Thomas Bradford of Woodlands and Elizabeth (Otter); brother of Captain and Lieutenant Colonel Sir Henry Hollis Bradford, 1st Foot Guards
Entry to Army: Ensign in 1st West Yorkshire Militia 30 Oct 1792; Ensign in Independent Company 20 Oct 1793
Regimental Field Officer Promotions: Major in Nottinghamshire Fencibles 9 Sep 1795; Major in 3rd Garrison Battalion 25 Feb 1805; Major in 87th Foot 30 May 1805 (vice Locke); Lieutenant Colonel in 34th Foot 18 May 1809 (vice Dodsworth); Lieutenant Colonel in 82nd Foot 21 Dec 1809 (vice McDonnell) by exchange; removed from the regiment as a general officer 1814
Brevets: Brevet Lieutenant Colonel 1 Jan 1801; Brigadier General (Portuguese service) 19 Dec 1811; Major General 4 Jun 1813; Lieutenant General 27 May 1825; General 28 Nov 1841
Colonelcies: 94th Foot 1 Dec 1823; 30th Foot 18 Apr 1829 (vice Montgomerie); 4th Foot 7 Feb 1846 (vice Hodgson)
Service 1793–1815: Served in Irish rebellion 1798; Assistant Adjutant General in Scotland 1801; served in Peninsula Aug 1808 to Jan 1809; commanded Portuguese brigade in Peninsula Dec 1811 to Apr 1814, severely wounded at Bayonne; temporary commander of 3rd Division in Belgium 18 Jul 1815; commanded brigades in Allied Army of Occupation in France 1815–1818
Later Service: Commander in Chief Bombay Presidency 1825–1829
Awards and Honours: AGC (Cor Sal Vitt SS Niv); KCTS (Portugal) 13 May 1813; KCB 2 Jan 1815; CD (Portugal) 28 May 1820; CM (Portugal) 1 Dec 1820; GCH 12 Aug 1831; GCB 15 Feb 1838
Residences: Eaton Square, Belgravia, London; Hartwell, Kent; Brunswick Terrace, Brighton, Sussex
Died: London 28 Nov 1853
Sources: ANCW; ARLI; CHAL; DINB; WEBC; WEOF; WO 25/744

96. *Chichester MACDONELL (1809–1810)*

Born: Inverness-shire 1761
Relations: Son of Alexander Macdonell of Aberchalder and Ann (Cuming); cousin of Lieutenant Colonel John Macdonell, York Militia; and Lieutenant Colonel George Macdonell, Glengarry Light Infantry Volunteers
Entry to Army: Lieutenant in Butler's Rangers (New York) 9 Oct 1781; Ensign in 17th Foot 7 Apr 1797
Regimental Field Officer Promotions: Major in 82nd Foot 2 Aug 1804; Lieutenant Colonel in 34th Foot 21 Dec 1809
Early Service: Served in American War of Independence 1778–1783
Service 1793–1815: Served in Peninsula Aug 1808 to Jan 1809; commanded 1/34th Foot in India 1809–1811
Awards and Honours: AGM (Cor)
Died: Jalna 22 Dec 1810
Sources: ANCB; ARLI; FMPW; WEOF; Madras Courier 15 Jan 1811; <https://www.noonans.co.uk/auctions/calendar/ 671/catalogue/452834/>

97. *Sir William THORNTON (1811–1812)*

Born: County Londonderry c.1779
Relations: Son of William Thornton of Muff and Anne (James); brother of Captain Robert Innes

Thornton, 21st Light Dragoons
Entry to Army: Ensign in 89th Foot 31 Mar 1796
Regimental Field Officer Promotions: Major in Royal York Rangers 13 Nov 1806 (vice Lloyd); Lieutenant Colonel in 34th Foot 1 Aug 1811 (vice McDonell); Lieutenant Colonel in Duke of York's Greek Light Infantry 23 Jan 1812 (vice Fouveaux); Lieutenant Colonel in 85th Foot 25 Jan 1813 (vice Cuyler); to half-pay of 85th Foot 30 Sep 1819 (vice Warburton) by exchange
Brevets: Brevet Lieutenant Colonel 28 Jan 1808; Brevet Colonel 4 Jun 1814; Major General 27 May 1825; Lieutenant General 28 Jun 1838
Colonelcies: 96th Foot 10 Oct 1834 (vice Smith); 85th Foot 9 Apr 1839 (vice Taylor)
Service 1793–1815: Served in Malta and Naples 1805–1806; ADC to James Henry Craig in British North America 1807; Inspecting Field Officer of Militia in Canada 28 Jan 1808; Assistant military secretary to Duke of York 1812–1813; commanded 85th Foot in Spain and France Jul 1813 to Apr 1814; served in North America Aug 1814 to Jan 1815
Awards and Honours: AGM (Niv); CB 4 Jun 1815; KCB 16 Sep 1836
Residence: Stanhope Lodge, Greenford, Middlesex
Died: Committed suicide at home 6 Apr 1840
Sources: ARLI; CHAL; DINB; GHLG; WEOF; WO 25/748

98. *John Matthias EVERARD (1812–1818)*
Born: County Meath 1778
Relations: Son of Thomas Everard of Randalstown and Barbara (O'Reilly); brother of Captain Thomas Everard RN; Lieutenant James Everard, 46th Foot; Lieutenant William Everard RN; Major General Matthias Everard; and Captain Richard Nugent Everard, 86th Foot
Entry to Army: Ensign in 66th Foot 30 Nov 1796 by purchase
Regimental Field Officer Promotions: Major in 34th Foot 10 Jul 1806 (vice Dodsworth) by purchase; Lieutenant Colonel in 34th Foot 23 Jan 1812 (vice Thornton); Lieutenant Colonel in 77th Foot 5 Mar 1818 (vice Dunkin); to half-pay of 77th Foot 5 Mar 1818; Captain and Lieutenant Colonel in 1st Foot Guards 12 Jun 1840 (vice Lyster)
Brevets: Brevet Colonel 22 Jul 1830
Service 1793–1815: Commanded 1/34th Foot in India 1812–1818
Retired: 12 Jun 1840
Residence: Randalstown, County Meath
Died: Ricoaro, Pisa, Italy 25 Jul 1845
Sources: ANCB; ANCD; ANCW; ARLI; WEOF

99. *Henry ROBERTS (1814–1816)*
Born: Caernarvonshire 1772
Relations: Son of Rev. John Roberts of Llanrug and Catherine (Jones)
Entry to Army: Ensign in 15th Foot 20 Jan 1792 by purchase
Regimental Field Officer Promotions: Major in 34th Foot 19 Jan 1809 (vice Fenwick); Lieutenant Colonel in 34th Foot 27 Jan 1814 (vice Fenwick) by purchase
Service 1793–1815: Served in West Indies 1794; served in Gibraltar 1795–1800; served in Egypt 1801; Brigade Major to John Moore 1802; served in East Indies 1803–1816
Died: Cuddalore, India 1 Apr 1816
Sources: ARLI; FMPW; WEOF; WO 25/748; List of Inscriptions on Tombs or Monuments in Madras Possessing Historical or Archaeological Interest

Majors

100. *Robert WOOD (1792–1797)*
Born: London 1763
Relations: Son of Robert Wood of Lime Grove, Under Secretary of State, and Ann (Skottowe); nephew of Captain Nicholas Skottowe, EIC naval service; John George Skottowe, Governor of St Helena; and Thomas Skottowe, Secretary of the Province of South Carolina
Education: Christ Church, Oxford
Entry to Army: Cornet in 1st Dragoon Guards 23 Jan 1784
Regimental Field Officer Promotions: Major in 34th Foot 25 Jul 1792 (vice Ancram) by purchase
Brevets: Brevet Lieutenant Colonel 3 May 1796
Service 1793–1815: Received letter of service to raise a battalion of fencible infantry 1 Dec 1794; received letter of service to raise two battalions of fencible infantry in Europe at own expense 8 May 1795; commission sold to defray expenses when fencibles not delivered
Retired: Majority sold out from under him 22 Nov 1797
Political Career: MP (Minehead) 1786–1790; MP (East Looe) 1790–1796
Residence: Putney, Surrey
Died: Putney 20 Dec 1841
Sources: ANCB; ANCD; ARLI; HPON; The Life and Works of Robert Wood; English Chronicle and Whitehall Evening Post 27 Jun 1822

101. *George ANDERSON (1797–1800)*
Born: Northumberland 1760
Relations: Son of George Anderson of Anderson Place, master builder

Entry to Army: Ensign in 28th Foot 17 Oct 1778 by purchase
Regimental Field Officer Promotions: Major in 34th Foot 22 Nov 1797 (vice Wood) by purchase
Retired: 9 May 1800
Later Service: Deputy Lieutenant and Magistrate for the county of Northumberland
Awards and Honours: FSA
Residences: Anderson Place, Newcastle-Upon-Tyne, Northumberland; Hawthorn Hive Cottage, near Easington, County Durham
Died: Anderson Place 6 Sep 1831
A noted church benefactor and author; he rescued the crew of a wrecked ship near his cottage in Durham with the aid of his Newfoundland dog and servants in 1824
Sources: ANCW; ARLI; LFBI; WEOF; A Descriptive and Historical Account of the Monuments & Tombstones in the Church of St. Nicholas, Newcastle-upon-Tyne

102. *Robert GORDON (1800–1806)*
Born: Scotland c.1768
Entry to Army: 2nd Lieutenant in Marines 3 Dec 1781
Regimental Field Officer Promotions: Major in 34th Foot 9 May 1800 (vice Anderson) by purchase; temporary Lieutenant Colonel unattached 7 May 1808
Service 1793–1815: Brigade Major in South Britain 27 Feb 1798; Inspecting Field Officer of Yeomanry 7 May 1808
Retired: 17 Jul 1806
Died: Inverness, Inverness-shire 2 Mar 1832
Sources: ARLI; UNSM (1832); WEOF

103. *John BROMHEAD (1805–1809)*
Born: Lincolnshire 1776
Relations: Son of John Bromhead of Lincoln and Anne (Darwin); cousin of Lieutenant General Sir Gonville Bromhead, Bt
Entry to Army: Ensign in 24th Foot 13 Nov 1793
Regimental Field Officer Promotions: Major in 34th Foot 16 May 1805; Lieutenant Colonel in 77th Foot 3 Aug 1809 (vice Whitelocke) by purchase
Brevets: Brevet Colonel 12 Aug 1819
Service 1793–1815: Served in British North America 1794–1800; Deputy Quartermaster General in British North America; served in Egypt 1801; served in Hanover 1805; commanded 77th Foot in Peninsula Jul to Oct 1811, and Apr 1812 to Apr 1814
Retired: 26 Dec 1822
Awards and Honours: AGM (Bad); CB 4 Jun 1815
Residences: Grecian Terrace, Lincoln, Lincolnshire; Washingborough, Lincolnshire
Died: Lincoln 7 Feb 1837
Sources: ANCB; ANCD; ANCW; ARLI; CHAL; WEOF; WO 25/744

104. *Richard DIGGENS (1806)*
Born: Sussex 1774
Relations: Son of Richard Diggens, merchant of Chichester, and Mary (Tiszard)
Entry to Army: Cornet in 11th Light Dragoons 18 Aug 1796 by purchase
Regimental Field Officer Promotions: Major in 34th Foot 17 Jul 1806 (vice Gordon) by purchase; Major in 11th Light Dragoons 14 Aug 1806 (vice Browne) by exchange; Lieutenant Colonel in 5th Portuguese Dragoons 3 Aug 1811; Lieutenant Colonel in 6th Portuguese Dragoons 23 Dec 1811; Lieutenant Colonel in 11th Light Dragoons 5 Nov 1818
Brevets: Brevet Lieutenant Colonel 4 Jun 1813
Service 1793–1815: Served in Helder 1799; ADC to Henry Paget in Egypt 1801; ADC to Edward Paget 1806–1810; served in Peninsula with 11th Light Dragoons Jun and Jul 1811; served in Peninsula in Portuguese service Aug 1811 to Apr 1814
Later Service: Barrack Master in Barbados
Awards and Honours: AGM (Vit)
Retired: 21 Sep 1820
Residences: Chichester, Sussex; Le Havre, Haute-Normandie, France
Died: Le Havre 29 Nov 1835
Sources: ANCB; ANCD; ARLI; CHAL; PHIL; WEOF; Bonhams (sale of ornamental sabre)

105. *Thomas BROWNE (1806)*
Born: Devon 1775
Relations: Son of John Browne of Canonsleigh Abbey and Margaret (Clarke); father of Lieutenant Colonel Barton Parker Browne, 11th Light Dragoons
Entry to Army: Cornet in 11th Light Dragoons 17 Feb 1794 by purchase
Regimental Field Officer Promotions: Major in 11th Light Dragoons 29 Jan 1802 (vice Anderson) by purchase; Major in 34th Foot 14 Aug 1806 (vice Diggens) by exchange; to half-pay in 9th Foot 16 Oct 1806; rank stationary thereafter
Service 1793–1815: Served at Helder 1799
Residences: Canonsleigh Abbey, Burlescombe, Devon; St. Peter Port, Guernsey, Channel Islands
Died: Guernsey 3 Apr 1845
Sources: ANCB; ANCD; ARLI; PHIL; WEOF

106. *Thomas BODKIN (1806–1807)*
Born: County Galway c.1770
Relations: Son of John Bodkin of Rahoon
Entry to Army: Ensign in 9th Foot 19 Oct 1787 by purchase
Regimental Field Officer Promotions: Major in 9th Foot 16 Jul 1803 (vice Molesworth); Major in 8th Battalion of Reserve 2 Jun 1804 (vice Molle) by exchange; to half-pay of 9th Foot 25 Jun 1804; Major in 34th Foot 16 Oct 1806 (vice Browne) by exchange
Retired: 30 Apr 1807
Residence: Kilcloony, County Galway
Died: Kilcloony 1834
Sources: ARLI; HPON (son); GHLG; WEOF

107. *James Tomlinson TERREWEST (1807–1810)*
Born: Lincolnshire 1776
Relations: Son of John Terrewest of Stamford and Mary (Tomlinson)
Entry to Army: Ensign in 34th Foot 17 Jan 1799 by purchase
Regimental Field Officer Promotions: Major in 34th Foot 30 Apr 1807 (vice Bodkin) by purchase
Service 1793–1815: Served at Cape of Good Hope 1800–1802; served in East Indies 1803–1808
Retired: 1 Feb 1810
Residence: Newark-upon-Trent, Nottinghamshire
Died: Newark-upon-Trent 10 Oct 1854
Sources: ANCB; ANCD; ARLI; WEOF; WO 25/748; Annual Military Obituary 1854

108. *Henry Charles DICKENS (1809–1816)*
Born: London c.1786
Relations: Son of Lieutenant Colonel Richard Mark Dickens, 34th Foot, and Mary Ann (Hoar)
Entry to Army: Ensign in 35th Foot 1 Sep 1795
Regimental Field Officer Promotions: Major in 34th Foot 26 Jun 1809 (vice Bromhead) by purchase; Lieutenant Colonel in 34th Foot 2 Apr 1816 (vice Roberts)
Brevets: Brevet Lieutenant Colonel 4 Jun 1814
Service 1793–1815: Served in Peninsula Jul 1809 to Aug 1811
Retired: 28 Oct 1824
Residence: Boulogne-sur-Mer, Pas-de-Calais, France
Died: Boulogne-sur-Mer 30 Dec 1833
Sources: ANCD; ARLI; PHIL; WEOF

109. *Rev. Walter HOVENDEN (1810–1812)*
Born: Staffordshire 1783
Relatives: Son of Colonel Walter Hovenden of Wolverhampton and Catherine (Eykyn); brother of Captain John Eykyn Hovenden, 69th Foot; and Major Frederic Hovenden, 34th Foot
Education: St Peter's, Cambridge (BD) 1818
Entry to Army: Ensign in 87th Foot Jan 1796 by purchase
Regimental Field Officer Promotions: Major in 34th Foot 1 Feb 1810 (vice Terrewest) by purchase
Service 1793–1815: Served in East Indies 1803–1811
Retired: 26 Mar 1812
Later Service: Took holy orders; Deacon (Norwich) 16 Nov 1817; Priest 24 May 1818; Chaplain and Secretary to the Bengal Military Orphan Institution
Residence: Kolkata, West Bengal, India
Died: On board *Sea Horse* pilot vessel off Kolkata 30 Sep 1832
Sources: ANCB; ARLI; ANCD; FMPW; Cambridge University Alumni 1261-1900; The Bengal Obituary Booklet

110. *Henry WORSLEY (1812–1820)*
Born: Isle of Wight 1783
Relations: Son of Rev. James Worsley, rector of Gatcombe and Ann (Hayles); brother of Captain James Worsley RA; Lieutenant Frederick Worsley RN; and Lieutenant William Worsley RN; brother-in-law of Captain Henry Hill RN
Entry to Army: Ensign in North Hants Militia; Ensign in 5th Foot 13 Aug 1799
Regimental Field Officer Promotions: Major in 4th Garrison Battalion 13 Jun 1811 (vice Knight); Major in 34th Foot 23 Jan 1812 (vice Everard)
Brevets: Brevet Lieutenant Colonel 13 May 1812
Service 1793–1815: Served in Helder 1799; served in Walcheren 1809; served in Peninsula with 85th Foot Apr to Aug 1811; served in Peninsula with 2/34th Foot Jun 1812 to Apr 1814; commanded 2/34th Foot in Peninsula 1813–1814
Later Service: Served in East Indies 1816–1817; Captain of Yarmouth Castle 1818
Awards and Honours: AGM (Pyr Nlle Niv Ort); CB 4 Jun 1815
Residence: Newport, Isle of Wight
Died: Newport 13 May 1820
Sources: ARLI; CHAL; DINB; GEMA (1820); WEOF; <https://www.warmemorialsonline.org.uk/memorial/179115/>

111. *George Edward PRATT-BARLOW (1812–1823)*

Born: George Edward Barlow in London 1784; added Pratt- surname in 1803
Relations: Son of Robert Barlow (later Robert Pratt-Barlow) of Turnham Green, solicitor, and Elizabeth Emma (Barlow); cousin of Sir George Hilario Barlow, Governor of Madras
Entry to Army: Ensign in 22nd Foot 24 Apr 1803
Regimental Field Officer Promotions: Major in 34th Foot 26 Mar 1812 (vice Hovenden) by purchase; Lieutenant Colonel in 61st Foot 4 Dec 1823 (vice Royall) by purchase; to half-pay unattached 24 Aug 1832 (vice Darley) by exchange
Brevets: Brevet Colonel 28 Jun 1838
Service 1793–1815: Served in East Indies 1803–1810; served in capture of Mauritius 1810
Later Service: Served in Ceylon 1828–1832
Retired: 28 Jun 1838
Residence: Leonard Place, Kensington, London
Died: London 6 Mar 1865
Conducted a scandalous affair with the (much older) wife of his cousin, Sir George Barlow, Governor of Madras, whilst serving as ADC to the Governor
Sources: ANCB; ANCD; ANCW; ARLI; PHIL; WEOF

112. *James Harrison BAKER (1814)*

Born: Norfolk 1781
Relations: Son of Richard Baker of Cawston, DD, theologian, and Elizabeth (Oakes)
Entry to Army: Ensign in 65th Foot 1 Feb 1798 by purchase
Regimental Field Officer Promotions: Major in 34th Foot 10 Mar 1814 (vice Roberts) by purchase
Service 1793–1815: Served in Peninsula Dec 1812 to Apr 1814, wounded at Toulouse
Residence: Cawston-with-Portland, Norfolk
Died: Of wounds in Toulouse 11 Apr 1814
Sources: ANCB; ARLI; CHAL; WEOF

113. *Charles Ramus FORREST (1814–1817)*

Born: Berkshire 1786
Relations: Son of Lieutenant Charles Forrest, Governor of the Poor Knights of Windsor, and Anne (unk.); son-in-law of Lieutenant General William Charles St Leger; father of Lieutenant Colonel Charles Forrest, 35th Foot
Education: Eton College
Entry to Army: Ensign in 3rd Foot 1 Oct 1802 by purchase
Regimental Field Officer Promotions: Major in 34th Foot 2 Jun 1814 (vice Baker) by purchase; to half-pay of 34th Foot 25 Jun 1817
Brevets: Brevet Lieutenant Colonel 29 Jun 1815
Service 1793–1815: Served in Peninsula Apr 1812 to Apr 1814, on staff as Assistant Deputy Quartermaster General Aug 1813 to Apr 1814; served on staff in New Orleans 1815
Later Service: Served on staff in British North America 1821–1823
Residence: Spent his last years in a lunatic asylum
Died: Fort Pitt, Chatham, Kent 26 Jan 1827
Sources: ANCB; ANCD; ANCW; WEOF

Selected Regimental Histories

Sutherland, Douglas, *Tried and Valiant: The History of the Border Regiment (the 34th and 55th Regiments of Foot) 1702–1959* (London: Leo Cooper, 1972)
Cannon, Richard, *Historical Record of the Thirty-fourth, or the Cumberland Regiment of Foot: An Account of the Formation of the Regiment in 1702 and of Its Subsequent Services to 1844* (London: Parker, Furnivall and Parker, 1844)

Regimental Museum

Cumbria's Museum of Military Life, Alma Block, Carlisle Castle, Carlisle, Cumbria

---

35th Regiment of Foot

Secondary Title:	Dorsetshire (to Jul 1805) Sussex (Jul 1805 on)
Nicknames:	Prince of Orange's Own The Orange Lilies
Jacket:	Red
Facings:	Orange
Badge:	White (Rousillon) plume

Regimental Lineage, 35th Regiment of Foot

1701: Raised as marines by Arthur Chichester, 3rd Earl of Donegall; also called the Belfast Regiment of Foot
1706: Gorges's Regiment of Foot
1717: Otway's Regiment of Marines
1718: Otway's Regiment of Foot
1747: Ranked as 35th Regiment of Foot
1751: 35th Regiment of Foot
1774: 35th Regiment of Foot (The Prince of Orange's Own Regiment)
1782: 35th (Dorsetshire) Regiment of Foot
1799: Aug – 2nd Battalion formed in Barham Downs
1803: May – 2nd Battalion disbanded in Malta
1805: Jul – 35th (Sussex) Regiment of Foot
1805: Apr – 2nd Battalion re-formed in Winchester
1817: Apr – 2nd Battalion disbanded in Ireland
1832: 35th (Royal Sussex) Regiment of Foot
1881: 1st Battalion, The Royal Sussex Regiment (on amalgamation with 107th (Bengal Infantry) Regiment of Foot)
1966: 3rd Battalion, The Queen's Regiment (Royal Sussex) (on amalgamation with the Queen's Royal Surrey Regiment, the Queen's Own Buffs, The Royal Kent Regiment, and the Middlesex Regiment (Duke of Cambridge's Own))
1968: 3rd Battalion, The Queen's Regiment
1992: The Princess of Wales's Royal Regiment (Queen's and Royal Hampshires) (on amalgamation with the Royal Hampshire Regiment)

Service History, 1st Battalion 35th Regiment of Foot

1793: Dublin; Oct – flank companies to West Indies
1794: Jan – flank companies in Barbados; Feb – Martinique; Mar – St Lucia; Apr – Guadeloupe; to Barbados; Mar – eight companies from Cork to West Indies; May – flank companies to St Domingue; Jun – eight companies in Guadeloupe; Fort Matilda
1795: Martinique; Feb to May – drafted out to other regiments; cadre to England; diverted to Gibraltar
1796: Gibraltar; Sep – to England; Portsmouth; Nov – Hilsea
1797: Hilsea; Apr – Leeds; Jun – Beverley
1798: Beverley; Feb – Durham; May – Monkswearmouth and South Shields; Jun – Chester-le-Street and Blyth; Dec – Chester-le-Street and Durham
1799: Chester-le-Street and Durham; Apr – Chester-le-Street; South Shields; May – Jersey; Aug – Canterbury; Barham Downs, received militia volunteers; Sep – to Helder; Bergen; Oct – Egmont-op-Zee; Nov – to England; Deal; Dec – Canterbury
1800: Canterbury; Mar – Deal; to Mediterranean; Minorca; Jul – eight companies to MALTA; Sep – St Elmo Barracks
1801: Malta – Vittoriosa
1802–1804: Malta
1805: Malta – Floriana; Nov – to Naples
1806: Naples; Feb – Messina; Mar – Melazzo; Jun – flank companies to Calabria; MAIDA; Scylla; to Sicily – Melazzo; recruited Sicilian company
1807: Sicily – Messina; Mar – to Egypt; Aboukir Bay; Apr – El Hamet [Al-Hammad]; POWs to Cairo; retreat to Rosetta; Sep – to Sicily; Melazzo
1808: Melazzo
1809: Melazzo; May – flank companies to Capri; Sep – Ionian Islands; Zante
1810: Zante; Santa Maura
1811: Zante
1812: Zante; Jul – capture of Cape Ceste; Lissa

1813: Zante; capture of Lagosta; two companies with Austrian Army at Trieste and Apennines campaign
1814: Zante; Feb – capture of Paxo; capture of Lessina and Brazza; Corfu
1815: Corfu and Ionian Islands
1816: Corfu and Ionian Islands; Sep – Malta
1817: Malta; Nov – to England after 17 years away

Service History, 2nd Battalion 35th Regiment of Foot

1799: Aug – formed at Barham Downs from militia volunteers; Sep – Deal; to Helder; Bergen; Oct – Egmont-op-Zee; Nov – to England; Deal; Dec – Canterbury
1800: Canterbury; Mar – Deal; to Mediterranean; Minorca; Jul – eight companies to Malta; Sep – St Elmo Barracks
1801: Malta – Vittoriosa
1802: Malta
1803: Malta; May – disbanded in Malta, fit men into 1st Battalion
1805: Apr – re-formed in Winchester from militia volunteers; Jul – Weymouth; Nov – Lewes
1806: Blatchington; Feb – Lewes; May – to Sicily; Dec – Sicily; recruited Sicilian company
1807: Sicily – Messina; Mar – to Egypt; Aboukir Bay; Apr – El Hamet [Al-Hammad]; POWs to Cairo; retreat to Rosetta; Sep – to Sicily; Oct – to England
1808: Portsmouth; Ashford; Jun – Danbury Camp; Sep – Chichester
1809: Chichester; Jul – Portsmouth; to Walcheren; Flushing; Nov – to England
1810: Chichester; Dec – Shorncliffe
1811: Shorncliffe; Jun – to Guernsey
1812: Guernsey
1813: Guernsey; Portsmouth; Chichester; Nov – Deal; to Netherlands
1814: Merxcem; Mar – Bergen-op-Zoom; Jun – Ostend garrison
1815: Ostend; May – Courtrai; Grammont; Jun – Hal; advance on Paris; Jul – Paris; Allied Army of Occupation; Dec – to Ireland
1817: Apr – disbanded in Ireland

Establishments, 1st Battalion 35th Regiment of Foot

Year	Subunits	Field Off	Off/ Staff	Sjts	Mus	Corp/ Pvts	Total
Dec 1792	10co	3	32	22	12	330	399
Jan 1793	10co	3	32	32	22	600	689
Sep 1795	10co+2r	3	40	42	30	610	725
Dec 1795	10co+2r	5	51	62	30	1,010	1,158
Dec 1797	10co	5	32	53	22	600	712
Dec 1798	10co	5	38	53	22	600	718
Dec 1799	11co	5	46	47	24	880	1002
Dec 1800	10co	5	47	53	22	1,000	1,127
Jun 1802	10co	5	33	34	22	750	844
Oct 1803	10co	5	46	54	22	1,000	1,127
Dec 1806	10co	4	46	54	22	1,000	1,126
Aug 1809	10co+r	4	50	62	26	1,008	1,150
Dec 1809	10co	4	46	54	22	1,000	1,126
Dec 1810	10co	4	46	64	22	1,200	1,337
Dec 1811	10co	4	46	65	22	1,200	1,337
Dec 1813	10co+r	4	49	73	22	1,208	1,356
Dec 1815	10co	4	46	55	22	1,000	1,127

Establishments, 2nd Battalion 35th Regiment of Foot

Year	Subunits	Field Off	Off/ Staff	Sjts	Mus	Corp/ Pvts	Total
Dec 1799	11co	5	46	47	24	880	1,002
Dec 1800	10co	5	46	43	22	800	916
Apr 1805	10co	3	35	34	22	600	694
Dec 1807	10co	3	39	42	26	608	718
Dec 1808	10co	3	35	34	22	600	694
Sep 1809	10co+r	3	40	52	26	808	929
Dec 1809	10co	3	36	44	22	800	905
Dec 1810	10co	3	35	34	22	600	694
Dec 1811	10co	3	35	35	22	600	695
Dec 1813	10co+r	3	38	43	22	608	714

Service Statistics, 35th Regiment of Foot

	Lieutenant Colonels	Majors
Number of officers in period 1793–1815	12	24
Average age on appointment to substantive rank	35	33
Average time in rank in regiment (years)	5.5	4
Total field officers by nationality	13 E / 10 I / 7 S	
Demographics of other ranks 1809	2/35th: 94% EW / 6% I	
Months of overseas service 1793–1815	1/35th: 224 2/35th: 88	

Significant Militia/Volunteer Intakes

1799: Dorset, South Middlesex, West Middlesex, Leicestershire, North Lincolnshire, Nottinghamshire, East Suffolk, 1st Surrey, 1st Sussex, 2nd Sussex, 5th West Yorkshire
1800: Oxfordshire, County Kildare, County Sligo
1805: South Gloucestershire, Oxfordshire, Sussex, North Yorkshire
1806: Cheshire, Sussex, North Yorkshire
1807: Bedfordshire, Nottinghamshire, 2nd Somerset, Sussex, King's County
1809: South Gloucestershire, West Middlesex
1810: West Middlesex
1811: Sussex, County Longford

Regimental Colonels

114. *Henry FLETCHER CAMPBELL (1764–1803)*

Born: Edinburgh 1724
Relations: Son of Andrew Fletcher, Lord Milton, Chief Justice Clerk for Scotland and Keeper of the Signet, and Elizabeth (Kinloch); brother of General John Fletcher Campbell
Entry to Army: Ensign in 5th Foot 2 May 1739 by purchase
Regimental Field Officer Promotions: Major in 35th Foot 25 Dec 1755; Lieutenant Colonel in 35th Foot 16 Feb 1758
Brevets: Brevet Colonel 20 Jun 1762; Major General 25 May 1772; Lieutenant General 29 Aug 1777; General 12 Oct 1793
Colonelcies: 35th Foot 10 Aug 1764 (vice Otway)
Early Service: Commanded 35th Foot at Louisburg and Heights of Abraham 1758
Residences: Saltoun Hall, near Pencaitland, East Lothian
Died: Saltoun Hall 13 Mar 1803
Sources: ANCB; ANCW; ARLI; GEMA (1803)

115. *Rt Hon. Charles LENNOX, 4th Duke of Richmond (1799–1819)*

Born: 'In a barn' in Scotland 1764
Relations: Son of General Lord George Henry Lennox and Lady Louisa (Kerr); son-in-law of Alexander Gordon, 4th Duke of Gordon; brother-in-law of Henry Bathurst, Earl Bathurst
Entry to Army: Ensign in 100th Foot 6 Apr 1785 by purchase
Regimental Field Officer Promotions: Captain and Lieutenant Colonel in Coldstream Foot Guards 26 Mar 1789 by purchase; Lieutenant Colonel in 35th Foot 15 Jun 1789 by exchange

Brevets: Brevet Lieutenant Colonel 16 Mar 1789; Brevet Colonel 28 Jan 1795; Major General 1 Jan 1798; Lieutenant General 1 Jan 1805; General 4 Jun 1814
Colonelcies: Colonel Commandant of 2/35th Foot 5 Aug 1799; 35th Foot 17 Mar 1803 (vice Fletcher)
Political Career: MP (Sussex) 1790–1806; House of Lords 1806–1819; Lord Lieutenant of Ireland 19 Apr 1807 to 26 Aug 1813 (vice Russell)
Service 1793–1815: Quartermaster General at Toulon 1793; served in West Indies; present at Waterloo in civilian capacity
Later Service: Lord Lieutenant of Sussex 1816–1819; Governor of Lower Canada 29 Jul 1818 to 28 Aug 1819
Creations and Dignities: 4th Duke of Richmond 29 Dec 1806; also Earl of March, Baron of Suttington, Duke of Lennox, Earl of Darnley and Baron of Methuen 29 Dec 1806; Duke of Aubigny (France) 18 Mar 1818
Awards and Honours: PC 1 Apr 1807; KG 31 Mar 1812
Residences: Privy Garden, London; Goodwood Park, Chichester, Sussex; West Stoke House, Chichester, Sussex
Died: Of rabies in Québec 28 Aug 1819
Sources: ARLI; DICB; HPON; MENA; ODNB; WOST

Lieutenant Colonels

116. *Colin CAMPBELL (1795–1797)*

Born: Argyllshire c.1739
Relations: Reputedly of the Campbells of Corries
Entry to Army: Ensign in 35th Foot 11 Apr 1756 by purchase
Regimental Field Officer Promotions: Major in 35th Foot Apr 1789 (vice Lord Strathaven) by purchase; Lieutenant Colonel in 35th Foot 1 Sep 1795
Brevets: Brevet Lieutenant Colonel 1 Mar 1794
Early Service: Served in British North America 1757–1760
Retired: 30 Mar 1797
Residence: Dean Street, Soho, London
Died: London Jun 1800
Sources: ANCD; ARLI; An Historical Memoir of the 35th Royal Sussex Regiment of Foot

117. *Sir John OSWALD (1797–1811)*

Born: Fifeshire 1771
Relations: Son of James Townsend Oswald of Dunnikier, MP and Janet (Grey); brother of Lieutenant Colonel Robert Oswald, Greek Light Infantry; brother-in-law of Lieutenant General Thomas Bruce, 7th Earl of Elgin; and Lieutenant Colonel Robert Smythe, 52nd Foot
Education: Brienne-le-Château military academy
Entry to Army: 2nd Lieutenant in 23rd Foot 1 Feb 1788 by purchase
Regimental Field Officer Promotions: Major in 35th Foot 1 Sep 1795; Lieutenant Colonel in 35th Foot 30 Mar 1797 (vice Campbell) by purchase
Brevets: Brevet Colonel 30 Oct 1805; Major General 4 Jun 1811; Lieutenant General 12 Aug 1819; General 10 Jan 1837
Colonelcies: 1st Greek Light Infantry 25 Feb 1811; Colonel Commandant of 3/Rifle Brigade 2 Jul 1818 (vice Spencer); 35th Foot 9 Oct 1819 (vice Duke of Richmond)
Early Service: Served in Gibraltar 1790
Service 1793–1815: Served in West Indies 1794; badly wounded in Helder 1799; served in Malta 1800; served in Maida and Calabria 1806; served in Egypt 1807; British Civil Commissioner in Ionian Islands 16 Oct 1809 to Feb 1811; commanded 5th Division in Peninsula Oct to Dec 1812; commanded 5th Division in Peninsula Mar 1813 to Apr 1814
Awards and Honours: AGM (Mai Vitt SS); KCB 4 Jan 1815; GCB 25 Feb 1824; GCMG 9 Nov 1839
Residence: Dunnikier House, Kirkcaldy, Fifeshire
Died: Dunnikier House 8 Jun 1840
Sources: *ANCB; ANCD; ARLI; CHAL; DINB; PHIL; WEOF; WOST; WO 25/747*

118. *Archibald MacALISTER (1799–1801)*

Born: Argyllshire 1756
Relations: Son of Lieutenant General Charles MacAlister of Loup and Christina (Lamont); father of Lieutenant Colonel Charles MacAlister, Ceylon Rifle Regiment; Ensign John MacAlister, 35th Foot; and Lieutenant William MacAlister, 35th Foot
Entry to Army: Lieutenant in 35th Foot 4 May 1767
Regimental Field Officer Promotions: Major in 35th Foot 1 Sep 1795 (vice Campbell) by purchase; Lieutenant Colonel in 35th Foot 5 Aug 1799
Brevets: Brevet Major 18 Nov 1790; Brevet Lieutenant Colonel 1 Mar 1794; Brevet Colonel 1 Jan 1798
Early Service: Served in American War of Independence 1775–1776; served in St Lucia 1778
Service 1793–1815: Commanded 35th Foot in Guadeloupe 1794; commanded 2/35th Foot in Helder 1799
Retired: 10 Aug 1801
Residence: Canterbury, Kent
Died: Canterbury early 1802

Sources: ANCW; ARLI; GHLG; The Scottish Nation Vol.2

119. *Rt Hon. Nathaniel Williams MASSEY, 2nd Baron Clarina (1799–1800)*
Born: Dublin 1773
Relations: Son of General Eyre Massey, 1st Baron Clarina and Catherine (Clements); father of Colonel Hon. Nathaniel Henry Charles Massey
Education: Trinity College, Dublin
Entry to Army: Ensign in 27th Foot 3 Jul 1793 by purchase
Regimental Field Officer Promotions: Lieutenant Colonel in 33rd Light Dragoons 15 Dec 1794 by purchase; to half-pay1 Mar 1798; Lieutenant Colonel in 35th Foot 6 Aug 1799; Lieutenant Colonel in 27th Foot 30 May 1800 (vice Brown) by exchange; to half-pay of 27th Foot 25 Oct 1802
Brevets: Brevet Colonel 1 Jan 1801; Major General 25 Apr 1808
Service 1793–1815: Lieutenant Governor in Barbados 1809 to 26 Jan 1810
Creations and Dignities: 2nd Baron Clarina of Elm Park 17 May 1804
Residences: Elm Park, near Clarina, County Limerick; The Promenade, Cheltenham, Gloucestershire
Died: Of fever at Bridgetown, Barbados 26 Jan 1810
Sources: ANCB; ANCD; ARLI; PEER; WEOF; WOST; Monumental inscriptions of the British West Indies from the earliest date

120. *John BAYLIS (1799–1802)*
Born: County Wexford c.1758
Relations: Son of John Baylis of Enniscorthy and Diana (unk.)
Entry to Army: Ensign in 63rd Foot 25 Oct 1776 by purchase
Regimental Field Officer Promotions: Major in 63rd Foot 1 Apr 1795 (vice Ashe) by purchase; Lieutenant Colonel in 35th Foot 7 Aug 1799
Service 1793–1815: Commanded combined grenadier battalion at Helder 1799; served at capture of Malta 1800; tried for murder of Captain Richard Newman (20th Foot) in a duel in Malta May 1802 and acquitted
Retired: Dismissed 17 Sep 1802, allowed to receive the value of his majority
Residence: Enniscorthy, County Wexford
Died: Enniscorthy 1804
Sources: ANCW; ARLI; <https://www.maltaramc.com/regmltgar/35th.html>

121. *Lyde BROWN (1800–1801)*
Born: London 1759
Relations: Son of Lyde Browne, banker and antiquary, and Margaret (Barwell)
Entry to Army: Cornet in 3rd Dragoons 11 Jun 1777 by purchase
Field Officer Promotions: Major in 4th West India Regiment 18 Jan 1797 (vice Cranston); Major in 90th Foot 11 Jul 1798 (vice Houstoun); Lieutenant Colonel in 27th Foot 17 May 1800; Lieutenant Colonel in 35th Foot 30 May 1800 (vice Massey) by exchange; Lieutenant Colonel in 85th Foot 10 Apr 1801; Lieutenant Colonel in 21st Foot 25 Jun 1802 (vice Stuart)
Brevets: Brevet Major 1 Mar 1794; Brevet Lieutenant Colonel 1 Jan 1798
Service 1793–1815: Served in West Indies 1794–1798; served in Malta 1800–1801
Residence: Wimbledon, Surrey
Died: Murdered in Dublin riots 23 Jul 1803
Sources: ANCB; ANCD; DINB; WEOF

122. *Sir Francis John WILDER, Kt (1801–1814)*
Born: London 1775
Relations: Son of Peter Bigot Wilder of Islington and Elizabeth (Connor)
Education: Eton College
Entry to Army: Ensign in 16th Foot 15 Apr 1794 by purchase
Regimental Field Officer Promotions: Major in 106th Foot 18 Sep 1794; to half-pay of 106th Foot 1 Mar 1798; Major in 88th Foot 14 Apr 1798 (vice Duff); Major in 9th Foot 1 Jan 1799 (vice Hayman); Lieutenant Colonel in Banffshire Fencibles 23 Jul 1799; Lieutenant Colonel in 35th Foot 10 Apr 1801 (vice Browne); removed from the regiment as a general officer 1814
Brevets: Brevet Lieutenant Colonel 29 Dec 1798; Brevet Colonel 25 Apr 1808; Major General 4 Jun 1811; Lieutenant General 19 Jul 1821
Service 1793–1815: Served in Gibraltar; served in Malta and Sicily 1801–1811; served on home staff at Ipswich 1811–1815
Political Career: MP (Horsham) 1807; MP (Arundel) 1807–1818
Awards and Honours: Knight Bachelor 29 May 1817
Residences: Binfield Manor, Binfield, Buckinghamshire; Grosvenor Place, Belgravia, London
Died: Binfield 23 Jan 1824
Sources: ANCB; ANCD; ARLI; HPON; PHIL; WEOF

123. *William Howe CAMPBELL (1801–1802)*

See 13.
Major in 35th Foot 11 Dec 1800 (vice Quin) by purchase; Lieutenant Colonel in 35th Foot 10 Aug 1801 (vice McAlister) by purchase; to half-pay of 35th Foot 25 Oct 1802

124. *Charles STICKLAND (1802)*

Born: Dorset 1776
Relations: Son of Robert Stickland, Bailiff of Dorchester and Jane (Mitchell); brother of Captain Nathaniel Stickland, Dorset Militia
Entry to Army: Ensign in 43rd Foot May 1793
Regimental Field Officer Promotions: Major in 35th Foot 7 Aug 1801 (vice Hay) by purchase; Lieutenant Colonel in 35th Foot 17 Sep 1802 (vice Baylis) by purchase; to half-pay of 35th Foot 25 Sep 1802; Lieutenant Colonel in 2nd Garrison Battalion 9 Jul 1803; Lieutenant Colonel in 59th Foot 12 Jan 1805
Service 1793–1815: Served in Guadeloupe 1794; served in Helder 1799
Retired: 20 Jan 1805
Later Service: Magistrate and Mayor of Dorchester
Residence: South Street, Dorchester, Dorset
Died: Dorchester 6 Jul 1845
Officer's surname is based upon his will signature and father's marriage license, rather than the 'Strickland' usually found in Army Lists
Sources: ANCB; ANCD; ANCW; GEMA (1845); WEOF; <https://www.opcdorset.org/fordingtondorset/Files2/DorchesterStrays1.html#charlesstickland>

125. *Peter Hayes PETIT (1805–1809)*

Born: London 1773
Relations: Son of Dr John Lewis Petit of Bloomsbury Square and Katherine Letitia (Serces)
Entry to Army: Ensign in 12th Foot 3 Nov 1790
Regimental Field Officer Promotions: Major in 35th Foot 30 Mar 1797 (vice Oswald) by purchase; Lieutenant Colonel in 35th Foot 1 May 1805
Brevets: Brevet Lieutenant Colonel 29 Apr 1802
Service 1793–1815: Served in West Indies 1794; wounded and POW at Helder Sep 1799; served in capture of Malta 1800; served in Egypt 1807; served in Walcheren 1809, mortally wounded at Flushing
Residence: Deal, Kent
Died: Of wounds at Deal 2 Sep 1809
Sources: *ANCB; ANCD: ANCW; HPON (brother); WEOF*

126. *Sir George Henry Frederick BERKELEY (1808–1817)*

Born: Sussex 1785
Relations: Son of Admiral Sir George Cranfield Berkeley and Emily Charlotte (Lennox); cousin of General Charles Lennox, 4th Duke of Richmond
Education: Harrow School
Entry to Army: Cornet in Royal Horse Guards 21 Jan 1802 by purchase
Regimental Field Officer Promotions: Major in 9th Garrison Battalion 28 Jan 1808 (vice Edwards); Major in 35th Foot 25 Mar 1808 (vice O'Keefe) by exchange; Lieutenant Colonel in 35th Foot 13 Jun 1811; to half-pay of 35th Foot 29 Jul 1817
Brevets: Brevet Colonel 27 May 1825; Major General 10 Jan 1837; Lieutenant General 23 Nov 1841; General 20 Jun 1854
Colonelcies: 81st Foot 15 Jan 1844 (vice O'Connell); 35th Foot 11 Jul 1845 (vice Jackson)
Service 1793–1815: Served in Sicily 1806; served in Egypt 1807; Assistant Adjutant General in Peninsula Apr 1809 to Apr 1814; Assistant Adjutant General in Netherlands Aug 1814; Assistant Adjutant General in Waterloo campaign
Later Service: Commander in Chief of Madras Army 1847; commanded forces in Kaffir War 1847; Surveyor General of the Ordnance 3 Jul 1852
Political Career: MP (Devonport) 1852–1857
Awards and Honours: AGM (Bus FDO Bad Sal Vitt SS Niv); KCB 2 Jan 1815; WatM 23 Apr 1816; MGSM (Tal)
Residence: Stratton Street, Piccadilly, London
Died: London 25 Sep 1857
Sources: ANCB; ANCD; ANCW; ARLI; CHAL; DALT; WEOF; WO 25/744

127. *Sir Lorenzo MOORE (1809–1830)*

Born: Dublin c.1765
Relations: Son of John Moore of Summerhill, Deputy Registrar of Deeds in Ireland, and Mary Anne (Moore); nephew of Lorenzo Moore, Colonel of the Battle-Axe Guards; brother of George Ogle Moore KC MP, Registrar of Deeds in Ireland; father of Major John Hildebrand Oakes Moore, 4th Foot
Entry to Army: Cornet in 14th Light Dragoons 26 Aug 1786 by purchase
Regimental Field Officer Promotions: Major in 35th Foot 1 May 1805; Lieutenant Colonel in 35th Foot 14 Sep 1809 (vice Petit); removed from the regiment as a general officer 22 Jul 1830
Brevets: Brevet Colonel 12 Aug 1819; Major General 22 Jul 1830
Early Service: Served in Gibraltar 1792–1794
Service 1793–1815: Served in West Indies

1794–1796; Brigade Major to Sir John Moore in Ireland 1798; served at Cape of Good Hope 1799–1803; served in Mediterranean 1806–1808 and 1809–1817; British Resident of the Lord High Commissioner in Zante 1815
Later Service: Acting Governor of St Lucia Nov 1827 to 17 Jan 1829
Awards and Honours: CB 4 Jun 1815; KCH 12 Aug 1834
Residence: Dresden, Saxony, Germany
Died: Dresden 18 Mar 1837
Sources: ANCW; HPON (brother); UNSM (1837); WEOF; WO 25/747

Majors

128. *George STEWART (1799–1806)*

Born: [spec.] Ireland c.1760
Entry to Army: Ensign in 82nd Foot 5 Jan 1778
Regimental Field Officer Promotions: Major in 35th Foot 5 Aug 1799; Major in Ramsay's Regiment 31 Jul 1806 (vice Morrice); to half-pay of 9th Garrison Battalion 30 Nov 1805 (vice Chaplin) by exchange
Brevets: Brevet Lieutenant Colonel 1 Jan 1798; Brevet Colonel 25 Apr 1808
Service 1793–1815: Assistant Adjutant General in Ireland 1808–1809
Died: Dublin May 1809
Sources: ANCW; ARLI; FMPW

129. *Adam HAY (1799–1801)*

Born: Cromarty c.1767
Relations: Son of James Hay of Davidston and Ann (Gordon); cousin of General Sir James Hay
Entry to Army: Ensign in 35th Foot 18 Jan 1778
Regimental Field Officer Promotions: Major in 35th Foot 6 Aug 1799
Service 1793–1815: Served in Guadeloupe 1794; severely wounded in Helder 1799
Retired: 7 Aug 1801
Residence: Broughton Park, Edinburgh, Midlothian
Died: Edinburgh 25 May 1836
Sources: ANCW; GEMA (1836); GHLG; WEOF

130. *George QUIN (1799–1800)*

Born: Ireland c.1754
Entry to Army: Ensign in 49th Foot 10 Mar 1777
Regimental Field Officer Promotions: Major in 35th Foot 7 Aug 1799
Retired: 16 Dec 1800
Service 1793–1815: Fort Major of Duncannon Fort 1812–1820
Residence: Duncannon Fort, County Wexford
Died: Duncannon Fort 2 Jul 1820
Sources: ARLI; EDMA (1820); FMPD

131. *Christopher St Leger CLARGES (1801–1803)*

Born: King's County 1772
Relations: Son of George Clarges of Birr and Levina (St Leger); nephew of Major General Anthony St Leger; and Brigadier General Barrimore Matthew Pennefather St Leger; cousin of Colonel Christopher Clarges Patrickson, 43rd Foot
Entry to Army: Ensign in 35th Foot 29 Jun 1793 by purchase
Regimental Field Officer Promotions: Major in 35th Foot 10 Aug 1801 (vice Campbell) by purchase; to half-pay of 35th Foot 25 Oct 1802; Major in 69th Foot 9 Jul 1803
Brevets: Brevet Lieutenant Colonel 25 Apr 1808
Service 1793–1815: Served in West Indies 1794; served in Helder 1799; served in capture of Java 1811
Died: Killed in action in Java 22 Aug 1811
Sources: ANCB; ANCW; ARLI; WEOF

132. *William SIBBALD (1802)*

Born: London 1771
Relations: Son of John Sibbald of Edinburgh, merchant, and Anne (Franks); brother-in-law of Captain John Mein RN; father of Captain John Sibbald, Madras service; Commander Thomas Sibbald RN; Midshipman James Sibbald RN; and Lieutenant Colonel Hugh Sibbald, Bengal service
Entry to Army: Ensign in 35th Foot 11 Nov 1795 by purchase
Regimental Field Officer Promotions: Major in 35th Foot 1 Oct 1802 (vice Strickland) by purchase; to half-pay of 35th Foot 1 Oct 1802; Major in 15th Foot 1 Aug 1804; Lieutenant Colonel in 15th Foot 31 Jan 1807 (vice Pearse) by purchase
Service 1793–1815: Commanded 2/15th Foot 1807–1812
Retired: 4 Feb 1813
Residence: Whiterig, Roxburghshire; Eildon Hall, Melrose, Roxburghshire
Died: Whiterig 12 Dec 1835
Sources: ARLI; GHLG; WEOF; A History of the 15th (East Yorkshire) Regiment, the Duke of York's Own, 1685 to 1914

133. *George Duncan ROBERTSON (1805–1807)*

Born: Yorkshire 1766

Relations: Son of Colonel Alexander Robertson of Struan and Mary (Best); father of Lieutenant Colonel George Duncan Robertson, 42nd Foot
Entry to Army: Ensign in Independent Company Jun 1782
Regimental Field Officer Promotions: Major in 35th Foot 29 Apr 1805; Lieutenant Colonel in Sicilian Regiment Mar 1807; to half-pay of Sicilian Regiment 25 Mar 1816; Lieutenant Colonel in 89th Foot 4 Apr 1816 (vice Morrison) by exchange; to half-pay of 89th Foot 25 Jan 1817
Brevets: Brevet Major 1 Jan 1805; Brevet Colonel 4 Jun 1814; Major General 19 Jul 1821
Service 1793–1815: Served in Guadeloupe 1794; served in Helder 1799; served in Italy 1805; commanded light company of 35th Foot at Maida 1806; commanded Castle of Scylla 1808; captured Lagosta and Courzola 1812; served in Trieste 1813
Awards & Honours: CB 4 Jan 1815; GCOL (Habsburg)
Residences: Dunalastair Estate, near Pitlochry, Perthshire; Edinburgh, Midlothian
Died: Edinburgh 1 Jul 1842
Sources: ANCB; ANCD; ARLI; GHLG; PHIL; WEOF

134. *Welch Hamilton BUNBURY (1805–1806)*

Born: County Carlow 1772
Relations: Son of Captain Thomas Henry Bunbury of Cranavonane and Mary (Milles); brother of Major Benjamin Bunbury, 2nd West India Regiment; Lieutenant Harrison Charles Bunbury, RN; Lieutenant John Monseer Bunbury, RN; and Lieutenant General Sir Thomas Bunbury
Entry to Army: Ensign in 3/60th Foot 24 Oct 1787 by purchase
Regimental Field Officer Promotions: Major in 35th Foot 30 Apr 1805; Lieutenant Colonel in 3rd Foot 1 Jan 1806 (vice Scott) by purchase
Brevets: Brevet Major 1 Jan 1805
Service 1793–1815: Deputy Quartermaster General in Maida 1806; served in Peninsula Sep 1808 to Feb 1810; commanded 1st Battalion of Detachments in Peninsula Feb to Sep 1809; commanded 1/3rd Foot in Peninsula Jun 1812 to Dec 1813
Retired: 16 May 1814
Residences: Paris, France; Dover, Kent; Wandsworth, Surrey
Died: Wandsworth 30 Apr 1833
This officer is shown in Army Lists as 'William Henry' and occasionally 'W.H.' however Burke et al show him as Welch Hamilton. Ordered his battalion to retire in the face of French attacks at St Pierre on 12 Dec 1813; was subjected to a court of enquiry, after which he resigned from the army
Sources: ANCB; ANCD; ANCW; ARLI; CHAL; GHLG; WEOF

135. *Jeremiah O'KEEFFE (1806–1808)*

Born: County Cork c.1778
Relations: [spec.] Son of Manus O'Keeffe of Mt Keeffe and Charity (Yelverton); cousin of Lieutenant Manus O'Keeffe, 35th Foot
Entry to Army: Ensign in 57th Foot 2 Apr 1794 by purchase
Regimental Field Officer Promotions: Major in Baillie's Corps (3rd Ceylon Regiment) 8 Apr 1804; Major in 35th Foot 31 Jul 1806 (vice Stewart); Major in 9th Garrison Battalion 25 Mar 1808 (vice Berkeley) by exchange; Major in 1st Foot 22 Sep 1809 (vice Hunter) by exchange; Major in 12th Foot 8 Feb 1810 (vice Nixon) by exchange
Service 1793–1815: Served in Flanders 1794–1795; served in West Indies 1796–1799; served in Ferrol 1800; served in Egypt 1801; served in Ceylon 1804–1806; served in Calabria 1806–1807; served in Egypt 1807; served in capture of Mauritius 1810
Died: Killed in action in Mauritius 29 Nov 1810
Sources: ARLI; WEOF; WO 25/747

136. *Charles William CLARKE (1806–1810)*

Born: County Cork 1785
Relations: Son of William Clarke of Crosses Green House, merchant, and Anne (Fogharty); brother of Major General Sir William Clarke, Bt
Entry to Army: Ensign in 84th Foot 19 Nov 1794
Regimental Field Officer Promotions: Major in 35th Foot 31 Dec 1806 (vice Bunbury) by purchase
Service 1793–1815: Served in Cape of Good Hope 1797; served in East Indies 1798–1806; served in Egypt 1807; served in Sicily and in Mediterranean 1807–1810
Died: Of wounds at Santa Maura Apr 1810
Sources: ARLI; GHPB; WEOF; WO 25/744

137. *Richard WESTERMAN (1807–1808)*

Born: County Kilkenny 1761
Relations: Son of Richard Westerman of Kilkenny and Lucy (Reade)
Entry to Army: Serjeant Major in 35th Foot; Quartermaster in 35th Foot 14 Nov 1787; Ensign in 35th Foot 23 Jun 1789
Regimental Field Officer Promotions: Major in 35th Foot 12 Mar 1807 (vice Robertson)
Service 1793–1815: Served in Guadeloupe 1794; served in Helder 1799; Town Major in Malta 1805
Retired: 26 May 1808

Residence: Spring Gardens, Doncaster, Yorkshire
Died: Doncaster 24 Oct 1820
Sources: ANCW; ARLI; An Historical Memoir of the 35th Royal Sussex Regiment of Foot

138. *Cæsar Colclough ARMETT (1808–1819)*

Born: Cheshire 1781
Relations: Son of Charles Armett of Buglawton and Mary (Scott)
Entry to Army: Ensign in 35th Foot 14 Apr 1798 by purchase
Regimental Field Officer Promotions: Major in 35th Foot 26 May 1808 (vice Westerman) by purchase
Brevets: Brevet Lieutenant Colonel 4 Jun 1814
Service 1793–1815: Served in Helder 1799; served at capture of Malta 1800; served in Egypt 1807; served in Walcheren 1809; served at capture of Ionian Islands 1810
Residence: Lancaster, Lancashire
Died: Lost with wife and family in shipwreck off Ireland 24 Jan 1819
Sources: ANCB; ANCD; ARLI; WEOF; WO 25/744

139. *Robert John Charles HERRIES (1809–1813)*

Born: Dumfriesshire 1773
Relations: Son of William Herries of Halldyke and Susanna (Braun)
Entry to Army: Ensign in 52nd Foot 29 Jun 1792
Regimental Field Officer Promotions: Major in 35th Foot 14 Sep 1809 (vice Moore); Lieutenant Colonel in 102nd Foot 16 Sep 1813 (vice Napier); to half-pay of 100th Foot 25 Jun 1818; Lieutenant Colonel in 96th Foot 29 Jan 1824
Service 1793–1815: Joined East India Company as cadet; served in Pondicherry 1793; served in Ceylon 1795–1796; served in Helder 1799; served in Malta and Italy 1805–1806; served in Maida 1806; served in Egypt 1807; served at capture of Ionian Islands 1809–1810
Retired: 30 Dec 1826
Residence: Edinburgh, Midlothian
Died: Cheltenham, Gloucestershire 6 Nov 1832
Sources: ANCW; ARLI; PHIL; WEOF; WO 25/746

140. *Robert OSWALD (1810–1813)*

Born: Fifeshire 1784
Relations: Son of James Townsend Oswald of Dunnikier, MP and Janet (Grey); brother-in-law of Lieutenant General Thomas Bruce, 7th Earl of Elgin; brother of General Sir John Oswald
Entry to Army: Ensign in 35th Foot 31 Dec 1799
Regimental Field Officer Promotions: Major in 35th Foot 19 Apr 1810 (vice Clarke); Lieutenant Colonel in Greek Light Infantry 18 May 1813 (vice Church); to half-pay of Greek Light Infantry 24 Feb 1816; Captain and Lieutenant Colonel in 1st Foot Guards 26 Apr 1827 (vice Hardinge) by exchange
Service 1793–1815: Served in Egypt 1807; ADC to Sir John Stuart; served in Mediterranean 1810–1811, wounded in capture of Ionian Islands; commanded 1st Greek Light Infantry in Genoa 1814
Awards & Honours: CB 4 Jun 1815
Retired: 30 Apr 1827 (name to be retained on Army List)
Residence: Kirkcaldy, Fifeshire
Died: Kirkcaldy 26 Feb 1848
Sources: ANCB; ANCD; ARLI; PHIL; WEOF

141. *Charles Archibald MacALISTER (1811–1826)*

Born: Yorkshire 1787
Relations: Son of Colonel Archibald MacAlister, 35th Foot, and Sarah (unk.); grandson of General Charles MacAlister; brother of Ensign John MacAlister, 35th Foot; and Lieutenant William MacAlister, 35th Foot
Entry to Army: Ensign in 35th Foot 19 Sep 1795
Regimental Field Officer Promotions: Major in 35th Foot 13 Jun 1811; to half-pay of 35th Foot 8 Jun 1826; Lieutenant Colonel in Ceylon Rifle Regiment 19 Nov 1829
Brevets: Brevet Lieutenant Colonel 12 Aug 1819
Service 1793–1815: Served in Helder 1799; served at capture of Malta 1800; served in Maida 1806; wounded and POW in Egypt 1807; served in Mediterranean 1810–1811; commanded 2/35th Foot in Flanders 1813–1814; served in Waterloo campaign
Later Service: Served in Ceylon 1830–1834; Magistrate of the county of Devon
Retired: 27 Feb 1835
Awards and Honours: WatM 23 Apr 1816; KH 12 Aug 1833
Residence: Loup Cottage, Axminster, Devon
Died: Axminster 25 Aug 1869
Sources: ANCW; DALT; PHIL; WEOF; Modern English Biography Vol.2

142. *Joseph PHILLOTT (1813–1817)*

Born: Somerset 1771
Relations: Son of Henry Phillott of Bath and Anne (Haycock); brother of Major General Henry Phillott RA; and Vice Admiral Charles George Rodney Phillott RN

Entry to Army: Ensign in 35th Foot 12 Jan 1796
Regimental Field Officer Promotions: Major in 35th Foot 27 May 1813 (vice Oswald); to half-pay of 35th Foot 25 Jun 1817
Brevets: Brevet Lieutenant Colonel 22 Jul 1830
Service 1793–1815: Served and wounded in Helder 1799; served at capture of Malta 1800; served in Maida 1806; served in Egypt 1807; served at capture of Ionian Islands 1809–1810
Residence: Kensington Gore, Kensington, London
Died: London 16 Nov 1846
Sources: ANCB; ANCD; ANCW; ARLI; PHIL; WEOF

143. *John Henry SLESSOR (1813–1817)*
Born: Portugal 1781
Relations: Son of General John Slessor, Governor of Oporto, and Harriot Elizabeth (Bristow); brother of Major William Edward Slessor, Bengal service; and Lieutenant Henry Thomas Slessor RN
Entry to Army: 1st Lieutenant in Royal Irish Artillery 14 Jun 1794
Regimental Field Officer Promotions: Major in 35th Foot 7 Oct 1813 (vice Herries)
Brevets: Brevet Major 25 Apr 1808; Brevet Lieutenant Colonel 4 Jun 1814; Brevet Colonel 10 Jan 1837; Major General 9 Nov 1846
Service 1793–1815: Served in Royal Irish Artillery in 1798 rebellion; served in Scylla 1806; served in Egypt 1807; wounded at capture of Ionian Islands 1809; Civil Governor of Zante and Commandant of the Island Militia Oct 1809 to Jun 1812; served in Trieste with Austrian Army 1813–1814; served in Flanders 1814; served in Waterloo campaign 1815
Retired: On full pay of Royal Irish Artillery 25 Jun 1817
Awards and Honours: WatM 23 Apr 1816
Residence: Broadway, Sidmouth, Devon
Died: Sidmouth 11 Oct 1850
This officer's father was a general in the Portuguese service and at one time Governor of Oporto
Sources: ANCB; ANCD; ANCW; ARLI; DALT; PHIL; WEOF

Selected Regimental Histories
Trimen, Richard (ed.), *An Historical Memoir of the 35th Royal Sussex Regiment of Foot* (Southampton: Southampton Times Newspaper and Printing and Publishing Company (Limited), 1873)
Glover, Gareth, *Fighting Napoleon: The Recollections of Lieutenant John Hildebrand 35th Foot in the Mediterranean and Waterloo Campaigns* (Barnsley: Pen & Sword Books, 2017)

Regimental Museum
West Sussex Record Office, 3 Orchard Street, Chichester, Sussex

---

36th Regiment of Foot

Secondary Title:	Herefordshire
Nicknames:	The Grasshoppers The Saucy Greens
Jacket:	Red
Facings:	Green
Motto:	Firm

Regimental Lineage, 36th Regiment of Foot

1701:	Raised in Ireland by Major General William Caulfield, 2nd Viscount Charlemont
1706:	Alnutt's Regiment of Foot
1709:	Earl of Islay's Regiment of Foot
1710:	Disney's Regiment of Foot
1715:	Egerton's Regiment of Foot
1719:	Hotham's Regiment of Foot
1720:	Pocock's Regiment of Foot
1721:	Lenoe's Regiment of Foot
1732:	Moyle's Regiment of Foot
1737:	Bland's Regiment of Foot
1741:	Fleming's Regiment of Foot
1747:	Ranked as 36th Regiment of Foot

1751: 36th Regiment of Foot
1782: 36th (Herefordshire) Regiment of Foot
1804: Nov – 2nd Battalion formed in Sunderland
1814: Oct – 2nd Battalion disbanded in Portsmouth
1881: 2nd Battalion, the Worcestershire Regiment (on amalgamation with the 29th (Worcestershire) Regiment of Foot)
1970: The Worcestershire and Sherwood Foresters Regiment (29th/45th Foot) (on amalgamation with the Sherwood Foresters)
2007: 2nd Battalion, The Mercian Regiment (on amalgamation with The Cheshire Regiment and The Staffordshire Regiment (Prince of Wales'))

Service History, 1st Battalion 36th Regiment of Foot

1793: India – Bangalore [Bengaluru]; Jun – to Pondicherry [Puducherry]; Aug – siege of Pondicherry; Dec – Warriore [Woraiyur]
1794–1795: Warriore
1796: Warriore; Mar – Nagapatam; Apr – Warriore
1797: Warriore; Pondicherry
1798: Pondicherry; Sep – Wallahjabad [Walajabad]; fit men into 76th Foot; Oct – cadre home to England
1799: St Helena; Jul – England; Winchester; Sep – Cirencester; Dec – Cirencester and Liverpool
1800: Winchester and Liverpool; to Ireland; Cork; Fermoy; Clonmel; Cork; Jun – to Isle de Houat; Quiberon; Jul – Minorca
1801: Minorca
1802: Minorca; Jul – to Ireland; Aug – Cork; Sep – Galway
1803: Galway; Jul – Dublin riots; Aug – Athlone; Sep – Dublin
1804: Dublin
1805: Dublin; Aug – Curragh camp; Oct – Bandon; Cork; to Hanover
1806: Hanover; Mar – to England; Hastings; Apr – Battle; Oct – Portsmouth; to South America
1807: At sea; Jul – Monte Video; assault on Buenos Ayres; taken POW; Aug – to Ireland; Dec – Cork
1808: Cork; May – Fermoy; Jul – Cork; to Portugal; Aug – Figuera; ROLICA; VIMEIRO; Lisbon; Oct – advance into Spain; Elvas; Abrantes; Nov – Salamanca; Dec – Mayorga; Astorga
1809: Retreat to Corunna; CORUNNA; to England; Feb – Playdon; Apr – Battle; Jul – Portsmouth; to Walcheren; Flushing; Nov – Woolwich
1810: Battle Barracks
1811: Battle; Feb – to Portugal; PENINSULA; Mar – Lisbon; Santa Comba Dão; Apr – Malpartida; May – Fuentes d'Onoro; Mealhada; Barba del Puerco; Jun – Arronches; Jul – St Vincente; Aug – Barquillas; Sep – Espeja; Ronda; Oct – Pinzio; Nov – Gallegos de Argañán; Dec – Mangualde
1812: Mangualde; Nave de Haver; Feb – Meada; Mar – Almendralejo; Apr – Castelo de Vide; Pedrógão; May – Puebla de Argeme; Jun – Salamanca Forts; Jul – SALAMANCA; Nava de Arévalo; Aug – Cuéllar; Sep – Burgos; Oct – retreat from Burgos; Dec – Folgosa de Medelina
1813: Folgosa de Medelina; Feb – Tourais; May – Malhadas; Jun – Vittoria; Mondragón; Jul – San Estevan; Vittoria; blockade of Pamplona; Aug – PYRENEES; Pass of Maya; Oct – Maya; Nov – NIVELLE; Larressore; Dec – NIVE; Saint-Pierre-d'Irube
1814: Villafranque; Feb – Montfort-en-Chalosse; ORTHEZ; Mar – Sainte-Foy-de-Peyrolières; Apr – TOULOUSE; Auch; Jun – Bordeaux; to Ireland; Jul – Cork; Kilkenny; Sep – Birr
1815: Birr; May – Cork; Jun – to Flanders; Jul – advance on Paris; Paris; Allied Army of Occupation; Dec – Calais; to England; Portsmouth

Service History, 2nd Battalion 36th Regiment of Foot

1804:	Nov – formed at Sunderland from Additional Force Act men from County Durham
1805:	Sunderland; Jun – Durham; Jul – Colchester; Aug – Chelmsford; Nov – Nottingham
1806:	Nottingham; Aug – Scarborough; Sep – Beverley; Oct – Bedale; Dec – Richmond
1807:	Richmond; Dec – Worcester
1808:	Worcester; May – Gosport; Jun – Jersey; Jul – Isle of Wight; Aug – Worcester
1809:	Worcester
1810:	Worcester; May – Kidderminster; Aug – Cirencester; Oct – Horsham
1811:	Horsham; Feb – reduced to six companies
1812:	Horsham; increased to ten companies; Apr – Blatchington; Dec – Lewes
1813:	Lewes; Apr – Blatchington
1814:	Lewes; Aug – Plymouth; Sep – Dartmoor; Oct – disbanded in Portsmouth

Establishments, 1st Battalion 36th Regiment of Foot

Year	Subunits	Field Off	Off/ Staff	Sjts	Mus	Corp/ Pvts	Total
Dec 1792	10co+r	3	47	48	26	1,008	1,132
Dec 1794	10co+r	5	47	48	26	1,008	1,134
Dec 1797	10co+r	5	46	48	26	1,008	1,133
Dec 1798	10co	5	35	53	22	600	715
Dec 1799	10co	5	43	53	22	1,000	1,123
Dec 1801	10co	5	47	53	22	1,000	1,127
Aug 1802	10co	5	36	34	22	750	847
Feb 1805	10co	5	36	44	22	800	907
Nov 1805	10co	5	36	44	22	1,000	1,107
Dec 1805	10co	5	46	54	22	1,000	1,127
Dec 1806	10co	4	46	54	22	1,000	1,126
Dec 1809	10co	4	36	44	22	800	906
Dec 1811	10co	4	36	45	22	800	907
Jul 1814	10co	6	36	55	22	800	929
Dec 1815	10co	4	46	45	22	800	917

Establishments, 2nd Battalion 36th Regiment of Foot

Year	Subunits	Field Off	Off/ Staff	Sjts	Mus	Corp/ Pvts	Total
Dec 1804	10co	3	35	23	22	400	483
Dec 1810	6co	1	23	16	14	198	252
Dec 1811	10co	3	35	25	22	400	485

Service Statistics, 6th Regiment of Foot

	Lieutenant Colonels	Majors
Number of officers in period 1793–1815	8	18
Average age on appointment to substantive rank	38.5	34.5
Average time in rank in regiment (years)	8.5	5
Total field officers by nationality	7 E / 7 S / 6 I / 1 W / 1 F	
Demographics of other ranks 1809	1/36th: 85% EW / 13% I / 2% S	
Demographics of other ranks 1810	1/36th: 81% EW / 16% I / 3% S 2/36th: 80% EW / 18% I / 2% S	
Months of overseas service 1793–1815	1/36th: 177 2/36th: no overseas service	

Significant Militia/Volunteer Intakes

1799: 1st Lancashire, 1st Shropshire, 2nd Shropshire, Westminster, 1st Worcestershire, Monmouth and Breconshire, Montgomeryshire
1805: Cornwall, 3rd Lincolnshire, County Carlow, County Sligo
1806: County Kilkenny, King's County, County Westmeath
1807: Northumberland, 3rd West Yorkshire
1808: West Kent, North Lincolnshire, Carmarthenshire
1809: Herefordshire, Shropshire, Cardiganshire, Glamorganshire
1812: County Louth

Regimental Colonels

144. *Hon. Henry ST JOHN (1778–1818)*
Born: London 1737
Relations: Son of John St John, 2nd Viscount St John and Anne (Furnese); brother of Frederick St John, 2nd Viscount Bolingbroke; brother-in-law of William Bagot, 1st Baron Bagot; uncle of Lieutenant General Hon. Frederick St John
Education: Eton College
Entry to Army: Ensign in Coldstream Foot Guards 31 Dec 1754 by purchase
Regimental Field Officer Promotions: Major in 91st Foot 12 Jan 1760; Lieutenant Colonel in 121st Foot 13 Feb 1762; to half-pay of 121st Foot 1763; Lieutenant Colonel in 67th Foot 9 Nov 1767
Brevets: Brevet Colonel 11 Jan 1776; Major General 19 Feb 1779; Lieutenant General 28 Sep 1787; General 26 Jan 1797
Colonelcies: 36th Foot 27 Nov 1778 (vice Pierson)
Early Service: Groom of Bedchamber to Duke of York 1767; served in Minorca 1768–1771; Groom of Bedchamber to King George III 1771–1784
Political Career: MP (Wootton Bassett) 1761–1784 and 1802
Residences: Rockley, Wiltshire; Audley Street, Mayfair, London
Died: London 3 Apr 1818
Sources: ANCB; ANCD; ANCW; ARLI; HPON; WEOF

Lieutenant Colonels

145. *Allan CAMPBELL (1778–1794)*
Born: Argyllshire c.1725
Relations: Son of Patrick Campbell, 4th Laird of Barcaldine, and Lucy (Cameron); brother of Major Archibald Campbell, 43rd Foot; uncle of Colonel Alexander Campbell, 48th Foot; and Major Patrick Campbell, 42nd Foot
Entry to Army: Served in Hanoverian army c.1745
Regimental Field Officer Promotions: Major in 42nd Foot 15 Aug 1762; to half-pay of 42nd Foot 1763; Major in 36th Foot 27 Mar 1770; Lieutenant Colonel in 36th Foot 26 Jan 1778
Brevets: Brevet Lieutenant Colonel 25 May 1772; Brevet Colonel 17 Nov 1780; Major General 28 Sep 1787
Early Service: Served and captured at the Battle of Prestonpans 1745; served in East Indies 1783
Residence: Norton Street, Marylebone, London
Died: London 13 Nov 1794
Sources: ANCB; ANCD; ANCW; ARLI

146. *Hon. John KNOX (1795–1799)*
Born: County Tyrone 1758
Relations: Son of Thomas Knox, 1st Viscount Northland and Dungannon, and Anne (Vesey); brother of Thomas Knox, 1st Earl of Ranfurly
Entry to Army: Cornet in 18th Light Dragoons 14 Nov 1775 by purchase
Regimental Field Officer Promotions: Major in 36th Foot 23 Nov 1780 (vice Bannerman) by purchase; Lieutenant Colonel in 36th Foot 1 Aug 1795 (vice Campbell)
Brevets: Brevet Lieutenant Colonel 18 Nov 1790; Brevet Colonel 21 Aug 1795; Brigadier General (West Indies) 6 Sep 1795; Major General 18 Jun 1798
Colonelcies: Colonel Commandant of 3/9th Foot Nov 1799
Service 1793–1815: Commanded advanced guard in Helder 1799; appointed Governor and Commander in Chief in Jamaica 1800
Political Career: MP (Ire) 1777–1783 and 1790–1794
Residence: Grafton Square, Fitzroy Square, London
Died: Lost at sea aboard *HMS Babet* off Martinique late Oct 1800
Sources: ANCB; ANCD; ANCW; ARLI; WEOF

147. *Hay McDOWALL (1795–1797)*
Born: Dumfries and Galloway, c.1752
Relations: Son of William MacDowell, MP for Renfrewshire and Elizabeth (Graham); brother of Captain David McDowall-Grant, RN; uncle of Lieutenant General Day Hort MacDowall

Entry to Army: Ensign in 25th Foot 4 Aug 1774 by purchase
Regimental Field Officer Promotions: Major in 73rd Foot 24 Mar 1784; Lieutenant Colonel in 57th Foot 6 Apr 1791 by purchase; Lieutenant Colonel in 36th Foot 19 Aug 1795; Lieutenant Colonel in 78th Foot 22 May 1797 (vice Mackenzie) by exchange; to half-pay of 78th Foot 24 Aug 1802
Brevets: Brevet Colonel 21 Aug 1795; Major General 30 Oct 1805; Lieutenant General 16 May 1808
Colonelcies: Colonel Commandant of 2/40th Foot 24 Mar 1802; 41st Foot 16 May 1808 (vice Stirling)
Service 1793–1815: Served in Flanders 1793; General Officer Commanding Ceylon 22 Jul 1799 to Mar 1804; Commander in Chief Madras 17 Sep 1807 to 16 Mar 1809; at centre of White Mutiny scandal 1809 and ordered home
Died: Lost at sea aboard the *Jane, Duchess of Gordon* near Cape of Good Hope c.16 Mar 1809
Sources: ANCB; ARLI; GHLG; WEOF

148. *Alexander MacKENZIE (1797–1814)*
Born: Ross-shire 1771
Relations: Son of Roderick Mackenzie of Fairburn and Catherine (Baillie)
Entry to Army: Ensign in 1/1st Foot 30 Jun 1787 by purchase
Regimental Field Officer Promotions: Major in 78th Foot 24 Jul 1793; Lieutenant Colonel in 78th Foot 10 Feb 1794; Lieutenant Colonel in 36th Foot 22 May 1797 (vice McDowall) by exchange; removed from the regiment as a general officer 1814
Brevets: Brevet Colonel 26 Jan 1797; Brigadier General (Mediterranean) 25 Aug 1800; Major General 25 Sep 1803; Lieutenant General 25 Jul 1810; General 19 Jul 1821
Service 1793–1815: Served in Flanders 1793; served in Cape of Good Hope 1796; commanded 36th Foot 1797–1798; commanded division in Italy 1806; served on staff in Sicily 1810–1811
Residence: Bath, Somerset
Died: Bath 17 Oct 1853
Sources: ANCB; ANCD; ARLI; PHIL; WEOF

149. *Robert BURNE (1799–1814)*
Born: County Westmeath 1755
Relations: [spec.] Son of James Burne of Athlone
Entry to Army: Ensign in 36th Foot 28 Sep 1773 by purchase
Regimental Field Officer Promotions: Major in 36th Foot 15 Apr 1796 by purchase; Lieutenant Colonel in 36th Foot 13 Nov 1799; removed from the regiment as a general officer 1814
Brevets: Brevet Major 1 Mar 1794; Brevet Lieutenant Colonel 1 Jan 1798; Brevet Colonel 25 Apr 1808; Brigadier General (Spain) 31 Jan 1811; Major General 4 Jun 1811; Lieutenant General 19 Jul 1821
Early Service: Served in East Indies 1783–1798
Service 1793–1815: Commanded 36th Foot 1798–1809; served in Minorca 1800; served in Hanover 1805; served in Buenos Aires 1807; Governor of Carlisle 18 Sep 1808; served in Peninsula Aug 1808 to Jan 1809; served on staff in Walcheren 1809; commanded brigade in 6th Division in Peninsula Mar 1811 to Mar 1812; sent home due to health; held staff positions 1812–1815
Awards and Honours: AGM (Rol&Vim Cor)
Residence: Berkeley Cottage, Stanmore, Hertfordshire
Died: Hertfordshire 16 Jun 1825
Burne '...loved to sit [in the regimental mess] habitually from five to ten o'clock swallowing glass after glass of port and never being himself the slightest degree affected except that his nose was then assuming the purple colour and bottle shape which rendered him so conspicuous in the Peninsular War...'
Sources: ANCB; ANCD; ANCW; ARLI; CHAL; PHIL; WEOF

150. *George HART (1804–1806)*
Born: Dublin c.1763
Relations: Brother of Lieutenant William Sterne Hart, Dublin Attorneys Corps (a volunteer unit made up entirely of lawyers!)
Entry to Army: Lieutenant in 36th Foot 2 Jun 1778
Regimental Field Officer Promotions: Major in 36th Foot 30 Dec 1798 (vice Colman); Lieutenant Colonel in 36th Foot 1 Aug 1804
Brevets: Brevet Major 6 May 1795; Brevet Lieutenant Colonel 1 Jan 1800
Service 1793–1815: Deputy Paymaster General to HM Forces in Madras; commanded 2/36th Foot 1804–1806
Retired: 9 Oct 1806
Residences: Rathmines Road, Rathmines, Dublin
Died: Rathmines 7 Apr 1811
Sources: ARLI; The Parish of Taney – A History of Dundrum

151. *Hon. Basil COCHRANE (1806–1816)*
Born: Fifeshire 1779
Relations: Son of Archibald Cochrane, 9th Earl of Dundonald, and Anne (Gilchrist); brother of Admiral of the Fleet Thomas Cochrane, 10th Earl of Dundonald, Marquess of Maranhão
Entry to Army: Midshipman in Royal Navy Jan 1791; 2nd Lieutenant in 7th Foot 29 Jul 1795
Regimental Field Officer Promotions: Major in

96th Foot 10 Mar 1804 (vice Coast) by purchase; Lieutenant Colonel in 36th Foot 9 Oct 1806 (vice Hart) by purchase
Brevets: Brevet Colonel 4 Jun 1814
Service 1793–1815: Served in British North America 1795–1798; commanded 2/36th Foot 1806–1811; present at naval battle of Basque Roads Apr 1809; commanded 1/36th Foot 1811–1816; served in Peninsula Mar to Nov 1811
Residence: Lyndhurst, Hampshire
Died: Lyndhurst 14 May 1816
Censured by Wellington for his part in the escape of the French garrison of Almeida on 11 May 1811, he returned home a bitter man and in poor health
Sources: ANCB; ANCD; ARLI; CHAL; WEOF; WO 25/744

152. *Lewis DAVIES (1812–1814)*
Born: Cardiganshire 1776
Relations: Son of John Davies of Crugiau, estate agent, and Jane (Morris)
Entry to Army: Ensign in 31st Foot 3 Jun 1791 by purchase
Regimental Field Officer Promotions: Major in 36th Foot 14 Jun 1800 (vice Chambers); Lieutenant Colonel in 36th Foot 2 Jan 1812; to half-pay of 36th Foot 25 Oct 1814
Brevets: Brevet Lieutenant Colonel 25 Apr 1808; Brevet Colonel 4 Jun 1814; Major General 27 May 1825
Service 1793–1815: Served in Flanders 1794; served in West Indies 1796; served in Helder 1799; served in Hanover 1805; served in Cape of Good Hope 1806; served in Peninsula Aug 1808 to Jan 1809; served in Walcheren 1809; commanded 1/36th Foot 1812–1816; served in Peninsula May 1812 to Jul 1813, wounded at Salamanca
Awards and Honours: AGM (Sal); CB 4 Jun 1815
Residence: Tan-y-bwlch, Llanychaearn, Cardiganshire
Died: Llanychaearn 10 May 1828
Sources: ANCW; ARLI; CHAL; PHIL; WEOF; WO 25/745

Majors

153. *Andrew WIGHT (1795–1797)*
Born: East Lothian 1754
Relations: Son of Lieutenant Archibald Wright of Ormiston and Alison (Ramsay)
Entry to Army: Ensign in 92nd Foot 28 Dec 1779
Regimental Field Officer Promotions: Major in 36th Foot 1 Sep 1795 (vice Knox); Major in 45th Foot 9 Feb 1797 (vice Colman) by exchange
Brevets: Brevet Major 1 Mar 1794
Early Service: Served in West Indies 1781
Retired: 15 Nov 1797
Residence: Chapelerne, Kirkcudbrightshire
Died: Chapelerne 4 Sep 1806
Sources: ANCB; ANCD; ARLI

154. *John AUSTEN (1795–1796)*
Born: Kent 1761
Relations: Son of Francis Austen of Sevenoaks and Jane Chadwick (Lennard); second cousin of novelist Jane Austen
Entry to Army: Lieutenant in Independent Company 19 Apr 1781
Regimental Field Officer Promotions: Major in 36th Foot 2 Sep 1795
Brevets: Brevet Major 1 Mar 1794
Retired: 15 Apr 1796
Residence: Sevenoaks, Kent
Died: Hastings, Sussex 8 Feb 1831
Sources: ANCB; ANCD; ARLI; LFBI

155. *Edward Edwin COLMAN (1797–1798)*
Born: London 1770
Relations: Son of Major Edward Colman MP, 1st Dragoons & Martha (Provis); brother of Brigadier General Francis John Colman, Portuguese service
Entry to Army: Ensign in 32nd Foot 4 Jul 1787 by purchase
Regimental Field Officer Promotions: Major in 45th Foot 9 Dec 1795 (vice Haviland); Major in 36th Foot 9 Feb 1797 (vice Wight) by exchange; Major in 84th Foot 30 Dec 1798 (vice Orde)
Brevets: Brevet Major 12 Jan 1795; Brevet Lieutenant Colonel 1 Jan 1800
Service 1793–1815: Served in East Indies 1797–1807
Retired: 14 Feb 1807
Died: Southampton, Hampshire 10 Jan 1808
Sources: ANCB; ANCD; ANCW; ARLI; HPON; WEOF

156. *William CHAMBERS (1799–1800)*
Born: County Donegal c.1763
Relations: Son of Daniel Chambers of Rockhill and Isabel (Davis)
Entry to Army: Ensign in 36th Foot 12 Aug 1779 by purchase
Regimental Field Officer Promotions: Major in 36th Foot 13 Nov 1799; Lieutenant Colonel in 28th Foot 30 May 1800 (vice Hall) by purchase
Brevets: Brevet Major 1 Jan 1798
Service 1793–1815: Commanded 28th Foot in Alexandria 1801 after Paget wounded

Retired: 24 Jul 1802
Residence: Bomany, Letterkenny, County Donegal
Died: Bomany 13 Jun 1842
Was the officer who gave the order, 'Rear rank, 28th! Right about face!' when threatened by French cavalry from the rear at Alexandria
Sources: ANCB; ARLI; <https://www.findagrave.com/memorial/98428629/william-chambers>

157. *Duncan DARROCH (1804–1815)*

Born: Renfrewshire 1776
Relations: Son of Duncan Darroch, 2nd Laird of Gourock, and Mary (Rowan); father of Major Duncan Darroch, 86th Foot; and Major Donald George Angus Darroch, 51st Foot
Entry to Army: Ensign in 41st Foot 31 Mar 1792
Regimental Field Officer Promotions: Major in 104th Foot 18 Sep 1794; Major in Rothesay and Caithness Fencibles 1796; Lieutenant Colonel (temporary) in Glengarry Fencibles 7 Dec 1799; to half-pay of Rothesay and Caithness Fencibles Jul 1802; Major in 36th Foot 1 Aug 1804 (vice Hart); removed from the regiment as a general officer 1815
Brevets: Brevet Lieutenant Colonel 1 Jan 1800; Brevet Colonel 25 Jul 1810; Brigadier General (North America) 1812; Major General 4 Jun 1813; Lieutenant General 27 May 1825; General 23 Nov 1841
Service 1793–1815: Served in Irish rebellion 1798; Assistant Adjutant General in Hanover 1805; served in Cape of Good Hope 1806; served in Buenos Aires 1807; Assistant Adjutant General in Peninsula Aug 1808 to Sep 1809; served on staff in British North America 1812–1815
Residences: Gourock House, near Greenock, Renfrewshire; Torridon, Auchnasheen, Ross-shire
Died: Gourock House 16 Feb 1847
Sources: ARLI; CHAL; GEMA (1847); GHLG; PHIL; WEOF; WO 25/745

158. *William HUTCHINSON (1804–1808)*

Born: Yorkshire 1759
Relations: Son of Francis Hutchinson of Hunmansby and Jane (Ovinton)
Entry to Army: Ensign in 65th Foot 26 May 1780 by purchase
Regimental Field Officer Promotions: Major unattached 25 Sep 1794; Major in 36th Foot 2 Aug 1804
Brevets: Brevet Lieutenant Colonel 1 Jan 1800
Retired: 8 Dec 1808
Residence: Wold Newton, Yorkshire
Died: Wold Newton 17 Dec 1808
Sources: ANCD; ARLI; WEOF; <https://www.militaryimages.net/media/william-hutchinson.94745/>

159. *Alexander MacKENZIE (1804–1810)*

Born: Ross-shire 1763
Relations: Son of William Mackenzie of Gruinard and Lilias (Mackenzie); brother of Captain John Mackenzie, 73rd Foot; and Captain Simon Mackenzie, 78th Foot; father of Major General Alexander Mackay Mackenzie, Bengal staff corps
Entry to Army: Ensign in 2/73rd Foot 21 Aug 1779
Regimental Field Officer Promotions: Major in 36th Foot 3 Aug 1804; Lieutenant Colonel in York Light Infantry Volunteers 20 Dec 1810 (vice Henderson); to half-pay of York Light Infantry Volunteers 19 Mar 1817
Brevets: Brevet Colonel 12 Aug 1819
Early Service: Served in Gibraltar 1782–1785; served in East Indies 1783–1793
Service 1793–1815: Served in East Indies 1793–1798; served in Mediterranean 1800–1802; served in Peninsula 1809–1809; served in Walcheren 1809, wounded at Flushing; served in West Indies 1811–1817
Retired: 1825
Residence: St Helier, Jersey, Channel Islands
Died: Jersey 12 Jul 1831
There were 23 officers named Mackenzie serving in the 73rd Foot when this officer received his first commission, including four other Alexanders. This officer claims to have served in Portugal in 1808, although does not appear on Challis' Peninsular Roll Call
Sources: ANCD; ARLI; PHIL; WEOF; WO 25/747

160. *William CROSS (1808–1816)*

Born: Dorset 1779
Relations: Son of William Cross of Buckhorn Weston and Mary (Law); father of Lieutenant Colonel William Jennings Cross, unattached
Entry to Army: Lieutenant in East Yorkshire Militia; Ensign in 62nd Foot 5 Dec 1798
Regimental Field Officer Promotions: Major in 36th Foot 8 Dec 1808 (vice Hutchinson) by purchase; Lieutenant Colonel in 36th Foot 23 May 1816; to half-pay of 36th Foot 29 Apr 1824
Brevets: Brevet Lieutenant Colonel 22 Nov 1813; Brevet Colonel 22 Jul 1830; Major General 23 Nov 1841
Service 1793–1815: Served in Hanover 1805; served in Buenos Aires 1807; served in Peninsula Aug 1808 to Jan 1809; served in Peninsula Mar 1811 to May 1812; and again Sep 1813 to Apr 1814, wounded at Toulouse
Awards and Honours: AGM (Nlle Niv Ort Toul)
Residence: Paris, Île-de-France, France
Died: Paris 25 Nov 1843
Sources: ARLI; CHAL; PHIL; WEOF; WO 25/744

161. *George Ralph Payne JARVIS (1810–1811)*

Born: Antigua 1774
Relations: Son of Thomas Jarvis, Chief Justice of Antigua, and Rachel (Thibou)
Entry to Army: Ensign in 36th Foot 8 Feb 1792
Regimental Field Officer Promotions: Major in 36th Foot 24 1810 (vice Mackenzie); to half-pay of 36th Foot 25 Mar 1811; rank stationary thereafter
Brevets: Brevet Lieutenant Colonel 12 Aug 1819
Service 1793–1815: Served in East Indies 1793–1798; served in Mediterranean 1800–1802; served in Buenos Aires 1807; Deputy Assistant Adjutant General in Peninsula Aug 1808 to Jan 1809; served in Walcheren 1809; served on home staff 1813–1814
Later Service: Magistrate and Deputy Lieutenant for Lincolnshire
Awards and Honours: MGSM (Rol&Vim Cor)
Residences: Doddington Hall, Doddington, Lincolnshire; Brock St, Bath, Somerset
Died: Doddington Hall 14 Jun 1851
Sources: ANCB; ANCD; ARLI; GEMA (1851); WEMR

162. *Molyneux SMITH (1812)*

Born: County Westmeath c.1778
Relations: Of the Smiths of Moyvore; father of Lieutenant Molyneux Smith, Bombay service
Entry to Army: Ensign in 36th Foot 8 Feb 1792
Regimental Field Officer Promotions: Major in 36th Foot 30 Jan 1812 (vice Davies)
Service 1793–1815: Served in Peninsula Aug 1808 to Jan 1809; served in Peninsula Mar 1811 to Aug 1812, severely wounded at Salamanca
Died: Of wounds at Cuellar, Spain 21 Aug 1812
Sources: ANCB; ANCW; ARLI; CHAL; HALL; WEOF

163. *Martin LEGGATT (1812–1821)*

Born: [spec.] Sussex c.1760
Entry to Army: Ensign in 79th Foot 6 Nov 1780
Regimental Field Officer Promotions: Major in 36th Foot 30 Jan 1812; to half-pay of 101st Foot Jun 1821 (vice Browne) by exchange
Brevets: Brevet Lieutenant Colonel 21 Jun 1817
Service 1793–1815: Served in Peninsula with 50th Foot Sep 1808 to Jan 1809; served in Walcheren 1809; served in Peninsula as ADC to General Lumley Oct 1810 to Sep 1811; served in Peninsula with 1/36th Foot Jul 1813 to Apr 1814
Retired: 18 Feb 1826
Awards and Honours: AGM (Pyr Toul)
Residence: Charlton Kings, Gloucestershire
Died: Charlton Kings 3 Aug 1830
Sources: ANCD; ANCW; ARLI; GEMA (1830); PHIL; WEMR; WEOF

164. *John FOX (1812–1814)*

Born: Shropshire c.1771
Entry to Army: Ensign in 92nd Foot 27 Jun 1795
Regimental Field Officer Promotions: Major in 36th Foot 1 Oct 1812; to half-pay of 39th Foot 1814; Major in 10th Royal Veteran Battalion 9 Dec 1819; to retired full pay on disbandment 24 Mar 1821; Lieutenant Colonel in 3rd Royal Veteran Battalion 25 Dec 1821; to retired full pay on disbandment 24 Jun 1826
Brevets: Brevet Major 4 Jun 1811; Brevet Lieutenant Colonel 12 Aug 1819
Service 1793–1815: Served in Peninsula Aug 1808 to Jan 1809; served in Walcheren 1809; served in Peninsula Mar 1811 to Dec 1812, wounded at Salamanca
Residences: The Lees, Wellington, Shropshire; Bear Street, Barnstaple, Devon
Died: Barnstaple 21 Jan 1830
Sources: ANCW; ARLI; CHAL; HALL; WEOF; The Monthly Magazine Vol.19

165. *John Richard WARD (1812–1814)*

Born: County Down 1790
Relations: Son of Colonel Rt Hon. Robert Ward of Bangor Castle, South Down Militia, and Sophia Frances (Whaley); grandson of Bernard Ward, 1st Viscount Bangor; half-brother of Rear Admiral James Hamilton Ward RN
Entry to Army: Captain on half-pay of 62nd Foot 8 Dec 1794
Regimental Field Officer Promotions: Major in 36th Foot 26 Nov 1812; to half-pay of 36th Foot 25 Oct 1814; Lieutenant Colonel in 2nd Dragoons Dec 1838 (vice Sandys) by exchange
Brevets: Brevet Major 1 Jan 1805; Brevet Lieutenant Colonel 1 Jan 1812; Brevet Colonel 22 Jul 1830
Service 1793–1815: Served in Peninsula with 3/27th Foot Nov 1808 to Jul 1811; commanded 7th *Caçadores* in Peninsula with Portuguese forces Jan to Dec 1812, wounded at Badajoz; served in Peninsula with 36th Foot Feb to Sep 1813
Later Service: Assistant Quartermaster General in Ireland
Retired: 1856
Awards and Honours: AGM (Bad Sal Pyr); CB 4 Jun 1815; MGSM (Bus)
Residence: Tubber na Carrig, Strangford, County Down
Died: Strangford 30 Aug 1860
This officer appears to have been commissioned literally

from the cradle; he served on half-pay until joining his regiment in 1806 at age 16
Sources: ANCW; ARLI; CHAL; GEMA (1831) (father); PHIL; WEOF

Selected Regimental Histories

Cannon, Richard, *Historical Record of the Thirty-sixth, or the Herefordshire Regiment of Foot: Containing an Account of the Formation of the Regiment in 1701, and of its Subsequent Services to 1852* (London: Parker, Furnivall & Parker,1853)

Regimental Museum

Worcester City Art Gallery and Museum, Foregate Street, Worcester, Worcestershire
Herefordshire Light Infantry Museum, Harold St, Hereford, Herefordshire

---

37th Regiment of Foot

Secondary Title:	North Hampshire
Nickname:	The Mindens
Jacket:	Red
Facings:	Yellow

Regimental Lineage, 37th Regiment of Foot

1702:	Feb – raised in Ireland by Lieutenant General Thomas Meredyth
1710:	Windress's Regiment of Foot
1715:	Earl of Westmorland's Regiment of Foot
1717:	Viscount Hinchingbrooke's Regiment of Foot
1722:	Murray's Regiment of Foot
1735:	Ponsonby's Regiment of Foot
1745:	Munro's Regiment of Foot
1746:	Dejean's Regiment of Foot
1747:	Ranked as 37th Regiment of Foot
1751:	37th Regiment of Foot
1782:	37th (North Hampshire) Regiment of Foot
1813:	Mar – 2nd Battalion formed in Battle
1817:	Mar – 2nd Battalion disbanded in Cork
1881:	The Hampshire Regiment (on amalgamation with the 67th (South Hampshire) Regiment of Foot)
1946:	The Royal Hampshire Regiment
1992:	The Princess of Wales's Royal Regiment (Queen's and Royal Hampshires) (on amalgamation with The Queen's Regiment)

Service History, 1st Battalion 37th Regiment of Foot

1793:	Edinburgh Castle; Mar – Leith; Yarmouth; to Holland; Apr – flank companies to Marquain; May – Famars; Jul – Valenciennes; Sep – Dunkirk; Oct – Vervice
1794:	Wevelgem; Apr – Cateau; Premont; Landrecies; May – Tourcoing; TOURNAY; Antwerp; Oct – Nijmegen; Dec – line of River Waal
1795:	Geldermalsen; retreat to Bremen; Mar – Bremenlee; to England; May – Harwich; Jun – Sunderland; Aug – Whitley camp; Oct – Southampton; Nov – to West Indies; caught in storms; sheltered at Isle of Wight
1796:	Six companies at Isle of Wight, four companies to Barbados; Apr – Poole; May – to Gibraltar
1797–1799:	Gibraltar
1800:	Gibraltar; Mar – to West Indies; Apr – St Vincent
1801–1807:	St Vincent
1808:	St Vincent; Feb – Trinidad
1809:	Trinidad; Jul – to England; Oct – Portsmouth; Burton on Trent; Nov – Derby

1810:	Derby; Apr – Loughborough; May – Horsham; Jul – Blatchington; Oct – Lewes; Dec – to Ireland
1811:	Cork; Dec – to England; Portsmouth; Chichester
1812:	Hastings; Mar – Hilsea; Portsmouth; to Gibraltar
1813:	Gibraltar
1814:	Gibraltar; Feb – to Spain, then France; PENINSULA; Mar – Pasaies; Apr – Boucau; May – Bordeaux; Jun – Pauillac, to England, then Upper Canada; Aug – Québec; Kingston; Nov – Burlington
1815:	Burlington; Jun – Queenston; Aug – Amherstburg

Service History, 2nd Battalion 37th Regiment of Foot

1813:	May – formed (four companies) at Battle from militia volunteers; Jun – augmented to six companies; Oct – Hastings; Nov – Battle; Dec – augmented to eight companies; Ramsgate; to Netherlands; Willemstad
1814:	Steenbergen and Tholen; Feb – Merxcem; Mar – Bergen-op-Zoom; Apr – Antwerp garrison
1815:	Antwerp; in garrison during Waterloo campaign; Dec – to Ireland; Cork
1817:	Mar – disbanded in Cork

Establishments, 1st Battalion 37th Regiment of Foot

Year	Subunits	Field Off	Off/ Staff	Sjts	Mus	Corp/ Pvts	Total
Dec 1792	10co	3	32	22	12	330	399
Jan 1793	10co	3	32	32	22	600	689
Dec 1793	10co	3	32	42	22	850	949
Dec 1795	10co+2r	5	51	62	30	1,010	1,158
Dec 1797	10co	5	38	53	22	600	718
Dec 1802	10co	5	43	34	22	750	854
May 1803	10co	5	46	34	22	750	857
Dec 1804	10co	5	46	54	22	1,000	1,127
Dec 1805	10co	5	46	44	22	800	917
Dec 1806	10co	4	46	44	22	800	916
Dec 1808	10co	4	46	34	22	600	706
Oct 1809	10co	4	36	44	22	800	906
Dec 1810	10co	4	46	54	22	1,000	1,126
Dec 1811	10co	4	46	55	22	1,000	1,127
Dec 1812	10co+r	4	50	73	26	1,208	1,361
Dec 1813	10co+r	4	49	63	22	1,008	1,146

Establishments, 2nd Battalion 37th Regiment of Foot

Year	Subunits	Field Off	Off/ Staff	Sjts	Mus	Corp/ Pvts	Total
Dec 1813	10co+r	3	39	53	22	808	925
Dec 1815	10co+r	3	39	43	22	608	715

Service Statistics, 37th Regiment of Foot

	Lieutenant Colonels	Majors
Number of officers in period 1793–1815	9	13
Average age on appointment to substantive rank	34.5	34.5
Average time in rank in regiment (years)	5	4.5
Total field officers by nationality	8 S / 6 E / 5 I / 1 F	
Demographics of other ranks 1808	62% EW / 32% I / 5% S / 1% F	
Demographics of other ranks 1810	66% EW / 31% I / 3% S	
Months of overseas service 1793–1815	1/37th: 229 2/37th: 24	

Significant Militia/Volunteer Intakes

1807: South Gloucestershire, North Hampshire
1809: 3rd Lancashire, Stirlingshire
1810: Worcestershire, South Cork, County Kilkenny, County Longford, County Meath, County Tipperary
1811: North Hampshire, Oxfordshire, County Limerick, County Meath, County Sligo
1812: 3rd Lancashire, East Middlesex, Northumberland, Oxfordshire, Radnorshire, South Cork, County Kerry, County Longford, North Mayo,
1813: 3rd Lancashire, North Hampshire, East Middlesex, Lanarkshire, Cork City, County Galway, County Kildare, County Kilkenny, County Wicklow
1814: Westmorland, South Cork, North Mayo

Regimental Colonels

166. *Sir John DALLING, 1st Bt (1783–1798)*
Born: Suffolk c.1731
Relations: Son of John Dalling of Bungay and Catherine (Windham); father of Lieutenant John Windham Dalling, 37th Foot; Sir William Windham Dalling, 2nd Baronet; Major Edward Lawford Dalling, Coldstream Foot Guards; and Captain John Windham Dalling RN; father-in-law of General Hon. Robert Meade
Education: Bury School
Entry to Army: Ensign in 20th Foot 1747 by purchase
Regimental Field Officer Promotions: Major in 28th Foot 2 Feb 1757; Lieutenant Colonel in 43rd Foot 27 Feb 1760 by purchase; Lieutenant Colonel in 36th Foot 4 Dec 1767; Lieutenant Colonel in 50th Foot 14 Aug 1772
Brevets: Brevet Colonel 25 May 1772; Major General 19 Aug 1777; Lieutenant General 20 Nov 1782; General 1796
Colonelcies: Colonel Commandant of 3/60th Foot 16 Jan 1776 (vice Taylor); 37th Foot 1783 (vice Coote)
Early Service: Served in British North America 1757–1759; served in Jamaica 1760–1782; commanded 43rd Foot at siege of Havana 1762; Lieutenant Governor of Jamaica 1767–1777; acting Captain General and Governor-in-Chief of Jamaica 11 Dec 1772 to 5 Jan 1774; Captain General and Governor-in-Chief of Jamaica 15 Jun 1777 to 25 Nov 1781; Commander in Chief of Madras forces 1784–1786
Creations and Dignities: 1st Baronet of Burwood 11 Mar 1783
Residence: Burwood Park, Hersham, Surrey
Died: Burwood Park 16 Jan 1798
Sources: *ARLI; ODNB; WOST; The American Revolution 1775–1783, An Encyclopedia Vol.1*

167. *Sir Hew Whitefoord DALRYMPLE, 1st Bt (1798–1810)*
Born: Ayrshire 1750
Relations: Son of Captain John Dalrymple of Ayr, 6th Dragoons and Mary (Ross)
Education: Edinburgh University
Entry to Army: Ensign in 31st Foot 8 Apr 1763 by purchase
Regimental Field Officer Promotions: Major in 77th Foot 17 Dec 1777 by purchase; Lieutenant Colonel in 68th Foot 21 Sep 1781 by purchase; Captain and Lieutenant Colonel in 1st Foot Guards 23 May 1783 (vice de Burgh) by exchange
Brevets: Brevet Colonel 18 Nov 1790; Major General 3 Oct 1794; Lieutenant General 1 Jan 1801; General 1 Jan 1812
Colonelcies: 81st Foot 8 Aug 1797 (vice Forbes); 37th Foot 18 Jan 1798 (vice Dalling); 19th Foot 25 Jun 1810 (vice Hulse); 57th Foot 7 Apr 1811 (vice Hutchinson)
Service 1793–1815: Commanded Guards grenadier battalion in Flanders 1793; Lieutenant Governor of Guernsey Mar 1796 to 1802; acting Commander in Chief and Governor of Gibraltar 2 Nov 1806 to 30 Jun 1808; appointed to command in Portugal Aug 1808; cleared after Convention of Cintra in 1808 but not employed again
Later Service: Governor of Blackness Castle 1818
Creations and Dignities: 1st Baronet of High Mark 27 Dec 1814
Awards and Honours: Knight Bachelor 19 May 1779
Residence: High Mark, near Glenluce, Wigtownshire
Died: London 9 Apr 1830
Sources: ARLI; DINB; ODNB; WEOF; WO 25/745; WOST

168. *Sir Charles LOCKHART ROSS, 7th Bt (1810–1814)*
Born: London 1763
Relations: Son of Vice Admiral Sir John Lockhart

Ross RN, 6th Baronet, and Elizabeth Baillie (Dundas); nephew of Lord Advocate Robert Dundas
Entry to Army: Cornet in 7th Dragoons 5 Jan 1780 by purchase
Regimental Field Officer Promotions: Major in 37th Foot 13 Jun 1787 by purchase; Lieutenant Colonel in 37th Foot 16 Mar 1791 by purchase; Lieutenant Colonel in 116th Foot 1 Sep 1795; to half-pay of 116th Foot 1 Mar 1798
Brevets: Brevet Colonel 21 Aug 1795; Major General 18 Jun 1798; Lieutenant General 30 Oct 1805
Colonelcies: Colonel Commandant of 2/85th Foot 9 May 1800; 86th Foot 30 Oct 1806 (vice Craig); 37th Foot 25 Jun 1810 (vice Dalrymple)
Service 1793–1815: Commanded 37th Foot 1791–1795
Political Career: MP (Tain Burghs) 1786–1796; MP (Ross-shire) 1796–1806; MP (Linlithgow Burghs) 1806–1807
Creations and Dignities: 7th Baronet of Balnagown 9 Jun 1790
Residence: Balnagown, Ross-shire
Died: Edinburgh 8 Feb 1814
Sources: *ANCB; ANCW; ARLI; HPON; WEOF*

169. *Sir Charles GREEN, 1st Bt (1814–1831)*

Born: Gibraltar 1749
Relations: Son of Captain Christopher Green, 31st Foot and Britania Maria (Hamilton); brother of Major General Christopher Green, Bengal service; and Lieutenant Nicholas Green, 37th Foot
Education: Royal Military Academy, Woolwich
Entry to Army: Gentleman cadet in RA 1760; Volunteer in 31st Foot; Ensign in 31st Foot 10 Aug 1765
Regimental Field Officer Promotions: Major in 31st Foot 25 Feb 1788 (vice Cotton) by purchase; Lieutenant Colonel in 85th Foot 30 Oct 1793; Lieutenant Colonel in 30th Foot 19 Feb 1794 (vice Maxwell) by exchange
Brevets: Brevet Major 19 Mar 1783; Brevet Colonel 26 Jan 1797; Brigadier General (Leeward Islands) 11 Oct 1798; Brigadier General (Ireland) 1803; Major General 25 Sep 1803; Lieutenant General 25 Oct 1809; General 12 Aug 1819
Colonelcies: York Light Infantry Volunteers 16 Jan 1804; 16th Foot 29 Aug 1808 (vice Bowyer); 37th Foot 17 Feb 1814 (vice Ross)
Early Service: Served in Florida 1766–1771; served in served in West Indies 1771–1773; served in American War of Independence 1776–1778, taken POW at Saratoga
Service 1793–1815: Commanded 30th Foot in Corsica 1794; Lieutenant Governor of Grenada 9 Mar 1797 to 8 Jun 1801; temporary Commander in Chief Windward and Leeward Islands Nov 1803 to Apr 1804; commanded forces at capture of Surinam Apr 1804; Governor of Surinam 9 May 1804 to 15 Apr 1805; commander of Malta garrison May 1807 to May 1808; commanded districts on home staff 1812–1814
Awards and Honours: Knight Bachelor 4 May 1803
Creations and Dignities: 1st Baronet of Milnrow 30 Nov 1805
Residence: Cheltenham, Gloucestershire
Died: Cheltenham 12 Jul 1831
Sources: ARLI; DEBA; GEMA (1831); PHIL; WEOF; WOST

Lieutenant Colonels

170. *Sir Charles LOCKHART ROSS, 7th Bt (1791–1795)*

See 168.
Lieutenant Colonel in 37th Foot 16 Mar 1791 by purchase

171. *Hon. Charles HOPE (1794–1799)*

Born: West Lothian 1768
Relations: Son of John Hope, 2nd Earl of Hopetoun and Lady Elizabeth (Leslie); brother of General Sir Alexander Hope; half-brother of General Sir John Hope, Earl of Hopetoun; brother-in-law of Henry Dundas, Viscount Melville
Entry to Army: Cornet in 3rd Dragoon Guards 11 May 1785 by purchase
Regimental Field Officer Promotions: Major in 37th Foot 12 Apr 1793 (vice Wemyss) by purchase; Lieutenant Colonel in 37th Foot 3 Jun 1794; Lieutenant Colonel in 28th Light Dragoons 19 Apr 1799 (vice J. Hope) by exchange; Lieutenant Colonel in 7th Dragoon Guards 5 Dec 1799 (vice E. Dunne) by purchase
Brevets: Brevet Lieutenant Colonel 3 Jun 1794; Brevet Colonel 1 Jan 1800; Brigadier General (Jersey) 27 May 1803; Major General 30 Oct 1805; Lieutenant General 1 Jan 1812; General 27 May 1825
Colonelcies: Colonel Commandant of 5/60th Foot 15 Feb 1813
Early Service: ADC to Alexander Leslie 1789–1790
Service 1793–1815: Served in Flanders 1793–1795; served in Portugal 1797; commanded brigade of cavalry in Southern District 1801; commanded Canterbury garrison Nov 1805 to Jun 1808;

commanded brigade of cavalry in Kent Jun 1808 to May 1809
Political Career: MP (Dysart Burghs) 1790–1796; MP (Haddingtonshire) 1800–1816
Residences: Welbeck Street, Cavendish Square, London; Waughton, Haddingtonshire
Died: Monimail, Fifeshire 1 Jul 1828
Sources: ARLI; FMPD; HPON; WEOF; WO 25/746

172. *Alexander BUCHANAN (1795–1801)*
Born: Lanarkshire c.1765
Relations: Of the Buchanans of Glasgow
Entry to Army: Ensign in 75th Foot 12 Mar 1783
Regimental Field Officer Promotions: Lieutenant Colonel in 116th Foot 10 Feb 1794; Lieutenant Colonel in 37th Foot 1 Sep 1795 (vice Lockhart Ross) by exchange
Brevets: Brevet Major 1 Mar 1794; Brevet Colonel 26 Jan 1797; Brigadier General (Leeward Islands) 10 May 1800
Service 1793–1815: Commanded 37th Foot 1795–1802; served in Gibraltar 1796–1802; served in West Indies 1800–1802
Residence: Trongate Street, Glasgow, Lanarkshire
Died: After falling from a window in St Vincent, West Indies Dec 1801
Sources: ANCW; ARLI;

173. *Sir John HOPE, Kt (1799–1804)*
Born: Middlesex 1765
Relations: Son of John Hope, author and MP and Mary (Breton); brother of Vice Admiral William Johnstone Hope; cousin of General Sir John Hope of Hopetoun
Entry to Army: Cadet in Houston's Regiment of Scots Brigade Dec 1778; Ensign in Scots Brigade Dec 1779
Regimental Field Officer Promotions: Major in 28th Light Dragoons 25 Mar 1795; Lieutenant Colonel in 28th Light Dragoons 20 Feb 1796 (vice Baird) by purchase; Lieutenant Colonel in 37th Foot 19 Apr 1799 (vice C. Hope) by exchange; Lieutenant Colonel in 60th Foot 30 Jun 1804 (vice Maclean) by exchange
Brevets: Brevet Lieutenant Colonel 20 Feb 1796; Brevet Colonel 1 Jan 1805; Brigadier General (North Britain) Apr 1808; Major General 25 Jul 1810; Lieutenant General 12 Aug 1819
Colonelcies: 92nd Highlanders 29 Jan 1820 (vice J. Hope); 72nd Highlanders 6 Sep 1823 (vice Murray)
Early Service: Served in Flanders 1778–1781
Service 1793–1815: ADC to William Erskine in Flanders 1793–1795; commanded 28th Light Dragoons at Cape of Good Hope 1796–1798; served in West Indies 1800–1804; Assistant Adjutant General in North Britain 1805–1807; Deputy Adjutant General in Hanover 1805; Assistant Adjutant General in Copenhagen 1807; Deputy Adjutant General in North Britain May 1809; commanded brigade in 5th Division in Peninsula May to Sep 1812
Later Service: Commander in Chief in Scotland 1816–1819
Awards and Honours: AGM (Sal); GCH 12 Aug 1820; Knight Bachelor 30 Mar 1821
Residence: Rothesay, Isle of Bute
Died: Rothesay 1 Aug 1836
Sources: ANCB; ANCD; ARLI; CHAL; DINB; ODNB; PHIL; WEOF; WO 25/746

174. *Sir Fitzroy Jefferies Grafton McLEAN, 8th Bt (1804–1815)*
Born: Edinburgh 1770
Relations: Son of Donald Maclean of Brolas and Margaret Wall; half-brother of Sir Hector Mclean, 23rd Clan Chief; father of Lieutenant Colonel Charles Fitzroy Maclean, 13th Light Dragoons
Entry to Army: Ensign in 29th Foot 24 Sep 1787 by purchase
Regimental Field Officer Promotions: Major in 110th Foot 8 Sep 1794; Major in 79th Foot 22 Jul 1795; Lieutenant Colonel in 2/82nd Foot 18 Nov 1795 (vice Barry) by purchase; to half-pay of 82nd Foot 1796; Lieutenant Colonel in 2/60th Foot 5 Feb 1801 (vice Cunynghame) by exchange; Lieutenant Colonel in 37th Foot 30 Jun 1804 (vice Hope) by exchange; removed from the regiment as a general officer 1815
Brevets: Brevet Colonel 25 Sep 1803; Brigadier General (West Indies) 12 Jan 1805; Major General 25 Jul 1810; Lieutenant General 4 Jun 1814; General 10 Jan 1837
Colonelcies: 84th Foot 28 July 1823 (vice Pack)
Service 1793–1815: Served in West Indies 1787–1801; served in West Indies 1803–1815; commanded 37th Foot 1804–1805; commanded Batavian troops after capture of Demerara 1804; Commandant of St Thomas and St John 21 Dec 1807 to 15 Apr 1815; served at capture of Guadeloupe 1810
Creations and Dignities: 8th Baronet of Duart and Morvern 2 Nov 1818; 24th Clan Chief of Clan Maclean 1818–1847
Awards and Honours: AGM (Guad)
Residence: Cadogan Place, Belgravia, London
Died: London 5 Jul 1847
Sources: ANCB; ANCD; ANCW; ARLI; PHIL; WEOF

175. *William SPREAD (1805–1812)*
Born: County Cork 1757
Relations: Son of John Spread of Forrest and Anstace (Earbery); brother of Captain John Matthias Spread RN; Captain Christopher Earbery Spread, Royal Marines; and Lieutenant Richard Spread, 87th Foot
Entry to Army: Ensign in 64th Foot 21 Nov 1778
Regimental Field Officer Promotions: Major in 37th Foot 5 Dec 1799 (vice Baird); Lieutenant Colonel in 37th Foot 13 Jun 1805
Brevets: Brevet Lieutenant Colonel 1 Jan 1805
Service 1793–1815: Served in West Indies 1795
Retired: 20 Feb 1812
Residence: Kinsale, County Cork
Died: Kinsale Apr 1836
Sources: ANCB; ANCD; ANCW; ARLI; WEOF

176. *Reginald JAMES (1812–1817)*
Born: Dublin c.1770
Relations: [spec.] Son of William James, Mayor of Dublin
Entry to Army: Lieutenant in 77th Foot 13 Jun 1796
Regimental Field Officer Promotions: Major in 37th Foot 5 Nov 1807 (vice Stewart); Lieutenant Colonel in 37th Foot 20 Feb 1812 (vice Spread) by purchase
Service 1793–1815: Superintendent of Indian Affairs in Sandwich, Ontario 1815
Retired: 3 Jul 1817
Residence: Queens Elm, Brompton, London
Died: Brompton 23 Oct 1824
Sources: ARLI; EDAR (1824); WEOF

177. *Simon HART (1813–1815)*
Born: India c.1780
Relations: Son of Colonel Simon Hart, Madras service and Margaret (Campbell)
Entry to Army: Ensign in 37th Foot 10 Jan 1798 by purchase
Regimental Field Officer Promotions: Major in 37th Foot 25 Oct 1805 (vice Beckwith); Lieutenant Colonel in 37th Foot 10 Jun 1813
Brevets: Brevet Lieutenant Colonel 1 Jan 1812
Service 1793–1815: Commanded 2/37th Foot in Netherlands and Belgium 1813–1815
Residence: Bray, County Wicklow
Died: Antwerp, Belgium 23 Nov 1815
Sources: ARLI; WEOF; WikiTree

178. *Andrew TILT (1815–1817)*
Born: Sussex 1780
Relations: Son of Thomas Tilt of Brighton, property developer, and Mary (Ker)
Entry to Army: Ensign in 37th Foot 1 Jan 1801 by purchase
Regimental Field Officer Promotions: Major in 37th Foot 20 Feb 1812 (vice James) by purchase; Lieutenant Colonel in 37th Foot 7 Dec 1815 (vice Hart); to half-pay of 37th Foot 25 Mar 1817
Service 1793–1815: Served in West Indies 1801–1809; served in Gibraltar 1812–1814; served in Peninsula Mar and Apr 1814; served in British North America 1814–1817
Retired: 1826
Died: Clapham, London 20 Oct 1853
Took his articles of clerkship in Apr 1795 – it appears he took a commission immediately after completion
Sources: ANCB; ARLI; CHAL; WEMR; WEOF

Majors

179. *David Douglas WEMYSS (1791–1793)*
Born: David Douglas in [spec.] Fifeshire c.1760; assumed Wemyss surname c.1790
Relations: Natural son of James Wemyss, 5th Earl of Wemyss; half-brother of Colonel Charles James Wemyss, RM; uncle of Lieutenant General Thomas James Wemyss; and Captain Hugo Wemyss, 19th Foot
Entry to Army: Ensign in 49th Foot 27 Apr 1777 by purchase
Regimental Field Officer Promotions: Major in 37th Foot 16 Mar 1791 (vice Ross) by purchase; Lieutenant Colonel in 18th Foot 12 Apr 1793 (vice Chapman)
Brevets: Brevet Colonel 3 May 1796; Brigadier General (Gibraltar) 5 Apr 1798; Major General 29 Apr 1802; Lieutenant General 25 Apr 1808; General 12 Aug 1819
Early Service: Served in Newfoundland 1777; served in West Indies 1778–1782; also 1786–1789
Service 1793–1815: Served in Flanders 1793; commanded 18th Foot at Toulon 1793; in Corsica 1794–1795; Governor of Calvi 1795; commanded force at Leghorn [Livorno] 1797; served on staff in Gibraltar 1797–1799 and again Apr 1800 to Nov 1802; General Officer Commanding Ceylon Mar 1804 to 19 Jul 1805; Governor of Tynemouth Castle and Cliffe Fort May 1809
Residences: Gore House, St Margaret Westminster; Cumberland Street, Pimlico, London
Died: London 29 Aug 1839
Sources: ARLI; DINB; PHIL; WEOF; WO 25/748; WOST

180. *Ferdinand Amelia Fairfax BECKWITH (1794–1805)*
Born: Yorkshire 1764
Relations: Son of Major General John Beckwith of Bluerly and Janet (Wishart); brother of General Sir George Beckwith; Captain John Beckwith, 23rd Light Dragoons; Major General William George Henry Beckwith; and Lieutenant General Sir Thomas Sydney Beckwith; uncle of Lieutenant John Ferdinand Beckwith, Rifle Brigade; Major General John Charles Beckwith; Lieutenant Colonel Sydney Beckwith, Rifle Brigade; and Lieutenant Colonel Henry Ferdinand Beckwith, Rifle Brigade
Entry to Army: Ensign in 33rd Foot 25 Oct 1779 by purchase
Regimental Field Officer Promotions: Major in 37th Foot 22 Nov 1794 (vice Hope) by purchase
Brevets: Brevet Lieutenant Colonel 13 May 1795; Brevet Colonel 29 Apr 1802; Brigadier General (West Indies) 28 Sep 1804
Early Service: Served with light battalion in American War of Independence
Service 1793–1815: Served in West Indies 1800–1804; Commissioner of Military Enquiry 27 Jun 1805
Residences: York Street, Marylebone, London
Died: London 14 Oct 1805
Sources: *ANCB; ANCD; ARLI; UNSM (1805); WEOF; The Beckwiths*

181. *Joseph BAIRD (1795–1799)*
Born: Edinburgh 1759
Relations: Son of William Baird of Newbyth and Alison (Johnston); brother of General Sir David Baird, 1st Bt; son-in-law of William Hull, 1st Baron Riversdale
Entry to Army: 2nd Lieutenant in 21st Foot 13 Sep 1782
Regimental Field Officer Promotions: Major in 37th Foot 1 Sep 1795; Lieutenant Colonel in 62nd Foot 25 Nov 1799; to half-pay of 62nd Foot 25 Jun 1802; Lieutenant Colonel in 83rd Foot 17 Mar 1803 (vice Skerrett) by exchange
Brevets: Brevet Colonel 25 Oct 1809; Major General 1 Jan 1812
Early Service: Served in British North America 1789–1792
Service 1793–1815: Served in Flanders 1793–1795; served in Gibraltar 1796–1799; served at Cape of Good Hope 1806–1808; second-in-command at Cape of Good Hope 1815–1816
Died: Cape Town 4 Mar 1816
Sources: *ANCB; ANCD; ANCW; ARLI; WEOF; WO 25/744*

182. *William STEWART (1805–1807)*
Born: Aberdeenshire 1771
Relations: Son of William Stewart of Lesmurdie and Barbara (King); brother of Major General Francis Stewart
Entry to Army: Lieutenant in 106th Foot 17 May 1794
Regimental Field Officer Promotions: Major in 37th Foot 13 Jun 1805 (vice Spread); Lieutenant Colonel in 8th West India Regiment 5 Sep 1807; Lieutenant Colonel in 40th Foot 26 Jun 1815; to half-pay of 40th Foot 5 Feb 1816
Brevets: Brevet Colonel 4 Jun 1814; Major General 19 Jul 1821
Service 1793–1815: Served in Gibraltar 1796–1800; served in West Indies 1800–1815; commanded 8th West India Regiment in Guadeloupe 1810
Awards and Honours: AGM (Guad); CB 4 Jun 1815
Residence: West Park, Elgin, Morayshire
Died: Elgin 20 Jun 1836
Sources: *ANCB; ANCD; ANCW; ARLI; PHIL; WEOF; WO 25/748*

183. *George Germaine COCHRANE (1813–1817)*
Born: Edinburgh 1776
Relations: Son of Captain Thomas John Cochrane, 23rd Foot, and Frances (Hay); brother of Lieutenant James Hay Cochrane, 1st Foot; and Lieutenant John Cochrane, 39th Foot; father of Colonel Hugh Stewart Cochrane VC, 43rd Foot
Entry to Army: Ensign in 28th Foot 8 Nov 1793
Regimental Field Officer Promotions: Major in 37th Foot 10 Jun 1813 (vice Hart); to half-pay of 3rd Provisional Battalion of Militia 25 May 1817
Brevets: Brevet Lieutenant Colonel 22 Jul 1830
Service 1793–1815: Served in Gibraltar 1796–1800; served in West Indies 1800–1805; served in France 1814; served in British North America 1814–1817
Retired: 1838
Later Service: Deputy Sheriff of Argyllshire; Commandant at Fort William 1841–1854
Died: Fort William 18 May 1854
Sources: *ANCB; ANCD; ARLI; PHIL; WEOF; WikiTree*

184. *Gabriel Louis BÜRER (1813–1817)*
Born: Netherlands 1774
Relations: Son of Jean Louis Bürer of Den Haag and Anna Catharina (Oudaan); brother of Lieutenant Colonel Joachim Joannes Christiaan Bürer, Kingdom of Holland service
Entry to Army: Lieutenant in Waldstein's

Regiment c.1795
Regimental Field Officer Promotions: Major in 37th Foot 1 Jul 1813; Lieutenant Colonel in 37th Foot 3 Jul 1817 (vice James) by purchase; to half-pay unattached 22 Mar 1827 (vice Le Blanc) by exchange; rank stationary thereafter
Service 1793–1815: Served in Egypt 1801; served in Copenhagen 1807; served in Peninsula with 71st Foot Aug to Nov 1808, and May 1811 to Jan 1813; ADC to Harry Burrard Sep to Nov 1813
Awards and Honours: MGSM (Egt Rol&Vim)
Residence: Gosport Street, Lymington, Hampshire
Died: Lymington, Hampshire 2 Apr 1864
Sources: *ANCB; ANCD; ANCW; CHAL; PHIL; WEOF*

185. *Edward BARWICK (1815–1821)*
Born: Ireland c.1767
Entry to Army: Adjutant in 37th Foot 19 Mar 1796; Ensign in 37th Foot 19 Apr 1796
Regimental Field Officer Promotions: Major in 37th Foot 12 Jan 1815
Brevets: Brevet Major (Continent) 6 Nov 1826 (noting this was after he had retired from the army)
Service 1793–1815: Served in British North America 1814–1817
Retired: 24 Oct 1821
Residence: Gerrard Street, Soho, London
Died: London 12 Apr 1830
Sources: *ARLI; FMPD; PHIL; WEOF*

186. *Temple FENTON (1815–1816)*
Born: County Cork c.1784
Relations: Son of Captain Thomas Temple Fenton of Kinsale, 48th Foot, and Barbara (Spread)
Entry to Army: Ensign in 37th Foot 12 Jan 1800
Regimental Field Officer Promotions: Major in 37th Foot 7 Dec 1815 (vice Tilt); to half-pay of 58th Foot 2 May 1816 (vice Druitt) by exchange
Service 1793–1815: Served in Peninsula Mar and Apr 1814
Died: Kinsale, County Cork 5 Aug 1820
Sources: *ARLI; CHAL; FMPD; PHIL; WEOF*

Selected Regimental Histories
Whitting, Captain John Everard, *Annals of the Thirty-Seventh North Hampshire Regiment* (Warren & Son, 1878)
Wykes, Alan, *The Royal Hampshire Regiment: (37th/67th Regiments of Foot)* (London: Hamilton, 1968)

Regimental Museum
The Royal Hampshire Regiment Trust, Serle's House, Southgate Street, Winchester, Hampshire

---

38th Regiment of Foot

Secondary Title:	1st Staffordshire
Nickname:	The Pump and Tortoise
Jacket:	Red
Facings:	Yellow
Badge:	Staffordshire Knot

Regimental Lineage, 38th Regiment of Foot

1688:	Raised in Gloucestershire by Sir John Guise
1689:	Foulkes's Regiment of Foot
1693:	Lillingston's Regiment of Foot
1694:	Disbanded
1694:	Re-raised as Lillingston's Regiment of Foot
1696:	Disbanded
1705:	Re-raised in Lichfield as Lillingston's Regiment of Foot
1708:	Jones's Regiment of Foot
1711:	Alexander's Regiment of Foot
1717:	Lucas's Regiment of Foot
1729:	Jones's Regiment of Foot
1735:	Murray's Regiment of Foot
1738:	Duke of Marlborough's Regiment of Foot
1739:	Dalzell's Regiment of Foot

1750: Philipps' Regiment of Foot
1747: Ranked at 38th Regiment of Foot
1751: 38th Regiment of Foot
1782: 38th (1st Staffordshire) Regiment of Foot
1804: Nov – 2nd Battalion formed in Lichfield
1814: Oct – 2nd Battalion disbanded in Hastings
1881: South Staffordshire Regiment (on amalgamation with the 80th (Staffordshire Volunteers) Regiment of Foot)
1959: Staffordshire Regiment (Prince of Wales') (on amalgamation with the North Staffordshire Regiment (Prince of Wales'))
2007: 3rd Battalion, Mercian Regiment (on amalgamation with the Cheshire Regiment and the Worcestershire and Sherwood Foresters Regiment)
2014: The Mercian Regiment (Cheshire, Worcesters and Foresters, and Staffords)

Service History, 1st Battalion 38th Regiment of Foot

1793: Dublin; Oct – flank companies to West Indies; Belfast
1794: Belfast; to England; Bristol; Mar – to Low Countries; Apr – Ostend; May – Courtrai; Ypres; Jun – garrison of Ostend; Jul – Walheim; Dec – line of the River Waal
Flank companies at capture of Martinique and Guadeloupe; Oct – Berville
1795: Buren; retreat to Bremen; to England; May – Harwich; Jun – Hockerill; Jul – King's Lynn; Aug – King's Lynn and Peterborough; Sep – Chelmsford; Oct – aboard ships off Southampton; Nov – to Barbados; delayed by storms
1796: Mar – to West Indies, detachment at Hilsea; May – four service companies in Barbados, six home companies to West Indies; Jun – six companies in Grenada; Morne Qua Qua; Vigie; Jul – battalion reunited in Barbados; Nov – Martinique
1797: Martinique and The Saintes; Feb – detachment at capture of Trinidad; May – St Lucia and The Saintes; Jul – Dominica and The Saintes; Oct – The Saintes
1798–1799: The Saintes
1800: The Saintes; Jun – Martinique; to England; Aug – Portsmouth; Chichester; Oct – Lichfield
1801: Lichfield; Apr – Liverpool; to Ireland; Newry
1802: Newry; Aug – Dublin
1803: Dublin; Jul – Dublin riots; Sep – Birr
1804: Birr; Aug – Curragh camp; Oct – Birr
1805: Birr; Jun – Fermoy; Aug – Cork; to Cape of Good Hope
1806: Cape of Good Hope; Saldanha Bay; Cape Town; to South America; Oct – Maldonado
1807: Maldonado; Feb – MONTE VIDEO; two companies left in reserve in Montevideo; Jul – eight companies in assault on Buenos Aires; to Ireland; Dec – Cork
1808: Bandon; Jun – Fermoy; Jul – Cork; to Portugal; Aug – Mondego Bay; ROLICA; VIMEIRO; Oct – advance into Spain; Viseu; Nov – Salamanca; Dec – Mayorga; Astorga
1809: Retreat to Corunna; CORUNNA; to England; Feb – Canterbury; Jul – Deal; to Walcheren; Nov – to England; Dec – Shorncliffe
1810: Jan – Shorncliffe; Apr – Hythe; May – Shorncliffe; Aug – to Ireland; Sep – Cork; Midleton; Dec – Birr
1811: Birr; Sep – Fermoy
1812: Fermoy; May – Cork; to Portugal; Lisbon; PENINSULA; Jul – joined field Army; SALAMANCA; Nava de Arévalo; Aug – El Escorial; Sep – siege of Burgos; Oct – Villarmero; retreat to Portugal; Nov – Campelo; Dec – Lamego
1813: Lamego; May – Outeiro; Jun – VITTORIA; Jul – SAN SEBASTIAN; Sep – Ozarzun; Oct – Croix de Bouquets; Nov – Nivelle; Dec – NIVE; Bidart
1814: Arcangues; siege of Bayonne; Feb – Villefranque; Mar – Bassussary; Apr – Bayonne; Aug – Bordeaux; to Ireland; Cork; Sep – Midleton; Nov – Charles Fort
1815: Kinsale; Mar – Charles Fort; Apr – Kinsale; May – Cork; Jun – to Flanders; Jul – advance into France; Paris; Allied Army of Occupation

Service History, 2nd Battalion 38th Regiment of Foot (1804-1814)

1804: Nov – formed in Lichfield from Staffordshire Limited Service men
1805: Lichfield
1806: Lichfield
1807: Lichfield; Jun – Portsmouth; Guernsey; Nov – to Ireland; Waterford
1808: Cork; Feb – New Geneva; Apr – Waterford; to England; May – Portsmouth; Stafford; Jul – Lichfield
1809: Lichfield; Feb – Walsingham; Mar – Guernsey
1810: Guernsey; Mar – to Portugal; Apr – Lisbon; Jun – Alcoentre; joined Field Army; Jul – Tomar; Sep – Penamacor; BUSACO; Oct – Heights of Sobral; Nov – Alcoentre; Dec – Torres Vedras
1811: Torres Vedras; Mar – Vendada; Apr – Barba de Puerca; siege of Almeida; May –Fuentes d'Onoro; Nave de Haver; Jun – Torre de Mouro; Jul – Portalegre; Aug – Navasfrias; Oct – Guarda; Nov – Paço de Melo; Dec – Travinhas
1812: Ciudad Rodrigo; Mar – Campo Maior; Apr – BADAJOZ; Casteleiro; May – Pinhel; Jun – Salamanca Forts; Jul – SALAMANCA; Nava de Arévalo; Aug – El Escorial; Sep – siege of Burgos; Oct – Villarmero; retreat to Portugal; Nov – Campillo; Dec – Lamego; fit men into 1st Battalion; Lisbon, cadre to England
1813: Feb – Portsmouth; Mar – Winchester
1814: Winchester; Jul – Isle of Wight; Aug – Fort Cumberland; Oct – disbanded in Hastings

Establishments, 1st Battalion 38th Regiment of Foot

Year	Subunits	Field Off	Off/ Staff	Sjts	Mus	Corp/ Pvts	Total
Dec 1792	10co	3	32	22	12	330	399
Jan 1793	10co	3	32	32	22	600	689
Apr 1794	12co	3	38	50	26	990	1,107
Jun 1795	10co	3	32	42	22	850	949
Dec 1795	10co+2r	5	51	62	30	1,010	1,158
Dec 1797	10co	5	38	53	22	600	718
Apr 1801	10co	5	43	53	22	1,000	1,123
Jul 1802	10co	5	33	34	22	750	844
Feb 1805	10co	5	36	44	22	800	907
Aug 1805	10co	5	36	44	22	1,000	1,107
Dec 1805	10co	5	46	54	22	1,000	1,127
Dec 1806	10co	4	46	54	22	1,000	1,126
Dec 1812	10co	4	46	55	22	1,000	1,127
Aug 1814	10co+r	4	49	63	22	1,008	1,146
Dec 1815	10co	4	46	45	22	800	917

Establishments, 2nd Battalion 38th Regiment of Foot

Year	Subunits	Field Off	Off/ Staff	Sjts	Mus	Corp/ Pvts	Total
Dec 1804	10co	3	35	23	22	400	483
Dec 1806	10co	3	35	33	22	600	693
May 1808	10co	3	35	23	22	400	483
Dec 1808	10co	3	35	33	22	600	693
Dec 1810	10co	3	35	34	22	600	694
Dec 1811	10co	3	35	35	22	600	695

Service Statistics, 38th Regiment of Foot

	Lieutenant Colonels	Majors
Number of officers in period 1793–1815	10	13
Average age on appointment to substantive rank	32	31
Average time in rank in regiment (years)	7	6
Total field officers by nationality	10 E / 8 I / 4 A / 2 S	
Demographics of other ranks 1809	1/38th: 84% EW / 13% I / 2% S / 1% F 2/38th: 87% EW / 13% I	
Demographics of other ranks 1814	2/38th: 78% EW / 20% I / 1% S / 1% F	
Months of overseas service 1793–1815	1/38th: 137 2/38th: 33	

Significant Militia/Volunteer Intakes

1803:	Irish Fencible volunteers
1804:	Additional Force Act men from Staffordshire
1807:	Cheshire, West Norfolk, Staffordshire, Warwickshire
1808:	Staffordshire, County Meath
1809:	West Middlesex, West Norfolk, Staffordshire, Warwickshire
1812:	Warwickshire
1813:	Warwickshire

Regimental Colonels

187. *Sir Robert PIGOT, 2nd Bt (1775–1796)*

Born: Staffordshire 1720
Relations: Son of Richard Pigot of Westminster and Frances (Goode); brother of George, 1st Baron Pigot, Governor of Madras; and Admiral Hugh Pigot RN; father of Lieutenant Colonel Robert Pigot, 30th Foot
Entry to Army: Ensign in 31st Foot 1741
Regimental Field Officer Promotions: Major in 70th Foot 5 May 1758; Lieutenant Colonel in 70th Foot 4 Feb 1760; Lieutenant Colonel in 38th Foot 1 Oct 1764
Brevets: Brevet Colonel 11 Dec 1775; Major General 29 Aug 1777; Lieutenant General 20 Nov 1782; General 26 Jan 1797
Colonelcies: 55th Foot 7 Sep 1775 (vice Earl of Cavan); 38th Foot 11 Dec 1775 (vice Lord Blayney)
Early Service: Served in North America 1774–1781; commanded British left wing at Bunker Hill 1775
Political Career: MP (Wallingford) 1768–1772; Warden of the Mint 1772–1796
Creations and Dignities: 2nd Baronet of Patshull 11 May 1777
Residence: Patshull Hall, near Pattingham, Staffordshire
Died: Patshull Hall 1 Aug 1796
Sources: ANCB; ANCD; ANCW; ARLI; DINB; HPON; WEOF

188. *James ROOKE (1796–1805)*

Born: Gloucestershire 1742
Relations: Son of Major James Rooke of St Briavels and Jane (Catchmay); father of Lieutenant Colonel James Rooke, 1st Regiment of Hussars of Venezuela
Entry to Army: Ensign in 69th Foot 15 May 1759
Regimental Field Officer Promotions: Major in 104th Foot 25 Nov 1762; to half-pay of 104th Foot 1763; Lieutenant Colonel in 75th Foot 14 Jan 1778; Lieutenant Colonel in 14th Foot 13 Oct 1779
Brevets: Brevet Lieutenant Colonel 25 May 1772; Brevet Colonel 17 Nov 1780; Major General 28 Sep 1787; Lieutenant General 26 Jan 1797; General 1802
Colonelcies: Colonel Commandant of 4/60th Foot 20 Oct 1788 (vice Gordon); 38th Foot 2 Aug 1796 (vice Pigot)
Early Service: Commandant at Goree 1779
Political Career: MP (Monmouthshire) 1785–1805
Residence: Ifton, Monmouthshire; Bigsweir House, St Briavels, Gloucestershire
Died: Whilst out hunting in St Briavels 4 Oct 1805
Sources: ANCB; ANCW; ARLI; HPON; WEOF

189. *Rt Hon. George James LUDLOW, 1st Baron Ludlow (1805–1836)*

Born: London 1758
Relations: Son of Peter Ludlow, 1st Earl Ludlow and Lady Frances (Lumley-Saunderson); grandson of Thomas Lumley-Saunderson, 3rd Earl of Scarborough
Entry to Army: Ensign in 1st Foot Guards 19 Mar 1778 by purchase

Regimental Field Officer Promotions: Captain and Lieutenant Colonel in 1st Foot Guards 24 Nov 1790 by purchase; Third Major in 1st Foot Guards 6 May 1799 (vice Asgill)
Brevets: Brevet Colonel 21 Aug 1795; Major General 18 Jun 1798; Lieutenant General 30 Nov 1805; General 4 Jun 1814
Colonelcies: Colonel Commandant of 2/52nd Foot 8 May 1801; 96th Foot 8 May 1801; 38th Foot Oct 10 Oct 1805 (vice Rooke); Scots Fusilier Guards 30 May 1836 (vice Gordon)
Early Service: Served in American War of Independence 1781–1782, POW at Yorktown
Service 1793–1815: Served in Flanders 1793–1794, lost left arm at Roubaix; commanded 2nd Guards Brigade in Ireland and Egypt 1800–1802; commanded division in Hanover 1805; Adjutant General in Copenhagen 1807
Creations and Dignities: 3rd Earl Ludlow 7 Nov 1811; 3rd Viscount Preston of Ardsallagh 7 Nov 1811; 3rd Baron Ludlow of Ardsallagh 7 Nov 1811; 1st Baron Ludlow (GB) 10 Sep 1831
Awards and Honours: KB 14 Nov 1804
Residence: Cople House, Cople, Bedfordshire
Died: Cople House 16 Apr 1842
Sources: ANCB; ARLI; DEPE; GEMA (1842); PHIL; WEOF; WO 25/746

Lieutenant Colonels

190. *Hon. Henry Edward FOX (1778–1795)*
Born: London 1755
Relations: Son of Henry Fox, 1st Baron Holland and Lady Caroline (Lennox); brother of Charles James Fox MP; grandson of Charles Lennox, 2nd Duke of Richmond; father of Henry Stephen Fox, envoy-extraordinary and minister-plenipotentiary to the United States of America; father-in-law of Lieutenant General Sir Henry Bunbury and General Sir William Francis Patrick Napier
Education: Westminster School; Strasbourg Military Academy
Entry to Army: Cornet in 1st Dragoon Guards 16 Sep 1770 by purchase
Regimental Field Officer Promotions: Major in 49th Foot 12 Jul 1777 by purchase; Lieutenant Colonel in 38th Foot 12 Oct 1778 by purchase
Brevets: Brevet Colonel 12 Mar 1783; Brigadier General (Nova Scotia) 1782; Major General 20 Dec 1793; Lieutenant General 26 Jun 1799; General (Mediterranean inc. Gibraltar) 2 Apr 1804; General 25 Apr 1808
Colonelcies: 10th Foot 23 Jun 1795 (vice Keith)
Early Service: Served in North America 1774–1783; ADC to Howe 1776; commanded 2nd battalion grenadiers in North America 1778–1781; Receiver and Paymaster of widow's pensions 1779–1781; ADC to King George III 12 Mar 1783; commander of the forces in Nova Scotia 1783–1789
Service 1793–1815: Quartermaster General in Flanders 1793; commanded brigade in Flanders 1794–1795; Inspector General of Recruiting Service 21 Oct 1795 to 1799; Lieutenant Governor of Minorca 18 Jul 1799 to 1801; Governor of Minorca 1801 to 27 Mar 1802 (vice Stuart); Commander in Chief Mediterranean (outside Gibraltar) 25 Jul 1801 to 1802 (vice Abercromby); Commander in Chief in Ireland 9 May to Oct 1803 (vice Medows); acting Commander in Chief and Governor of Gibraltar 18 Dec 1804 to 28 Jun 1806 (vice Trigge); Commander in Chief Mediterranean (outside Gibraltar) Oct 1806 to Feb 1808 (vice Stuart); Commander in Chief Sicily Jun 1807 to Jul 1807 (vice Stuart); Governor of Portsmouth 1810–1811
Residence: Sevenoaks, Kent
Died: Portsmouth, Hampshire 18 Jul 1811
Sources: ARLI; ODNB; WEOF; WO 25/745; WOST

191. *Thomas PITCAIRNE (1793–1795)*
Born: Fifeshire 1755
Relations: Son of Major John Pitcairne, Marines, and Elizabeth (Dalrymple); brother of Midshipman Robert Pitcairne RN; and Captain William Pitcairne, Royal Marines
Entry to Army: Lieutenant in 14th Foot 13 Jan 1776
Regimental Field Officer Promotions: Major in 82nd Foot 20 Feb 1783 by purchase; to half-pay of 82nd Foot 6 Jul 1784; Major in 17th Foot 17 Feb 1787 by exchange; Lieutenant Colonel in 38th Foot 14 Dec 1793 (vice Fox); Lieutenant Colonel in 92nd Foot 28 Oct 1795; to half-pay of 92nd Foot 1 Mar 1796
Brevets: Brevet Colonel 26 Jan 1797
Early Service: Served in American War of Independence
Residence: Chatham, Kent
Died: Chatham 27 Oct 1797
Sources: ANCB; ANCD; ARLI; WEOF

192. *Charles APTHORP (1795–1800)*
Born: Massachusetts 1756
Relations: Son of Charles Ward Apthorp of Boston, merchant, and Mary (McEvers)
Entry to Army: 2nd Lieutenant in 23rd Foot 19 Apr 1774 by purchase
Regimental Field Officer Promotions: Major in 39th Foot 28 Mar 1795 (vice Hislop); Lieutenant Colonel in 38th Foot 1 Sep 1795

Brevets: Brevet Major 1 Mar 1794
Early Service: Served in American War of Independence
Retired: 3 Apr 1800
Residence: Bloomingdale, New York State, USA
Died: Bloomingdale 2 Jun 1803
Sources: ANCB; ANCD; ARLI; WEOF

193. *Sir Miles NIGHTINGALL (1795–1802)*

Born: Middlesex 1768
Relations: Son of Miles Nightingale of Fulham, girdler, and Ann (unk.); rumoured to be natural son of Earl Cornwallis
Entry to Army: Ensign in 52nd Foot 4 Apr 1787
Regimental Field Officer Promotions: Major in 121st Foot 28 Feb 1795 by purchase; Lieutenant Colonel in 115th Foot 1 Sep 1795 by purchase; Lieutenant Colonel in 38th Foot 28 Oct 1795 (vice Pitcairne) by exchange; Lieutenant Colonel in 51st Foot 23 Jul 1802 (vice Pringle) by exchange; Lieutenant Colonel in 69th Foot 8 May 1806 (vice Darling) by exchange; removed from the regiment as a general officer 1814
Brevets: Brevet Lieutenant Colonel 9 Sep 1795; Brevet Colonel 25 Dec 1805; Brigadier General (home staff) Feb 1808; Major General 25 Jul 1810; Lieutenant General 4 Jun 1814
Colonelcies: 6th West India Regiment 20 Mar 1815 (vice Pakenham); 49th Foot 19 Feb 1820 (vice Maitland)
Early Service: Served in East Indies 1787–1795, ADC to Lord Cornwallis
Deputy Adjutant General in San Domingo 1797; served in Ireland 1798; served on staff in Helder 1799; Assistant Quartermaster General on home staff 1801; Quartermaster General in India 1 Jul 1802; commanded brigade in Portugal Aug and Sep 1808; commanded brigade in 1st Division in Peninsula Jan 1811 to Jul 1811; temporary commander of 1st Division in Peninsula May and Jun 1811, wounded at Fuentes d'Oñoro; served on staff in Bengal Nov 1812; Commander in Chief in Java Oct 1813 to Nov 1815
Later Service: Commander in Chief in Bombay Feb 1816 to Jan 1819
Political Career: MP (Eye) 1820–1829
Awards and Honours: AGM (Rol&Vim); KCB 2 Jan 1815
Residences: York Place, Portman Square, London; Redgrave Hall, Botesdale, Suffolk
Died: Gloucester, Gloucestershire 17 Sep 1829
Sources: ANCB; ANCD; ANCW; ARLI; CHAL; HPON; PHIL; WEBC; WEOF; WO 25/747

194. *Spencer Thomas VASSALL (1800–1807)*

Born: Massachusetts 1764
Relations: Son of Major John Vassall of Cambridge and Elizabeth (Oliver); father of Captain Sir Spencer Lambert Hunter Vassall RN; and General Sir Rawdon John Popham Vassall; distant cousin of Major John Lindall Borland, 38th Foot
Entry to Army: Ensign in 59th Foot 19 Aug 1778
Regimental Field Officer Promotions: Major in 59th Foot 1 Sep 1796 (vice Bruce) by purchase; Major in 58th Foot 30 Aug 1799 (vice Horsford) by exchange; Lieutenant Colonel in 38th Foot 3 Apr 1800 (vice Apthorpe) by purchase
Early Service: Served in West Indies; commanded 38th Foot 1800–1804; commanded 1/38th Foot 1804–1807; served in South America 1807
Residence: Newport, Isle of Wight
Died: Of wounds in Montevideo 5 Feb 1807
Sources: ANCB; ANCD; ANCW; ARLI; WEOF

195. *Robert PRINGLE (1802)*

Born: County Tyrone c.1762
Relations: Son of Rev. Robert Pringle of Madencourt and (Frances) Emery; brother of Lieutenant John Pringle, 51st Foot; nephew of Major General Henry Pringle; and Lieutenant Boyle Pringle, 40th Foot; cousin of Major General William Henry Pringle
Entry to Army: Ensign in 14th Foot 26 Dec 1770
Regimental Field Officer Promotions: Major in 51st Foot 15 Mar 1793 (vice FitzRoy) by purchase; Lieutenant Colonel in 51st Foot 1 Sep 1795; Lieutenant Colonel in 38th Foot 23 Jul 1802 (vice Nightingall) by exchange
Retired: 24 Jul 1802
Residence: Crosby Row, Newington, Surrey
Died: Newington 13 Feb 1837
Sources: ANCD; ANCW; ARLI; FMPB; WEOF; <https://pringle.info/contents/caledon/>

196. *Rt Hon. Lord William Charles Augustus CAVENDISH-BENTINCK (1802)*

Born: Nottinghamshire 1780
Relations: Son of William Henry Cavendish Bentinck, 3rd Duke of Portland, and Lady Dorothy (Cavendish); brother of Major General Lord Frederick Cavendish Bentick; William Henry Cavendish Bentinck, Marquess of Titchfield; and General William Henry Cavendish Bentinck
Entry to Army: Ensign in Coldstream Foot Guards 20 Jan 1796 by purchase
Regimental Field Officer Promotions: Major in

3rd West India Regiment 9 Jul 1802 (vice Coter) by purchase; Lieutenant Colonel in 38th Foot 24 Jul 1802 (vice Pringle) by purchase; Captain and Lieutenant Colonel in 1st Foot Guards 17 Sep 1802 (vice Colman) by exchange
Retired: 3 Apr 1811
Political Career: MP (Ashburton) 1807–1812; Treasurer of the Household July 1812 to Apr 1826
Awards and Honours: PC 13 Aug 1812
Residence: St George Hanover Square, Marylebone, London
Died: London 28 Apr 1826
Sources: ANCB; ANCD; ARLI; HPON; WEOF

197. *Francis John COLMAN (1802–1805)*

Born: London 1767
Relations: Son of Edward Colman of Gornhay, MP and Martha (Provis); brother of Lieutenant Colonel Edward Edwin Colman, 84th Foot
Entry to Army: Cornet in 1st Dragoons 13 Sep 1786 by purchase
Regimental Field Officer Promotions: Captain Lieutenant and Lieutenant Colonel in 1st Foot Guards 30 Oct 1799 (vice Dyer); Captain and Lieutenant Colonel in 1st Foot Guards 25 Nov 1799 (vice Asgill); Lieutenant Colonel in 38th Foot 17 Sep 1802 (vice Bentinck) by exchange
Brevets: Brigadier General (Portuguese service) 24 Sep 1809
Service 1793–1815: Served in Flanders 1794–1795; served in Helder 1799; commanded 2/38th Foot 1804–1805; commanded Portuguese brigade in Peninsula Sep 1809 to Dec 1811
Retired: Resigned 21 Mar 1805; appointed to Portuguese service Sep 1809
Political Career: Serjeant at Arms to the House of Commons Oct 1805 to Dec 1811
Awards and Honours: AGM (Bus)
Died: Of fever in Lisbon 12 Dec 1811
Sources: ANCB; ARLI; CHAL; WEOF; <https://www.bhsportugal.org/uploads/fotos_artigos/files/2012_BrigadierFrancisJohnColman.pdf>

198. *Hon. Sir Charles John GREVILLE (1805–1825)*

Born: Warwickshire 1780
Relations: Son of George De Brooke Greville, 2nd Earl of Warwick, and Henrietta (Vernon); brother of Colonel Henry Richard Greville, 3rd Earl of Warwick, Warwickshire Militia
Education: Winchester School
Entry to Army: Cornet in Warwickshire Fencibles 1795; Ensign in 6th Foot 27 Feb 1796 by purchase
Regimental Field Officer Promotions: Major in 38th Foot 13 Apr 1803 (vice Gordon) by purchase; Lieutenant Colonel in 38th Foot 21 Mar 1805 (vice Colman) by purchase; removed from the regiment as a general officer 2 Jun 1825
Brevets: Brevet Colonel 4 Jun 1813; Major General 12 Aug 1819
Colonelcies: 98th Foot 28 Feb 1832 (vice Hinde); 38th Foot 30 May 1836 (vice Ludlow)
Service 1793–1815: Served in India; served in Egypt 1801; commanded 2/38th Foot 1805–1808; commanded 1/38th in Peninsula Aug 1808 to Jan 1809; served in Walcheren 1809; commanded 1/38th in Peninsula Jun 1812 to Apr 1814; commanded a brigade in 1st Division in Peninsula Jul 1812 to Oct 1813; commanded brigade in Allied Army of Occupation in France 1815
Awards and Honours: AGC (Rol Vim Cor Sal Vit SS Nive); KCB 2 Jan 1815
Political Career: MP (Warwick) 1816–1831, 1832–1833 and 1835–1836
Residence: Chesterfield Street, Mayfair, Middlesex
Died: London 2 Dec 1836
Sources: ARLI; CHAL; HPON; PHIL; WEOF

199. *John NUGENT (1807–1814)*

Born: County Westmeath c.1774
Relations: Son of John Nugent of Clonlost and Elizabeth Poer (Trench); nephew of William Power Keating Trench, 1st Earl of Clancarty; nephew of Lieutenant General Eyre Power Trench; brother of Richard Nugent; and Lieutenant Colonel James Nugent, Westmeath Militia; father of Colonel Eyre Trench John Richard Nugent, Staffordshire Militia; cousin of Colonel Hon. Sir Robert Le Poer Trench, 74th Foot
Entry to Army: Ensign in 13th Foot 31 Jul 1789
Regimental Field Officer Promotions: Major in 38th Foot 1 Aug 1804; Lieutenant Colonel in 38th Foot 8 Feb 1807 (vice Vassall); to half-pay of 38th Foot 25 Oct 1814
Brevets: Brevet Major 29 Apr 1802; Brevet Colonel 4 Jun 1814; Major General 19 Jul 1821
Early Service: Served in Flanders 1793–1795; served in West Indies 1796–1797; commanded 1/38th in South America 1807; commanded 2/38th Foot 1807–1814; commanded 2/38th in Peninsula Apr 1810 to Jan 1813
Awards and Honours: AGM (Bus Bad Sal); CB 4 Jun 1815
Residence: St Germain-en-Laye, Île-de-France, Paris
Died: Paris Apr 1830
Sources: ANCD; ARLI; CHAL; HALL; PHIL; WEOF; WO 25/747

Majors

200. *Eyre Power TRENCH (1781–1793)*
Born: County Galway 1749
Relations: Son of Colonel Richard Trench of Garbally, MP, and Frances (Power); brother of William Power Keating Trench, 1st Earl of Clancarty; uncle of Colonel Sir Robert Le Poer Trench, 74th Foot; Major General John Nugent; Richard Nugent; and Lieutenant Colonel James Nugent, Westmeath Militia
Entry to Army: Cornet in 14th Dragoons 13 Apr 1768 by purchase
Field Officer Promotions: Major in 38th Foot 8 Sep 1781; Lieutenant Colonel in 102nd Foot 31 Oct 1793; to half-pay of 102nd Foot 1795; to half-pay of 27th Foot 25 Oct 1802
Brevets: Brevet Lieutenant Colonel 18 Nov 1790; Brevet Colonel 21 Aug 1795; Major General 18 Jun 1798; Lieutenant General 30 Oct 1805
Colonelcies: Colonel Commandant 2/27th Foot 9 May 1800; 5th Garrison Battalion 25 Nov 1806; 2nd West India Regiment 25 Mar 1808 (vice Cavan)
Early Service: Served in American War of Independence
Political Career: MP (Ire) 1798–1799
Residence: Kilkenny, County Kilkenny
Died: Kilkenny 20 Jun 1808
Sources: ANCB; ANCD; ARLI; WEOF

201. *Mungo NOBLE (1793–1794)*
Born: County Fermanagh c.1760
Relations: Son of Major Jerome Noble of Summerhill, 28th Foot, and Elizabeth (Crawford); cousin of Lieutenant Colonel Mungo Noble Paumier, 70th Foot
Entry to Army: 1st Lieutenant in 21st Foot 20 Sep 1777
Field Officer Promotions: Major in 38th Foot 1 Nov 1793 (vice Trench); Lieutenant Colonel in 84th Foot 2 Dec 1794 (vice Lord Newark); Lieutenant Colonel in 67th Foot 18 Mar 1795 (vice Fitter)
Brevets: Brevet Colonel 1 Jan 1801
Early Service: Served in American War of Independence 1778
Service 1793–1815: Deputy Adjutant General in Jamaica 10 Apr 1801
Political Career: Served in Flanders 1793–1795
Residence: Glassdrummond, County Fermanagh
Died: On passage to Jamaica 21 Jun 1801
Sources: ANCB; ARLI; GHLG

202. *David OSWALD (1794–1797)*
Born: Renfrewshire 1772
Relations: Son of George Oswald of Scotstoun, tobacco merchant, and Margaret (Smythe); brother of Captain James Oswald RN
Entry to Army: Lieutenant in 19th Foot 3 Mar 1791
Field Officer Promotions: Major in 38th Foot 2 Dec 1794 (vice Noble)
Residence: Scotstoun, Renfrewshire
Died: West Indies Sep 1797
Sources: ANCB; ARLI; History of the Counties of Ayr and Wigton, Pts.1-2

203. *John GORDON (1795–1803)*
Born: Dublin 1767
Relations: Son of Alexander Gordon of Swords and Catherine (Montgomery); brother of Hugh Loftus Gordon, Assistant Commissary General
Entry to Army: Ensign in 45th Foot 6 Jun 1783 by purchase
Field Officer Promotions: Major in 38th Foot 1 Sep 1795
Brevets: Brevet Lieutenant Colonel 1 Jan 1801
Retired: 13 Apr 1803
Later Service: Inspecting Field Officer of Volunteers 7 Feb 1804
Residence: Prince's Town, County Fermanagh
Died: Prince's Town 15 Oct 1846
Sources: ARLI; GEMA (1846); WEOF; Gordons Under Arms

204. *John Lindall BORLAND (1797–1807)*
Born: Massachusetts 1754
Relations: Son of John Borland of Cambridge and Anna (Vassall); distant cousin of Lieutenant Colonel Spencer Thomas Vassall, 38th Foot
Education: Harvard College
Entry to Army: Ensign in 22nd Foot 24 Nov 1775 by purchase
Field Officer Promotions: Major in 38th Foot 18 Oct 1797 (vice Oswald)
Brevets: Brevet Lieutenant Colonel 30 Oct 1799
Early Service: Served in American War of Independence 1775–1783
Retired: 9 Apr 1807
Residence: Gloucester Place, Camden Town, London
Died: London 16 Nov 1825
Sources: ANCB; ANCD; ANCW; ARLI; The Giles Memorial: Genealogical Memoirs of the Families Bearing the Names of Giles, Gould, Holmes

205. *Thomas BURROWES (1804–1807)*
Born: County Cavan c.1772
Relations: Son of Robert Burrowes of Stradone House and Sophia (Storey); cousin of Major James Burrowes, 7th Foot
Entry to Army: Ensign in Independent Company 19 Feb 1793
Regimental Field Officer Promotions: Major in 38th Foot 2 Aug 1804
Retired: 11 Jun 1807
Residence: Stradone House, Drumlanaght, County Cavan
Died: Stradone House 3 Apr 1836
Sources: *ARLI; GHLG; WEOF; Lord Belmont in Northern Ireland*

206. *Sir Edward MILES, Kt (1805–1818)*
Born: County Tipperary 1775
Relations: Son of Edward Lawford Miles of Roche's Town and Catherine (Evans); father of Captain Robert James Falconer Miles, 89th Foot
Entry to Army: Volunteer in 38th Foot; Ensign in 38th Foot 13 Aug 1794
Regimental Field Officer Promotions: Major in 38th Foot 21 Mar 1805 (vice Greville) by purchase; Lieutenant Colonel in 38th Foot 7 May 1818; to half-pay of 38th Foot 1818; Lieutenant Colonel in 89th Foot 12 Aug 1819
Brevets: Brevet Lieutenant Colonel 1 Jan 1812; Brevet Colonel 22 Jul 1830
Service 1793–1815: Served in Flanders 1794–1795; served in West Indies 1795–1797; served in Irish rebellion 1798; served Peninsula with 1/38th Foot Aug 1808 to Jan 1809; served in Walcheren 1809; served in Peninsula Jun 1812 to Nov 1813, wounded at Salamanca and San Sebastian; served in Peninsula Apr 1814; served in Allied Army of Occupation in France 1815
Later Service: Commanded brigade in Burma 1824
Retired: 8 Nov 1833
Awards and Honours: AGM (Sal SS); CB 4 Jun 1813; KTS 1820; Knight Bachelor 27 Nov 1826; MGSM (Rol Vim Cor Vit)
Residence: Boulogne-sur-Mer, Pas-de-Calais, France
Died: Boulogne-sur-Mer Dec 1848
Sources: ARLI; CHAL; GEMA (1848); PHIL; WEOF

207. *Rt Hon. John Thomas Fitzmaurice DEANE, 2nd Baron Muskerry (1807–1819)*
Born: Shropshire 1777
Relations: Son of Robert Deane, 1st Baron Muskerry, and Anne (Fitzmaurice); brother of Lieutenant Hon. William Fitzmaurice Deane, 38th Foot
Entry to Army: Ensign in 12th Foot 31 Dec 1793
Regimental Field Officer Promotions: Major in 38th Foot 8 Feb 1807 (vice Nugent); Lieutenant Colonel in 38th Foot 12 Aug 1819
Brevets: Brevet Lieutenant Colonel 2 Oct 1806; Brevet Colonel 4 Jun 1814; Major General 19 Jul 1821
Service 1793–1815: Served in West Indies 1796–1800; served in South America 1807; served in Peninsula Aug 1808 to Jan 1809; served in Walcheren 1809; served in Peninsula Jun and Jul 1812; served in Peninsula Aug 1813 to Apr 1814
Retired: 1823
Creations and Dignities: 2nd Baron Muskerry 25 Jun 1818
Awards and Honours: AGC (Rol Vim Cor SS Nive); CB 4 Jun 1815
Residence: Springfield Castle, Broadford, County Limerick
Died: Caen, Basse-Normandie, France 25 Dec 1824
Sources: *ANCB; ANCD; ARLI; CHAL; GHLG; HALL; WEOF*

208. *William Francis Bentinck LOFTUS (1807–1814)*
Born: Surrey 1784
Relations: Son of General William Loftus and Margaret (King); half-brother of Major George Colby Loftus, Dorsetshire Militia; General Charles Loftus; and Colonel Ferrars Loftus, Grenadier Guards
Entry to Army: Cornet in 15th Light Dragoons 30 Aug 1799
Regimental Field Officer Promotions: Major in 38th Foot 9 Apr 1807 (vice Borland) by purchase; to half-pay of 38th Foot 25 Dec 1814
Brevets: Brevet Lieutenant Colonel 4 Jun 1813; Brevet Colonel 22 Jul 1830; Major General 23 Nov 1841; Lieutenant General 11 Nov 1751
Colonelcies: 50th Foot 11 Apr 1851 (vice Willshire)
Service 1793–1815: Served in Peninsula with 2/38th Foot Apr 1810 to Jan 1813
Retired: MGSM (Bus FDO Bad Sal)
Residence: Chacombe Priory, Northamptonshire
Died: Chacombe Priory 13 Sep 1852
Sources: *ANCB; ANCD; CHAL; PHIL; WEOF; WO 25/746*

209. *William ORANGE (1807–1809)*
Born: Virginia 1764
Relations: Son of Major William Orange of Norfolk and Mary Malbone (Kenner); father of

Lieutenant Colonel William Nesbitt Orange, 67th Foot; and Colonel John Edward Orange, 34th Foot
Entry to Army: Ensign in Independent Company 1794
Regimental Field Officer Promotions: Major in 38th Foot 11 Jun 1807 (vice Burrowes)
Service 1793–1815: Served with 2/38th Foot 1807–1809
Retired: 19 Oct 1809
Residence: Barlaston Hall, near Stone, Staffordshire
Died: Barlaston Hall 8 Apr 1815
Sources: *ANCB; ANCD; ANCW; ARLI; WEOF*

210. *Arthur Chichester William CROOKSHANK (1809–1814)*

Born: Dublin 1777
Entry to Army: Son of Alexander Crookshank of Dublin, MP and Esther (Kennedy)
Regimental Field Officer Promotions: Major in 38th Foot 19 Oct 1809 (vice Orange); Lieutenant Colonel in 15th Portuguese Line 16 May 1810; Lieutenant Colonel in 12th *Caçadores* 6 Jun 1811; to half-pay of 38th Foot 25 Dec 1814; to half-pay in 11th Foot 25 Aug 1816; Major in 33rd Foot 11 Sep 1817 (vice Parkinson) by exchange; to half-pay of 35th Foot 31 Aug 1820 (vice Phillott) by exchange
Brevets: Brevet Lieutenant Colonel 4 Jun 1814
Service 1793–1815: Served in West Indies 1799–1800; served in Ireland 1803; served in South America 1807; served in Portugal with 2/38th Foot Aug 1808 to Mar 1809; served in Peninsula with 1st Battalion of Detachments Feb and Mar 1809; in Portuguese service in Peninsula May 1810 to Apr 1813
Retired: From Portuguese service 28 Sep 1813; from British service 1826
Awards and Honours: AGM (Sal)
Residence: Georgetown, Grenada
Died: Georgetown 24 Aug 1830
Sources: ANCB; ANCD; ANCW; ARLI; CHAL; WEOF

Selected Regimental Histories

Vale, Walter Leonard, *History of the South Staffordshire Regiment* (Aldershot: Gale & Polden, 1969)

Regimental Museum

The Staffordshire Regiment Museum, DMS Whittington, Lichfield, Staffordshire

---

39th Regiment of Foot

Secondary Title:	East Middlesex (to Oct 1807) Dorsetshire (Oct 1807 on)
Nickname:	Sankey's Horse The Green Linnets
Jacket:	Red
Facings:	Pea Green
Badge:	The Castle and Key
Motto:	*Primus in Indis* (First in India)

Regimental Lineage, 39th Regiment of Foot

1689:	Raised in Ireland by Adam Loftus, 1st Viscount Lisburne
1697:	Disbanded
1702:	Aug – re-raised in Ireland by Colonel Richard Coote
1703:	Sankey's Regiment of Foot
1719:	Ferrers Regiment of Foot
1722:	Newton's Regiment of Foot
1730:	Sir John Cope's Regiment of Foot
1732:	Wentworth's Regiment of Foot
1737:	Duke of Argyll's Regiment of Foot
1738:	Onslow's Regiment of Foot
1739:	Dalway's Regiment of Foot
1740:	Whitshed's Regiment of Foot
1743:	Richbell's Regiment of Foot

1747: Ranked as 39th Regiment of Foot
1751: 39th Regiment of Foot
1782: 39th (East Middlesex) Regiment of Foot
1803: Jul – 2nd Battalion formed in Bexhill
1807: Oct – 39th (Dorsetshire) Regiment of Foot
1814: Dec – 2nd Battalion disbanded in Winchester
1881: 1st Battalion, The Dorsetshire Regiment (on amalgamation with the 54th (West Norfolk) Regiment of Foot)
1951: The Dorset Regiment
1958: 2nd Battalion, The Devonshire and Dorset Regiment (on amalgamation with The Devonshire Regiment)
2005: The Devonshire and Dorset Light Infantry
2007: 1st Battalion, The Rifles (on amalgamation with 1st Battalion, Royal Gloucestershire, Berkshire and Wiltshire Light Infantry)

Service History, 1st Battalion 39th Regiment of Foot

1793: Galway; Aug – Downpatrick; Limerick; Cork; Sep – to West Indies
1794: Barbados; Feb – capture of MARTINIQUE; Apr – Guadeloupe; May – Pont Gabbare; Oct – Berville; evacuation of Guadeloupe
1795: Martinique; Feb to May – drafted out to other regiments, cadre to Ireland; Aug – absorbed men from 104th Foot in Dublin; Oct – to West Indies
1796: Mar – Barbados; Apr – capture of Demerara; Sep – Demerara and Berbice
1797: Demerara and Berbice; Oct – Demerara
1798: Demerara
1799: Berbice; Nov – Demerara
1800: Demerara; Oct – Surinam
1801: Surinam
1802: Surinam; Dec – Barbados
1803: Antigua; Mar – to England; Apr – Spithead; Jul – Silverhill; Sep – Worcester; Nov – Bexhill
1804: Bexhill; Nov – Hailsham
1805: Hailsham; Mar – Portsmouth; to Mediterranean; Jul – Malta; Nov – flank companies to Naples
1806: Malta; flank companies to Sicily; Feb – battalion re-united
1807: Malta
1808: Malta; May – flank companies to Sicily
1809: Malta; flank companies in Ischia, Procida and Scylla
1810: Malta; Jun – Sicily
1811: Sicily; Aug – to Peninsula; Oct – Lisbon; Nov – Gavião; Dec – Crato; received fit men from 2nd Battalion
1812: Lisbon; Feb – Alberquerque; Mar – Almandralejo; Apr – Fuente del Maestre; Badajoz; May – Almaraz; Merida; Jun – Albuera; Jul – Zafra; Aug – Huerta; Sep – Oropesa; Oct – Aranjuez; Nov – El Sahugo; Dec – Casas de Don Gómez
1813: Casillas de Coria; May – Montejo; Jun – VITTORIA; Huarte (Pamplona); Jul – Maya; Dona Maria; Aug – PYRENEES; Burguete-Auritz; Oct – Aldudes; Nov – NIVELLE; Larressore; Dec – NIVE; Bidart
1814: Mouqueron; Feb – Parenties; ORTHEZ; Mar – Saint-Élix-le-Château; Apr – Toulouse; Baziège; May – Casties; Jun – Bordeaux; to Lower Canada; Aug – Québec; Chambly; Sep – Plattsburg; Dec – Chambly
1815: Chambly; May – Québec; to England; Jun – Portsmouth; Jul – Belgium; Paris; Allied Army of Occupation
1818: Calais; to England

Service History, 2nd Battalion 39th Regiment of Foot

1803: Jul – formed in Bexhill; Nov – Battle
1804: Bexhill; Nov – Chichester; Nov – Plymouth; Dec – Guernsey
1805: Guernsey
1806: Guernsey; Feb – to Ireland; Cork; Apr – Cahir; Jun – Mallow; Sep – Fermoy; sent limited service men to 6th Garrison Battalion; Nov – Dublin
1807: Dublin; cadre to England; Liverpool; Feb – Edmonton; Jun – Broomsgrove; Aug – Kidderminster; Aug – Plymouth; Oct – Berryhead
1808: Berryhead; May – Guernsey
1809: Guernsey; Jun – to PENINSULA; Jul – Lisbon; to Field Army; Abrantes
1810: Sardoal; Feb – Portalegre; Apr – Alegrete; May – Portalegre; Jun – Alegrete; Jul – Atalaia; Aug – Castelo Branco; Sep – Penacova; Busaco; Oct – Bucelas; Nov – Almeirim
1811: Almeirim; Feb – Alpiarça; Mar – Campo Maior; Apr – Almendralejo; May – 1st siege of Badajoz; ALBUERA; Jun – Torre de Mouro; Jul – Vila Viçosa; Sep – Portalegre; Oct – Castillejo; Arroyomolinos; Casa Quinta Lana; Nov – Alberquerque; Dec – Crato; effectives into 1st Battalion, cadre home to recruit
1812: Lisbon; to England; Feb – Weymouth; Oct – Exeter; Dec – Weymouth
1813: Weymouth
1814: Weymouth; Apr – Colchester
1815: Weymouth; Apr – Winchester; Dec – disbanded in Winchester

Establishments, 1st Battalion 39th Regiment of Foot

Year	Subunits	Field Off	Off/ Staff	Sjts	Mus	Corp/ Pvts	Total
Dec 1792	10co	3	32	22	12	330	399
Jan 1793	10co	3	32	32	22	600	689
Aug 1795	10co+2r	5	53	62	30	1,010	1,160
Dec 1795	10co+2r	5	51	62	30	1,010	1,158
Dec 1797	10co	5	51	53	22	1,000	1,131
Dec 1798	10co	5	38	53	22	600	718
Dec 1801	10co	5	33	34	22	750	844
Dec 1802	10co	5	43	34	22	750	854
Jul 1803	10co	5	46	54	22	1,000	1,127
Dec 1803	10co	5	36	54	22	1,000	1,117
Dec 1804	10co	5	36	44	22	800	907
Dec 1805	10co	5	36	54	22	1,000	1,117
Dec 1806	10co	4	36	54	22	1,000	1,116
Dec 1807	10co	4	46	54	22	1,000	1,126
Jun 1809	10co+r	4	50	62	26	1,008	1,150
Dec 1811	10co+r	4	50	63	26	1,008	1,151
Dec 1812	10co	4	46	65	22	1,200	1,337
Dec 1814	10co	4	46	55	22	1,000	1,127
Dec 1815	10co+r	4	49	63	22	1,008	1,146

Establishments, 2nd Battalion 39th Regiment of Foot

Year	Subunits	Field Off	Off/ Staff	Sjts	Mus	Corp/ Pvts	Total
Dec 1803	10co	3	35	53	22	1,000	1,113
Dec 1804	10co	3	36	44	22	800	905
Dec 1805	10co	3	35	33	22	600	693
Dec 1807	10co	3	35	43	22	800	903
Dec 1808	10co	3	35	33	22	600	693
Jun 1809	10co+r	3	40	51	26	808	928
Dec 1810	10co+r	3	40	52	26	808	929

Dec 1811	10co+r	3	40	53	26	808	930
Dec 1812	10co	3	35	35	22	600	695
Dec 1813	10co	3	35	25	22	400	485

Service Statistics, 39th Regiment of Foot

	Lieutenant Colonels	Majors
Number of officers in period 1793–1815	9	13
Average age on appointment to substantive rank	35	32
Average time in rank in regiment (years)	7	6.5
Total field officers by nationality	8 E / 6 S / 5 I / 1 A / 1 F	
Demographics of other ranks 1807	1/39th: 92% EW / 6% I / 1% S / 1% F	
Demographics of other ranks 1809	2/39th: 90% EW / 9% I / 1% S	
Demographics of other ranks 1813	1/39th: 78% EW / 18% I / 3% S / 1% F	
Demographics of other ranks 1815	1/39th: 83% EW / 17% I 2/39th: 84% EW / 16% I	
Months of overseas service 1793–1815	1/39th: 239 2/39th: 32	

Significant Militia/Volunteer Intakes

1799:	Cornish Miners
1803:	Cheshire, Shropshire, Warwickshire, Worcestershire
1804:	South Gloucestershire, received Shropshire Additional Force Act men
1805:	South Gloucestershire, County Carlow
1806:	North Hampshire, County Sligo
1807:	Tower Hamlets
1808:	Leicestershire
1809:	County Donegal, County Limerick
1811:	Sussex
1812:	Hertfordshire, Sussex, County Donegal

Regimental Colonels

211. *Sir Robert BOYD (1766–1794)*
Born: Surrey 1710
Relations: Son of Major Ninian Boyd, storekeeper of ordnance at Port Mahon, Minorca and Susanna (Johnston)
Education: University of Glasgow
Entry to Army: Lieutenant Colonel (unattached) 25 Mar 1758
Field Officer Promotions: Captain and Lieutenant Colonel in 1st Foot Guards 13 Jan 1760
Brevets: Brevet Colonel 23 Jun 1762; Major General 15 May 1772; Lieutenant General 29 Aug 1777; General 12 Oct 1793
Colonelcies: 39th Foot 6 Aug 1766
Early Service: Served as volunteer at siege of Minorca 1756; Lieutenant Governor of Gibraltar May 1768 to 13 Oct 1790; second in command during defence of Gibraltar 1779–1783
Service 1793–1815: Commander in Chief and Governor of Gibraltar 13 Oct 1790 to 13 May 1794
Awards and Honours: KB 28 Jan 1785
Residence: Gibraltar
Died: Gibraltar 13 May 1794
Sources: ANCB; ARLI; DINB; ODNB; WOST

212. *Nisbett BALFOUR (1794–1823)*
Born: Fifeshire 1744
Relations: Son of Henry Balfour of Dunbog and Katherine (Porterfield)
Entry to Army: Ensign in 4th Foot 27 Jan 1761 by purchase
Field Officer Promotions: Major in 4th Foot 4 Jun 1777 by purchase; Lieutenant Colonel in 23rd Foot 31 Jan 1778 by purchase
Brevets: Brevet Major 6 Nov 1776; Brevet Colonel 20 Nov 1782; Major General 12 Oct 1793; Lieutenant General 1 Jan 1798; General 25 Sep 1803
Colonelcies: 93rd Foot 30 Oct 1793; 39th Foot 2 Jul 1794 (vice Boyd)
Early Service: Served in American War of Independence, wounded at Bunker Hill; ADC to King George III 20 Nov 1782
Service 1793–1815: Commanded brigade in Flanders 1794
Political Career: MP (Wigtown Burghs)

1790–1796; MP (Arundel) 1797–1802
Residence: Dunbog, Fifeshire
Died: Dunbog 10 Oct 1823
Sources: ANCB; ARLI; DINB; HPON; PHIL; WEOF

Lieutenant Colonels

213. *Henry BARRY (1790–1793)*
Born: [spec.] Worcestershire c.1750
Relations: Son of Captain Robert Barry, Worcestershire Militia, and Sarah (Baker)
Entry to Army: 2nd Lieutenant on half-pay 22 Feb 1763; Ensign in 52nd Foot 11 Mar 1768
Regimental Field Officer Promotions: Major in 52nd Foot 27 Feb 1786; Major in 19th Foot 9 May 1789 (vice Nesbitt) by exchange; Lieutenant Colonel in 71st Foot 28 May 1790 (vice Elphinstone); Lieutenant Colonel in 39th Foot 8 Dec 1790 (vice Mercier) by exchange
Brevets: Brevet Major 19 Feb 1783; Brevet Colonel 19 Jul 1793
Early Service: ADC to Lord Rawdon in North America 1775–1777; served in East Indies 1783–1790
Service 1793–1815: Commanded 39th Foot 1790–1793
Retired: 31 Mar 1793
Residence: Queen Square, Bath, Somerset
Died: Bath 2 Nov 1822
Sources: ANCD; ANCW; ARLI; DINB

214. *Stephen Francis William FREMANTLE (1793–1794)*
Born: London 1764
Relations: Son of John Fremantle of Aston Abbots and Frances (Edwards); brother of Vice Admiral Sir Thomas Francis Fremantle, RN; and Colonel John Edwards Fremantle, Coldstream Foot Guards; father of Major General John Fremantle, Coldstream Foot Guards
Entry to Army: Ensign in 2nd Foot 28 Mar 1778 by purchase
Regimental Field Officer Promotions: Major in 18th Light Dragoons 31 Dec 1791 by purchase; Lieutenant Colonel in 39th Foot 31 Mar 1793 by purchase
Brevets: Brevet Major 5 Dec 1787
Service 1793–1815: Deputy Adjutant General in Ireland 1789; Served at capture of Martinique and Guadeloupe 1794
Residence: Leeson Lane, St. Stephen Green, Dublin
Died: Of yellow fever aboard *HMS Vengeance* off Guadeloupe, Aug 1794
Sources: ANCB; ANCD; ANCW; ARLI; WEOF

215. *Hugh Henry MAGAN (1793–1805)*
Born: County Westmeath 1760
Relations: Son of Arthur Magan of Clonearl, High Sheriff of Westmeath, and Anne (Henry)
Entry to Army: Cornet in 14th Light Dragoons 4 Nov 1777 by purchase
Regimental Field Officer Promotions: Major in 39th Foot 31 Oct 1792 (vice Vaughan); Lieutenant Colonel in 39th Foot 1 Nov 1793 (vice Fremantle)
Brevets: Brevet Colonel 26 Jan 1797; Brigadier General (West Indies) 27 Dec 1797; Major General 25 Sep 1803
Service 1793–1815: Commanded 39th Foot in West Indies 1794–1797
Residence: Bath, Somerset
Died: Bath 4 Jul 1805
Sources: ANCD; ANCW; ARLI; GHLG; WEOF

216. *Sir Thomas HISLOP, 1st Bt (1795–1798)*
Born: London 1764
Relations: Son of Lieutenant Colonel William Hislop of Lasswade, RA and Janet (Jack)
Education: Royal Military Academy, Woolwich
Entry to Army: Ensign in 39th Foot 28 Dec 1778 by purchase
Field Officer Promotions: Lieutenant Colonel in 115th Foot 25 Mar 1795; Lieutenant Colonel in 39th Foot 1 Sep 1795; Lieutenant Colonel Commandant in 11th (later 8th) West India Regiment 6 Sep 1798
Brevets: Brevet Major 6 Aug 1794; Brevet Colonel 29 Apr 1802; Brigadier General (Leeward Islands) 3 Feb 1803; Major General 25 Oct 1809; Lieutenant General 4 Jun 1814; General 10 Jan 1837
Colonelcies: 8th West India Regiment 29 Apr 1802; 95th Foot 4 Apr 1818 (vice Don); 93rd Foot 8 Feb 1822 (vice Wemyss); 51st Foot 4 Jun 1822 (vice Morshead); 48th Foot 25 Dec 1829 (vice FitzRoy)
Early Service: Served in Gibraltar 1780–1783
Service 1793–1815: ADC to David Dundas at Toulon 1793; served in Corsica 1794; served in West Indies 1796–1803; commanded 39th Foot at capture of Demerara 1797; Lieutenant Governor of Grenada Mar 1803 to Jul 1803 (did not actually arrive); Governor of Trinidad 20 Jul 1803 to 9 Jan 1810; served at capture of Martinique and Guadeloupe 1809–1810; Commander in Chief Bombay 1812 but taken POW at sea by US Navy Dec 1813; Commander in Chief Madras 3 Dec 1813 to 15 Jun 1821 (vice Abercromby)
Later Service: Commanded forces in Third Anglo-Maratha War 1817–1818; Equerry to Duke of Cambridge

Creations and Dignities: 1st Baronet of Tothill 2 Nov 1813
Awards and Honours: AGM (Mart Guad); GCB 14 Oct 1818
Residence: Charlton, Kent
Died: Charlton 3 May 1843
Sources: ANCW; ARLI; ODNB; PHIL; WEOF; WO 25/746; WOST

217. *George BELL (1798–1803)*
Born: Midlothian 1758
Relations: Son of William Bell of South Leith and Alison (Straiton)
Entry to Army: Ensign in 39th Foot 26 Dec 1778
Regimental Field Officer Promotions: Major in 39th Foot 1 Sep 1795 (vice Apthorp); Lieutenant Colonel in 39th Foot 6 Sep 1798 (vice Hislop)
Service 1793–1815: Served in West Indies 1794–1795; commanded 39th Foot in South America 1798–1803
Retired: 16 Jul 1803
Residence: Feddinch, near St Andrews, Fifeshire
Died: Feddinch 12 May 1834
Sources: ARLI; FMPD; WEOF

218. *Hon. Sir Robert William O'CALLAGHAN (1803–1814)*
Born: County Tipperary 1777
Relations: Son of Cornelius, 1st Baron Lismore of Shanbally, and Frances (Ponsonby); brother of Cornelius O'Callaghan, 1st Viscount Lismore
Entry to Army: Ensign in 128th Foot 29 Nov 1794
Regimental Field Officer Promotions: Major in 40th Foot 17 Feb 1803 by purchase; Lieutenant Colonel in 39th Foot 16 Jul 1803 by purchase; removed from the regiment as a general officer Jun 1814
Brevets: Brevet Colonel 1 Jan 1812; Major General 4 Jun 1814; Lieutenant General 22 Jul 1830
Colonelcies: 97th Foot 7 Sep 1829; 39th Foot 4 Mar 1833
Service 1793–1815: Served in Egypt 1801; served in Maida 1806; commanded 1/39th Foot in Peninsula Oct 1811 to Apr 1814; commanded brigade in 2nd Division in Peninsula Jan to Jul 1813, and Feb to Apr 1814; commanded brigade in Army of Occupation in France 1815–1818
Later Service: Commander in Chief in Madras 17 Oct 1830; commanded forces in Coorg rebellion 1834
Political Career: MP (Ire) 1797–1800
Awards and Honours: AGC (Mai Vitt Pyr Nlle Nive Orth); KCB 2 Jan 1815; GCB 19 Jul 1838
Residences: Clarges Street, Westminster, London; Shanbally Castle, near Clogheen, County Tipperary
Died: London 9 Jun 1840
Sources: ANCD; ANCW; ARLI; CHAL; DINB; PHIL; WEBC; WEOF

219. *George WILSON (1803–1813)*
Born: Staffordshire 1767
Relations: Son of John Wilson of Tamworth and Frances (Broadley)
Entry to Army: Ensign in 39th Foot 18 Feb 1784 by purchase
Regimental Field Officer Promotions: Major in 39th Foot 1 Sep 1795; Lieutenant Colonel in 9th Battalion of Reserve 9 Jul 1803; Lieutenant Colonel in 39th Foot 15 Oct 1803
Brevets: Brevet Lieutenant Colonel 1 Jan 1801; Brevet Colonel 25 Jul 1810
Service 1793–1815: Served in West Indies 1794–1795; served in Demerara 1796–1800; commanded 39th Foot in Demerara 1800; commanded 2/39th Foot 1804–1809; commanded 2/39th Foot in Peninsula Jul 1809 to Sep 1811; served on staff in Peninsula Oct 1811 to Jan 1813
Residence: Tamworth, Staffordshire
Died: Of fever in Moraleja, Spain 6 Jan 1813
Sources: ANCB; ANCW; ARLI; CHAL; WEOF; WO 25/748

220. *Cavendish STURT (1813–1824)*
Born: Dorset 1768
Relations: Son of Humphrey Sturt of Crichel House, MP and Mary (Pitfield); brother of Lieutenant Colonel John Ashley Sturt, 69th Foot; and Captain Henry Evelyn Pitfield Sturt-Grindall RN; uncle of Captain Charles Sturt, noted explorer of Australia
Education: Wadham College, Oxford
Entry to Army: Ensign in 34th Foot 5 Jun 1790
Regimental Field Officer Promotions: Major in 39th Foot 9 Jul 1803; Lieutenant Colonel in 39th Foot 1 Apr 1813 (vice Wilson)
Brevets: Brevet Major 29 Apr 1802; Brevet Lieutenant Colonel 25 Oct 1809; Brevet Colonel 12 Aug 1819
Early Service: Served aboard fleet as marine 1791–1792; served in Gibraltar
Service 1793–1815: Served in West Indies and South America 1796–1803; commanded 1/39th Foot in Malta and Sicily 1810; served in Peninsula with 1/39th Foot Oct 1811 to May 1813; commanded 39th Foot in France 1815
Retired: 12 Aug 1824
Died: Bruges, Belgium 1847
Sources: ANCB; ANCD; CHAL; PHIL; WEOF; WO 25/748; Alumni Oxonienses

221. *Sir Charles BRUCE (1815–1816)*
Born: British East Indies 1777
Relations: Son of Colonel Thomas Bruce, Madras service and Sarah (Meetkerke); brother of Lieutenant General Henry Pasley Bruce
Entry to Army: Ensign in 52nd Foot 4 Jul 1793
Regimental Field Officer Promotions: Major in 39th Foot 21 Mar 1805 (vice Murray); Lieutenant Colonel in 39th Foot 29 Jun 1815; to half-pay of 39th Foot 25 Feb 1816; Lieutenant Colonel in 69th Foot 29 Mar 1821 (vice de la Douespe); to half-pay of 69th Foot 25 Apr 1826; Lieutenant Colonel in 6th Foot Apr 1827 (vice Napier) by exchange; Lieutenant Colonel in 64th Foot 1 May 1828 (vice Fearon) by exchange
Brevets: Brevet Major 25 Sep 1803; Brevet Lieutenant Colonel 25 Jul 1810; Brevet Colonel 12 Aug 1819; Major General 22 Jul 1830
Service 1793–1815: Served in West Indies 1794–1795; served in South America 1796–1803; served in Malta and Sicily 1805–1811; served in Peninsula with 1/39th Foot Oct 1811 to Apr 1814; commanded 1/39th 1813–1814, wounded at Garris; served in British North America 1814; served in France 1815
Later Service: Served in East Indies 1820–1825
Awards and Honours: AGC (Vitt Nlle Nive Orth); CB 4 Jun 1815; KCB 28 Sep 1831
Residence: Clay Hill, Beckenham, Kent
Died: London 7 Aug 1832
Sources: ANCB; ANCD; ARLI; CHAL; GEMA (1832); HALL; PHIL; WEOF; WO 25/744

Majors

222. *Charles APTHORP (1795)*
See 192.
Major in 39th Foot 28 Mar 1795 (vice Hislop)

223. *Matthew JENOUR (1798–1803)*
Born: London 1759
Relations: Son of Joshua Jenour of Fleet Street, newspaper proprietor, and Ann (Harding); uncle of Captain Matthew Jenour, 69th Foot
Entry to Army: Ensign in 102nd Foot 14 Dec 1781
Field Officer Promotions: Major in 4th West India Regiment 11 Jul 1798 (vice Browne); Major in 39th Foot 6 Sep 1798 (vice Bell); Lieutenant Colonel in 9th Battalion of Reserve 15 Oct 1803; to half-pay in 9th Garrison Battalion; Lieutenant Colonel in 7th West India Regiment 16 Jul 1807
Brevets: Brevet Major 6 May 1795; Brevet Lieutenant Colonel 1 Jan 1800
Died: Antigua 24 Jul 1808
Author of 'The route to India through France, Germany, Hungary [&c.] and the desart of Arabia, delineated with the distances, times, mode and expence of travelling', 1791
Sources: ANCB; ANCD; ARLI; GEMA (1853); WEOF; WikiTree

224. *John MAISTER (1803–1807)*
See 93.
Major in 39th Foot 9 Jul 1803 (vice Wilson)

225. *John MURRAY (1803–1805)*
Born: Jamaica c.1776
Relations: Son of Walter Murray of Dundee estate and Eliza (Tharp)
Entry to Army: Ensign in 37th Foot 9 Feb 1791 by purchase
Regimental Field Officer Promotions: Major in 4th Foot 18 Jul 1801 (vice Horndon) by purchase; to half-pay of 4th Foot 25 Nov 1802; Major in 39th Foot 9 Jul 1803; Lieutenant Colonel in 100th Foot 21 Mar 1805; to half-pay unattached 1816
Brevets: Brevet Major 18 Jul 1801; Brevet Colonel 4 Jun 1813; Major General 12 Aug 1819
Service 1793–1815: Served in Flanders 1794, taken POW; served in British North America 1805–1815; Inspecting Field Officer of Militia in British North America 18 Jul 1811
Awards and Honours: CB 4 Jun 1815
Retired: 1826
Residence: Brighton, Sussex
Died: Brighton 21 Feb 1832
Sources: ARLI; GEMA (1832); PHIL; WEOF

226. *Boyd HORSBURGH (1803–1808)*
Born: Gibraltar c.1770
Relations: Son of Captain James Horsburgh, 39th Foot, Adjutant General and Town Major of Gibraltar, and Margaret (Bell)
Entry to Army: Ensign in 39th Foot 1 Feb 1786
Field Officer Promotions: Major in 39th Foot 31 Oct 1803 (vice Jenour)
Retired: 25 Feb 1808
Residences: Pitbladdo, Fifeshire; Kilmany, Fifeshire
Died: Kilmany 15 Dec 1837
Sources: ANCB; ANCD; ARLI; A History of the Late Siege of Gibraltar

227. *Sir Patrick LINDESAY, Kt (1807–1824)*
Born: Midlothian 1778
Relations: Son of Lieutenant Colonel John Lindesay, 53rd Foot, and Margaret Maria (Craigie)
Education: Edinburgh University

Entry to Army: Ensign in 32nd Foot 7 Nov 1793 by purchase
Field Officer Promotions: Major in 39th Foot 1 Oct 1807 (vice Maister) by purchase; Lieutenant Colonel in 39th Foot 12 Aug 1824 (vice Sturt) by purchase; removed from the regiment as a general officer 10 Jan 1837
Brevets: Brevet Lieutenant Colonel 20 Jun 1811; Brevet Colonel 25 May 1825; Major General 10 Jan 1837
Early Service: Served in Flanders 1794–1795; served in West Indies 1796; served in Sicily 1805; served in Peninsula with 2/39th Foot Jul 1809 to Jan 1812; served in Peninsula with 1/39th Foot Oct 1813 to Apr 1814; served in British North America 1814–1815
Later Service: Served in New South Wales 1827–1832; Acting Governor of New South Wales 22 Oct to 2 Dec 1831; commanded forces in Bengaluru and Coorg 1832–1835
Creations and Dignities: *De jure* 8th Earl of Lindsay, 7th Lord Kilbirny and Drumry, 7th Viscount of Garnock, and 8th Lord Parbroath, May 1809
Awards and Honours: AGM (Alb); CB 4 Jun 1815; KCH 12 Aug 1834; KCB 28 Jun 1838
Residence: Brighton Crescent, Portobello, Midlothian
Died: Portobello 14 Jul 1839
Petitioned the king in 1838 for recognition of the ancient Lindsay/Lindesay titles, but died before any proceedings had been taken
Sources: ANCB; ANCD: ANCW; CHAL; PHIL; WEOF; WOST

228. *Roger PARKE (1808–1826)*
Born: County Sligo c.1780
Relations: Son of Colonel Roger Parke of Dunally, Sligo Militia, and Alice (Browne); brother of Major Andrew Parke, 8th Foot; Lieutenant Colonel Sir William Parke, 66th Foot; and Major Charles Parke, 3rd Foot; cousin of Major Alexander Duke, 8th Foot
Entry to Army: Ensign in 113th Foot 30 Jun 1795 by purchase
Field Officer Promotions: Major in 39th Foot 25 Feb 1808 (vice Horsburgh) by purchase; Lieutenant Colonel unattached on half-pay 18 May 1826; Lieutenant Colonel in 22nd Foot 6 Mar 1828 (vice Taylor); to half-pay unattached 25 Nov 1828 (vice Falconer) by exchange
Brevets: Brevet Lieutenant Colonel 4 Jun 1814; Brevet Colonel 10 Jan 1837; Major General 9 Nov 1846
Colonelcies: 86th Foot 26 May 1852 (vice Maister)
Early Service: Served in West Indies 1795–1796; served in Naples 1805; served in Peninsula with 1/39th Foot Jul 1809 to Jan 1812; served in British North America 1814
Political Career: MGSM (Alb)
Residence: Park Terrace, Regents Park, London
Died: London 1 May 1854
Sources: ANCB; ANCD; ARLI; CHAL; PHIL; WEOF

229. *Henry STANDISH (1813–1816)*
Born: Dublin c.1780
Relations: [spec.] Son of Henry Standish of Dublin, deputy Clerk of the Pells, and Frances Diana (Obree)
Entry to Army: Ensign in 27th Foot 21 Oct 1795
Field Officer Promotions: Major in 39th Foot 1 Apr 1813 (vice Sturt); to half-pay of 39th Foot 25 Feb 1816
Brevets: Brevet Major 1 Jan 1812; Brevet Lieutenant Colonel 19 Jul 1821; Brevet Colonel 10 Jan 1837
Early Service: Served in Egypt 1801; served in Peninsula with 1/39th Foot Oct 1811 to Jul 1813
Awards and Honours: MGSM (Egt)
Residence: Dublin, County Dublin
Died: Dublin 21 Apr 1853
Sources: ARLI; CHAL; PHIL; WEMR; WEOF; Annual Military Obituary (1854); The Journal of the Royal Society of Antiquaries of Ireland

230. *William Hart LAPSLIE (1815–1816)*
Born: Lanarkshire c.1778
Relations: Son of James Lapslie of Campsie and Elizabeth (Hart)
Entry to Army: Ensign in 40th Foot 4 Sep 1795
Field Officer Promotions: Major in 39th Foot 29 Jun 1815 (vice Bruce); to half-pay of 39th Foot 25 Feb 1816
Brevets: Brevet Major 4 Jun 1813; Brevet Lieutenant Colonel 22 Jul 1830
Residences: Wyke Regis, Dorset; Gloucester Cottage, Weymouth, Dorset
Died: Weymouth, Dorset 29 Apr 1831
Sources: ANCW; ANCD; ARLI; PHIL; WEOF

Selected Regimental Histories
Cannon, Richard, *Historical Record of the Thirty-Ninth, or the Dorsetshire Regiment of Foot: Containing an Account of the Formation of the Regiment in 1702, and of its Subsequent Services to 1853* (London: Parker, Furnivall, and Parker, 1853)

Regimental Museum
The Keep Military Museum, Barrack Road, Dorchester, Dorset

40th Regiment of Foot

Secondary Title:	2nd Somersetshire
Nickname:	The Excellers
Jacket:	Red
Facings:	Buff

Regimental Lineage, 40th Regiment of Foot

1717:	Raised by Colonel Richard Philipps in Annapolis from independent companies in Nova Scotia and Newfoundland
1747:	Ranked as 40th Regiment of Foot
1750:	Edward Cornwallis's Regiment of Foot
1751:	40th Regiment of Foot
1782:	40th (2nd Somersetshire) Regiment of Foot
1799:	Aug – 2nd Battalion formed in Taunton
1802:	Jul – 2nd Battalion disbanded in Hilsea
1804:	Aug – 2nd Battalion re-formed in Taunton
1815:	Dec – 2nd Battalion disbanded in Dover
1881:	1st Battalion, Prince of Wales's Volunteers (South Lancashire Regiment) (on amalgamation with the 82nd Regiment of Foot (Prince of Wales's Volunteers))
1958:	Lancashire Regiment (Prince of Wales's Volunteers) (on amalgamation with 1st Battalion, South Lancashire Regiment (The Prince of Wales's Volunteers))
1970:	1st Battalion, The Queen's Lancashire Regiment (30th, 40th, 47th, 59th, 81st and 82nd Regiments of Foot) (on amalgamation with the Loyal Regiment (North Lancashire))
2006:	1st Battalion, The Duke of Lancaster's Regiment (King's, Lancashire and Border) (on amalgamation with The King's Regiment and The King's Own Royal Border Regiment)

Service History, 1st Battalion 40th Regiment of Foot

1793:	Galway; flank companies to West Indies; Nov – battalion companies at Cork; to Vendée with Moira
1794:	Feb – battalion companies in Plymouth; Mar – Plymouth and Exeter; Jun – battalion companies in Southampton; to Flanders; Nov – Nijmegen; Dec – line of River Waal Flank companies in Barbados; Mar – capture of Martinique; St Lucia; Guadeloupe; flank companies ceased to exist
1795:	Battalion companies in retreat to Bremen; Apr – Bremen; to England; Jun – Romsey; Jul – Romsey; to West Indies; Sep – Martinique; Oct – St Vincent; La Vigie
1796:	St Vincent; Colonarie; May – St Vincent and Grenada; La Vigie; Jun – St Vincent
1797:	St Domingue
1798:	St Domingue; May – Jamaica; Dec – cadre to England
1799:	Portsmouth; Apr – Taunton; Aug – Deal; Sep – to Helder; Alkmaar; Oct – Bergen; Nov – to England; Yarmouth; Dec – Ramsgate
1800:	Margate, Ramsgate and Broadstairs; Mar – Ashford; to Mediterranean; May – Minorca; Jul – Livorno (Leghorn); Minorca; Aug – Gibraltar; Nov – Malta; flank companies to Egypt
1801:	Battalion companies in Malta; Nov – battalion reunited Mar – flank companies in EGYPT; Aboukir; Alexandria; Oct – flank companies to Malta
1802:	Minorca; Jun – to England; Aug – Winchester; absorbed fit men from 2nd Battalion; Oct – Portsmouth
1803:	Portsmouth; Jun – Battle; Oct – Fairlight; Nov – Hastings
1804:	Hastings
1805:	Hastings; Jul – Fairlight; Nov – Bexhill
1806:	Bexhill; Aug – Portsea; Sep – Portsmouth; to South America
1807:	Jan – MONTE VIDEO; Jun – San Pedro; Jul – assault on Buenos Aires; to Ireland; Dec – Cork

1808: Bandon; Apr – Fermoy; Jun – Cove of Cork; Jul – to PENINSULA; Aug – Roliça; Vimeiro; Nov – Elvas
1809: Elvas; Feb – Seville; May – Cadiz; Jun – Lisbon; Jul – Abrantes; TALAVERA; Aug – Merida; Sep – Badajoz; Nov – Abrantes; Dec – Ponte de Sor
1810: Guarda; Sep – Sula; Busaco; Oct – Patameira de Cima; Lines of Torres Vedras; Nov – Azambujeira
1811: Azambujeira; Mar – Redinha; Arronches; Apr – siege of Olivenca; Valverde; May – Fort San Cristoval; Aceuchal; Jun – Torra de Mouro; Jul – Estremoz; Aug – Aldea del Joao Perez; Sep – Fuenteguinaldo; Oct – Gallegos de Argañán; Nov – Fuenteguinaldo; Dec – Gallegos de Argañán
1812: Gallegos de Argañán; Villar del Puerco; Convent of San Francisco; Feb – Villar de Ciervo; Mar – Elvas; Apr – BADAJOZ; Quintas de São Bartolomeu; May – São João da Pesqueira; Jun –Salamanca; Jul – Medina del Campo; SALAMANCA; Nava de Arévalo; Aug – El Escorial; Oct – Ciempozuelos; Nov – Villar de Ciervo; Dec – Ceclavin
1813: Ceclavin; Mar – Mata de Lobos; May – Seudim; Jun – VITTORIA; Pamplona; Aug – PYRENEES; 2nd siege of San Sebastian; Oct – Vera; Nov – NIVELLE; Ascain; Dec – Nive; Ustaritz
1814: Ustaritz; Feb – ORTHEZ; Cames; Mar – Sainte-Foy-de-Peyrolières; Apr – TOULOUSE; Valence; May – Blanquefort; Jun – Bordeaux; to Ireland; Cork; Jul – Athlone; Aug – Mallow; Oct – Monkstown; to North America; Nov – Jamaica; to Louisiana
1815: Feb – Fort Mobile; Apr – to England; May – Spithead; to Belgium; Jun – WATERLOO; Jul – Paris; Allied Army of Occupation
1817: Mar – Calais; to Scotland; Glasgow

Service History, 2nd Battalion 40th Regiment of Foot

1799: Aug – formed at Taunton; Deal; to Helder; Sep – Bergen; Oct – Alkmaar; Nov – to England; Yarmouth; Dec – Ramsgate
1800: Margate, Ramsgate and Broadstairs; Feb – Ramsgate; Mar – Ashford; to Mediterranean; May – Minorca; Jul – Leghorn; Minorca; Aug – Gibraltar; Nov – Malta; flank companies to Egypt
1801: Battalion companies in Malta, flank companies in Egypt; Aboukir; Alexandria; Oct – flank companies to Malta; battalion reunited; Nov – Minorca
1802: Minorca; Jun – to England; Aug – Hilsea; disbanded in Hilsea
1804: Aug – re-formed in Taunton using Additional Forces Act men from Somerset and Dorset
1805: Taunton; Aug – Winchester; Oct – Portsmouth; Nov – Bexhill; Dec – Pevensey
1806: Pevensey; Sep – Hilsea; to Ireland; Oct – Kinsale
1807: Kinsale; Feb – Clonmel; Mar – New Geneva; Dec – Waterford
1808: Waterford; Feb – Cashel; Jun – Clonmel; Jul – Waterford
1809: Waterford; Mar – Clonmel; Sep – New Geneva
1810: New Geneva
1811: New Geneva; Feb – Clonmel; Jul – Cahir; Sep – New Geneva
1812: New Geneva
1813: New Geneva; Oct – Dublin; Chapelizod
1814: Dublin; Jul – Athlone; Aug – Mallow; Oct – to England; Nov – Plymouth
1815: Plymouth; Jun – Deal; Jul – Dover; Dec – disbanded in Dover

Establishments, 1st Battalion 40th Regiment of Foot

Year	Subunits	Field Off	Off/ Staff	Sjts	Mus	Corp/ Pvts	Total
Dec 1792	10co	3	32	22	12	330	399
Jan 1793	10co	3	32	32	22	600	689
Jun 1795	10co+2r	3	32	42	22	850	949
Oct 1795	10co+2r	5	51	62	30	1,010	1,158
Dec 1797	10co	5	38	53	22	600	718
Dec 1799	11co	5	46	47	24	880	1,002

Dec 1800	10co	5	46	43	22	800	916
Dec 1802	10co	5	33	34	22	750	844
May 1803	10co	5	36	34	22	750	847
Dec 1804	10co	5	46	54	22	1,000	1,127
Dec 1806	10co	4	46	54	22	1,000	1,126
Dec 1810	10co	4	47	63	22	1,200	1,336
Dec 1811	10co	4	47	64	22	1,200	1,337
Dec 1814	10co	4	36	45	22	800	907
Dec 1815	10co+r	4	49	63	22	1,008	1,146

Establishments, 2nd Battalion 40th Regiment of Foot

Year	Subunits	Field Off	Off/ Staff	Sjts	Mus	Corp/ Pvts	Total
Dec 1799	11co	5	46	47	24	880	1,002
Dec 1800	10co	5	46	43	22	800	916
Dec 1801	10co	5	33	34	22	750	844
Jun 1802	10co	5	46	43	22	800	916
Dec 1804	10co	3	35	23	22	400	483
Dec 1808	10co	3	35	34	22	600	694
Jan 1809	10co	3	36	44	22	800	905
Dec 1813	10co	3	36	35	22	600	696
Dec 1814	10co	3	35	25	22	400	485

Service Statistics, 40th Regiment of Foot

	Lieutenant Colonels	Majors
Number of officers in period 1793–1815	11	29
Average age on appointment to substantive rank	36.5	31
Average time in rank in regiment (years)	5.5	5
Total field officers by nationality	14 E / 12 I / 9 S / 2 F	
Demographics of other ranks 1793–1815 (based upon pension returns)	69% E / 23% I / 5% S / 2% W / 1% F	
Months of overseas service 1793–1815	1/40th: 192 2/40th: 31	

Significant Militia/Volunteer Intakes

1799: Bedfordshire, 1st Cornwall, North Devon, East Somerset, West Somerset, 1st Wiltshire, 2nd Wiltshire, Worcestershire, Irish Fencibles
1804: Additional Forces Act men from Somerset and Dorset
1805: Bedfordshire, East Middlesex, Edinburgh
1806: Ayrshire, County Sligo, County Tipperary
1807: Lincolnshire, Nottinghamshire, 1st Somerset, 2nd Somerset, County Derry, County Mayo South
1808: County Derry, County Monaghan, County Tyrone, County Wicklow
1809: Bedfordshire, Glamorganshire, 1st Somerset, 2nd Somerset, 3rd West Yorkshire, Ayrshire, County Wicklow
1810: County Derry, Limerick City, County Meath, County Wexford
1811: Leicestershire
1812: Bedfordshire
1813: County Limerick
1814: Bedfordshire, North Devon, Somerset

Regimental Colonels

231. *Sir George OSBORN, 4th Bt (1786–1818)*
Born: London 1742
Relations: Son of Sir Danvers Osborn, 3rd Bt, Governor of New York Province, and Lady Mary (Montagu); son-in-law of George, 1st Earl of Halifax; cousin of Lord North; nephew of General John Burgoyne
Education: Westminster School; Trinity College, Cambridge
Entry to Army: Ensign in 24th Foot 1759
Regimental Field Officer Promotions: Major in 18th Foot 13 Feb 1762 by purchase; Captain and Lieutenant Colonel in 3rd Foot Guards 19 Nov 1765 by purchase; Second Major in 3rd Foot Guards 7 Aug 1777; First Major in 3rd Foot Guards 20 Dec 1781; Lieutenant Colonel in 3rd Foot Guards 25 Mar 1782
Brevets: Brevet Colonel 7 Aug 1777; Brigadier General (home staff) 1778; Major General 19 Feb 1779; Lieutenant General 18 Sep 1787; General 26 Jan 1797
Colonelcies: 40th Foot 11 Aug 1786 (vice Hamilton)
Early Service: Groom of the Bedchamber 1770–1812; served in American War of Independence 1775–1777; Inspector of Foreign Troops
Political Career: MP (Northampton) 1768–1769; MP (Bossiney) 1769–1774; MP (Penryn) 1774–1780; MP Horsham (1780–1784)
Awards and Honours: 4th Baronet of Chicksands 27 Dec 1753
Residence: Chicksands Priory, Bedfordshire
Died: Chicksands Priory 29 Jun 1818
Sources: ANCB; ANCD; ARLI; HPON; WEOF

Colonels Commandant

232. *Rt Hon. John HELY-HUTCHINSON, 2nd Earl of Donoughmore (1st Battalion) (1799–1802)*
Born: County Tipperary 1757
Relations: Son of John Hely-[Hutchinson], 1st Earl of Donoughmore, MP, and Christiana (Nickson); brother of Lieutenant General Richard Hely-Hutchinson
Education: Eton College; Magdalen College, Oxford; Strasbourg military academy
Entry to Army: Cornet in 18th Dragoons 17 Jan 1774 by purchase
Regimental Field Officer Promotions: Major in 77th Foot 21 Sep 1781 (vice Dalrymple); Lieutenant Colonel in 77th Foot 13 Mar 1783 (vice Acklom) by purchase; to half-pay of 77th Foot 8 May 1783
Brevets: Brevet Colonel 1 Mar 1794; Major General 3 May 1796; Lieutenant General (Mediterranean) 29 Mar 1801; Lieutenant General 25 Sep 1803; General 4 Jun 1813
Colonelcies: Colonel Commandant of 2/40th Foot 5 Aug 1799; 74th Foot 24 Mar 1802 (vice O'Hara); 57th Foot 8 Sep 1806 (vice Campbell); 18th Foot 27 Apr 1811 (vice Murray-Pulteney)
Service 1793–1815: Served in Flanders 1793–1794 as ADC to Abercromby; served in Irish Rebellion 1798; commanded brigade in Helder 1799; second-in-command in Egypt 1801, commander in chief after Abercromby's death; Governor of Londonderry 1806; Governor of Stirling Castle 1806
Later Service: Lord Lieutenant of Tipperary 1831
Political Career: MP (Ire) 1776–1783, and 1789–1800; MP (Cork) 1801–1802; diplomatic mission to Berlin and St Petersburg 1806–1807
Creations and Dignities: 1st Baron Hutchinson 16 Dec 1801; 2nd Viscount Hutchinson and 2nd Earl of Donoughmore 22 Aug 1825
Awards and Honours: KB 28 May 1801; KCt (Ottoman) 1802; GCB 2 Jan 1815
Residences: Knocklofty House, near Clonmel, County Tipperary
Died: Knocklofty House 29 June 1832
Sources: ARLI; DINB; HPON; ODNB; PHIL; WEOF; WO 25/746

233. *Hay McDOWALL (2nd Battalion) (1802)*
See 147.
Colonel Commandant of 2/40th Foot 24 Mar 1802

Lieutenant Colonels

234. *Stephen BROMFIELD (1787–1795)*
Born: Berwickshire 1741
Relations: Son of Stephen Bromfield of Hassington Mains and Margaret Eliot (Paterson); brother of Lieutenant Colonel Andrew Bromfield, Jamaica Militia
Entry to Army: Lieutenant on half-pay 2 Mar 1763
Regimental Field Officer Promotions: Major in 40th Foot 7 Sep 1781; Lieutenant Colonel in 40th Foot 12 Oct 1787 (vice Musgrave); Lieutenant Colonel in 58th Foot 2 Jul 1795 (vice Cunninghame)
Brevets: Brevet Major 17 Nov 1780; Brevet Colonel 1 Mar 1794; Brigadier General (St Domingue) 1795
Early Service: Served in British North America 1781

Service 1793–1815: Commanded 40th Foot 1787–1795; served in Flanders 1794–1795; served in West Indies 1795–1796
Retired: 4 Jun 1796
Residence: Millington Lodge, Hassington Mains, Berwickshire
Died: Hassington Mains 16 May 1823
Sources: ANCB; ANCD; ARLI; WEOF

235. *Sir Brent SPENCER (1795–1806)*
Born: County Antrim 1760
Relations: Son of Conway Spencer of Trumery and Mary (Graham)
Entry to Army: Ensign in 15th Foot 18 Jan 1778 by purchase
Regimental Field Officer Promotions: Major in 13th Foot 6 Mar 1791 (vice Freeman) by purchase; Lieutenant Colonel in 115th Foot 2 May 1794; Lieutenant Colonel in 40th Foot 22 Jul 1795 (vice Bromfield)
Brevets: Brigadier General (St Domingue) 9 Jul 1797; Brevet Colonel 28 May 1798; Major General 1 Jan 1805; Lieutenant General (Spain and Portugal) 5 May 1810; Lieutenant General 4 Jun 1811; General 27 May 1828
Colonelcies: 9th Garrison Battalion 25 Nov 1806; 2nd West India Regiment 25 Jun 1808 (vice Trench); Colonel Commandant of 2/95th Rifles 31 Aug 1809; 40th Foot 2 Jul 1818 (vice Osborn)
Early Service: Served in West Indies 1779–1782, taken POW in St Kitts
Service 1793–1815: Commanded 13th Foot in West Indies 1791–1794; commanded flank battalion in St Domingue 1794; commanded brigade in West Indies 1797–1798; served in Helder 1799; served in Egypt 1801; Equerry extraordinary to King George III 1805–1815; commanded brigade in Copenhagen 1807; commanded troops near Cadiz Jul 1808; second in command in Peninsula early Aug 1808; commanded 1st Division in Peninsula May 1810 to Jul 1811
Later Service: Equerry in ordinary to King George III 1815–1819; Governor of Cork 1820–1828
Political Career: MP (Sligo) 1815–1818
Awards and Honours: KB 21 Apr 1809; AGM (Rol&Vim Bus FDO); KTS 29 Apr 1812; GCB 2 Jan 1815
Residence: Tremary, County Antrim; Lee, Great Missenden, Buckinghamshire
Died: Lee 29 Dec 1828
Sources: ANCW; ARLI; CHAL; DIIB; DINB; ODNB; PHIL; WEOF; WO 25/748

236. *George William Richard HARCOURT (1795–1799)*
Born: London 1775
Relations: Son of John Harcourt of Ankerwycke Priory and Margaret Irene (Meade)
Entry to Army: Volunteer in Flanders 1793; Captain in 24th Light Dragoons 23 Jul 1794
Regimental Field Officer Promotions: Major in 40th Foot 1 Sep 1795; Lieutenant Colonel in 40th Foot 1 Sep 1795; Lieutenant Colonel in 12th Foot 1 Mar 1799 (vice Aston)
Brevets: Brevet Lieutenant Colonel 1 Sep 1795; Brevet Colonel 1 Oct 1810; Major General 25 Jul 1810
Service 1793–1815: Served in St. Domingue 1797–1798; served in Helder 1799; served in India 1800–1807; Governor of St Croix 28 Apr 1808 to 20 Sep 1812; Commandant of St Martin 15 Feb 1810 to late 1810
Died: Of fever in St Croix 20 Sep 1812
Sources: ANCB; ANCW; ARLI; WEOF; WOST; Historical Records of the 40th (2nd Somersetshire) Regiment

237. *Gore BROWNE (1799–1813)*
Born: Ireland c.1764
Relations: Son of Thomas Browne and Jane Eliza (Armstrong); brother of Colonel Robert Gore Browne, Buckinghamshire Militia; uncle of Colonel Sir Thomas Robert Gore Browne, Governor of New Zealand, Governor of Tasmania and Governor of Bermuda
Education: Lochée's Military Academy, Chelsea
Entry to Army: Ensign in 35th Foot 5 Jul 1780 by purchase
Regimental Field Officer Promotions: Major in 83rd Foot 15 Jun 1794 (vice Hay); Lieutenant Colonel in 7th West India Regiment 30 Nov 1796; Lieutenant Colonel in 40th Foot 5 Aug 1799
Brevets: Brevet Colonel 1 Jan 1805; Brigadier General (Continent) 1809; Major General 25 Jul 1810; Lieutenant General 12 Aug 1819; General 10 Jan 1837
Colonelcies: 6th Garrison Battalion 21 May 1813 (vice Dalhousie); 44th Foot 29 Jan 1820 (vice Lord Suffolk)
Early Service: Served in British North America; served in West Indies
Service 1793–1815: Served in Jamaica and St Domingue 1795; commanded 2/40th Foot in Helder 1799; commanded 2/40th Foot in Mediterranean 1800–1802; commanded 1/40th Foot in South America 1807; Governor of Monte Video 1807; commanded brigade and wounded in Walcheren 1809; Lieutenant Governor of Plymouth

7 Nov 1812
Residence: Melcombe Regis, Dorset
Died: Melcombe Regis 18 Jan 1843
Sources: ANCB; ANCD; ARLI; WEOF; WO 25/744

238. *Rt Hon. William, 1st Earl of CRAVEN (1799–1802)*

Born: London 1770
Relations: Son of William Craven, 6th Baron Craven and Lady Elizabeth (Berkeley); father of Cornet Hon. George Augustus Craven, 8th Light Dragoons; brother-in-law of General Hon. Frederick. St John
Entry to Army: Ensign in 45th Foot 4 Sep 1793 by purchase
Regimental Field Officer Promotions: Major in 84th Foot 28 Feb 1794 by purchase; Lieutenant Colonel in 84th Foot 31 May 1794 by purchase; Lieutenant Colonel in 3rd Foot 25 Sep 1794 (vice Newark) by exchange; Lieutenant Colonel in 40th Foot 1 Sep 1799 (vice Harcourt); to half-pay of 40th Foot 25 Aug 1802
Brevets: Brevet Colonel 1 Jan 1798; Major General 1 Jan 1805; Lieutenant General 4 Jun 1811
Colonelcies: 9th Battalion of Reserve 9 Jul 1803
Service 1793–1815: Served in Flanders 1794–1795; served in West Indies 1796–1797; ADC to King George III 1 Jan 1798; served in Helder 1799; served on home staff 1805–1811
Later Service: Lord Lieutenant of Berkshire 1819–1825
Creations and Dignities: 7th Baron Craven 26 Sep 1791; 1st Viscount Uffington 18 Jun 1801; 1st Earl of Craven 18 Jun 1801
Residences: Coombe Abbey, near Coventry, Warwickshire; Hamstead Marshall, Berkshire
Died: Cowes, Isle of Wight, 30 Jul 1825
Sources: ANCB; ANCD; ARLI; CRAC; DEPE; PHIL; WEOF; WO 25/744

239. *William Waldegrave Pelham CLAY (1799–1802)*

Born: Nottinghamshire 1760
Relations: Son of William Clay of Southwell, attorney, and Jemima (Pelham); brother of General John Granby Clay; and Rear Admiral Edward Sneyd Clay RN
Entry to Army: Ensign in 40th Foot 27 May 1777 by purchase
Regimental Field Officer Promotions: Major in 40th Foot 1 Sep 1795 (vice Adlam); Lieutenant Colonel in 40th Foot 6 Aug 1799; to half-pay of 40th Foot 24 Aug 1802
Brevets: Brevet Major 1 Mar 1794; Brevet Lieutenant Colonel 1 Jan 1798; Brevet Colonel 25 Apr 1808; Major General 4 Jun 1811; Lieutenant General 19 Jul 1821
Early Service: Served in West Indies 1779–1781; served in American War of Independence 1781–1783
Service 1793–1815: Served in West Indies 1794–1795; commanded 1/40th Foot in Malta 1801–1802; Inspecting Field Officer of Recruiting District in Ireland Nov 1804; served on staff in West Indies 1813–1815, court-martialled in Barbados for alleged financial irregularities in 1813
Residence: Southwell, Nottinghamshire
Died: Southwell 27 Sep 1822
Sources: ANCB; ANCD; ANCW; ARLI; WEOF; WO 25/744

240. *James KEMMIS (1804–1814)*

Born: Queen's County 1751
Relations: Son of Thomas Kemmis of Shaen Castle and Susannah (Long)
Entry to Army: Ensign in 9th Foot 7 Jul 1775 by purchase
Regimental Field Officer Promotions: Major in 40th Foot 5 Aug 1799 (vice Clay); Lieutenant Colonel in 40th Foot 1 Aug 1804; removed from the regiment as a general officer 1815
Brevets: Brevet Major 1 Mar 1794; Brevet Lieutenant Colonel 1 Jan 1798; Brevet Colonel 25 Apr 1808; Brigadier General (Peninsula staff) 23 Jan 1811; Major General 4 Jun 1811
Early Service: Served in American War of Independence 1777–1781, taken POW
Service 1793–1815: Served in Flanders 1794–1795; served in West Indies 1798; served in Helder 1799; served in Mediterranean 1800–1802; commanded 2/40th Foot 1804–1807; commanded 1/40th Foot in Peninsula Aug 1808 to Jun 1809; commanded brigade in 4th Division in Peninsula Jul 1809 to Mar 1812; temporary commander of 4th Division in Peninsula Jul to Oct 1809 and May to Jul 1811
Awards and Honours: AGM (Rol&Vim Tal)
Retired: 1819
Residence: Cheltenham, Gloucestershire
Died: Cheltenham 2 Apr 1820
He and his wife being childless, adopted the orphaned daughter of Private William Curtis of the 50th Foot in Spain in 1811 and raised her as their own
Sources: ANCB; ANCD; ANCW; ARLI; CHAL; WEBC; WEOF

241. *Amédée Louis André Marie Charles François, 3rd Marquess D'HARCOURT-OLONDE (1810–1814)*

Born: Paris 1771
Relations: Son of Charles Louis Hector D'Harcourt-Olonde, Marquess D'Harcourt, and Anne Louise Catherine (D'Harcourt-Beuvron)
Entry to Army: Volunteer in Flanders 1793; Ensign in 127th Foot 11 Dec 1794 by purchase
Regimental Field Officer Promotions: Major in 40th Foot 25 Dec 1802 (vice Gore) by purchase; to half-pay of 40th Foot 25 Dec 1802; Lieutenant Colonel in 40th Foot 25 Jan 1810; to half-pay of 40th Foot 14 Apr 1814
Brevets: Brevet Lieutenant Colonel 1 Nov 1804; Brevet Colonel 4 Jun 1813; Major General 12 Aug 1819
Service 1793–1815: Served in Flanders 1793–1794; served on staff in Helder 1799; on mission to Russia 1800; Assistant Quartermaster General in Ireland 1803–1809; Deputy Quartermaster General at Cape of Good Hope 1809; commanded 1/40th Foot in Peninsula May 1810 to May 1811; served in Peninsula Oct 1811 to Apr 1812; commanded brigade in 4th Division and wounded at Badajoz 1812
Creations and Dignities: 3rd Marquess d'Harcourt-Olonde 5 Jun 1820
Awards and Honours: AGM (Bad); CB 4 Jun 1815
Residence: St Leonard's Hill, Berkshire
Died: Thrown from his horse at Windsor 14 Sep 1831
Served as an ADC to Major General William Harcourt in Flanders in 1793, an officer who claimed a distant kinship with the French d'Harcourts
Sources: ANCB; ANCD; ARLI; CHAL; PHIL; WEOF; WO 25/746

242. *Henry Charles THORNTON (1811–1827)*

Born: Leicestershire 1779
Relations: Son of Thomas Lee Thornton of Brockhall and Mary (Reeve)
Entry to Army: Ensign 8 Oct 1794
Regimental Field Officer Promotions: Major in 40th Foot 2 Aug 1804; Lieutenant Colonel in 40th Foot 13 Jun 1811 (vice Kemmis); Lieutenant Colonel in 82nd Foot 7 Jun 1827 (vice Valiant) by exchange
Brevets: Brevet Lieutenant Colonel 4 Jun 1811; Brevet Colonel 27 May 1825
Service 1793–1815: Served in West Indies 1796; served in Helder 1799; commanded 1/40th Foot in Peninsula Aug 1808 to May 1810; again in Peninsula Jul 1813 to Apr 1814, wounded at Nivelle; commanded 1/40th Foot after Waterloo
Later Service: Commanded 40th Foot in New South Wales 1824–1827
Awards and Honours: AGC (Tal Nlle Ort Toul); CB 4 Jan 1815; MGSM (Rol Vim Bus Pyr)
Retired: 17 Jan 1828
Residence: Southampton Place, Camberwell, London
Died: Camberwell 26 Feb 1856
Sources: ANCB; ANCD; ARLI; CHAL; HALL; PHIL; WEOF; WO 25/748

243. *Rt Hon. Sir Henry, 1st Viscount HARDINGE (1814)*

Born: Kent 1785
Relations: Son of Rev. Henry Hardinge of Ketton, rector of Stanhope, and Frances (Best); son-in-law of Robert Stewart, 1st Marquess of Londonderry
Education: Durham School; Royal Military College
Entry to Army: Ensign in Queen's Rangers 23 Jul 1799
Regimental Field Officer Promotions: Major in 57th Foot 7 Apr 1809; Major in Portuguese service 13 Apr 1809; Lieutenant Colonel in Portuguese service 30 May 1811; Lieutenant Colonel in 40th Foot 14 Apr 1814 (vice Harcourt); Captain and Lieutenant Colonel in 1st Foot Guards 25 Jul 1814; to half-pay of 1st Greek Light Infantry 26 Apr 1827 (vice Oswald) by exchange
Brevets: Brevet Colonel 10 Jul 1813; Major General 22 Jul 1830; Lieutenant General 23 Nov 1841; General (staff) 28 Sep 1852; General 20 Jun 1854; Field Marshal 2 Oct 1855
Colonelcies: 97th Foot 4 Mar 1833 (vice O'Callaghan); 57th Foot 31 May 1843 (vice Adam)
Service 1793–1815: Served in Peninsula as Deputy Assistant Quartermaster General Aug 1808 to Jan 1809, wounded at Vimeiro; Deputy Quartermaster General in Peninsula 15 Apr 1809; commanded 5th Portuguese Line Apr 1809 to Apr 1814, wounded at Vittoria; British liaison officer at Prussian HQ during Waterloo campaign 1815, lost left hand at Ligny
Later Service: Clerk of the Ordnance Apr 1823 to May 1827, and Jan to May 1828; Governor General of British East Indies 23 Jul 1844 to 12 Jan 1848; Commander in Chief in First Sikh War 1845; Master General of the Ordinance Mar to Sep 1852; Commander in Chief of British Army Sep 1852 to Sep 1856
Political Career: MP (Durham City) 1820–1830; Secretary at War May 1828 to Jul 1831; Chief Secretary for Ireland Jul to Nov 1830; MP (St

Germans) 1830; MP (Newport) 1830–1832; MP (Launceston) 1832–1844; Chief Secretary for Ireland Dec 1834 to Apr 1835; Secretary at War Aug 1841 to Jul 1844
Awards and Honours:
AGC (Bus Alb Bad Sal Vit Pyr Nlle Nive Ort); KCB 2 Jan 1815; PC 30 May 1828; GCB 1 Jul 1844; MGSM (Rol Vim Cor CR Tal)
Creations and Dignities: 1st Viscount Hardinge of Lahore 2 May 1846
Residences: Ketton, County Durham; Sackville Street, Mayfair, London; South Park, Penshurst, Kent
Died: Penshurst 24 Sep 1856
Succeeded Wellington as commander in chief of the British army in September 1852, and commanded during the Crimean war; was considered the last 'political general' to be put in charge of the army (HPON)
Sources: ANCB; ANCD; ARLI; CHAL; HPON; ODNB; PHIL; WEOF

244. *William STEWART (1815–1816)*
See 182.
Lieutenant Colonel in 40th Foot 26 Jun 1815 (vice Hardinge); to half-pay 5 Feb 1816

Majors

245. *John Erasmus ADLAM (1787–1795)*
Born: [spec.] Wiltshire c.1745
Relations: Son of Captain John Adlam, 40th Foot; brother of Major General William Adlam, Royal Marines
Entry to Army: Ensign in 40th Foot 30 Sep 1761
Regimental Field Officer Promotions: Major in 40th Foot 12 Oct 1787
Brevets: Brevet Lieutenant Colonel 1 Mar 1794
Service 1793–1815: Served in American War of Independence
Retired: 1 Sep 1795
Residence: Oystermouth, Glamorganshire
Died: Oystermouth 1 Sep 1809
Invariably (and incorrectly) shown as John Edward Adlam on Army Lists
Sources: ANCD; ANCW; ARLI

246. *Edward BOLAND (1795–1801)*
Born: County Cork c.1761
Relations: Son of Jonathan Boland of Cork and Elizabeth (Parsons); brother of Lieutenant Colonel John Boland, 40th Foot
Entry to Army: Ensign in 40th Foot 18 Aug 1778 by purchase
Regimental Field Officer Promotions: Major in 40th Foot 1 Sep 1795
Brevets: Brevet Lieutenant Colonel 1 Jan 1801
Early Service: Served in American War of Independence
Service 1793–1815: Commanded 40th Foot 1798–1799
Residence: Bath, Somerset
Died: Bath 18 Oct 1801
Sources: ANCB; ANCD; ARLI

247. *Hon. Edward WINGFIELD (1799–1803)*
Born: County Wicklow 1772
Relations: Son of Richard Wingfield, 3rd Viscount Powerscourt, and Lady Amelia (Stratford)
Entry to Army: Ensign in 69th Foot 30 Jul 1791 by purchase
Regimental Field Officer Promotions: Major in 2/84th Foot 24 Jun 1795; to half-pay of 84th Foot 1796; Major in 40th Foot 6 Aug 1799
Brevets: Brevet Lieutenant Colonel 1 Jan 1801
Service 1793–1815: Served in Helder 1799, wounded at Bergen
Retired: 17 Feb 1803
Residence: Cork Abbey, Bray, County Dublin
Died: Bray 24 Aug 1859
Sources: ANCB; ANCD; ANCW; ARLI; BUPE; WEOF

248. *Alexander Cosby JACKSON (1799–1802)*
Born: Bombay 1772
Relations: Son of Lieutenant Colonel Robert Jackson, Bombay service, and Charlotte Jane Emma (Cosby)
Entry to Army: Ensign in 40th Foot 31 Jul 1790 by purchase
Regimental Field Officer Promotions: Major in 94th Foot 23 Dec 1795; to half-pay 1796; Major in 40th Foot 7 Aug 1799; to half-pay of 40th Foot 24 Aug 1802; Major in 67th Foot 9 Jul 1803; Lieutenant Colonel in 66th Foot 27 Dec 1810; removed from the regiment as a general officer 1815
Brevets: Brevet Lieutenant Colonel 1 Jan 1801; Brevet Colonel 25 Jul 1810; Major General 4 Jun 1813; Lieutenant General 27 May 1825
Service 1793–1815: Served in Helder 1799, wounded at Alkmaar; served in Malta; served in East Indies 1805–1810; served on staff in Ceylon 1810–1815
Residences: Bath, Somerset; Dawlish, Devon
Died: Dawlish 29 Jan 1827
Sources: ANCB; ANCD; ANCW; ARLI; WEOF

249. *Arthur GORE (1802)*
See 66.
Major in 40th Foot 9 Jul 1802 (vice Boland)

250. *Hon. Sir Robert William O'CALLAGHAN (1803)*
See 218.
Major in 40th Foot 17 Feb 1803 (vice Wingfield)

251. *Hon. George Augustus Frederick LAKE (1803)*
Born: London 1771
Relations: Son of General Gerard, Viscount Lake, and Elizabeth (Baker)
Entry to Army: Cornet in 8th Light Dragoons 10 Aug 1796 by purchase
Regimental Field Officer Promotions: Major in 40th Foot 24 Sep 1803 (vice O'Callaghan) by purchase; Lieutenant Colonel in 29th Foot 12 Nov 1803 (vice Montagu) by purchase; to half-pay of 29th Foot 20 Dec 1804; Lieutenant Colonel in 29th Foot 5 Nov 1807 (vice Vesey) by exchange
Service 1793–1815: ADC to General Lake in Ireland 1798; Assistant Adjutant General and military secretary to General Lake in British East Indies 1801; wounded at Laswaree 1803; Deputy Quartermaster General in British East Indies 20 Dec 1804; commanded 29th Foot in Peninsula Jul to Aug 1808
Died: Killed in action at Roliça 17 Aug 1808
Sources: ANCB; ANCD; ANCW; WEOF; Everard; The European Magazine, and London Review (1808)

252. *John DALRYMPLE (1803–1807)*
Born: Edinburgh c.1774
Relations: Son of Colonel William Dalrymple of Fordell and Diana (Molyneux); brother of Lieutenant Hew Dalrymple RN; nephew of Lieutenant General Samuel Dalrymple
Entry to Army: Lieutenant in Scotch Brigade 27 Oct 1794
Regimental Field Officer Promotions: Major in 40th Foot 22 Dec 1803 (vice Lake)
Service 1793–1815: Served in South America 1807
Died: Killed in action at Monte Video 3 Feb 1807
Sources: ANCB; ARLI

253. *Donald CAMPBELL (1804–1808)*
Born: Isle of Lewis c.1774
Relations: Son of John Campbell of Mishnish; brother of Colonel Archibald Campbell, 46th Foot
Entry to Army: Lieutenant in Argyllshire Fencibles; Ensign in Independent Company 16 Oct 1793
Regimental Field Officer Promotions: Major in Cape Regiment 25 Jun 1801; Major in 10th Garrison Battalion 9 Jul 1803; Major in 40th Foot 1 Aug 1804 (vice Kemmis); Lieutenant Colonel on staff in British North America 28 Jan 1808; Lieutenant Colonel in 63rd Foot 22 Dec 1808 (vice St George)
Service 1793–1815: Served in South America, wounded at Monte Video 1807; Inspecting Field Officer of Militia in Canada 28 Jan 1808
Retired: 28 Jun 1810
Residence: Knock, Isle of Lewis
Died: Knock 23 Jun 1843
Sources: *ARLI; WEOF; The History of the Late 63rd, West Suffolk Regiment*

254. *Paul ANDERSON (1804–1805)*
Born: County Waterford 1767
Relations: Son of James Anderson of Grace Dieu and Suzanna (Paul); brother of Lieutenant Henry Anderson, RN; and Captain Alexander Anderson, 95th Foot
Entry to Army: Ensign in 51st Foot 31 Mar 1788 by purchase
Regimental Field Officer Promotions: Major in 9th Foot 25 Jul 1801 (vice Lorraine); to half-pay of 9th Foot 25 Jun 1802; Major in 7th Foot 25 Nov 1802 (vice Cliffe) by exchange; to half-pay of Corsican Rangers 14 Apr 1803; Major in 40th Foot 5 Oct 1804; Lieutenant Colonel in Nova Scotia Fencibles 16 Oct 1805 (vice Brinley); to half-pay of 4th Foot 30 Oct 1806; Lieutenant Colonel in 4/60th Foot 14 Jan 1808 (vice Gordon); to half-pay of 60th Foot 25 Feb 1817
Brevets: Brevet Colonel 4 Jun 1813; Major General 12 Aug 1819; Lieutenant General 10 Jan 1837; General 11 Nov 1851
Colonelcies: 78th Foot 9 Feb 1837 (vice Smith)
Early Service: Served in Gibraltar 1792–1793
Service 1793–1815: Served in Toulon and in Corsica 1793–1795; Brigade Major in West Indies 1795–1796; served in Irish Rebellion 1798; ADC to Sir John Moore in Helder 1799; ADC to Sir John Moore and wounded in Egypt 1801; served in Sicily 1806; Deputy and Assistant Adjutant General in Peninsula Aug 1808 to Jan 1809; served in Walcheren 1809
Later Service: Lieutenant Governor of Gravesend and Tilbury Fort 13 Dec 1827; Governor of Pendennis Castle 23 Jul 1832
Awards and Honours: Sultan's medal (Ottoman) 1802; AGM (Cor); CB 4 Jun 1815; MGSM (Egt)
Residence: Paragon Buildings, Bath, Somerset
Died: Bath 17 Dec 1851
Sources: ANCB; ANCD; CHAL; LFBI; PHIL; WEOF; WO 25/744

255. *Hon. George CARLETON (1805)*
Born: Surrey 1781
Relations: Son of General Guy Carleton, 1st Baron Dorchester, and Lady Maria (Howard); grandson of Thomas Howard, 2nd Earl of Effingham; nephew of Colonel Thomas Carleton; brother of Lieutenant Guy Carleton, 3rd Foot Guards; Captain Thomas Carleton, 1st Dragoons; Lieutenant Colonel Cristopher Carleton, 25th Light Dragoons; and Midshipman Charles Carleton, RN
Entry to Army: Ensign in 9th Foot 11 Jul 1798 by purchase
Field Officer Promotions: Major in 40th Foot 17 Oct 1805 (vice Anderson); Major in 27th Foot 29 Oct 1805 (vice Shaw) by exchange; Lieutenant Colonel as Inspecting Field Officer of Militia in British North America 28 Jan 1808; Lieutenant Colonel in 44th Foot 22 Aug 1811 (vice Egerton) by exchange
Service 1793–1815: Served in Helder 1799; served in Ferrol and Lisbon 1800–1801; served in Hanover 1805–1806; served in Sicily and Malta 1806–1808; served on staff in British North America 1808–1811; commanded 2/44th Foot in Peninsula December 1811 to April 1812, wounded at Badajoz; commanded 2/44th Foot in Netherlands 1814
Awards and Honours: AGM (Bad)
Died: Killed in action at Bergen-op-Zoom 8 Mar 1814
Sources: ARLI; CHAL; WEOF; WO 25/744

256. *John SHAW (1805–1806)*
Born: Inverness-shire 1769
Relations: Son of Alexander Shaw of Tordarroch and Charlotte (Stewart)
Entry to Army: Ensign on half-pay of 42nd Foot 15 Aug 1783; Ensign in 42nd Foot 18 Jan 1786
Field Officer Promotions: Major in Champagné's Corps 5 May 1804 (vice Brownrigg); Major in 27th Foot 11 Sep 1805; Major in 40th Foot 25 Oct 1805 (vice Carleton) by exchange; to half-pay of 15th Garrison Battalion 8 May 1806 (vice Thompson) by exchange
Brevets: Brevet Lieutenant Colonel 3 Apr 1806; Brevet Colonel 4 Jun 1814; Major General 19 Jul 1821
Early Service: Served in British North America 1786; served in East Indies 1791–1793
Service 1793–1815: Served in East Indies 1793–1799; Deputy Barrackmaster General in Cape of Good Hope 1806–1809
Residence: Baker Street, Marylebone, London
Died: London 21 Oct 1835
Sources: ANCB; ANCD; ARLI; PHIL; WEOF; WO 25/748

257. *Joseph THOMPSON (1806)*
Born: Berwickshire 1764
Relations: Son of John Thompson of Brooklyn and Berwick-Upon-Tweed and Jane (Hall); brother of Surgeon John Vaughan Thompson, 37th Foot; father of Lieutenant Colonel John Hall Thompson, Ontario County Militia
Entry to Army: Ensign in 46th Foot 12 Aug 1778 by purchase
Regimental Field Officer Promotions: Major in 15th Garrison Battalion 9 Jul 1803; to half-pay of 15th Garrison Battalion 24 Jan 1805; Major in 40th Foot 8 May 1806 (vice Shaw) by exchange
Brevets: Brevet Major 29 Apr 1802
Early Service: Served in American War of Independence
Service 1793–1815: Served in West Indies
Retired: 21 Aug 1806
Residence: Brock, Ontario, Canada
Died: Brock 22 Nov 1843
Sources: ARLI; Find A Grave; Death Notices of Ontario

258. *Richard ARCHDALL (1806–1813)*
Born: London 1783
Relations: Son of Richard Archdall of Spondon MP, and Anna Maria (Montague); cousin of Lieutenant General Mervyn Archdall; Lieutenant Colonel William Archdall, 4th Foot; and Captain Henry Archdall, 6th Dragoon Guards
Entry to Army: Ensign in 40th Foot 18 Apr 1800
Regimental Field Officer Promotions: Major in 40th Foot 21 Aug 1806 (vice Thompson); allowed to sell out following court-martial in Spain 22 Jul 1813; re-enlisted as Cornet in 3rd Dragoons 3 Mar 1814; to half-pay of 17th Foot 25 Dec 1822
Brevets: Brevet Lieutenant Colonel 17 Aug 1812
Service 1793–1815: Served in Malta and Minorca 1801–1802; served in Baltic and Peninsula Aug to Nov 1808; served in Peninsula Apr 1810 to Jan 1813; commanded 1/40th Foot May 1812 to Jan 1813
Later Service: Assistant Inspector General of Barracks Department 1818–1828
Awards and Honours: AGM (Sal)
Residences: St Helier, Jersey
Died: St Helier 27 Jan 1829
Sources: ANCB; ANCD; ANCW; ARLI; CHAL; WEOF; WO 25/744

259. *John GILLIES (1807–1816)*
Born: Inverness-shire 1778
Relations: Son of Donald Gillies of Morar
Entry to Army: Private in 40th Foot; Ensign in 40th Foot 28 Oct 1795

Regimental Field Officer Promotions: Major in 40th Foot 8 Feb 1807 (vice Dalrymple); to half-pay of 40th Foot 25 Feb 1816
Brevets: Brevet Lieutenant Colonel 4 Jun 1813; Brevet Colonel 22 Jul 1830
Service 1793–1815: Served in Peninsula Sep 1811 to Jul 1812, wounded at Badajoz
Awards and Honours: AGM (Bad); CB 8 Sep 1831
Residences: Kinlochmorar, Inverness-shire
Died: Kinlochmorar Jun 1836
Sources: ANCB; CHAL; HALL; GEMA (1836); PHIL; WEOF

260. *William BALFOUR (1808–1828)*

Born: Edinburgh 1784
Relations: Son of David Coventry Balfour and Marion (McIntosh); father of Lieutenant Colonel David William Balfour-Ogilvy; Lieutenant Charles Anthony Balfour RA; and Captain George McIntosh Balfour RN
Education: Royal Military Academy, Woolwich
Entry to Army: Ensign on half-pay of 125th Foot 1798; Ensign in 40th Foot 25 Jul 1799
Regimental Field Officer Promotions: Major in 40th Foot 4 Feb 1808 (vice Campbell); to half-pay of 40th Foot 10 Nov 1814; Major in 3rd Foot 8 Jul 1819 (vice Morris) by purchase; Major in 40th Foot 22 Jun 1820 (vice Browne); Lieutenant Colonel in 82nd Foot 17 Jan 1828 (vice Thornton) by purchase; to Lieutenant Colonel unattached 28 Jun 1833 (vice Philips)
Brevets: Brevet Lieutenant Colonel 12 Apr 1814
Service 1793–1815: Served in Helder 1799; served on staff in Mediterranean; served in Copenhagen 1807; served in Peninsula Oct 1813 to Apr 1814
Later Service: Commanded 40th Foot in New South Wales 1823–1824; commanded 82nd Foot in Mauritius 1828–1832
Retired: 28 Jun 1833
Awards and Honours: AGM (Nlle)
Residences: Regent Street, St James's, London
Died: London 10 Feb 1838
Sources: ANCB; ANCW; ARLI; CHAL; DINB; LFBI; WEOF

261. *John WHETHAM (1811–1815)*

Born: Gloucestershire 1783
Relations: Son of Rev. John Whetham, Dean of Lismore, and Agatha (Moore); brother of Major General Arthur Whetham; cousin of Lieutenant General Arthur Whetham, Lieutenant Governor of Portsmouth
Entry to Army: Ensign on half-pay of East Yorkshire Militia; Lieutenant in 40th Foot 30 Aug 1799
Regimental Field Officer Promotions: Major in 40th Foot 13 Jun 1811 (vice Thornton); to half-pay of 1st Garrison Battalion 30 Mar 1815 (vice Oglander) by exchange
Brevets: Brevet Lieutenant Colonel 12 Aug 1819; Brevet Colonel 10 Jan 1837; Major General 9 Nov 1846
Service 1793–1815: Served in Helder 1799; served in Mediterranean; ADC to Lieutenant General Whetham; served in South America, lost right leg at Montevideo; Brigade Major on staff in Portsmouth 1807–1811
Residence: Kirklington Hall, Kirklington, Nottinghamshire
Died: Kirklington Hall 13 May 1853
Sources: ANCB; ANCD; ANCW; ARLI; CHAL; PHIL; WEOF

262. *Peter Augustus LAUTOUR (1813–1814)*

Born: India 1788
Relations: Son of Louis Francois Joseph de Lautour, banker of Madras, and Anne (Hordle); brother of Lieutenant Joseph Andrew Lautour, 1st Foot Guards; and Ensign James Oliver Lautour, 1st Foot Guards; brother-in-law of General Henry John Cumming; uncle of Colonel Henry Wedderburn Cumming, Coldstream Foot Guards; and Admiral Sir Arthur Cumming, RN
Entry to Army: Cornet in 11th Light Dragoons 31 Mar 1804
Regimental Field Officer Promotions: Major in 40th Foot 20 May 1813 (vice Archdall) by purchase; Major in 23rd (late 26th) Light Dragoons 6 Jan 1814 (vice Moore) by exchange; to half-pay of 23rd Light Dragoons 25 Jan 1818; retired to France in 1828 but returned to army on same rank and seniority in 1834
Brevets: Brevet Major 20 May 1813; Brevet Lieutenant Colonel 18 Jun 1815; Brevet Colonel 10 Jan 1837; Major General 9 Nov 1846; Lieutenant General 20 Jun 1854; General 9 Mar 1861
Colonelcies: 3rd Light Dragoons 26 May 1855 (vice Manners)
Service 1793–1815: Served in Peninsula Jun 1811 to Dec 1812; served at Waterloo, commanded 23rd Light Dragoons and eventually brigade late in the day
Awards and Honours: CB 22 Jun 1815; KH 5 Apr 1816; WatM 23 Apr 1816; MGSM (Sal)
Residences: Little Staughton Park, Bedfordshire; Staughton Villa, Bromley Common, Kent
Died: Bromley Common 11 Jan 1866
Lautour was a heavy investor in overseas speculations (mainly Australia and New Zealand) but went

bankrupt in 1830 and served time in debtor's prisons between 1831 and 1834
Sources: ANCB; ANCD; ANCW; ARLI; CHAL; DALT; GHLG; WEOF

263. *James MOORE (1814–1815)*

Born: County Tyrone c.1761
Relations: Son of John Moore of Cottage Hill
Entry to Army: Ensign in 11th Foot 1 Jun 1778 by purchase
Regimental Field Officer Promotions: Major in 26th Light Dragoons 1 Nov 1796; Major in 40th Foot 6 Jan 1814 (vice Latour) by exchange; removed from the regiment as a general officer 1815
Brevets: Brevet Lieutenant Colonel 29 Jun 1802; Brevet Colonel 4 Jun 1811; Brigadier General (Channel Islands) 1812; Major General 4 Jun 1814; Lieutenant General 22 Jul 1830
Early Service: Served at Gibraltar 1783–1792
Service 1793–1815: Served in West Indies 1795–1797; served on staff in Egypt 1801; Assistant Adjutant General in Sicily 1804–1809, wounded at Maida
Later Service: Equerry to HRH Duke of Kent 1793–1820
Awards and Honours: KC
Residence: The Pavilions, Home Park, Hampton, Middlesex
Died: Hampton 24 Apr 1838
Sources: ANCD; ANCW; ARLI; GEMA (1838); WEOF

264. *Arthur Rowley HEYLAND (1814–1815)*

Born: County Londonderry 1781
Relations: Son of Rowley Heyland of Castle Roe and Mary (McDonnell); father of Lieutenant Colonel John Rowley Kyffin Lloyd Heyland, 7th Foot; Captain Kyffin Heyland, 25th Foot; and General Alfred Thomas Heyland
Education: Eton College
Entry to Army: Ensign in 49th Foot 22 Apr 1802 by purchase
Regimental Field Officer Promotions: Major in 40th Foot 10 Nov 1814 (vice Balfour)
Brevets: Brevet Major 26 Aug 1813
Service 1793–1815: Served in Peninsula Aug 1808 to Apr 1814; commanded 1/40th Foot at Vittoria and in Pyrenees; wounded at 1st Badajoz and Pyrenees; commanded 1/40th Foot at Waterloo 1815
Awards and Honours: AGM (Vit); WatM 23 Apr 1816
Residence: Bangor, Caernarvonshire
Died: Killed in action at Waterloo 18 Jun 1815
Sources: ANCW; CHAL; HALL; LGBI; WEOF

265. *Fielding BROWNE (1815–1820)*

Born: County Galway 1788
Relations: Son of Major Robert Browne of Headford and Elizabeth (Swift); brother of Major Thomas Browne, 67th Foot; and Richard Browne, Royal Marines
Entry to Army: Ensign in 40th Foot 7 Mar 1800
Regimental Field Officer Promotions: Major in 40th Foot 19 Jan 1815; to half-pay of Rifle Brigade 22 Jun 1820
Brevets: Brevet Major 4 Jun 1814; Brevet Lieutenant Colonel 18 Jun 1815; Brevet Colonel 10 Jan 1837; rank stationary thereafter
Service 1793–1815: Served in Peninsula Aug 1808 to Nov 1812, commanded 1/40th Foot after Badajoz; served in New Orleans 1815; commanded 1/40th Foot at start of Waterloo campaign and after Waterloo
Later Service: Barrackmaster in Malta; Barrackmaster at Regent's Park
Creations and Dignities: AGM (Sal); CB 22 Jun 1815; WatM 23 Apr 1816; MGSM (Rol Vim Tal Bus Alb CR Bad Sal)
Residence: Gloucester Crescent, Regent's Park, London
Died: London 22 Jul 1864
Sources: ANCB; ANCD; ANCW; ARLI; CHAL; DALT; PHIL; WEOF

266. *Henry OGLANDER (1815)*

Born: Isle of Wight 1788
Relations: Son of Sir William Oglander, 5th Baronet, and Sukey (Serle); brother of Sir William Oglander, 6th Baronet
Entry to Army: Ensign in 43rd Foot 20 Aug 1806 by purchase
Regimental Field Officer Promotions: Major in 1st Garrison Battalion 27 Oct 1814 (vice Nestor); to half-pay of 2nd Garrison Battalion 1814; Major in 40th Foot 30 Mar 1815 (vice Whetham) by exchange; Lieutenant Colonel in Watteville's Regiment 14 Dec 1815 (vice Fischer); to half-pay of Watteville's Regiment 24 Oct 1816; Lieutenant Colonel in 26th Foot 23 Oct 1817 (vice Wauchope) by exchange
Brevets: Brevet Major 14 Oct 1813; Brevet Colonel 10 Jan 1837
Service 1793–1815: Served in Copenhagen 1807; served in Peninsula with 43rd Foot Jan 1809; served in Peninsula with 43rd Foot Jul 1810 to Jun 1812, lost left arm at Badajoz; served in Peninsula with 47th Foot Feb 1813 to Apr 1814, wounded at San Sebastian

Later Service: Served in East Indies 1828–1840
Awards and Honours: AGM (SS); CB 28 Jun 1838
Residence: Nunwell, Isle of Wight
Died: At sea off Chusan, China 23 Jun 1840
Sources: ANCB; ANCW; ARLI; CHAL; WEOF; The Journals of Captain Henry Oglander

267. *Sempronius STRETTON (1815–1824)*
Born: Nottinghamshire 1781
Relations: Son of William Stretton of Nottingham, builder, and Susanna (Lynam); brother of Lieutenant Colonel Severus William Lynam Stretton, 68th Foot; son-in-law of Major General Nathaniel William Massey, 2nd Baron Clarina; son-in-law of Richard Handcock, 2nd Baron Castlemaine
Entry to Army: Ensign in Nottinghamshire Militia Apr 1800; Ensign in 6th Foot Nov 1800
Regimental Field Officer Promotions: Major in 40th Foot 20 Jul 1815 (vice Heyland); to half-pay of 84th Foot 19 Feb 1824 (vice Chamberlain) by exchange
Brevets: Brevet Lieutenant Colonel 21 Jun 1817; Brevet Colonel 10 Jan 1837
Service 1793–1815: Served in British North America 1801–1806; served in Peninsula Feb 1813 to Apr 1814, commanded 1/40th Foot in Pyrenees; served at New Orleans 1815; served in Waterloo campaign 1815; served in advance on Paris and in Allied Army of Occupation in France
Awards and Honours: AGM (Pyr); WatM 23 Apr 1816; CB 19 Jul 1838
Residences: Lenton Priority, Lenton, Nottinghamshire (but never lived there); Athlone, County Westmeath
Died: Croydon, London 6 Feb 1842
A noted artist; his siblings were named Stella, Salacia, Sabina and Severus
Sources: ANCB; ANCD; ANCW; CHAL; PHIL; WEOF

Selected Regimental Histories

Smythies, Raymond Henry Raymond, *Historical Records of the 40th (2nd Somersetshire) Regiment* (Devonport: A.H. Swiss, 1894)

Regimental Museum

Lancashire Infantry Museum, Fulwood Barracks, Preston, Lancashire

---

41st Regiment of Foot

Secondary Title:	none
Nicknames:	The Invalids Warder's Regiment
Jacket:	Red
Facings:	Red

Regimental Lineage, 41st Regiment of Foot

1719:	Raised as Colonel Edmund Fielding's Regiment of Invalids at Chelsea Hospital
1743:	Wardour's Regiment of Invalids
1747:	Ranked as 41st Regiment of Foot (Royal Invalids)
1751:	41st Regiment of Foot (Invalids)
1782:	41st (Invalids) Regiment of Foot
1787:	41st Regiment of Foot
1812:	Aug – 2nd Battalion formed in Winchester
1814:	Oct – 2nd Battalion disbanded in Kingston (Ontario)
1831:	41st (Welsh) Regiment of Foot
1881:	The Welsh Regiment (on amalgamation with the 69th (South Lincolnshire) Regiment of Foot)
1921:	The Welch Regiment
1969:	1st Battalion, the Royal Regiment of Wales (on amalgamation with the South Wales Borderers)
2006:	2nd Battalion, The Royal Welsh (Royal Regiment of Wales) (on amalgamation with 1st Battalion, the Royal Welch Fusiliers (23rd Foot))

Service History, 1st Battalion 41st Regiment of Foot

1793: Ireland – Carrick on Shannon; May – civil disturbance at Drumkeerin; Sep – Cork; flank companies to West Indies; Dec – battalion companies to West Indies

1794: Battalion companies delayed by storms; Apr – battalion companies in Barbados; Martinique; May – St Domingue; Jul – battalion reunited; Dec – Fort Bizzotto
Flank companies in Barbados; Mar – flank companies at capture of Martinique; Apr – St Lucia; Guadeloupe; Jul – flank companies to St Domingue

1795: St Domingue

1796: St Domingue; Jun – Jamaica; Aug – cadre home; Dec – Gosport; to Ireland; Cork

1797: Cork

1798: Cork

1799: Limerick; Feb – Cork; Aug – to British North America; Oct – Québec; Nov – Montréal; detachment to Three Rivers

1800–1801: Montréal

1802: York, Kingston and Fort George; Aug – St John's and Fort George

1803: St John's and Fort George; Aug – Québec

1804: Québec

1805: York; detachments at various forts

1806–1808: Fort George; detachments at various forts

1809: Fort George; Aug – Montréal

1810: Montréal

1811: Montréal; Sep – Fort George; detachments at Amherstburg, Québec and York

1812: Fort George; various detachments in outposts; Jul – Aux Canards Bridge; Aug – capture of DETROIT; Sep – Fort Wayne; Oct – QUEENSTOWN

1813: Frenchtown; Apr – Amherstburg; May – Fort Meigs (MIAMI); Jun – Amherstburg; Aug – Fort Stephenson; Amhertsburg; Sep – detachments aboard ships as marines and crewmen on Lake Erie; Oct – retreat to Moraviantown – several companies taken POW; remnants merged with 2nd Battalion in Niagara; Dec – detachment at Fort Niagara; Black Rock

1814: Fort Niagara; Jul – light company at Lundy's Lane; NIAGARA; Aug – Fort Erie; Sep – Fort George; Nov – Kingston; Three Rivers

1815: Three Rivers; Mar – Québec; to England; Jul – Spithead; Ostend; Paris; Allied Army of Occupation; Nov – to England; Ramsgate

Service History, 2nd Battalion 41st Regiment of Foot

1812: Aug – formed in Winchester from militia volunteers; Chichester; Nov – Brighton

1813: Brighton; Mar – Portsmouth; to British North America; May – Québec; Kingston; Jul – Black Rock; Goose Creek; York and Kingston; Oct – Fort Niagara; merged with remnants of 1st Battalion; Dec – detachment at Fort Niagara; Black Rock

1814: Fort Niagara; Aug – Fort Erie; Sep – Fort George; Oct – disbanded in Kingston

Establishments, 1st Battalion 41st Regiment of Foot

Year	Subunits	Field Off	Off/ Staff	Sjts	Mus	Corp/ Pvts	Total
Dec 1792	10co	3	32	22	12	330	399
Jan 1793	10co	3	32	32	22	600	689
Apr 1793	10co	3	32	42	22	790	889
Dec 1795	10co+2r	5	51	62	30	1,010	1,158
Jan 1798	10co	5	49	52	22	600	728
Dec 1799	10co	5	38	53	22	600	718
Dec 1801	10co	5	33	34	22	750	844
May 1803	10co	5	36	34	22	750	847
Dec 1804	10co	5	36	44	22	800	907
Dec 1806	10co	4	36	44	22	800	906
Dec 1807	10co	4	36	34	22	600	696

May 1809	10co+r	4	40	42	26	608	720
Dec 1809	10co+r	4	50	62	26	1,008	1,150
Dec 1810	10co+r	4	40	52	26	808	930
Dec 1811	10co+r	4	50	73	26	1,208	1,361
Dec 1812	10co	4	46	55	22	1,000	1,127
Dec 1813	10co+r	4	49	63	22	1,008	1,146
Dec 1814	10co+r	4	49	53	22	808	936

Establishments, 2nd Battalion 41st Regiment of Foot

Year	Subunits	Field Off	Off/ Staff	Sjts	Mus	Corp/ Pvts	Total
Dec 1812	6co	2	23	35	12	600	672
Dec 1813	6co+r	2	26	43	12	608	691

Service Statistics, 41st Regiment of Foot

	Lieutenant Colonels	Majors
Number of officers in period 1793–1815	6	14
Average age on appointment to substantive rank	34	33
Average time in rank in regiment (years)	9.5	4.5
Total field officers by nationality	9 I / 6 S / 5 E / 1 F	
Demographics of other ranks 1810	76% EW / 15% I / 5% S / 4% F	
Demographics of other ranks 1815	87% EW / 11% I / 2% S	
Months of overseas service 1793–1815	1/41st: 228 2/41st: 19	

Significant Militia/Volunteer Intakes

1799: 100 prisoners from Irish rebellion
1807: Wiltshire
1808: Wiltshire
1809: Staffordshire, Wiltshire, 1st West Yorkshire
1810: Brunswick Fencibles, Newfoundland Fencibles, Nova Scotia Fencibles
1811: Cheshire, Cornwall, 2nd Lancashire, Nottinghamshire, 1st Somerset, Wiltshire
1812: Cheshire, South Gloucestershire, Somerset, Staffordshire, County Limerick, County Louth
1813: Shropshire

Regimental Colonels

268. *Sir Thomas STIRLING, 5th Bt (1790–1808)*

Born: St Petersburg 1731
Relations: Son of Sir Henry Stirling, 3rd Bt, and Anna (Gordon); brother of Sir William Stirling, 4th Bt
Entry to Army: Captain in 42nd Foot 20 Jul 1757 by purchase
Regimental Field Officer Promotions: Major in 42nd Foot 12 Dec 1770; Lieutenant Colonel in 42nd Foot 7 Sep 1771
Brevets: Brevet Colonel 19 Feb 1779; Major General 20 Nov 1782; Lieutenant General 3 May 1796; General 1 Jan 1801
Colonelcies: 71st Foot 13 Feb 1782 (vice Fraser); 41st Foot 13 Jan 1790 (vice McNab)
Early Service: In Dutch service 1747–1757; served in West Indies 1762; ADC to King George III 1779; commanded 42nd Foot in American War of Independence, wounded in 1781
Creations and Dignities: 5th Baronet of Ardoch 26 Jul 1799
Residence: Strowan, Upper Strathearn, Perthshire
Died: Strowan 9 May 1808
Sources: ANCB; ANCD: ANCW; ARLI; A History of the Services of the 41st (the Welch) Regiment

269. *Hay McDOWALL (1808–1809)*

See 147.
Colonel of 41st Foot 16 May 1808 (vice Stirling)

270. *Sir Josiah CHAMPAGNÉ (1810–1819)*

Born: Ireland 1753
Relations: Son of Very Rev. Arthur Champagné of Clonmacnoise and Marianne (Hamon); elder brother of Lieutenant General Forbes Champagné;

brother-in-law of Earl of Uxbridge; nephew of Generals Henry and Edward Paget
Entry to Army: Ensign in 31st Foot 29 Jan 1775 by purchase
Regimental Field Officer Promotions: Major in 80th Foot 13 Sep 1793; Lieutenant Colonel in 80th Foot 19 Dec 1793 by purchase
Brevets: Brevet Colonel 26 Jan 1797; Brigadier General (East Indies) 1800; Major General 25 Sep 1803; Lieutenant General 25 Jul 1810
Colonelcies: 1st Ceylon Regiment 25 Apr 1801; 41st Foot 25 Feb 1810 (vice MacDowall); 17th Foot 14 Jun 1819 (vice G. Garth)
Early Service: Served in American War of Independence 1776–1781; served in West Indies 1784–1786
Service 1793–1815: Commanded 80th Foot in Flanders 1794; commanded 80th Foot at Quiberon 1795; commanded 80th Foot at Cape of Good Hope and in India 1796–1799; General Officer Commanding and Governor of Ceylon 14 Mar 1799 to 22 Jul 1799; second in command of Baird's Anglo-Indian force from India to Egypt 1801
Awards and Honours: GCH 26 Jan 1832
Residence: Harley Street, Marylebone, London
Died: London 31 Jan 1840
Sources: ARLI; GEMA (1840); PHIL; WEOF; WO 25/744; WOST; Protestant Exiles from France in the Reign of Louis XIV

Lieutenant Colonels

271. *Sir Charles GORDON (1787–1794)*
Born: Aberdeenshire 1756
Relations: Son of Charles Gordon, 12th of Abergeldie and Alison (Hunter); brother of Captain Peter Gordon, 81st Foot; Captain Alexander Sinclair Gordon, London and Westminster Volunteers; and Major William Gordon, 60th Foot
Entry to Army: Ensign in 1/71st Foot 2 Dec 1775 by purchase
Regimental Field Officer Promotions: Major in 83rd Foot 3 Apr 1782 (vice Whyte); Lieutenant Colonel in 83rd Foot 17 Apr 1782 (vice Fanshawe) by purchase; to half-pay of 83rd Foot 8 May 1783; Lieutenant Colonel in 41st Foot 25 Dec 1787
Brevets: Brevet Lieutenant Colonel 17 Apr 1783; Colonel (North America) 15 Nov 1790; Brevet Colonel 20 Dec 1793; Brigadier General (West Indies) 1794
Early Service: Served in American Revolution 1777–1780; served in Germany and Holland 1787–1790; British Commissioner on continent 1791–1792
Service 1793–1815: Commanded 41st Foot 1787–1794; served in West Indies 1793; commanded brigade at capture of Martinique and Guadeloupe 1794; Governor of St Lucia 4 Apr 1794 to Oct 1794, rescinded and cashiered due to alleged improprieties
Retired: Resigned 1 Sep 1795 (allowed to sell commission)
Later service: Active in British intelligence in Europe
Awards and Honours: Knight of the Prussian Order of Military Merit Oct 1790
Residence: Ely Place, Camden, London
Died: London 26 Mar 1835
'There is little doubt that he should never have been tried; on his retirement he was continually employed on missions of secrecy by the British Government' – Lomax, 41st Ft., pp.367–8
Sources: ANCB; ANCD; ANCW; ARLI; DINB; WEOF; WOST; The House of Gordon; A History of the Services of the 41st (the Welch) Regiment

272. *William THOMAS (1795–1810)*
Born: County Dublin c.1760
Relations: Son of Vigors Thomas of Dublin and Mary (Gabbett); uncle of Lieutenant Colonel William Evans, 41st Foot; and Lieutenant Nicholas Evans, 41st Foot
Entry to Army: Volunteer in 55th Foot 1776; Ensign in 5th Foot 31 May 1777
Regimental Field Officer Promotions: Major in 41st Foot 21 Dec 1793 (vice Ellis); Lieutenant Colonel in 41st Foot 20 Aug 1795 (vice Gordon) by purchase
Brevets: Brevet Colonel 29 Apr 1802; Major General 25 Oct 1809; Lieutenant General 4 Jun 1814
Colonelcies: 3rd Ceylon Regiment 22 Feb 1810 (vice Baillie)
Early Service: Served in American War of Independence 1776–1778; served in West Indies 1778–1779
Service 1793–1815: Served in St Domingue 1794–1796; served in Irish rebellion 1798; served in British North America 1799–1800
Later Service: Lieutenant Governor of Tynemouth 6 Sep 1826
Retired: 28 Aug 1827
Residence: Westleigh, Devon
Died: Westleigh Jan 1848
Sources: ANCB; ANCD' ANCW; ARLI; PHIL; WEOF; A History of the Services of the 41st (the Welch) Regiment

273. *Coote MANNINGHAM (1795–1800)*

Born: Surrey 1765
Relations: Son of Charles Manningham of Thorpe and Ann (Hutchinson); nephew of Lieutenant General Sir Robert Boyd; brother-in-law of Charles Philips Yorke, Secretary at War and First Lord of the Admiralty
Entry to Army: Ensign in 39th Foot 5 Jun 1782
Regimental Field Officer Promotions: Major in 45th Foot 23 Feb 1791; Lieutenant Colonel in 41st Foot 1 Sep 1795
Brevets: Brevet Lieutenant Colonel 18 Apr 1794; Brevet Colonel 1 Jan 1798; Major General 1 Jan 1805
Colonelcies: Experimental Corps of Riflemen (later 95th Foot) 25 Aug 1800
Early Service: Served in Gibraltar 1782; served in West Indies
Service 1793–1815: ADC to King George III 1 Jan 1798; served in Ferrol 1800; commanded brigade in Peninsula Nov 1808 to Jan 1809
Awards & Honours: AGM (Cor)
Residence: Little Bookham, Surrey
Died: Of disease after Corunna campaign in Maidstone, Kent 26 Aug 1809
Sources: ANCB; ANCD; ARLI; CHAL; HALL; WEOF; WIKI

274. *Henry Patrick PROCTOR (1800–1815)*

Born: County Kilkenny 1764
Relations: Son of Surgeon Richard Proctor of Kilkenny, 5th Foot, and Anne (Gregory)
Entry to Army: Ensign in 43rd Foot 5 Apr 1781 by purchase
Regimental Field Officer Promotions: Major in 43rd Foot 13 May 1795; Lieutenant Colonel in 41st Foot 9 Oct 1800 (vice Manningham); removed from the regiment as a general officer 1815
Brevets: Brevet Lieutenant Colonel 1 Jan 1800; Brevet Colonel 25 Jul 1810; Brigadier General (North America) 8 Feb 1813; Major General 4 Jun 1813
Service 1793–1815: Commanded 1/41st Foot in Canada 1802–1813; suspended for six months following reverse at Moraviantown 1813
Residence: South Parade, Bath, Somerset
Died: Bath 31 Oct 1822
By all accounts an extremely capable battalion CO; but 'He (was)… merely a victim of circumstances, a brave officer but weak, capable enough except in moments of stress, a man of modest pretensions… The prisoner of events beyond his control, Procter dallied and equivocated until he was crushed.' – Pierre Berton
Sources: ANCB; ANCD; ARLI; PHIL; WEOF; A History of the Services of the 41st (the Welch) Regiment

275. *William EVANS (1812–1821)*

Born: County Dublin c.1769
Relations: Son of Captain Nicholas Evans of Baymount, 45th Foot, and Mary Anne (Thomas); nephew of Lieutenant Colonel William Thomas, 41st Foot; brother of Lieutenant Nicholas Evans, 41st Foot; nephew of Lieutenant William Evans, 41st Foot
Entry to Army: Ensign in 41st Foot 26 May 1795
Regimental Field Officer Promotions: Major in 41st Foot 14 Apr 1808 (vice Campbell); Lieutenant Colonel in 41st Foot 13 Aug 1812
Service 1793–1815: Commanded 2/41st Foot in British North America 1812–1813, POW at Moraviantown; commanded 1/41st Foot 1813–1814; commanded 41st Foot in France 1815
Later Service: Commanded 41st Foot 1815–1821
Retired: 26 Jul 1821
Residence: Swindon, Wiltshire
Died: Swindon 12 Jun 1843
Sources: ANCD; ANCW; GHLG; PHIL; WEOF; A History of the Services of the 41st (the Welch) Regiment

276. *Augustus Frederick WARBURTON (1813–1819)*

Born: County Cork 1783
Relations: Son of Rt Rev. Terence Charles Mongan Warburton, Lord Bishop of Cloyne, and Frances (Marston)
Entry to Army: Ensign in Buckinghamshire Militia; Ensign in 4th Foot 28 Aug 1799
Regimental Field Officer Promotions: Major in 91st Foot 18 Dec 1806 (vice Campbell) by purchase; Inspecting Field Officer of Militia in Canada 1 Aug 1811; Lieutenant Colonel in 41st Foot 30 Sep 1813; to half-pay of 85th Foot Oct 1814; Lieutenant Colonel in 85th Foot 30 Sep 1819 (vice Thornton) by exchange
Brevets: Brevet Colonel 27 May 1825
Service 1793–1815: Served in Helder 1799; served in Copenhagen 1807; served in Walcheren 1809; served in British North America 1811–1814, taken POW at Moravianstown 1813; commanded 2/41st Foot 1813–1814
Later Service: Acting Governor of Malta 1 Aug 1831 to 22 Oct 1831
Residence: Kill, Naas, County Kildare; Cheltenham, Gloucestershire
Died: Cheltenham 20 May 1836
Sources: ANCW; ARLI; PHIL; WEOF; WOST; WO 25/748; <https://warburton.one-name.net/>

Majors

277. *John Joynour ELLIS (1787–1793)*
Born: John Joynour in Gloucestershire c.1748, adopted Ellis surname when adopted by Governor Henry Ellis of Georgia in 1758
Relations: Son of John Joynour of Berkeley and Hannah (Poole); father of Colonel Sir Henry Walton Ellis, 23rd Foot
Entry to Army: Ensign in 18th Foot 6 Apr 1770 by purchase
Field Officer Promotions: Major in 93rd Foot 7 Feb 1780; Major in 89th Foot 16 Feb 1780; to half-pay of 89th Foot 17 Mar 1783; Major in 3rd Foot 6 Oct 1787; Major in 41st Foot 29 Dec 1787; Lieutenant Colonel in 23rd Foot 6 Dec 1793 (vice Balfour)
Brevets: Brevet Lieutenant Colonel 18 Nov 1790; Brevet Colonel 21 Aug 1795; Major General 18 Jun 1798
Early Service: Served in British North America 1770–1775
Residences: Kempsey, Worcestershire; Lansdown Place, Bath, Somerset
Died: Bath 30 Oct 1803
Sources: ANCW; DINB; Protecting the Empire's Frontier – Officers of the 18th (Royal Irish) Regiment of Foot During Its North American Service

278. *Thomas Auchmuty DANIEL (1795–1798)*
Born: County Westmeath c.1765
Relations: Son of John Daniel of Auburn and Dorcas (Auchmuty); brother of Captain Nicholas Charles Daniel, Royal Horse Guards
Entry to Army: Ensign in 36th Foot 30 Apr 1781 by purchase
Regimental Field Officer Promotions: Major in 41st Foot 1 Sep 1795 (vice Thomas)
Early Service: Served in East Indies
Service 1793–1815: Served in St Domingue 1795–1796, wounded at Fort Bizetton
Retired: 22 Sep 1798
Residence: Dublin, County Dublin
Died: Dublin Nov 1798
Sources: ARLI; GHLG

279. *John GREY (1795–1802)*
Born: Ireland c.1762
Entry to Army: Ensign in 28th Foot 11 Jun 1778 by purchase
Regimental Field Officer Promotions: Major in 41st Foot 30 Sep 1795; to half-pay of York Fencibles 3 Dec 1802 (vice Campbell) by exchange; rank stationary thereafter
Brevets: Brevet Lieutenant Colonel 1 Jan 1801
Early Service: Served aboard ship in West Indies 1782
Service 1793–1815: Major of Brigade to Duke of Kent in West Indies 1794; Assistant Deputy Adjutant General in St Domingue 1794–1796; Assistant Quartermaster General in Ireland 1799; commanded division of light infantry in Ireland 1803–1805
Died: 4 Jan 1837
Not to be confused with Lieutenant General John Grey of Ruddington, Nottinghamshire, who died the same month
Sources: ANCW; ARLI; UNSM (1837)

280. *Jasper GRANT (1798–1812)*
Born: County Cork 1762
Relations: Son of Thomas Grant of Kilmurry and Elizabeth (Campion)
Entry to Army: Ensign in 4th Foot 21 Sep 1781 by purchase
Regimental Field Officer Promotions: Major in 41st Foot 22 Sep 1798 (vice Daniel)
Brevets: Brevet Lieutenant Colonel 25 Sep 1803; Brevet Colonel 1 Jan 1812
Service 1793–1815: Served in West Indies 1796–1797; served in British North America 1800–1809; Lieutenant Governor of Carlisle 20 Feb 1812
Residence: Lismore, County Waterford
Died: Lismore 5 Mar 1812
Sources: ANCW; ARLI; DIIB

281. *Alexander CAMPBELL (1802–1808)*
Born: Lanarkshire c.1779
Relations: Son of John Campbell of Morriston, West Indian trader, and Marion (Murdoch); father of Captain John Campbell, 7th Dragoon Guards; father-in-law of General George Campbell, Bengal artillery
Entry to Army: Lieutenant in Independent Company 29 Jan 1794
Regimental Field Officer Promotions: Major in York Fencibles 20 Jul 1800; Major in 41st Foot 3 Dec 1802 (vice Grey) by exchange; Lieutenant Colonel in 20th Foot 25 Mar 1808 (vice Clephane) by purchase
Service 1793–1815: Served at Cape of Good Hope 1806; served in Peninsula Aug 1808 to Jan 1809, commanded 20th Foot at Vimeiro and Corunna
Retired: 8 Jun 1809
Residences: Abercromby Place, New Town, Edinburgh; Possil, Lanarkshire; Achnacroish, Mull, Argyllshire
Death: Craigie Hall, Glasgow, Lanarkshire 1849
Sources: ARLI; GHLG; WEOF

282. *George Hay, 8th Marquess of TWEEDDALE (1812–1814)*

Born: East Lothian 1787
Relations: Son of George Hay, 7th Marquess of Tweeddale and Lady Hannah (Maitland); brother of General Lord James Hay; Rear Admiral Lord John Hay RN; and Colonel Lord Edward George Hay; father of Colonel Arthur Hay, 9th Marquess of Tweeddale; William Montagu Hay, 10th Marquess of Tweeddale; Admiral of the Fleet Lord John Hay RN; and George Hay, Earl of Gifford; father-in-law of Lieutenant General Arthur Richard Wellesley, 2nd Duke of Wellington
Education: Royal High School, Edinburgh
Entry to Army: Ensign in 88th Foot 9 Aug 1804
Regimental Field Officer Promotions: Major in 41st Foot 14 May 1812 (vice Grant) by purchase; Lieutenant Colonel in 100th Foot 20 Jan 1814 (vice McPherson) by purchase
Brevets: Brevet Lieutenant Colonel 21 Jun 1813; Brevet Colonel 27 May 1825; Major-General 10 Jan 1837; Lieutenant General 9 Nov 1846; General 20 Jun 1854; Field Marshal 29 May 1875
Colonelcies: 30th Foot 7 Feb 1846 (vice Bradford); 42nd Foot 7 Mar 1862 (vice Douglas); 2nd Life Guards 9 Sep 1863 (vice Earl Beauchamp)
Service 1793–1815: Served on staff in Sicily 1806; served in Peninsula as ADC to Paget Jun to Oct 1809; Deputy Assistant Quartermaster General in Peninsula Nov 1809 to Jan 1811, wounded at Busaco, and again Jul 1811 to May 1812; Assistant Quartermaster General in Peninsula 14 May 1812 until Oct 1813, wounded at Vittoria; served in British North America 1814, wounded at Niagara
Later Service: Governors of the Presidency of Fort St George and Commander in Chief in Madras 24 Sep 1842 to 23 Feb 1848
Creations and Dignities: 8th Marquess of Tweeddale, 8th Earl of Gifford, and 8th Viscount Walden 9 Aug 1804
Awards and Honours: AGM (Vit); CB 4 Jun 1815; KT 22 May 1820; KCB 9 Nov 1862; GCB 13 Mar 1867
Residence: Yester, East Lothian
Died: Due to injuries sustained in house fire at Yester 10 Oct 1876
Sources: ANCB; ANCD; ARLI; CHAL; HALL; ODNB; WEOF; WOST

283. *Rt Hon. Robert Cotton St John Trefusis, 18th Baron CLINTON (1812–1814)*

Born: Cornwall 1787
Relations: Son of Robert George William Trefusis, 17th Baron Clinton, and Albertina Marianna (Gaulis); brother of Charles Rodolph Trefusis, 19th Baron Clinton; and Captain George Rolle Walpole Trefusis RN
Education: Harrow School
Entry to Army: Cornet in 16th Light Dragoons 21 Feb 1805
Regimental Field Officer Promotions: Major in 41st Foot 13 Aug 1812 (vice Evans); to half-pay of 8th Garrison Battalion 27 Jan 1814 (vice Tucker) by exchange
Brevets: Brevet Lieutenant Colonel 20 Aug 1812; Brevet Colonel 27 May 1825
Service 1793–1815: ADC to King George III; served in Peninsula Mar 1810 to Mar 1811; served in Peninsula Oct 1811 to Jul 1812 as extra ADC to Wellington; carried victory despatches for Salamanca 1812
Later Service: Lord Gentleman of the Bedchamber 22 Aug 1827
Creations and Dignities: 18th Baron Clinton of Trefusis and Heanton Satchville 25 Aug 1797
Residence: Heanton Satchville, Petrockstowe, Cornwall
Died: Florence, Italy 8 Oct 1832
Sources: ARLI; CHAL; DEPE; PHIL; WEOF; The Visitations of Cornwall

284. *Holt McKENZIE (1813)*

Born: Edinburgh 1765
Relations: Son of Dr Joshua McKenzie of Drumsleugh and Jean (McKenzie)
Entry to Army: Ensign in 26th Foot 13 Mar 1782 by purchase
Regimental Field Officer Promotions: Major in 41st Foot 7 Jan 1813
Brevets: Brevet Lieutenant Colonel 1 Jan 1813
Service 1793–1815: Served in British North America
Residence: Richmond Place, Edinburgh, Midlothian
Died: On passage to England 28 Aug 1813
Sources: ANCB; ANCD; ARLI; WEOF

285. *Richard O'Farrell FREND (1813–1821)*

Born: County Kildare 1777
Relations: Son of Captain Richard Frend, 1st Foot, and Eleanor (Sampson); brother of Captain Albert Frend, 55th Foot
Entry to Army: Ensign in 41st Foot 31 Dec 1793
Regimental Field Officer Promotions: Major in 41st Foot 9 Dec 1813 (vice McKenzie); Lieutenant Colonel in 41st Foot 8 Dec 1819
Brevets: Brevet Lieutenant Colonel 12 Aug 1819

Service 1793–1815: Served in West Indies 1794–1796; commanded 2/41st Foot 1812–1814
Retired: 3 May 1821
Residence: Portarlington, County Laois
Died: Portarlington 1 Nov
Sources: ANCB; ARLI; WEOF; A History of the Services of the 41st (the Welch) Regiment

286. *John Goulston Price TUCKER (1814–1815)*

Born: Bermuda 1777
Relations: Son of Henry Tucker of Port Royal and Frances (Bruere); brother of Lieutenant Colonel George James Bruere Tucker; Rear Admiral Thomas Tudor Tucker RN; Major Charlton Browne Tucker, 3rd Light Dragoons; and Captain Nathaniel Butterfield Tucker; father of Major General Auchmuty Tucker, Bengal service
Entry to Army: Ensign in 78th Foot 29 Apr 1795 by purchase
Regimental Field Officer Promotions: Major in 72nd Foot 13 Jan 1805 (vice McDougall) by purchase; Major in 8th Garrison Battalion 2 Oct 1808 (vice Waldegrave) by exchange; to half-pay of 8th Garrison Battalion 25 Jun 1810; Major in 41st Foot 27 Jan 1814 (vice Clinton) by exchange; Major in 5th West India Regiment 30 Nov 1815 (vice Godwin) by exchange; to half-pay of 5th West India Regiment 18 Jan 1816
Brevets: Brevet Lieutenant Colonel 16 Apr 1807; Brevet Colonel 4 Jun 1814
Service 1793–1815: Served in Cape of Good Hope 1795–1796; Served in East Indies 1796–1798; ADC and Assistant Quartermaster General in South America 1807; Assistant Adjutant General in Peninsula 24 Nov 1808 to Jan 1809; Deputy Adjutant General in Cape of Good Hope 1811; served on staff in British North America Oct 1814 to Jan 1815
Retired: Retaining rank 1827
Awards & Honours: AGM (Rol Vim)
Residence: Paris, Île-de-France, France
Died: Paris 9 Feb 1841
Sources: ANCB; ARLI; CHAL; PHIL; WEOF; WO 25/748

287. *Hon. Henry Cecil LOWTHER (1814)*

Born: Westmoreland 1790
Relations: Son of Lieutenant Colonel William Lowther, Earl of Lonsdale and Lady Augusta (Fane); grandson of John Fane, 9th Earl of Westmoreland; son-in-law of Philip Sherard, 5th Earl of Harborough
Education: Westminster School
Entry to Army: Cornet in 7th Light Dragoons 16 Jul 1807 by purchase
Regimental Field Officer Promotions: Major in 41st Foot 14 Apr 1814 (vice Tweeddale); Major in 10th Light Dragoons 12 Nov 1814 (vice Robarts); Lieutenant Colonel in 12th Foot 20 Apr 1817 (vice Stirke) by purchase; to half-pay of 12th Foot 25 Jan 1818; Lieutenant Colonel in 44th Foot 11 Jun 1830 by exchange
Service 1793–1815: Served in Peninsula Nov 1808 to Jan 1809; served in Peninsula Aug 1813 to Apr 1814
Retired: 25 Jun 1830
Political Career: MP (Westmoreland) 1812–1867, the 'father of the House'
Awards and Honours: MGSM (Sah&Ben Ort Toul)
Residences: Bruton Street, Mayfair, London; Barleythorpe Hall, Barleythorpe, Rutland; Lowther Castle, Penrith, Cumberland
Died: Barleythorpe Hall 4 Dec 1867
Sources: ANCB; ANCD; ARLI; BUPB; CHAL; GEMA (1868); HPON; PHIL; WEOF

288. *Sir Henry Thomas GODWIN (1815–1821)*

Born: London 1781
Relations: Son of Henry Godwin of Lambeth and Elizabeth (unk.)
Entry to Army: Ensign in 9th Foot 30 Oct 1799
Regimental Field Officer Promotions: Major in 5th West India Regiment 26 May 1814 (vice Arbuthnot) by purchase; Major in 41st Foot 30 Nov 1815 (vice Tucker) by exchange; Lieutenant Colonel in 41st Foot 26 Jul 1821 (vice Evans) by purchase; Lieutenant Colonel in 87th Foot 5 Apr 1829 (vice Chambers) by exchange; to half-pay of 87th Foot 25 Jun 1827
Brevets: Brevet Colonel 10 Jan 1837; Major General 9 Nov 1846
Colonelcies: 20th Foot 25 Oct 1853 (vice Chalmers)
Service 1793–1815: Served in Ferrol 1800; served in Hanover 1805; served in Peninsula with 2/9th Foot Nov 1808 to Jun 1809; served in Gibraltar Jul 1809 to Sep 1811, wounded at Barrosa
Later Service: Served in Madras and Burma; commanded division in Bengal 1850; Commander in Chief in Second Burma War 1852–1853
Awards and Honours: KCB 9 Dec 1853
Residence: Pall Mall, St James's, London
Died: Simla, Bengal 26 Oct 1853
Died before knowing that he had been awarded colonelcy of the 20th Foot the day before, and awarded the KCB before London knew of his passing
Sources: ANCB; ANCW; CHAL; DINB; PHIL;

WEOF; A History of the Services of the 41st (the Welch) Regiment

Selected Regimental Histories

Lomax, David Alexander Napier, *A History of the Services of the 41st (the Welch) Regiment, (now 1st Battalion the Welch Regiment) from Its Formation, in 1719, to 1895* (Devonport: Hiorns & Miller, 1899)

Regimental Museum

The Royal Welsh Regimental Museum, The Barracks, The Watton, Brecon, Breconshire

---

42nd Regiment of Foot

Secondary Title:	Royal Highland
Nicknames:	The Black Watch The Forty-Twa The Black Jocks
Jacket:	Red
Facings:	Dark blue
Badge:	The star of the Order of the Thistle
Motto:	*Nemo me impune lacessit* (No one assaults me with impunity)

Regimental Lineage, 42nd Regiment of Foot

1739: Raised by Earl of Crawford from independent companies (originally raised for crime-watching in 1725) as 43rd Highland Regiment of Foot

1749: Re-numbered 42nd Highland Regiment of Foot

1758: 42nd (Royal Highland) Regiment of Foot

1803: Jul – 2nd Battalion formed in Perth

1814: Oct – 2nd Battalion disbanded in Aberdeen

1861: 42nd (Royal Highland) Regiment of Foot, The Black Watch

1881: 1st Battalion, The Black Watch (Royal Highlanders) (on amalgamation with the 73rd (Perthshire) Regiment of Foot)

1931: The Black Watch (Royal Highland Regiment)

2006: The Black Watch, 3rd Battalion, Royal Regiment of Scotland (on amalgamation with The Royal Scots (The Royal Regiment), The King's Own Scottish Borderers, The Royal Highland Fusiliers (Princess Margaret's Own Glasgow and Ayrshire Regiment), The Highlanders (Seaforth, Gordons and Camerons) and The Argyll and Sutherland Highlanders (Princess Louise's))

Service History, 1st Battalion 42nd Regiment of Foot

1793: Fort George, Aberdeen and Dundee; Apr – Aberdeen, Dundee and Montrose; Jun – Edinburgh Castle; Jul – Tynemouth; to Flanders; Oct – Menin; Nieuwpoort; to England; Portsmouth; Nov – to West Indies, orders rescinded; Guernsey

1794: Portsmouth and Newport; Jun – to Flanders; Ostend; Alost; Oct – Nijmegen; Dec – Tuyl; line of River Waal

1795: Geldermalsen; Feb – retreat to Bremen; Apr – Bremen; to England – Harwich; May – Chelmsford; Danbury; Jun – Royston; received red hackle; Jul – Portsmouth; Aug – Nursling camp; Nov – Portsmouth; to West Indies; storms in channel – some ships returned to port

1796: Jan – five companies in Gibraltar; Feb – other five companies reach Barbados; Apr – five companies in St Lucia; Morne Chabot; Morne Fortunée; Jun – five companies in St Vincent; Vigie

1797: Five companies in Gibraltar, five companies in St Vincent; Feb – five companies in St Christopher; Apr – five companies in Puerto Rico; Truxillo raid; Jun – five West Indies companies to England; Jul – five West Indies companies in Portsmouth; Sep – Hilsea; to Gibraltar; Dec – battalion reunited in Gibraltar

1798:	Gibraltar; Nov – to Minorca; Citadella
1799:	Minorca; Jun – to Genoa; Minorca; Sep – Gibraltar
1800:	Gibraltar; Oct – Cadiz; Nov – Malta; to Egypt
1801:	Bay of Marmorice [Marmaris]; Mar – EGYPT; Aboukir; Mandora; Alexandria; Jun – Cairo; Sep – to England; Dec – Portsmouth
1802:	Winchester; May – Ashford; to Scotland; Jun – Carlisle; Jul – Edinburgh Castle
1803:	Edinburgh Castle; received new colours; Apr – Leith; Jul – Weeley barracks
1804:	Weeley barracks; Sep – Lexden camp; Nov – Weeley
1805:	Weeley barracks; Oct – Hilsea; Plymouth; to Gibraltar
1806:	Gibraltar
1807:	Gibraltar
1808:	Gibraltar; Aug – to PENINSULA; Sep – Lisbon; Oct – advance into Spain; Castelo Branco; Ciudad Rodrigo; Nov – Salamanca; Dec – Mayorga; Astorga
1809:	Retreat to Corunna; CORUNNA; to England – Portsmouth; Shorncliffe; Jul – to Walcheren; Sep – Dover; Canterbury
1810:	Canterbury; Jul – to Scotland; Aug – Musselburgh
1811:	Musselburgh; Aug – to England; Gravesend; Sep – Lewes
1812:	Lewes; Apr – Portsmouth; to Peninsula; Lisbon; joined field army; May – Castelo de Vide; received fit men from 2/42nd; Jun – San Cristóbal de la Cuesta; Jul – Fort St Michel; SALAMANCA; Valladolid; Aug – Olmedo; Sep – siege of Burgos; Oct – Dueñas; Nov – Junça; Dec – Seia
1813:	Seia; Apr – São Romão; May – Malhadas; Jun – Vittoria; Aug – PYRENEES; Sorauren; Oct – Erratzu; Nov – NIVELLE; Ustaritz; Dec – NIVE; Bayonne
1814:	Bayonne; Feb – ORTHEZ; Apr – TOULOUSE; Auch; Jun – Bordeaux; to Ireland; Cork; Jul – Naas; Aug – Kilkenny
1815:	Kilkenny; May – Cork; to Belgium; Brussels; Jun – Quatre Bras; WATERLOO; Jul – Paris; Allied Army of Occupation; Dec – to England

Service History, 2nd Battalion 42nd Regiment of Foot

1803:	Jul – formed in Perth; Oct – Fort George; Dec – Weeley Barracks
1804:	Weeley Barracks; Aug – Lexden Heath; Oct – Liverpool; to Ireland; Nov – Athlone; Dec – Tuam
1805:	Tuam; May – Loughrea; Aug – Curragh camp; Oct – Birr; Nov – Ballinasloe
1806:	Ballinasloe; Mar – Tuam; Apr – Birr; May – Tuam
1807:	Dundalk; Feb – Donaghadee; to Scotland – Portpatrick; Glasgow; Mar – Fort George
1808:	Fort George; May – Perth; Portpatrick; to Ireland; Jun – Armagh; Dec – Newry
1809:	Dublin; Jun – Cork; to Peninsula; Lisbon; Jul – to Field Army; Aug – Guadiana; Nov – Arroyo de San Serván; Dec – Elvas
1810:	Mangualde; Mar – Cassurrães; May – Linhares; Jul – Minhocal; Aug – Baraçal; Sep – Santa Comba Dão; BUSACO; Oct – Malga; Nov – Cartaxo; Dec – Ribeira de São João
1811:	Ribeira de São João; Mar – Foz de Arouce; Sarzedas; Mar – Aldeia da Ponte; May – FUENTES D'ONORO; St Olaia; Jul – Portalegre; Aug – Santo Estevão; Sep – Nave de Haver; Oct – Carnicães; Dec – Escarigo
1812:	Ciudad Rodrigo; Fuentes de Oñoro; Feb – Pago de San Clemente; Mar – Fuente del Maestre; Apr – Benquerencia; May – Castelo de Vide; fit men into 1/42nd, cadre home; Lisbon; to England; Jul – Portsmouth; to Scotland; Aug – Inverness
1813:	Inverness
1814:	Aberdeen; Aug – ordered to Ireland, did not embark; Oct – disbanded in Aberdeen

Establishments, 1st Battalion 42nd Regiment of Foot

Year	Subunits	Field Off	Off/ Staff	Sjts	Mus	Corp/ Pvts	Total
Dec 1792	10co	3	32	22	12	430	499
Jan 1793	10co	3	32	32	22	600	689
Dec 1793	10co	3	32	42	22	850	949
Dec 1795	10co+2r	5	51	62	30	1,010	1,158
Dec 1797	10co	5	51	53	22	1,000	1,131
Jun 1802	10co	5	33	34	22	750	844
May 1803	10co	5	36	34	22	750	847
Jul 1803	10co	5	36	54	22	1,000	1,117
Dec 1804	10co	5	36	44	22	800	907
Aug 1805	10co	5	46	54	22	1,000	1,127
Dec 1806	10co	4	46	54	22	1,000	1,126
Dec 1808	10co	4	36	44	22	800	906
Dec 1811	10co	4	46	55	22	1,000	1,127
Dec 1812	10co	4	46	65	22	1,200	1,337
Jul 1814	10co	5	46	65	22	1,200	1,338
Dec 1815	10co	4	46	35	22	600	707

Establishments, 2nd Battalion 42nd Regiment of Foot

Year	Subunits	Field Off	Off/ Staff	Sjts	Mus	Corp/ Pvts	Total
Oct 1803	10co	3	35	53	22	1,000	1,113
Dec 1804	10co	3	36	43	22	800	904
Feb 1807	10co	3	35	23	22	400	483
Dec 1807	10co	3	35	43	22	800	903
Jun 1809	10co	3	36	44	22	800	905
Dec 1809	10co	3	36	43	22	800	904
Dec 1810	10co	3	35	33	22	600	693
Dec 1811	10co	3	35	34	22	600	694
Dec 1812	10co	3	35	25	22	400	485

Service Statistics, 42nd Regiment of Foot

	Lieutenant Colonels	Majors
Number of officers in period 1793–1815	9	22
Average age on appointment to substantive rank	42.5	34
Average time in rank in regiment (years)	8	4
Total field officers by nationality	25 S / 1 I	
Demographics of other ranks 1807	2/42nd: 95% S / 4% I / 1% E	
Demographics of other ranks 1809	1/42nd: 84% S / 8% E / 8% I	
Months of overseas service 1793–1815	1/42nd: 146 2/42nd: 37	

Significant Militia/Volunteer Intakes

1799: Aberdeenshire
1805: Suffolk, Stirlingshire
1808: Inverness-shire, Perthshire
1809: Argyllshire
1811: Edinburgh, Inverness-shire

Regimental Colonels

289. *Sir Hector MUNRO (1787–1806)*
Born: Ross-shire 1726
Relations: Son of Hugh Munro, 7th Laird of Novar, merchant, and Isobel (Gordon); father of Ensign Hector Sutherland Munro, Madras service
Entry to Army: Ensign in Loudon's Regiment 28 May 1747
Regimental Field Officer Promotions: Major in 89th Foot 13 Oct 1759; to half-pay of 89th Foot 1765
Brevets: Brevet Lieutenant Colonel 8 Oct 1765; Brevet Colonel 19 Aug 1777; Major General (East Indies) 9 May 1777; Major General 20 Nov 1782; Lieutenant General 12 Oct 1793; General 1 Jan 1798
Colonelcies: 42nd Foot 1 Jun 1787 (vice Murray)
Early Service: Served in Jacobite rebellion 1746; served in East Indies 1761–1765; Commander in Chief in Madras 1777–1780
Political Career: MP (Inverness Burghs) 1768–1802
Awards and Honours: KB 23 Mar 1779
Residence: Novar House, near Evanton, Ross-shire
Died: Novar House 27 Dec 1805
Sources: ARLI; DINB; HPON; ODNB; WEOF

290. *George Gordon, 9th Marquess of HUNTLY (1806–1820)*
Born: Edinburgh 1761
Relations: Son of Charles Gordon, 4th Earl of Aboyne, and Lady Margaret (Stewart); half-brother of Major Lord Douglas Gordon-Hallyburton, 1st Foot Guards; father of Charles Gordon, 10th Marquess of Huntly; Admiral Lord John Frederick Gordon-Hallyburton RN; Major Lord Henry Gordon, Bengal service; and Lieutenant Colonel Francis Arthur Gordon, 1st Life Guards
Education: Eton College
Entry to Army: Ensign in 1st Foot Guards 2 Sep 1777 by purchase
Regimental Field Officer Promotions: Major in Independent Company 12 Mar 1783; to half-pay 1784; Lieutenant Colonel in 35th Foot 9 Apr 1789 (vice Shee) by purchase; Captain and Lieutenant Colonel in Coldstream Foot Guards 15 Jun 1789 (vice Lennox) by exchange
Colonelcies: 92nd Foot 3 May 1796; 42nd Foot 3 Jan 1806 (vice Munro)
Militia Career: Colonel of Aberdeenshire Militia 23 May 1798
Political Career: House of Lords 1807–1819
Creations and Dignities: Lord Strathavon 1761; Earl of Aboyne 28 Dec 1794; Baron Meldrum of Morven 11 Aug 1815; 9th Marquess of Huntly 28 May 1836
Awards and Honours: KT 10 May 1827
Residence: Aboyne Castle, near Aboyne, Aberdeenshire; Chapel Street, Grosvenor Square, London
Died: London 17 Jun 1853
Sources: ANCB; ANCD; ARLI; DINB; ODNB; WEOF

Lieutenant Colonels

291. *Charles GRAHAM (1782–1796)*
Born: Inverness-shire c.1743
Relations: Son of Lieutenant Colonel Gordon Graham of Drynie, 42nd Foot, and unk. (McKenzie); nephew of Colonel Mungo Graham, Scotch Brigade
Entry to Army: Ensign in 42nd Foot 17 Sep 1760 by purchase
Regimental Field Officer Promotions: Major in 42nd Foot 25 Aug 1778 by purchase; Lieutenant Colonel in 42nd Foot 28 Apr 1782
Brevets: Brevet Colonel 12 Oct 1793; Major General 26 Feb 1795
Colonelcies: 5th West India Regiment 30 Nov 1796 (vice Howe)
Early Service: Commanded 42nd Foot in latter stages of American War of Independence
Service 1793–1815: Commanded a brigade and second in command to Abercromby in West Indies 1796; commanded southern district in Ireland 1800
Died: Cork, County Cork Jul 1800
Sources: ANCW; ARLI; Sketches of the Character, Manners, and Present State of the Highlanders of Scotland

292. *William DICKSON (1795–1808)*
Born: Peeblesshire 1748
Relations: Son of David Dickson of Kilbucho and Anna (Gillon)
Entry to Army: Volunteer in British North America; Ensign in 42nd Foot 15 May 1780
Regimental Field Officer Promotions: Major in 42nd Foot 14 Jan 1795 (vice Dalrymple); Lieutenant Colonel in 42nd Foot 1 Sep 1795 by purchase
Brevets: Brevet Major 1 Mar 1794; Brevet Colonel 25 Sep 1803
Early Service: Served in American War of Independence
Service 1793–1815: Served in Egypt 1801; commanded 42nd Foot and wounded at Mandora; Lieutenant Governor of Cork 8 May 1808
Retired: Retaining rank 3 Mar 1808
Political Career: MP (Linlithgow Burghs) 1802–1806
Awards and Honours: KCt (Ottoman) 1802

Residence: Kilbucho Castle, Kilbucho, Peeblesshire
Died: Edinburgh, Midlothian 18 May 1815
Sources: ANCB; ANCD; ARLI; HPON

293. *James STEWART (1796–1804)*

Born: Kirkcudbrightshire 1758
Relations: Son of Charles Stewart of Shambelly and Ann (Hay)
Entry to Army: Ensign in 5th Foot 15 Aug 1775 by purchase
Regimental Field Officer Promotions: Major in 42nd Foot 21 Oct 1795; Lieutenant Colonel in 42nd Foot 14 Dec 1796 (vice Graham)
Early Service: Served in American War of Independence 1777, badly wounded at Piscataway
Service 1793–1815: Served in Egypt 1801, wounded at Aboukir; commanded 42nd Foot at Alexandria 1801
Retired: 19 Sep 1804
Later Service: Inspector of Volunteers in Aberdeen 17805
Awards and Honours: KCt (Ottoman) 1802
Residence: Moffat, Dumfriesshire
Died: Moffat 9 Aug 1819
Sources: ANCB; ANCD; ARLI; WEOF; History of the lands and their owners in Galloway

294. *James STIRLING (1804–1814)*

Born: [spec.] Lanarkshire c.1756
Relations: Father of Captain James Stirling, 42nd Foot; father-in-law of Paymaster John Home, 42nd Foot
Entry to Army: Volunteer in British North America 1776; Ensign in 42nd Foot 22 Apr 1777 by purchase
Regimental Field Officer Promotions: Major in 42nd Foot 14 Dec 1796 (vice Stewart); Lieutenant Colonel in 42nd Foot 7 Sep 1804; removed from the regiment as a general officer 1814
Brevets: Brevet Lieutenant Colonel 11 May 1802; Brevet Colonel 4 Jun 1811; Major General 4 Jun 1814; rank stationary thereafter
Early Service: Served in American war of Independence 1776–1783; served in British North America 1783–1789
Service 1793–1815: Served in Flanders 1793–1795; served in Minorca 1798; served in Egypt 1801, wounded at Alexandria; commanded 1/42nd Foot in Peninsula Aug 1808 to Jan 1809; served in Walcheren 1809; served in Peninsula Apr to Nov 1812; commanded brigade in 6th Division in Peninsula Nov 1812 to Jul 1813; commanded brigade in 1st Division in Peninsula Sep and Oct 1813
Later Service: Lieutenant Governor of Cork 8 Jun 1815
Awards and Honours: KCt (Ottoman) 1802; AGM (Cor Sal Pyr)
Residence: Eskbank, Dalkeith, Midlothian
Died: Eskbank 12 Dec 1834
Sources: ANCD; ARLI; CHAL; PHIL; WEMR; WEOF

295. *Rt Hon. Robert Walter STUART, 11th Baron Blantyre (1804–1813)*

Born: Edinburgh 1777
Relations: Son of Alexander Stuart, 10th Lord Blantyre and Catherine (Lindsay); brother of Lieutenant General Hon. William Stuart, 1st Foot Guards; father of Lieutenant and Captain Charles Walter Stuart, 12th Lord Blantyre, Grenadier Guards
Entry to Army: Ensign in 3rd Foot Guards 13 Mar 1795 by purchase
Regimental Field Officer Promotions: Major in 17th Light Dragoons 7 Apr 1804 (vice Jephson) by purchase; Lieutenant Colonel in 42nd Foot 19 Sep 1804 (vice Stewart) by purchase; to half-pay of 8th Garrison Battalion 6 May 1813
Brevets: Brevet Colonel 4 Jun 1813
Service 1793–1815: Served in Portugal 1796–1798; served at Helder 1799; ADC to John Stuart in Egypt 1801; Assistant Adjutant General in Copenhagen 1807; commanded 1/42nd Highlanders in Peninsula Jul 1809 to Apr 1812; commanded brigade in 1st Division in Peninsula Aug 1810 to Jan 1812
Creations and Dignities: 11th Baron Blantyre 5 Nov 1783
Awards and Honours: AGM (FDO); CB 4 Jun 1815
Residence: Erskine House, Erskine, Renfrewshire
Died: Killed by a musket-ball during a street riot in Brussels 22 Sep 1830
Sources: ANCB; ANCD; ARLI; CHAL; PHIL; WEOF; WO 25/744

296. *John FARQUHARSON (1808–1812)*

Born: Aberdeenshire 1753
Relations: Son of Alexander Farquharson of Crathie and Margaret (Fisher); brother of Lieutenant Charles Farquharson, Independent Company
Entry to Army: Lieutenant in 77th Foot 30 Dec 1777
Regimental Field Officer Promotions: Major in 8th Garrison Battalion 16 Jul 1803; Major in 42nd Foot 9 Sep 1803; Lieutenant Colonel in 42nd Foot 3 Mar 1808 (vice Dickson) by purchase
Service 1793–1815: Served in Flanders 1793–1795; served in West Indies 1795–1797; served in Egypt

1801; Assistant Adjutant General in Northern District 1 Nov 1804; served in Peninsula Aug 1808 to Jan 1809; Assistant Adjutant General in Walcheren 1809; Assistant Adjutant General at Horse Guards 1810; Lieutenant Governor of Carlisle 16 Apr 1812
Retired: Retaining rank 16 Apr 1812
Awards and Honours: KCt (Ottoman) 1802
Residence: Newington, Edinburgh, Midlothian
Died: Edinburgh 3 Nov 1835
Sources: ANCB; ANCD; ARLI; CHAL; WEOF; WO 25/745; <https://www.findagrave.com/memorial/146596718/john-farquharson>

297. *Sir Robert MACARA (1812–1815)*
Born: Perthshire 1759
Relations: Son of Rev. Duncan Macara of Fortingall and Susanna (Robertson)
Education: United College, University of St Andrews
Entry to Army: Ensign in 95th Foot 17 Aug 1782 by purchase
Regimental Field Officer Promotions: Major in 42nd Foot 14 Nov 1805 (vice Grant) by purchase; Lieutenant Colonel in 42nd Foot 16 Apr 1812 (vice Farquharson) by purchase
Brevets: Brevet Lieutenant Colonel 1 Jan 1812
Early Service: Ship's surgeon in EIC service 1785–1803
Service 1793–1815: Served in Peninsula Jul and Aug 1809; commanded 1/42nd Foot in Peninsula Apr 1812 to Apr 1814, wounded at Toulouse; commanded 1/42nd Foot at Quatre Bras 1815
Awards and Honours: AGM (Pyr Nlle Niv Ort Toul); KCB 2 Jan 1815; WatM 23 Apr 1816
Died: Killed by Lancers whilst being carried wounded from the field at Quatre Bras 16 Jun 1815
Sources: ANCW; CHAL; DALT; WEMR; WEOF; <https://pdfs.semanticscholar.org/359b/0f62d8d6a262c334c376d762850d49a772b8.pdf>

298. *Sir George Alexander William LEITH, 2nd Bt (1813–1814)*
Born: Aberdeenshire 1766
Relations: Son of Lieutenant Colonel Sir Alexander Leith, 1st Bt, 88th Foot and Margaret (Hay)
Entry to Army: Ensign in 88th Foot 12 Oct 1779
Regimental Field Officer Promotions: Major in 17th Foot 14 May 1804 (vice Thorley); Lieutenant Colonel in 2nd West India Regiment 13 Jun 1805; to half-pay of 8th Garrison Battalion 25 Oct 1806 (vice Irving) by exchange; Lieutenant Colonel in 42nd Foot 6 May 1813 (vice Blantyre) by exchange; to half-pay of 42nd Foot 1814
Brevets: Brevet Major 1 Jan 1800; Brevet Colonel 4 Jun 1813; Major General 12 Aug 1819
Colonelcies: 9th Royal Veteran Battalion 20 Nov 1819
Early Service: Served in Jamaica 1779–1781; served in British East Indies 1786–1793
Service 1793–1815: Served in British East Indies 1793–1804; ADC to Governor General in British East Indies 1793; Lieutenant Governor of Penang 20 Apr 1800 to 1 Jan 1804; Assistant Adjutant General in Ireland 1806–1809
Creations and Dignities: 2nd Baronet of Burgh St Peter 3 Oct 1780
Residences: Melville Street, Edinburgh, Midlothian; Sanbant, Norfolk; Burgh St Peter, Norfolk
Died: London 25 Jan 1842
Sources: ANCB; ARLI; DEBA; WEOF; WOST; WO 25/746

299. *Sir Robert Henry DICK (1815–1828)*
Born: Perthshire 1787
Relations: Son of Dr William Dick of Tullimet, Bengal service, and Charlotte (MacLaren); nephew of General Alexander Dick
Entry to Army: Ensign in 75th Foot 22 Nov 1800
Regimental Field Officer Promotions: Major in Bradshaw's Levy 24 May 1808; Major in 42nd Foot 14 Jul 1808 (vice Johnston) by exchange; Lieutenant Colonel in 42nd Foot 18 Jun 1815 (vice Macara); to half-pay unattached 25 Nov 1828
Brevets: Brevet Lieutenant Colonel 8 Oct 1812; Brevet Colonel 27 May 1825; Major General 10 Jan 1837
Colonelcies: 73rd Foot 10 Jun 1845 (vice Harris)
Service 1793–1815: Served in Calabria and Sicily 1806; served in Egypt 1807; served in Peninsula Jul 1809 to Dec 1812; commanded 1/42nd Foot and wounded at Waterloo 1815
Later Service: ADC to King George IV 1825; acting Commander in Chief in Madras 1841–1842; commanded division in 3rd Sikh War 1846
Awards and Honours: AGM (Bus FDO Sal); CB 4 Jun 1815; KMT (Habsburg) 1816; KSW (Russia) 1816; KCH 12 Aug 1832; KCB 19 Jul 1838
Residence: Tulliemet, Perthshire
Died: Killed in action at Sobraon 10 Feb 1846
Sources: ANCW; CHAL; DALT; DINB; PHIL; WEOF; WO 25/745; List of Inscriptions on Tombs & Monuments in Madras, Vol 1

Majors

300. *George DALRYMPLE (1791–1794)*

Born: Berkshire 1757
Relations: Son of Colonel Campbell Dalrymple, Governor of Grenada, and Margaret (Douglas); brother of Major Hew Dalrymple, Champagné's Regiment
Entry to Army: Ensign in 42nd Foot 12 Jul 1773
Regimental Field Officer Promotions: Major in 42nd Foot 16 Mar 1791.(vice Home) by purchase; Lieutenant Colonel in 19th Foot 31 Dec 1794 (vice Coates)
Brevets: Brevet Colonel 1 Jan 1801
Early Service: Served in American War of Independence
Service 1793–1815: Commanded 42nd Foot in descent on French coast 1793; commanded 19th Foot 1794–1803
Residence: North Berwick, East Lothian
Died: North Berwick 19 Jan 1804
Sources: ANCW; ARLI; WEOF

301. *William Hector MUNRO (1794)*

Born: Stirlingshire 1769
Relations: Son of Dr. George Munro of Auchinbowie and Jane (McComish); brother of Captain George Munro, 41st Foot; father of Captain Edmund Augustus Munro, Bengal service
Entry to Army: Ensign in 51st Foot 30 Jul 1778 by purchase
Regimental Field Officer Promotions: Major in 42nd Foot 2 Sep 1794 by purchase; Lieutenant Colonel in Caithness Legion 15 Nov 1794; to half-pay1802; Inspecting Field Officer of Volunteers Mar 1804
Brevets: Brevet Colonel 1 Jan 1801; Brigadier General (home staff); Major General 25 Apr 1808; Lieutenant General 4 Jun 1813
Early Service: Served in Minorca
Service 1793–1815: Served in Flanders 1794; acting Governor of Trinidad 25 Apr 1811 to 14 Jun 1813 (vice Tolley)
Residence: Edmondsham House, near Wimborne Minster, Dorset
Died: Bath, Somerset 3 Jan 1821
Sources: ANCW; ARLI; PHIL; WEOF; WOST; The Monros of Auchinbowie and Cognate Families

302. *Robert Pigot CHRYSTIE (1795–1796)*

Born: London 1764
Relations: Son of Captain Robert Christie, army agent in London
Entry to Army: Ensign in 24th Foot 12 Apr 1783
Regimental Field Officer Promotions: Major in 42nd Foot 1 Sep 1795
Brevets: Brevet Major 6 May 1795
Service 1793–1815: Served in West Indies 1795–1796
Died: Of fever in Barbados 23 Jun 1796
Sources: ARLI; GEMA (1796); WEOF; Scottish Soldiers in Colonial America; Caledonian Mercury 6 Aug 1796

303. *Alexander STEWART (1796–1804)*

Born: Perthshire 1756
Relations: Son of Robert Stewart of Cloichfoldich and Susan (Fleming)
Entry to Army: Ensign in 42nd Foot 28 Aug 1775 by purchase
Regimental Field Officer Promotions: Major in 42nd Foot 24 Jun 1796 (vice Christie)
Brevets: Brevet Lieutenant Colonel 24 Jan 1797
Service 1793–1815: Served in Egypt 1801; commanded 42nd Foot after Aboukir
Awards and Honours: KCt (Ottoman) 1802
Retired: 7 Sep 1804
Residence: Cloichfoldich, Perthshire
Died: Cloichfoldich 23 May 1808
Sources: ARLI; GEMA (1808); <https://breadalbane-heritage.org.uk/projects/killiechassie-burial-ground/lineage-of-stewarts-of-fothergill/descendants-of-rev-robert-stewart-of-killiechassie-and-pitcastle/>

304. *Archibald Argyle CAMPBELL (1803–1809)*

Born: New York c.1768
Relations: Son of Captain Duncan Campbell, 84th Foot, and Eleanor (Baker); brother of Lieutenant Colonel John Campbell, 33rd Foot; brother-in-law of Lieutenant General Sir James Hay
Entry to Army: Lieutenant in 42nd Foot 26 Mar 1792
Regimental Field Officer Promotions: Major in 42nd Foot 9 Jul 1803
Service 1793–1815: Served in in Egypt 1801, wounded at Mandora; served in Peninsula Aug 1808 to Jan 1809
Awards and Honours: KCt (Ottoman) 1802
Died: Of wounds in Plymouth 27 Jan 1809
Sources: ANCB; ANCW; ARLI; CHAL; HALL; WEOF

305. *Charles MACQUARIE (1804–1811)*

Born: Isle of Mull 1771
Relations: Son of Lachlan Macquarie of Ulva and Margaret Maclaine; Brother of Major General Lachlan Macquarie

Entry to Army: Lieutenant in 116th Foot 1795
Regimental Field Officer Promotions: Major in 42nd Foot 7 Sep 1804 (vice Stirling)
Brevets: Brevet Lieutenant Colonel 25 Jul 1810
Service 1793–1815: Served in Egypt 1801, wounded at Aboukir; served in Peninsula Aug 1808 to Jan 1809; served in Walcheren 1809
Retired: 2 May 1811
Awards and Honours: KCt (Ottoman) 1802
Residence: Ulva, Isle of Mull
Died: Ulva 27 Mar 1835
Sources: ANCB; ANCD; ANCW; CHAL; WEMR; WEOF; <https://www.jbhawkinsantiques.com/wp-content/uploads/2022/05/Macquarie-Part-III.pdf>

306. *James GRANT (1804–1805)*
Born: Edinburgh 1770
Relations: Son of Gregor Grant of Abernethy and Margaret (Urquhart)
Entry to Army: Lieutenant in 97th Foot 17 Jul 1795
Regimental Field Officer Promotions: Major in 42nd Foot 7 Sep 1804 (vice Stewart) by purchase
Retired: 14 Nov 1805
Residence: Brixton Hill, Surrey
Died: Brixton Hill May 1829
Sources: ANCB; ANCD; ANCW; WEOF

307. *Thomas JOHNSTON (1808)*
Born: Dumfries-shire 1770
Relations: Son of Alexander Johnston of Kirkpatrick-Fleming
Entry to Army: Ensign in 34th Foot 24 Oct 1795
Field Officer Promotions: Major in 42nd Foot 3 Mar 1808 (vice Farquharson) by purchase; to Major on half-pay of Bradshaw's Levy 14 Jul 1808; Major in 27th Foot 21 Jan 1813 (vice Knight-Erskine) by exchange
Service 1793–1815: Served in Peninsula with 3/27th Foot Aug to Nov 1813
Residences: Newport, Isle of Wight; Springfield, Dumfries-shire
Died: Killed in action at Nivelle 10 Nov 1813
According to will documents, this officer was a naval surgeon before joining the army. He may also have been a bigamist!
Sources: ANCW; CHAL; HALL; WEMR

308. *Hamilton ROSE (1809–1811)*
Born: Wigtownshire 1776
Relations: Son of Rev. John Rose of Leswalt
Entry to Army: Ensign in 78th Foot 2 May 1794
Regimental Field Officer Promotions: Major in 42nd Foot 9 Feb 1809 (vice Campbell)
Service 1793–1815: Served in Flanders 1794–1795; served in Minorca 1798; served in Egypt 1801, wounded at Alexandria; served in Peninsula Aug 1808 to Jan 1809; served in Peninsula Jul 1809 to Sep 1811
Awards and Honours: KCt (Ottoman) 1802
Died: Lisbon 5 Oct 1811
Sources: ARLI; CHAL; HALL; WEOF; WO 25/748

309. *James Jonathan FRASER (1810)*
Born: London 1775
Relations: Son of Angus Fraser, Fort Major of Plymouth, and Susanna (Charnly)
Entry to Army: Ensign in 42nd Foot 7 Jun 1793
Regimental Field Officer Promotions: Major in 42nd Foot 4 Jan 1810; Major in 7th Royal Veteran Battalion 27 Dec 1810
Service 1793–1815: Served in Flanders 1794–1796; served in West Indies 1795–1796; served in Gibraltar 1804–1807, and 1810–1822; Town Major of Gibraltar 13 Mar 1814 to 4 Jul 1822
Retired: Receiving full pay 17 Aug 1814
Residence: Jemappes, Hainault, Belgium
Died: Jemappes 26 Jun 1842
Sources: ANCB; ANCD; ANCW; ARLI; PHIL; WEOF; The Annual Biography: Being Lives of Eminent or Remarkable Persons, who Have Died Within the Year 1842

310. *William MUNRO (1811)*
Born: Argyllshire c.1769
Relations: Son of Duncan Munro of Inveraray and Mary (Sinclair)
Entry to Army: Ensign in 91st Foot 12 Feb 1794
Regimental Field Officer Promotions: Major in 42nd Foot 2 May 1811 (vice Macquarie) by purchase; to half-pay of Royal Regiment of Malta 30 May 1811 (vice Cowell) by exchange
Brevets: Brevet Lieutenant Colonel 12 Aug 1819
Residence: Inveraray, Argyllshire
Died: Stamford Baron, Northamptonshire 9 Feb 1828
Sources: ANCW; EDMA (1842); WEOF

311. *William COWELL (1811–1826)*
Born: County Kildare 1778
Relations: Son of George Cowell of Harristown and Amelia (White); brother of Major George Cowell, 76th Foot; Captain James Gifford Cowell, 71st Foot; Lieutenant Colonel Henry Clayton Cowell, 1st Foot; Lieutenant Frederick Luke Gardiner Cowell, 23rd Foot; and Lieutenant John Cowell, 1st Foot; nephew of Major Robert Cowell;

Lieutenant Colonel William Henry Clayton Cowell, 26th Foot; and Lieutenant Colonel John Clayton Cowell, 1st Foot
Entry to Army: Ensign in 89th Foot 1 Apr 1797
Regimental Field Officer Promotions: Major in Royal Regiment of Malta 16 Mar 1809; Major in 42nd Foot 30 May 1811 (vice Munro) by exchange
Brevets: Brevet Lieutenant Colonel 3 Mar 1814
Service 1793–1815: Served in Ireland 1798; served in Egypt 1801; served in Sicily and Malta 1806–1811; served in Peninsula Apr 1812 to Apr 1814, wounded at Orthez
Retired: 8 Apr 1826
Awards and Honours: CB 4 Jun 1815
Residence: Rathmines, County Dublin
Died: Rathmines 21 Sep 1827
Sources: ANCW; ARLI; CHAL; PHIL; WEOF; Irish Pedigrees

312. *Sir Maxwell GRANT (1811–1813)*
Born: Aberdeenshire 1780
Relations: Son of John Grant of Rippachie and Elizabeth (Lumsden)
Entry to Army: Lieutenant in 42nd Foot 4 Sep 1793
Regimental Field Officer Promotions: Major in 6th Portuguese Line 26 Aug 1809; Lieutenant Colonel in 6th Portuguese Line 3 Jul 1810; Major in 42nd Foot 10 Oct 1811; to half-pay of Portuguese service 26 Aug 1813
Brevets: Brevet Lieutenant Colonel 26 Aug 1813
Service 1793–1815: Served in Minorca 1798; served in Egypt 1801, wounded at Alexandria; served in Peninsula with 1/42nd Foot Aug 1808 to Jan 1809, wounded at Corunna; served in Peninsula with Portuguese army Aug 1809 to Apr 1814, wounded in Pyrenees and at Nive
Awards and Honours: KCt (Ottoman) 1802; AGC (Vitt Pyr Nlle Niv Ort); KCB 2 Jan 1815; KTS (Portugal) 4 Apr 1816
Residence: Lynlish, near Grantown-on-Spey, Morayshire
Died: Lynlish 22 Oct 1823
Sources: ANCB; ANCD; ANCW; ARLI; CHAL; PHIL; WEOF

313. *Robert Charles ANSTRUTHER-THOMSON (1812–1814)*
Born: Fifeshire 1785
Relations: Son of Colonel John Anstruther of Charleton and Grizel Maria (Thomson); father took -Thomson surname after 1774
Entry to Army: Ensign in 58th Foot 15 Dec 1800 by purchase
Regimental Field Officer Promotions: Major in 42nd Foot 16 Apr 1812 (vice Macara) by purchase; to half-pay of 42nd Foot 25 Dec 1814; Major in 102nd Foot 7 Sep 1815 (vice Russell); to half-pay of 100th Foot 25 Feb 1817
Service 1793–1815: Served in Peninsula Jul to Dec 1809; served in Peninsula Apr and May 1812
Residence: St Andrews, Fifeshire
Died: St Andrews 20 Sep 1824
Sources: ARLI; FMPD; GHLG; History of the Family of Anstruther

314. *John CAMPBELL (1815)*
Born: Edinburgh 1788
Relations: Son of Lieutenant General Colin Campbell and Mary (Johnson); brother of Major General Sir Guy Campbell, Bt
Education: Christ Church, Oxford
Entry to Army: Ensign in 42nd Foot 30 Jun 1804
Regimental Field Officer Promotions: Captain in 42nd Foot 3 Dec 1807 by purchase; to half-pay Major unattached 6 Jul 1826
Brevets: Brevet Major 12 Apr 1815; Brevet Lieutenant Colonel 18 Jun 1815; Brevet Colonel 10 Jan 1837
Service 1793–1815: Served in Peninsula Jul 1809 to Nov 1810; served in Peninsula Apr 1812 to Mar 1813; again in Peninsula Sep 1813 to Apr 1814, wounded at Orthez; served in Waterloo campaign 1815, commanded 1/42nd Foot as the only unwounded captain at the end of Waterloo
Later Service: Inspecting Field Officer of a Recruiting District 1836
Awards and Honours: AGM (Ort Toul); CB 4 Jun 1815; WatM 23 Apr 1816
Residence: Marseille, Bouches-du-Rhône, France
Died: Marseille 31 Mar 1841
Sources: ANCB; ANCD; ARLI; CHAL; DALT; PHIL; WEOF

Selected Regimental Histories
Groves, John Percy, *History of the 42nd Royal Highlanders: The Black Watch, now the First Battalion The Black Watch (Royal Highlanders) 1729–1893* (Edinburgh: W. & A.K. Johnston, 1893)
Cannon, Richard, *Historical Record of the Forty-second, or the Royal Highland Regiment of Foot: Containing an Account of the Formation of Six Companies of Highlanders in 1729, and of the Subsequent Services of the Regiment to 1844* (London: Parker, Furnivall and Parker, 1845)

Regimental Museum
The Black Watch Castle and Museum, Hay Street, Perth, Perthshire

43rd Regiment of Foot

Secondary Title: Monmouthshire
Nicknames: The Light Bobs
Jacket: Red
Facings: White
Badge: A hunting horn below the crown

Regimental Lineage, 43rd Regiment of Foot

1741: Raised in Winchester as Thomas Fowke's Regiment of Foot
1741: Graham's Regiment of Foot
1746: Kennedy's Regiment of Foot
1747: Ranked as 54th Regiment of Foot
1751: 43rd Regiment of Foot
1782: 43rd (Monmouthshire) Regiment of Foot
1803: Jul – 43rd (Monmouthshire) Regiment of Foot (Light Infantry)
1804: Nov – 2nd Battalion formed in Bromsgrove
1817: Apr – 2nd Battalion disbanded in Baupaume
1881: 1st Battalion, Oxfordshire Light Infantry (on amalgamation with the 52nd (Oxfordshire) Regiment of Foot (Light Infantry))
1908: 1st Battalion, Oxfordshire and Buckinghamshire Light Infantry
1958: 1st Green Jackets (43rd and 52nd) (on amalgamation with The King's Royal Rifle Corps and The Rifle Brigade)
1966: 1st Battalion, The Royal Green Jackets (43rd and 52nd)
1968: 1st Battalion, The Royal Green Jackets
1992: 1st Battalion disbanded, lineage perpetuated by 2nd Battalion, which became 1st Battalion
2007: 2nd Battalion, The Rifles (on amalgamation with the Devonshire and Dorset Light Infantry, Royal Gloucestershire, Berkshire and Wiltshire Light Infantry, and the Light Infantry)

Service History, 1st Battalion 43rd Regiment of Foot

1793: Kilkenny; Nov – Cork; to West Indies
1794: Jan – Barbados; Feb – MARTINIQUE; Fort Bourbon; Apr – St Lucia; May – Guadeloupe; Oct – Berville; evacuation of Guadeloupe
1795: Martinique; Feb to May – drafted out to other regiments, cadre to England; Jun – Plymouth; Jul – Plympton; Sep – Fareham and Titchfield; Nov – Exeter; received new colours
1796: Wells; May – Hilsea; Jun – to Isle of Wight; Jul – West Cowes; Aug – Newport; Oct – Eling; Dec – Portsmouth
1797: Cowes; Mar – to West Indies; Jun – Martinique; Fort George; Sep – Fort Edward
1798: Martinique; St Pierre
1799: St Pierre
1800: St Pierre; Feb – Fort George; Apr – cadre to England; Jun – Portsmouth; Jul – Hilsea; Aug – Gloucester; Oct – Stroud; Nov – Tilbury
1801: Tilbury; Portsmouth; Isle of Wight; Feb – Guernsey
1802: Guernsey
1803: Guernsey; Jul – became Light Infantry
1804: Guernsey; Dover; Feb – Ashford; Jul – Shorncliffe; Nov – Hythe
1805: Hythe; Jul – Shorncliffe; Nov – Hythe; Dec – Shorncliffe
1806: Shorncliffe; Jul – Brabourne Lees
1807: Hythe; Jul – Ramsgate; to Copenhagen; Kjøge; Oct – to England; Nov – Dover; Hythe
1808: Maldon; Jun – Colchester; Sep – Harwich; to Spain; Oct – Corunna; Nov – Astorga; Dec – Mayorga; Astorga

1809:	Retreat to Vigo; Vigo; to England; Feb – Colchester; May – Harwich; Jun – to Portugal; PENINSULA; Lisbon; Villada; Jul – Coria; march to Talavera; Aug – Almaraz; Sep – Campo Maior; Dec – Celorico da Beira
1810:	Villa Torpin; Feb – Azinhal; in Light Division; Mar – Malpartida; Apr – Villar de Ciervo; May – Espeja; Jun – Gallegos de Argañán; Jul – retreat across Coa; Carvalhal; Aug – Freixadas; Sep – BUSACO; Oct – Arruda dos Vinhos; Nov – Quinta de Valle
1811:	Quinta de Valle; Mar – Pombal; Cazal Novo; Foz d'Arouce; Melo; Apr – Sabugal; Fuentes de Oñoro; May – FUENTES D'ONORO; Espeja; Jun – Reguengo; Jul – Castelo de Vide; Aug – Martiago; Sep – Herguijuela de Ciudad Rodrigo; Oct – Fuenteguinaldo; Nov – Martiago; Dec – Fuenteguinaldo
1812:	CIUDAD RODRIGO; La Encina; Feb – Espeja; Mar – Elvas; Apr – BADAJOZ; Puebla de Azaba; May – La Encina; Jun – Aldealengua; Jul –SALAMANCA; Flores de Ávila; Aug – Madrid; Villaverde; Oct – Alcala de Henares; Nov – Saelices el Chico; Ciudad Rodrigo; Dec – Gallegos de Argañán
1813:	Gallegos de Argañán; May – San Muñoz; Jun – VITTORIA; Villava; Jul – Bera; Aug – PYRENEES; volunteers to siege of San Sebastian; Sep – Santa Barbara Kalea; Oct – Puerta de Bera; Etxalar; Nov – NIVELLE; Ustaritz; Dec – NIVE; Arbonne
1814:	Arrauntz; Feb – Charre; Mar – Samatan; Apr – TOULOUSE; Montech; May – Montech; Jun – Blanquefort; Jul – Bordeaux; to England; Portsmouth; Hythe; Oct – to North America; Dec – New Orleans
1815:	New Orleans; Feb – Mobile Bay; Apr – to England; Jun – Dover; Deal; to Netherlands; Ostend; Jul – Ghent; Paris; Allied Army of Occupation
1818:	Valenciennes; Oct – Calais; to England; Canterbury

Service History, 2nd Battalion 43rd Regiment of Foot

1804:	Nov – formed in Broomsgrove
1805:	Broomsgrove; Jun – Hythe; Oct – Dover; Hythe
1806:	Hythe; Aug – Shorncliffe; Nov – Brabourne Lees
1807:	Hythe
1808:	Hythe; Aug – Ramsgate; to Portugal; VIMEIRO; Sep – Quelus; Oct – advance into Spain; Viseu; Nov – Salamanca; Dec – Mayorga; Astorga
1809:	Retreat to Corunna; CORUNNA: to England; Feb – Plymouth; Colchester; Aug – Shorncliffe; Deal; to Walcheren; Oct – to England; Colchester; Nov – Weeley barracks
1810:	Weeley barracks; Feb – Colchester
1811:	Colchester
1812:	Brabourne Lees; Nov – Hythe
1813:	Hythe
1814:	Hythe; Aug – Plymouth
1815:	Plymouth
1817:	Apr – disbanded in Baupaume, France

Establishments, 1st Battalion 43rd Regiment of Foot

Year	Subunits	Field Off	Off/ Staff	Sjts	Mus	Corp/ Pvts	Total
Dec 1792	10co	3	32	22	12	330	399
Jan 1793	10co	3	32	32	22	600	689
Dec 1793	10co	3	32	42	22	850	949
Dec 1795	10co+2r	5	51	62	30	1,010	1,158
Dec 1797	10co	5	38	53	22	600	718
Dec 1801	10co	5	33	34	22	750	844
May 1803	10co	5	36	34	22	750	847
Apr 1804	10co	5	46	44	22	760	877
Dec 1805	10co	5	46	54	22	1,000	1,127
Dec 1806	10co	4	46	54	22	1,000	1,126

Aug 1808	10co+r	4	50	62	26	1,008	1,150
Dec 1809	10co	4	46	64	22	1,010	1,146
Dec 1811	10co	4	46	65	22	1,010	1,147
Dec 1812	10co	4	46	75	22	1,210	1,357
Dec 1814	10co	4	46	65	22	1,010	1,147

Establishments, 2nd Battalion 43rd Regiment of Foot

Year	Subunits	Field Off	Off/ Staff	Sjts	Mus	Corp/ Pvts	Total
Dec 1804	10co	3	35	23	22	400	483
Sep 1806	10co	3	35	33	22	600	693
Oct 1807	10co	3	36	43	22	800	904
Oct 1809	10co+r	3	50	61	26	1,008	1,148
Dec 1809	10co	3	46	53	22	810	934
Dec 1810	10co	3	46	54	22	810	935
Dec 1812	10co	3	45	44	22	610	724
Dec 1815	10co	3	45	35	22	420	515

Service Statistics, 43rd Regiment of Foot

	Lieutenant Colonels	Majors
Number of officers in period 1793–1815	12	26
Average age on appointment to substantive rank	36.5	33
Average time in rank in regiment (years)	6	3.5
Total field officers by nationality	13 E / 9 S / 8 I / 2 F	
Demographics of other ranks 1801	64% EW / 33% I / 2% S / 1% F	
Demographics of other ranks 1808	1/43rd: 65% EW / 32% I / 3% S	
Demographics of other ranks 1810	2/43rd: 67% EW / 30% I / 2% S / 1% F	
Months of overseas service 1793–1815	1/43rd: 141 2/43rd: 8	

Significant Militia/Volunteer Intakes

1795:	Londonderry Fencibles
1802:	Tarbet Fencibles, Loyal Irish Fencibles
1804:	Fifeshire
1805:	Worcestershire
1806:	County Tyrone, County Wicklow
1808:	Cumberland, East Essex, Leicestershire
1809:	Shropshire, East Suffolk, Caernarvonshire, Monmouth and Breconshire, Radnorshire
1811:	Cornwall, Shropshire, East Suffolk
1812:	East Suffolk
1813:	East Suffolk

Regimental Colonels

315. *Edward SMITH (1792–1809)*

Born: Kent c.1734
Relations: Son of Captain Edward Smith RN and Elizabeth (Douglass); brother of Captain and Lieutenant Colonel John Smith, 3rd Foot Guards; brother-in-law of Lieutenant General Henry Bowyer; uncle of Admiral Sir William Sidney Smith RN
Entry to Army: Cornet in 3rd Horse 9 Feb 1751 by purchase
Regimental Field Officer Promotions: Major in 60th Foot 14 Oct 1761; Lieutenant Colonel in 6th Foot 24 Oct 1770; Lieutenant Colonel in 4th Horse 29 Jun 1771; Lieutenant and Lieutenant Colonel in Horse Grenadier Guards 12 Dec 1777
Brevets: Brevet Colonel 19 Feb 1779; Major General 20 Nov 1782; Lieutenant General 3 May 1796; General 1 Jan 1801
Colonelcies: 43rd Foot 26 Apr 1792 (vice Cary)
Early Service: Served in British North America 1758; Governor of Fort George in Jamaica; Governor of Isle of Man 1777–1793

Residence: Clifton, Gloucestershire
Died: Bath, Somerset 5 Jan 1809
Sources: ANCW; UNSM (1838); WEOF

316. *Rt Hon. Sir John Francis CRADOCK [CARADOC], 1st Baron Howden (1809–1839)*

Born: Dublin 1762
Relations: Son of John Cradock, Bishop of Dublin, and Mary (Blaydwin); son-in-law of John Meade, 1st Earl of Clanwilliam; changed surname to Caradoc by Royal Licence 19 Dec 1831
Education: Trinity College, Dublin; St John's College, Cambridge (MA 1777)
Entry to Army: Cornet in 4th Horse 15 Dec 1777 by purchase
Regimental Field Officer Promotions: Major in 12th Dragoons 26 Apr 1783 by purchase; Major in 13th Foot 16 Sep 1786 by exchange; Lieutenant Colonel in 13th Foot 16 Jun 1789 (vice Nugent); to half-pay1795
Brevets: Major General 1 Jan 1798; Lieutenant General (Madras) 21 Dec 1803; Lieutenant General 1 Jan 1805; General 4 Jun 1814
Colonelcies: 127th Foot 16 Apr 1795; Colonel Commandant of 2/54th Foot 8 May 1801; 71st Foot 6 Aug 1803 (vice Gordon); 43rd Foot 7 Jan 1809 (vice Smith)
Early Service: Commanded 13th Foot in West Indies 1790–1791; QMG in Ireland 1792
Service 1793–1815: Commanded flank battalion and ADC to Charles Grey in West Indies 1794, wounded in Martinique; Quartermaster General in Ireland 1797; served and wounded in Irish rebellion 1798; commanded brigade in Egypt 1801; served on staff in Mediterranean 1802–1803; Deputy Quartermaster General in Ireland 1803; Commander in Chief Madras 21 Dec 1803 to 17 Sep 1807 (vice Stuart); Commander in Chief British forces remaining in Portugal after Corunna 16 Jan 1809 to Apr 1809; Commander of Gibraltar 1 Jan 1809 to 20 Aug 1809 (vice Drummond); Governor of Cape Colony 6 Sep 1811 to 6 Apr 1814 (vice Grey)
Political Career: MP (Ire) 1785–1790, 1790–1797 and 1799–1800
Creations and Dignities: 1st Baron Howden (Ire) 19 Oct 1819; 1st Baron Howden (GB) 7 Sep 1831
Awards and Honours: KB 16 Feb 1803; KC 1812; GCB 2 Jan 1815
Residences: Grimston Park, near Tadcaster, Yorkshire; Spaldington Hall, near Howden, Yorkshire; Cradocks Town, County Kildare
Died: Grimston Hall 6 Jul 1839
Sources: ARLI; DIIB; DINB; MENA; PHIL; WEOF; WOST

Lieutenant Colonels

317. *Rt Hon. Sir George HEWETT, 1st Bt (1787–1799)*

Born: Leicestershire 1750
Relations: Son of Major Shuckburgh Hewett, 3rd Foot and Anne (Ward); father of Colonel Sir George Henry Hewett, 2nd Bt
Education: Wimborne Grammar School; Royal Military Academy, Woolwich
Entry to Army: Ensign in 70th Foot 27 Apr1762 by purchase
Regimental Field Officer Promotions: Major in 43rd Foot 31 Dec 1781 by purchase; Lieutenant Colonel in 43rd Foot 12 Oct 1787
Brevets: Brevet Colonel 1 Mar 1794; Major General 3 May 1796; Lieutenant General 25 Sep 1803; General 4 Jun 1813
Colonelcies: Colonel Commandant of 2/5th Foot 5 Aug 1799; 61st Foot 4 Apr 1800 (vice Morris)
Early Service: Served in West Indies 1764–1774; served in North America 1775–1781; Adjutant General in Ireland 1793–1799
Service 1793–1815: Inspector General of Army of Reserve 1803–1804; Barrackmaster General 11 Nov 1804 to 24 Dec 1806 (vice De Lancey); Commander in Chief in British East Indies 17 Oct 1807 to 14 Jan 1812 (vice Lake); Commander in Chief Madras 10 Apr 1810 to 27 Sep 1810; Commander in Chief in Ireland Dec 1813 to 1816 (vice Hope)
Creations and Dignities: 1st Baronet of Nether Seale 6 Nov 1813
Awards and Honours: PC (Ire) 1813; GCB 20 May 1820
Residences: Freemantle Park, near Southampton, Hampshire; Nether Seale, Leicestershire
Died: Freemantle Park 21 Mar 1840
Sources: ARLI; ODNB; PHIL; WEOF

318. *James DRUMMOND (1793–1807)*

Born: Perthshire c.1758
Relations: Son of George Drummond of Drummawhance and Barbara (McGruther)
Entry to Army: Ensign in 40th Foot 10 Oct 1776 by purchase
Regimental Field Officer Promotions: Major in 43rd Foot 2 Dec 1793 (vice Cameron) by purchase; Lieutenant Colonel in 43rd Foot 31 Dec 1793 (vice Hewitt) by purchase
Brevets: Brevet Colonel 26 Jan 1797; Brigadier General (West Indies) 29 May 1797; Brigadier General (Guernsey) May 1803; Major General 25 Sep 1803; Lieutenant General 25 Jul 1810; General 12 Aug 1819

Colonelcies: 7th Garrison Battalion 14 Jun 1807 (vice Wauchope)
Early Service: Served in American War of Independence 1777–1783
Service 1793–1815: Commanded 43rd Foot in West Indies 1793–1794; taken POW in Guadeloupe 1794 but escaped prison hulk in 1795; commanded 43rd Foot and later brigade in West Indies 1797–1798; Lieutenant Governor and Commander in Chief St. Lucia Jan 1797 to Jul 1798; on Irish staff Dec 1798 to 1802; served on Guernsey May to Sep 1803; on staff in Malta Mar to Nov 1804; acting Commander in Chief and Governor of Gibraltar 28 Jun 1806 to 2 Nov 1806; acting Commander in Chief and Governor of Gibraltar 13 Aug 1808 to 1 Jun 1809 (vice Dalrymple)
Residence: Drummawhance, Perthshire
Died: 22 Jun 1831
Sources: ARLI; GEMA (1831); WEOF; WO 25/745; WOST; A genealogical memoir of the... house of Drummond

319. *George Hamson DENNISS (1794–1799)*
Born: Jamaica 1758
Relations: Son of Digby Dennis of Port Royal, member of Jamaican Assembly, and Sarah (Sandys); father of Lieutenant Colonel George Gladwin Denniss, Bengal service
Entry to Army: Ensign in 43rd Foot 18 Aug 1778
Regimental Field Officer Promotions: Major in 43rd Foot 12 May 1794 (vice Drummond) by purchase; Lieutenant Colonel in 43rd Foot 1 May 1794 (backdated)
Service 1793–1815: Commanded 43rd Foot in West Indies 1797–1799
Retired: 25 Jul 1799
Later Service: Assistant Barrackmaster General at Cape of Good Hope 21 Jan 1804
Died: Cape Town 15 May 1821
'Notes and Queries' (22 Nov 1952) p.524 states that this officer was forced to retire from the 43rd by the Duke of York in 1799 for 'court martialling two officers'
Sources: ANCB; ANCD; ARLI; GEMA (1821)

320. *William MONTGOMERY (1799–1800)*
Born: Peeblesshire 1764
Relations: Son of Sir James William Montgomery of Stobo, 1st Bt Stanhope, and Margaret (Scott); brother of Sir James Montgomery, 2nd Bt
Entry to Army: Ensign in 98th Foot 25 Dec 1781 by purchase
Regimental Field Officer Promotions: Major in 2/78th Foot 15 Jul 1795; to half-pay of 2/78th Foot; Major in 3rd West India Regiment 4 Oct 1797 (vice O'Meara); Lieutenant Colonel in 43rd Foot 25 Jul 1799 (vice Denniss) by purchase
Service 1793–1815: Served in West Indies 1797–1800
Political Career: MP (Peeblesshire) 1790–1800
Residence: Stanhope, Peeblesshire
Died: Hounslow, London 25 Oct 1800
Sources: ARLI; DINB (father); EDMA (1800); HPON; WEOF; The Baronetage of England

321. *Richard STEWART (1800–1810)*
See 51.
Lieutenant Colonel in 43rd Foot 5 Nov 1800 (vice Montgomery)

322. *Edward HULL (1808–1810)*
Born: Jamaica c.1773
Relations: Son of Trevor Hull, Gentlemen Usher of the Privy Chamber, and Ann (Gibbons); cousin of Captain James Watson Hull, 43rd Foot
Entry to Army: Ensign on half-pay of Independent Company 1790; Lieutenant in 43rd Foot 31 Dec 1791
Regimental Field Officer Promotions: Major in 43rd Foot 10 Aug 1804; Lieutenant Colonel in 43rd Foot 8 Sep 1808
Service 1793–1815: Commanded 2/43rd Foot in Peninsula Aug 1808 to Jan 1809; commanded 1/43rd Foot in Peninsula Jul 1810
Died: Killed in action at Coa River 24 Jul 1810
Sources: ANCW; ARLI; WEOF; WikiTree

323. *William GIFFORD (1804–1814)*
Born: Yorkshire 1770
Relations: Father of James Gifford of Giggleswick and Agnes (Walker); brother of Rear Admiral James Gifford RN
Entry to Army: Ensign in 50th Foot 9 Apr 1789
Regimental Field Officer Promotions: Major in 87th Foot Aug 1804; Lieutenant Colonel in 43rd Foot 19 Sep 1804; removed from the regiment as a general officer 1814
Brevets: Brevet Major 26 Dec 1798; Brevet Lieutenant Colonel 19 Jul 1802; Brevet Colonel 4 Jun 1811; Major General 4 Jun 1814; rank stationary thereafter
Early Service: Served in Gibraltar 1789–1793
Service 1793–1815: Served in Corsica 1794–1795; served in Portugal 1797; served in Minorca 1798; served in Egypt 1801; Deputy Adjutant General in Malta 1802–1806; commanded 2/43rd Foot 1807–1809 and in Copenhagen 1807; commanded 1/43rd

in Peninsula Oct 1808 to Jan 1809; commanded 1/43rd in Peninsula Jul 1809 and Jun 1810
Residence: Swansea, Glamorganshire
Died: Swansea 9 Aug 1825
Sources: ANCB; ANCD; ARLI; PHIL; WEMR; WEOF; WO 25/745; The Monthly Repository of Theology and General Literature 1825

324. *Charles MacLEOD (1810–1812)*
Born: Kent 1784
Relations: Son of Lieutenant General Sir John MacLeod, Director General of RA, and Emily Wilhelmina Frances (Kerr)
Entry to Army: Ensign in 71st Foot 5 Sep 1799
Regimental Field Officer Promotions: Major in 4th Garrison Battalion 26 Nov 1806; Major in 43rd Foot 26 Nov 1806 (vice Sorell) by exchange; Lieutenant Colonel in 43rd Foot 16 Aug 1810 (vice Hull)
Service 1793–1815: Served in Copenhagen 1807; served in Peninsula with 1/43rd Foot Oct 1808 to Jan 1809; served in Peninsula Jul 1809 to Dec 1810; commanded 1/43rd Foot after Coa 1810; served in Peninsula May 1811 to Apr 1812
Died: Killed in action in Badajoz 6 Apr 1812
Sources: ANCB; ANCD; ARLI; CHAL; WEMR; WEOF

325. *Daniel James HEARN (1812–1814)*
Born: County Westmeath 1768
Relations: Son of Major Robert Thomas Hearn of Correagh and Frances (Cooksey); father of Major Robert Thomas Hearn, 76th Foot; and Surgeon Major Charles Bush Hearn, 1st Foot
Entry to Army: Ensign in 43rd Foot Jun 1795
Regimental Field Officer Promotions: Major in 43rd Foot 25 Mar 1808 (vice MacDonald) by purchase; Lieutenant Colonel in 43rd Foot 14 May 1812 (vice MacLeod)
Service 1793–1815: Served in West Indies 1798–1799; served in Copenhagen 1807; served in Peninsula with 2/43rd Foot Aug 1808; wounded at Vimeiro; served in Peninsula Jul 1811 to May 1812; commanded 1/43rd Foot in Peninsula Oct 1812 to Nov 1813
Retired: 4 Aug 1814
Later Service: High Sheriff of Westmeath
Residence: Correagh, County Westmeath
Died: Correagh 1 Jan 1837
Sources: ARLI; CHAL; HALL; WEOF; WO 25/746; WikiTree

326. *Christopher Clarges PATRICKSON (1813–1826)*
Born: Dublin c.1778
Relations: Son of John Patrickson of Dublin and Helena (Clarges)
Entry to Army: Ensign in 31st Foot 31 Aug 1793
Regimental Field Officer Promotions: Major in 43rd Foot 28 Sep 1809 (vice Proctor); Lieutenant Colonel in 43rd Foot 17 Jun 1813
Brevets: Brevet Lieutenant Colonel 30 May 1811; Brevet Colonel 19 Jul 1821
Service 1793–1815: Served in Irish rebellion 1798; served in Copenhagen 1807; served in Peninsula with 1/43rd Foot Oct 1808 to Jan 1809; served in Peninsula Jul 1809 to Aug 1811; again in Peninsula Feb to Aug 1813; commanded 1/43rd Foot in Peninsula Mar to Apr 1814; commanded 1/43rd Foot in New Orleans 1815
Retired: 29 Aug 1822
Residence: Kildare Street, Dublin
Died: Dublin 25 Sep 1856
Sources: ANCB; ANCD; ANCW; ARLI; CHAL; PHIL; WEOF

327. *Joseph WELLS (1814–1815)*
Born: London 1773
Relations: Son of Joseph Wells and Mary (Nicklin); father of Lieutenant Colonel Frederick Wells, 1st Foot
Entry to Army: Ensign in 43rd Foot Jan 1798
Regimental Field Officer Promotions: Major in 43rd Foot 10 Oct 1811 (vice Elers); Lieutenant Colonel in 43rd Foot 4 Aug 1814 (vice Hearn) by purchase; Inspecting Field Officer in Canada 16 Nov 1815 (vice Pearson) by exchange
Service 1793–1815: Served in West Indies 1799–1800; served in Copenhagen 1807; served in Peninsula with 1/43rd Foot Oct 1808 to Jan 1809; served in Peninsula Jul 1809 to Jul 1812; commanded 2/43rd Foot 1814–1815
Later Service: Member of Legislative Assembly for Upper Canada
Retired: Mar 1827
Awards and Honours: AGM (Bad); MGSM (Bus CR Bad)
Residence: Davenport, York, Canada West
Died: Davenport 4 Feb 1853
Sources: ANCB; ANCD; ARLI; CHAL; PHIL; WEOF

328. *Sir Thomas PEARSON, Kt (1815–1817)*

Born: Somerset 1781
Relations: Son of Rev. Thomas Horner Pearson of Queen Camel and Temperance (Andrews); brother of Lieutenant George Pearson RN; brother-in-law of Admiral John Aylmer RN; father of Captain Thomas Aylmer Pearson, 43rd Foot
Entry to Army: 2nd Lieutenant in 23rd Foot 2 Oct 1796
Field Officer Promotions: Major in 23rd Foot 8 Dec 1804; Inspecting Field Officer of Militia in British North America Jun 1812; Lieutenant Colonel in 43rd Foot 16 Nov 1815 (vice Wells) by exchange; to half-pay of 43rd Foot 1817; Lieutenant Colonel in 23rd Foot 24 Jul 1817 (vice Dalmer) by exchange; removed from the regiment as a general officer 22 Jul 1830
Brevets: Brevet Lieutenant Colonel 4 Jun 1811; Brevet Colonel 19 Jul 1821; Major General 22 Jul 1830; Lieutenant General 23 Nov 1841
Colonelcies: 85th Foot 21 Nov 1843 (vice Fitzgerald)
Service 1793–1815: Served in Helder 1799; served in Egypt 1801, wounded at Aboukir; served in Copenhagen 1807; served in Martinique 1809; served in Peninsula Dec 1810 to Nov 1811, severely wounded at Aldea de Ponte 27 Sep 1811; served on staff in British North America Jun 1812 to Apr 1814; commanded wing of forces Apr 1814 to Sep 1814, wounded at Fort Erie; commanded 2/43rd Foot 1815–1817
Awards and Honours: AGM (Alb CF); CB 4 Jun 1815; Knight Bachelor 13 Mar 1835; KCH 12 Aug 1835
Residence: Sandford Orcas, Somerset
Died: Bath, Somerset 21 May 1847
Sources: ANCB; ANCD; ANCW; CHAL; ODNB; PHIL; WEOF

Majors

329. *Duncan CAMERON (1787–1793)*

Born: Inverness-shire c.1745
Relations: Son of Allan Cameron of Callart and Helen (Stewart); brother of Captain Charles Cameron, 76th Foot
Entry to Army: Ensign in 43rd Foot 15 Oct 1761 by purchase
Regimental Field Officer Promotions: Major in 43rd Foot 12 Oct 1787; Lieutenant Colonel in 91st Foot 30 Oct 1793; Lieutenant Colonel Commandant in 132nd Foot 11 Sep 1794; to half-pay of 132nd Foot 1 Mar 1798
Brevets: Brevet Major 19 Feb 1783; Brevet Colonel 26 Jan 1797; Brigadier General (West Indies) 7 Jun 1797
Early Service: Served in North America
Service 1793–1815: Quartermaster General in West Indies 1797–1798
Residence: Callart, Inverness-shire
Died: Martinique 2 Oct 1798
The son of a Jacobite exile who died in France in 1754
Sources: ANCW; ARLI; WEOF; WikiTree

330. *Henry Patrick PROCTOR (1795–1800)*

See 274.
Major in 43rd Foot 13 Feb 1795

331. *John BURNET (1795–1797)*

Born: [spec.] British North America 1748
Relations: Natural son of Captain Thomas Burnet RN
Entry to Army: Served in Royal Navy 1756–1762; Ensign in 28th Foot 26 Jul 1762
Regimental Field Officer Promotions: Major in 43rd Foot 13 May 1795 (vice Dennis); Lieutenant Colonel in 17th Foot 14 Sep 1797 (vice Hallam); Lieutenant Colonel in 1st Foot 31 Oct 1805 (vice Hardyman) by exchange; to half-pay of 11th Garrison Battalion 27 Feb 1806
Brevets: Brevet Major 1 Mar 1794; Brevet Colonel 30 Oct 1805; Major General 4 Jun 1811
Early Service: Served in Havana 1762; served in North America 1768–1775; served in American War of Independence 1776–1781
Service 1793–1815: Assistant Quartermaster General and Deputy Judge Advocate in Leeward Islands 1794, severely wounded in Guadeloupe; Military Superintendent of Hospitals in South Britain May 1800
Residences: Durham Place, Chelsea, London; Armagh, Ireland
Died: Armagh 29 Oct 1817
Sources: ANCB; ANCW; ARLI; WEOF; WO 25/744; More Than Nelson (father)

332. *William ROBINS (1797–1799)*

Born: Cornwall c.1775
Relations: [spec.] Natural son of Lieutenant Colonel John Robins of Tregony, 20th Light Dragoons
Education: Rugby School
Entry to Army: Ensign in 3/60th Foot 14 Nov 1787
Regimental Field Officer Promotions: Major in 43rd Foot 14 Sep 1797 (vice Burnett)
Service 1793–1815: Served in West Indies 1794–1799

Residence: Hinckley, Leicestershire
Died: Martinique Apr 1799
A possible alternative family background for this officer is as a son of Thomas Robyns Esq. of Trenere, which would make him the brother of Major General John Robyns RM
Sources: ANCB; ANCW (putative father); ARLI; Historical Records of the Forty-third Regiment, Monmouthshire Light Infantry

333. *John Godfrey DREW (1799–1800)*
Born: County Dublin 1768
Relations: Son of George Purdon Drew of High Park and Letitia (Godfrey); brother of Major George Purdon Drew, 45th Foot; Captain Barry Drew, 45th Foot; and Captain Francis Drew, 45th Foot
Entry to Army: Ensign in 45th Foot 1 Oct 1784 by purchase
Regimental Field Officer Promotions: Major in 43rd Foot 12 Apr 1799 (vice Robbins); Lieutenant Colonel in 3rd West India Regiment 23 Jan 1800 (vice Stuart)
Brevets: Brevet Lieutenant Colonel 30 Mar 1797
Service 1793–1815: Served in West Indies 1797–1801
Died: Charlotte Town (Roseau), Dominica 26 Feb 1801
Sources: ANCW; ARLI; GHLG; Miscellanea Genealogica Et Heraldica

334. *Patrick MacKENZIE (1800–1804)*
Born: Perthshire 1758
Relations: Son of Colin MacKenzie of Finnagand and Jean (Small)
Entry to Army: Ensign in 77th Foot 28 Dec 1777
Regimental Field Officer Promotions: Major in 43rd Foot 23 Jan 1800 (vice Drew); Lieutenant Colonel in 81st Foot 28 Aug 1804
Brevets: Brevet Colonel 4 Jun 1813; Major General 12 Aug 1819
Colonelcies: 3rd Royal Veteran Battalion 1 Nov 1819
Service 1793–1815: Served in Gibraltar and Toulon 1793; served and wounded in Corsica 1794–1795; served on staff in West Indies 1798; commanded 2/81st Foot 1808; commanded 1/81st Foot 1811–1813; served in Peninsula (east coast of Spain) Aug 1812 to Apr 1814; commanded brigade in Catalonia Apr 1813 to Apr 1814
Residence: Sharrow Head House, Sharrow, Sheffield, Yorkshire
Died: Sharrow 7 Mar 1820
Sources: ANCB; ANCD; ANCW; ARLI; WEOF

335. *Sir John CAMERON (1800–1807)*
Born: Inverness-shire 1773
Relations: Son of John Cameron of Culchenna and Anne (Crocket); brother of Captain Ewen Cameron, 43rd Foot; father of General Sir Duncan Alexander Cameron; and Major General John Cameron RE
Education: Eton College
Entry to Army: Ensign in 43rd Foot 25 Sep 1787 by purchase
Regimental Field Officer Promotions: Major in 43rd Foot 28 Oct 1800 (vice Proctor); Lieutenant Colonel in 7th West India Regiment 28 May 1807 (vice Conran); Lieutenant Colonel in 9th Foot 3 Sep 1807
Brevets: Brevet Colonel 4 Jun 1814; Major General 19 Jul 1821; Lieutenant General 10 Jan 1837
Service 1793–1815: Served in Leeward Islands 1794, wounded and taken POW; served in Peninsula with 2/9th Foot Aug to Sep 1808; commanded 2/9th Foot at Vimeiro; commanded 1/9th Foot in Peninsula Oct 1808 to Jan 1809; commanded 1/9th Foot in Walcheren 1809; commanded 1/9th Foot in Peninsula Mar 1810 to Dec 1810; and again Apr 1811 to Aug 1812; finally Dec 1812 to Apr 1814; wounded in San Sebastian 1813 commanded brigade in North America 1814; commanded brigade in Allied Army of Occupation in France 1815
Awards and Honours: KCB 2 Jan 1815
Residence: St Peter Port, Guernsey
Died: Guernsey 23 Nov 1844
Sources: ARLI; CHAL; DINB; PHIL; WEOF; WO 25/744

336. *William SORELL (1804–1807)*
Born: London 1773
Relations: Son of Major General William Alexander Sorell and Jane (Binslow)
Education: Westminster School
Entry to Army: Ensign in 31st Foot 18 Aug 1790
Regimental Field Officer Promotions: Major in 43rd Foot 11 Aug 1804; Major in 4th Garrison Battalion 28 May 1807 (vice MacLeod) by exchange; to half-pay of Hompesch's Mounted Riflemen 19 May 1808 (vice Hamilton) by exchange; Major in 46th Foot 12 Nov 1812 (vice Payne) by exchange
Brevets: Brevet Lieutenant Colonel 17 Apr 1807
Service 1793–1815: Served in West Indies 1793–1795 and 1795–1797; served in Helder 1799; commanded 2/43rd Foot 1804–1807; Deputy Adjutant General in Cape of Good Hope 1807–1811
Retired: 4 Feb 1813

Later Service: Lieutenant Governor of Van Diemen's Land (Tasmania) 3 Apr 1816 to 14 May 1824
Residence: George Street, Marylebone, London
Died: London 4 Jun 1848
Sources: ANCB; ANCD; ANCW; ARLI; WEOF; WO 25/748; Australian Dictionary of Biography, Vol.2

337. *Sir Neil CAMPBELL, Kt (1805–1806)*

Born: Argyllshire 1776
Relations: Son of Captain Neil Campbell of Duntroon and Jean (Campbell); brother of Lieutenant Colonel Patrick Campbell, 52nd Foot, later Consul General to Egypt and Syria
Education: Royal Military College, Great Marlow
Entry to Army: Ensign in 6th West India Regiment 2 Apr 1797
Regimental Field Officer Promotions: Major in 43rd Foot 24 Jan 1805 (vice MacKenzie) by purchase; Major in 54th Foot 20 Feb 1806 (vice Pye); Lieutenant Colonel in 54th Foot 20 Jun 1808; Colonel of 16th Portuguese Infantry 2 May 1811; Colonel of 7th Portuguese Infantry 6 Oct 1812; retired from Portuguese service 26 Feb 1814; Lieutenant Colonel in 4th West India Regiment 19 Dec 1816 (vice Eddins); to half-pay of Royal Corsican Rangers 2 Jan 1817 (vice McCombe) by exchange
Brevets: Brevet Lieutenant Colonel 18 Aug 1808; Brevet Colonel 4 Jun 1814; Major General 27 May 1825
Service 1793–1815: Served in West Indies 1798–1800 and 1806–1808; Deputy Adjutant General in West Indies 1808–1810; served at capture of Martinique 1809 and Guadeloupe 1810; in Portuguese service in Peninsula Apr 1811 to Jan 1813, military commission to Russian forces in Poland and Saxony 1813–1814; British commissioner on Elba 1814–1815; commanded 54th Foot in Waterloo campaign 1815; served in Allied Army of Occupation in France 1815–1818
Later Service: Governor of Sierra Leone 23 Aug 1826 to 14 Aug 1827
Awards and Honours: AGC (Mart Guad CR Sal); Knight Bachelor 7 Oct 1814; CB 4 Jun 1815; KSW (Russia) 1815; WatM 23 Apr 1816
Died: Freetown, Sierra Leone 14 Aug 1827
Unfairly derided as 'the man who let Boney go'; his official orders required him and his entourage to travel away from Elba to Italy on a regular basis, of which the exiled Emperor was acutely aware
Sources: ANCB; ANCD; ARLI; DINB; CHAL; PHIL; WEOF; WOST

338. *Sir John MacDONALD (1806–1808)*

Born: Inverness-shire 1776
Relations: Son of Norman MacDonald of Scalpay and Susannah (MacAllister); brother of Lieutenant General Alexander MacDonald RA; and Colonel Archibald MacDonald, Adjutant General of HM Forces in India
Entry to Army: Ensign in 89th Foot 15 Apr 1795
Regimental Field Officer Promotions: Major in 99th Foot 28 Feb 1805; to half-pay of 10th West India Regiment 21 Mar 1805; Major in 43rd Foot 20 Feb 1806 (vice Campbell); Lieutenant Colonel in 51st Foot 17 Mar 1808 (vice Logan) by purchase; Lieutenant Colonel in 90th Foot 21 Apr 1808 (vice Mainwaring) by exchange; to half-pay of 5th Garrison Battalion 16 Jun 1808 (vice Smyth) by exchange
Brevets: Brevet Lieutenant Colonel 17 Mar 1808; Brevet Colonel 4 Jun 1814; Major General 27 May 1825; Lieutenant General 28 Jun 1838
Colonelcies: 67th Foot 25 Aug 1828 (vice Keppel); 42nd Foot 16 Mar 1844 (vice Murray)
Service 1793–1815: Served in Irish rebellion 1798; served in Malta 1799–1800; served in Egypt 1801; Military Secretary to Lord Cathcart in Copenhagen 1807; Adjutant General of Reserve in Walcheren 1809; Assistant Adjutant General in Cadiz 1810–1812; Military Secretary to John Hope in Ireland 1812–1813; Assistant Adjutant General to Hope in Peninsula Sep 1813 to Apr 1814
Later Service: Adjutant General to HM Forces 27 Jul 1830 to 28 Mar 1850
Awards and Honours: CB 4 Jun 1815; KCB 13 Sep 1831; GCB 17 Sep 1847
Residence: Bruton Street, Berkeley Square, London
Died: London 28 Mar 1850
'He did not exercise power – and at one time it was almost unlimited over the army – as a mere machine… His official demeanour was courteous and kind, and his sincerity and candour were seldom found to border on abruptness or roughness, and never on rudeness or insult' – Nav. and Mil. Gazette, 30 Mar 1850
Sources: ANCW; ARLI; CHAL; DINB; PHIL; WEOF; WO 25/747

339. *Thomas PROCTOR (1807–1809)*

Born: Ireland c.1768
Relations: Son of Surgeon Richard Proctor of Kilkenny, 5th Foot, and Anne (Gregory); brother of Major General Henry Patrick Proctor
Entry to Army: Ensign in 105th Foot 21 Mar 1782
Regimental Field Officer Promotions: Major in 43rd Foot 4 Jun 1807 (vice Cameron)
Service 1793–1815: Served in Peninsula with 1/43rd Foot Jul to Aug 1809
Died: Campo Maior, Portugal 15 Aug 1809
Sources: ARLI; CHAL; WEOF

340. *Hungerford Richard ELERS (1808–1811)*
Born: London c.1773
Relations: Son of Lieutenant Paul George Elers, 70th Foot, and Elizabeth (Debonnaire); brother of Captain George Elers, 12th Foot; and Lieutenant Edward Elers RN
Entry to Army: Ensign in 43rd Foot 26 Mar 1794
Regimental Field Officer Promotions: Major in 43rd Foot 8 Sep 1808 (vice Hull)
Service 1793–1815: Served in West Indies; served in Copenhagen 1807; served in Peninsula with 2/43rd Foot Oct 1808 to Jan 1809; served in Peninsula with 1/43rd Foot Apr to Aug 1811, commanded 1/43rd Foot at Fuentes d'Onoro
Residence: Marylebone, London
Died: Celorico da Beira, Portugal 29 Aug 1811
Was apprenticed to be an attorney in London in 1788, but joined the army at the completion of his articles of clerkship
Sources: ANCB; ANCW; ARLI; CHAL; WEOF

341. *Peter DESHON (1810–1813)*
Born: St Vincent 1776
Relations: Son of Captain John Deshon of New London and St Vincent, and Sarah (Starr); father of Major Charles John Deshon, 17th Foot; and Lieutenant General Fredrick George Thomas Deshon
Entry to Army: Ensign in 43rd Foot 14 Mar 1789
Regimental Field Officer Promotions: Major in 43rd Foot 16 Aug 1810 (vice MacLeod); Major in 85th Foot 25 Jan 1813 (vice Mein) by exchange
Service 1793–1815: Served in West Indies 1794–1795, taken POW; served in Peninsula with 1/43rd Foot Oct 1808 to Jan 1809; served in Peninsula Jul 1809 to Dec 1810, wounded at Coa; served in Peninsula with 85th Foot Aug to Dec 1813
Retired: 22 May 1817
Awards and Honours: AGM (Niv); MGSM (Bus SS Nlle)
Residence: Warwick Street, Leamington Priors, Warwickshire
Died: Royal Leamington Spa 27 Jun 1852
Sources: ANCB; ANCD; ANCW; ARLI; CHAL; WEOF; <https://www.noonans.co.uk/auctions/archive/lot-archive/results/187850/>

342. *Sir William Francis Patrick NAPIER (1812–1819)*
Born: County Kildare 1785
Relations: Son of Colonel Hon. George Napier and Lady Sarah (Lennox); brother of General Sir Charles James Napier; General Sir George Thomas Napier; and Captain Henry Edward Napier RN; grandson of Charles Lennox, 2nd Duke of Richmond; cousin of Admiral Sir Charles Napier RN; brother-in-law of Sir Henry Bunbury, 7th Bt
Entry to Army: 2nd Lieutenant in Royal Irish Artillery 14 Jun 1800
Regimental Field Officer Promotions: Major in 43rd Foot 14 May 1812 (vice Hearn); to half-pay of 43rd Foot 17 Jun 1819 (vice Haverfield) by exchange
Brevets: Brevet Major 30 May 1811; Brevet Lieutenant Colonel 22 Nov 1813; Major General 23 Nov 1841; Lieutenant General 11 Nov 1851; General 17 Oct 1857
Colonelcies: 27th Foot 5 Jul 1848 (vice Maclean); 22nd Foot 18 Sep 1853 (vice C.J. Napier)
Service 1793–1815: Served in Copenhagen 1807; served in Peninsula with 1/43rd Foot Oct 1808 to Jan 1809; served in Peninsula Jul 1809 to Aug 1811, wounded at Coa; served in Peninsula Apr 1812 to Feb 1813, badly wounded at Cazal Nova; again in Peninsula Aug 1813 to Mar 1814, wounded at Nive; served in advance on Paris 1815; commanded 43rd Foot in Army of Occupation in France 1815–1818
Later Service: Wrote *History of the War in the Peninsula and the South of France from the Year 1807 to the Year 1814* (6 vols.) 1828–1840; Lieutenant Governor and Colonel on Staff, Guernsey 1 Apr 1842 to Dec 1847
Awards and Honours: AGM (Sal Nlle Niv); MGSM (Bus FDO Ort); KCB 27 Apr 1848
Residence: Scinde House, Clapham Park, London
Died: Clapham Park 12 Feb 1860
Sources: ARLI; CHAL; DINB; HALL; PHIL; WEMR; WEOF; WOST

343. *Nichol Alexander MEIN (1813–1819)*
Born: Dumfriesshire 1777
Relations: Son of Andrew Mein of Canonbie and Elizabeth (Dalzell); brother of Lieutenant Colonel William Mein, 52nd Foot; and Surgeon Pulteney Mein, 73rd Foot; cousin of Colonel John Alexander Mein, 74th Foot
Entry to Army: Ensign in 52nd Foot 13 May 1797
Regimental Field Officer Promotions: Major in 85th Foot 21 Sep 1809 (vice Hill); Major in 43rd Foot 25 Jan 1813 (vice Deshon) by exchange
Brevets: Brevet Lieutenant Colonel 4 Jun 1813
Service 1793–1815: Served in India 1799–1800; served in Walcheren 1809; served in Peninsula Dec 1813 to Apr 1814; served in New Orleans 1815
Retired: 9 Sep 1819
Residence: Marsh House, Canonbie, Dumfriesshire
Died: Canonbie 8 Jun 1847
Sources: ANCB; ANCD; ARLI; CHAL; WEOF

344. *John DUFFY (1813–1815)*

Born: County Monaghan c.1780
Relations: Son of Bernard Duffy of Coothill and Anne (Jeffares); son-in-law of Major General Sir Archibald Campbell
Entry to Army: Ensign in 10th Foot 21 Oct 1795
Regimental Field Officer Promotions: Major in 43rd Foot 17 Jun 1813 (vice Patrickson); Lieutenant Colonel in 95th Foot 21 Sep 1815; Lieutenant Colonel in 8th Foot 9 Sep 1819; to half-pay unattached 29 Mar 1828
Brevets: Brevet Major 6 Feb 1812; Brevet Colonel 22 Jul 1830; Major General 23 Nov 1845; Lieutenant General 11 Nov 1851
Colonelcies: 28th Foot 18 May 1849 (vice Paget); 8th Foot 10 Oct 1854 (vice Drummond)
Service 1793–1815: Served in West Indies 1796; served in Helder 1799; served in Egypt 1807; served in Copenhagen 1807; served in Peninsula with 1/43rd Foot Oct 1808 to Jan 1809; served in Peninsula Jul to Dec 1809; again in Peninsula Mar to Jul 1810; again in Peninsula Dec 1810 to May 1812; again in Peninsula Feb 1813 to Jan 1814, wounded at Vittoria
Awards and Honours: KCt (Ottoman) 1802; AGM (Bad); CB 26 Sep 1831; MGSM (Egt FDO CR Vitt Pyr Nlle Niv)
Residence: Jermyn Street, Piccadilly, London
Died: London 17 Mar 1855
Sources: ANCW; CHAL; GEMA (1855); HALL; PHIL; WEOF

345. *William HAVERFIELD (1814–1817)*

Born: Somerset c.1788
Relations: Son of Rev. William Haverfield of Lyncombe and Elizabeth (Roberts); cousin of Lieutenant Colonel John Haverfield, 48th Foot; and Captain Robert Tunstall Haverfield RN
Entry to Army: Ensign in 43rd Foot 25 Jul 1805
Regimental Field Officer Promotions: Major in 43rd Foot 11 Aug 1814 (vice Wells) by purchase; to half-pay of 43rd Foot Mar 1817; to full-pay of 43rd Foot 17 Jun 1819; Lieutenant Colonel in 43rd Foot 29 Aug 1822 (vice Patrickson) by purchase
Service 1793–1815: Served in Copenhagen 1807; served in Peninsula with 2/43rd Foot Aug 1808 to Jan 1809; served in Walcheren 1809; served in Peninsula Dec 1810 to Dec 1811; served in Peninsula Jun to Nov 1812; again in Peninsula Apr 1813 to Apr 1814
Residence: Devonshire Buildings, Lyncombe, Somerset
Died: Bath, Somerset 1 Jun 1830
Sources: ANCB; ANCD; ANCW; ARLI; CHAL; PHIL; WEOF

346. *Saumarez BROCK (1815–1817)*

Born: Guernsey 1785
Relations: Son of Henry Brock of St Peter Port and Susannah (Saumarez); brother of Major George Brock, 37th Foot; cousin of Major General Sir Isaac Brock; Lieutenant Colonel John Brock, 81st Foot; Lieutenant Ferdinand Brock, 60th Foot; and Paymaster John Savery Brock, 49th Foot; nephew of Admiral James Saumarez RN, 1st Baron de Saumarez; and Midshipman John Brock RN
Entry to Army: Ensign in 52nd Foot 1803 by purchase
Regimental Field Officer Promotions: Major in 43rd Foot 12 Dec 1815 (vice Duffy) by purchase; to half-pay of 43rd Foot 25 Mar 1817; Major in 55th Foot 29 Aug 1822 (vice Rolt); Lieutenant Colonel in 55th Foot 12 Jun 1830; Lieutenant Colonel in 48th Foot 30 Mar 1833 (vice Schoedde) by exchange; to half-pay of 48th Foot 13 May 1835
Brevets: Brevet Colonel 9 Nov 1846
Service 1793–1815: Served in Peninsula with 2/43rd Foot Aug 1808 to Jan 1809, wounded at Vimeiro; served in Peninsula with 1/43rd Foot Feb 1813 to Apr 1814; served in Louisiana 1814–1815; served in Army of Occupation in France 1815
Later Service: Commanded 48th Foot in East Indies 1834
Awards and Honours: KH 12 Aug 1836; MGSM (Vim Vitt Pyr Nlle Niv Toul)
Residence: Vimiera Lodge, St Peter Port, Guernsey
Died: Guernsey 23 Apr 1854
Sources: ANCB; ANCD; ARLI; CHAL; UNSM (1854); WEMR; WEOF; The History of Guernsey and Its Bailiwick

Selected Regimental Histories

Levinge, R.G.A., *Historical Records of the 43rd Regiment, Monmouthshire Light Infantry* (London: W. Clowes, 1868).
Glover, Gareth & Burnham, Robert, *The Men of Wellington's Light Division: Unpublished Memoirs from the 43rd Light Infantry in the Peninsular War* (Barnsley: Pen & Sword Books, 2022)

Regimental Museum

Soldiers of Oxfordshire Museum, Park Street, Woodstock, Oxfordshire

44th Regiment of Foot

Secondary Title:	East Essex
Nicknames:	The Two Fours
	Little Fighting Fours
Jacket:	Red
Facings:	Yellow
Badge:	The Sphinx superscribed Egypt

Regimental Lineage, 44th Regiment of Foot

1741:	Raised as Colonel James Long's Regiment of Foot
1743:	Lee's Regiment of Foot
1747:	Ranked as 55th Regiment of Foot
1751:	44th Regiment of Foot
1782:	44th (East Essex) Regiment of Foot
1803:	Jul – 2nd Battalion formed in Ireland
1816:	Oct – 2nd Battalion disbanded in Dover
1881:	1st Battalion, Essex Regiment (on amalgamation with the 56th (West Essex) Regiment of Foot)
1958:	3rd East Anglian Regiment (16th/44th Foot) (on amalgamation with 1st Battalion, Bedfordshire and Hertfordshire Regiment)
1964:	3rd Battalion, Royal Anglian Regiment (on amalgamation with 1st East Anglian Regiment (Royal Norfolk and Suffolk), 2nd East Anglian Regiment (Duchess of Gloucester's Own Royal Lincolnshire and Northamptonshire), and Royal Leicestershire Regiment)
1992:	3rd Battalion disbanded, lineage perpetuated by 1st and 2nd Battalions

Service History, 1st Battalion 44th Regiment of Foot

1793:	Dublin; Sep – Kilkenny; flank companies to Barbados
1794:	Battalion companies in Dublin; to England; Liverpool; Jun – to Flanders; Ostend; Malines; Breda; Sep – Boxtel; Dec – line of River Waal Flank companies in Martinique, St Lucia and Guadeloupe
1795:	Retreat to Bremen; Bremenlee; Apr – to England; Harwich; Jun – Sunderland; Aug – Seaton camp; Oct – Tynemouth; to Southampton; Nov – to Barbados; storms in English Channel
1796:	Feb – part of battalion in Barbados; Apr – remainder of battalion in Barbados; May – capture of St Lucia; Morne Fortunee; La Vigie
1797:	St Lucia; Jun – fit men drafted into 87th Foot, cadre to England; Jul – Gravesend; Sep – Sudbury
1798:	Sudbury and Ballington; Feb – Staines and Egham; May – Farnham; Jun – Farnham and Canterbury; Jul – Hilsea and Canterbury; Aug – Hilsea; Oct – Portsmouth; to Gibraltar
1799:	Gibraltar
1800:	Gibraltar; Oct – to Egypt; Dec – Bay of Marmorice [Marmaris];
1801:	Mar – EGYPT; Aboukir; Alexandria; Jun – Cairo; siege of Alexandria; Sep – to Malta; Oct – Malta; Dec – to England
1802:	At sea; Apr – Hilsea; May – Bristol; to Ireland; Jun – Waterford; Jul – Wexford
1803:	Wexford; Sep – New Geneva; Oct – to England; Portsmouth; Nov – Portchester; Dec – Winchester
1804:	Winchester; Apr – Isle of Wight; Aug – Shorncliffe; Sep – Fairlight; Nov – Battle
1805:	Battle; Apr – Hilsea; May – to Mediterranean; Jul – Malta
1806–1807:	Malta
1808:	Malta; May – flank companies to Sicily; Sep – battalion companies to Sicily
1809:	Sicily; Jun – Ischia; Procida; Aug – Sicily; Messina; Scylla; Sep – detachment to Ionian Islands
1810:	Messina
1811:	Messina; Mar – Salvadore dei Greci; Aug – to Malta

1812: Malta; Jun – five companies to Sicily
1813: Malta; Mar – five companies to Sicily; May – Malta companies to Minorca; Minorca companies to east coast of Spain; Aug – Tarragona; Sep – Sicily companies to Spain; battalion reunited at Villafranca
1814: Tarragona; Mar – Vilafranca del Penedes; Saragossa; Apr – to France; Bourdeaux; Jun – to North America; Jul – Bermuda; Aug – Chesapeake; Washington; BLADENSBURG; Sep – Baltimore; to West Indies; Oct – Jamaica; Dec – to Louisiana
1815: Jan – New Orleans; Feb – Mobile; Bermuda; May – Portsmouth; Jul – Cork

Service History, 2nd Battalion 44th Regiment of Foot

1803: Jul – formed in Ireland from Irish Army of Reserve men; Oct – New Geneva
1804: New Geneva; Mar – to England; Apr – Isle of Wight; Aug – Sandown; Oct – Guernsey
1805–1808: Guernsey
1809: Guernsey; Aug – Alderney
1810: Alderney; Mar – to Cadiz; Isla de Leon; Sep – to Portugal; PENINSULA; Lisbon; Oct – Heights of Sobral; Nov – Alcoentre; Dec – Torres Vedras
1811: Torres Vedras; Mar – Venda do Valle; Apr – Aldea del Obispo; May – Fuentes d'Onoro; Nave de Haver; Jun – Arronches; Jul – Quinta Lameira; Aug – Villasrubias; Oct – Guarda; Nov – Alfaiates; Dec – Vila Nova de Oliveirinha
1812: Ciudad Rodrigo; Feb – Penacova; Mar – Campo Maior; Apr – BADAJOZ; Sortelha; May – Lamego; Jun – Heights of San Cristóbal; Jul – SALAMANCA; Flores de Ávila; Aug – Villacastin; Sep – siege of Burgos; Oct – retreat from Burgos; Villamuriel de Cerrato; Nov – Vila de Rei; Dec – Martinhal; fit men into four service companies, other six companies to England; into 4th Provisional Battalion with 2/30th Foot
1813: Feb – home companies in Portsmouth; Mar – Horsham; Jun – Steyning
Service companies in Vila de Rei; Apr – Lisbon; Jun – to England; Jul – Portsmouth; Aug – battalion reunited in Steyning; Sep – Brighton; Oct – Steyning; Nov – Ramsgate; to Netherlands; Dec – Tholen
1814: Antwerp; Merxcem; Mar – Bergen-op-Zoom – most of battalion taken POW; May – Ostend; POWs released
1815: Ostend; Apr – Brussels; Jun – Quatre Bras; WATERLOO; advance on Paris; Nov – Allied Army of Occupation
1816: Jan – Calais; to England; Dover; Mar – disbanded in Dover

Establishments, 1st Battalion 44th Regiment of Foot

Year	Subunits	Field Off	Off/ Staff	Sjts	Mus	Corp/ Pvts	Total
Dec 1792	10co	3	32	22	12	330	399
Jan 1793	10co	3	32	32	22	600	689
Apr 1794	12co	3	38	50	26	990	1,107
Jun 1795	10co	3	32	42	22	850	949
Dec 1795	10co+2r	5	51	62	30	1,010	1,158
Dec 1797	10co	5	38	53	22	600	718
Jul 1802	10co	5	33	34	22	750	844
May 1803	10co	5	33	53	22	700	813
Oct 1803	10co	5	36	54	22	1,000	1,117
Dec 1804	10co	5	36	44	22	800	907
Aug 1805	10co	5	46	54	22	1,000	1,127
Dec 1806	10co	4	46	54	22	1,000	1,126
Sep 1807	10co	4	46	64	22	1,200	1,336
Dec 1810	10co+r	4	50	72	26	1,208	1,360
Dec 1811	10co+r	4	50	73	26	1,208	1,361
Dec 1812	10co+r	4	50	63	26	1,008	1,151
Dec 1813	10co+r	4	49	63	22	1,008	1,146

Establishments, 2nd Battalion 44th Regiment of Foot

Year	Subunits	Field Off	Off/ Staff	Sjts	Mus	Corp/ Pvts	Total
Apr 1804	10co	3	35	53	22	1,000	1,113
Dec 1805	10co	3	36	43	22	800	904
Dec 1806	10co	3	35	33	22	600	693
Aug 1808	10co+r	3	39	41	26	608	717
Dec 1808	10co	3	35	33	22	600	693
Dec 1810	10co+r	3	40	51	26	808	928
Dec 1811	10co+r	3	39	43	26	608	719
Dec 1813	10co+r	3	39	53	22	808	925
Dec 1814	10co+r	3	38	43	22	608	714

Service Statistics, 44th Regiment of Foot

	Lieutenant Colonels	Majors
Number of officers in period 1793–1815	14	15
Average age on appointment to substantive rank	38.5	32.5
Average time in rank in regiment (years)	5.5	6
Total field officers by nationality	14 E / 9 S / 7 I	
Demographics of other ranks 1807	1/44th: 86% I / 11% EW / 3% S	
Demographics of other ranks 1808	2/44th: 91% I / 8% EW / 1% S	
Months of overseas service 1793–1815	1/44th: 192 2/44th: 65	

Significant Militia/Volunteer Intakes

1799: 2nd Surrey
1801: 1st Devonshire
1804: Additional Force Act men from County Kildare, County Wicklow, County Carlow, County Westmeath, King's County, Queen's County
1807: Queen's County
1808: County Down South
1810: County Tipperary
1811: Worcestershire
1812: West Kent, Worcestershire, County Wicklow
1813: West Kent, 1st Lancashire, County Clare, County Longford

Regimental Colonels

347. *Charles Alexander RAINSFORD (1781–1809)*
Born: Essex 1728
Relations: Son of alderman Francis Rainsford of West Ham and Isabella (Bale); father of Colonel William Henry Rainsford, 18th Foot
Entry to Army: Cornet in 3rd Dragoons Mar 1744 by purchase
Field Officer Promotions: Captain and Lieutenant Colonel in Coldstream Foot Guards 5 Mar 1761 by purchase; 2nd Major in Coldstream Foot Guards 21 Nov 1777
Brevets: Brevet Colonel 5 Aug 1774; Major General 29 Aug 1777; Lieutenant General 20 Nov 1782; General 3 May 1796
Colonelcies: 44th Foot 4 May 1781
Early Service: Served in War of Austrian Succession; served in Jacobite Rising 1745; Equerry to Duke of Gloucester 1766–1780; Governor of Chester 1776–1796; raised troops in Germany for service in American War of Independence 1776; ADC to King George III 1777–1782
Service 1793–1815: Lieutenant Governor of Gibraltar 1793 to May 1794; Commander in Chief and Governor of Gibraltar 13 May 1794 to 28 Nov 1795 (vice Boyd); Governor of Cliff Fort, Tynemouth 1796 to May 1809
Political Career: MP (Maldon) 1772–1774; MP (Bere Alston) 1787–1788; MP (Newport) 1790–1796
Awards and Honours: FRS 1779
Residence: King's Square, Westminster, London
Died: London 24 May 1809
Sources: ARLI; ODNB; WOST

348. *Sir Thomas TRIGGE (1809–1814)*
Born: Cambridgeshire 1740
Relations: Son of Thomas Trigge of Bassingbourn and Martha (Hills); uncle of Captain and Lieutenant Colonel William Henry Raikes, Coldstream Foot Guards
Entry to Army: Ensign in 12th Foot 6 Oct 1757 by purchase
Regimental Field Officer Promotions: Major in 12th Foot 17 Nov 1773; Lieutenant Colonel in 12th Foot 6 Jun 1778
Brevets: Brevet Colonel 20 Nov 1782; Major General 12 Oct 1793; Lieutenant General (Mediterranean) Mar 1795; Lieutenant General 1 Jan 1798; General 25 Sep 1803
Colonelcies: 68th Foot 25 Mar 1795 (vice C. Stewart); 44th Foot 27 May 1809 (vice Rainsford)
Early Service: Served in Germany at Emden and Minden 1758–1762; served in Gibraltar 1769–1770; commanded 12th Foot at the Great Siege of Gibraltar 1782; Lieutenant Governor of Portsmouth 8 Sep 1790
Service 1793–1815: Second in command in Corsica 1794, then commander Mar 1795; Lieutenant Governor of Gibraltar 12 Jan 1796; Commander in Chief West Indies 22 Nov 1798; commanded ground troops at capture of Surinam Aug 1799 and The Saints Mar 1801; Commander of St Barthélemy 20 Mar 1801 to 10 Jul 1802; acting Lieutenant Governor of St Lucia Mar 1802 to May 1802 (vice Prévost); acting Commander in Chief and Governor of Gibraltar 1 Apr 1803 to 15 Dec 1804; Lieutenant Governor of Royal Hospital, Chelsea 2 Apr 1804 to 19 Oct 1804; Lieutenant General of the Ordnance 22 Nov 1804 to 11 Jan 1814
Awards and Honours: KB 6 Jun 1801
Residences: Savile Row, London; Bromley, Kent
Died: London 11 Jan 1814
Sources: ARLI; WEOF; WO 25/748; WOST; An Historical Description of Westminster Abbey: Its Monuments and Curiosities

349. *Rt Hon. John Howard, 15th Earl of SUFFOLK (1814–1820)*
Born: County Kerry 1739
Relations: Son of Captain Philip Howard, HM Marines, and Margaret (Skreen); brother of Captain and Lieutenant Colonel Thomas Howard, 1st Foot Guards; father of Captain and Lieutenant Colonel Hon. John Howard, Foot Guards; and Captain and Lieutenant Colonel Thomas Howard, 16th Earl of Suffolk, 1st Foot Guards; distant cousin of Thomas Howard, 14th Earl of Suffolk
Entry to Army: Ensign in 1st Foot Guards 13 Jun 1756 by purchase
Regimental Field Officer Promotions: Captain and Lieutenant Colonel in 1st Foot Guards 22 Feb 1773 by purchase
Brevets: Brevet Colonel 17 Nov 1780; Major General 28 Sep 1787; Lieutenant General 26 Jan 1789; General 29 Apr 1802
Colonelcies: 97th Foot 13 Sep 1782 (vice Stanton); 70th Foot 16 Aug 1783 (vice Tryon); 44th Foot 12 Jan 1814 (vice Trigge)
Early Service: Served in American War of Independence 1779–1781
Service 1793–1815: Governor of Londonderry and Culmore 1806–1820
Creations and Dignities: 15th Earl of Suffolk, 8th Earl of Berkshire, Viscount Andover and Baron Howard of Charleton 3 Feb 1783
Awards and Honours: FRSA 1785
Residences: Charlton House, near Malmesbury, Wiltshire; Harley Street, Marylebone, London
Died: Charlton House 23 Jan 1820
Sources: ANCB; ANCD: ANCW; ARLI; DEPE; GHLG

Lieutenant Colonels

350. *William John DARBY (1789–1793)*
Born: Kent 1751
Relations: Son of Lieutenant Colonel John Darby, 17th Foot, and Frances (Lawrence); brother of Captain George Darby, Independent Company; nephew of Vice Admiral George Darby RN; cousin of Major General Matthew Chitty Darby; father of Lieutenant William John Darby, Madras service; and Lieutenant Charles Anne William Darby, RA
Entry to Army: Ensign in 17th Foot 6 May 1762 by purchase
Regimental Field Officer Promotions: Major in 7th Foot 10 Aug 1780 (vice Crosbie); Lieutenant Colonel in 44th Foot 13 Jun 1789 (vice Hope) by purchase
Early Service: Served in American War of Independence
Service 1793–1815: Commanded 44th Foot 1789–1793
Retired: 26 Nov 1793
Residence: Green Park Buildings, Bath, Somerset
Died: Bath 24 Sep 1826
Sources: ANCB; ANCD; ANCW; ARLI; WEOF

351. *Robert RIDDELL (1793–1796)*
Born: Kirkcudbrightshire 1755
Relations: Son of Walter Riddell of Newhouse and Anne (Riddell)
Entry to Army: Cornet in 9th Dragoons 16 Dec

1775 by purchase
Regimental Field Officer Promotions: Major in 18th Light Dragoons 31 Mar 1793 (vice Fremantle) by purchase; Lieutenant Colonel in 44th Foot 26 Nov 1793 (vice Darby) by purchase
Brevets: Brevet Colonel (West Indies) 20 Oct 1796
Service 1793–1815: Commanded 44th Foot 1793–1796
Residence: Friar's Carse House, Dunscore, Dumfriesshire
Died: Of yellow fever on St Lucia 27 Sep 1796
The Dictionary of National Biography (Volume 16) has this officer dying at home at Friars Carse on 21 Apr 1794, which is at odds with the 'Regimental Lineage of the 44th Foot'
Sources: ANCB; ANCD; ANCW; ARLI; ODNB

352. *David OGILVY (1795–1801)*
Born: Aberdeenshire 1762
Relations: Son of Sir John Ogilvy, 5th Baronet of Inverquharity, and Charlotte (Tulliedeph); brother of Rear Admiral Sir William Ogilvy, 8th Bt; and Lieutenant Ramsay Ogilvy, 45th Foot
Education: United College, University of St Andrews
Entry to Army: Cornet in 4th Dragoons 28 Apr 1779
Regimental Field Officer Promotions: Major in 44th Foot 20 May 1795 (vice Blundell); Lieutenant Colonel in 44th Foot 1 Sep 1795
Brevets: Brevet Major 1 Mar 1794
Service 1793–1815: Commanded 44th Foot 1796–1801; served in West Indies; served in Egypt 1801, wounded at Alexandria
Residence: Inverquharity, Aberdeenshire
Died: Of wounds in Alexandria 4 Apr 1801
Sources: ANCB; ARLI; BUPE; WEOF

353. *Charles William BAILLIE (1797–1798)*
Born: Ross and Cromarty c.1750
Relations: Son of William Baillie of Rose Hall and Robina (Mackay); brother of Lieutenant General Sir Ewen Baillie, Bengal service; and Major General Mackay Hugh Baillie
Entry to Army: Lieutenant in 81st Foot 24 Dec 1777 by purchase
Regimental Field Officer Promotions: Lieutenant Colonel in 23rd Light Dragoons 27 Aug 1794 by purchase; Lieutenant Colonel in 101st Foot 22 Oct 1794 (vice Hardy) by exchange; to half-pay of 101st Foot 1795; Lieutenant Colonel in 44th Foot 18 Jan 1797 (vice Riddell); Lieutenant Colonel in 50th Foot 25 Jul 1798 (vice Erskine) by exchange; Lieutenant Colonel in 51st Foot 6 Sep 1798 (vice Moore)
Brevets: Brevet Colonel 1 Jan 1800; Brigadier General (Ceylon) 9 Aug 1806; Major General 25 Apr 1808
Colonelcies: 3rd Ceylon Regiment 7 Apr 1804
Service 1793–1815: Commanded 51st Foot 1798–1800; commanded brigade in Kandian War 1803
Died: Lost at sea aboard the Jane, Duchess of Gordon near Cape of Good Hope c.16 Mar 1809
Sources: ANCB; ANCD; ARLI; Notes and Queries S11 V8

354. *Francis ERSKINE (1798–1799)*
Born: Angusshire 1760
Relations: Son of Francis Erskine of Kirkbuddo and Jean (Guthrie)
Entry to Army: 2nd Lieutenant in 23rd Foot 23 Nov 1775 by purchase
Regimental Field Officer Promotions: Major in 50th Foot 1 Sep 1795 (vice Rose); Lieutenant Colonel in 50th Foot 2 Jan 1796 (vice Rose); Lieutenant Colonel in 44th Foot 25 Jul 1798 (vice Baillie) by exchange; to half-pay of 99th Foot 24 Jan 1799 (vice Tilson) by exchange
Brevets: Brevet Major 1 Mar 1794
Service 1793–1815: Served in Gibraltar
Residence: Kirkbuddo, Angusshire
Died: Kirkbuddo 8 Jun 1833
Sources: ANCB; ANCD; ARLI; WEOF

355. *Christopher TILSON [-CHOWNE] (1799–1814)*
Born: Oxfordshire 1771
Relations: Son of John Tilson of Watlington Park, banker, and Maria (Lushington); brother of Lieutenant Colonel John Tilson; and Lieutenant George Tilson RN; took -Chowne surname 14 Jan 1812
Entry to Army: 2nd Lieutenant in 23rd Foot 13 Feb 1788 by purchase
Regimental Field Officer Promotions: Lieutenant Colonel in 99th Foot 15 Nov 1794; to half-pay of 99th Foot 1796; Lieutenant Colonel in 44th Foot 24 Jan 1799 (vice Erskine) by exchange
Brevets: Brevet Colonel 1 Jan 1801; Brigadier General (Mediterranean) 25 Mar 1805; Major General 25 Apr 1808; Lieutenant General 4 Jun 1813; General 22 Jul 1830
Colonelcies: 76th Foot 17 Feb 1814 (vice Prevost)
Service 1793–1815: Commanded 99th Foot in West Indies 1796–1797; served in Helder 1799; commanded 44th Foot in Egypt 1801, wounded at Mandora; commanded brigades in Peninsula Apr to Dec 1809; deputy commander of 2nd Division in Peninsula Apr to Dec 1812
Awards and Honours: AGM (Tal)

Residence: Eaton Place, Pimlico, London
Died: London 15 Jul 1834
Colonel Henry Torrens wrote of him that 'the habitual want of energy in his character, and his indifference to his profession, have rendered him a burden to the army,' hence his lack of employment after 1812
Sources: ANCB; ANCD; ANCW; ARLI; CHAL; PHIL; WEOF

356. *Sir Kenneth MacKENZIE [DOUGLAS], 1st Bt (1801–1803)*

Born: Dundee 1754
Relations: Son of Kenneth Mackenzie of Kilcoy and Janet (Douglas); grandson of Sir Robert Douglas, 6th Baronet of Glenbervie (first creation); changed surname to Douglas 30 Sep 1831
Entry to Army: Ensign in 33rd Foot 26 Aug 1767 by purchase
Regimental Field Officer Promotions: Major in 90th Foot 13 May 1794 (vice Hill); Lieutenant Colonel in 44th Foot 5 Apr 1801 (vice Ogilvy); Lieutenant Colonel in 52nd Foot 24 Feb 1803 (vice Dirom) by exchange; Lieutenant Colonel in 91st Foot 18 Feb 1808 (vice Ross) by exchange; to half-pay of 15th Foot 7 Apr 1808 (vice Robinson) by exchange
Brevets: Brevet Lieutenant Colonel 19 Oct 1798; Brevet Colonel 25 Apr 1808; Major General 4 Jun 1811; Lieutenant General 19 Jul 1821
Colonelcies: 58th Foot 1 Mar 1828 (vice Bentinck)
Early Service: Served in West Indies 1788–1791
Service 1793–1815: Served in Flanders 1793, wounded at Dunkirk; served in Quiberon 1795; commanded flank battalion in Portugal 1797; Deputy Adjutant General in Mediterranean 1798–1800; trainer of light infantry at Shorncliffe; retired from duty after fall from horse Nov 1803, reinstated in 1810; served in Cadiz 1810; served on staff in Flanders 1813; commanded Antwerp garrison in 1815
Creations and Dignities: 1st Baronet Douglas of Glenbervie 30 Sep 1831 (second creation)
Residence: Holles Street, Cavendish Square, London
Died: London 22 Nov 1833
Sources: ARLI; CHAL; ODNB; WEOF; A New General Biographical Dictionary, Vol 9

357. *Alexander DIROM (1803–1814)*

Born: Banffshire 1757
Relations: Son of Alexander Dirom of Muiresk and Ann (Fotheringham)
Entry to Army: Ensign in 61st Foot 5 Dec 1778
Regimental Field Officer Promotions: Major in 52nd Foot 3 Sep 1795; Lieutenant Colonel in 52nd Foot 6 Jun 1799 (vice Lumley); Lieutenant Colonel in 44th Foot 24 Feb 1803 (vice MacKenzie) by exchange; removed from the regiment as a general officer 1814
Brevets: Brevet Major 12 Feb 1791; Brevet Lieutenant Colonel 13 Apr 1795; Brevet Colonel 29 Apr 1802; Brigadier General (home staff) 27 May 1807; Major General 25 Oct 1809; Lieutenant General 4 Jun 1814
Early Service: Served in West Indies 1780–1784; served in East Indies 1790–1792
Service 1793–1815: Served on staff at home 1795–1814
Awards and Honours: FRS 10 Jul 1794
Residences: Mount Annan, Dumfries and Galloway; Charlotte Square, Edinburgh
Died: Mount Annan 6 Oct 1830
Sources: ANCB; ANCD: ARLI; DINB; ODNB; WEOF; WO 25/745

358. *Thomas NICOLL (1803–1804)*

Born: Middlesex 1754
Relations: Son of Thomas Inwood Nicoll of Neasdon and Mary (Coome)
Entry to Army: Ensign in 33rd Foot 4 Mar 1771 by purchase
Regimental Field Officer Promotions: Major in 70th Foot 1 Sep 1795 (vice Johnstone); Lieutenant Colonel in 70th Foot 9 Aug 1799 (vice Coote); Lieutenant Colonel in 44th Foot 8 Oct 1803
Brevets: Brevet Major 1 Mar 1794; Brevet Lieutenant Colonel 1 Jan 1798
Service 1793–1815: Commanded 2/44th Foot 1803–1804
Retired: 15 Jun 1804
Residence: Copt Hall, Hendon, Middlesex
Died: Hendon 20 Nov 1824
Sources: ANCW; ARLI; WEOF; WikiTree

359. *Sir Arthur BROOKE (1804–1825)*

Born: County Fermanagh 1772
Relations: Son of Francis Brooke of Colebrooke and Hannah (Prittie); brother of Sir Henry Brooke, Bt; Major General Richard Prittie Brooke; and Lieutenant Colonel Francis Brooke, 4th Foot; great granduncle of Field Marshal Viscount Alanbrooke
Entry to Army: Ensign in 44th Foot 31 Oct 1792
Regimental Field Officer Promotions: Major in 44th Foot 26 Dec 1802 (vice Johnstone) by purchase; Lieutenant Colonel in 44th Foot 15 Jun 1804 (vice Nicoll) by purchase; to Lieutenant Colonel unattached 1825
Brevets: Brevet Colonel 4 Jun 1813; Major General 12 Aug 1819; Lieutenant General 10 Jan 1837
Colonelcies: 86th Foot 24 May 1837 (vice Watson)

Service 1793–1815: Served in Flanders 1793–1795; served in West Indies 1796; served in Egypt 1801; commanded 1/44th Foot in Mediterranean 1804–1812; served in Peninsula Aug 1813 to Apr 1814; served in North America 1814–1815
Later Service: Governor of Yarmouth 1822–1825
Awards and Honours: KCB 16 Sep 1833
Residence: George Street, Portman Square, London
Died: London 26 Jul 1843
Sources: ARLI; CHAL; DINB; WEOF; WO 25/744

360. *Robert GARDEN (1804–1809)*
Born: Aberdeenshire c.1763
Relations: Son of Robert Garden of Laurencekirk and Betty (Moir)
Entry to Army: Lieutenant in 81st Foot 20 Dec 1777
Regimental Field Officer Promotions: Major in 54th Foot 5 Jan 1799 (vice Montgomery); to half-pay of 54th Foot 25 Jul 1802; Lieutenant Colonel in 10th Battalion of Reserve 16 Jan 1804 (vice Skerrett); Lieutenant Colonel in 44th Foot 1 Dec 1804; Lieutenant Colonel in 89th Foot 5 Jan 1809 (vice Egerton) by exchange
Brevets: Brevet Major 1 Mar 1794; Brevet Lieutenant Colonel 1 Jan 1798; Brevet Colonel 25 Apr 1808
Service 1793–1815: Inspecting Field Officer of Yeomanry 1803; commanded 2/44th Foot 1804–1809; served in East Indies 1809–1810, commandant of Fort St George
Died: Madras [Chennai] 30 Jun 1810
Sources: ARLI; FMPW; WEOF; List of Inscriptions on Tombs or Monuments in Madras Possessing Historical or Archaeological Interest; <https://www.findagrave.com/memorial/263494428/ robert-garden>

361. *Sir Charles Bulkeley EGERTON (1809–1811)*
Born: Cheshire 1774
Relations: Son of Philip Egerton of Egerton and Mary Haskins Eyles (Styles); brother of Major Thomas Egerton, 29th Foot; and Lieutenant General Richard Egerton
Entry to Army: Ensign in 29th Foot 16 Nov 1791 by purchase
Regimental Field Officer Promotions: Major in 89th Foot 1 Jun 1798 (vice Boyle) by purchase; Lieutenant Colonel in 89th Foot 14 Nov 1802 (vice Stewart) by purchase; Lieutenant Colonel in 44th Foot 5 Jan 1809 (vice Garden) by exchange; Lieutenant Colonel on staff and Field Officer of Militia in British North America 22 Aug 1811 (vice Carleton) by exchange
Brevets: Brevet Colonel 4 June 1811; Major General 4 June 1814; Lieutenant General 22 July 1830; General 9 November 1846
Colonelcies: 89th Foot 26 Sep 1837 (vice Macfarlane)
Service 1793–1815: Served as a marine officer at Glorious 1st of June 1794; served in Irish rebellion 1798; served in Malta 1800; served in Egypt 1801; commanded 2/89th Foot 1804–1809; commanded 2/44th
Foot in Peninsula Jun 1810 to Sept 1811; commanded brigade in 5th Division in Peninsula Mar and Apr 1811
Awards & Honours: KCH 12 Aug 1832; GCMG 10 May 1837; MGSM (Egt FDO); NGSM (1 June)
Residences: Chesham Place, Belgravia, London; Portland Square, Marylebone, London
Died: London 8 July 1857
Sources: ANCB; ANCD; ANCW; CHAL; PBKN; PHIL; WEOF; WO 25/745

362. *Hon. George CARLETON (1811–1814)*
See 255.
Lieutenant Colonel in 44th Foot 22 Aug 1811 (vice Egerton)

363. *John Millet HAMERTON (1814–1816)*
Born: County Tipperary c.1777
Relations: Son of John Hamerton of Rathronan and Mary (Millet)
Entry to Army: Ensign in 44th Foot 31 Oct 1792
Regimental Field Officer Promotions: Major in 44th Foot 15 Jun 1804 (vice Brooke) by purchase; Lieutenant Colonel in 44th Foot 31 Mar 1814 (vice Carleton); to half-pay of 44th Foot 25 Mar 1816
Brevets: Brevet Lieutenant Colonel 4 Jun 1811; Brevet Colonel 27 May 1825; Major General 10 Jan 1837; Lieutenant General 9 Nov 1846; General 20 Jun 1854
Colonelcies: 55th Foot 7 Dec 1848 (vice Wardlaw)
Service 1793–1815: Served in Flanders 1794; served in West Indies 1796; served in Egypt 1801; commanded 2/44th Foot in Belgium 1814–1815; commanded 2/44th Foot and wounded at Quatre Bras; commanded 2/44th Foot and wounded at Waterloo 1815
Awards nd Honours: CB 22 Jun 1815; WatM 23 Apr 1816
Residence: Orchardstown House, near Clonmel, County Tipperary
Died: Clonmel 28 Jan 1855
Sources: ARLI; DALT; GEMA (1855); WEOF; WO 25/746

Majors

364. *Bryan BLUNDELL (1783–1795)*

Born: Liverpool 1757
Relations: Son of Jonathan Blundell of Lark Hill, manufacturer, and Alice (Townsend)
Entry to Army: Ensign in 46th Foot 1 May 1775 by purchase
Regimental Field Officer Promotions: Major in 79th Foot 12 Nov 1780; Major in 44th Foot 4 Apr 1783 (vice Lumm) by exchange; Lieutenant Colonel in 45th Foot 20 May 1795 (vice Nicolls)
Brevets: Brevet Lieutenant Colonel 18 Nov 1790; Brevet Colonel 21 Aug 1795; Major General 18 Jun 1798
Early Service: Served in West Indies 1778–1784
Service 1793–1815: Commanded light infantry battalion in West Indies 1794–1795
Residence: Exeter, Devon
Died: Exeter 23 Sep 1799
Sources: ANCB; ANCD; ANCW; ARLI; WEOF

365. *Sir Rufane Shaw DONKIN (1795–1798)*

Born: Devon 1773
Relations: Son of General Robert Donkin of Morpeth and Mary (Collins); father of Lieutenant George David Donkin, 7th Foot
Entry to Army: Ensign in 44th Foot 21 Mar 1778 by purchase
Regimental Field Officer Promotions: Major in 44th Foot 1 Sep 1795 (vice Ogilvy); Lieutenant Colonel in 11th Foot 24 May 1798 (vice Hely)
Brevets: Brevet Colonel 25 Apr 1808; Major General 4 Jun 1811; Lieutenant General 1821; General 28 Jun 1838
Colonelcies: 80th Foot 20 Apr 1825 (vice Campbell); 11th Foot 15 Mar 1837 (vice Montresor)
Service 1793–1815: Served in Leeward Islands 1794; served in Ostend 1798; commanded 11th Foot in West Indies 1802; permanent Assistant Quartermaster General 18 May 1805; served in Copenhagen 1807; Assistant Quartermaster General in Portugal Aug 1808 to Jan 1809; commanded brigade in 3rd Division in Peninsula Jun to Nov 1809; Quartermaster General on east coast of Spain Jul 1812 to Sep 1813
Later Service: Served in Mahratta War 1817–1818; acting Governor of Cape Colony 13 Jan 1820 to 30 Nov 1821; Surveyor General of the Ordnance 1835–1841
Political Career: MP (Berwick-upon-Tweed) 1832–1837; MP (Sandwich) 1839–1841
Awards and Honours: AGM (Tal); KCB 14 Oct 1818; GCH 12 Aug 1821; FRGS 1830; FRS 1832
Residences: Lower Caversham, Oxfordshire; Park Street, Grosvenor Square, London
Died: Committed suicide in Southampton, Hampshire 1 May 1841
Sources: ARLI; CHAL; GHHC; PHIL; WEOF; WO 25/745

366. *Edward WILSON (1795–1796)*

Born: Norfolk 1770
Relations: Son of Henry William Wilson of Kirby Cane and Didlington, and Mary (Miller); brother of Robert Wilson, 9th Baron Berners; Rev. Henry Wilson, 10th Baron Berners; and Major Knyvett Wilson, 27th Foot
Entry to Army: Ensign in 44th Foot 28 Feb 1787 by purchase
Regimental Field Officer Promotions: Major in 44th Foot 21 Oct 1795
Service 1793–1815: Served in West Indies 1796
Died: St Lucia 11 Dec 1796
Sources: ANCB; ANCD; ANCW (father); ARLI

367. *Alexander MALL (1797–1802)*

Born: Berwickshire 1741
Relations: Son of Alexander Mall of Whitsome and Mary (Watts)
Entry to Army: Ensign in 29th Foot 3 Jul 1765 by purchase
Regimental Field Officer Promotions: Major in 44th Foot 17 Jan 1797 (vice Wilson)
Brevets: Brevet Major 1 Mar 1794; Brevet Lieutenant Colonel 1 Jan 1798
Early Service: Served in British North America; served in American War of Independence
Service 1793–1815: Served in Flanders 1794–1795; served in West Indies 1796–1797
Retired: 14 Jan 1802
Residence: Whitsome, Berwickshire
Died: Berlin, Germany Apr 1802
Sources: ANCB; ARLI; FMPD; British Officers in America 1754–1774

368. *George JOHNSTON (1798–1802)*

Born: Fifeshire 1767
Relations: Son of Alexander Johnston of Rennyhill and Euphame (Clephane); cousin of Major General William Douglas Maclean Clephane, 3rd Foot Guards; and Captain Robert Clephane RN
Entry to Army: Ensign in 44th Foot 7 Dec 1785 by purchase
Regimental Field Officer Promotions: Major in 44th Foot 24 May 1798 (vice Donkin); Lieutenant Colonel in 58th Foot 27 Nov 1802 (vice Douglas) by purchase

Service 1793–1815: Served in West Indies; served in Egypt 1801, commanded 44th Foot after Alexandria; served in Mediterranean 1802–1806
Died: Messina, Sicily 28 Jul 1806
Sources: ANCB; ANCW; ARLI; FMPB; UNSM (1806); WEOF

369. *Sir Charles PHILLIPS, Kt (1802–1815)*
Born: Berkshire 1773
Relations: Son of Major General William Phillips of Windsor and Elizabeth Colleton (Browne)
Entry to Army: Ensign in 33rd Foot 20 Jun 1783 by purchase
Regimental Field Officer Promotions: Major in 44th Foot 14 Jan 1802 (vice Mall) by purchase; removed from the regiment as a general officer 27 Apr 1815
Brevets: Brevet Lieutenant Colonel 9 Mar 1803; Brevet Colonel 1 Jan 1812; Major General 4 Jun 1814; Lieutenant General 22 Jul 1830
Service 1793–1815: Served in West Indies 1794; served in Egypt 1801; Deputy Quartermaster General in Malta 9 Mar 1803; served on Mediterranean staff 1803–1815
Awards and Honours: GCSJ (Sicily) 20 Jan 1817; Knight Bachelor 6 Mar 1817
Residence: Linwood, Hampshire
Died: Linwood 20 Jun 1846
Sources: ANCW; GEMA (1846); PHIL; WEOF

370. *Henry POWLETT (1803–1806)*
Born: Devon 1769
Relations: Son of Thomas Norton Powlett of Rotherfield and Ann (Poore)
Entry to Army: Ensign in 4/60th Foot 14 Oct 1789 by purchase
Regimental Field Officer Promotions: Major in 20th Foot 27 Mar 1801 (vice Williams) by purchase; to half-pay of 20th Foot 25 Feb 1803; Major in 44th Foot 9 Jul 1803; Lieutenant Colonel in 7th Garrison Battalion 25 Nov 1806; Lieutenant Colonel in 12th Royal Veteran Battalion 28 Dec 1809; Lieutenant Colonel in 11th Royal Veteran Battalion 5 Sep 1811 (vice Christie) by exchange; Lieutenant Colonel in 5th Royal Veteran Battalion 25 May 1815
Early Service: Served in West Indies 1789–1792
Service 1793–1815: Served in Helder 1799, wounded twice; served and wounded at Maida 1806; wounded at St Euphemia 1806
Residence: Alderley, Gloucestershire
Died: Alderley 8 Feb 1817
Sources: ANCB; ANCD; ARLI; PHIL; WEOF

371. *Thomas DANSER (1803–1805)*
Born: Yorkshire 1769
Relations: Son of John Danser of Howden and Elizabeth (Hall); brother of Lieutenant Colonel William Danser, 1st Foot
Entry to Army: Ensign in 40th Foot 31 May 1792 by purchase
Regimental Field Officer Promotions: Major in 44th Foot 9 Jul 1803
Service 1793–1815: Served in Mediterranean 1805
Died: Jumped from a window in Malta 6 Aug 1805
Sources: ANCB; ANCW; ARLI; Records and Family Notices of Military and Naval Officers who are, or have been, Connected with Doncaster

372. *George HARDINGE (1805–1822)*
Born: County Kildare c.1776
Relations: Father of Lieutenant Henry Hardinge, 39th Foot
Entry to Army: Ensign in 44th Foot 31 Dec 1793 by purchase
Regimental Field Officer Promotions: Major in 44th Foot 16 Aug 1805 (vice Danser); Lieutenant Colonel in 44th Foot 25 May 1822; Lieutenant Colonel in 99th Foot 28 Mar 1824
Brevets: Brevet Lieutenant Colonel 1 Jan 1812
Service 1793–1815: Served in Flanders 1794–1795; served in West Indies 1796–1797; served in Peninsula Jul 1811 to Feb 1813, wounded at Villa Muriel; wounded and taken POW at Bergen-op-Zoom 1814
Later Service: Served in Mauritius 1825–1829
Awards and Honours: AGM (Sal)
Residence: Brompton, near Chatham, Kent
Died: Port Louis, Mauritius, 8 Mar 1829
Sources: ARLI; GEMA (1829); CHAL; HALL; PHIL; WEMR; WEOF

373. *Edward GREGORY (1806–1821)*
Born: Dublin c.1777
Relations: [spec.] Son of Edward Gregory of Dublin and Joanna (Smith)
Entry to Army: Ensign in 44th Foot 31 Dec 1793
Regimental Field Officer Promotions: Major in 44th Foot 27 Nov 1806 (vice Poulett)
Brevets: Brevet Lieutenant Colonel 4 Jun 1813
Service 1793–1815: Served in Flanders 1794–1795; served in West Indies 1795–1797, wounded in St Lucia; served in Egypt 1801; served in Peninsula Apr 1810 to Sep 1811; commandant of Ostend 1814–1815
Retired: Retaining rank 1821
Residence: York Street, Marylebone, London
Died: From the effects of his wound in London 12 Jul 1834
Sources: ARLI; FMPD; PHIL; WEOF

374. *Fountain ELWIN (1814–1816)*
Born: Middlesex 1780
Relations: Son of Fountain Elwin of Enfield, attorney, and Ann Maria (Gibson)
Entry to Army: Ensign in 44th Foot 14 Apr 1798 by purchase
Regimental Field Officer Promotions: Major in 44th Foot 31 Mar 1814 (vice Hamerton); to half-pay of 44th Foot 25 Mar 1816
Brevets: Brevet Major 4 Jun 1813; Brevet Lieutenant Colonel 22 Jul 1830
Service 1793–1815: Served in Naples 1806; served in Sicily 1813; served in Peninsula Sep 1813 to Apr 1814, wounded at Tudela; Assistant Adjutant General in east Spain 1813–1814; commanded 2/44th Foot in Allied Army of Occupation in France 1815
Awards and Honours: KCt (Ottoman) 1802
Residence: Peckham Rye, Surrey
Died: Peckham Rye 8 Dec 1846
Sources: ANCB; ANCD; ANCW; ARLI; GEMA (1847); WEMR; WEOF

375. *George O'MALLEY (1815–1816)*
Born: County Mayo 1780
Relations: Son of George O'Malley of Castlebar and Elizabeth (Clarke); brother of Surgeon James O'Malley, 11st Light Dragoons; and Major Owen O'Malley, South Mayo Militia
Entry to Army: Volunteer in Castlebar Yeomanry; Lieutenant in North Mayo Militia; Ensign in 13th Foot 23 Feb 1800
Regimental Field Officer Promotions: Major in 101st Foot 21 Aug 1806; Major in 44th Foot 27 Apr 1815; to half-pay of 44th Foot 25 Mar 1816; Major in 38th Foot 12 Aug 1819 (vice Lord Muskerry); to half-pay of 60th Foot 2 Mar 1820 (vice Cuyler) by exchange; to half-pay unattached 1823; Lieutenant Colonel in 88th Foot 2 Jun 1825 (vice Ferguson)
Brevets: Brevet Lieutenant Colonel 4 Jun 1813; Brevet Colonel 22 Jul 1830; Major General 23 Nov 1841
Service 1793–1815: Served as volunteer in Irish rebellion 1798; served in Egypt 1801; served in Mediterranean 1802–1803; served in British North America and West Indies; commanded 2/44th Foot at Waterloo 1815, wounded twice
Awards and Honours: CB 22 Jun 1815; WatM 23 Apr 1816
Residence: St Alban's Place, St James', London
Died: London 16 May 1843
Sources: ANCW; ARLI; GEMA (1843); WEOF; <https://irelandxo.com/ireland-xo/history-and-genealogy/ancestor-database/major-george-omalley>

376. *Hon. Thomas MULLINS (1812–1815)*
Born: County Kerry c.1770
Relations: Son of Thomas Mullins of Burnham House, 1st Baron Ventry, and Elizabeth (Gunn); brother of Major Hon. Edward Mullins, 28th Foot; and William Townsend Mullins, 2nd Baron Ventry
Entry to Army: Ensign in 24th Foot 30 Jun 1788
Regimental Field Officer Promotions: Captain in 44th Foot 9 Jul 1803
Brevets: Brevet Major 1 Jan 1805; Brevet Lieutenant Colonel 1 Jan 1812
Service 1793–1815: Served in Peninsula Aug 1813 to Apr 1814; commanded 1/44th Foot in North America 1814–1815
Retired: Cashiered 1 Aug 1815 after New Orleans
Residence: Leigh Street, St Pancras, London
Died: London 1 Feb 1823
Sources: ANCD; ARLI; GHPB; WEOF

Selected Regimental Histories
Carter, Thomas, *Historical Record of the Forty-Fourth: Or the East Essex Regiment* (Chatham: Gale & Polden, 1887)
Roworth, Vivien, *Not So Easy, Lads: Wearing the Red Coat 1786–1797* (Warwick: Helion, 2023)

Regimental Museum
Essex Regiment Museum, Oaklands Park, Moulsham Street, Chelmsford, Essex

45th Regiment of Foot

Secondary Title:	1st Nottinghamshire
Nicknames:	The Old Stubborns The Fire Eaters
Jacket:	Red
Facings:	Deep green

Regimental Lineage, 45th Regiment of Foot

1741:	Raised in Buckinghamshire as Daniel Houghton's Regiment of Foot
1745:	Warburton's Regiment of Foot
1747:	Ranked as 46th Regiment of Foot
1751:	45th Regiment of Foot
1782:	45th (1st Nottinghamshire) Regiment of Foot
1804:	Aug – 2nd Battalion formed in Mansfield
1814:	Oct – 2nd Battalion disbanded in Plymouth
1881:	1st Battalion, The Sherwood Foresters (Derbyshire Regiment) (on amalgamation with the 95th (Derbyshire) Regiment of Foot)
1902:	The Sherwood Foresters (Nottinghamshire and Derbyshire Regiment)
1970:	The Worcestershire and Sherwood Foresters Regiment (29th/45th Foot) (on amalgamation with The Worcestershire Regiment)
2007:	2nd Battalion, The Mercian Regiment (on amalgamation with The Cheshire Regiment and The Staffordshire Regiment)

Service History, 1st Battalion 45th Regiment of Foot

1793:	West Indies – Grenada; May – Grenada and Tobago; Jun – Grenada and Dominica
1794:	Grenada and Dominica; Feb to Apr – drafted out on Barbados and cadre home to England; Jun – Bristol; Guernsey; Nov – Hilsea
1795:	Hilsea; Feb – Portsmouth; to West Indies; Apr – Martinique; Sep – seven companies in The Saints, three companies in Martinique
1796:	Seven companies in Martinique, three companies in The Saints; May – Martinique, The Saintes and St Kitts; Jul – Dominica, The Saintes and St Kitts
1797:	Dominica, The Saintes and St Kitts; Feb – Dominica and The Saintes; Jun – Dominica
1798–1799:	Dominica
1800:	Dominica; Jun – The Saintes
1801:	The Saintes; Apr – St Kitts; drafted out and to England, one transport kidnapped en route; Jul – Portsmouth; Hilsea; Aug – Horsham; Oct – Winchester; Nov – Portsmouth and Portsea
1802:	Portsmouth; Apr – to Ireland; May – Charles Fort; Aug – Kinsale
1803:	Kinsale; Sep – Limerick
1804:	Limerick; Jul – Boyle; Aug – Ballyshannon
1805:	Ballyshannon; Aug – Enniskillen; Sep – Curragh camp; Oct – Fermoy; Dec – Cork; embarked on Hanover expedition
1806:	Disembarked in England; Feb – Brabourne Lees; Jul – Shorncliffe; Aug – Portsmouth; to South America
1807:	Cape Verde Islands; Mar – Cape Town; Jun – Monte Video; Jul – Buenos Ayres; to Ireland; Dec – Cork
1808:	Cork; Jul – to Portugal; PENINSULA; Aug – ROLICA; VIMEIRO; Oct – Peniche; Dec – Oporto
1809:	Almeida; Feb – Lisbon; May – Villa Velha; Jul – TALAVERA; Aug – Arroyo; Sep – Campo Mayor; Nov – Villa del Rey; Dec – Thomar
1810:	Jan – Pinhel; Feb – Lameiros; Jul – Val de Madeira; Aug – Vila Franca das Naves; Sep – BUSACO; Oct – Cardozes; Nov – Tagarro

1811:	Tagarro; Mar – Celorico; Apr – Nave d'Aver; May – FUENTES D'ONORO; Jun – Campo Mayor; Jul – Castelo Branco; Aug – Aldea de Ponte; Sep – Fuenteguinaldo
1812:	CIUDAD RODRIGO; Zamarra; Feb – Quadrazais; Mar – BADAJOZ; Apr – La Alberguería de Argañán; May – Rendo; Jul – SALAMANCA; Nava de Arévalo; Aug – Madrid; Oct – Valdemoro; Nov – Fuenteguinaldo; Dec – Moimenta de Beira
1813:	Moimenta de Beira; May – Vimiosa; Jun – VITTORIA; Irunzun; Jul – Ulague; PYRENEES; Aug – Arizkun; Sep – Zugarramurdi; Nov – NIVELLE; Arrauntz; Dec – Urcuray
1814:	Hasparren; Feb – Sauveterre-de-Béarn; ORTHEZ; Mar –Vic-en-Bigorre; Samatan; Apr – TOULOUSE; Grenade; Jun – Bordeaux; to Ireland; Jul – Cork; Sep – Enniskillen
1815:	Enniskillen; Feb – Belfast; ordered to Belgium but did not sail

Service History, 2nd Battalion 45th Regiment of Foot

1804:	Aug – formed in Mansfield
1805:	Mansfield; May – Nottingham; Nov – Chelmsford; Dec – Colchester
1806:	Colchester; Feb – Chelmsford; Apr – Maldon; Jun – Chelmsford
1807:	Nottingham
1808:	Nottingham; Jun – Manchester; Jul – Nottingham
1809:	Nottingham
1810:	Nottingham; May – Portsmouth; Jun – Guernsey
1811:	Guernsey; Jun – Portsmouth; Oct – Steyning
1812:	Horsham; Apr – Blatchington; Dec – Lewes
1813:	Lewes; Nov – Blatchington
1814:	Blatchington; Sep – Plymouth; Dartmoor; Oct – disbanded in Plymouth

Establishments, 1st Battalion 45th Regiment of Foot

Year	Subunits	Field Off	Off/ Staff	Sjts	Mus	Corp/ Pvts	Total
Dec 1792	10co	3	32	22	12	430	499
Jan 1793	10co	3	32	32	22	600	689
Oct 1795	10co+2r	5	51	62	30	1,010	1,158
Dec 1797	10co	5	38	53	22	600	718
Jul 1802	10co	5	33	34	22	750	844
May 1803	10co	5	33	53	22	700	813
Feb 1805	10co	5	36	44	22	800	907
Dec 1806	10co	4	36	44	22	800	906
Dec 1808	10co	4	46	54	22	1,000	1,126
Dec 1810	10co	4	36	44	22	800	906
Dec 1813	10co	4	36	45	22	800	907
Jul 1814	10co+r	4	49	53	22	808	936

Establishments, 2nd Battalion 45th Regiment of Foot

Year	Subunits	Field Off	Off/ Staff	Sjts	Mus	Corp/ Pvts	Total
Dec 1805	10co	3	35	23	22	400	483
Dec 1807	10co	3	35	43	22	800	903
Dec 1808	10co	3	35	23	22	400	483
Dec 1810	10co	3	35	24	22	400	484
Dec 1811	10co	3	35	25	22	400	485

Service Statistics, 45th Regiment of Foot

	Lieutenant Colonels	Majors
Number of officers in period 1793–1815	12	22
Average age on appointment to substantive rank	34	31.5
Average time in rank in regiment (years)	5.5	3.5
Total field officers by nationality	16 E / 8 S / 6 I / A 1 / F 1	
Demographics of other ranks 1808	2/45th: 83% EW / 14% I / 3% S	
Demographics of other ranks 1810	2/45th: 90% EW / 8% I / 2% S	
Demographics of other ranks 1793–1815 (based upon pension returns)	59% E / 35% I / 5% S / 1% W	
Months of overseas service 1793–1815	1/45th: 182 2/45th: no overseas service	

Significant Militia/Volunteer Intakes

1802: Northumberland Fencibles
1805: County Antrim, County Donegal, County Limerick, County Louth
1807: Derbyshire, Nottinghamshire
1808: Nottinghamshire, Worcestershire, County Limerick
1809: Derbyshire, Nottinghamshire, Leicestershire, South Lincolnshire, 2nd Tower Hamlets
1811: Inverness-shire, City of Dublin
1812: Inverness-shire
1813: Nottinghamshire

Regimental Colonels

377. *James Whorwood ADEANE (1788-1802)*

Born: Oxfordshire 1740
Relations: Son of Simon Whorwood Adeane of Chalgrove and Mary (Brydges); nephew of James Brydges, 1st Duke of Chandos
Education: Westminster School
Entry to Army: Lieutenant in 71st Foot 29 Sep 1757 by purchase
Regimental Field Officer Promotions: Major in 1st Troop Horse Grenadier Guards 8 Jun 1768; Lieutenant and Lieutenant Colonel in 1st Troop Horse Grenadier Guards 1 Aug 1770
Brevets: Brevet Colonel 19 Feb 1779; Major General 20 Nov 1782; Lieutenant General 3 May 1796; General 1 Jan 1801
Colonelcies: 45th Foot 11 Sep 1788 (vice Cuninghame)
Early Service: Groom of the Bedchamber of King George III 1784–1793
Service 1793–1815: Groom of the Bedchamber of King George III 1793–1802
Political Career: MP (Cambridge) 1780–1789; MP (Cambridgeshire) 1789–1802
Residences: Babraham, near Cambridge, Cambridgeshire; Chalgrove, Oxfordshire; Harley Street, Cavendish Square, London
Died: Babraham 15 Apr 1802
Sources: *ANCW; ARLI; HPON; WEOF; WIKI*

378. *William Cavendish LISTER (1802-1823)*

Born: Leicestershire 1735
Relations: Son of John Lister of Syson and Dorothy (Robinson)
Entry to Army: Cornet in 16th Light Dragoons 22 Aug 1760 by purchase; Ensign in 3rd Foot Guards 1 Apr 1761 by purchase
Regimental Field Officer Promotions: Captain and Lieutenant Colonel in 3rd Foot Guards 1 Sep 1777 by purchase; Second Major in 3rd Foot Guards 13 Sep 1791 (vice Grinfield); First Major in 3rd Foot Guards 31 Jul 1793 (vice Grinfield); Lieutenant Colonel in 3rd Foot Guards 1 Apr 1795 (vice Grinfield)
Brevets: Brevet Colonel 20 Nov 1782; Major General 12 Oct 1793; Lieutenant General 1 Jan 1798; General 25 Sep 1803
Colonelcies: 45th Foot 27 Apr 1802 (vice Adeane)
Early Service: Served in Seven Years War in Germany 1760–1761; served in American War of Independence 1775–1777
Service 1793–1815: Governor of Landguard Fort 1801–1823
Residences: Colwick, Nottinghamshire; Coln St Alwyns, Gloucestershire
Died: Coln St Alwyns 2 Feb 1823
Lister was apprenticed to a merchant in Leeds in 1753 but later decided to pursue a military career
Sources: ANCB; ANCD; ARLI; PHIL; WEOF; WO 25/746

Lieutenant Colonels

379. *Oliver Anthony NICOLLS (1787-1795)*

Born: County Wexford 1742
Relations: Son of Jasper Nicolls, storekeeper of Duncannon Fort and Mary (Darby); son-in-law of General Sir William Green, Bt; brother of General Gustavus Nicolls, RE; father of Lieutenant William Jasper Nicolls, 45th Foot; Captain Oliver Justly Nicolls, RA; and Lieutenant Colonel George Green Nicolls, 1st Dragoon Guards; uncle of Lieutenant General Sir Jasper Nicolls
Entry to Army: Ensign in 1st Foot 22 Nov 1756
Regimental Field Officer Promotions: Major in 1/1st Foot 14 Mar 1781 by purchase; Lieutenant Colonel in 1st Foot 5 Feb 1787; Lieutenant Colonel in 45th Foot 31 Mar 1787 (vice Dundas) by exchange
Brevets: Brevet Colonel 1 Mar 1794; Brigadier General (West Indies) 25 Dec 1794; Major General 3 May 1796; Lieutenant General 25 Sep 1803; General 4 Jun 1813
Colonelcies: 4th West India Regiment 20 May 1795; 54th Foot 19 Jul 1807 (vice Baird); 66th Foot 3 Aug 1808 (vice Clanricarde)
Early Service: Served at Gibraltar 1768; served in West Indies 1780–1783; commanded 45th Foot in West Indies 1787–1794
Service 1793–1815: Commanded 45th Foot 1787–1795; Commander in Chief in Grenada 1792–1794; Quartermaster General in West Indies 1795; Commander in Chief Bombay 22 Jan 1802 to 1808 (vice Stuart); Governor of Anhalt 1813
Residence: Chichester, Sussex
Died: Chichester 3 Dec 1829
Sources: ANCB; ANCD; ANCW; ARLI; PHIL; WEOF; WO 25/747

380. *Bryan BLUNDELL (1795-1799)*

See 364.
Lieutenant Colonel in 45th Foot 20 May 1795 (vice Nicolls)

381. *Alexander FRASER (1795-1797)*

Born: Inverness-shire c.1741
Relations: Reputedly of the Frasers of Balnain
Entry to Army: Ensign in 38th Foot 13 Feb 1757 by purchase
Regimental Field Officer Promotions: Lieutenant Colonel in 45th Foot 1 Sep 1795
Brevets: Brevet Major 18 Nov 1790; Brevet Lieutenant Colonel 1 Mar 1794
Early Service: Assistant Superintendent of Indian Affairs in British North America 1776–1777
Service 1793–1815: Served in West Indies 1795–1797
Died: Of fever in Dominica 6 Aug 1797
Sources: ANCB; ARLI; Hadden's Journal and Orderly Books; A Memoir of the Exploits of Captain Alexander Fraser and his Company of British Marksmen 1776-1777

382. *James MONTGOMERIE (1797-1804)*

Born: Ayrshire 1755
Relations: Son of Alexander Montgomerie of Coilsfield & Lilias (Montgomerie); grandson of Sir Robert Montgomerie of Skelmorlie, Bt; brother of Colonel Hugh Montgomerie, 12th Earl of Eglinton
Entry to Army: Ensign in 51st Foot 13 Sep 1773 by purchase
Regimental Field Officer Promotions: Major in 6th West India Regiment May 1795; Lieutenant Colonel in 6th West India Regiment 20 May 1795; Lieutenant Colonel in 45th Foot 4 Oct 1797 (vice Fraser); Lieutenant Colonel in 64th Foot 5 May 1804 (vice Pakenham)
Brevets: Brevet Major 1 Mar 1794; Brevet Colonel 29 Apr 1802; Brigadier General (Leeward Islands) 1804; Major General 25 Oct 1809; Lieutenant General 4 Jun 1814
Colonelcies: 74th Foot 26 Apr 1813 (vice A. Hope); 30th Foot 13 Jun 1823 (vice Manners)
Early Service: Served in Minorca 1774
Service 1793–1815: Commanded 45th Foot 1798–1804; Commander in Chief Tobago 1804–1805; acting Lieutenant Governor of Demerara 19 Oct 1805 to 8 May 1806; Lieutenant Governor of Berbice 23 Oct 1806 to 26 Nov 1808; acting Lieutenant Governor of Demerara 2 May 1807 to 14 Sep 1807; Governor of Dominica 12 Dec 1808 to Jun 1809
Political Career: MP (Ayrshire) 1818–1829
Residence: Wrighthill, Ayrshire
Died: Bath, Somerset 13 Apr 1829
Sources: ARLI; HPON; PHIL; WEOF

383. *William GUARD (1799-1814)*

Born: Devon 1773
Relations: Son of John Guard of Honiton and Susan (Baker)
Entry to Army: Ensign in 45th Foot 13 Jun 1789 by purchase
Regimental Field Officer Promotions: Major in 45th Foot 15 Nov 1797 (vice Wight) by purchase; Lieutenant Colonel in 45th Foot 3 Oct 1799 (vice Blundell) by purchase
Brevets: Brevet Colonel 25 Oct 1809; Major General

4 Jun 1812; Lieutenant General 27 May 1825
Service 1793–1815: Served in West Indies 1794–1801; commanded 1/45th Foot 1804–1809; commanded 1/45th Foot in Buenos Ayres; commanded 1/45th Foot in Peninsula Aug 1808 to Jul 1809, wounded and POW at Talavera; released Apr 1814
Later Service: Governor of Kinsale Dec 1827 to Jul 1830
Awards & Honours: AGM (Rol Vim Tal)
Residence: Southernhay, Exeter, Devon
Died: Exeter 13 Jul 1830
Sources: ANCB; ANCD; ARLI; PHIL; WEOF

384. *Lord Frederick CAVENDISH BENTINCK (1804-1805)*

Born: Nottingham 1781
Relations: Son of William Henry Cavendish Bentinck, 3rd Duke of Portland and Lady Dorothy (Cavendish); brother of Lieutenant Colonel Lord Charles Augustus Cavendish Bentinck, 1st Foot Guards; Lord William Cavendish Bentinck, 4th Duke of Portland; and General Lord William Henry Cavendish Bentinck
Education: Westminster School
Entry to Army: Ensign in 32nd Foot 1 Feb 1798
Regimental Field Officer Promotions: Major in 45th Foot 24 Mar 1804 (vice Vachell) by purchase; Lieutenant Colonel in 7th Foot 21 Apr 1804 (vice King) by purchase; Lieutenant Colonel in 45th Foot 5 May 1804 (vice Montgomerie); Captain and Lieutenant Colonel in 1st Foot Guards 31 Jan 1805 (vice Fitzroy) by exchange; Lieutenant Colonel in 1st Foot Guards 25 Jul 1814 (vice Leslie)
Brevets: Brevet Colonel 4 Jun 1813; Major General 12 Aug 1819
Colonelcies: 58th Foot 6 Sep 1826 (vice Lord Lynedoch)
Service 1793–1815: Served in Irish rebellion 1798; attached to Austrian Army at Marengo 1800; served in Peninsula with 1/1st Foot Guards Oct 1808 to Jan 1809; served in Peninsula with 1/1st Foot Guards Jul 1812 to Apr 1813; Deputy Adjutant General in Peninsula Apr 1813 to Apr 1814
Political Career: MP (Weobley) 1816–1824; MP (Queenborough) 1824–1826
Awards & Honours: CB 4 Jun 1815
Residence: St. James's Square, St. James's, London
Died: Rome, Italy 11 Feb 1828
Bentinck was promoted to lieutenant colonel in 1814 jumping 15 places on the seniority list in so doing. Obviously being the son of a former Prime Minister had its perks
Sources: ARLI; HPON; PHIL; WEOF; WO 25/744

385. *Hon. Charles FITZROY (1805)*

Born: Hampshire 1762
Relations: Son of Charles FitzRoy, 1st Baron Southampton & Anne (Warren); grandson of Admiral Sir Peter Warren; brother of George Ferdinand FitzRoy, 2nd Baron Southampton; and Lieutenant General William FitzRoy
Entry to Army: Cornet in 11th Light Dragoons 27 Aug 1779 by purchase
Regimental Field Officer Promotions: Captain and Lieutenant Colonel in 1st Foot Guards 21 Feb 1794 (vice Colquhoun) by purchase; Lieutenant Colonel in 45th Foot 31 Jan 1805 (vice Bentinck) by exchange
Brevets: Brevet Colonel 26 Jan 1797; Major General 25 Sep 1803; Lieutenant General 25 Jul 1810; General 19 Jul 1821
Colonelcies: 25th Foot 25 Mar 1805 (vice Lennox)
Service 1793–1815: Served in Flanders 1793–1794; served in Helder 1799; commanded 3/1st Foot Guards 1803; ADC to King George III 25 Sep 1803; Equerry to King George III 1809–1811
Residence: Harley Street, Marylebone, London
Died: London 18 Oct 1831
Reputedly a lover of King George's favourite daughter, Princess Amelia
Sources: ANCB; ANCD; ARLI; PHIL; WEOF; WIKI

386. *Hon. John MEADE (1805-1813)*

Born: County Down 1775
Relations: Son of John Meade, 1st Earl of Clanwilliam, and Theodosia (Hawkins-Magill); brother of General Hon. Robert Meade; and Richard Meade, 2nd Earl of Clanwilliam; father of Major Richard Raphael Meade, 8th Foot
Entry to Army: Lieutenant in 12th Foot 12 Nov 1794
Regimental Field Officer Promotions: Major in 30th Foot 4 Jun 1801 (vice Reynolds) by purchase; Lieutenant Colonel in 16th Garrison Battalion 1 Dec 1804; to half-pay of 16th Garrison Battalion 24 Feb 1805; Lieutenant Colonel in 45th Foot 28 Mar 1805 (vice Fitzroy); to half-pay of 45th Foot 4 Jun 1813
Brevets: Brevet Colonel 4 Jun 1813; Major General 12 Aug 1819; Lieutenant General 10 Jan 1837
Service 1793–1815: Served in Flanders 1794–1795; served in Helder campaign 1799; commanded 2/45th Foot 1805–1810; commanded 1/45th Foot in Peninsula Jul to Nov 1810
Later Service: British Consul-General in Spain 1817–1849
Political Career: MP (County Down) 1805–1817
Awards & Honours: AGM (Bus)

Residences: Gill Hall, Dromore, County Down
Died: Madrid, Spain 6 Aug 1849
An art lover; whilst in Madrid he amassed one of the largest and most eclectic collections of Spanish art of his day
Sources: ANCB; ANCD; ARLI; HPON; PHIL; WEOF; WO 25/747

387. *Henry Richard RIDEWOOD (1811-1813)*

Born: Sussex 1781
Relations: Son of Quartermaster Richard Ridewood, 52nd Foot, and Elizabeth (Barber); stepson of Major William Molesworth Hatch Madden, 52nd Foot; step-brother of Lieutenant Edward Marcell Madden, 95th Rifles; Lieutenant Monsoon Molesworth Madden, 43rd Foot; Lieutenant William Sterling Madden, 52nd Foot; and Lieutenant Wyndham Carlyon Madden, 43rd Foot
Entry to Army: Ensign in 52nd Foot 28 Jun 1792 by purchase
Regimental Field Officer Promotions: Major in 52nd Foot 29 May 1806 (vice Barclay); Lieutenant Colonel in 45th Foot 27 Jun 1811
Service 1793–1815: Served in East Indies 1794–1798; served in Copenhagen 1807; served in Peninsula with 52nd Foot Aug 1808 to Jan 1809; served in Peninsula with 1/52nd Foot Jul 1809 to Apr 1811; served in Peninsula with 2/52nd Foot Apr to Jul 1811; commanded 1/45th Foot in Peninsula Jul 1812 to Jul 1813, mortally wounded at Vittoria
Awards & Honours: AGM (Sal Vit)
Residence: Horsham, Sussex
Died: Of wounds after Vittoria 11 Jul 1813
Sources: ANCB; ANCD; ARLI; CHAL; HALL; WEOF; WO 25/748

388. *Henry CRAUFURD (1813)*

Born: Renfrewshire 1774
Relations: Son of Archibald Craufurd of Greenock and Annabella (Maxwell)
Entry to Army: Ensign in 81st Foot 18 Aug 1794 by purchase
Regimental Field Officer Promotions: Major in 9th Foot 13 Nov 1801 (vice Marriott) by purchase; to half-pay of 9th Foot 25 Jun 1802; Major in 9th Foot 1 Aug 1804; Lieutenant Colonel in 45th Foot 26 Aug 1813 (vice Ridewood)
Brevets: Brevet Major 25 Apr 1808; Brevet Lieutenant Colonel 25 Apr 1808
Service 1793–1815: Served in Peninsula with 1/9th Foot Aug 1808 to Jan 1809; served at Walcheren 1809; served in Peninsula with 1/9th Foot Mar 1810 to Aug 1813; killed before could take up appointment with 45th Foot
Awards & Honours: AGM (Rol Vim Bus SS)
Died: Killed in action at San Sebastian 31 Aug 1813
Sources: ANCB; ANCD; ARLI; CHAL; HALL; WEOF; WO 25/744

389. *Thomas FORBES (1813-1814)*

Born: Aberdeenshire 1774
Relations: Son of Rev. George Forbes of Lochell and Katherine (Stewart)
Entry to Army: Ensign in 80th Foot 8 Jul 1794
Regimental Field Officer Promotions: Major on half-pay of McDonald's Recruiting Corps 3 Dec 1800; Major in 6th West India Regiment 23 Jun 1808 (vice Dales) by exchange; Major in 45th Foot 20 Oct 1808 (vice Browne) by exchange; Lieutenant Colonel in 45th Foot 7 Oct 1813 (vice Craufurd)
Brevets: Brevet Lieutenant Colonel 25 Apr 1808
Service 1793–1815: Served in Peninsula Jan 1812 to Jan 1813; commanded 1/45th in Peninsula Jul 1813 to Apr 1814, wounded Salamanca and Orthez
Awards & Honours: AGM (Bad Nlle Ort Toul)
Residence: Strathdon, Aberdeenshire
Died: Killed in action at Toulouse 10 Apr 1814
Sources: ANCB; ANCD; ARLI; CHAL; HALL; WEOF; WO 25/745

390. *Sir Leonard GREENWELL, Kt (1814-1827)*

Born: Durham 1781
Relations: Son of Joshua Greenwell of Kibblesworth and Mary (Robinson)
Entry to Army: Ensign in 45th Foot 7 Aug 1801 by purchase
Regimental Field Officer Promotions: Major in 45th Foot 25 Oct 1810 (vice Smith); Lieutenant Colonel in 45th Foot 19 May 1814 (vice Forbes)
Brevets: Brevet Lieutenant Colonel 17 Aug 1812; Brevet Colonel 25 May 1825; Major General 10 Jan 1837
Service 1793–1815: Served in South America 1807, wounded at Buenos Ayres; served in Peninsula Aug 1808 to Jul 1811; served in Peninsula Mar to Sep 1812; served in Peninsula Nov 1813 to Apr 1814, commanded light companies of 3rd Division and wounded five times; commanded 1/45th Foot Apr 1814 to 1825
Later Service: Served in East Indies 1819–1825; ADC to King George IV, King William IV and Queen Victoria; Commandant at Chatham 1831–1837
Retired: Due to ill-health and effects of wounds 8 Nov 1827

Awards & Honours: AGM (FDO Bad Ort); CB 4 Jun 1815; Knight Bachelor 22 Feb 1832; KCB 28 Jun 1838
Residence: Chatham, Kent; Harley Street, Marylebone, London
Died: London 11 Nov 1844
Sources: ANCB; ANCD; ARLI; CHAL; DINB; HALL; PHIL; WEOF

Majors

391. *Coote MANNINGHAM (1791-1795)*
See 273.
Major in 45th Foot 23 Feb 1791 (vice St John)

392. *Thomas HAVILAND (1794-1795)*
Born: Buckinghamshire c.1755
Relations: Son of General William Haviland of Penn, 45th Foot, and Salusbury (Aston)
Entry to Army: Ensign in 14th Foot 3 Mar 1773
Regimental Field Officer Promotions: Major in 45th Foot 19 Apr 1794 (vice Manningham)
Service 1793–1815: Served in West Indies 1794–1795
Residence: Penn, near Burnham, Buckinghamshire
Died: Of fever in Martinique Dec 1795
Sources: ARLI; CHAL; GHLG; WEOF

393. *Henry HAWLEY (1795-1802)*
Born: Nottinghamshire c.1757
Relations: Son of Thomas Hawley of Southwell and Hannah (unk.)
Entry to Army: Ensign in 45th Foot 15 Aug 1775
Regimental Field Officer Promotions: Major in 45th Foot 1 Sep 1795
Brevets: Brevet Lieutenant Colonel 1 Jan 1801
Retired: 16 Sep 1802
Later Service: Captain in Loyal Southwell Volunteer Infantry Apr 1804
Died: Southwell, Nottinghamshire 13 Jan 1833
Sources: ANCD; ARLI; The History of Southwell, in the County of Nottingham

394. *Edward Edwin COLMAN (1795-1797)*
See 155.
Major in 45th Foot 9 Dec 1795 (vice Haviland)

395. *Andrew WIGHT (1797)*
Born: East Lothian 1754
Relations: Son of Lieutenant Archibald Wright of Ormiston and Alison (Ramsay)
Entry to Army: Ensign in 92nd Foot 28 Dec 1779
Regimental Field Officer Promotions: Major in 45th Foot 9 Feb 1797 (vice Colman) by exchange
Early Service: Served in West Indies 1781
Retired: 15 Nov 1797
Residence: Chapelerne, Kirkcudbrightshire
Died: Chapelerne 4 Sep 1806
Sources: ANCB; ANCD; ARLI

396. *Sir William Howe DE LANCEY (1799-1802)*
Born: New York City 1781
Relations: Son of Stephen De Lancey, Governor of Tobago and Cornelia (Barclay); grandson of Major General Oliver De Lancey
Entry to Army: Cornet in 16th Light Dragoons 7 Jul 1792
Regimental Field Officer Promotions: Major in 45th Foot 17 Oct 1799 (vice Guard) by purchase; Major on permanent staff of Quartermaster General's Department 26 May 1802; Lieutenant Colonel on permanent staff of Quartermaster General's Department 14 May 1807 (vice Harcourt)
Brevets: Brevet Lieutenant Colonel 1 Jan 1805; Brevet Colonel 4 Jun 1813
Service 1793–1815: Served in Flanders 1794–1795; served in West Indies 1795; served in Cape of Good Hope 1796; served in East Indies 1797–1798; to permanent staff of the Quartermaster General's Department as Deputy Assistant Quartermaster General 1802; Deputy Quartermaster General in Peninsula Aug 1808 to Jan 1809; Deputy Quartermaster General in Peninsula May 1809; acting Quartermaster General in Peninsula Dec 1811 to Aug 1812; acting Quartermaster General in Peninsula Dec 1812 to Mar 1813; head of Quartermaster Department May 1813 to Apr 1814; Deputy Quartermaster General in North Britain 1814–1815; Quartermaster General in Waterloo campaign 1815; mortally wounded at Waterloo
Awards & Honours: AGC (Cor Tal Bus FDO Bad Sal Vit SS Nive); KCB 2 Jan 1815
Residence: Maitland Street, Edinburgh, Midlothian
Died: Of wounds after Waterloo 28 Jun 1815
Sources: ANCD; ARLI; CHAL; DALT; WEOF; WO 25/745

397. *William VACHELL (1802-1804)*
Born: Cambridgeshire 1772
Relations: Son of William Vachell of Hinxton and Mary (Jones)
Entry to Army: Ensign in 45th Foot 27 Oct 1790
Regimental Field Officer Promotions: Major in 45th Foot 16 Sep 1802 (vice Hawley) by purchase
Retired: 24 Mar 1804
Residence: Catton, Norfolk

Died: Catton 5 Feb 1826
Sources: AJMM; ANCB; ANCD; ARLI

398. *Sir Jasper NICOLLS (1804-1807)*
Born: Kent 1778
Relations: Son of Colonel Gustavus Nicolls of East Farleigh, 1st Foot, and Elizabeth (Dann); brother of General Gustavus Nicolls, RE; and Captain William Dann Nicolls, RA; nephew of General Oliver Anthony Nicolls; cousin of Lieutenant William Jasper Nicolls, 45th Foot; Captain Oliver Justly Nicolls, RA; and Lieutenant Colonel George Greene Nicolls, 1st Dragoon Guards
Education: Trinity College, Dublin
Entry to Army: Ensign in 45th Foot 24 May 1793
Regimental Field Officer Promotions: Major in 45th Foot 6 Jul 1804 (vice Bentinck) by purchase; Lieutenant Colonel in Royal York Rangers 29 Oct 1807; Lieutenant Colonel in 14th Foot 31 Mar 1808 (vice Dyer) by exchange; to half-pay of 14th Foot 24 Dec 1817
Brevets: Brevet Colonel 4 Jun 1814; Major General 19 Jul 1821; Lieutenant General 10 Jan 1837
Colonelcies: 93rd Foot 31 May 1833 (vice Cameron); 38th Foot 15 Jun 1840 (vice Pigot); 5th Foot 4 Apr 1843 (vice Colville)
Service 1793–1815: Served in West Indies 1795–1800; served in British East Indies 1802–1804; served in Hanover 1805; served in South America 1806; commanded 2/14th Foot 1808–1811; served in Peninsula Nov 1808 to Jan 1809; served in Walcheren 1809; Assistant Adjutant General at Horse Guards 1811; Quartermaster General in Ireland 1812; Quartermaster General in East Indies 1813; served in Nepal 1815
Later Service: Served in British East Indies 1815–1821; commanded division in Madras 1825–1829; commanded division in Bengal 1829–1831; Commander in Chief Madras 1838; Commander in Chief in British East Indies 1839–1843
Awards and Honours: AGM (Cor); CB 4 Jun 1815; KCB 26 Dec 1826
Residence: Goodrest Lodge, near Reading, Berkshire
Died: Goodrest Lodge 4 May 1849
Sources: ANCW; ARLI; CHAL; DINB; GEMA (1849); ODNB; PHIL; WEOF; WO 25/747

399. *John STODDART (1804-1805)*
Born: [spec.] Midlothian 1763
Relations: Son of Thomas Stoddart of South Leith and Rebecca (Tod); brother of Rear Admiral Pringle Stoddart RN
Entry to Army: Ensign in 80th Foot 22 Jan 1778
Regimental Field Officer Promotions: Major in 45th Foot 1 Aug 1804
Brevets: Brevet Major 25 Sep 1803
Retired: 8 Aug 1805
Residence: Ballyshannon, County Donegal
Died: Ballyshannon 1 Jan 1814
Sources: ANCB; ARLI; SCMA

400. *William GWYN (1804-1810)*
Born: [spec.] Kent 1773
Relations: [spec.] Son of Rev. William Gwyn of Lewisham and Anna Maria (unk.)
Entry to Army: Ensign in 45th Foot 1 Aug 1788 by purchase
Regimental Field Officer Promotions: Major in 45th Foot 2 Aug 1804; Lieutenant Colonel in 89th Foot 27 Dec 1810 (vice Blaney)
Early Service: Served in West Indies 1789–1794
Service 1793–1815: Served in West Indies 1795–1801; served in West Indies 1804–1805; served in Buenos Aires 1807; served in Peninsula Aug 1808 to Dec 1810; commanded 1/45th Jul 1809 to Jul 1810, wounded at Talavera and Busaco; Inspecting Field Officer of Militia in North Britain 1814–1815
Awards & Honours: AGM (Tal)
Died: Of wound complications at Govan, Lanarkshire 30 Aug 1815
Sources: ANCW; ARLI; WEMR; WEOF; WO 25/745

401. *Andrew PATTON (1804-1809)*
Born: Fifeshire 1771
Relations: Son of Henry Patton of Chatto and Mary (Bethune)
Entry to Army: Ensign on half-pay of 93rd Foot; Ensign in 10th Foot 15 May 1789
Regimental Field Officer Promotions: Major in 45th Foot 1 Sep 1804
Service 1793–1815: Served in Helder 1799; served in Egypt 1801; served in Buenos Aires 1807; served in Peninsula Aug 1808 to Mar 1809
Retired: 13 Jul 1809
Later Service: Migrated to Canada in 1816; Barrackmaster at Fort Wellington 1821–1829; Barrackmaster at Fort York 1829–1836
Residence: Fort Wellington, Prescott, Ontario
Died: Toronto 15 Aug 1838
Sources: ANCB; ANCD: ARLI; WEOF; St. Alban the Martyr UEL Memorial Church

402. *Francis Frye BROWN (1805-1808)*
Born: Antigua c.1775
Relations: Son of Joseph Brown of Antigua, merchant, and Mary (Weston)
Entry to Army: Ensign in 3rd Foot 25 Sep 1798

Regimental Field Officer Promotions: Major in 45th Foot 8 Aug 1805 (vice Stoddart) by purchase; Major in 6th West India Regiment 20 Oct 1808 (vice Forbes) by exchange; Lieutenant Colonel in 6th West India Regiment 16 May 1816 (vice Dolphin); to half-pay of 6th West India Regiment 24 Oct 1817
Brevets: Brevet Lieutenant Colonel 1 Jan 1812
Service 1793–1815: Served in West Indies 1808–1817; dismissed in Dominica in 1813 for insubordination but eventually reinstated
Retired: 1827
Awards & Honours: AGM (Guad)
Died: Antigua Apr 1842
Sources: ARLI; The history of the island of Antigua

403. *George Purdon DREW (1808-1811)*
Born: County Clare 1772
Relations: Son of George Purdon Drew of Dublin, clerk, and Letitia (Godfrey); brother of Lieutenant Colonel John Godfrey Drew, 45th Foot; Captain Barry Drew, 45th Foot; and Captain Francis Drew, 45th Foot
Entry to Army: Ensign in 45th Foot 25 Jan 1792 by purchase
Regimental Field Officer Promotions: Major in 45th Foot 7 Jan 1808 (vice Nicolls)
Service 1793–1815: Served in West Indies 1794–1801; served in Buenos Ayres 1807; served in Peninsula Sep to Dec 1809
Retired: 27 Jun 1811
Residence: Limerick, County Limerick
Died: Limerick 20 Mar 1843
Sources: ANCB; ANCD; ARLI; CHAL; GHHI; WEOF; WO 25/745

404. *William SMITH (1809-1810)*
Born: Berwickshire 1776
Relations: Son of James Smith of Ninewell Mains and Elizabeth (Thomson)
Entry to Army: Ensign in 45th Foot 26 Feb 1793 by purchase
Regimental Field Officer Promotions: Major in 45th Foot 13 Jul 1809 (vice Patton) by purchase
Service 1793–1815: Served in West Indies 1794–1801; served in Buenos Ayres 1807; served in Peninsula Aug 1808 to Sep 1810; Observing Officer in Peninsula Jan to Jun 1809
Awards & Honours: AGM (Tal)
Died: Killed in action at Busaco 27 Sep 1810
Sources: ARLI; CHAL; HALL; WEOF; WO 25/748

405. *David LECKY (1811-1816)*
Born: County Derry 1774
Relations: Son of Thomas Lecky of Londonderry and Elizabeth (Squire)
Entry to Army: Captain in Londonderry Regiment 8 Dec 1794
Regimental Field Officer Promotions: Major in 45th Foot 28 Feb 1811 (vice Gwyn)
Brevets: Brevet Lieutenant Colonel 1 Jan 1812
Service 1793–1815: Served in Buenos Aires 1807; served in Peninsula Aug 1808 to Oct 1811, taken POW at Talavera and exchanged; commanded 1/45th in Peninsula Nov 1810 to Jul 1812, wounded at Fuentes d'Oñoro
Retired: 19 Dec 1816
Residence: Newtownlimavady, near Londonderry, County Derry
Died: Newtownlimavady 27 Mar 1821
Sources: ANCB; ANCW; ARLI; CHAL; HALL; WEMR; WEOF

406. *Hugh STACPOOLE (1811-1826)*
Born: County Clare 1784
Relations: Son of George Hogan Stacpoole of Cragbrien and Jane (Lysaght); brother of Lieutenant Colonel John Massey Stacpoole, 45th Foot; and Commander Michael Stacpoole RN
Entry to Army: Ensign in 46th Foot 1 May 1800
Regimental Field Officer Promotions: Major in 45th Foot 18 Jul 1811 (vice Drew) by purchase; Lieutenant Colonel in 30th Foot 20 Dec 1826 (vice Vigoureux)
Brevets: Brevet Lieutenant Colonel 12 Aug 1819
Retired: 18 Oct 1827
Residence: Clanville Lodge, Penton Grafton, Hampshire
Died: Clanville Lodge 18 Jan 1840
Sources: ANCB; ANCD; ANCW; ARLI; WEOF

407. *Thomas LIGHTFOOT (1813-1831)*
Born: Warwickshire 1777
Relations: Son of John Lightfoot of Birmingham and Anchoret (Herbert); father of Colonel Thomas Lightfoot, 84th Foot
Education: Royal Military College 1818
Entry to Army: Ensign in Warwickshire Militia; Ensign in 5th Foot 11 Aug 1799
Regimental Field Officer Promotions: Major in 45th Foot 7 Oct 1813 (vice Forbes); to half-pay of 45th Foot 25 Oct 1814
Brevets: Brevet Lieutenant Colonel 19 May 1814; Brevet Colonel 6 May 1831; Major General 23 Nov 1841; Lieutenant General 20 Jun 1854
Colonelcies: 62nd Foot 11 Apr 1851 (vice Smelt)
Service 1793–1815: Served in Buenos Aires 1807; served in Peninsula Aug 1808 to Apr 1814, wounded at Badajoz, Salamanca and Toulouse

Later Service: Assistant Quartermaster General in British North America 1819; extra ADC to King William IV 6 May 1831
Awards & Honours: AGM (Pyr Toul); CB 4 Jun 1815; MGSM (Rol Vim Tal Bus FDO CR Bad Sal Nlle Niv Ort)
Residence: Barbourne House, Worcester, Worcestershire
Died: Barbourne House 15 Nov 1858
Sources: ANCW; ARLI; CHAL; PHIL; WEOF

408. *John O'FLAHERTY (1814-1829)*

Born: County Mayo c.1775
Relations: Son of Edmund O'Flaherty of Roscommon and Barbara (Dillon); brother of Captain Francis O'Flaherty, 23rd Foot
Entry to Army: Ensign in Galway Militia; Ensign in 68th Foot Feb 1800
Regimental Field Officer Promotions: Major in 45th Foot 19 May 1814 (vice Greenwell); to half-pay of 45th Foot 25 Oct 1814
Service 1793–1815: Served in Buenos Aires 1807; served in Peninsula Nov 1810 to Apr 1814, wounded at Badajoz
Awards & Honours: AGM (Vit)
Residences: Ballyhaunis, County Mayo
Died: Ballyhaunis 6 Mar 1829
Sources: ANCW (brother); ARLI; CHAL; HALL; WEMR; WEOF

Selected Regimental Histories

Wyllie, H.C., *History of the 1st and 2nd Battalions, The Sherwood Foresters, Nottinghamshire and Derbyshire Regiment 1740-1914* (Frome: Butler & Tanner, 1929)
Brown, Steve, *Wellington's Redjackets: The 45th (Nottinghamshire) Regiment on Campaign in South America and the Peninsula, 1805–14* (Barnsley: Pen & Sword Books, 2015)

Regimental Museum

Nottingham Castle, Lenton Road, Nottingham, Nottinghamshire

46th Regiment of Foot

Secondary Title:	South Devonshire
Nicknames:	The Lacedemonians The Surprisers
Jacket:	Red
Facings:	Yellow

Regimental Lineage, 46th Regiment of Foot

1741:	Jan – raised as a marine Regiment by Major General John Price in Newcastle-upon-Tyne
1743:	Murray's Regiment of Foot
1747:	Ranked as 57th Regiment of Foot
1751:	46th Regiment of Foot
1782:	46th (South Devonshire) Regiment of Foot
1800:	May – 2nd Battalion formed in Plymouth
1802:	May – 2nd Battalion disbanded in Ireland
1881:	Duke of Cornwall's Light Infantry (on amalgamation with 32nd (Cornwall) Regiment of Foot)
1959:	Somerset and Cornwall Light Infantry (on amalgamation with the Somerset Light Infantry)
1968:	1st Battalion, The Light Infantry (on amalgamation with the King's Own Yorkshire Light Infantry, the King's Shropshire Light Infantry and the Durham Light Infantry)
2007:	5th Battalion, The Rifles

Service History, 1st Battalion 46th Regiment of Foot

1793:	Gibraltar
1794:	Gibraltar; Nov – to West Indies; Dec – Martinique
1795:	Martinique; Mar – to St Vincent; Dorsetshire Hill; May – Calliaqua; Jun – La Vigie; Mount Young

1796:	Martinique; Mar – Martinique, St Vincent and St Kitts; Fort Charlotte; Jun – New Vigie; Mount Young; Mount William; Jul – men drafted in Martinique, cadre to England; Oct – Portsmouth; Nov – Hilsea; Tiverton
1797:	Poole; Apr – Doncaster; Jun – York
1798:	York; Chelmsford; Feb – Reading; Jun – Reading and Ashford; Jul – Warminster; Oct – Warminster and Westbury
1799:	Warminster and Westbury; Aug – Poole; Dec – Plymouth and Exeter
1800:	Plymouth; to Ireland; Feb – Cork; Fermoy; Mar – Cork; Aug – Limerick
1801:	Limerick
1802:	Limerick; May – absorbed 2md Battalion men; Aug – Tarbert; Sep – Cork
1803:	Cork
1804:	Cork; Feb – to West Indies; Apr – Barbados; Jun – DOMINICA
1805:	Dominica; Feb – Pont Michel
1806–1808:	Dominica
1809:	Dominica; Jan – flank companies in Martinique; Fort Bourbon
1810:	Dominica; Jan – flank companies in Guadeloupe; Bellair
1811:	Dominica; Nov – HQ and five companies to England, four service companies remained in West Indies
1812:	Plymouth; Feb – Kingsbridge; Apr – Jersey; Jun – four West Indies companies arrived in Jersey, battalion reunited
1813:	Jersey; Jun – Portsmouth; Cowes; Aug – to New South Wales
1814:	Feb – Sydney; detachment to Van Diemen's Land
1815:	Sydney

Service History, 2nd Battalion 46th Regiment of Foot

1800:	May – formed in Plymouth; Aug – to Ireland; Limerick
1801:	Limerick
1802:	Limerick; Jan – ordered disbanded; May – amalgamated with 1/46th in Limerick

Establishments, 1st Battalion 46th Regiment of Foot

Year	Subunits	Field Off	Off/ Staff	Sjts	Mus	Corp/ Pvts	Total
Dec 1792	10co	3	32	22	12	430	499
Dec 1793	10co	3	32	32	22	600	689
Dec 1795	10co+2r	5	51	62	30	1,010	1,158
Dec 1797	10co	5	32	53	22	600	712
Dec 1798	10co	5	38	53	22	600	718
Dec 1799	10co	5	43	53	22	1,000	1,123
May 1801	10co	5	42	43	22	800	912
Jul 1802	10co	5	33	34	22	750	844
Jan 1804	10co	5	36	34	22	750	847
Dec 1804	10co	5	46	44	22	800	917
Dec 1806	10co	4	46	44	22	800	916
Dec 1807	10co	4	45	24	22	400	495
May 1809	10co	4	50	32	26	408	520
Dec 1809	10co	4	46	34	22	410	516
Dec 1811	10co	4	46	45	22	610	727
Dec 1812	10co	4	35	35	22	600	696
Dec 1813	10co+r	4	38	43	22	608	715
Dec 1814	11co+r	5	52	48	24	708	837
Dec 1815	11co+r	5	53	58	24	908	1,048

Establishments, 2nd Battalion 46th Regiment of Foot

Year	Subunits	Field Off	Off/ Staff	Sjts	Mus	Corp/ Pvts	Total
May 1801	10co	5	42	43	22	800	912

Service Statistics, 46th Regiment of Foot

	Lieutenant Colonels	Majors
Number of officers in period 1793–1815	13	15
Average age on appointment to substantive rank	38.5	34.5
Average time in rank in regiment (years)	6.5	4.5
Total field officers by nationality	14 E / 9 S / 3 I / 1 W / 1 A	
Demographics of other ranks 1799	91% EW / 5% I / 4% S	
Demographics of other ranks 1810	42% EW / 42% I / 16% S	
Demographics of other ranks 1815	55% EW / 26% I / 19% S	
Months of overseas service 1793–1815	1/46th: 175 2/46th: no overseas service	

Significant Militia/Volunteer Intakes

1799: Buckinghamshire, Cambridgeshire, East Devon, Dorset, 1st Somerset, 1st Staffordshire, Sussex, Cardiganshire
1801: Cambridgeshire, Cheshire
1807: Forfarshire
1811: South Devon
1812: 1st Somerset
1814: Shropshire

Regimental Colonels

409. *Hon. Sir John VAUGHAN (1775–1795)*

Born: Northumberland 1729
Relations: Son of Wilmot Vaughan, 3rd Viscount Lisburne and Elizabeth (Watson)
Entry to Army: 2nd Lieutenant in 9th Marines 30 Apr 1746; cornet in 10th Dragoons 9 Apr 1748
Field Officer Promotions: Major in 94th Foot 15 Oct 1759; Lieutenant Colonel Commandant in 94th Foot 12 Jan 1760; Lieutenant Colonel in 46th Foot 25 Nov 1762
Brevets: Brevet Colonel 25 May 1772; Major General 29 Aug 1777; Lieutenant General 20 Nov 1782
Colonelcies: 46th Foot 11 May 1775 (vice Howe)
Early Service: Served in Seven Years War; served at capture of Martinique 1762; served in American War of Independence 1776–1779; Governor of Fort William 1779–1780; Commander in Chief Leeward Islands 1780–1782; Governor of Berwick-upon-Tweed
1780–1795
Service 1793–1815: Commander in Chief Leeward and Windward Islands and Governor of Martinique 22 Nov 1794 to 30 Jun 1795
Political Career: MP (Berwick-upon-Tweed) 1774–1795; MP (Ire) 1776–1783
Awards and Honours: KB 15 Aug 1792
Died: Martinique 30 Jun 1795
Sources: ARLI; HPON; ODNB; WEOF; WOST

410. *Sir James Henry CRAIG (1795–1804)*

Born: Gibraltar 1748
Relations: Son of Captain Hew Craig, judge of civil and military courts in Gibraltar, and Margaret Frances (Dumas); brother of General Peter William Craig
Education: Military school in France
Entry to Army: Ensign in 30th Foot 1 Jun 1763 by purchase
Regimental Field Officer Promotions: Major in 82nd Foot 22 Dec 1777; Lieutenant Colonel in 82nd Foot 31 Dec 1781; Lieutenant Colonel in 16th Foot 30 Jun 1783 by purchase
Brevets: Brevet Colonel 18 Nov 1790; Major General 3 Oct 1794; Lieutenant General 1 Jan 1801; General (Mediterranean) Mar 1805; General 1 Jan 1812
Colonelcies: 46th Foot 1 Aug 1795 (vice Vaughan); 86th Foot 5 Jan 1804 (vice Grinfield); 22nd Foot 30 Oct 1806 (vice Simcoe); 78th Foot 15 Sep 1809 (vice Fraser)
Early Service: Served in Gibraltar 1763; ADC to Boyd in Gibraltar 1770–1771; served in American War of Independence 1773–1782, wounded at Bunker's Hill

Service 1793–1815: Commander in Chief and Lieutenant Governor of Jersey 31 Jan 1793 to Oct 1793; Lieutenant Governor of Guernsey Oct 1793 to Dec 1793; Adjutant General in Flanders 1794; commanded forces at capture of Cape of Good Hope 1795; Commandant of Cape Colony 15 Nov 1795 to 5 May 1797; Commander in Chief in British East Indies Feb 1801; commanded Eastern District at home 1803–1805; Commander in Chief in Mediterranean 25 Mar 1805 to Apr 1806 (vice Villettes); Commander in Chief of British Forces in Sicily 17 Feb 1806 to Apr 1806; Governor of Blackness Castle 29 Sep 1806; Governor General of British North America and Governor of Lower Canada 24 Oct 1807 to 19 Jun 1811
Awards and Honours: KB 14 Jan 1797
Residence: St. Pancras, London
Died: London 12 Jan 1812
Sources: ARLI; ANCW; DICB; DINB; WEOF; WO 25/744; WOST

411. *John WHYTE (1804–1816)*

Born: England c.1740
Entry to Army: Probably promoted from the ranks; Quartermaster in 38th Foot 1 Jun 1761
Regimental Field Officer Promotions: Major in 83rd Foot 23 Dec 1777; Lieutenant Colonel in 6th Foot 3 Apr 1782 (vice Home) by purchase
Brevets: Brevet Colonel 12 Oct 1793; Brigadier General (West Indies) 1794; Major General 26 Feb 1795
Colonelcies: 1st West India Regiment 24 Apr 1795; 46th Foot 5 Jan 1804 (vice Craig)
Early Service: Served in Havana 1762; served in Nova Scotia 1786–1793
Service 1793–1815: Served in West Indies 1793–1796; commanded brigades in St. Domingue and Martinique 1794; commander in Chief in Demerara Apr 1796; Governor of St Domingue Jul 1797 to Apr 1798
Residence: Walburton House, Walburton, Sussex
Died: 31 Mar 1816
Sources: ANCD; ARLI; WEOF; WO 25/748; WOST

Colonel Commandant

412. *Sir Charles ASGILL, 2nd Bt (2nd Battalion) (1800–1802)*

Born: London 1762
Relations: Son of Sir Charles Asgill, Bt and Sarah Theresa (Pratviel); son-in-law of Admiral Sir Chaloner Ogle, Bt.
Education: Westminster School; University of Göttingen
Entry to Army: Ensign in 1st Foot Guards 27 Feb 1778 by purchase
Regimental Field Officer Promotions: Captain and Lieutenant Colonel in 1st Foot Guards 3 Mar 1790 by purchase; Third Major in 1st Foot Guards 25 Nov 1799 (vice Burrard); to half-pay25 Jun 1802
Brevets: Brevet Colonel 26 Feb 1795; Brigadier General (Ireland) Jun 1797; Major General 1 Jan 1798; Lieutenant General 1 Jan 1805; General 4 Jun 1814
Colonelcies: Colonel Commandant of 2/46th Foot 9 May 1800; 5th West India Regiment 8 Feb 1806 (vice Calvert); 85th Foot 30 Oct 1806 (vice Ross); 11th Foot 25 Feb 1807 (vice Fitzpatrick)
Early Service: Served in the American War of Independence 1781–1782; POW at Yorktown, sentenced to hang but had his life spared on appeal from King Louis XVI; Equerry to Duke of York
Service 1793–1815: Served in Flanders 1794–1795; served on Irish staff during Rebellion 1797–1798; served on staff in Ireland 1803–1812
Creations and Dignities: 2nd Baronet of London 15 Sep 1788
Awards and Honours: GCH 12 Aug 1820
Residences: Old Burlington Street, Mayfair, London; York Street, St James's Square, London; Park Place South, Chelsea, London
Died: London 23 Jul 1823
Sources: ARLI; DINB; PHIL; WEOF; WO 25/744

Lieutenant Colonels

413. *Hon. Colin LINDSAY (1783–1795)*

Born: Fifeshire 1755
Relations: Son of James Lindsay, 5th Earl of Balcarres, and Anne (Dalrymple); brother of General Alexander Lindsay, 6th Earl of Balcarres; Captain Hon. James Stair Lindsay, 73rd Foot; and Lieutenant Colonel Hon. John Lindsay, 71st Foot
Entry to Army: Ensign in 4th Foot 14 Nov 1771 by purchase
Regimental Field Officer Promotions: Major in 2/73rd Foot 13 Sep 1780 (vice MacLeod); Lieutenant Colonel in 82nd Foot 30 Jun 1783 (vice Craig); Lieutenant Colonel in 46th Foot 11 Jul 1783 (vice Markham) by exchange
Brevets: Brevet Colonel 20 Dec 1793; Brigadier General (Grenada) Mar 1795
Early Service: Commanded 46th Foot 1783–1795
Service 1793–1815: ADC to King George III 20 Dec 1793
Died: Committed suicide in Grenada 23 Mar 1795
Sources: ANCB; ARLI; Ashby, T., 'Fédon's Rebellion I', Journal of the Society for Army Historical Research, Vol.62, pp154–168

414. *Sir Baldwin LEIGHTON, 6th Bt (1795–1809)*
Born: Shropshire 1747
Relations: Son of Captain Baldwin Leighton of Shrewsbury and Anne (Smith); brother of Colonel Burgh Leighton, 4th Dragoons; and Lieutenant General Thomas Leighton, Madras service
Entry to Army: Lieutenant in 96th Foot 28 Oct 1760
Regimental Field Officer Promotions: Major in 46th Foot 20 Dec 1787 (vice Johnson); Lieutenant Colonel in 46th Foot 27 Mar 1795 (vice Lindsay)
Brevets: Brevet Major 12 Jun 1782; Brevet Lieutenant Colonel 12 Oct 1793; Brevet Colonel 26 Jan 1797; Brigadier General (Portugal) 11 Oct 1798; Brigadier General (West Indies) 22 Jan 1801; Major General 25 Sep 1803; Lieutenant General 29 Oct 1809; General 12 Aug 1819
Colonelcies: 3rd Garrison Battalion 18 Sep 1809 (vice Hill)
Early Service: Served in East Indies 1761–1765; served in American War of Independence 1775–1778, wounded at Monmouth
Service 1793–1815: Served in West Indies 1794–1796; commanded 1/46th Foot 1795–1801; served in Portugal 1797–1802; on staff in Jersey Jan 1807 to acting Lieutenant Governor of Jersey 17 Oct 1809 to 1810
Later Service: Governor of Carrickfergus 30 Jan 1817
Creations and Dignities: 6th Baronet of Wattlesborough 21 Feb 1819
Residence: Loton Park, near Alberbury, Shropshire
Died: Loton Park 13 Nov 1828
Sources: ARLI; GEMA (1829); PHIL; WEOF; WOST; WO 25/746; Complete Baronetage, Vol.4

415. *Bryan BELL (1795–1798)*
Born: Northumberland c.1746
Relations: Son of Matthew Bell of Lowick and Frances (Grey)
Entry to Army: Ensign in 44th Foot 5 Jul 1772 by purchase
Regimental Field Officer Promotions: Major in 46th Foot 27 Mar 1795 (vice Leighton); Lieutenant Colonel in 46th Foot 1 Sep 1795; to half-pay of 97th Foot 1 Feb 1798
Brevets: Brevet Major 1 Mar 1794
Early Service: Served in American War of Independence; served in West Indies 1779–1783
Retired: Court martialled in Aug 1797 for the manslaughter of Surgeon Crigan in a duel; told 'not to expect any further promotion in the army'
Residence: Bowsden, Northumberland
Died: Killed by his gun going off whilst loading, Bowsden 22 Sep 1809
Sources: ARLI; FMPD; The Sun, 12 Feb 1808

416. *James GRANT (1798–1800)*
Born: Scotland c.1758
Entry to Army: Volunteer in British North America; Ensign in 14th Foot 18 Jun 1775
Regimental Field Officer Promotions: Major in 3rd West India Regiment 20 May 1795; Lieutenant Colonel in 3rd West India Regiment 5 Aug 1796; Lieutenant Colonel in 46th Foot 1 Feb 1798 (vice Bell)
Brevets: Brevet Lieutenant Colonel 5 Oct 1795
Early Service: Served in American War of Independence
Service 1793–1815: Served in West Indies 1796–1800; Deputy Adjutant General in Jamaica 2 May 1799
Died: Jamaica 5 Jan 1800
Sources: ARLI; EDMA (1801)

417. *Edward McDONNELL (1800)*
Born: County Clare 1766
Relations: Son of Lieutenant Colonel Charles McDonnell of Killone and Catherine (O'Brien)
Entry to Army: Ensign in 24th Foot 3 Apr 1786
Regimental Field Officer Promotions: Major in 46th Foot 2 Sep 1795; Lieutenant Colonel in 46th Foot 24 Apr 1800; to half-pay of 105th Foot 7 Jul 1800 (vice Cockell) by exchange
Service 1793–1815: Deputy Quarter Master General in British North America
Residence: Newhall, Killone, County Clare; Montréal, Québec, Canada
Died: Montréal 20 Oct 1812
Sources: ANCB; ANCD; ARLI; WEOF; <https://landedestates.ie/estate/1903>

418. *Crofton VANDELEUR (1800–1806)*
Born: County Clare c.1770
Relations: Son of Crofton Vandeleur of Kilrush and Alice (Burton); brother of Major Richard Vandeleur, 38th Foot; and Captain Frederick Vandeleur, 87th Foot; cousin of Colonel John Ormsby Vandeleur, 5th Dragoon Guards; and Lieutenant Colonel Thomas Pakenham Vandeleur, 8th Light Dragoons
Entry to Army: Ensign in 24th Foot 20 Dec 1787 by purchase
Regimental Field Officer Promotions: Major in 107th Foot 8 Apr 1794; Lieutenant Colonel in 107th Foot 8 Feb 1795; to half-pay of 107th Foot 1 Mar 1798; Lieutenant Colonel in 46th Foot 1 May 1800

Brevets: Brevet Colonel 29 Apr 1802; Brigadier General (Leeward Islands) 31 Dec 1803
Service 1793–1815: Commanded 1/46th Foot 1800–1803; served in West Indies 1804–1806
Residence: Clooncoose, County Clare
Died: Died of fever in Antigua 30 Oct 1806
Sources: ARLI; LHHI; WEOF; Vandeleurs of Kilrush County Clare

419. *William COCKELL (1800–1802)*

Born: Yorkshire 1759
Relations: [spec.] Son of Marmaduke Coghill of Leeds and Mercy (Mann); father of Captain William Wetherall Cockell, 16th Foot
Entry to Army: Ensign in 1st West Yorkshire Militia 1780; Ensign in 31st Foot 12 Jul 1782 by purchase
Regimental Field Officer Promotions: Major in 105th Foot 18 Apr 1794 by purchase; Lieutenant Colonel in 105th Foot 16 Sep 1795 (vice Manningham); to half-pay of 105th Foot 1795; Lieutenant Colonel in 46th Foot 7 Jul 1800 (vice McDonnell) by exchange; to half-pay of 46th Foot 24 Jun 1802; Lieutenant Colonel in 5th Foot 3 Oct 1802 (vice Lindsey) by exchange; removed from the regiment as a general officer 1815
Brevets: Brevet Lieutenant Colonel 16 Sep 1795; Brevet Colonel 25 Sep 1803; Brigadier General (Guernsey) 24 Aug 1804; Brigadier General (Cape of Good Hope) 25 Oct 1806; Major General 25 Jul 1810; Lieutenant General 4 Jun 1814
Early Service: Served in American War of Independence as volunteer in 33rd Foot 1776–1780; served in Gibraltar 1783–1789
Service 1793–1815: Assistant Adjutant General in Ireland 1796; Inspector of Recruiting District in Ireland Aug 1802; served in capture of Mauritius 1810
Residence: Sandleford Lodge, near Newbury, Berkshire
Died: Sandleford Lodge 6 Jun 1831
Sources: ANCW; ARLI; PHIL; WEOF; WO 25/744

420. *William RAYMOND (1801–1802)*

Born: Essex 1760
Relations: Son of James Raymond of Saffron Walden and Mary (Collin); father-in-law of Lieutenant General Sir William Inglis
Entry to Army: Ensign in 33rd Foot 28 Aug 1775 by purchase
Regimental Field Officer Promotions: Major in 89th Foot 18 Jul 1799 (vice Boyle); Lieutenant Colonel in 46th Foot 28 Mar 1801; to half-pay of 46th Foot 25 Jun 1802
Brevets: Brevet Lieutenant Colonel 29 Jul 1799; Brevet Colonel 25 Aug 1808; Major General 1 Jan 1812; Lieutenant General 27 May 1825
Colonelcies: 13th Royal Veteran Battalion 19 Nov 1812
Early Service: Served in American War of Independence 1777–1781, POW at Yorktown
Service 1793–1815: Deputy Adjutant General in Ireland 1798; commanded 2/46th Foot 1801–1802; Deputy Adjutant General in Ireland 1808
Residences: Bath, Somerset; The Lee, Littlebury, Essex
Died: York Street, Portman Square, London 9 Jun 1830
Sources: ANCB; ANCD; ARLI; WEOF; WO 25/748

421. *Sir Edward BARNES (1807–1814)*

Born: Middlesex 1776
Relations: Son of John Barnes of Enfield, former Governor of Senegal, and Anne (Parke); father of Captain Edward Barnes, 27th Foot
Entry to Army: Ensign in 47th Foot 8 Nov 1792
Field Officer Promotions: Major in 99th Foot 16 Nov 1794; to half-pay of 99th Foot 1797; Major in 79th Foot 17 Feb 1800 (vice Stewart) by exchange; Lieutenant Colonel in 46th Foot 23 Apr 1807 (vice Vandeleur); removed from the regiment as a general officer Feb 1814
Brevets: Brevet Lieutenant Colonel 1 Jan 1800; Brevet Colonel 25 Jul 1810; Major General 4 Jun 1813; Lieutenant General (Ceylon) 20 Mar 1823; Lieutenant General 27 May 1825; General (India) 7 Jun 1831
Colonelcies: 2nd Garrison Battalion 27 Nov 1815 (vice Torrens); 99th Foot 24 Oct 1816 (vice Howard); Colonel Commandant of 2/Rifle Brigade 13 May 1820; 78th Foot 25 Aug 1822 (vice Auchmuty); 31st Foot 10 Oct 1834 (vice Warde)
Service 1793–1815: Served in Egypt 1801; commanded 46th Foot 1807–1811; acting Governor of Dominica 31 Jul 1808 to 12 Dec 1808; acting Governor of Dominica 3 Jul 1809 to 15 Apr 1812; commanded brigades in Peninsula Oct 1812 to Apr 1814; Adjutant General in Waterloo campaign 1815; Adjutant General in Army of Occupation in France Nov 1815 to Nov 1818
Later Service: Acting Governor of Ceylon Feb 1820 to Feb 1822; Governor Ceylon Jan 1824 to Oct 1831; Commander in Chief India 1831–1833
Political Career: MP (Sudbury) 1834–1835; MP (Sudbury) 1837–1838
Awards and Honours: Sultan's Egypt medal; KCB 2 Jan 1815; AGC (Mart Guad Vitt Pyr Nlle Niv Ort); WatM 23 Apr 1816; KMT 1816; KSA 1816; GCB 24 Feb 1831
Residences: Beech Hill Park, Hadley Wood,

Middlesex; Berkeley Square, London; Piccadilly, London; Walthamstow, Essex
Died: Walthamstow 19 Mar 1838
Sources: ANCW; ARLI; CHAL; DALT; HPON; PHIL; WEBC; WEOF; WOST

422. *Sir John BROWN (1812–1813)*

Born: Surrey 1774
Relations: Son of Captain Samuel Brown of Dulwich, RN and Elizabeth (Penn)
Entry to Army: Cornet in 6th Dragoons 27 May 1795 by purchase
Regimental Field Officer Promotions: Lieutenant Colonel in 5th Portuguese Dragoons 1809; Lieutenant Colonel in 8th Portuguese Dragoons 23 Mar 1811; Lieutenant Colonel in 13th Portuguese Infantry 14 Mar 1811; Lieutenant Colonel in 46th Foot 13 Aug 1812; Lieutenant Colonel in 1st Greek Light Infantry 25 Jan 1813 (vice Thornton); Lieutenant Colonel in 21st Light Dragoons 6 Apr 1815 (vice Pritzler); Lieutenant Colonel in 13th Light Dragoons 9 May 1820
Brevets: Brevet Major (Portuguese service) 16 Feb 1809; Brevet Colonel (Portuguese service) 5 Feb 1812; Brevet Colonel 19 Jul 1821; Major General 22 Jul 1830; Lieutenant General 23 Nov 1841; General 20 Jun 1854
Colonelcies: 8th Hussars 4 Apr 1843 (vice Philpot)
Service 1793–1815: ADC to Whitelocke in South America 1806–1807; served on staff in Peninsula Nov 1808 to Jan 1809; served in Peninsula with Portuguese army Feb 1809 to Apr 1814
Later Service: Commanded Cavalry Depot at Maidstone 1820
Awards and Honours: AGM (Rol Vim Cor); KTS (Portugal) 25 Jan 1813; GCCT (Spain); KCH 12 Aug 1831
Residence: Pall Mall, St. James's, London
Died: London 16 Nov 1856
Sources: ANCB; ANCM; ANCD; ARLI; CHAL; PHIL; WEOF; WO 25/744; Hardwicke's Annual Biography

423. *Henry CUYLER (1813)*

Born: New York State 1769
Relations: Son of Henry Cuyler of Greenbush and Catherine (Lydius); brother of Major William Howe Cuyler, US Army
Entry to Army: Ensign in 30th Foot 1 Dec 1782 by purchase
Regimental Field Officer Promotions: Major in 27th Foot 3 Nov 1797 (vice Rutherford); Lieutenant Colonel in 27th Foot 16 May 1800; to half-pay of 27th Foot 24 Oct 1803; Lieutenant Colonel in 1st Garrison Battalion 14 Nov 1804; Lieutenant Colonel in 3rd Foot 6 Feb 1805; Lieutenant Colonel in 85th Foot 18 Nov 1806 (vice Mellifont); Lieutenant Colonel 46th Foot 25 Jan 1813 (vice Brown)
Brevets: Brevet Major 9 Sep 1797; Brevet Colonel 25 Jul 1810
Early Service: Served in West Indies 1783
Service 1793–1815: Served aboard ship as a marine 1792–1793; served in Toulon 1793, taken POW; prisoner in France 1793–1795; Deputy Adjutant General in West Indies 1797–1798; Inspecting Field Officer of Militia 1803–1804; commanded 85th Foot in Walcheren 1809; commanded 85th Foot in Peninsula Mar to Oct 1811
Retired: 1 Feb 1813
Residence: Rochester, Kent
Died: Rochester 22 Nov 1841
Cuyler was prodded to 'retire' after the excoriation of the officer corps of the 85th Foot in 1813 following numerous courts martial involving that regiment
Sources: ANCD; ARLI; CHAL; WEOF; WO 25/744

424. *George James MOLLE (1813–1823)*

Born: George James Mow in Berwickshire 1773; changed surname to Molle in 1789
Relations: Son of John Mow of Chirnside and Margaret (Crow)
Entry to Army: Ensign in Scotch Brigade Jun 1793
Regimental Field Officer Promotions: Major in 8th Battalion of Reserve 3 Mar 1803; Major in 9th Foot 2 Jun 1804 (vice Bodkin) by exchange; Lieutenant Colonel in 9th Foot 2 Sep 1808 (vice Stewart); Lieutenant Colonel in 46th Foot 3 Jun 1813 (vice MacGregor) by exchange
Brevets: Brevet Colonel 4 Jun 1814
Service 1793–1815: Served in British East Indies 1799, wounded at Seringapatam; served in Peninsula with 1/9th Foot Aug to Sep 1808, severely wounded at Roliça; commanded 2/9th Foot 1809–1813; commanded 46th Foot in New South Wales 1813–1817; Lieutenant Governor of New South Wales Jun 1813 to Sep 1817
Died: Belgaum, India 9 Sep 1823
Sources: ARLI; HALL; PHIL; WEOF

425. *Archibald CAMPBELL (1814–1840)*

Born: Isle of Lewis c.1777
Relations: Son of John Campbell of Mishnish; brother of Lieutenant Colonel Donald Campbell, 40th Foot; father of Lieutenant Colonel Colin Frederick Campbell, 46th Foot
Entry to Army: Ensign in 25th Foot 9 Nov 1797
Regimental Field Officer Promotions: Major in 46th Foot 3 Sep 1812 (vice D. Campbell); Major in 15th Portuguese Line 29 Oct 1811; retired from

Portuguese service 4 May 1814; Lieutenant Colonel in 46th Foot 17 Feb 1814 (vice Barnes)
Brevets: Brevet Lieutenant Colonel 13 Dec 1813; Brevet Colonel 6 May 1831
Service 1793–1815: Served in West Indies 1804–1805; in Portuguese service in Peninsula Oct 1811 to Dec 1813, severely wounded at Nive
Later Service: Served in East Indies 1820–1827
Awards and Honours: AGM (Niv); CB 26 Sep 1831
Residence: Knock, Isle of Lewis
Died: Knock 13 Nov 1840
Sources: ANCW; ARLI; CHAL; PHIL; WEOF; Morvern, A Highland Parish

Majors

426. *James Phillips LLOYD[-PHILLIPS] (1795–1796)*
Born: James Phillips Lloyd in Pembrokeshire 1762; adopted additional -Phillips surname later in life
Relations: Son of James Phillips Lloyd of Mabws, Cardiganshire, and Anna Maria (Lloyd); nephew of General Vaughan Lloyd, RA
Entry to Army: Cadet in Royal Artillery; Lieutenant in 75th Foot 24 Jan 1778
Regimental Field Officer Promotions: Major in 46th Foot 1 Sep 1795 (vice Leighton) by purchase; Lieutenant Colonel in 86th Foot 8 Jun 1796 (vice Campbell) by purchase; Lieutenant Colonel in 10th Foot 17 Apr 1805 (vice Fraser) by exchange; rank stationary after Jun 1805
Brevets: Brevet Colonel 1 Jan 1805
Retired: Retaining rank 6 Jun 1805
Later Service: Governor of Fishguard Fort 31 May 1821
Residence: Mabws, Llanrhystud, Cardiganshire; Penty Park, near Haverfordwest, Pembrokeshire
Died: Mabws 11 Apr 1837
Sources: ANCB; ANCD; ANCW; ARLI; PHIL; WEOF

427. *William CLARKE (1796–1802)*
Born: [spec.] Shropshire c.1769
Entry to Army: Ensign in 65th Foot 6 Mar 1783 by purchase
Regimental Field Officer Promotions: Major in 46th Foot 28 Sep 1796 (vice Lloyd) by purchase
Brevets: Brevet Lieutenant Colonel 29 Jun 1802
Retired: 28 Jul 1802
Residence: Portland Square, Bristol; Buckingham Street, St Martin in the Fields, London
Died: London 23 Jun 1839
Sources: ANCD; ANCW; ARLI; GEMA (1815) (wife)

428. *Dugald CAMPBELL (1800–1812)*
Born: Argyllshire 1764
Relations: Son of James Campbell of Silvercraigs, Provost of Inveraray and Jean (Campbell); brother of Captain John Campbell, Paymaster of 46th Foot; and Lieutenant Colonel Colin Campbell, 1st Foot
Entry to Army: Ensign in 57th Foot 30 Apr 1783 by purchase
Regimental Field Officer Promotions: Major in 46th Foot 27 Apr 1800; to Lieutenant Colonel in 3rd West India Regiment 13 Aug 1812 (vice Viscount Petersham); removed from the regiment as a general officer 1814
Brevets: Brevet Major 1 Jan 1798; Brevet Lieutenant Colonel 25 Sep 1803; brevet Colonel 1 Jan 1812; Major General 4 Jun 1814
Early Service: Served in British North America 1784–1786
Service 1793–1815: Served in West Indies 1794–1796; commanded 46th Foot 1803–1807; served in West Indies 1804–1814
Residence: Inveraray, Argyllshire
Died: Inveraray 11 Jul 1824
Sources: *ARLI; WEOF; WO 25/744; The Kist, No.27, Spring 1984*

429. *Richard BUCKBY (1800–1802)*
Born: County Armagh 1765
Relations: Son of Richard Buckby of Seagoe and Elizabeth (Hesilrige)
Entry to Army: Ensign in 56th Foot 22 Sep 1787
Regimental Field Officer Promotions: Major in 46th Foot 1 May 1800; to half-pay of 46th Foot 25 Jun 1802; Major in 58th Foot 9 Jul 1803; Lieutenant Colonel in 58th Foot 8 Nov 1810 (vice Fitzgerald); to half-pay of 58th Foot 25 Feb 1816
Brevets: Brevet Lieutenant Colonel 25 Apr 1808; Brevet Colonel 4 Jun 1813; Major General 27 May 1825
Service 1793–1815: Served in West Indies 1794–1795; served in Helder 1799; served in Malta, Naples and Sicily; served in Maida 1806; commanded 2/58th Foot in Peninsula Jan 1811 to Jun 1812
Residences: Midhurst, Sussex; Guilsborough, Northamptonshire
Died: Guilsborough 2 Jun 1830
Sources: ANCB; ANCD; CHAL; PHIL; WEOF; WO 25/744

430. *Archibald DRUMMOND (1800–1802)*
Born: Scotland c.1767
Entry to Army: Ensign in 16th Foot 30 Apr 1787

Regimental Field Officer Promotions: Major in 46th Foot 2 May 1800; to half-pay of 46th Foot May 1802; Major in 3rd Foot 9 Jul 1803; Lieutenant Colonel in 3rd Foot 17 Aug 1809 (vice Muter)
Brevets: Brevet Major 2 May 1800; Brevet Lieutenant Colonel 25 Apr 1806
Service 1793–1815: Served in Peninsula Sep 1808 to Jul 1810, commanded 1/3rd Foot Mar to Jun 1809; served in Peninsula Jul 1809 to Jul 1810
Awards and Honours: AGM (Tal)
Died: At sea on passage from Lisbon 22 Jul 1810
Sources: ARLI; CHAL; WEOF

431. *Hastings FRASER (1802–1804)*

Born: Vellore, British East Indies 1771
Relations: Son of Captain Charles Fraser, Madras service, and Isabella (Hook)
Entry to Army: Ensign in 74th Foot 9 Apr 1788 by purchase
Regimental Field Officer Promotions: Major in 46th Foot Jul 1802 (vice Clarke) by purchase; Lieutenant Colonel in 10th Foot 15 Sep 1804 by purchase; Lieutenant Colonel in 86th Foot 18 Apr 1805 (vice Lloyd) by exchange
Brevets: Brevet Colonel 4 Jun 1813; Major General 12 Aug 1819; Lieutenant General 10 Jan 1837
Colonelcies: 83rd Foot 30 Sep 1835 (vice Hodgson); 61st Foot 1 Sep 1848 (vice Dickson)
Early Service: Served in British East Indies 1790–1793
Service 1793–1815: Served in Penang 1797; served in British East Indies 1799–1802; served in West Indies 1803–1805; served in British East Indies 1805–1810; commanded brigade at capture of Bourbon 1810
Awards and Honours: CB 4 Jun 1815
Residence: Bury Street, St James's, London
Died: London 29 Sep 1852
Sources: ARLI; GEMA (1852); PHIL; WEOF; WO 25/745; <https://blogs.ucl.ac.uk/eicah/the-attar-casket-of-tipu-sultan/casket-case-study-the-fraser-family-living-between-britain-and-india/>

432. *Richard PAYNE (1804–1812)*

Born: Devon 1765
Relations: Son of Richard Payne of Tiverton and Sarah (Jones)
Entry to Army: Cornet in Warwickshire Fencible Cavalry May 1794; Ensign in 1/78th Foot Apr 1795
Regimental Field Officer Promotions: Major in 46th Foot 29 Dec 1804 (vice Fraser) by purchase; to half-pay of Hompesch Mounted Rifles 12 Nov 1812 (vice Sorell) by exchange
Brevets: Brevet Lieutenant Colonel 4 Jun 1811; Brevet Colonel 27 May 1825
Service 1793–1815: Served in Quiberon 1795; served in West Indies 1797; served in West Indies 1800–1810
Later Service: Second in command of Army Depot on Isle of Wight
Awards and Honours: AGM (Mart); CB 26 Sep 1831
Residences: Great Dorweeke, Silverton, Devon; Bath, Somerset; Marine Place, Dover, Kent
Died: Dover 20 Jan 1833
Sources: ANCW; ARLI; FMPD; GEMA (1833); WEOF; WO 25/747

433. *William SORELL (1812–1813)*

See 336.
Major in 46th Foot 12 Nov 1812 (vice Payne) by exchange

434. *Alexander OGILVIE (1813–1823)*

Born: Aberdeenshire 1783
Relations: Son of George Ogilvie of Auchiries and Rebecca (Irvine); brother of Major William Ogilvie, Bombay service
Entry to Army: Ensign in 92nd Foot 9 Jul 1803
Regimental Field Officer Promotions: Major in 46th Foot 4 Feb 1813 (vice Sorell) by purchase; Lieutenant Colonel in 46th Foot 10 Sep 1823 (vice Molle)
Service 1793–1815: Served in West Indies 1809–1810; commanded 46th Foot 1813
Later Service: Served in East Indies; commanded at Secunderabad 1832
Died: Secunderabad, India 22 Oct 1832
Sources: ANCB; ANCD; ARLI; PHIL; WEOF

435. *William Gordon MacGREGOR (1813)*

Born: Inverness-shire 1778
Relations: Son of James MacGregor of Ballimore and Margaret (Grant); brother of Sir Patrick MacGregor, Bt, royal surgeon; and Major George MacGregor, Madras service
Entry to Army: Ensign in 11th Foot 16 Oct 1793
Regimental Field Officer Promotions: Major in 11th Foot 26 Nov 1807 (vice Raleigh) by purchase; Major in 46th Foot 4 Feb 1813 (vice Cuyler) by purchase; Lieutenant Colonel in 9th Foot 3 Jun 1813 (vice Molle) by exchange; to half-pay of 9th Foot 24 Dec 1815
Brevets: Brevet Lieutenant Colonel 4 Feb 1813; Brevet Colonel 4 Jun 1813
Service 1793–1815: Served in Corsica 1794; served aboard fleet as marine 1795–1796; served in Madeira 1807–1808; served in Peninsula Aug 1809 to Sep 1812, severely wounded at Salamanca

Residence: St James's, Westminster, London
Died: London 6 Jan 1840
Sources: ANCD; ANCW; ARLI; CHAL; WEOF; WO 25/747

436. *John MacKENZIE (1814–1821)*
Born: Midlothian 1775
Relations: Son of Alexander Mackenzie of Duddingston and Elizabeth (Drew)
Entry to Army: Ensign in 88th Foot 19 Apr 1800 by purchase
Regimental Field Officer Promotions: Major in 46th Foot 17 Feb 1814 (vice Campbell)
Service 1793–1815: Served in West Indies
Later Service: Served in New South Wales 1814–1817; Commandant of Port Dalrymple
Retired: 1 Mar 1821
Residence: Wester Duddingston, Edinburgh
Died: Edinburgh 2 Sep 1830
Sources: ANCB; ANCD; ARLI; PHIL; WEOF

Selected Regimental Histories

Cannon, Richard, *Historical Record of the Forty-sixth, Or the South Devonshire, Regiment of Foot* (London: Parker, Furnivall and Parker, 1851)

Regimental Museum

Cornwall Army Museum, The Keep, Bodmin, Cornwall

47th Regiment of Foot

Secondary Title:	Lancashire
Nicknames:	The Cauliflowers Wolfe's Own The Lancashire Lads
Jacket:	Red
Facings:	White

Regimental Lineage, 47th Regiment of Foot

1741:	Raised in Scotland as Colonel John Mordaunt's Regiment of Foot
1743:	Lascelles' Regiment of Foot
1747:	Ranked as 58th Regiment of Foot
1751:	47th Regiment of Foot
1782:	47th (Lancashire) Regiment of Foot
1803:	Jun – 2nd Battalion formed in Colchester
1814:	Oct – 2nd Battalion disbanded in Liverpool
1881:	1st Battalion, Loyal North Lancashire Regiment (on amalgamation with 81st Regiment of Foot (Loyal Lincoln Volunteers))
1970:	Queen's Lancashire Regiment (on amalgamation with The Lancashire Regiment (Prince of Wales's Volunteers))
2006:	1st Battalion, The Duke of Lancaster's Regiment (King's, Lancashire and Border) (on amalgamation with The King's Own Royal Border Regiment and The King's Regiment)

Service History, 1st Battalion 47th Regiment of Foot

1793–1796:	New Providence, Bahamas; detachment on Turks and Caicos Islands
1797:	Bahamas; Mar – Bermuda
1798–1801:	Bermuda
1802:	Bermuda; Nov – to England
1803:	Gosport; Jun – Battle; Jul – Lewes; Aug – Battle; Oct – Colchester; Dec – Woodbridge; Liverpool; to Ireland; Dublin
1804:	Kilkenny; Aug – Curragh camp; Oct – Kilkenny
1805:	Kilkenny; Oct – Cork
1806:	Cork; Apr – to England; Portsmouth; May – to East Indies; Aug – Cape of Good Hope; to South America; Oct – Rio de la Plata; Montevideo

1807:	Maldonado; Feb – capture of Montevideo; Mar – Canelones and Santa Lucia; Jun – Montevideo garrison, light company at Buenos Aires; Jul – to Cape of Good Hope; Oct – to East Indies; Dec – Madras
1808:	Madras; Apr – Bombay [Mumbai]; Jun – Surat; Dec – Demaan [Daman]
1809:	Demaan and Diu; Apr – Butcher Island [Jawahar Dweep]; Jul – Bombay; Sep – flank companies to Muscat on anti-pirate expedition; Dec – flank companies return to Bombay
1810–1811:	Bombay
1812:	Bombay; flank companies to Nava Nagar; Aug – Poona [Pune]; Sep – Serdie [Shirdi]; Oct Erapoor [Arapur]; Nov – Mullingaum [Malangaon]; Dec – Bombay
1813:	Bombay; Mar – Colabah [Colaba]
1814:	Bombay; Nov – Surat; flank companies to Gujarat
1815:	Surat; Jun – battalion reunited at Surat; Jul – Baruchi [Bharuch]; Oct – Bombay (in East Indies until 1829)

Service History, 2nd Battalion 47th Regiment of Foot

1803:	Jul – formed at Colchester; Dec – Woodbridge; Liverpool; to Ireland
1804:	Clonmel; Apr – Cahir; Aug – Kildare; Sep – Curragh camp; Oct – Cahir
1805:	Cahir; Sep – Belfast
1806:	Belfast; Jul – Aughnacloy; Dec – Enniskillen
1807:	Enniskillen; Feb – Omagh; May – to England; Liverpool; Preston; Sep – Manchester; Oct – Chelmsford
1808:	Chelmsford; May – Jersey
1809:	Jersey; Oct – to Gibraltar; Nov – Gibraltar
1810:	Gibraltar
1811:	Gibraltar; Feb – flank companies to Tarifa; PENINSULA; flank companies at Barrosa; Jun – battalion companies in Tarragona; Cadiz; Isla de Leon; Oct – battalion reunited in Tarifa
1812:	Siege of TARIFA; Feb – Cadiz; to main field army; Oct – Trujillo; Talavera de la Reina; Nov – Castillejo de Dos Casas; Dec – Portelo
1813:	Portelo; May – Outeiro; Jun – VITTORIA; Salvatierra; siege of San Sebastian; Aug – SAN SEBASTIAN; Oct – Irun; Nov – St Jacques; Dec – NIVE; Bidart
1814:	Arcangues; Feb – sortie from Bayonne; Mar – Arcangues; Apr – Bayonne; Jul – Bordeaux; Aug – to England; Portsmouth; Chichester; Oct – disbanded in Liverpool

Establishments, 1st Battalion 47th Regiment of Foot

Year	Subunits	Field Off	Off/ Staff	Sjts	Mus	Corp/ Pvts	Total
Dec 1792	10co	3	32	22	12	430	499
Jan 1793	10co	3	32	32	22	600	689
Dec 1795	10co+2r	5	51	62	30	1,010	1,158
Dec 1797	10co	5	38	53	22	600	718
Dec 1799	10co	5	43	53	22	1,000	1,123
Dec 1801	10co	5	47	53	22	1,000	1,127
Jun 1802	10co	5	33	34	22	750	844
Jul 1803	10co	5	36	54	22	1,000	1,117
Jan 1804	10co	4	36	54	22	1,000	1,116
Feb 1805	10co	5	36	44	22	800	907
Dec 1805	10co	5	46	54	22	1,000	1,127
Dec 1806	10co	4	46	54	22	1,000	1,126
Oct 1807	10co	4	46	64	22	1,200	1,336
Dec 1807	10co	5	46	64	22	1,200	1,337
Dec 1809	10co+r	5	50	62	26	1,008	1,151
Dec 1810	10co+r	5	50	52	26	808	941
Dec 1811	10co+r	5	50	53	26	808	942
Dec 1813	10co+r	5	49	53	22	808	937

Dec 1814	10co+r	5	49	73	22	1,208	1,357
Dec 1815	10co+r	5	49	63	22	1,008	1,147

Establishments, 2nd Battalion 47th Regiment of Foot

Year	Subunits	Field Off	Off/ Staff	Sjts	Mus	Corp/ Pvts	Total
Dec 1803	10co	3	35	53	22	1,000	1,113
Dec 1804	10co	3	36	43	22	800	904
Jul 1807	10co	3	35	23	22	400	483
Oct 1807	10co	3	35	33	22	600	693
Jul 1808	10co	3	35	43	22	800	903
Dec 1808	10co	3	36	43	22	800	904
Jun 1809	10co	3	46	53	22	1,000	1,124
Dec 1809	10co+r	3	40	51	26	808	928
Dec 1810	10co+r	3	49	61	22	1,008	1,148
Dec 1811	10co+r	3	50	62	26	1,008	1,149
Dec 1813	10co+r	3	49	62	22	1,008	1,144

Service Statistics, 47th Regiment of Foot

	Lieutenant Colonels	Majors
Number of officers in period 1793–1815	9	20
Average age on appointment to substantive rank	39.5	35.5
Average time in rank in regiment (years)	10.5	4
Total field officers by nationality	11 E / 9 S / 7 I	
Demographics of other ranks 1798	52% I / 39 % EW / 6% S / 3% F	
Demographics of other ranks 1807	2/47th: 58% I / 38% EW / 4% S	
Demographics of other ranks 1811	2/47th: 58% EW / 40% I / 2% S	
Demographics of other ranks 1815	58% EW / 41% I / 1% S	
Months of overseas service 1793–1815	1/47th: 234 2/47th: 59	

Significant Militia/Volunteer Intakes

1798: Irish Brigade
1803: Army of Reserve men from Essex, Norfolk and Suffolk
1805: County Cork, County Mayo, County Monaghan, County Wexford
1807: North Devon, 1st Lancashire, 3rd Lancashire, County Tipperary
1809: 2nd Lancashire, North Lincolnshire, County Galway
1810: Dumfriesshire; County Meath
1811: County Louth
1812: County Galway

Regimental Colonels

437. *Sir Adam WILLIAMSON (1790–1794)*

Born: London 1736
Relations: Son of Lieutenant General George Williamson RA and Jane (Redley); brother of Colonel John Williamson RA; father-in-law of Major General William Mudge RA
Education: Royal Military Academy, Woolwich
Entry to Corps: Practitioner Engineer in Royal Engineers 1 Jan 1753
Regimental Field Officer Promotions: Major in 61st Foot 16 Aug 1770 by purchase; Lieutenant Colonel in 18th Foot 9 Dec 1775 by purchase
Brevets: Brevet Lieutenant Colonel 12 Sep 1775; Major General 28 Apr 1790; Lieutenant General (West Indies) 12 Oct 1793; Lieutenant General 26 Jan 1797
Colonelcies: 47th Foot 16 Jul 1790 (vice Carleton); 72nd Foot 19 Mar 1794 (vice Murray)
Early Service: Served in North America 1755–1760; served in West Indies 1762; served in North America 1775–1776; Deputy Adjutant General in South Britain 23 Sep 1778
Service 1793–1815: Commander in Chief

and acting Governor of Jamaica (including St. Domingue) 17 Nov 1791 to 29 Apr 1795; Governor of St. Domingue May 1795 to Mar 1796
Awards and Honours: KB 18 Nov 1794
Residence: Avebury House, near Marlborough, Wiltshire
Died: After a fall at home 21 Oct 1798
Sources: ANCB; ARLI; DINB; WEOF; WOST

438. *William DALRYMPLE (1794–1807)*

Born: Edinburgh 1736
Relations: Son of Hon. George Dalrymple of Dalmahoy and Euphame (Myrton); nephew of Field Marshal John Dalrymple, 2nd Earl of Stair; brother of Captain John Dalrymple, 5th Earl of Stair, 87th Foot
Education: Glasgow University
Entry to Army: Ensign in 52nd Foot 21 Jan 1756 by purchase
Regimental Field Officer Promotions: Major in 91st Foot 13 Feb 1762; to half-pay 1763; Lieutenant Colonel in 14th Foot 27 Mar 1765
Brevets: Brevet Colonel 29 Aug 1777; Major General 20 Nov 1782; Lieutenant General 12 Oct 1793; General 1 Jan 1798
Colonelcies: 47th Foot 19 Mar 1794 (vice Williamson)
Early Service: Served in Portugal 1762; served in British North America 1766–1772; Quartermaster General in North America 1779–1783
Service 1793–1815: Lieutenant Governor of Royal Hospital Chelsea 22 Mar 1798 to 16 Feb 1807
Political Career: MP (Wigton Burghs) 1784–1790 and 1796–1797
Residence: Royal Hospital, Chelsea
Died: Chelsea 16 Feb 1807
Sources: ANCB; ANCD; ANCW; ARLI; HPON; WEOF

439. *Rt Hon. Richard FITZPATRICK (1807–1813)*

Born: County Cork 1748
Relations: Son of John FitzPatrick, 1st Earl of Upper Ossory and Lady Evelyn (Leveson-Gower); grandson of John Leveson-Gower, 1st Earl Gower; brother of John Fitzpatrick, 2nd Earl of Upper Ossory
Education: Westminster School; Caen Military Academy
Entry to Army: Ensign in 1st Foot Guards 12 Jun 1765 by purchase
Regimental Field Officer Promotions: Captain and Lieutenant Colonel in 1st Foot Guards 23 Jan 1778 by purchase
Brevets: Brevet Colonel 20 Nov 1782; Major General 12 Oct 1793; Lieutenant General 1 Jan 1798; General 25 Sep 1803
Colonelcies: 11th Foot 20 Apr 1806 (vice Grant); 47th Foot 25 Feb 1807 (vice Dalrymple)
Early Service: Served in North America 1777–1778
Political Career: MP (Okehampton) 1770–1774; MP (Tavistock) 1774–1807; Chief Secretary for Ireland 1782; Secretary at War Apr 1783 to Dec 1783; Secretary at War Feb 1806 to Mar 1807; MP (Bedfordshire) 1807–1812; MP (Tavistock) 1812–1813
Awards and Honours: PC (Ire) 4 May 1782; PC 14 Apr 1783
Residences: Arlington Street, St. James's, London; Sunninghill, Berkshire
Died: London 25 Apr 1813
Apparently a 'solo balloonist, inveterate gambler, bon viveur, wit and first rate satirical versifier'
Sources: ARLI; HPON; MENA; ODNB; WEOF

440. *Hon. Sir Alexander HOPE (1813–1835)*

Born: West Lothian 1769
Relations: Son of John Hope, 2nd Earl of Hopetoun and Lady Elizabeth (Leslie); brother of General Hon. Charles Hope; half-brother of General Sir John Hope, Earl of Hopetoun; father of Lieutenant Colonel John Thomas Hope, Fifeshire Militia
Education: Honorary DCL (Oxon) 30 Jun 1824
Entry to Army: Ensign in 63rd Foot 6 Mar 1786 by purchase
Regimental Field Officer Promotions: Major in 81st Foot 19 Aug 1794 (vice Lindsay) by purchase; Lieutenant Colonel in 2/90th Foot 27 Aug 1794; Lieutenant Colonel in 14th Foot 17 Dec 1794 (vice Ross)
Brevets: Brevet Colonel 1 Jan 1800; Brigadier General (home staff) 11 Feb 1804; Major General 25 Apr 1808; Lieutenant General 4 Jun 1813; General 22 Jul 1830
Colonelcies: Cape Regiment 25 Jan 1806; 5th West India Regiment 30 Oct 1806 (vice Asgill); 47th Foot Apr 1813 (vice FitzPatrick); 14th Foot 25 Mar 1835 (vice Colville)
Service 1793–1815: Brigade Major in Foot Guards in Flanders 1794; commanded 14th Foot and severely wounded (lamed left arm) at Geldermalsen 1795; Governor of Tynemouth 1797; Lieutenant Governor of Edinburgh Castle 1798; Assistant and Deputy Adjutant General in Helder 1799; Deputy Quartermaster General at Horse Guards 1802; Governor of Royal Military College 1812–1819
Later Service: Lieutenant Governor of Edinburgh Castle 1819–1826; Lieutenant Governor of Royal

Hospital, Chelsea 1826 –1837
Militia Career: Colonel of Loyal Nottinghamshire Fencibles 19 Dec 1801
Political Career: MP (Dumfries Burghs) 1796–1800; MP (Linlithgowshire) 1800–1834
Awards and Honours: GCB 2 Jan 1815
Residences: Craighall, Linlithgowshire
Died: Royal Hospital, Chelsea 19 May 1837
Sources: ANCW; HPON; ODNB; PHIL; WEOF

Lieutenant Colonels

441. *Sir Paulus Æmilius IRVING, 1st Bt (1781–1802)*

Born: Dumfriesshire 1751
Relations: Son of Lieutenant Colonel Paulus Æmilius Irving and Judith (Westfield)
Entry to Army: Lieutenant in 47th Foot 28 Sep 1762 by purchase
Field Officer Promotions: Major in 47th Foot 31 Mar 1775; Lieutenant Colonel in 47th Foot 3 Aug 1781
Brevets: Brevet Lieutenant Colonel 17 Nov 1780; Brevet Colonel 18 Nov 1790; Major General 3 Oct 1794; Lieutenant General 1 Jan 1801; General 1 Jan 1812
Colonelcies: 2nd (later 6th) Royal Veteran Battalion 25 Dec 1802
Early Service: Served in American War of Independence 1775–1781, POW at Saratoga; Lieutenant Governor of Guernsey 1776–1783; commanded 47th Foot in West Indies 1790–1795
Service 1793–1815: Commander in Chief Leeward and Windward Islands Jun to Sep 1795 (vice Vaughan); Commander and Lieutenant Governor of St. Vincent Sep 1795
Creations and Dignities: 1st Baronet of Woodhouse and Robgill Tower 19 Sep 1809
Residence: Woodhouse Mains, near Kirkpatrick-Fleming, Dumfriesshire
Died: Carlisle 31 Jan 1828
Sources: ANCB; ARLI; DEBA; DINB; PHIL; WEOF; WOST

442. *Robert DOUGLAS (1795–1798)*

Born: Dumfriesshire c.1744
Relations: Of Garlieston; cousin of Major James Sholto Douglas, Consul General of Morocco; father of Captain Robert Sholto Douglas RA; Lieutenant Charles Douglas RHA; and Captain John Douglas, 54th Foot
Entry to Army: 2nd Lieutenant in 23rd Foot 7 Feb 1759 by purchase
Field Officer Promotions: Major in 47th Foot 31 May 1788 (vice Coote); Lieutenant Colonel in 47th Foot 1 Sep 1795
Brevets: Brevet Lieutenant Colonel 22 Aug 1783; Colonel (America) 17 Nov 1790; Brevet Colonel 1 Mar 1794; Major General 3 May 1796
Early Service: Served in American War of Independence
Service 1793–1815: Commanded 47th Foot in Bermuda 1795–1798
Residence: Taunton, Somerset
Died: Bermuda 7 Jun 1798
Sources: ANCW; WEOF; <https://www.douglashistory.co.uk/history/robertdouglas7.htm>

443. *Thomas Joseph BACKHOUSE (1798–1814)*

Born: Manila, Philippines 1764
Relations: Natural son of Captain Thomas Backhouse of Great Missenden
Entry to Army: Ensign in 13th Foot 22 Mar 1780
Field Officer Promotions: Major in 47th Foot 26 Jan 1797 (vice Alcock); Lieutenant Colonel in 47th Foot 6 Jun 1798 (vice Douglas) by purchase; removed from the regiment as a general officer 1814
Brevets: Brevet Major 3 May 1796; Brevet Colonel 25 Apr 1808; Major General 4 Jun 1811; Lieutenant General 19 Jun 1821
Early Service: Served in West Indies 1781
Service 1793–1815: Commanded 1/47th Foot 1798–1807; commanded brigade in Montevideo 1807; commanded garrison in Bombay [Mumbai] 1808–1811; on staff in Bombay 1811–1813
Residence: Wimpole Street, Cavendish Square, London
Died: London 22 May 1828
Sources: ANCD; ARLI; WEOF; Reports of Cases Decided in the High Court of Chancery

444. *Fielder KING (1803–1804)*

Born: Sussex 1753
Relations: Son of John King of Wisborough Green and Elizabeth (Fielder)
Entry to Army: Ensign in Independent Company 7 Nov 1793
Regimental Field Officer Promotions: Major in 98th Foot 17 May 1796; Lieutenant Colonel in 98th Foot 2 Mar 1797 (vice Veitch) by purchase; Lieutenant Colonel in 47th Foot 9 Jul 1803; Lieutenant Colonel in 7th Foot 21 Jan 1804 (vice Layard)
Service 1793–1815: Commanded 2/7th Foot 1804; Inspecting Field Officer of Yeomanry Sep 1804
Retired: 21 Apr 1804
Residence: High Street, Godalming, Surrey
Died: Godalming 10 Apr 1831
Sources: ANCB; ANCD; ARLI; WEOF

445. *John Byne SKERRETT (1804–1814)*
Born: Cheshire 1777
Relations: Son of Lieutenant General John Nicholas Skerrett of Nantwich and Anne (Byne)
Entry to Army: Volunteer in 86th Foot; Ensign in 86th Foot 26 Apr 1783
Field Officer Promotions: Major in 83rd Foot 29 Mar 1798 (vice Edwards) by purchase; Lieutenant Colonel in 83rd Foot 23 Oct 1800 (vice Godley) by purchase; to half-pay of 62nd Foot 17 Mar 1803 (vice Baird) by exchange; Lieutenant Colonel in 10th Battalion of Reserve 9 Jul 1803; Lieutenant Colonel in 47th Foot 16 Jan 1804 (vice King)
Brevets: Brevet Colonel 25 Jul 1810; Major General 4 Jun 1813
Service 1793–1815: Served in West Indies 1794; served in West Indies 1798–1803; served in Cape of Good Hope 1806; served in East Indies 1807–1811; served in Peninsula Jan to Apr 1811; commanded brigade in Peninsula May 1811 to Jul 1812; commanded brigade in 4th Division in Peninsula Nov 1812 to Jun 1813; commanded brigade in Light Division in Peninsula Jul to Oct 1813; commanded brigade in Netherlands 1813–1814
Awards and Honours: AGM (Vitt)
Residence: Newcastle-Upon-Tyne, Northumberland
Died: Killed in action at Bergen-op-Zoom 10 Mar 1814
Sources: ANCB; ANCD; ANCW; CHAL; WEBC; WEOF

446. *William WARDROBE (1806–1810)*
Born: Edinburgh 1762
Relations: Son of David Wardrope of Edinburgh, merchant, and Eleanora (Irvine); brother of Captain John Wardrobe
Entry to Army: Ensign in 86th Foot 25 Aug 1780
Field Officer Promotions: Major in 52nd Foot 23 Sep 1800 (vice Master) by purchase; Lieutenant Colonel in 96th Foot 1 Feb 1803 (vice Manners) by purchase; to half-pay of York Hussars 13 Jun 1805 (vice Leathes) by exchange; Lieutenant Colonel in 47th Foot 8 May 1806
Early Service: Served in West Indies 1781–1783; served in East Indies 1787–1792
Service 1793–1815: Served in East Indies 1793–1798; served at capture of Ceylon 1795; served at Cadiz 1800; Assistant Adjutant General in Ireland 13 Jun 1805
Retired: 3 May 1810
Residence: St Simons Island, Georgia, United States
Died: St Simons Island 11 Nov 1812
Sources: ANCB; ANCD; ANCW; WEOF; WO 25/748; A Compilation of the Laws of the State of Georgia

447. *Humphrey Dalrymple BLAND (1810–1816)*
Born: County Laois 1770
Relations: Son of Captain Neville Bland of Dublin and Charlotte (Smith); brother of Captain Loftus Otway Bland RN; nephew of General Thomas Bland; and Captain Humphrey Bland, 62nd Foot
Entry to Army: Ensign in 47th Foot 19 Apr 1796 by purchase
Field Officer Promotions: Major in 47th Foot 28 Aug 1804 (vice Burroughs) by purchase; Lieutenant Colonel in 47th Foot 3 May 1810 (vice Wardrobe) by purchase
Service 1793–1815: Served in Bahamas 1796–1797; served in Bermuda 1797–1802; commanded 2/47th in Cadiz Nov 1809 to Apr 1811; served in East Indies 1813–1815
Residence: Dublin, County Dublin
Died: Bombay [Mumbai], India 21 Sep 1815
Sources: ARLI; GHLG; WEOF; WO 25/744

448. *James CUMING (1811–1815)*
Born: Isle of Man c.1769
Relations: Son of James Cuming of Castletown and Grissel (Stevenson)
Entry to Army: Ensign in 47th Foot 21 Jan 1784 by purchase
Field Officer Promotions: Major in 47th Foot 16 Jun 1798 (vice Backhouse) by purchase; Lieutenant Colonel in 47th Foot 13 Jun 1811; removed from the regiment as a general officer 1815
Brevets: Brevet Lieutenant Colonel 25 Sep 1803; Brevet Colonel 1 Jan 1812; Major General 4 Jun 1814; Lieutenant General 22 Jul 1830
Service 1793–1815: Served in West Indies 1793–1802; served in Cape of Good Hope 1806; served in South America 1807; commanded 1/47th in East Indies 1808–1813
Residence: Castletown, Isle of Man
Died: Castletown 16 Aug 1839
Sources: ANCW; ARLI; GEMA (1839); WEOF

449. *Richard Goodall ELRINGTON (1813–1841)*
Born: Worcestershire 1776
Relations: Son of Colonel Thomas Elrington of Low Hill and Rebecca (Goodall); brother of Major General Thomas Gerard Elrington; Lieutenant Colonel John Hamilton Elrington, Scots Fusilier Guards; Major William Sandys Elrington, 11th Foot; and Lieutenant Colonel George Esdaile Elrington, 39th Foot
Entry to Army: Ensign in 14th Foot 27 Jul 1791 by purchase

Field Officer Promotions: Major in 47th Foot 3 May 1810 (vice Bland) by purchase; Lieutenant Colonel in 47th Foot 4 Jun 1813; removed from the regiment as a general officer 23 Nov 1841
Brevets: Brevet Major 25 Apr 1808; Brevet Colonel 22 Jul 1830; Major General 23 Nov 1841
Service 1793–1815: Served in Flanders 1793–1794, wounded at Dunkirk; served in West Indies 1795–1796, wounded in Jamaica; served in South America 1807; served in Est Indies 1808–1826, commanded anti-pirate operations in 1809; commanded 1/47th in East Indies 1813–1815
Later Service: Commanded force in Pindari War 1817; commanded brigade in Persian Gulf 1819; commanded brigade in Burmese War 1824–1825; court-martialled in 1832 for neglect of duty and acquitted
Awards and Honours: CB 26 Dec 1827
Residence: Kempsey, White Ladies Aston, Worcestershire
Died: London 2 Aug 1845
Sources: ANCB; ANCD; ANCW; ARLI; GEMA (1845); PHIL; WEOF

Majors

450. *John Dormer ALCOCK (1795–1797)*
Born: County Kildare 1750
Relations: Son of Rev. John Alcock and Catherine (Burgh)
Entry to Army: Ensign in 47th Foot 13 Mar 1767
Regimental Field Officer Promotions: Major in 47th Foot 1 Sep 1795 (vice Douglas)
Brevets: Brevet Major 7 Jun 1782; Brevet Lieutenant Colonel 12 Oct 1793
Service 1793–1815: Served in West Indies
Residence: Kinsale, County Cork
Died: Kinsale 20 Jan 1797
Sources: ARLI; GHLG

451. *John IRVING (1795–1803)*
Born: Dumfriesshire c.1757
Relations: Son of Henry Irving of Dumfries; cousin of General Sir Paulus Æmilius Irving, 1st Bt; and Lieutenant Colonel Robert Irving, 70th Foot; father of Major Paulus Æmilius Irving, 62nd Foot
Entry to Army: Ensign in 2/60th Foot 25 Sep 1778 by purchase
Regimental Field Officer Promotions: Major in 47th Foot 2 Sep 1795; Lieutenant Colonel in 8th Battalion of Reserve 9 Jul 1803; to half-pay of 8th Garrison Battalion 15 Mar 1805; Lieutenant Colonel in 2nd West India Regiment 25 Oct 1806 (vice Leith) by exchange; Lieutenant Colonel in 1st West India Regiment 9 Jan 1808 (vice D'Urban) by exchange
Brevets: Brevet Major 1 Mar 1794; Brevet Lieutenant Colonel 1 Jan 1798
Early Service: Served in Gibraltar 1779–1783
Service 1793–1815: Served in West Indies 1793–1802, and 1806–1808
Retired: 14 Jan 1808
Residence: Bath, Somerset
Died: Bath 4 Feb 1808
Sources: ANCB; ANCD; ANCW; GEMA (1808); WEOF

452. *Henry David FRASER (1803–1804)*
Born: Aberdeenshire 1767
Relations: Son of William Fraser of Fraserfield and Rachel (Kennedy)
Entry to Army: Ensign in 64th Foot 20 Sep 1776 by purchase
Regimental Field Officer Promotions: Major in 47th Foot 1 Jul 1803 (vice Irving)
Brevets: Brevet Major 1 Jan 1798; Brevet Lieutenant Colonel 17 May 1799
Service 1793–1815: Deputy Adjutant General in Portugal 17 May 1799
Retired: 7 Apr 1804
Residence: Aberdeen, Aberdeenshire
Died: Aberdeen 4 Aug 1810
Several sources note this officer as being a Brigadier General in Portuguese service, even suggesting that he died as 'the senior general in the Portuguese army', which is demonstrably untrue
Sources: ANCB; ANCD; ARLI; WEOF; The Peerage, Baronetage, Knightage & Companionage of the British Empire for 1907

453. *Rt Hon. Sir Edward BLAKENEY (1803–1804)*
Born: Newcastle-upon-Tyne 1778
Relations: Son of Colonel William Blakeney, MP and Sarah (Shields); brother of Lieutenant Colonel Thomas Blakeney; and Captain Samuel Blakeney, RN; son-in-law of Colonel Thomas Gardiner, EIC service
Entry to Army: Cornet in 8th Light Dragoons 28 Feb 1794 by purchase
Regimental Field Officer Promotions: Major in 17th Foot 17 Sep 1801 (vice Wallace) by purchase; Major in 47th Foot 9 Jul 1803; Major in 7th Foot 24 Mar 1804 (vice Burroes) by exchange; Lieutenant Colonel in 7th Foot 20 Jun 1811 (vice Myers)
Brevets: Brevet Lieutenant Colonel 25 Apr 1808; Brevet Colonel 4 Jun 1814; Major General 27 May 1825; Lieutenant General 26 Aug 1836; General 20 Jun 1854; Field Marshal 9 Nov 1862
Colonelcies: 7th Foot 20 Sep 1832 (vice Clarke); 1st Foot 21 Dec 1854 (vice Kempt); Colonel

Commandant of Rifle Brigade 28 Aug 1865 (vice Brown)
Service 1793–1815: Served in West Indies 1796–1799, taken POW by privateers three times; served in Helder 1799; served in Copenhagen 1807; served in Martinique 1808; commanded 1/7th Foot in Peninsula Aug to Oct 1810; commanded 2/7th Foot in Peninsula Nov 1810 to Jun 1811, wounded at Albuera; commanded 1/7th Foot in Peninsula Jul 1811 to May 1812, severely wounded at Badajoz; served in Peninsula Jan 1813 to Jan 1814; commanded 1/7th Foot in North America and France 1814–1815
Later Service: Commanded brigade in Portugal 1826; Commander in Chief in Ireland 1836–1855; Lieutenant Governor of Chelsea Hospital 6 Feb 1855; Governor of Chelsea Hospital 25 Sep 1856
Awards and Honours: AGC (Mart Alb Bad Vit Pyr); KTS (Portugal) 6 Apr 1813; KCB 2 Jan 1815; PC (Ire) 7 May 1836; GCB 7 May 1840; GCH 12 Aug 1836; MGSM (Bus CR Niv Nlle)
Residence: Richmond House, Twickenham, Middlesex
Died: Chelsea Hospital 3 Aug 1868
Sources: ARLI; BRFM; GHLG; ODNB; PHIL; WEOF; WO 25/744

454. *William JOHNSON (1803–1811)*
Born: Ireland c.1754
Entry to Army: Ensign in 29th Foot 29 Mar 1776 by purchase
Regimental Field Officer Promotions: Major in 47th Foot 9 Jul 1803
Brevets: Brevet Major 29 Apr 1802; Brevet Lieutenant Colonel 25 Oct 1809
Early Service: Served in American War of Independence
Service 1793–1815: Lieutenant Governor of Québec 8 Nov 1810 to 7 Feb 1811 (vice Callow)
Retired: 7 Feb 1811
Residence: Bath, Somerset
Died: Bath 23 Dec 1812
Sources: ARLI; FMPD; GEMA (1813)

455. *James BURROWES (1804)*
Born: County Cavan c.1763
Relations: Son of Thomas Burrowes of Drung and Jane (Nesbitt)
Entry to Army: Lieutenant in 7th Foot 24 Jul 1775 by purchase
Regimental Field Officer Promotions: Major in 7th Foot 16 Apr 1795; Major in 47th Foot 24 Mar 1804 (vice Blakeney) by exchange
Brevets: Brevet Major 1 Mar 1794; Brevet Lieutenant Colonel 1 Jan 1798
Retired: 28 Aug 1804
Residence: Drung and Larah, County Cavan
Died: Drung 23 Aug 1816
Sources: ARLI; FMPD

456. *John Burges HAFFEY (1804–1807)*
Born: Essex 1773
Relations: Son of John Haffey of Walthamstow and Elizabeth (Stevenson)
Entry to Army: Cornet in 11th Light Dragoons 5 Dec 1795 by purchase
Field Officer Promotions: Major in 47th Foot 7 Apr 1804 (vice Fraser) by purchase; Major in 18th Foot 5 Nov 1807 (vice Yates) by exchange
Brevets: Brevet Lieutenant Colonel 4 Jun 1811
Service 1793–1815: Acting Governor of Curaçao 11 Sep 1813 to 15 Sep 1813 (vice Hodgson)
Died: Jamaica 6 Jul 1814
Sources: ANCB; WEOF; WOST

457. *Jonathan YATES (1807–1810)*
Born: Lancashire 1780
Relations: Son of William Yates of Bury and Ann (Haworth)
Entry to Army: Ensign in 81st Foot 14 Feb 1799 by purchase
Regimental Field Officer Promotions: Major in 18th Foot 18 Dec 1806 (vice Dunlop) by purchase; Major in 47th Foot 5 Nov 1807 (vice Haffey) by exchange; Lieutenant Colonel in 1st West India Regiment 19 Jul 1810 (vice Wemyss) by purchase; Lieutenant Colonel in 49th Foot 13 May 1813; to half-pay of Royal York Rangers 9 Aug 1821
Brevets: Brevet Colonel 12 Aug 1819; Major General 22 Jul 1830; Lieutenant General 23 Nov 1841; General 20 Jun 1854
Retired: Served in Egypt and Malta 1801; served in West Indies 1803–1807 and 1810–1813; taken POW in West Indies Feb 1807
Residence: East Tytherley House, near Stockbridge, Hampshire
Died: East Tytherley House 3 Oct 1854
Sources: ANCB; ANCD; ANCW; ARLI; PHIL; WEOF; WO 25/748

458. *William Edmondstone CHEYNE (1810–1816)*
Born: Midlothian 1774
Relations: Son of John Cheyne of South Leith, surgeon, and Margaret (Edmondstone); brother of Captain Alexander Cheyne RE
Entry to Army: Ensign in 76th Foot 1 Jul 1797 by purchase
Field Officer Promotions: Major in 47th Foot 9

Aug 1810 (vice Yates) by purchase; Lieutenant Colonel in 47th Foot Jul 1816 (vice Bland)
Service 1793–1815: Served in East Indies 1808–1815
Retired: 29 Jun 1820
Residence: Cheyne Street, Stockbridge, Edinburgh, Midlothian
Died: Edinburgh 21 Jan 1843
Sources: ANCB; ANCD; ARLI; WEOF

459. *Richard BROAD (1811–1812)*

Born: [spec.] Cornwall c.1776
Entry to Army: Ensign and Adjutant in Royal Cornwall and Devon Miners Militia Jun 1799; Adjutant in 85th Foot 21 Aug 1801
Regimental Field Officer Promotions: Major in 10th Foot 17 Jan 1811 (vice Cashell) by purchase; Major in 47th Foot 7 Feb 1811 (vice Johnson)
Service 1793–1815: Commanded 2/47th Foot on east coast of Spain Jun 1811 to Oct 1812
Residence: Colby House, Kensington Gore, London
Died: Of fever at Trujillo, Spain 31 Oct 1812
Sources: ANCW; ARLI; CHAL; HALL; WEOF

460. *Robert KELLY (1811–1813)*

Born: County Galway c.1767
Relations: Son of Denis Kelly of Aghrane and Anne (Armstrong); brother of Captain John Kelly, Athlone Militia; Captain Charles Kelly; Lieutenant William Kelly, 24th Foot; and Captain Dennis Kelly, 64th Foot
Entry to Army: Ensign in 47th Foot 25 Feb 1791 by purchase
Regimental Field Officer Promotions: Major in 47th Foot 13 Jun 1811 (vice Cuming)
Brevets: Brevet Major 25 Jul 1810
Service 1793–1815: Commanded 2/47th in Peninsula Apr to Aug 1813
Awards and Honours: AGM (Vitt SS)
Died: Killed in action at San Sebastian 31 Aug 1813
Sources: ARLI; CHAL; HALL; WEOF; Tribes and Customs of Hy-Many, Commonly Called O'Kellys Country

461. *Richard CHETHAM [STRODE] (1813–1814)*

Born: London 1771
Relations: Son of Thomas Chetham of Mellor Hall and Ann (Strode); brother of Colonel Thomas Chetham Strode, East Somerset Militia; and Colonel John Chetham, 61st Foot; added Strode surname 24 Oct 1827
Entry to Army: Ensign in 47th Foot 26 Oct 1796
Regimental Field Officer Promotions: Major in 47th Foot 14 Jan 1813 (vice Broad); to half-pay of 47th Foot Oct 1814
Brevets: Brevet Major 1 Jan 1812; Brevet Lieutenant Colonel 19 Jul 1821
Service 1793–1815: Commanded 2/47th in Peninsula Sep 1813 to Apr 1814
Awards and Honours: AGM (Nive)
Residence: Southill House, West Cranmere, Somerset
Died: Southill House 27 Jul 1828
Sources: ARLI; GEMA (1828); GHLG; PHIL; WEOF; <https://www.noonans.co.uk/auctions/calendar/566/catalogue/ 381479/>

462. *Charles HAYNES (1813–1816)*

Born: England c.1776
Entry to Army: Ensign in 47th Foot 24 May 1793
Regimental Field Officer Promotions: Major in 47th Foot 4 Jun 1813 (vice Elrington)
Service 1793–1815: Served in East Indies 1808–1816
Residence: Southampton, Hampshire
Died: Of the effects of fatigue in Bombay [Mumbai] 26 Nov 1816
Sources: ANCW; GEMA (1817); WEOF

463. *Bysse Cole MOLESWORTH (1813–1819)*

Born: Dublin c.1775
Relations: Son of Robert Molesworth and Catherine Elizabeth (Rose); brother of Colonel Arthur Molesworth, Madras service
Entry to Army: Ensign in 38th Foot 21 Dec 1797
Regimental Field Officer Promotions: Major in 47th Foot 29 Sep 1813 (vice Kelly); to half-pay of 47th Foot 25 Mar 1816; reinstated in 47th Foot 27 Nov 1816
Service 1793–1815: Served in East Indies
Later Service: Served in Pindari War 1817–1819
Residence: Dublin, County Dublin
Died: Killed in action at Ras-el-Kimah 4 Dec 1819
Sources: ARLI; PBBE; WEOF

Selected Regimental Histories

Purdon, Henry, *An Historical Sketch of the 47th (Lancashire) Regiment: and of the Campaigns through which they Passed* (Preston: Guardian Printing Works, 1907)
Wylly, H.C., *Loyal North Lancashire Regiment 1741–1914* (Uckfield: Naval & Military Press, 2014)

Regimental Museum

Lancashire Infantry Museum, Fulwood Barracks, Preston, Lancashire

48th Regiment of Foot

Secondary Title:	Northamptonshire
Nicknames:	The Heroes of Talavera
Jacket:	Red
Facings:	Buff

Regimental Lineage, 48th Regiment of Foot

1741:	Raised in Norwich as James Cholmondeley's Regiment of Foot
1743:	Beauclerk's Regiment of Foot
1745:	Ligonier's Regiment of Foot
1746:	Conway's Regiment of Foot
1747:	Ranked as 59th Regiment of Foot
1749:	Viscount Torrington's Regiment of Foot
1751:	48th Regiment of Foot
1782:	48th (Northamptonshire) Regiment of Foot
1803:	Jul – 2nd Battalion formed in Manchester
1814:	Oct – 2nd Battalion disbanded in Chelmsford
1881:	1st Battalion, Northamptonshire Regiment (on amalgamation with the 58th (Rutlandshire) Regiment of Foot)
1960:	2nd East Anglian Regiment (Duchess of Gloucester's Own Royal Lincolnshire and Northamptonshire) (on amalgamation with 1st Battalion, Royal Lincolnshire Regiment)
1964:	2nd Battalion, Royal Anglian Regiment (Duchess of Gloucester's Own Royal Lincolnshire and Northamptonshire) (on amalgamation with 1st East Anglian Regiment (Royal Norfolk and Suffolk Regiment), 3rd East Anglian Regiment (16th/44th Foot) and the Royal Leicestershire Regiment)

Service History, 1st Battalion 48th Regiment of Foot

1793:	Antigua; Feb – nine companies in St Vincent, one company in Dominica; Jun – seven companies in St Vincent, three companies in Dominica
1794:	Jan – Barbados; Feb to May – drafted out to other regiments, cadre to England; Oct – Harwich
1795:	Plymouth; Sep – Portsmouth; Oct – Nursling camp; Nov – two companies to West Indies, rest detained by storms
1796:	Feb – remainder to West Indies; Barbados; Apr – St Lucia; May – Castries; Vigie; Morne Fortune; St Lucia garrison
1797:	St Lucia; Jun – drafted fit men into 87th Foot, cadre returned home; Aug – Portsmouth; Sep – Huntingdon; Oct – Norwich
1798:	Chelmsford; Feb – Worcester; Jul – Poole; Aug – to Mediterranean; Oct – Gibraltar
1799:	Gibraltar
1800:	Gibraltar; May – Minorca; Jun – Leghorn; to Malta; Jul – Gudja; Sep – capture of Fort St Angelo; Fort St Elmo
1801–1802:	Malta, Fort St Elmo
1803:	Malta; May – to England; Aug – Portsmouth; Sep – Manchester; Nov – Horsham; Dec – Eastbourne
1804:	Eastbourne; Sep – Hailsham; Nov – Isle of Wight
1805:	Isle of Wight; Feb – Winchester; Mar – Portsmouth; Mar – to Gibraltar; May – Gibraltar
1806–1808:	Gibraltar
1809:	Gibraltar; Jun – to Portugal; Lisbon; Jul – TALAVERA; Sep – Montijo; Dec – Punhete
1810:	Punhete; Apr – Alegrete; May – Portalegre; Jul – Atalaia; Aug – Sarzedas; Sep – São Miguel de Poiares; Oct – Alhandra; Nov – Chamusca

1811:	Chamusca; Mar – Campo Maior; Apr – Almendralejo; May – ALBUERA; Almendralejo; Jun – Torre de Mouro; absorbed fit men from 2/48th; Jul – Estremoz; Aug – Pedrogão; Sep – Fuenteguinaldo; Oct – Villar de Ciervo; Nov – Ituero de Azaba; Dec – San Felices de los Gallegos
1812:	Castillejo de Dos Casas; Feb – Barquilla; Mar – Badajoz; Apr – BADAJOZ; Sabugal; May – Vale de Póvoa; Jun – Salamanca forts; Jul – SALAMANCA; Nava de Arévalo; Aug – El Escorial; Oct – Ciempozuelos; Nov – Villar de Ciervo; Dec – Mêda
1813:	Mêda; Feb – Freixeda do Torrão; Mar – Escarigo; May – Miranda do Douro; Jun – VITTORIA; Pamplona; Aug – PYRENEES; Sorauren; Oct – Vera; Nov – NIVELLE; Ustaritz; Dec – Arrauntz
1814:	Ustarritz; Feb – Came; ORTHEZ; Mar – Sainte-Foy-de-Peyrolières; Apr – TOULOUSE; Briscan; May – Éauze; Jun – Bordeaux; to Ireland; Jul – Monkstown; Clonmel; Aug – Clonooney; Nov – Templemore
1815:	Templemore; Mar – Limerick; Aug – Dublin

Service History, 2nd Battalion 48th Regiment of Foot

1803:	Jul – formed in Manchester from Army of Reserve volunteers; Nov – Horsham
1804:	Hailsham; Feb – Portsmouth; to Ireland; Mar – Cork; Apr – Mallow; Sep – Killady camp; Oct – Mallow
1805:	Mallow; Jun – Clonooney; Sep – Curragh camp; Oct – Dublin
1806:	Dublin; Nov – Birr
1807:	Jan – Dublin; to England; Liverpool; Northampton; Sep – Chelmsford; Nov – Liverpool; to Ireland; Dec – Dublin
1808:	Clonooney; Jul – Curragh camp; Sep – Dublin
1809:	Dublin; Mar – Monkstown; to Portugal; PENINSULA; Apr – Lisbon; May – Porto; DOURO; Jul – TALAVERA; Sep – Montijo; Dec – Abrantes
1810:	Abrantes; Feb – Portalegre; Apr – Alegrete; May – Portalegre; Jul – Atalaia; Aug – Sarzedas; Sep – São Miguel de Poiares; Oct – São João dos Montes; Nov – Chamusca
1811:	Santa Margarida da Coutada; Mar – Campo Maior; Apr – Almendralejo; May – ALBUERA; Almendralejo; Jun – Estremoz; fit men absorbed into 1st Battalion; Jul – cadre to Lisbon; to England; Aug – Portsmouth; Sep – Northampton; Dec – Weedon
1812:	Weedon; Mar – Maldon; Apr – Danbury; Jul – Chelmsford
1813:	Chelmsford
1814:	Chelmsford; Oct – disbanded in Chelmsford

Establishments, 1st Battalion 48th Regiment of Foot

Year	Subunits	Field Off	Off/ Staff	Sjts	Mus	Corp/ Pvts	Total
Dec 1792	10co	3	32	22	12	430	499
Jan 1793	10co	3	32	32	22	600	689
Aug 1795	10co+2r	5	53	62	30	1,010	1,160
Dec 1795	10co+2r	5	51	62	30	1,010	1,158
Dec 1797	10co	5	38	53	22	600	718
Jun 1802	10co	5	33	34	22	750	844
Jul 1803	10co	5	36	54	22	1,000	1,117
Dec 1804	10co	5	36	44	22	800	907
Dec 1805	10co	5	36	54	22	1,000	1,117
Dec 1806	10co	4	36	44	22	800	906
Dec 1807	10co	4	46	54	22	1,000	1,126
May 1809	10co+r	4	50	62	26	1,008	1,150
Dec 1810	10co+r	4	40	52	26	808	930
Dec 1811	10co	4	46	55	22	1,000	1,127
Jul 1814	10co	5	46	55	22	1,000	1,128

Establishments, 2nd Battalion 48th Regiment of Foot

Year	Subunits	Field Off	Off/ Staff	Sjts	Mus	Corp/ Pvts	Total
Oct 1803	10co	3	35	53	22	1,000	1,113
Dec 1804	10co	3	36	43	22	800	904
Jan 1807	10co	3	35	23	22	400	483
Sep 1807	10co	3	46	53	22	1,000	1,124
Dec 1807	10co	3	46	54	22	1,000	1,125
Mar 1809	10co	3	36	44	22	800	905
May 1809	10co+r	3	40	52	26	808	929
Dec 1809	10co+r	3	40	51	26	808	928
Dec 1810	10co+r	3	39	41	26	608	717
Dec 1811	10co	3	35	25	22	400	485

Service Statistics, 48th Regiment of Foot

	Lieutenant Colonels	Majors
Number of officers in period 1793–1815	14	18
Average age on appointment to substantive rank	42.5	38.5
Average time in rank in regiment (years)	6	4
Total field officers by nationality	11 E / 7 S / 7 I / 2 F / 1 unk.	
Demographics of other ranks 1807	1/48th: 91% EW / 7% I / 2% S	
Demographics of other ranks 1809	1/48th: 83% EW / 16% I / 1% S	
Months of overseas service 1793–1815	1/48th: 199 2/48th: 29	

Significant Militia/Volunteer Intakes:

1794: Bedfordshire, North Lincolnshire
1803: Army of Reserve men from Cumberland, Westmoreland and Lancashire
1806: 1st West Yorkshire
1807: Hertfordshire, East Middlesex, West Suffolk, County Londonderry
1808: South Cork, Dublin City, King's County, County Limerick
1809: 3rd West Yorkshire
1812: West Essex
1813: 2nd Lancashire, South Mayo

Regimental Colonels

464. *Patrick George TONYN (1787–1804)*

Born: [spec.] Berwickshire 1725
Relations: Son of Colonel Charles William Tonyn and Jane Lydia (Billingham); brother of Major John Columbine Tonyn, Madras service; and Captain George Anthony Tonyn RN; father of Lieutenant Colonel George Augustus Tonyn, 31st Foot
Entry to Army: Cornet in 6th Dragoons 16 Apr 1744 by purchase
Regimental Field Officer Promotions: Lieutenant Colonel Commandant in 104th Foot 12 Aug 1761; to half-pay 1763
Brevets: Brevet Colonel 29 Aug 1777; Major General 9 Oct 1781; Lieutenant General 12 Oct 1793; General 1 Jan 1798
Colonelcies: 48th Foot 23 May 1787 (vice Skene)
Early Service: Served in Germany 1758–59; Governor of East Florida 1 Mar 1774 to 12 Jul 1784
Service 1793–1815: On home staff 1793
Residence: Park Street, St George Hanover Square, London
Died: London 30 Dec 1804
Sources: ANCB; ANCD; ANCW; ARLI; WOST; <https://allthingsliberty.com/2018/03/patrick-tonyn-britains-most-effective-revolutionary-era-royal-governor/>

465. *Charles, Lord FITZROY (1805–1829)*

Born: Suffolk 1764
Relations: Son of Augustus FitzRoy, 3rd Duke of Grafton and Anne (Liddell); grandson of Henry Liddell, 1st Baron Ravensworth; brother of Colonel George Henry Fitzroy, Earl of Euston, West Suffolk Militia; and Admiral William, Lord Fitzroy RN; father of Lieutenant Colonel Sir Charles Augustus FitzRoy; and Lieutenant Colonel George

FitzRoy; cousin of General Charles FitzRoy; brother-in-law of General Godfrey Basil Meynell Mundy; brother-in-law of Robert Stewart, Lord Castlereagh; and General Sir Charles William Vane Stewart, Earl Vane
Education: Harrow School; Trinity College, Cambridge
Entry to Army: Ensign in 3rd Foot Guards 27 Nov 1782 by purchase
Regimental Field Officer Promotions: Captain and Lieutenant Colonel in 3rd Foot Guards 21 Jul 1789 by purchase; Lieutenant Colonel in 129th Foot Sep 1795; to half-pay of 129th Foot 9 Dec 1795
Brevets: Brevet Colonel 26 Feb 1795; Major General 1 Jan 1797; Lieutenant General 1 Jan 1805; General 4 Jun 1814
Colonelcies: Colonel Commandant of 2/20th Foot 5 Aug 1799; Colonel Commandant of 4/60th Foot 15 Jun 1804 (vice Hunter); 48th Foot 1 Jan 1805 (vice Tonyn)
Service 1793–1815: Equerry to Duke of York; served in Flanders 1793–1794; ADC to King George III 26 Feb 1795
Political Career: MP (Bury St Edmunds) 1787–1796; MP (Bury St Edmunds) 1802–1818
Residences: Wickens, Northamptonshire; Berkeley Square, Mayfair, London
Died: London 20 Dec 1829
Sources: ARLI; DEPE; DIMB; HPON; ODNB; WEOF

Lieutenant Colonels

466. *Benjamin GORDON (1769–1803)*
Born: Aberdeenshire 1719
Relations: Son of James Gordon of Balbithan and Jean (Innes); granduncle of Major General Benjamin Forbes Gordon
Education: Marischal College, Aberdeen
Entry to Army: 2nd Lieutenant in 1st Foot 25 May 1742
Field Officer Promotions: Major in 48th Foot 2 Sep 1762; Lieutenant Colonel in 48th Foot 4 Mar 1769
Brevets: Brevet Colonel 19 Feb 1779; Major General 20 Nov 1782; Lieutenant General 3 May 1796; General 1 Jan 1801
Early Service: Served in Belgium 1744–1747, wounded at Fort Sandberg
Service 1793–1815: Commanded 48th Foot 1769–1803
Residence: Balbithan House, near Inverurie, Aberdeenshire
Died: Balbithan House 20 Nov 1803
Sources: ANCB; ANCD; ARLI; WEOF; Gordons Under Arms

467. *Archibald CAMPBELL (1795–1796)*
Born: Argyllshire c.1751
Relations: Son of Alexander Campbell of Stralachlan and Catherine (White)
Entry to Army: Ensign in 1st Foot 25 Sep 1762
Field Officer Promotions: Major in 69th Foot 31 Jul 1792 (vice Yorke) by purchase; Lieutenant Colonel in 48th Foot 19 Sep 1795 (vice Skerrett)
Brevets: Brevet Lieutenant Colonel 1 Mar 1794
Service 1793–1815: Commanded 48th Foot in West Indies 1795–1796
Died: St Lucia 23 Oct 1796
Sources: ANCB; ANCD; ARLI; History of the Northamptonshire Regiment

468. *William HORNE (1797)*
Born: Antigua 1746
Relations: Son of Captain William Horne, 38th Foot, and Elizabeth (Osborn)
Entry to Army: Ensign in 63rd Foot 6 Feb 1762 by purchase
Field Officer Promotions: Major in 48th Foot 2 Sep 1795; Lieutenant Colonel in 27th Foot 17 Nov 1796 (vice Drummond); Lieutenant Colonel in 48th Foot 24 Oct 1797 (vice Campbell)
Brevets: Brevet Major 1 Mar 1794
Service 1793–1815: Served in West Indies 1796–1797
Residence: Bath, Somerset
Died: Bath 8 Dec 1797
Sources: ANCD; ANCW; The History of the Island of Antigua

469. *Sir Martin HUNTER (1797–1803)*
Born: County Durham 1757
Relations: Son of Cuthbert Hunter of Medomsley and Anne (Nixon)
Entry to Army: Ensign in 52nd Foot 30 Aug 1771 by purchase
Field Officer Promotions: Major in 91st Foot 30 Oct 1793; Lieutenant Colonel in 91st Foot 19 Jul 1794; Lieutenant Colonel in 3/60th Foot 12 Jan 1796; Lieutenant Colonel in 48th Foot 13 Dec 1797 (vice Horne)
Brevets: Brevet Colonel 1 Jan 1800; Brigadier General (West Indies) 1801; Brigadier General (North America) 1803; Major General 30 Oct 1805; Lieutenant General 1 Jan 1812; General 27 May 1825
Colonelcies: New Brunswick Fencibles 9 Jul 1803
Early Service: Served in British North America 1773; served in American War of Independence 1775–1778; served in India 1783–1793; commanded 52nd Foot at Seringapatam 1792
Service 1793–1815: Commanded brigade at

capture of Trinidad 1797; commanded 48th Foot in Gibraltar 1797–1800 and at siege of Malta 1800; served in West Indies 1801–1802; served in British North America 1803–1817; Administrator of New Brunswick 24 May 1808 to 17 Dec 1808; Administrator of New Brunswick 26 Apr 1809 to 10 Sep 1811; Administrator of New Brunswick 14 Nov 1811 to 15 Jun 1812
Later Service: Governor of Pendennis Castle 1823–1832; Governor of Stirling Castle 1832–1846
Awards and Honours: GCH 12 Aug 1832; GCMG 10 May 1837
Residence: Anton's Hill, near Coldstream, Berwickshire
Died: Anton's Hill 9 Dec 1846
At the time of his death, Hunter was the last British survivor of Lexington and Concord
Sources: ARLI; DICB; DINB; PHIL; WEOF; WO 25/746

470. *William SINCLAIR-WEMYSS (1803–1808)*

Born: William Wemyss in Midlothian 1759
Relations: Son of William Wemyss of Edinburgh, writer, and Robina (Hamilton); took additional surname Sinclair- at marriage in 1784; brother of Captain John Wemyss, 59th Foot
Entry to Army: Ensign in 76th Foot 27 Dec 1777
Field Officer Promotions: Major in 48th Foot 24 Oct 1796 (vice Horne); Lieutenant Colonel in 48th Foot 9 Jul 1803; Lieutenant Colonel in 1st West India Regiment 16 Jun 1808 (vice Duckworth) by exchange
Brevets: Brevet Lieutenant Colonel 29 Apr 1802
Service 1793–1815: Commanded 48th Foot 1803–1808
Retired: 19 Jul 1810
Residence: Southdun, Caithness; Raebank, Selkirk, Selkirkshire
Died: Raebank 27 Jul 1834
Sources: ANCB; ANCD; ARLI; WEOF

471. *Hon. David LESLIE-MELVILLE (1803–1814)*

Born: Fifeshire c.1754
Relations: Son of David Leslie, 6th Earl of Leven and 5th Earl of Melville, and Wilhelmina (Nisbet); nephew of Major General Hon. Alexander Leslie; brother of General Hon. John Leslie-Melville-Cuming; and Hon. William Leslie, 17th Foot
Entry to Army: Ensign in 59th Foot 1 Aug 1770 by purchase
Field Officer Promotions: Lieutenant Colonel in Loyal Tay Fencibles 25 Oct 1795; Lieutenant Colonel in 48th Foot 9 Jul 1803; removed from the regiment as a general officer 1814
Brevets: Brevet Major 1 Mar 1794; Brevet Colonel 1 Jan 1801; Brigadier General (Irish staff) 29 Feb 1804; Major General 25 Apr 1808; Lieutenant General 4 Jun 1813; General 22 Jul 1830
Early Service: Served in Gibraltar 1782–1791
Service 1793–1815: Served in Irish rebellion 1798
Residence: Jedbank, Jedburgh, Roxburghshire
Died: Edinburgh 21 Oct 1838
Sources: ARLI; FMPD; WEOF; Historical Records of the Family of Leslie from 1067 to 1868-9

472. *Charles DONNELLAN (1804–1809)*

Born: County Galway c.1770
Relations: [spec.] Son of Charles Donnellan of Ballydonnellan; father of Colonel Anthony Donnellan, York Chasseurs; uncle of Captain Anthony Henry Donnellan, 58th Foot
Entry to Army: Ensign in 15th Foot 31 Jul 1789
Field Officer Promotions: Major in 62nd Foot 26 Nov 1799 (vice Fisher); Lieutenant Colonel in York Rangers 12 Oct 1804 (vice Minet); Lieutenant Colonel in 48th Foot 14 Nov 1804
Brevets: Brevet Lieutenant Colonel 28 Sep 1804
Service 1793–1815: Commanded 1/48th Foot in Peninsula May to Sep 1809
Awards and Honours: AGM (Tal)
Died: Of wounds after Talavera 1 Aug 1809
The historical spelling for the surname is as shown, however this officer spelt it 'Donelan' on his will
Sources: ANCW; ARLI; CHAL; WEOF

473. *George Henry DUCKWORTH (1808–1811)*

Born: Devonshire 1782
Relations: Son of Admiral Sir John Thomas Duckworth Bt, and Anne (Wallis); half-brother of Sir John Thomas Buller Duckworth, 2nd Bt
Entry to Army: Ensign in 39th Foot 25 Apr 1801
Regimental Field Officer Promotions: Major in York Light Infantry Volunteers 25 Jul 1806 (vice Erskine) by purchase; Major in 67th Foot 2 Oct 1806 (vice Stuart) by exchange; Lieutenant Colonel in 1st West India Regiment 14 Jan 1808 (vice Irving) by purchase; Lieutenant Colonel in 48th Foot 16 Jun 1808 (vice Wemyss) by exchange
Service 1793–1815: Served in Peninsula Apr to Sep 1809; commanded brigade in 2nd Division in Peninsula Dec 1809 to Jul 1810; commanded 1/48th Foot in Peninsula Jul 1810 to May 1811
Awards and Honours: AGM (Tal Alb)
Residence: Topsham, Devon
Died: Killed in action at Albuera 16 May 1811
This officer worked his way up through eleven different

regiments in seven years before ending up in the 48th Foot in 1808
Sources: ANCB; ANCW; ARLI; CHAL; HALL; WEOF

474. *George MIDDLEMORE (1809–1811)*

Born: Cumberland 1770
Relations: Son of William Richard Middlemore of Grantham Hall and Mary (Douglas); father of Captain Robert Frederick Middlemore, 91st Foot
Entry to Army: Ensign in 48th Foot 16 Jan 1793 by purchase
Regimental Field Officer Promotions: Major in 48th Foot 14 Sep 1804 (vice Pearse); Lieutenant Colonel in 48th Foot 2 Nov 1809 (vice Donnellan); to half-pay of 8th Garrison Battalion 21 Mar 1811 (vice Ross) by exchange
Brevets: Brevet Colonel 12 Aug 1819; Major General 22 Jul 1830; Lieutenant General 23 Nov 1841
Colonelcies: 76th Foot 2 Jan 1843 (vice Maitland); 48th Foot 31 May 1843 (vice Hislop)
Service 1793–1815: Served aboard ship as marine 1795; served in East Indies 1799; served in Egypt 1801; served in East Indies 1803; served in Malta 1804; served in Gibraltar 1804–1809; served in Peninsula Jul 1809 to Apr 1810; commanded 1/48th Foot in Peninsula Aug 1809 to Apr 1810; Assistant Quartermaster General in Severn District 1814; Inspecting Field Officer in Nottingham 1814
Later Service: Lieutenant Governor of Grenada 9 May 1833 to 4 Jul 1835; Governor of St Helena 5 Mar 1836 to 6 Jan 1842 – oversaw repatriation of Napoleon's remains to France in 1840; Governor of Windward & Leeward Islands 1843
Awards and Honours: AGM (Tal); CB 4 Jun 1815; MGSM (Egt)
Residence: Royal Tunbridge Wells, Kent
Died: Tunbridge Wells 18 Nov 1850
Sources: ANCB; ANCD; ANCW; CHAL; DINB; WEOF; WOST

475. *Sir Patrick ROSS (1810–1811)*

Born: London 1778
Relations: Son of General Patrick Ross of Invernethie, Chief Engineer at Madras and Mary Clara (Maule); brother of Lieutenant Colonel Archibald Ross, 91st Foot; father of Captain Patrick William Sydenham Ross, 85th Foot
Entry to Army: Ensign in Independent Company 12 May 1794
Regimental Field Officer Promotions: Major in 26th Foot 2 Jan 1806 (vice Mitchell) by purchase; Major in 23rd (late 26th) Light Dragoons 26 Mar 1806 (vice Freeth) by exchange; Lieutenant Colonel in 23rd (late 26th) Light Dragoons 9 Apr 1807 (vice Lumley) by purchase; Lieutenant Colonel in 10th Foot 6 Apr 1809 (vice Dawson) by exchange; to half-pay of 8th Garrison Battalion 18 Feb 1810 (vice Travers) by exchange; Lieutenant Colonel in 48th Foot 21 Mar 1811 (vice Middlemore) by exchange; to half-pay of 12th Garrison Battalion 24 Oct 1811 (vice Hutchinson) by exchange; Lieutenant Colonel in 75th Foot 12 Oct 1815 (vice Swinton) by exchange
Brevets: Brevet Major 25 Sep 1803; Brevet Colonel 4 Jun 1814; Major General 19 Jul 1821
Colonelcies: 1st Portuguese Cavalry 22 Sep 1810
Service 1793–1815: Served in Ireland 1794–1796; served in India 1797–1805; commanded 2/48th Foot in Peninsula Jun to Sep 1810; served with Portuguese forces Sep 1810 to Feb 1811; Assistant Adjutant General on Home staff 1813–1814; served in Malta and Ionian Islands 1815–1825
Later Service: Governor of Antigua, Montserrat and Barbuda 23 May 1825 to Jan 1832; Governor of St. Helena 23 Nov 1846 to 28 Aug 1850
Awards and Honours: KCMG 9 Nov 1819; KCH 12 Aug 1834; GCMG 19 May 1837
Died: St. Helena 28 Aug 1850
Sources: ANCB; ANCD; ARLI; CHAL; PHIL; WEOF; WO 25/748; WOST

476. *James ERSKINE (1811–1825)*

Born: Queen's County 1765
Relations: Son of Captain Archibald Erskine, 3rd Horse, and Jane (Paget); father of Lieutenant Colonel Archibald Erskine, 45th Foot; Lieutenant James Andrews Erskine, 48th Foot; Captain John Erskine, 17th Foot; and General George Erskine
Entry to Army: Ensign in 103rd Foot 2 Feb 1782
Field Officer Promotions: Major in 22nd Foot 3 Nov 1804 (vice Parr); Major in 48th Foot 14 Feb 1805 (vice Frome) by exchange; Lieutenant Colonel in 48th Foot 20 Jun 1811 (vice Duckworth)
Brevets: Brevet Lieutenant Colonel 25 Jul 1810; Brevet Colonel 12 Aug 1819
Early Service: Served in West Indies 1791–1793
Service 1793–1815: Served in West Indies 1793–1797; served in Irish rebellion 1798; ADC to King George III 1808; served in Peninsula May 1809, wounded at Douro; and Dec 1811 to May 1812, wounded at Badajoz; served in Peninsula Jul to Dec 1813
Later Service: Lieutenant Governor of New South Wales 12 Sep 1817 to 25 Feb 1823; served in British East Indies Jun 1825 (for 4 days)
Awards and Honours: AGM (Bad); CB 14 Jun 1815
Died: Madras 7 Jun 1825

Sources: ANCB; ANCD; ARLI; WEOF; WO 25/745; Australian Dictionary of Biography, Vol.1; Family Records (Burke)

477. *Sir William HUTCHINSON (1811–1814)*

Born: Ireland c.1765
Relations: Father of General William Nelson Hutchinson; and Captain Frederick James Taggart Hutchinson, unattached
Entry to Army: Volunteer in West Indies; Ensign in 46th Foot 1 Jun 1780
Regimental Field Officer Promotions: Major unattached 25 Sep 1794; Major in 2nd West India Regiment 20 May 1795; Major in 49th Foot 11 Jul 1798 (vice Rooke) by purchase; Lieutenant Colonel in 83rd Foot 9 Jun 1803 (vice Gibson) by purchase; to half-pay of 12th Garrison Battalion 6 May 1805 (vice Gordon) by exchange; Lieutenant Colonel in 48th Foot 24 Oct 1811 (vice Ross) by exchange; removed from the regiment as a general officer 1814
Brevets: Brevet Lieutenant Colonel 1 Jan 1800; Brevet Colonel 25 Jul 1810; Major General 4 Jun 1813; Lieutenant General 27 May 1825; General 23 Nov 1841
Colonelcies: 75th Foot 26 Oct 1841 (vice Fuller)
Early Service: Served in West Indies 1780–1782; served in West Indies 1790–1793
Service 1793–1815: Served in West Indies 1793–1794; served in Helder 1799, wounded at Egmont-op-Zee; served in Copenhagen 1801; Inspecting Field Officer of Volunteers 1805; appointed to staff in Peninsula 25 Nov 1812 (according to Phillipart, unsupported by evidence); served on staff in Malta
Later Service: Governor of Carrickfergus 12 Feb 1830; Equerry to King William IV 6 Jun 1831
Awards and Honours: KCH 12 Aug 1831
Residence: Kenilworth House, Cheltenham, Gloucestershire
Died: Cheltenham 28 Aug 1845
Sources: ANCD; ANCW; ARLI; PHIL; WEOF; WO 25/746

478. *William BROOKE (1813)*

Born: Middlesex c.1756
Relations: Father of Captain John Bolingbroke Brooke, 48th Foot; and Captain William Henry Brooke, 48th Foot
Entry to Army: Ensign in 48th Foot 6 Sep 1779
Regimental Field Officer Promotions: Major in 48th Foot 2 Nov 1809 (vice Middlemore); Lieutenant Colonel in 48th Foot 4 Jun 1813
Brevets: Brevet Major 25 Apr 1808; Brevet Lieutenant Colonel 20 Jun 1811
Early Service: Served in West Indies 1787–1793
Service 1793–1815: Served in West Indies 1795–1797; served in Malta 1800–1803; served in Peninsula Jul 1809 to Apr 1812; commanded 2/48th Foot, wounded and taken POW at Albuera, escaped Aug 1811; Assistant Quartermaster General and badly wounded at Badajoz 1812
Awards and Honours: AGM (Alb)
Retired: 8 Dec 1813
Residence: Sloane Street, Chelsea, London
Died: London May 1828
Wrote a journal of his time as a POW, published as part of Oman's 'Studies in the Napoleonic Wars' in 1929
Sources: ANCD; ANCW; ARLI; CHAL; HALL; WEMR; WEOF; WO 25/744

479. *William WAUCHOPE (1813–1814)*

Born: Edinburgh 1780
Relations: Son of Captain Andrew Wauchope of Niddrie and Alicia (Baird); brother of Lieutenant Colonel Andrew Wauchope, 20th Foot; nephew of General Sir David Baird
Entry to Army: Ensign in 93rd Foot 14 Apr 1803
Field Officer Promotions: Major in Meuron's Regiment 14 Jan 1813 (vice Zweifel) by purchase; Lieutenant Colonel in 48th Foot 8 Dec 1813 (vice Brooke) by purchase; to half-pay of 48th Foot 24 Oct 1814; Lieutenant Colonel in 31st Foot 25 May 1815 (vice Leith) by exchange; Lieutenant Colonel in 26th Foot 8 Jun 1815 (vice L'Estrange) by exchange; to half-pay of Watteville's Regiment 23 Oct 1817 (vice Oglander) by exchange
Service 1793–1815: ADC to Thomas Maitland in Ceylon 1809
Residences: Genoa, Liguria, Italy
Died: Genoa Apr 1825
Sources: ANCB; ANCD; ARLI; PHIL; History and Genealogy of the Family of Wauchope of Niddrie-Merschell

Majors

480. *John Nicholas SKERRETT (1791–1795)*

Born: Cheshire 1743
Relations: Son of Joseph Skerrett of Nantwich and Sarah (Shenton); father of Major General John Byne Skerrett
Entry to Army: Volunteer in 30th Foot 1759; Ensign in 19th Foot 1 Oct 1761 by purchase
Field Officer Promotions: Major in 48th Foot 30 Nov 1791 (vice D'Arcy) by purchase; Lieutenant Colonel Commandant 7th West India Regiment 15 Sep 1795; to half-pay1 Mar 1798
Brevets: Brevet Major 14 Nov 1790; Brevet Lieutenant Colonel 1 Mar 1794; Brevet Colonel

1 Jan 1798; Brigadier General (Newfoundland) 2 Aug 1798; Major General 1 Jan 1805; Lieutenant General 4 Jun 1811
Colonelcies: Loyal Durham Fencibles Apr 1798; Royal Newfoundland Fencibles 9 Jul 1803
Early Service: Served in Belle Isle 1761; served in Gibraltar 1768–1774; served in American War of Independence 1780–1783; served in West Indies 1783–1798
Service 1793–1815: Served in Irish rebellion 1798; Commander of Newfoundland 1 Aug 1799 to 31 Dec 1805; served on staff in Jamaica 1807; served in Sicily
Residence: Heavitree, Devon
Died: Heavitree 18 Aug 1813
Sources: ANCB; ANCD; ANCW; ARLI; WEOF; WO 25/748

481. *James CAMPBELL (1795–1796)*
Born: New York 1738
Relations: Son of Captain Lachlan Campbell of Islay and New York, and Martha (Campbell); brother of Major General George Campbell; father of Lieutenant Donald Campbell, Bombay service
Entry to Army: Ensign in 48th Foot 23 Aug 1758
Regimental Field Officer Promotions: Major in 48th Foot 1 Sep 1795 (vice Skerrett) by purchase
Brevets: Brevet Major 19 Mar 1783; Brevet Lieutenant Colonel 1 Mar 1794
Retired: 14 Dec 1796
Residence: Glasgow, Lanarkshire
Died: Glasgow 6 Feb 1801
Sources: ANCB: ARLI; FMPD; Sun (newspaper) 11 Feb 1801; Records of Clan Campbell in the Military Service of the Honourable East India Company

482. *Sir Nathaniel Levett PEACOCKE, 2nd Bt (1796–1804)*
Born: County Clare 1769
Relations: Son of Sir Joseph Peacocke of Grange, 1st Bt, and Elizabeth Susanna (Cuffe); cousin of General Warren Marmaduke Peacocke
Entry to Army: Ensign in 88th Foot 15 Jan 1783 by purchase
Regimental Field Officer Promotions: Major in 48th Foot 14 Dec 1796 (vice Campbell) by purchase; to half-pay of Limerick Fencibles 24 May 1804; Major in 71st Foot 25 Jun 1807 (vice Hamilton) by exchange; Lieutenant Colonel in 71st Foot 4 Jun 1813
Brevets: Brevet Lieutenant Colonel 29 Apr 1802; Brevet Colonel 4 Jun 1811
Service 1793–1815: Served in Peninsula with 1/71st Foot Sep to Nov 1810; commanded 2/71st Foot 1810–1813; commanded 1/71st Foot in Peninsula Jun 1813 to Mar 1814; wounded at Nive and under suspicion of cowardice Dec 1813
Retired: Removed from the service 24 Mar 1814
Creations and Dignities: 2nd Baronet Peacocke of Barntick 17 Jun 1812
Residence: Barntick, County Clare; Upper Montague Street, Marylebone, London
Died: London 1 Nov 1847
Sources: ANCW; ARLI; CHAL; DEBA; GHPB; WEOF

483. *William PEARSE (1803–1804)*
Born: Cambridgeshire 1756
Relations: Son of Best Pearse of Hatley St George, Sheriff of Cambridgeshire and Huntingdonshire, and Sarah (Butler)
Entry to Army: Ensign in Huntingdonshire Militia; Ensign in 75th Foot 23 Jun 1778
Regimental Field Officer Promotions: Major in 123rd Foot 1795; to half-pay of 123rd Foot 1795; Major in 48th Foot 11 Jul 1803 (vice Wemyss); Lieutenant Colonel in 15th Foot 1 Aug 1804
Brevets: Brevet Lieutenant Colonel 1 Jan 1800
Retired: 31 Jan 1807
Residence: Charles Street, Kensington, London
Died: Kensington 23 Apr 1829
Sources: ANCD; ARLI; WEOF

484. *Arthur AYLMER (1803–1804)*
Born: County Kildare 1772
Relations: Son of Sir Fitzgerald Aylmer, 6th Bt, MP and Elizabeth (Cole); brother of Captain John Aylmer, 89th Foot
Entry to Army: Ensign in 49th Foot 19 Oct 1787 by purchase
Field Officer Promotions: Major in 108th Foot 21 Jun 1794; Major in Manx Fencibles 1 Jul 1798; to half-pay of Manx Fencibles 1802; Major in 48th Foot 11 Jul 1803; Lieutenant Colonel in 25th Foot 16 Aug 1804; to half-pay of 68th Foot 21 May 1807
Brevets: Brevet Lieutenant Colonel 1 Jan 1800; Major General 4 Jun 1813; Lieutenant General 27 May 1825
Service 1793–1815: Commanded 2/25th Foot 1804–1807; Inspecting Field Officer of Yeomanry and Volunteers 1807
Residence: Walworth Castle, near Darlington, County Durham
Died: Durham 5 Feb 1831
Sources: ANCW; ARLI; LFBI; PHIL; WEOF

485. *William Castle FROME (1804–1805)*
Born: Wiltshire 1769
Relations: Son of Rev. Thomas Frome of East

Woodhay and Theodosia (Kinneir)
Entry to Army: Cornet in 13th Light Dragoons 30 Apr 1792
Field Officer Promotions: Major in 48th Foot 16 Jun 1804 (vice Brooke); Major in 22nd Foot 14 Feb 1805 (vice Erskine) by exchange
Brevets: Brevet Lieutenant Colonel 1 Jan 1805
Service 1793–1815: Served in British East Indies 1805–1807
Residence: West Woodhay, Berkshire
Died: Mathura, Uttar Pradesh, British East Indies 19 Jul 1807
Sources: ANCB; ANCD; ANCW; ARLI

486. *Robert SEWELL (1804–1810)*

Born: Jamaica 1777
Relations: Son of Robert Sewell, attorney general of Jamaica, and Sarah (Lewis); brother of General Sir William Henry Sewell; and Lieutenant Henry Frederick Sewell RN; father of Captain Arthur Henry Cole Sewell, Bengal service
Entry to Army: Ensign in 51st Foot 30 Sep 1795
Regimental Field Officer Promotions: Major in 6/60th Foot 16 Jun 1803 (vice Forster) by purchase; Major in 48th Foot 24 Nov 1804; Lieutenant Colonel in 89th Foot 3 May 1810 (vice Garden); to unattached list 1825
Brevets: Brevet Lieutenant Colonel 26 Oct 1804; Brevet Colonel 4 Jun 1813; Major General 12 Aug 1819
Service 1793–1815: Served in Corsica 1796; served in Elba and in Portugal 1797; served on staff in Corfu 1799; served in Egypt 1801; ADC to Sir John Moore 1803; Deputy Adjutant General in Malta 26 Oct 1804 until 1809; served in Gibraltar 1810–1812; commanded brigade in East Indies 1812–1819
Later Service: Served on staff in East Indies 1819–1826
Residence: Twyford Lodge, near Horsted Keynes, Sussex
Died: Twyford Lodge 20 Oct 1835
Sources: ANCB; ANCD; ANCW; ARLI; WEOF; <http://www.sole.org.uk/sole2/sirthom.htm>

487. *George MORRISON (1805–1809)*

Born: Isle of Man c.1771
Entry to Army: Ensign in 48th Foot 31 May 1787
Regimental Field Officer Promotions: Major in 48th Foot 12 Jan 1805
Service 1793–1815: Served in Peninsula Apr to Jul 1809
Retired: 25 Nov 1809
Residence: St George's Street, Douglas, Isle of Man
Died: Douglas 2 Feb 1827
Sources: ANCD; ARLI; Liverpool Abion, 5 Feb 1827

488. *William Grove WHITE (1809–1814)*

Born: County Cork c.1776
Relations: Son of James White of Kilbyrne and Sarah (Garde); brother of Captain John Grove White, 73rd Foot
Entry to Army: Ensign in Ward's Corps 14 Apr 1795
Regimental Field Officer Promotions: Major in 48th Foot 25 Nov 1809 (vice Morrison) by purchase; to half-pay of 48th Foot 24 Oct 1814; Lieutenant Colonel in 94th Foot 1 Dec 1823
Brevets: Brevet Lieutenant Colonel 26 Aug 1813
Service 1793–1815: Served in West Indies 1795–1797; served in Gibraltar 1798–1800; served in Malta 1800–1802; served in Gibraltar 1805–1809; served in Peninsula Apr to Jul 1810; served in Peninsula May to Aug 1811; again in Peninsula Jul 1812 to Dec 1813; commanded 1/48th at Vittoria and Pyrenees, wounded 28 Jul 1813
Later Service: Served in New South Wales and Van Diemen's Land 1820–1823
Retired: 10 Jun 1826
Awards and Honours: AGM (Vitt Pyr); CB 4 Jun 1815
Residence: Newton Cottage, Swanage, Dorset
Died: Swanage 3 Mar 1844
Sources: ANCD; ANCW; ARLI; GHLG; PHIL; WEOF

489. *Molyneux MARSTON (1810–1817)*

Born: County Dublin c.1778
Relations: Son of Daniel Marston of Leixlip, iron merchant, and Catherine (Corry)
Entry to Army: Ensign in 86th Foot 8 Jul 1794
Regimental Field Officer Promotions: Major in 48th Foot 9 May 1810 (vice Sewell); to half-pay of 37th Foot 25 May 1817 (vice Druitt) by exchange
Brevets: Brevet Major 1 Jan 1805; Brevet Lieutenant Colonel 1 Jan 1812; Brevet Colonel 22 Jul 1830
Service 1793–1815: Served in Peninsula Jul 1809 to Nov 1811, wounded at Talavera; Deputy Assistant Quartermaster General in Peninsula 8 May 1810 to Nov 1811; also Mar 1812 to Apr 1814
Residences: Stafford Place, Pimlico, London; Bordeaux, France
Died: London 15 May 1834
Sources: ANCW; ARLI; CHAL; GEMA (1834); PHIL; WEOF; The Topographer and Genealogist, Vol.2

490. *Sir James WILSON (1811–1814)*
Born: Hampshire c.1782
Entry to Army: Ensign in 27th Foot 12 Dec 1798 by purchase
Regimental Field Officer Promotions: Major in 48th Foot 20 Jun 1811 (vice Erskine); to half-pay of 48th Foot 25 Sep 1814
Brevets: Brevet Lieutenant Colonel 27 Apr 1812; Brevet Colonel 22 Jul 1830; Major General 28 Jun 1838
Service 1793–1815: Served in Helder 1799; served in Ferrol and Cadiz 1800; served in Egypt 1801; served in Peninsula Jul 1809 to Apr 1814, wounded at Albuera, Badajoz, Pyrenees and Toulouse; commanded 1/48th in Peninsula after Albuera
Retired: No active military service after 1814 due to wounds
Awards and Honours: AGC (Alb Bad Sal Vit Toul); KCB 22 May 1830
Residences: Burnett, near Bath, Somerset; Kingsdown House Asylum, Box, Wiltshire
Died: Box 7 Feb 1847
Was admitted to Kingsdown House Asylum in 1841 and remained there until his death
Sources: ANCD; ANCM; ANCW; DINB; GEMA (1847); ODNB; PHIL; WEMR; <https://www.batharchives.co.uk/sites/www.bathvenues.co.uk/files/2022-07/BUR%2520Memorials%2520Issue%25201_0.pdf>

491. *Sir Stephen Arthur GOODMAN (1813–1814)*
Born: Surrey 1779
Relations: Son of Samuel Goodman of Camberwell and Sarah (unk.); father of Captain Charles Arthur Goodman, 36th Foot
Entry to Army: Ensign in 48th Foot Oct 1794
Regimental Field Officer Promotions: Major in 48th Foot 4 Jun 1813 (vice Brooke); to half-pay of 48th Foot 25 Oct 1814
Brevets: Brevet Lieutenant Colonel 6 Dec 1813; Brevet Colonel 22 Jul 1830; Major General 23 Nov 1841
Served in Minorca 1800; served in Peninsula May 1809 to Apr 1814; Deputy Judge Advocate in Peninsula 25 Aug 1809 to Apr 1814; acting Adjutant General in Peninsula Aug to Dec 1812; Deputy Judge Advocate in Waterloo campaign and occupation of Paris 1815
Later Service: Colonial Secretary in Berbice 1819; Vendue Master of Demerara and Essequibo 1821; Inspector General of Militia in British Guiana 1823–1844; Governor of Berbice May 1835 to Oct 1836
Awards and Honours: KH 12 Aug 1836; CB 19 Jul 1838
Residence: George Town, Demerara, British Guiana
Died: British Guiana 2 Jan 1844
Sources: ANCW; CHAL; DALT; DINB; GEMA (1844); PHIL; WEMR; WEOF

Selected Regimental Histories
Gurney, Russell, *History of the Northamptonshire Regiment: 1742–1934* (Aldershot: Gale & Polden, 1935)

Regimental Museum
Abington Park Museum, Park Avenue South, Northampton, Northamptonshire

---

49th Regiment of Foot

Secondary Title:	Hertfordshire
Nicknames:	The Green Tigers
Jacket:	Red
Facings:	Full green

Regimental Lineage, 49th Regiment of Foot

1743:	Raised from independent companies in Jamaica as Edward Trelawney's Regiment of Foot
1747:	Ranked as 63rd Regiment of Foot
1751:	49th Regiment of Foot
1782:	49th (Hertfordshire) Regiment of Foot
1813:	2nd Battalion formed in Maldon
1814:	2nd Battalion disbanded in Chelmsford
1816:	49th (Princess of Wales's Hertfordshire) Regiment

1881: 1st Battalion, Princess Charlotte of Wales's (Royal Berkshire Regiment) (on amalgamation with the 66th (Berkshire) Regiment of Foot)
1921: Royal Berkshire Regiment (Princess Charlotte of Wales's)
1959: Duke of Edinburgh's Royal Regiment (Berkshire and Wiltshire) (on amalgamation with the Wiltshire Regiment (Duke of Edinburgh's))
1994: Royal Gloucestershire, Berkshire and Wiltshire Regiment (on amalgamation with the Gloucestershire Regiment)
2005: Royal Gloucestershire, Berkshire and Wiltshire Light Infantry
2007: 1st Battalion, The Rifles (on amalgamation with the Devonshire and Dorset Regiment, the Royal Green Jackets and The Light Infantry)

Service History, 1st Battalion 49th Regiment of Foot

1793: St Domingue; Aug – Jamaica; flank companies to St Domingue; Jeremie
1794: Jamaica; Feb – flank companies at Tiburon; Fort L'Acul; Bombarde
1795: Jamaica
1796: Jamaica; two companies to St Domingue; Maroon rebellion; Apr – to England; Jun – Watford; Nov – Chatham; Dec – Chelmsford
1797: Chelmsford; Jun – Tilbury; Jul – Chelmsford and Gravesend; Sep – Chelmsford
1798: Norwich; Feb – Yarmouth; Apr – Yarmouth and Lowestoft; May – Broadstairs; Ostend raid, large number of POWs taken; Jun – Jersey
1799: Jersey; Feb – Portsmouth; Mar – Hilsea; Jun – Winchester; POWs returned; Aug – Barham Downs; to Helder; Sep – Bergen; Oct – EGMONT OP ZEE; Nov – to England; Yarmouth; Silverhill; Dec – Norwich
1800: King's Lynn; Feb – Bungay and Beccles; May – Colchester; Jun – Portsmouth; Jul – Jersey
1801: Jersey; Portsmouth; Feb – Horsham; Mar – Yarmouth; to COPENHAGEN as marines; Jul – Portsmouth; Aug – Colchester; Nov – Chelmsford
1802: Chelmsford; Jun – Tilbury; to British North America; Aug – Québec; Montréal
1803: Montréal; Jul – York (Toronto); Oct – Fort George
1804: Fort George
1805: Fort George; NCO revolt
1806–1810: Fort George
1811: Fort George; ordered home, but retained in British North America
1812: Fort George; Jul – Montréal; Aug – four companies to Kingston, six companies in Fort George; Oct – QUEENSTOWN; Nov – Fort Erie; Salmon River; Dec – Fort Erie, Kingston and Fort George
1813: Fort George; May – Beaver Dams; Fort George; Burlington Heights; Jun – Stoney Creek; Forty Mile Creek; Jul – Fort Schlosser; Aug – Queenston Heights; Oct – Kingston; Nov – Chrysler's Farm; Dec – Montréal
1814: Montréal and Isle au Noix; Mar – St Johns; Aug – Isle au Noix; Sep – Plattsburgh; Three Rivers
1815: Three Rivers; May – to England; Jul – Portsmouth; Aug – Gosport; Sep – Radipole; Nov – Weymouth

Service History, 2nd Battalion 49th Regiment of Foot

1813: Jul – formed at Maldon (four companies only)
1814: Maldon; Aug – Chelmsford; Oct – disbanded in Chelmsford

Establishments, 1st Battalion 49th Regiment of Foot

Year	Subunits	Field Off	Off/ Staff	Sjts	Mus	Corp/ Pvts	Total
Dec 1792	10co	3	32	22	12	430	499
Jan 1793	10co	3	32	32	22	600	689
Oct 1795	10co+2r	5	51	62	30	1,010	1,158
Dec 1797	10co	5	32	53	22	600	712

Dec 1798	10co	5	38	53	22	600	718
Aug 1799	11co	5	38	58	24	660	785
Dec 1800	10co	5	46	43	22	800	916
Dec 1802	10co	5	33	34	22	750	844
Dec 1803	10co	5	36	34	22	750	847
Dec 1804	10co	5	36	44	22	800	907
Dec 1806	10co	4	36	44	22	800	906
May 1809	10co+r	4	40	52	26	808	930
Dec 1811	10co+r	4	40	53	26	808	931
Dec 1813	10co	4	46	45	22	800	917
Dec 1814	10co+r	4	49	53	22	808	936
Dec 1815	10co	4	46	35	22	600	707

Establishments, 2nd Battalion 49th Regiment of Foot

Year	Subunits	Field Off	Off/ Staff	Sjts	Mus	Corp/ Pvts	Total
Dec 1813	4co	1	17	25	8	400	451

Service Statistics, 49th Regiment of Foot

	Lieutenant Colonels	Majors
Number of officers in period 1793–1815	8	11
Average age on appointment to substantive rank	38	31.5
Average time in rank in regiment (years)	6.5	6
Total field officers by nationality	6 E / 5 S / 4 I / 1 A	
Demographics of other ranks 1807	59% I / 37% EW / 3% S / 1% F	
Demographics of other ranks 1815	49% I / 38% EW / 12% S / 1% F	
Months of overseas service 1793–1815	1/49th: 198 2/49th: no overseas service	

Significant Militia/Volunteer Intakes

1799: South Middlesex, Suffolk Fencibles, Elgin Fencibles, Tarbert Fencibles
1800: Elgin Fencibles, County Monaghan
1806: Lanarkshire, County Monaghan
1809: Canadian Fencibles
1813: County Meath

Regimental Colonels

492. *Hon. Sir Alexander MAITLAND, 1st Bt (1768–1820)*
Born: Edinburgh 1728
Relations: Son of Rt Hon. Charles Maitland, 6th Earl of Lauderdale, and Lady Elizabeth (Ogilvy); brother of James Maitland, 7th Earl of Lauderdale; Colonel Hon. Richard Maitland, Deputy Adjutant General in North America; Captain Hon. Frederick Lewis Maitland RN; Lieutenant Colonel Hon. John Lauderdale Maitland, 71st Foot; father of General Frederick Maitland; and Captain and Lieutenant Colonel Augustus Maitland, 1st Foot Guards
Entry to Army: Midshipman in RN; Lieutenant in 3rd Foot Guards 20 Jan 1747
Regimental Field Officer Promotions: Captain and Lieutenant Colonel in 1st Foot Guards 6 Jun 1756
Brevets: Brevet Colonel 19 Feb 1762; Major General 25 May 1772; Lieutenant General 29 Aug 1777; General 12 Oct 1793
Colonelcies: 49th Foot 25 May 1768 (vice Graeme)
Early Service: Served in Flanders and France 1744–1745; served in Jacobite rebellion 1745
Service 1793–1815: Groom of the Bedchamber to HRH Frederick, Prince of Wales
Creations and Dignities: 1st Baronet of Clifton 30 Nov 1818
Residence: Totteridge, Hertfordshire
Died: Totteridge 15 Feb 1820
Sources: ANCW; DINB; GEMA (1820); PHIL; WEOF; The Peerage, Baronetage, Knightage & Companionage of the British Empire for 1907

Lieutenant Colonels

493. *William Collins DANSEY (1790–1793)*

Born: Herefordshire c.1744
Relations: Son of William Collins Dansey of Brinsop Court and Harriett (Sawyer); father of Captain William Mallet Dansey, 65th Foot; Colonel Charles Cornwallis Dansey RA; and Lieutenant Colonel George Henry Dansey, 76th Foot; father-in-law of Lieutenant Colonel Sydney Edward Scroggs, 53rd Foot
Entry to Army: Lieutenant 17 Jan 1763
Field Officer Promotions: Major in 33rd Foot 15 Oct 1778; Lieutenant Colonel in 49th Foot 21 Jul 1790 (vice Calder)
Brevets: Brevet Lieutenant Colonel 22 Aug 1783; Colonel (America) 17 Nov 1790
Early Service: Served in American War of Independence
Service 1793–1815: ADC to King George III; commanded 49th Foot 1790–1794; garrison commander at Mole St Nicolas 1793–1794
Residences: Brinsop Court, Brinsop, Herefordshire; Taunton, Somerset
Died: San Domingo 18 Nov 1793
Sources: ANCB; ANCD; ANCW; ARLI; GHLG

494. *James Ogilvie GRANT (1794–1797)*

Born: Aberdeenshire 1746
Relations: Son of Captain Alexander Grant of Grantsfield, Sherriff of Aberdeenshire, and Margaret (Farquharson)
Entry to Army: Lieutenant in 49th Foot 14 Aug 1765
Field Officer Promotions: Major in 49th Foot 18 Aug 1790; Lieutenant Colonel in 49th Foot 12 Feb 1794 (vice Dansey)
Brevets: Brevet Major 19 Mar 1783
Early Service: Served in American War of Independence
Service 1793–1815: Commanded 49th Foot 1794–1797
Retired: 25 Oct 1797
Residence: Fordington, Dorset
Died: Fordington 17 Aug 1801
Sources: ANCD; ANCW; ARLI; WikiTree

495. *Frederick KEPPEL (1795–1798)*

Born: Norfolk 1762
Relations: Son of Rt Rev. Frederick Keppel, Bishop of Exeter, and Laura (Walpole); nephew of Lieutenant General George Keppel, 3rd Earl of Albemarle; Admiral Augustus Keppel RN, 1st Viscount Keppel; and Lieutenant General William Keppel; brother-in-law of Lieutenant General William Stapleton; and George FitzRoy, 2nd Baron Southampton; father of Colonel Edward George Walpole Keppel, 48th Foot
Education: Westminster School
Entry to Army: Ensign in 1/1st Foot 20 May 1780 by purchase
Field Officer Promotions: Major in 88th Foot 25 Sep 1793; Lieutenant Colonel in 88th Foot 28 Mar 1794; Lieutenant Colonel in 49th Foot 1 Sep 1795
Brevets: Brevet Lieutenant Colonel 28 Mar 1794
Service 1793–1815: Served in Flanders 1794–1795; Inspecting Field Officer of Volunteers 1803
Retired: 22 Mar 1798
Residence: Lexham Hall, East Lexham, Norfolk; Pall Mall, St James's, London
Died: Lexham Hall 12 Apr 1830
Sources: ANCB; ANCD; ANCW; ARLI; GHPB; WEOF

496. *Sir Isaac BROCK (1797–1812)*

Born: Guernsey 1769
Relations: Son of Midshipman John Brock RN of St. Peter Port and Elizabeth (De Lisle); brother of Lieutenant Colonel John Brock, 81st Foot; Lieutenant Ferdinand Brock, 60th Foot; and Paymaster John Savery Brock, 49th Foot; cousin of Major George Brock, 37th Foot; and Major Saumarez Brock, 43rd Foot
Entry to Army: Ensign in 8th Foot 2 Mar 1785 by purchase
Regimental Field Officer Promotions: Major in 49th Foot 24 Jun 1795 (vice Gibson) by purchase; Lieutenant Colonel in 49th Foot 25 Oct 1797 (vice Grant) by purchase
Brevets: Brevet Colonel 30 Oct 1805; Major General 4 Jun 1811
Early Service: Served in West Indies 1791–1793
Service 1793–1815: Commanded 49th Foot in Helder 1799; commanded 49th Foot in Copenhagen 1801; served in British North America 1802–1812; acting Lieutenant Governor and Commander of Upper Canada 9 Oct 1811 to 13 Oct 1812
Awards and Honours: KB 10 Oct 1812
Died: Killed in action at Queenston Heights 13 Oct 1812
Sources: ARLI; ODNB; WEOF; WOST; The Life and Correspondence of Major-General Sir Isaac Brock

497. *Sir Roger Hale SHEAFFE, 1st Bt (1798–1814)*

Born: Massachusetts 1763
Relations: Son of William Sheaffe, deputy collector

of customs in Boston, and Susannah (Child); uncle of Captain Roger-Hale Sheaffe, 55th Foot
Education: Locke's Military Academy, Chelsea
Entry to Army: Ensign in 5th Foot May 1778 by purchase
Regimental Field Officer Promotions: Major in 81st Foot 13 Dec 1797 (vice Parry) by purchase; Lieutenant Colonel in 49th Foot 22 Mar 1798 (vice Keppel) by purchase; removed from the regiment as a general officer 1814
Brevets: Brevet Colonel 25 Apr 1808; Major General 4 Jun 1811; Lieutenant General 19 Jul 1821; General 28 Jun 1837
Colonelcies: 36th Foot 21 Dec 1829 (vice Don)
Early Service: Served in British North America May 1787 to Sep 1797
Service 1793–1815: Served in Helder 1799; served in Copenhagen 1801; served in British North America Jun 1802 to Jun 1813; acting Lieutenant Governor and Commander of Upper Canada 13 Oct 1812 to 19 Jun 1813 (vice Brock)
Creations and Dignities: 1st Baronet of Edswale 16 Jan 1813
Awards and Honours: NGSM (Cop); MGSM (CF)
Residence: Melville Street, Edinburgh, Midlothian
Died: Edinburgh 17 Jul 1851
Sources: ARLI; DEBA; DICB; WEOF; WOST; WO 25/748

498. *John VINCENT (1811–1815)*

Born: County Limerick 1764
Relations: Son of John Vincent of Mardyke, Sheriff of Limerick, and Catherine (Love)
Entry to Army: Ensign in 66th Foot 16 Jul 1781 by purchase
Regimental Field Officer Promotions: Major in 49th Foot 1 Sep 1795; Lieutenant Colonel in 49th Foot 13 Jun 1811; removed from the regiment as a general officer 1815
Brevets: Brevet Major 6 May 1795; Brevet Lieutenant Colonel 1 Jan 1800; Brevet Colonel 25 Jul 1810; Brigadier General (North America) Feb 1813; Major General 4 Jun 1813; Lieutenant General 27 May 1825; General Nov 1841
Colonelcies: 69th Foot 2 Jan 1836 (vice Hamilton)
Service 1793–1815: Served in St Domingue 1794; served in Helder 1799; served in Copenhagen 1801; served in British North America Aug 1802 to Jul 1814, commanded brigade in Niagara 1813–1814
Later Service: Lieutenant Governor of Dumbarton Castle 15 Apr 1824
Residence: Pall Mall, St James's, London
Died: London 21 Jan 1848
Sources: ANCD; ANCW; ARLI; DICB; WEOF; WO 25/748

499. *Jonathan YATES (1813–1821)*

See 457.
Lieutenant Colonel in 49th Foot 13 May 1813

500. *Charles PLENDERLEATH (1813–1814)*

Born: Peeblesshire c.1780
Relations: Son of Major John Plenderleath of The Glen in Tweeddale and Janet (Smith); brother of Dr John Plenderleath, physician to the forces in Portugal
Entry to Army: Ensign in 89th Foot 29 May 1796 by purchase
Regimental Field Officer Promotions: Major in 49th Foot 16 Oct 1806 (vice Bleamire) by purchase; Lieutenant Colonel in 49th Foot 4 Jun 1813; to half-pay of 49th Foot 1814
Service 1793–1815: Served as marine in Copenhagen 1801; served in British North America 1802–1815, wounded 25 Jul 1813
Awards and Honours: AGM (CF); CB 4 Jun 1815; NGSM (Cop)
Residences: Wolfe, Québec, Canada; Richmond Terrace, Clifton, Gloucestershire
Died: Florence, Tuscany, Italy 1 Jan 1854
Sources: ANCD; ANCW; ARLI; WEOF; WO 25/747

Majors

501. *Thomas GIBSON (1794–1795)*

Born: Fifeshire c.1755
Relations: Son of John Gibson of Durie and Helen (Carmichael)
Entry to Army: Ensign in 63rd Foot 14 Dec 1774 by purchase
Regimental Field Officer Promotions: Major in 49th Foot 12 Feb 1794 (vice Grant); Lieutenant Colonel in 83rd Foot 27 May 1795 (vice Sleigh)
Brevets: Brevet Colonel 29 Apr 1802
Service 1793–1815: Served in Jamaica 1795–1799
Retired: 9 Jun 1803
Residence: Scoonie, Fifeshire
Died: Scoonie 11 Dec 1838
Sources: ARLI; FMPD; WEOF; Monuments and Monumental Inscriptions in Scotland Vol.2

502. *James ROOKE (1797–1798)*

Born: Oxfordshire 1776
Relations: Son of Lieutenant General James Rooke of Brize Norton and Elizabeth (Brown)
Education: Oriel College, Cambridge
Entry to Army: Ensign in 49th Foot 13 Jun 1791
Regimental Field Officer Promotions: Major in 49th Foot 25 Oct 1797 (vice Brock) by purchase;

Major in 16th Light Dragoons 20 Jun 1798 (vice Anson) by purchase
Retired: 1 Jun 1799
Later Service: Commanded 1st Regiment of Hussars of Venezuela in Bolivar's Patriot army 1817–1819; commanded British Legion in Colombia 1819
Died: Of wounds at Belén de Chámeza, Colombia 28 Jul 1819
Rooke moved to France and was kept captive there between 1802 and 1813. Considered a Colombian national hero, he has a bronze statue in the town of Paipa and a unit of the Colombian army is named after him (Infantry Battalion 18 Cr Jaime Rooke)
Sources: ANCB; ANCD; ANCW; ARLI; WEOF; Freedom's mercenaries: British volunteers in the wars of independence of Latin America

503. *Sir William HUTCHINSON (1799–1802)*

See 477.
Major in 49th Foot 11 Jul 1798 (vice Rooke)

504. *William Bird BLEAMIRE (1803–1806)*

Born: London 1778
Relations: Son of William Bleamire of Hampstead, barrister, and Mary (Harrison)
Entry to Army: Ensign in 49th Foot 3 Sep 1795
Regimental Field Officer Promotions: Major in 49th Foot 6 Aug 1803 (vice Hutchinson) by purchase
Service 1793–1815: Served as marine in Copenhagen 1801
Retired: 16 Oct 1806
Militia Career: Captain in Royal Middlesex (East) Militia 22 Dec 1807
Awards and Honours: NGSM (Cop)
Residence: Bath, Somerset
Died: Bath 21 Mar 1850
Sources: ANCB; ANCD; ANCW; ARLI; GEMA (1850); WEOF

505. *Adam ORMSBY (1811–1820)*

Born: County Mayo 1777
Relations: Son of Thomas Ormsby of Ballinamore, High Sheriff of Mayo, and Elizabeth (Rutledge); uncle of Captain Thomas Ormsby, 92nd Foot; and Lieutenant Colonel Owen Lloyd Ormsby, 88th Foot
Entry to Army: Ensign in 49th Foot 8 Aug 1791
Regimental Field Officer Promotions: Major in 49th Foot 13 Jun 1811 (vice Vincent)
Brevets: Brevet Major 25 Apr 1808; Brevet Lieutenant Colonel 4 Jun 1814
Service 1793–1815: Served in San Domingo and Martinique; served in Helder 1799; served in British North America 1803–1808; served in British North America and commanded 'division' at Queenston Heights 1813; wounded 25 Jul 1813
Retired: 9 Mar 1820
Residence: Killeshin, County Mayo
Died: Killeshin 28 Apr 1835
Sources: ARLI; GHLG; PHIL; WEMR; WEOF

506. *Alexander CLERK (1813–1815)*

Born: Aberdeenshire c.1779
Relations: Son of Alexander Clerk of Aberdeen, merchant
Entry to Army: Volunteer in 49th Foot; Ensign in 49th Foot 27 Feb 1796
Regimental Field Officer Promotions: Major in 49th Foot 4 Jun 1813 (vice Plenderleath); Major on half-pay of Glengarry Fencibles 24 Aug 1815 (vice Bunbury) by exchange
Service 1793–1815: Served in British North America 1812–1815, badly wounded at Stoney Creek
Brevets: Brevet Major 25 Jul 1810; Brevet Lieutenant Colonel 12 Aug 1819
Residence: Aberdeen, Aberdeenshire
Died: Aberdeen 25 Jul 1836
Sources: ANCD; ANCW; ARLI; WEOF

507. *Sir Thomas BUNBURY (1815–1821)*

Born: County Carlow 1783
Relations: Son of Captain Thomas Bunbury of Cranavonane and Mary (Mill); brother of Major Benjamin Bunbury, 2nd West India Regiment; Lieutenant Harrison Charles Bunbury RN; Colonel Hamilton Welch Bunbury, 3rd Foot; and John Monseer Bunbury RN; father of Thomas Lieutenant Charles Bunbury, 60th Foot; and Lieutenant Colonel Stonehouse George Bunbury, 67th Foot
Entry to Army: Ensign in 8th West India Regiment 25 Mar 1804
Regimental Field Officer Promotions: Major in Glengarry Fencibles 14 Apr 1814 (vice Macdonnell); Major in 49th Foot 24 Aug 1815 (vice Clerk) by exchange; Lieutenant Colonel in 83rd Foot 5 Jul 1821 (vice Brunt) by purchase; to half-pay of 83rd Foot 25 Oct 1821
Brevets: Brevet Colonel 10 Jan 1837; Major General 9 Nov 1846; Lieutenant General 20 Jun 1854
Colonelcies: Colonel Commandant of 1/60th Foot 9 Feb 1855 (vice Eustace)
Service 1793–1815: Served in West Indies 1804–1808; served in British North America 1814–1815

Later Service: Lieutenant Governor of St Lucia 5 Apr 1837 to Feb 1838; acting Governor of British Guyana 9 Mar to 27 Jun 1838
Awards and Honours: KH 12 Aug 1835
Residences: Kingston, Jamaica; Lower James Street, St James's, London
Died: London 13 Apr 1857
Sources: ANCW; ARLI; GEMA (1857); GHHI; WEOF; WOST

Selected Regimental Histories

Myatt, Frederick, *The Royal Berkshire Regiment (the 49th/66th Regiment of Foot)* (London: Hamish Hamilton, 1968)

Regimental Museum

The Rifles: Berkshire and Wiltshire Museum, The Wardrobe, 58 The Close, Salisbury, Wiltshire

---

50th Regiment of Foot

Secondary Title:	West Kent
Nicknames:	The Dirty Half-Hundred The Blind Half-Hundred
Jacket:	Red
Facings:	Black

Regimental Lineage, 50th Regiment of Foot

1755:	Raised as the 52nd Regiment of Foot by Colonel James Abercrombie
1756:	50th Regiment of Foot
1782:	50th (West Kent) Regiment of Foot
1804:	Oct – 2nd Battalion formed in Cirencester
1814:	Oct – 2nd Battalion disbanded in Chatham
1827:	50th (Duke of Clarence's) Regiment of Foot
1831:	50th (Queen's Own) Regiment of Foot
1881:	1st Battalion, Queen's Own Royal West Kent Regiment (on amalgamation with the 97th (The Earl of Ulster's) Regiment of Foot)
1921:	Jan – Royal West Kent Regiment (Queen's Own) Regiment
1921:	Apr – Queen's Own Royal West Kent Regiment
1961:	Queen's Own Buffs, The Royal Kent Regiment (on amalgamation with The Buffs (Royal East Kent Regiment))
1966:	2nd Battalion, The Queen's Regiment (on amalgamation with The Queen's Royal Surrey Regiment, The Royal Sussex Regiment and The Middlesex Regiment (Duke of Cambridge's Own))
1992:	1st Battalion, The Princess of Wales's Royal Regiment (on amalgamation with the Royal Hampshire Regiment)

Service History, 1st Battalion 50th Regiment of Foot

1793:	Gibraltar (since 1784)
1794:	Gibraltar; Feb – Hyeres Bay; Corsica – San Fiorenzo; Apr – Bastia; Jun – Calvi; Jul – Fort Mozello; Bastia
1795:	Ajaccio
1796:	Ajaccio; Oct – Elba; Portoferraio
1797:	Portoferraio; to Gibraltar; Jun – to Portugal; Lisbon; Fort St Julien
1798:	Fort St Julien
1799:	Fort St Julien; to Minorca
1800:	Minorca; Nov – to Egypt; Dec – Malta
1801:	Bay of Marmorice [Marmaris]; Mar – EGYPT; Aboukir Bay; Alexandria; Lake Mareotis; May – Rhamanieh [Rahmaniyyah]; Jun – Cairo; Jul – siege of Alexandria; Oct – to Malta
1802:	Malta; Mar – to Ireland; May – Cork; Jun – Belfast

1803:	Belfast; Dec – Ballyshannon
1804:	Ballyshannon; Aug – Omagh
1805:	Omagh; May – Enniskillen; Aug – Curragh camp; Oct – Fermoy; Dec – Clonmel
1806:	Midleton; Mar – Fermoy; Apr – Mallow; Jun – Cork; Aug – ordered on foreign service but did not sail
1807:	Cork; Jun – to England; Ramsgate; Deal; Jul – to Copenhagen; Aug – Copenhagen; Nov – to England; Deal; Dec – Portsmouth; to Gibraltar
1808:	Gibraltar; May – Cadiz; Jul – to Portugal; Aug – Figueras; Roliça; VIMEIRO; Monte Santo; Oct – Villa Franca; Santarem; Nov – Salamanca; Dec – Mayorga; Astorga
1809:	Retreat to Corunna; CORUNNA; to England; Feb – Eastbourne; May – Reading; Jun – Ramsgate; Jul – Portsmouth; to Walcheren; Aug – South Beveland; Middelburg; Oct – to England; Horsham
1810:	Silverhill; Feb – Hastings; Jul – Silverhill; Sep – Lewes; to Portugal; PENINSULA; Lisbon; Oct – Sobral de Monte Agraço; Zibreira de Fetais; Nov – Alcoentre
1811:	Zibrera; Mar – Casal Nova; Foz de Arouce; Sarzedas; Apr – La Alberguería de Argañán; May – Fuentes d'Onoro; Jun – Torre de Mouro; Jul – Borba; Sep – Portalegre; Oct – Aliseda; Arroyomolinos; Nov – Portalegre
1812:	Nisa; Feb – Portalegre; Mar – Mérida; Apr – Almendralejo; May – ALMARAZ; Trujillo; San Pedro de Mérida; Jun – Albuera; Jul – Zafra; Aug – Feria; Sep – Lagartera; Oct – Fuentidueña de Tajo; Nov- Robleda; Dec – Coria
1813:	Coria; Montehermoso; Feb – Béjar; Apr – Puente de Baños; May – Salamanca; Jun – VITTORIA; Uharte Arakil; Pamplona; Jul – PYRENEES; Maya; Aug – Valley of Bastan; Oct – Roncesvalles; Nov – Nivelle; Ustaritz; Dec – NIVE; Bayonne
1814:	Bayonne; Feb – Loubieng; ORTHEZ; Aire; Mar – Saint-Julien-sur-Garonne; Apr – TOULOUSE; Baziège; Jun – Bordeaux; Jul – Paulliac; to Ireland; Cork; Nov – Aughnacloy
1815:	Aughnacloy; Apr – Enniskillen

Service History, 2nd Battalion 50th Regiment of Foot

1804:	Oct – formed in Cirencester
1805:	Cirencester; Jul – Worcester; Aug – Cirencester
1806:	Cirencester; Mar – Worcester; May – Bognor
1807:	Bognor; May – Jersey; Jul – Deal; Dec – Ashford
1808:	Ashford; Aug – Brabourne; Nov – Hythe
1809:	Hythe; Mar – Eastbourne; May – Reading; Aug – Ospringe; Dec – Shorncliffe
1810:	Silverhill; Oct – Eastbourne
1811:	Eastbourne; Nov – Jersey
1812:	Jersey; Mar – Portsmouth; May – Littlehampton; Jun – Eastbourne
1813:	Eastbourne
1814:	Eastbourne; Aug – Chatham; Oct – disbanded in Chatham

Establishments, 1st Battalion 50th Regiment of Foot

Year	Subunits	Field Off	Off/ Staff	Sjts	Mus	Corp/ Pvts	Total
Dec 1792	10co	3	32	22	12	430	499
Jan 1793	10co	3	32	32	22	600	689
Dec 1795	10co+2r	5	51	62	30	1,010	1,158
Dec 1797	10co	5	38	53	22	600	718
Jul 1802	10co	5	33	34	22	750	844
May 1803	10co	5	33	53	22	700	813
Feb 1805	10co	5	36	44	22	800	907
Jul 1807	10co	4	36	44	22	800	906
Dec 1807	10co	4	46	64	22	1,200	1,336
Dec 1808	10co	4	46	54	22	1,000	1,126
Dec 1809	10co	4	36	44	22	800	906

Dec 1810	10co	4	46	54	22	1,000	1,126
Dec 1811	10co	4	46	55	22	1,000	1,127
Aug 1814	10co	4	46	55	22	1,000	1,127

Establishments, 2nd Battalion 50th Regiment of Foot

Year	Subunits	Field Off	Off/ Staff	Sjts	Mus	Corp/ Pvts	Total
Dec 1804	10co	3	35	23	22	400	483
Oct 1807	10co	3	35	33	22	600	693
Dec 1810	10co	3	35	24	22	400	484
Dec 1811	10co	3	35	25	22	400	485

Service Statistics, 50th Regiment of Foot

	Lieutenant Colonels	Majors
Number of officers in period 1793–1815	12	21
Average age on appointment to substantive rank	41	36.5
Average time in rank in regiment (years)	4.5	3.5
Total field officers by nationality	14 E / 9 S / 4 I / 1 F	
Demographics of other ranks 1807	2/50th: 88% EW / 10% I / 1% S / 1% F	
Demographics of other ranks 1812	1/50th: 63% EW / 33% I / 3% S / 1% F	
Demographics of other ranks 1813	2/50th: 72% EW / 24% I / 4% S	
Months of overseas service 1793–1815	1/50th: 196 2/50th: no overseas service	

Significant Militia/Volunteer Intakes

1800: North Hampshire, Herefordshire, 1st Yorkshire
1801: Drafts from Maltese garrison
1804: Additional Force Act men from Gloucestershire
1806: County Leitrim, County Tyrone
1807: Dorset, South Gloucestershire, East Kent, West Yorkshire, County Wicklow
1809: 1st Devonshire, County Galway, County Louth
1810: East Middlesex
1812: Inverness-shire

Regimental Colonels

508. *Sir Thomas Spencer WILSON, 6th Bt (1777–1798)*
Born: Sussex 1727
Relations: Son of Sir Thomas Wilson of Uckfield, 4th Bt, and Elizabeth (Hutchinson); father-in-law of Prime Minster Spencer Perceval
Education: Charterhouse School
Entry to Army: Ensign in 8th Foot 1744
Regimental Field Officer Promotions: Captain Lieutenant and Lieutenant Colonel in Coldstream Foot Guards 14 Apr 1762 by purchase; Captain and Lieutenant Colonel in Coldstream Foot Guards 28 Jun 1761
Brevets: Brevet Lieutenant Colonel 18 Jan 1761; Brevet Colonel 31 Dec 1772; Major General 29 Aug 1777; Lieutenant General 20 Nov 1782; General 3 May 1796
Colonelcies: 50th Foot 30 Apr 1777 (vice Monson)
Early Service: Served in Jacobite rebellion 1746; served in Germany during Seven Years War; ADC to Lord Waldegrave at Minden 1759; wounded in action four times; served in American War of Independence 1777–1779
Political Career: MP (Sussex) 1774–1780
Creations and Dignities: 6th Baronet of Eastbourne 24 Jun 1760
Residence: Uckfield, Sussex
Died: Uckfield 29 Aug 1798
Sources: ARLI; HPON; County Genealogies: Pedigrees of the Families in the County of Sussex

509. *Sir James DUFF, Kt (1798–1839)*
Born: Banffshire 1753
Relations: Natural son of James Duff, 2nd Earl of Fife and Margaret (Adam); half-brother of General Hon. Alexander Duff
Education: King's College, Aberdeen (MA 1771)
Entry to Army: Ensign in 1st Foot Guards 18 Apr

1769 by purchase
Regimental Field Officer Promotions: Captain and Lieutenant Colonel in 1st Foot Guards 18 Jul 1780 by purchase; Third Major in 1st Foot Guards 7 Mar 1795 (vice D'Oyly); Second Major in 1st Foot Guards 28 Sep 1797 (vice D'Oyly); First Major in 1st Foot Guards 11 Oct 1797 (vice D'Oyly)
Brevets: Brevet Colonel 18 Nov 1790; Major General 4 Oct 1794; Lieutenant General 1 Jan 1801; General 25 Oct 1809
Colonelcies: 50th Foot 1 Jan 1798 (vice Wilson)
Service 1793–1815: Commanded Guards flank battalion in Flanders 1793; Major General in Ireland during the 1798 rebellion
Political Career: MP (Banffshire) 1784–1789
Awards and Honours: Knight Bachelor 30 Apr 1779
Residence: Funtington, near Chichester, Sussex
Died: Funtington 5 Dec 1839
Sources: ARLI; DINB; HPON; ODNB; PHIL; WEOF

Lieutenant Colonels

510. *William EDMESTON (1783–1793)*

Born: Northumberland 1728
Relations: Son of Andrew Edmeston of Berwick-upon-Tweed and Margaret (Alder); brother of Captain Robert Edmeston, 48th Foot
Entry to Army: Ensign in 48th Foot 7 Jul 1747
Regimental Field Officer Promotions: Major in 50th Foot 12 Feb 1782; Lieutenant Colonel in 75th Foot 12 Jun 1782; to half-pay of 75th Foot 10 May 1783 (vice Shee); Lieutenant Colonel in 50th Foot 13 Jun 1783 (vice Shee)
Brevets: Brevet Lieutenant Colonel 29 Aug 1777; Brevet Colonel 20 Nov 1782; Major General 12 Oct 1793; Lieutenant General 1 Jan 1798; General 25 Sep 1803
Colonelcies: 95th Foot 30 Oct 1793; 1st Royal Garrison Battalion 25 Dec 1802
Early Service: Served in British North America 1753–1775; served in American War of Independence 1775–1779
Service 1793–1815: Commanded 50th Foot 1783–1793
Residences: Hanwell, Middlesex; Mount Edmeston, Otsego County, New York State
Died: Hanwell 29 Jun 1804
Sources: ANCB; ANCD; ARLI; WEOF

511. *Patrick WAUCHOPE (1794–1807)*

Born: Edinburgh 1750
Relations: Son of James Wauchope of Edmonstone and Christian (Inglis)
Entry to Army: Ensign in 43rd Foot 13 Apr 1768 by purchase
Regimental Field Officer Promotions: Major in 50th Foot 9 Apr 1789 (vice Ogilvie); Lieutenant Colonel in 50th Foot 17 Feb 1794 (vice Edmeston) by purchase
Brevets: Brevet Major 7 Jun 1782; Brevet Lieutenant Colonel 12 Oct 1793; Brevet Colonel 26 Jan 1797; Brigadier General (West Indies) 22 Jan 1801; Major General 25 Sep 1803
Colonelcies: 7th Garrison Battalion 25 Nov 1806
Early Service: Served in Gibraltar
Service 1793–1815: Commanded 50th Foot in Corsica 1794; Governor of Ajaccio 1795; commanded brigade in Egypt 1807
Residence: Edmonstone, Midlothian
Died: Killed in action at Rosetta 31 Mar 1807
Sources: ANCB; ANCW; ARLI; WEOF

512. *John ROSE (1795)*

Born: Sutherland 1746
Relations: [spec.] Son of Roderick Rose of Dornoch and Jean (Munro)
Entry to Army: Ensign in 50th Foot 28 Jan 1763
Regimental Field Officer Promotions: Major in 50th Foot 17 Feb 1794 (vice Wauchope) by purchase; Lieutenant Colonel in 50th Foot 1 Sep 1795
Brevets: Brevet Major 18 Nov 1790; Brevet Lieutenant Colonel 1 Mar 1794
Died: [spec.] Corsica Dec 1795
Sources: ARLI; Caledonian Mercury 16 Mar 1797

513. *Francis ERSKINE (1796–1798)*

See 354.
Major in 50th Foot 1 Sep 1795 (vice Rose); Lieutenant Colonel in 50th Foot 2 Jan 1796 (vice Rose)

514. *Charles William BAILLIE (1798)*

See 353.
Lieutenant Colonel in 50th Foot 25 Jul 1798

515. *Sir George Townshend WALKER, 1st Bt (1798–1812)*

Born: Isle of Wight 1764
Relations: Son of Major Nathaniel Walker of Cowes, Royal American Rangers, and Henrietta (Bagster); brother of General Sir Frederick Nathaniel Walker RA; and Captain Charles Walker RN; father of Captain and Lieutenant Colonel Sir George Ferdinand Radziwill Forestier-Walker, Coldstream Foot Guards, 2nd Bt
Education: Rugby School

Entry to Army: Ensign in 95th Foot 4 Mar 1783
Regimental Field Officer Promotions: Major in 1/60th Foot 28 Aug 1794; Lieutenant Colonel in 50th Foot 6 Sep 1798 (vice Baillie)
Brevets: Brevet Colonel 25 Apr 1808; Brigadier General (Spain) Dec 1810; Major General 4 Jun 1811; Lieutenant General 19 Jul 1821; General 28 Jun 1838
Colonelcies: De Meuron's Regiment 24 Oct 1812 (vice de Meuron); 3/Rifle Brigade 21 May 1816 (vice Champagné); 2/Rifle Brigade 2 Jul 1818; 84th Foot 13 May 1820 (vice Bernard); 52nd Foot 19 Sep 1822 (vice Oakes); 50th Foot 23 Dec 1839 (vice Duff)
Early Service: Served in East Indies 1784–1787
Service 1793–1815: Served on staff in Flanders 1793; served in Portugal 1797; served in Helder 1799, Military Commissary to Russian Troops; commanded 1/50th Foot in Copenhagen 1807; commanded 1/50th Foot in Peninsula Aug 1808 to Jan 1809; served on staff at Walcheren 1809; served in Peninsula Sep 1810 to Aug 1812; commanded brigade in 5th Division in Peninsula Oct 1811 to Apr 1812, wounded at Badajoz; served in Peninsula Jul 1813 to Apr 1814; commanded brigade in 2nd Division in Peninsula Aug to Oct 1813; commanded 7th Division in Peninsula Nov 1813 to Mar 1814, wounded at Orthez
Later Service: Acting Governor of Grenada 7 Apr 1815 to 17 Feb 1816; Groom of the Bedchamber to the Duke of Sussex 1817; Commander in Chief Madras 11 May 1825 to May 1831; Lieutenant Governor of Chelsea Hospital 24 May 1837
Creations and Dignities: 1st Baronet of Castleton 28 Mar 1835
Awards and Honours: AGM (Vim Bad Ort); KCTS (Portugal) 17 Dec 1814; KCB 2 Jan 1815; GCB 11 Mar 1817
Residence: Royal Hospital, Chelsea
Died: Chelsea Hospital 14 Nov 1842
Sources: ANCB; ANCD; ARLI; CHAL; DINB; PHIL; WEBC; WEOF; WO 25/748

516. *Benjamin ROWE (1804–1805)*

Born: [spec.] Devon c.1750
Relations: Father of Major Benjamin Rowe, 50th Foot
Entry to Army: Ensign in 50th Foot 12 Apr 1777
Regimental Field Officer Promotions: Major in 50th Foot 2 Sep 1795 by purchase; Lieutenant Colonel in 50th Foot 1 Aug 1804
Brevets: Brevet Lieutenant Colonel 1 Jan 1801
Service 1793–1815: Commanded 50th Foot in Egypt 1801; commanded 2/50th Foot 1804–1805
Retired: 17 Feb 1805
Residence: Bristol, Gloucestershire
Died: Bristol 2 Aug 1805
Sources: ANCW; GEMA (1805)

517. *Charles STEWART (1805–1812)*

Born: Banffshire 1775
Relations: Son of Lieutenant Thomas Stewart of Keithmore, 56th Foot, and Anne (Gordon)
Entry to Army: Ensign in Duke of Gordon's Fencibles 18 Dec 1782; Lieutenant in 71st Foot Jan 25 1791
Regimental Field Officer Promotions: Major in 53rd Foot 4 Apr 1800 (vice Brisbane) by purchase; Lieutenant Colonel in 50th Foot 17 Feb 1805 (vice Rowe)
Early Service: Served in East Indies 1791–1794
Service 1793–1815: Served in West Indies 1795–1796; served in Seringapatam 1799; commanded 1/50th Foot in Walcheren 1809; commanded 1/50th Foot in Peninsula Sep 1810 to Oct 1812; commanded brigade in 2nd Division in Peninsula Oct 1811 and Nov to Dec 1812
Died: Coria, Spain 11 Dec 1812
Sources: ANCW; ARLI; CHAL; DINB; GHLG; HALL; WEOF; WO 25/748

518. *Charles HILL (1811–1819)*

Born: Yorkshire c.1763
Relations: Of the Hills of Halifax
Entry to Army: Ensign in 50th Foot 27 Dec 1778
Regimental Field Officer Promotions: Major in 50th Foot 1 Aug 1804 (vice Rowe); Lieutenant Colonel in 50th Foot 13 Jun 1811
Brevets: Brevet Major 25 Sep 1803; Brevet Lieutenant Colonel 25 Jul 1810
Service 1793–1815: Served in Copenhagen 1807; served in Peninsula Aug 1808 to Jan 1809, wounded at Vimeiro; served in Walcheren 1809; commanded 1/50th in Peninsula May 1813 to Apr 1814, wounded in Pyrenees
Later Service: Served in West Indies
Awards and Honours: AGM (Vit); CB
Residence:
Died: Of fever in Jamaica 31 Aug 1819
Sources: ANCW; ARLI; WO 25/746

519. *Charles MORLAND (1812–1813)*

Born: Kent 1773
Relations: Son of Thomas Morland of Lamberhurst and Ann (Matson)
Entry to Army: Cornet in 12th Light Dragoons 6 Apr 1796
Regimental Field Officer Promotions: Major in 17th Light Dragoons 20 Jul 1809 (vice Davis);

Major in 9th Light Dragoons 8 Feb 1810 (vice Orde); Lieutenant Colonel in 50th Foot 29 Oct 1812 (vice Walker) by purchase; Lieutenant Colonel in 9th Light Dragoons 4 Mar 1813 (vice Chabot) by exchange; to half-pay unattached 6 Mar 1828
Brevets: Brevet Colonel 27 May 1825
Service 1793–1815: Served in Portugal 1797–1800; served in Egypt 1801; ADC to Earl of Rosslyn in Baltic 1807; ADC to Earl of Rosslyn 1803–1805 and in Walcheren 1809; commanded 9th Light Dragoons in Peninsula Apr to Nov 1812
Later Service: ADC to King George IV 27 May 1825
Residence: Lamberhurst, near Tunbridge Wells, Kent
Died: Paris, France 14 Jun 1828
Sources: ANCB; ANCD; ARLI; PHIL; WEOF; WO 25/747

520. *Louis Guy Charles Guillaume de Rohan-CHABOT, Viscount (1813)*

Born: Paris 1780
Relations: Son of Charles Rosalie de Rohan-Chabot, comte de Jarnac and Elizabeth (Smith); son-in-law of William Fitzgerald, 2nd Duke of Leinster; father of Philippe Ferdinand Auguste de Rohan-Chabot, comte de Jarnac
Entry to Army: Cornet in 18th Light Dragoons 30 Apr 1793 by purchase
Regimental Field Officer Promotions: Major in 27th Foot 24 Oct 1802 (vice Stewart) by purchase; to half-pay of 27th Foot 25 Oct 1802; Major in 18th Light Dragoons 18 Nov 1802 (vice Butter) by exchange; Major in 9th Light Dragoons 16 Mar 1809 (vice Ellice) by exchange; Lieutenant Colonel in 9th Light Dragoons 24 Jan 1811; Lieutenant Colonel in 50th Foot 4 Mar 1813 (vice Morland) by exchange; to half-pay of 50th Foot 2 Sep 1813
Brevets: Brevet Lieutenant Colonel 12 Feb 1807; Brevet Colonel 4 Jul 1814; Major General 19 Jul 1821
Service 1793–1815: Served at Helder 1799; served at Ferrol 1800; served at Walcheren 1809; commanded 9th Light Dragoons in Peninsula Jul to Sep 1811
Later Service: Deputy Adjutant General in British North America
Awards and Honours: Comte de Jamac and Vicomte de Rohan-Chabot 1813 (not recognised by France until 1815); Member of French Chamber of Peers 11 Sep 1835 to 1848
Residences: Thomastown Castle, Thomastown, County Tipperary; Rue Beaujon, Faubourg-du-Roule, Paris
Died: Paris 12 Jul 1875 (aged 94)
Chabot's son, Philippe Ferdinand Auguste de Rohan-Chabot, led the expedition which returned Napoleon's remains from Saint Helena to Paris
Sources: ANCB; ANCD; ANCW; ARLI; PHIL; WEOF

521. *Sir Charles James NAPIER (1813–1814)*

Born: London 1782
Relations: Son of Colonel Hon. George Napier and Lady Sarah (Lennox); brother of General Sir William Patrick Francis Napier; Lieutenant General Sir George Thomas Napier; and Captain Henry Edward Napier RN
Entry to Army: Ensign in 33rd Foot 31 Jan 1794
Regimental Field Officer Promotions: Major in Cape Regiment 29 May 1806; Major in 50th Foot 6 Nov 1806 (vice Lyster) by exchange; Lieutenant Colonel in 102nd Foot 27 Jun 1811 (vice Paterson); Lieutenant Colonel in 50th Foot 2 Sep 1813 (vice Chabot); to half-pay of 50th Foot Oct 1814
Brevets: Brevet Colonel 27 May 1825; Major General 10 Jan 1837; Lieutenant General 9 Nov 1846; General (East Indies) 6 Mar 1849
Colonelcies: 97th Foot 31 May 1843 (vice Hardinge); 22nd Foot 21 Nov 1843 (vice Finch)
Service 1793–1815: Served in Irish rebellion 1798; served with 2/50th Foot 1806–1808; commanded 1/50th Foot in Peninsula Sep 1808 to Jan 1809; wounded and taken POW at Corunna, released Mar 1809; served in in Peninsula Aug 1809 to Jul 1811; served on staff and wounded at Busaco; served in British North America 1813; served in Army of Occupation in France 1815
Political Career: Inspecting Field Officer in Corfu 1819; British Resident of the Lord High Commissioner in Cephalonia Mar 1822 to 1830; Commander in Chief Bombay Apr 1841 to Oct 1847; Governor of Sindh Jun 1843 to Oct 1847; Commander in Chief in East Indies May 1849 to Nov 1850
Awards and Honours: AGM (Cor); KCB 20 Jul 1838; GCB 4 Jul 1843; MGSM (Bus FDO)
Residence: Oaklands, Waterlooville, Hampshire
Died: Oaklands 29 Aug 1853
'Generous to a fault, a radical in politics yet an autocrat in government, hot-tempered and impetuous, he was a man to inspire strong affection or the reverse, and his enemies were as numerous as his friends' – DINB
Sources: ARLI; CHAL; DINB; PHIL; WEOF; WOST; WO 25/747

Majors

522. *Thomas RUDSDELL (1796–1798)*
Born: Northamptonshire 1750
Relations: Son of Jeremiah Rudsdell of Northampton, wool stapler, and Sarah (Minor)
Entry to Army: Ensign in 11th Foot 31 Dec 1773 by purchase
Regimental Field Officer Promotions: Major in 50th Foot 2 Jan 1796 (vice Erskine); Lieutenant Colonel in 6th West India Regiment 20 Jun 1798 (vice O'Meara); Lieutenant Colonel in 65th Foot 10 May 1799 (vice Johnstone); Lieutenant Colonel in 61st Foot 23 Oct 1800 (vice Hastings) by exchange
Service 1793–1815: Lieutenant Governor of Sheerness 1806–1813
Residence: Limpsfield, Surrey
Died: Limpsfield 11 May 1813
Sources: ANCB; ANCD; ARLI; Roll of the Officers of the York and Lancaster Regiment

523. *James IMRIE (1798–1801)*
Born: Fifeshire 1756
Relations: Son of William Imrie of Denmuir and Marjory (Young); brother of Lieutenant Colonel Ninian Imrie, 1st Foot
Entry to Army: Lieutenant in 82nd Foot 14 Jan 1778
Regimental Field Officer Promotions: Major in 50th Foot 4 Jul 1798 (vice Rudsdell)
Brevets: Brevet Major 1 Jan 1798
Early Service: Served in American War of Independence
Service 1793–1815: Served in Egypt 1801
Died: Egypt Jun 1801
Sources: ANCB; ARLI; FMPW

524. *John Gordon HAVEN (1801–1807)*
Born: Belfast 1761
Relations: Son of William Haven of Shankill and Margery (Gordon); nephew of Lieutenant Colonel John Gordon, 50th Foot; cousin of Captain John Craford Gordon, 50th Foot; and Captain Robert Wallace, 50th Foot
Entry to Army: Ensign in 50th Foot 22 Apr 1778 by purchase
Regimental Field Officer Promotions: Major in 50th Foot 18 Jun 1801 (vice Imrie)
Retired: 10 Dec 1807
Service 1793–1815: Served in Egypt 1801
Residence: Old Steyne, Brighton, Sussex
Died: Brighton Dec 1848
Sources: ANCD; ARLI; FMPD; GHLG; WEOF

525. *Cholmley OVEREND (1804–1808)*
Born: Yorkshire 1766
Relations: Son of George Overend of Fangfoss and Catherine (Cholmley)
Entry to Army: Ensign in 50th Foot 24 Sep 1787 by purchase
Regimental Field Officer Promotions: Major in 50th Foot 2 Aug 1804 by purchase
Brevets: Brevet Major 29 Apr 1802
Retired: 22 Sep 1808
Residence: Micklegate, York, Yorkshire
Died: York 20 Oct 1852
Sources: ANCB; ANCD; ARLI; GEMA (1852); WEOF

526. *Thomas LYSTER (1804–1806)*
Born: County Roscommon 1764
Relations: Son of John Lyster of Rocksavage and Jane (Ducasse); brother of Captain William John Lyster, 8th Garrison Battalion
Entry to Army: Ensign in 50th Foot 20 Jul 1784
Regimental Field Officer Promotions: Major in 50th Foot 28 Sep 1804; Major in Cape Regiment 6 Nov 1806
Brevets: Brevet Lieutenant Colonel 4 Jun 1811
Service 1793–1815: Served in Cape of Good Hope 1806–1813
Retired: 21 Oct 1813; reinstated as Lieutenant Colonel (St Helena) 16 Nov 1815
Later Service: Inspector of Coast Militia and Volunteers on St Helena 1815–1821
Residences: Rocksavage House, Knockadangan, County Roscommon; Wexford, County Wexford
Died: Wexford 20 Nov 1844
On St Helena 'He was the senior officer, having special charge of the person of the Emperor, and it fell to his lot to carry out the somewhat uncompromising orders issued to or by Sir Hudson (Lowe), to which Napoleon and his Staff offered strenuous resistance'
Sources: ARLI; FMPW; WEOF; Memorials of an Ancient House: A History of the Family of Lister or Lyster

527. *Sir Henry James RIDDELL (1807–1808)*
Born: Berwickshire 1782
Relations: Son of Captain Thomas Riddell of Bessborough, EIC naval service, and Elizabeth (Maclauchlan)
Education: Royal Military College 1801–1803
Entry to Army: Ensign in 58th Foot 8 Mar 1798 by purchase
Regimental Field Officer Promotions: Major in 50th Foot 16 Dec 1807 (vice Haven) by purchase;

Major in 79th Foot 21 Apr 1808 (vice Hamilton); Lieutenant Colonel in Quartermaster General's Department 4 Jan 1810
Brevets: Brevet Lieutenant Colonel 4 Jun 1813; Brevet Colonel 22 Jul 1830; Major General 23 Nov 1841; Lieutenant General 11 Nov 1851; General 26 Sep 1857
Colonelcies: 6th Foot 25 Jun 1851 (vice Gardiner)
Service 1793–1815: Served in British North America 1799–1802; Assistant Quartermaster General in Ireland 1804–1807; Assistant Quartermaster General in Copenhagen 1807; Assistant Quartermaster General on staff in Peninsula Nov 1810 to Apr 1814
Later Service: Commander in Chief Scotland 1847–1852; Governor of Edinburgh Castle 1847–1852
Awards & Honours: KH 12 Aug 1832
Residences: Renton House, Coldingham, Berwickshire; Oxendean, Duns, Berwickshire
Died: Oxendean 8 Mar 1861
Sources: ANCB; ANCD; ANCW; ARLI; CHAL; GEMA (1861); PHIL; WEOF; WO 25/748

528. *Hon. Charles Banks STANHOPE (1808–1809)*
Born: Kent 1785
Relations: Son of Charles Stanhope, 3rd Earl Stanhope, and Louisa (Grenville); brother of Captain and Lieutenant Colonel Hon. James Hamilton Stanhope, 1st Foot Guards; nephew of Richard Grenville-Temple, 2nd Earl Temple
Entry to Army: Ensign in 25th Foot 9 Feb 1802
Regimental Field Officer Promotions: Major in 6th Garrison Battalion 6 Feb 1808 (vice Crigan); Major in 50th Foot 21 Apr 1808 (vice Riddell)
Service 1793–1815: Registrar and Secretary of the Order of the Bath 1805; served in Sicily 1806–1807; ADC to Sir John Moore in Peninsula Aug 1808 to Jan 1809
Died: Killed in action at Corunna 16 Jan 1809
Sources: ANCB; ANCW; CHAL; PHIL; WEMR; WEOF; The Royal Military Panorama or Officer's Companion, 1814

529. *Sir Frederick HANKEY (1808–1809)*
Born: London 1774
Relations: Son of John Hankey, alderman of London, and Elizabeth (Thomson)
Entry to Army: Ensign in 90th Foot 18 Sep 1800
Regimental Field Officer Promotions: Major in 50th Foot 22 Sep 1808 (vice Overend) by purchase; Major in 2nd Ceylon Regiment 13 Jul 1809; Major in 15th Foot 21 Sep 1815 (vice Spawforth) by exchange; to half-pay of 15th Foot 25 Mar 1816
Brevets: Brevet Lieutenant Colonel 15 Aug 1811; Brevet Colonel 27 May 1825
Service 1793–1815: Served in Ceylon 1800–1811, severely wounded in Kandy 1803; Inspector General of Colonial Troops in Ceylon 1811; Deputy Adjutant General in Malta
Later Service: Secretary to Thomas Maitland in Corfu 1814–1824; served in Malta 1825–1838
Retired: Aug 1826
Awards and Honours: KCMG 18 Nov 1818; GCMG 4 May 1833
Residence: Montague Square, Marylebone, London
Died: London 13 Mar 1855
Sources: ANCB; ANCD; ARLI; GEMA (1855); WEOF; Frederick Hankey (1821-1882), A Biographical Sketch

530. *John Bacon HARRISON (1809–1819)*
Born: Mumbai [Bombay] 1778
Relations: Son of Richardson Harrison, surgeon in EIC Bombay service, and Ann (Grant); brother of Major James Hall Harrison RM
Entry to Army: Ensign in 50th Foot 30 Dec 1794 by purchase
Regimental Field Officer Promotions: Major in 50th Foot 23 Feb 1809 (vice Stanhope); Lieutenant Colonel in 50th Foot 4 Nov 1819 (vice Hill)
Brevets: Brevet Lieutenant Colonel 19 Jun 1812
Service 1793–1815: Served in Corsica 1795; served in Egypt 1801; served in Copenhagen 1807; served in Peninsula Aug 1808 to Jan 1809; served at Walcheren 1809; commanded light company in Peninsula Aug 1810 to 1812; commanded 1/50th in Peninsula Dec 1812 to Apr 1814
Retired: 2 Sep 1824
Awards and Honours: AGM (Pyr Nive Ort); CB 4 Jun 1815
Residence: Clarence Square, Cheltenham, Gloucestershire
Died: Cheltenham 15 Apr 1863
Sources: ANCB; ANCD; ANCW; ARLI; CHAL; PHIL; WEOF; WO 25/746

531. *James ARMSTRONG (1809–1812)*
Born: County Fermanagh c.1761
Relations: Son of Thomas Armstrong of Castle Balfour; brother of Major John Armstrong; son-in-law of Cadwallader, 9th Baron Blayney
Entry to Army: Ensign in 74th Foot 20 Jan 1798
Regimental Field Officer Promotions: Major in 2nd Ceylon Regiment 30 Mar 1809 (vice Buchan); Major in 50th Foot 13 Jul 1809 (vice Hankey) by exchange
Brevets: Brevet Lieutenant Colonel 28 Aug 1811

Service 1793–1815: Military Secretary to Wellesley in East Indies; Quartermaster General in East Indies 1805; military agent in Spain 1809–1810; ADC to Duke of York 28 Aug 1811; served on staff in Peninsula Aug 1811 to early 1812, ADC to Wellington
Residence: Lisgoole, County Fermanagh; North Audley Street, Mayfair, London
Died: London 15 Aug 1812
Admitted to the Middle Temple 27 Jan 1781; many sources incorrectly refer to this officer as 'John Armstrong'; Major John Armstrong was in fact his brother
Sources: ARLI; FMPW; The European Magazine and London Review Vol.62; <https://www.nidirect.gov.uk/sites/default/files/publications/ armstrong-of-lisgoole-papers-d4073.pdf>

532. *Thomas Dundas CAMPBELL (1811–1821)*
Born: Argyllshire 1767
Relations: Son of Patrick Campbell of Ardchattan and Lilias (MacFarlane); brother of Captain Charles Campbell, 71st Foot; Lieutenant Colin Campbell, Bengal service; and Lieutenant Patrick Campbell, EIC service
Entry to Army: Ensign in 82nd Foot 28 Nov 1794
Regimental Field Officer Promotions: Major in 50th Foot 13 Jun 1811 (vice Hill)
Brevets: Brevet Lieutenant Colonel 12 Aug 1819
Service 1793–1815: Served in Sicily; served in Peninsula Sep 1810 to Dec 1813; commanded 1/50th Foot after Maya Aug 1813
Retired: 18 Oct 1821
Residence: Maddox Street, St George Hanover Square, London
Died: London 6 Feb 1846
Sources: ANCB; ANCD; ANCW; ARLI; CHAL; WEOF

533. *Edward Thomas ABBOTT (1811)*
Born: Montréal 1766
Relations: Son of Captain Thomas Abbott RA and Angelique Trotier (Desrivieres)
Entry to Army: Ensign in 34th Foot 22 Oct 1779
Regimental Field Officer Promotions: Major in 50th Foot 18 Jul 1811 (vice Napier) by exchange
Brevets: Brevet Major 25 Apr 1808
Service 1793–1815: Served in New South Wales 1790–1796 and 1799–1810; commandant at Parramatta 1803–1807
Retired: 29 Aug 1811
Later Service: Deputy Judge Advocate in Van Diemen's Land 1815–1824; civil commandant at Port Dalrymple, Tasmania 1825–1832
Residence: Newstead, Launceston, Tasmania
Died: Launceston 31 Jul 1832
Sources: ANCB; ANCD; ARLI; WEOF; A Genealogical and Heraldic History of the Colonial Gentry

534. *Hamilton ARCHDALL (1811–1814)*
Born: Dublin c.1775
Relations: Son of Hamilton Archdall of Dublin and Anna Maria (Osborne)
Entry to Army: Cornet in 5th Dragoons 6 Sep 1794
Regimental Field Officer Promotions: Major in 50th Foot 29 Aug 1811 (vice Abbott); to half-pay of 50th Foot 25 Oct 1814
Service 1793–1815: Served in Peninsula Aug to Sep 1808; served in Peninsula Sep 1810 to Dec 1811
Residence: Philipsburgh Avenue, Dublin, County Dublin
Died: Dublin 20 Dec 1815
Sources: ANCD; ANCW; ARLI; FMPW (mother); WEOF

535. *Herman STAPLETON (1812–1814)*
Born: Yorkshire c.1784
Relations: Son of Charles Stapleton of Carlton MD and Elizabeth (Fallowfield); brother of Major Charles Stapleton, 3rd West Yorkshire Militia
Entry to Army: Ensign in 50th Foot 19 Nov 1802 by purchase
Regimental Field Officer Promotions: Major in 50th Foot 3 Sep 1812 (vice Armstrong); to half-pay of 50th Foot 25 Oct 1814
Brevets: Brevet Major 19 Jun 1812; Brevet Lieutenant Colonel 27 May 1825; Brevet Colonel 28 Aug 1838
Service 1793–1815: Served in Walcheren 1809; served in Peninsula Sep 1810 to Nov 1812
Residence: Carlton, near Snaith, Yorkshire
Died: Carlton 23 Jun 1847
Sources: ANCD; ARLI; CHAL; PHIL; WEOF

Selected Regimental Histories
Fyler, Arthur Evelyn, *The History of the 50th Or (the Queen's Own) Regiment from the Earliest Date to the Year 1881* (London: Chapman and Hall, 1895)

Regimental Museum
Queen's & Princess of Wales's Royal Regiment Museum, Dover Castle, Dover, Kent

51st Regiment of Foot

Secondary Title:	2nd Yorkshire West Riding
Jacket:	Red
Facings:	Deep green
Badge:	A hunting horn below the crown

Regimental Lineage, 51st Regiment of Foot

1755:	Dec – raised by Marquess of Rockingham and Sir George Savile as 53rd Foot in Yorkshire
1757:	51st Regiment of Foot
1782:	51st (2nd Yorkshire West Riding) Regiment of Foot
1809:	May – 51st (2nd Yorkshire West Riding) Regiment of Foot (Light Infantry)
1821:	51st (2nd Yorkshire West Riding) or The King's Own Light Infantry Regiment
1881:	1st Battalion, King's Own Light Infantry (South Yorkshire Regiment) (on amalgamation with 105th (Madras Light Infantry) Regiment)
1897:	1st Battalion, King's Own (Yorkshire Light Infantry) Regiment
1968:	2nd Battalion, The Light Infantry (on amalgamation with the Somerset and Cornwall Light Infantry, King's Shropshire Light Infantry and Durham Light Infantry)
1993:	The Light Infantry (reduced to two battalions)
2007:	3rd or 5th Battalion, The Rifles (on amalgamation with 1st Battalion, The Light Infantry, 1st Battalion, Devonshire and Dorset Light Infantry, 1st Battalion Royal Gloucestershire, Berkshire and Wiltshire Light Infantry, and Royal Green Jackets)

Service History, 51st Regiment of Foot

1793:	Gibraltar; Dec – to Toulon; Hyères
1794:	Hyères; Mar – to Corsica; Tower of Fornelli; Bastia; Jun – siege of Calvi
1795:	Corsica
1796:	Corsica; Oct – to Elba; Porteferraio
1797:	Elba; May – Gibraltar; Jul – to Portugal; Lisbon
1798:	Lisbon; Oct – to East Indies
1799:	Jan – Cape of Good Hope; Apr – Madras; to Ceylon, but did not disembark; May – Fort St George; Jul – St Thomas' Mount; Sep – Fort St George
1800:	Fort St George; Feb – to Ceylon; Trincomalee; Feb – Colombo; Dec – Trincomalee; Colombo
1801–1802:	Colombo
1803:	Colombo; Jan – Kandian War; Feb – Kandy; May – Colombo; Aug – detachment at Hangwele [Hanwella]; Sep – Rowanelly [Ruwanwella]; Colombo
1804–1806:	Colombo
1807:	Colombo; Mar – fit men into 22nd Foot in India, cadre to England; Sep – Gravesend; Chatham; Oct – Chichester
1808:	Silverhill; Feb – Gosport; May – Guernsey; Jul – Portsmouth; Aug – Chichester; Portsmouth; Sep – Falmouth; to Spain; Oct – Corunna; Nov – Astorga; Dec – Mayorga; Astorga
1809:	Retreat to Corunna; CORUNNA; to England; Feb – Portsmouth; Isle of Wight; Sandown; May – Kingsbridge; Jun – Berryhead; May – became Light Infantry; Jul – Portsmouth; to Walcheren; Aug – Middelburg; Sep – Portsmouth; Oct – Horsham; Steyning Barracks
1810:	Horsham; May – Croydon; Jun – Steyning; Jul – Ashford; Sep – Shorncliffe; Dec – Lewes
1811:	Steyning Barracks; Feb – Portsmouth; to Portugal; PENINSULA; Lisbon; Mar – Carapinha; Apr – Vilar Maior; May – FUENTES D'ONORO; Campo Maior; Jul – Nisa; Aug – Vilar Maior; Sep – La Alamedilla; Oct – Penamacor

1812: El Payo; Feb – Penamacor; Mar – Ribeira de Nisa; Apr – Santo Estevão; May – Castelo Branco; Jun – SALAMANCA; Nava de Arévalo; Aug – El Escorial; Sep – siege of Burgos; Olmos de Atapuerca; Oct – retreat from Burgos; Cabezón de Pisuerga; Nov – La Alamedilla; Dec – Moimenta da Beira

1813: Moimenta da Beira; May – Malhadas; Jun –VITTORIA; Pamplona; Jul – Ostitz; Doña Maria; Aug – Etxalar; Sep – Bera; Oct – Etxalar; Nov – NIVELLE; Saint-Pée-sur-Nivelle; Nov – Arbonne; Dec – Ustaritz

1814: Jatxou; Feb – Gave d'Oloron; ORTHEZ; Mar – Langon; Apr – Bordeaux; Jun – to England; Plymouth; Aug – Portsmouth

1815: Portsmouth; Mar – to Netherlands; Ostend; Apr – Grammont; Jun – WATERLOO; Jul – Paris; Allied Army of Occupation

1816: Jan – Calais; to England; Dover

Establishments, 51st Regiment of Foot

Year	Subunits	Field Off	Off/ Staff	Sjts	Mus	Corp/ Pvts	Total
Dec 1792	10co	3	32	22	12	430	499
Jan 1793	10co	3	32	32	22	600	689
Dec 1795	10co+2r	5	51	62	30	1,010	1,158
Dec 1797	10co+r	5	46	70	26	1,208	1,355
Dec 1800	10co+r	5	46	78	30	1,216	1,375
Dec 1802	10co+r	5	50	62	30	1,008	1,155
Dec 1803	10co+r	5	50	62	26	1,008	1,151
Dec 1806	10co+r	4	50	52	26	808	940
Dec 1807	10co	4	36	34	22	600	696
Aug 1808	10co	4	36	44	22	800	906
Aug 1809	10co+r	4	50	62	26	818	960
Dec 1809	10co	4	46	54	22	810	936
Dec 1811	10co+r	4	50	63	26	818	961
Dec 1813	10co+r	4	49	63	22	818	956
Dec 1814	10co	4	46	55	22	810	937

Service Statistics, 51st Regiment of Foot

	Lieutenant Colonels	Majors
Number of officers in period 1793–1815	9	14
Average age on appointment to substantive rank	38.5	35
Average time in rank in regiment (years)	5	3.5
Total field officers by nationality	9 E / 8 I / 5 S / 1 A	
Demographics of other ranks 1809	78% E / 20% I / 1% S / 1% W	
Demographics of other ranks 1812	62% EW / 36% I / 2% S	
Months of overseas service 1793–1815	225	

Significant Militia/Volunteer Intakes

1807: Oxfordshire, Sussex, 2nd Tower Hamlets, 2nd West Yorkshire, 3rd West Yorkshire, County Galway

1808: County Armagh

1809: 1st Devon, South Gloucestershire, 1st Surrey, 2nd Surrey, County Galway, County Louth

1810: County Armagh

1811: South Gloucestershire

1812: 2nd Surrey

Regimental Colonels

536. *Rt Hon. Archibald MONTGOMERIE, 11th Earl of Eglinton (1767–1795)*

Born: Ayrshire 1726
Relations: Son of Alexander Montgomerie, 9th Earl of Eglinton, and Susanna (Kennedy); son-in-law of George, 21st Earl of Crawford
Education: Eton College; Winchester College
Entry to Army: Cornet in 2nd Dragoons 1739 by purchase
Regimental Field Officer Promotions: Major in 36th Foot 28 Jun 1751 by purchase; Lieutenant Colonel Commandant in 62nd Foot 4 Jan 1757
Brevets: Brevet Colonel 19 Feb 1762; Major General 25 May 1772; Lieutenant General 29 Aug 1777; General 12 Oct 1793
Colonelcies: 51st Foot 24 Jun 1767; 2nd Dragoons 2 Dec 1795 (vice Johnston)
Early Service: Served in Minorca 1753; served in North America 1757–1760; Governor of Edinburgh Castle 1782–1796
Service 1793–1815: Lord Lieutenant of Ayrshire 1794–1796
Political Career: MP (Ayrshire) 1761–1768
Creations and Dignities: 11th Earl of Eglinton 24 Oct 1769
Residence: Eglinton Castle, near Kilwinning, Ayrshire
Died: Eglinton Castle 30 Oct 1796
A good companion, hard drinking, genial but hot tempered, Montgomerie had few intellectual interests. A 'violent Scotsman', with a contempt for Englishmen… – HPON
Sources: ARLI; DINB; HPON

537. *Anthony George MARTIN (1795–1800)*

Born: [spec.] Essex c.1730
Relations: Son of Anthony Martin of Colchester
Entry to Army: Ensign in Coldstream Foot Guards 23 Jul 1748 by purchase
Regimental Field Officer Promotions: Captain and Lieutenant Colonel in Coldstream Foot Guards 11 Jan 1769 by purchase; Second Major in Coldstream Foot Guards Jun 1780; First Major in Coldstream Foot Guards 23 Nov 1785; Lieutenant Colonel in Coldstream Foot Guards 26 May 1789
Brevets: Major General 20 Nov 1782; Lieutenant General 3 May 1796
Colonelcies: 51st Foot 2 Dec 1795 (vice Montgomerie)
Early Service: Served in American War of Independence
Residence: Leicester Square, Westminster, London
Died: London 1 May 1800
Sources: ANCW; ARLI; GEMA (1800); WEOF

538. *William MORSHEAD (1800–1822)*

Born: Cornwall 1748
Relations: Son of William Morshead of Cartuther and Olympia (Treise)
Entry to Army: Ensign in Coldstream Foot Guards 23 Apr 1771 by purchase
Regimental Field Officer Promotions: Captain and Lieutenant Colonel in Coldstream Foot Guards 11 Jul 1785 by purchase; Second Major in Coldstream Foot Guards 23 Jun 1795 (vice Pennington); First Major in Coldstream Foot Guards 2 Dec 1795 (vice Stanwix)
Brevets: Brevet Colonel 20 Oct 1793; Major General 26 Feb 1795; Lieutenant General 29 Apr 1802; General 1 Jan 1812
Colonelcies: Colonel Commandant of 5/60th Foot 30 Dec 1797; 51st Foot 9 May 1800 (vice Martin)
Service 1793–1815: Served in Flanders 1793–1795; ADC to King George III 20 Oct 1793; second in command under Sir Ralph Abercromby in West Indies 1795–1798; served at Ferrol 1800
Residences: Lavethan, near Bodmin, Cornwall
Died: Lavethan 24 May 1822
As the first officer appointed in the new 5th Battalion of the 60th Foot in 1797, Morshead later claimed to be 'the first rifleman in the British Army'
Sources: ANCB; ANCD; ANCW; ARLI; PHIL; WEOF; WO 25/747

Lieutenant Colonels

539. *Sir John MOORE (1790–1798)*

Born: Glasgow 1761
Relations: Son of Dr John Moore and Jean (Simpson); brother of Admiral Sir Graham Moore RN
Education: Glasgow High School
Entry to Army: Ensign in 51st Foot 2 Mar 1776 by purchase
Regimental Field Officer Promotions: Major in 102nd Foot 23 Nov 1785 (vice Jones); Major in 4/60th Foot 16 Jan 1788; Major in 51st Foot 1 Oct 1788 (vice Boothby) by exchange; Lieutenant Colonel in 51st Foot 30 Nov 1790 (vice Jaques)
Brevets: Brevet Colonel 21 Aug 1795; Brigadier General (West Indies) 9 Sep 1795; Major General 18 Jun 1798; Lieutenant General 30 Oct 1805
Colonelcies: 9th West India Regiment 6 Sep 1798; Colonel Commandant of 2/52nd Foot 25 Nov 1799; 52nd Foot 8 May 1801 (vice Trapaud)

Early Service: Served in Nova Scotia 1778–1783
Service 1793–1815: Commanded 51st Foot in Corsica 1794; Lieutenant Governor of St. Lucia May 1796 to Jan 1797 (vice Abercromby); commanded brigade in Irish Rebellion 1798; President of the government of Connaught 31 Aug 1798 to 8 Sep 1798; commanded brigade in Helder 1799; Commander in Chief Sicily Jul 1807 to Sep 1807 (vice Fox); commanded force to Swedish Pomerania 1808; served in Peninsula Sep 1808 to Jan 1809; General Office Commanding Spain Oct 1808 to Jan 1809
Political Career: MP (Linlithgow Burghs) 1784–1790
Awards and Honours: KB 26 Sep 1804
Died: Died of wounds at Corunna 16 Jan 1809
Sources: ARLI; CHAL; DINB; HALL; HPON; ODNB; WEOF

540. *Robert PRINGLE (1795–1802)*

See 195.
Major in 51st Foot 15 Mar 1793 (vice FitzRoy) by purchase; Lieutenant Colonel in 51st Foot 1 Sep 1795

541. *Charles William BAILLIE (1798–1804)*

See 353.
Lieutenant Colonel in 51st Foot 6 Sep 1798 (vice Moore)

542. *Sir Miles NIGHTINGALL (1802–1806)*

See 193.
Lieutenant Colonel in 51st Foot 23 Jul 1802 (vice Pringle) by exchange

543. *James LOGAN (1804–1808)*

Born: Ayrshire 1757
Relations: Son of John Logan of Straiton and Mary (unk.)
Entry to Army: Ensign in 51st Foot 9 Feb 1780 by purchase
Regimental Field Officer Promotions: Major in 51st Foot 1 Sep 1795; Lieutenant Colonel in 51st Foot 22 Dec 1804 (vice Baillie)
Brevets: Brevet Lieutenant Colonel 1 Jan 1801
Service 1793–1815: Commanded 51st Foot in Ceylon 1803–1808
Retired: 17 Mar 1808
Residence: Blackfield House, Kirkdale, Lancashire
Died: Blackfield House 6 Feb 1822
Reputedly a friend of Lord Nelson
Sources: ANCB; ANCD; ARLI; WEOF; History of the King's Own Yorkshire Light Infantry

544. *Sir Ralph DARLING, Kt (1806–1811)*

Born: County Cork 1772
Relations: Son of Adjutant Christopher Darling, 45th Foot, and Ann (Jones); brother of Major General Henry Charles Darling; and Major General William Lindsay Darling; son-in-law of Colonel John Dumaresq, 22nd Foot; brother-in-law of Lieutenant Colonel Henry Dumaresq, 9th Foot; Captain William John Dumaresq, Royal Staff Corps; and Captain Edward Dumaresq, RE
Entry to Army: Private in 45th Foot 1786; Ensign in 45th Foot 15 May 1793
Regimental Field Officer Promotions: Major in 4th West India Regiment 2 Feb 1800 (vice Hewey); Lieutenant Colonel in 69th Foot 17 Jul 1801 (vice Fancourt) by purchase; Lieutenant Colonel in 51st Foot 8 May 1806 (vice Nightingall) by exchange; removed from the regiment as a general officer 1814
Brevets: Brevet Colonel 25 Jul 1810; Major General 4 June1813; Lieutenant General 27 May 1825; General 23 Nov 1841
Colonelcies: 90th Foot 9 Oct 1823 (vice R. Meade); 41st Foot 26 Sep 1837 (vice Stopford); 69th Foot 5 Feb 1848 (vice Vincent)
Service 1793–1815: Served in West Indies 1793–1799; served in Peninsula Oct 1808 to Jan1809; Deputy Assistant Adjutant General in Walcheren 1809; commanded 51st Foot 1806–1811; on staff positions 1810– 1813; Deputy Adjutant General on staff 1814
Later Service: Acting Governor and Commander in Chief Mauritius 6 Feb 1819 to 6 Jul 1820, and 20 May to 12 Jun 1823; Governor of New South Wales 19 Dec 1825 to 22 Oct 1831
Awards and Honours: AGM (Cor); GCH 2 Sep 1835; Knight Bachelor 2 Sep 1835
Residence: Brunswick Square, Brighton, Sussex
Died: Brighton 2 Apr 1858
Sources: ANCD; ARLI; CHAL; DINB; FMPB; WEOF; WOST; WO 25/745; Australian Dictionary of Biography, Vol.1

545. *Sir John MacDONALD (1808)*

See 338.
Lieutenant Colonel in 51st Foot 17 Mar 1808 (vice Logan) by purchase

546. *John Montagu MAINWARING (1808–1811)*

Born: Dublin 1761
Relations: Son of Captain Benjamin Mainwaring of Dublin, attorney, and Dorothy (Dixon); brother of Lieutenant Edward Mainwaring, 119th Foot;

Captain Jemmett Brown Mainwaring RN; uncle of Major Frederick Jennet Mainwaring, 51st Foot
Entry to Army: Ensign in 67th Foot 31 May 1784 by purchase
Field Officer Promotions: Major in 67th Foot 14 Aug 1801 (vice Gordon); Lieutenant Colonel in 90th Foot 23 Nov 1804; Lieutenant Colonel in 51st Foot 21 Apr 1808 (vice MacDonald) by exchange; to half-pay of 26th Foot 13 Jun 1811 (vice Mitchell) by exchange
Brevets: Brevet Colonel 4 Jun 1813; Major General 12 Aug 1819; Lieutenant General 10 Jan 1837
Early Service: Served in West Indies 1785–1794
Service 1793–1815: Served in West Indies 1794; Deputy Adjutant General in Plymouth 1795; served in Jamaica 1800–1808; commanded 51st Foot in Spain Oct 1808 to Jan 1809; served in Walcheren 1809; commanded 51st Foot in Peninsula Feb to Aug 1811; sent home for burning colours of the 51st Foot at Fuentes d'Oñoro; commandant of Depot at Hilsea 1812–1815; commandant of Isle of Wight 1814–1819
Later Service: Governor of St Lucia 18 Jul 1821 to Feb 1823; acting Governor of St Lucia 23 Apr 1823 to 21 Jan 1824; Governor of St Lucia 11 Jan 1826 to Nov 1827
Residence: West Cowes, Isle of Wight
Died: West Cowes 11 Jan 1842
Sources: ANCW; CHAL; FMPB; PHIL; WEOF; WOST; WO 25/747

547. *Hugh Henry MITCHELL (1811–1817)*

Born: Dublin 1770
Relations: Son of Hugh Henry Mitchell of Glasnevin, banker, and Margaret (Gordon); son-in-law of Henry, 5th Duke of Beaufort
Entry to Army: Ensign in 101st Foot 2 Jan 1782 by purchase
Field Officer Promotions: Major in 26th Foot 17 Mar 1804 (vice Green); Lieutenant Colonel in 26th Foot 12 Dec 1805 (vice Hope) by purchase; to half-pay25 Mar 1811; Lieutenant Colonel in 51st Foot 13 Jun 1811
Brevets: Brevet Colonel 4 Jun 1813
Early Service: Served in East Indies 1783; served in British North America 1786–1796
Service 1793–1815: Served in Egypt 1801; commanded 2/26th Foot 1805–1811; served in Peninsula Nov 1811 to Mar 1813; commanded 51st Foot in Peninsula Aug 1813 to Apr 1814; commanded brigade in 4th Division at Waterloo 1815
Awards and Honours: AGM (Sal Ort); CB 4 Jun 1815; WatM 23 Apr 1816; KSW (Russia) 1816
Residence: Merrion Castle, Dublin; Queen Anne Street, Marylebone, London
Died: London 20 Apr 1817
Sources: ANCB; ANCD; CHAL; DALT; PHIL; WEMR; WEOF

Majors

548. *Rt Hon. George Ferdinand FITZROY, 2nd Baron Southampton (1792–1793)*

Born: London 1761
Relations: Son of General Rt Hon. Charles Fitzroy, 1st Baron Southampton, and Anne (Warren); brother of General Charles FitzRoy; and Lieutenant General William Fitzroy; brother-in-law of Lieutenant Colonel Frederick Keppel, 49th Foot
Education: Eton College
Entry to Army: Ensign in 3rd Foot Guards 29 May 1778 by purchase
Regimental Field Officer Promotions: Major in 51st Foot 25 Apr 1792 (vice Fisher); Captain and Lieutenant Colonel in Coldstream Foot Guards 1 Feb 1793 (vice Pennington) by purchase
Brevets: Brevet Colonel 3 May 1796; Major General 1 Jan 1801; Lieutenant General 25 Apr 1808
Early Service: Groom of the Bedchamber to the Prince of Wales 1783–1797
Political Career: MP (Bury St. Edmunds) 1784–1787
Creations and Dignities: 2nd Baron Southampton 21 Mar 1797
Residence: Highgate, Middlesex
Died: Highgate 14 Jun 1810
Sources: ANCB; ANCD; ARLI; DEPE; HPON; WEOF

549. *John ELFORD (1795–1797)*

Born: Cornwall c.1742
Relations: Son of Isaac Elford of Duloe and Frances (Matthew)
Entry to Army: Ensign in 51st Foot 3 Aug 1760 by purchase
Regimental Field Officer Promotions: Major in 51st Foot 1 Sep 1795 (vice Pringle); Major in 81st Foot 22 May 1797 (vice Brinley) by exchange
Brevets: Brevet Major 13 Sep 1782; Brevet Lieutenant Colonel 12 Oct 1793; Brevet Colonel 26 Jan 1797
Early Service: Served in Germany during Seven Years War; served in siege of Minorca 1781
Service 1793–1815: Lieutenant Governor of St John's Newfoundland 1788–1797
Retired: 7 Sep 1797
Residence: Norton Street, St Marylebone, London
Died: London Jun 1818
Most sources show this officer born in Cornwall in 1770, which cannot be the case given his promotion dates; far

more likely he was born one generation earlier into the same Elford of Duloe family
Sources: ANCD; ANCW; ARLI; History of the King's Own Yorkshire Light Infantry; <https://www.findagrave.com/memorial/259730371/john-elford>

550. *Thomas BRINLEY (1797–1799)*
Born: Massachusetts 1765
Relations: Son of George Brinley, Commissary and Storekeeper General in Halifax and Mary (Wentworth); brother of Paymaster William Birch Brinley, 45th Foot
Entry to Army: Ensign in 76th Foot 1 Dec 1781 by purchase
Regimental Field Officer Promotions: Major in 81st Foot 9 Nov 1796 (vice Watling); Major in 51st Foot 22 May 1797 (vice Elford) by exchange; Major in 2nd West India Regiment 17 Jan 1799 (vice Williams) by exchange; Major in 4th Foot 5 Aug 1799; Lieutenant Colonel in 4th Foot 7 Oct 1799 (vice Dickson); Lieutenant Colonel in Nova Scotia Fencibles 1 Aug 1805 (vice Smith)
Brevets: Brevet Lieutenant Colonel 13 Oct 1796; Brevet Colonel 1 Jan 1805
Service 1793–1815: Commanded 1/4th Foot 1803–1804; Quartermaster General in Leeward Islands 7 Nov 1805 (vice Maitland)
Died: Of fever on Barbados 5 Aug 1806
Sources: ANCB; ANCD; ARLI; The Church of England in Nova Scotia and the Tory Clergy of the Revolution

551. *John WILLIAMS (1799–1800)*
Born: London c.1763
Entry to Army: Volunteer; Ensign in 97th Foot 13 Sep 1780
Regimental Field Officer Promotions: Major in 2nd West India Regiment 8 Aug 1798 (vice Hutchinson) by purchase; Major in 51st Foot 17 Jan 1799 (vice Brinley) by exchange; Lieutenant Colonel in Royal Newfoundland Regiment 21 Feb 1800; to half-pay of Royal Newfoundland Regiment Mar 1802
Service 1793–1815: Served in British North America 1800–1802; Superintendent of Militia in Newfoundland; taken POW at sea, held at Verdun 1806–1812
Died: Verdun, Meuse, France 18 Apr 1812
Sources: ANCW; ARLI; FMPD; FMPS; History of the King's Own Yorkshire Light Infantry

552. *John Alexander CASTLEMAN (1800–1803)*
Born: Gloucestershire 1758
Relations: Son of Paul Castleman of Horsley and Margaret (Colville); brother of Captain Paul Colville Castleman, 84th Foot
Entry to Army: Ensign in 69th Foot 28 Dec 1778
Regimental Field Officer Promotions: Major in 51st Foot 21 Feb 1800; to half-pay of 9th Foot 25 Jun 1803
Brevets: Brevet Major 3 May 1796; Brevet Lieutenant Colonel 29 Apr 1802
Early Service: Served in American War of Independence
Service 1793–1815: Served in Ceylon 1803
Residence: Corsham, Wiltshire
Died: Corsham 11 Nov 1827
Sources: ANCB; ANCD; ARLI; History of the King's Own Yorkshire Light Infantry

553. *John Henry DUNKIN (1803–1809)*
Born: County Antrim 1778
Relations: Son of Sir William Dunkin, supreme court judge in Bengal, and Eliza (Blacker); son-in-law of Lieutenant Colonel Joseph O'Halloran, Bengal service
Entry to Army: Cornet in 12th Light Dragoons 19 Feb 1794 by purchase
Regimental Field Officer Promotions: Major in 9th Foot 27 May 1802 (vice Siree) by purchase; to half-pay of 9th Foot 25 Jun 1802; Major in 51st Foot 25 Jun 1803 (vice Castleman) by exchange; Lieutenant Colonel in 77th Foot 18 Nov 1809 (vice Maddison) by purchase; Lieutenant Colonel in 34th Foot 5 Mar 1818 (vice Everard); to half-pay of 34th Foot 26 Sep 1823; Lieutenant Colonel in 44th Foot 25 Mar 1824 (vice Hardinge)
Brevets: Brevet Colonel 12 Aug 1819; Brigadier General (India) 1825
Service 1793–1815: Served in Cape of Good Hope 1796–1799; commanded 51st Foot in Ceylon 1804–1807; served in Peninsula Oct 1808 to Jan 1809; served in Walcheren 1809; commanded 77th Foot in Peninsula Jul 1811 to Jun 1812, wounded at Salamanca; commanded 77th Foot in Peninsula Dec 1812 to Apr 1812
Later Service: Served in British East Indies 1818–1825
Awards and Honours: AGM (CR); CB 3 Feb 1817
Died: Decca, India 11 Oct 1825
Sources: ANCW; ARLI; CHAL; HALL; UNSM (1869); WEOF; WO 25/745; History of the King's Own Yorkshire Light Infantry

554. *George NAPPER (1804)*
Born: County Limerick c.1764
Relations: [spec.] Son of John Napper of Limerick and Bridget (Creagh); brother of Lieutenant Colonel John Napper, 83rd Foot

Entry to Army: Ensign in 51st Foot 4 Dec 1782 by purchase
Regimental Field Officer Promotions: Major in 51st Foot 22 Dec 1804 (vice Logan)
Service 1793–1815: Served in Ceylon 1800–1804
Died: Trincomalee, Ceylon 21 Dec 1804
This officer died the day before his promotion to major was gazetted
Sources: ARLI; Limerick Gazette 19 Sep 1805; History of the King's Own Yorkshire Light Infantry

555. *Robert BLACKALL (1805–1809)*
Born: Dublin c.1768
Relations: Of the Blackalls of Dublin
Entry to Army: Ensign in 51st Foot 31 Jul 1788
Regimental Field Officer Promotions: Major in 51st Foot 14 Mar 1805 (vice Napper)
Service 1793–1815: Served in Ceylon 1803–1807; Town Major of Trincomalee 1807; served in Peninsula Oct 1808 to Jan 1809
Retired: 13 Jul 1809
Residence: Nelson Street, Dublin
Died: Dublin 29 Jun 1840
Not to confused with a contemporary, Major Robert Blackall of Coolamber (1765–1855), who served in the EIC Bengal Artillery
Sources: ARLI; FMPD; WEOF; History of the King's Own Yorkshire Light Infantry

556. *Samuel RICE (1809–1817)*
Born: Surrey 1775
Relations: Son of John Rice of Tooting and Frances (Plumbe)
Entry to Army: Ensign in 51st Foot 12 Feb 1793 by purchase
Regimental Field Officer Promotions: Major in 51st Foot 13 Jul 1809 (vice Blackall) by purchase; Lieutenant Colonel in 51st Foot 24 Apr 1817 (vice Mitchell); to half-pay unattached 5 Jul 1831 (vice Synge) by exchange
Brevets: Brevet Lieutenant Colonel 22 Nov 1813; Brevet Colonel 22 Jul 1830
Service 1793–1815: Served in Gibraltar and Corsica 1793–1794; served in Portugal 1798; served in Cape of Good Hope 1806; served in Peninsula Oct 1808 to Jan 1809; served in Peninsula Feb 1811 to Dec 1812; served in Peninsula Sep 1813 to Apr 1814; commanded 51st Foot in Waterloo campaign 1815
Later Service: Inspecting Field Officer of Leeds Recruiting District Sep 1834 to Nov 1835
Awards and Honours: AGM (Nlle); CB 22 Jun 1815; WatM 23 Apr 1816; KH 12 Aug 1835
Residence: Tooting, Surrey
Died: London 7 Mar 1840
The subject of a memoir entitled 'The Life of a Regimental Officer During the Great War, 1793-1815' by A.F. Mockler-Ferryman
Sources: ANCB; ANCD; ARLI; CHAL; DALT; WEOF; WO 25/748; History of the King's Own Yorkshire Light Infantry

557. *Frederick James SPARKS (1809–1811)*
Born: Dublin 1777
Relations: Son of Captain Frederick Sparks of Curough and Ann (unk.)
Entry to Army: Ensign in 44th Foot 6 Mar 1794
Regimental Field Officer Promotions: Major in 51st Foot 24 Nov 1809 by exchange
Service 1793–1815: Served in Peninsula Oct 1808 to Jan 1809; served in Peninsula Feb to Nov 1811
Residence: James Street, Dublin, County Dublin
Died: Castelo Branco, Portugal 13 Nov 1811
Sources: ARLI; CHAL; FMPB; HALL; WEOF; Miscellanea Genealogica Et Heraldica Vol.2; History of the King's Own Yorkshire Light Infantry

558. *David ROBERTS (1811–1815)*
Born: England c.1757
Relations: Father of Lieutenant Harry Harvey Roberts, 51st Foot
Entry to Army: Ensign in Independent Company 16 Apr 1794
Regimental Field Officer Promotions: Major in 51st Foot 12 Dec 1811 (vice Sparks)
Brevets: Brevet Major 4 Jun 1811; Brevet Lieutenant Colonel 21 Jun 1813
Service 1793–1815: Served in Peninsula Oct 1808 to Jan 1809; wounded at Lugo and Corunna (lost arm); served in Peninsula Sep 1812 to Apr 1814, badly wounded at Bidassoa
Retired: 22 Jun 1815
Awards and Honours: AGM (Vitt Pyr)
Residence: Brompton, Middlesex
Died: Le Havre, France 30 Apr 1819
Sources: ANCW; CHAL; HALL; WEMR; History of the King's Own Yorkshire Light Infantry

Selected Regimental Histories
Wheater, William, *A Record of the Services of the Fifty-first (Second West York), the King's Own Light Infantry Regiment. With a list of Officers from 1755 to 1870 (reprinted from The United Service Magazine for 1869)* (London: Longmans, Green & Company, 1870)

Regimental Museum
King's Own Yorkshire Light Infantry Regimental Museum, Danum Gallery, Library and Museum, Waterdale, Doncaster, Yorkshire

52nd Regiment of Foot

Secondary Title:	Oxfordshire
Nicknames:	The Light Bobs
Jacket:	Red
Facings:	Buff
Badge:	A hunting horn below the crown

Regimental Lineage, 52nd Regiment of Foot

1755:	Dec – raised as 54th Regiment of Foot by Colonel Hedworth Lambton in Coventry
1757:	Feb – renumbered 52nd Foot
1782:	52nd (Oxfordshire) Regiment of Foot
1799:	Dec – 2nd Battalion formed in Chelmsford
1803:	Jan – 2nd Battalion became 96th Regiment of Foot
1803:	Jan – 52nd (Oxfordshire) Regiment of Foot (Light Infantry)
1804:	Aug – 2nd Battalion re-formed in Newbury
1816:	Mar – 2nd Battalion disbanded in Canterbury
1881:	2nd Battalion, Oxfordshire Light Infantry (on amalgamation with the 43rd (Monmouthshire) Regiment of Foot)
1908:	2nd Battalion, Oxfordshire and Buckinghamshire Light Infantry
1958:	1st Green Jackets (43rd and 52nd) (on amalgamation with The King's Royal Rifle Corps and The Rifle Brigade)
1966:	1st Battalion, The Royal Green Jackets (43rd and 52nd)
1968:	1st Battalion, The Royal Green Jackets
1992:	1st Battalion disbanded, lineage perpetuated by 2nd Battalion, which became 1st Battalion
2007:	2nd Battalion, The Rifles (on amalgamation with the Devonshire and Dorset Light Infantry, Royal Gloucestershire, Berkshire and Wiltshire Light Infantry, and the Light Infantry)

Service History, 1st Battalion 52nd Regiment of Foot

1793:	Madras [Chennai]; Poonamallee; Jul – siege of Pondicherry [Puducherry]; Poonamallee
1794:	Poonamallee; Sep – Secundermally [Sikander Malai]
1795:	Secundermally; Aug – Nagapatam; Sep – to Ceylon; Oct – Trincomalee
1796:	Trincomalee; Mar – Colombo; to India; Apr – Nagapatam; Oct – Tanjore [Thanjavur]
1797:	Tanjore
1798:	Tanjore; Feb – Madras; fit men into 77th Foot, cadre to England; one ship lost en route; Sep – Chatham; Dec – Colchester
1799:	Colchester; Jun – Barking; Aug – Ashford; Nov – Horsham, Brighton and Lewes; Dec – Horsham
1800:	Chelmsford; Mar – Chelmsford and Maldon; Apr – Canterbury; Jun – Netley camp; Jul – Southampton; to Quiberon; Isle de Houat; Aug – Ferrol; Oct – Cadiz; Gibraltar; Nov – Lisbon; to England
1801:	Jan – Ramsgate; Feb – Ashford; Mar – Canterbury; Nov – Deal
1802:	Deal; Dec – Chatham
1803:	Chatham; Jan – became Light Infantry; Apr – Chatham and Sheerness; Jun – Canterbury; Jul – Riding Street; Aug – Shorncliffe; Dec – Hythe
1804:	Hythe; Jul – Shorncliffe; Nov – Hythe; Dec – Shorncliffe
1805:	Shorncliffe; Nov – Hythe
1806:	Hythe; Jul – Brabourne Lees; Aug – Deal; Plymouth; Sep – to Sicily; Melazzo; incorporated company of Sicilian recruits
1807:	Melazzo; Oct – to Gibraltar; Dec – Gibraltar; to England
1808:	Portsmouth; Canterbury; discharged Sicilians to foreign regiment; Apr – Ramsgate; to Sweden (did not disembark); Jul – Spithead; Aug – to Portugal; Lisbon; Oct – advance into Spain; Elvas; Alcantara; Nov – Salamanca; Dec – Mayorga; Astorga

1809: Retreat to Corunna; CORUNNA; to England; Feb – Deal; May – to Portugal; PENINSULA; Jul – Lisbon; Villada; Jul – Coria; march to Talavera; Aug – Almaraz; Sep – Campo Maior; Dec – Pinhel

1810: Pinhel; Mar – La Alameda de Gardón; Apr – Malpartida; May – Espeja; Jun – Gallegos de Argañán; Jul – retreat across Coa; Carvalhal; Aug – Freixadas; Sep – BUSACO; Oct – Arruda dos Vinhos; Nov – Quinta de Valle

1811: Quinta de Valle; Mar – Pombal; Casal Novo; Foz d'Arouce; Nabainhos; Apr – Sabugal; Gallegos de Argañán; May – FUENTES D'ONORO; Espeja; Jun – Reguengo; Jul – Castelo de Vide; Aug – El Sahugo; Sep – Herguijuela de Ciudad Rodrigo; Oct – Zamarra; Dec – Agallas

1812: CIUDAD RODRIGO; El Bodon; Feb – Fuenteguinaldo; Mar – Badajoz; Apr – BADAJOZ; Fuenteguinaldo; May – El Bodon; Jun – Salamanca forts; Jul – SALAMANCA; Flores de Ávila; Aug – Madrid; Gáfete; Oct – Vicálvaro; Nov – San Muñoz; Saelices el Chico; Dec – Fuenteguinaldo

1813: Fuenteguinaldo; May – San Muñoz; Jun – VITTORIA; Arre; Jul – Bera; Aug – PYRENEES; volunteers to siege of San Sebastian; Sep – Santa Barbara Kalea; Oct – Puerta de Bera; Etxalar; Nov – NIVELLE; Arbonne; Dec – NIVE; Arbonne

1814: Sala; Feb – ORTHEZ; Charre; Mar – Tarbes; Seysses-Savès; Apr – TOULOUSE; Castelsarracin; Jun – Bordeaux; to England; Plymouth; Aug – Hythe; Sep – Chatham; ordered to North America

1815: Jan – Portsmouth; to Ireland; Cork; recalled to Plymouth; Mar – to Netherlands; Apr – Brussels; Grammont; May – Quevre-au-Camps; Jun – WATERLOO; advance on Paris; Jul – Paris; Allied Army of Occupation

1818: Nov – Calais; to England; Ramsgate

Service History, 2nd Battalion 52nd Regiment of Foot

1799: Dec – formed in Chelmsford from militia volunteers; Horsham

1800: Chelmsford; Apr – Ashford; Jun – Netley camp; Aug – Southampton; to Spain – Ferrol; Cadiz; Gibraltar; Nov – Lisbon; to England

1801: Jan – Ramsgate; Feb – Ashford; May – Ashford and Riding Street; Aug – Ashford and Shorncliffe; Nov – Dover Castle

1802: Dover Castle; Jun – Dover Castle and Shorncliffe; Nov – Dover Castle and Dungeness; Dec – Chatham

1803: Jan – Chatham; became 96th Regiment of Foot

1804: Aug – re-formed in Newbury; Nov – Banbury; Dec – Newbury

1805: Newbury; Jul – Hythe

1806: Hythe; Jun – Riding Street; Jul – Maidstone; Aug – Riding Street

1807: Shorncliffe; Jul – Ramsgate; Aug – to Denmark; Copenhagen; Kjóge; Nov – to England; Deal

1808: Deal; Ospringe; Feb – Ramsgate; Jul – to Portugal; Aug – VIMEIRO; Lisbon; Oct – advance into Spain; Viseu; Nov – Salamanca; Dec – Mayorga; Astorga

1809: Retreat to Corunna; Vigo; to England; Feb – Ramsgate; Deal; Jul – Portsmouth; to Walcheren; Aug – Flushing; to England; Oct – Horsham

1810: Fort Pitt; Mar – Chatham; Apr – London (Burdett riots); Chatham; Jul – Ashford; Sep – Shorncliffe; Dec – Lewes

1811: Lewes; Feb – Portsmouth; to Portugal; Lisbon; Mar – Naves; Apr – Espeja; May – Gallegos de Argañán; Jun – Reguengo; Jul – Castelo de Vide; Aug – El Sahugo; Sep – Herguijuela de Ciudad Rodrigo; Oct – Martiago; Nov – Zamarra; Dec – Martiago

1812: CIUDAD RODRIGO; El Bodon; Feb – Fuenteguinaldo; Mar – to England; Lisbon; Apr – Portsmouth; Jul – Brabourne Lees; Nov – Shorncliffe

1813: Shorncliffe; Jul – Hythe; Dec – Ramsgate; to Netherlands; Stevense

1814: Merxcem; Mar – Bergen-Op-Zoom; May – Brussels; Aug – Antwerp; Sep – Tournay; Nov – Ypres

1815: Ostend; to England; Apr – Dover; Jul – Canterbury; Dec – reduced to six companies

1816: Canterbury; Mar – disbanded in Canterbury

Establishments, 1st Battalion 52nd Regiment of Foot

Year	Subunits	Field Off	Off/ Staff	Sjts	Mus	Corp/ Pvts	Total
Dec 1792	10co+r	3	47	48	26	1,008	1,132
Dec 1794	10co+r	5	47	48	26	1,008	1,134
Dec 1797	10co+r	5	46	48	26	1,008	1,133
Dec 1798	10co	5	35	53	22	600	715
Dec 1799	10co	5	43	53	22	1,000	1,123
Dec 1801	10co	5	33	34	22	750	844
Oct 1803	10co	5	46	44	22	1,000	1,117
Jun 1804	10co	5	46	54	22	1,000	1,127
Dec 1806	10co	4	46	54	22	1,000	1,126
Sep 1807	11co	4	50	59	24	1,100	1,237
Dec 1807	10co	4	46	54	22	1,000	1,126
Aug 1808	10co+r	4	50	62	26	1,018	1,150
Dec 1809	10co	4	46	64	22	1,010	1,146
Dec 1811	10co+r	4	50	73	26	1,018	1,171
Dec 1812	10co	4	46	65	22	1,010	1,147
Dec 1813	10co+r	4	49	73	22	1,018	1,166
Dec 1815	10co	4	46	65	22	1,010	1,147

Establishments, 2nd Battalion 52nd Regiment of Foot

Year	Subunits	Field Off	Off/ Staff	Sjts	Mus	Corp/ Pvts	Total
Dec 1799	10co	5	43	53	22	1,000	1,123
Dec 1801	10co	5	47	53	22	1,000	1,127
Dec 1804	10co	3	35	23	22	400	483
Jun 1805	10co	3	35	43	22	800	903
Dec 1805	10co	3	35	33	22	600	693
Dec 1806	10co	3	36	43	22	800	904
Dec 1807	10co	3	46	53	22	1,000	1,124
Aug 1808	10co+r	3	50	71	26	1,208	1,358
Dec 1808	10co+r	3	40	51	26	808	928
Dec 1809	10co	3	46	53	22	810	934
Dec 1810	10co	3	46	54	22	810	935
Dec 1811	10co+r	3	50	63	26	818	960
Dec 1812	10co	3	45	45	22	610	725
Dec 1813	10co+r	3	48	53	22	618	744
Dec 1814	10co+r	3	48	43	22	418	534
Dec 1815	6co	3	23	25	12	400	463

Service Statistics, 52nd Regiment of Foot

	Lieutenant Colonels	Majors
Number of officers in period 1793–1815	15	28
Average age on appointment to substantive rank	36	31
Average time in rank in regiment (years)	4	3
Total field officers by nationality	19 E / 10 I / 8 S	
Demographics of other ranks 1799	97% EW / 2% I / 1% S	
Demographics of other ranks 1806	1/52nd: 68% E / 22% I / 8% S / 2% W	
Demographics of other ranks 1807	2/52nd: 64% EW / 33% I / 3% S	
Demographics of other ranks 1810	2/52nd: 61% EW / 34% I / 5% S	
Months of overseas service 1793–1815	1/52nd: 166 2/52nd: 46	

Significant Militia/Volunteer Intakes

1799:	Derbyshire, West Essex, North Gloucestershire, South Gloucestershire, 3rd Kent, North Middlesex, Northamptonshire, West Suffolk, East Yorkshire, Caernarvonshire
1800:	South Middlesex, Westminster, Carmarthenshire, Lowland Fencibles
1801:	Cambridgeshire
1802:	Argyllshire
1805:	East Essex, 1st West Yorkshire, County Londonderry
1806:	Berkshire, County Cavan
1809:	Cheshire, 1st Lancashire, North Yorkshire, County Galway
1810:	Cheshire

Regimental Colonels

559. *Cyrus TRAPAUD (1778–1801)*

Born: Dublin 1715
Relations: Son of Jean Trapaud and Marianne Guinebauld (De La Milliere); brother of Alexander Trapaud, Deputy Governor of Fort Augustus; half-brother of Lieutenant General Jean de St Julian Adlercron-Trapaud
Entry to Army: Ensign in 3rd Foot 20 Jun 1735
Regimental Field Officer Promotions: Lieutenant Colonel in 3rd Foot 13 Feb 1750
Brevets: Brevet Colonel 10 Jul 1760; Major General 10 Jul 1762; Lieutenant General 25 May 1772; General 19 Feb 1783
Colonelcies: 70th 10 Jul Foot 1760 (vice Parslow); 52nd Foot 14 May 1778 (vice Clavering)
Early Service: Served in Netherlands 1742–1743; reputedly saved the life of King George II at Dettingen 1743; served in Jacobite rebellion 1745, served at Quiberon 1757; served in West Indies 1759
Residence: Mansfield Street, Marylebone, London
Died: London 3 May 1801
The son of a French Huguenot refugee, and was the most senior general in the British Army at the time of his death
Sources: ANCB; ANCD; ANCW; ARLI; <https://web.archive.org/web/20110518164438/http:// www.queensroyalsurreys.org.uk/colonels/063.html>

560. *Sir John MOORE (1801–1809)*

See 539.
Colonel of 52nd Foot 8 May 1801 (vice Trapaud)

561. *Sir Hildebrand OAKES, 1st Bt (1809–1820)*

Born: Devon 1754
Relations: Son of Lieutenant Colonel Hildebrand Oakes of Exeter, 33rd Foot and Sarah (Cornelison); brother of Lieutenant General Sir Henry Oakes, Bombay service
Entry to Army: Ensign in 33rd Foot 23 Dec 1767 by purchase
Regimental Field Officer Promotions: Major in 66th Foot 13 Sep 1791 (vice Castle) by purchase; Lieutenant Colonel in 66th Foot 1 Sep 1795; Lieutenant Colonel in 26th Foot 22 Sep 1795 (vice Gordon)
Brevets: Brevet Major 18 Nov 1790; Brevet Lieutenant Colonel 1 Mar 1794; Colonel (Portugal) 30 Nov 1796; Brevet Colonel 1 Jan 1798; Brigadier General (Forces under General Stuart) 29 Aug 1798; Major General 1 Jan 1805; Lieutenant General (Malta) 30 Apr 1810; Lieutenant General 4 Jun 1811
Colonelcies: 1st Battalion of Reserve 22 Oct 1803; to half-pay25 Feb 1805; 3rd West India Regiment 24 Apr 1806 (vice Keppel); 52nd Foot 25 Jan 1809 (vice Moore)
Early Service: Served in American War of Independence 1775–1784; served in West Indies 1792
Service 1793–1815: Served in Gibraltar 1793; Deputy Quartermaster General in Corsica May 1794 to Jun 1796; Quartermaster General in Portugal 1797–1798; commanded brigade at capture of Minorca 1798; served in Egypt 1801; Commissioner of Royal Hospital, Chelsea 5 Jun 1805; Commissioner of Royal Military College 5 Jun 1805; Quartermaster General in Mediterranean Jul 1806 to Dec 1807; acting Commissioner for the Civil Affairs of Malta 25 Oct 1809 to 12 May 1810; Commissioner for the Civil Affairs of Malta 12 May 1810 to 4 Oct 1813; Lieutenant General of the Ordnance 1814 to 1822
Creations and Dignities: 1st Baronet of the Army 2 Nov 1813; 1st Baronet of Hereford 1 Jun 1815
Awards and Honours: GCB 20 May 1820
Residence: Hereford Street, Mayfair, London
Died: London 9 Sep 1822
Sources: ANCB; ANCD; ANCW; ARLI; DINB; GEMA (1822); ODNB; PHIL; WEOF

Colonels Commandant

562. *Sir John MOORE (2nd Battalion) (1799–1801)*
See 539.
Colonel Commandant of 2/52nd Foot 25 Nov 1799

563. *Rt Hon. George James LUDLOW, 1st Baron Ludlow (2nd Battalion) (1801–1803)*
See 189.
Colonel Commandant of 2/52nd Foot 8 May 1801

Lieutenant Colonels

564. *Colebrook NESBITT (1789–1798)*
Born: [spec.] Sussex c.1755
Relations: Natural son of Arnold Nesbitt of Winchelsea, army victualler and MP
Entry to Army: Ensign in 32nd Foot 7 Jun 1773 by purchase
Regimental Field Officer Promotions: Major in 19th Foot 3 May 1782 (vice Lloyd); Major in 52nd Foot 9 May 1789 (vice Barry) by exchange; Lieutenant Colonel in 52nd Foot 21 Jun 1789 (vice Straubenzee) by purchase
Brevets: Brevet Colonel 26 Feb 1795; Major General 1 Jan 1798
Service: Served in East Indies 1791–1792
Residence: St James Place, Westminster, London
Died: London 21 Jul 1798
Sources: ANCD; ANCW; ARLI; ODNB; WikiTree

565. *George BRODIE (1795–1798)*
Born: Morayshire 1745
Relations: Son of James Joseph Brodie of Spynie, advocate, and Emilia (Brodie)
Entry to Army: 2nd Lieutenant in 21st Foot 11 Jan 1769 by purchase
Regimental Field Officer Promotions: Major in 52nd Foot 9 May 1789 (vice Nesbitt); Lieutenant Colonel in 52nd Foot 1 Sep 1795
Brevets: Brevet Lieutenant Colonel 1 Mar 1794; Brevet Colonel 1 Jan 1798
Service: Lieutenant Governor of Fort Augustus Dec 1796
Retired: 29 Nov 1798
Residence: Fort Augustus, Inverness-shire
Died: Fort Augustus 11 Jan 1812
Sources: ANCW; ARLI; SCMA (1812)

566. *Alexander DIROM (1799–1803)*
See 357.
Lieutenant Colonel in 52nd Foot 6 Jun 1799 (vice Lumley)

567. *John Agmondisham VESEY (1798–1803)*
Born: County Galway 1761
Relations: Son of John Vesey of Cross and Jane (Hickman); brother of Lieutenant Colonel Poole Hickman Vesey, Madras service; and Captain Francis Vesey RN
Entry to Army: Ensign in 11th Foot 5 Jun 1778 by purchase
Regimental Field Officer Promotions: Major in 83rd Foot 20 Dec 1796 (vice Browne); Lieutenant Colonel in 52nd Foot 6 Sep 1798 (vice Nesbitt) by purchase; Lieutenant Colonel in Nova Scotia Fencibles 13 Dec 1803; Lieutenant Colonel in 29th Foot 31 Jan 1805; to half-pay of 29th Foot 7 Feb 1807 (vice Lake)
Brevets: Brevet Lieutenant Colonel 22 Jul 1795; Brevet Colonel 25 Apr 1808; Major General 4 Jun 1811
Service: Served in Irish Rebellion 1798; Deputy Barrackmaster General in British North America 1802; served on staff in British North America
Died: Messina, Sicily 2 Dec 1811
Sources: ANCB; GHLG; WEOF

568. *Henry Lewis CONRAN (1799–1806)*
Born: Essex 1766
Relations: Son of Major Henry Poole Conran EIC and Jane Penelope Mary (Marcell); brother of Captain James Samuel Conran, 17th Light Dragoons
Entry to Army: Ensign in 49th Foot 4 Oct 1780 by purchase
Regimental Field Officer Promotions: Major in 52nd Foot 21 Dec 1797 (vice Monson); Lieutenant Colonel in 2/52nd (later 96th) Foot 25 Nov 1799; Lieutenant Colonel in 7th West India Regiment 15 May 1806 (vice McCreagh) by exchange; Lieutenant Colonel in 1st Foot 7 May 1807; removed from the regiment as a general officer 25 Jul 1814
Brevets: Brevet Major 6 May 1795; Brevet Colonel 25 Oct 1809; Major General 1 Jan 1812; Lieutenant General 27 May 1825
Colonelcies: 98th Foot 25 Mar 1824
Early Service: Served in West Indies 1787–1790; served in British East Indies 1791–1793
Service 1793–1815: Served in British East Indies 1793–1800; served in Ceylon 1795; served in Ferrol and Cadiz 1800; commanded 2/52nd (later 96th) Foot in West Indies 1804–1806; commanded 2/1st Foot in British East Indies 1807–1812; commanded brigade in Upper Canada 1814; served in Gibraltar 1815
Later Service: Groom of the Bedchamber to Duke

of Kent; served in West Indies 1816–1821; acting Captain General and Governor in Chief in Jamaica 31 Jul 1821 to 22 Dec 1822; Lieutenant Governor and Commander in Chief in Jamaica 1822–1827
Residences: Covent Garden, Westminster, London; Bury St Edmunds, Suffolk
Died: Near Epping 17 Jul 1829
Conran's nickname was 'Tiger' – due to his having rescued a brother officer who had been snatched by a tiger in India. Conran ran after the animal shouting to drop the man – it did, and fled
Sources: ANCB; ANCD; ANCW; ARLI; GAES; PHIL; WEOF; WOST; WO 25/744

569. *Hon. Saville Henry LUMLEY[-SAUNDERSON] (1798–1799)*
Born: Yorkshire 1768
Relations: Son of Richard, 4th Earl of Scarborough and Barbara (Saville); brother of Captain Richard Lumley-Saunderson, 5th Earl of Scarborough; and General Hon. William Lumley(-Saunderson); took the name Saville in 1784; took the surname -Saunderson in 1807 (but seems not to have used it)
Entry to Army: Cornet in 3rd Dragoons 28 Jul 1784 by purchase
Regimental Field Officer Promotions: Major in 2nd Dragoon Guards 26 Oct 1797 (vice Gordon); Lieutenant Colonel in 52nd Foot 4 Dec 1798 (vice Brodie) by purchase; Lieutenant Colonel in 26th (later 23rd) Light Dragoons 6 Jun 1799 (vice De Grey)
Retired: 9 Apr 1807
Residence: Ollerton, Nottinghamshire
Died: Ollerton 14 Nov 1846
Sources: ANCB; ANCD; ARLI; DEPE; WEOF

570. *James KIRKMAN (1799–1801)*
Born: Dublin c.1759
Relations: Son of James Kirkman; brother of Major Thomas Kirkman, Paymaster General to the forces in Ireland.; father of Captain James Kirkman, 6th Foot
Entry to Army: Ensign in 29th Foot 14 Mar 1775
Regimental Field Officer Promotions: Major in 29th Foot 10 Feb 1796 (vice Ramsay); Lieutenant Colonel in 52nd Foot 25 Nov 1799
Brevets: Brevet Major 6 May 1795
Early Service: Served in British North America 1776–1780
Service 1793–1815: Served in marine detachments 1793; served in West Indies 1794; served in Flanders as ADC to Cathcart 1795; served in Helder 1799; Inspecting Field Officer of Yeomanry Sep 1803
Retired: 27 May 1801
Residence: Bideford, Devon
Died: Bideford 20 Feb 1816
Sources: ANCW; ARLI; WEOF; Everard; The Peerage, Baronetage, Knightage & Companionage of the British Empire for 1907

571. *Frederick MANNERS (1801–1803)*
Born: Hampshire 1768
Relations: Natural son of Henry Hervey Hervey-Aston of Aston-by-Sutton and Teresa Giuseppa (Ravizza), half-brother of Colonel Henry Hervey-Aston, 12th Foot
Entry to Army: Quartermaster in 10th Light Dragoons; Cornet in 10th Light Dragoons 15 May 1793
Regimental Field Officer Promotions: Major in 52nd Foot 25 Nov 1799; Lieutenant Colonel in 52nd Foot 27 May 1801 (vice Kirkman) by purchase; Lieutenant Colonel in 96th Foot 27 May 1801
Service: Served in Helder 1799, wounded at Texel
Residence: Watton at Stone, Hertfordshire
Died: Watton at Stone 6 Feb 1803
Sources: ANCB; ANCW; ARLI; FMPD; LFBI

572. *John Lawrence STUART (1805–1806)*
Born: Hertfordshire 1776
Relations: Natural son of Colonel William Stuart, 9th Lord Blantyre, and Catherine Harriet (Teasdale); brother of Major Charles Nicholas Stuart
Entry to Army: Ensign in 72nd Foot 18 Dec 1790 by purchase
Regimental Field Officer Promotions: Major in 52nd Foot 27 May 1801 (vice Manners) by purchase; Major in 96th Foot 10 Jan 1803; Major unattached 1 Feb 1803; Lieutenant Colonel unattached 13 Dec 1803; Lieutenant Colonel in 52nd Foot 13 Dec 1805 (vice Vesey); Lieutenant Colonel in 9th Foot 29 May 1806 (vice Shairpe)
Service 1793–1815: Commanded 1/9th Foot in Peninsula Aug 1808
Died: Killed in action at Roliça 17 Aug 1808
Sources: ANCB; ANCD; ARLI; WEOF

573. *Sir Kenneth MacKENZIE [DOUGLAS], 1st Bt (1803–1808)*
See 356.
Lieutenant Colonel in 52nd Foot 24 Feb 1803 (vice Dirom) by exchange

574. *Robert BARCLAY (1806–1811)*
Born: Edinburgh 1774
Relations: Son of William Barclay of Edinburgh

and Ann (Rose)
Entry to Army: Ensign in 3/60th Foot 24 Jun 1783
Regimental Field Officer Promotions: Major in 52nd Foot 1 Feb 1803 (vice Beckwith); Lieutenant Colonel in 52nd Foot 26 May 1806 (vice Stuart)
Service 1793–1815: Served in West Indies 1794–1795, taken POW; served in West Indies 1796–1800; served in Sweden 1808; commanded 1/52nd in Peninsula Aug 1808 to Jan 1809; served in Peninsula Jul 1809 to Nov 1810; commanded brigade in Light Division in Peninsula Aug to Sep 1810, wounded at Busaco
Died: Of wounds in London 3 May 1811
A lot of the early career details of this officer in the Dictionary of National Biography are incorrect
Sources: ANCB; ANCD; ARLI; CHAL; DINB; HALL; WEOF; WO 25/744

575. *John ROSS (1808–1820)*

Born: Scotland c.1778
Relations: Son-in-law of General Sir Robert Brownrigg, Bt; brother-in-law of Lieutenant Colonel Robert James Brownrigg, 2nd Ceylon Regiment
Entry to Army: Ensign in 36th Foot 2 Jun 1793
Regimental Field Officer Promotions: Major in 52nd Foot 15 Aug 1804; Lieutenant Colonel in 91st Foot 28 Jan 1808 (vice Loraine) by purchase; Lieutenant Colonel in 52nd Foot 18 Feb 1808 (vice MacKenzie) by exchange; Lieutenant Colonel in 66th Foot 18 Jul 1811 (vice Colborne) by exchange; to half-pay of 66th Foot 25 Dec 1818
Brevets: Brevet Lieutenant Colonel 28 Jan 1808; Brevet Colonel 4 Jun 1814; Major General 27 May 1825; Lieutenant General 28 Jun 1838
Colonelcies: 46th Foot 1 Aug 1839 (vice Keane)
Service: Served in East Indies 1793–1798; served in Ferrol 1800; served in Sicily 1806–1808; commanded 2/52nd in Peninsula Aug 1808 to Jan 1809; commanded 1/52nd in Peninsula Nov 1810 to Jul 1811; Deputy Adjutant General in Ceylon 1811–1814
Later Service: Deputy Adjutant General in Ireland 1815–1818; commandant at the depot on Isle of Wight 1819; Lieutenant Governor of Guernsey 14 Aug 1828 to Mar 1837
Awards and Honours: AGM (Vim); CB 4 Jun 1815
Residences: St Peter Port, Guernsey; Anglesea Place, Southampton, Hampshire
Died: Southampton 17 May 1843
Many sources confuse this officer with the Major General John Ross who commanded the 95th Rifles and died in 1835
Sources: ANCW; ARLI; CHAL; PHIL; WEMR; WEOF; WOST; WO 25/748

576. *Hon. Sir Hugh ARBUTHNOTT (1811–1813)*

See 25.
Lieutenant Colonel in 52nd Foot 9 May 1811 (vice Barclay)

577. *Rt Hon. Sir John COLBORNE, 1st Baron Seaton (1811–1825)*

Born: Hampshire 1778
Relations: Son of Samuel Colbourne of Lyndhurst and Cordelia Ann (Garstin); father of Major General James Colborne; and General Sir Francis Colborne
Education: Winchester College
Entry to Army: Ensign in 20th Foot 10 Jul 1794
Regimental Field Officer Promotions: Major in 20th Foot 21 Jan 1808 (vice Ross); Lieutenant Colonel in 5th Garrison Battalion 2 Feb 1809 (vice Shaw); Lieutenant Colonel in 66th Foot 2 Nov 1809 (vice Murray) by exchange; Lieutenant Colonel in 52nd Foot 18 Jul 1811 (vice Ross) by exchange; removed from the regiment as a general officer 1825
Brevets: Brevet Colonel 4 Jun 1814; Major General 27 May 1825; Lieutenant General 28 Jun 1838; General 20 Jun 1854; Field Marshal 1 Apr 1860
Colonelcies: 94th Foot 12 Dec 1834 (vice Campbell); 26th Foot 28 Mar 1838 (vice Dalhousie); 2nd Life Guards 24 Mar 1854 (vice Vane); Rifle Brigade Feb 1862 (vice Prince Albert)
Service 1793–1815: Served in Helder 1799, wounded at Krabbendam; served in Egypt 1801; served in Sicily and in Maida 1806; served in Copenhagen 1807; served in Peninsula as military secretary to Sir John Moore Sep 1808 to Jan 1809; commanded brigade in 2nd Division in Peninsula May 1811; served in Peninsula with 1/52nd Foot Dec 1811 to Apr 1812, wounded at Ciudad Rodrigo; commanded 1/52nd Foot in Peninsula Sep 1813 to Apr 1814; commanded 1/52nd Foot in Waterloo campaign 1815
Later Service: ADC to King George IV 1820; Lieutenant Governor of Guernsey 23 Jul 1821 to Aug 1828 (vice Bayly); Lieutenant Governor of Upper Canada 4 Nov 1828 to 26 Jan 1836 (vice Maitland); Chancellor of King's College, Toronto 1828–1835 (vice Maitland); commanded troops at Battle of Saint-Eustache in Lower Canada 14 Dec 1837; Commander in Chief and acting Governor of Québec 27 Feb 1838 to 29 May 1838, and 1 Nov 1838 to 19 Oct 1839 (vice Gosford); High Commissioner of Ionian Islands 1 Apr 1843 to 2 Jun 1849 (vice Mackenzie); Commander in Chief in Ireland Jan 1855 to Mar 1860 (vice Blakeney)
Creations and Dignities: 1st Baron Seaton 14 Dec 1839

Awards and Honours: AGM (Cor Alb CR Nlle Niv Ort Toul); KCB 4 Jan 1815; KMT (Habsburg) 2 Aug 1815; WatM 23 Apr 1816; KStG 4th Class (Russia) 1816; GCB 29 Jan 1838; GCMG 3 Jul 1843; MGSM (Egt Mai Ben Bus Pyr); PC (Ire) 1855
Residences: Deerpark, Buckerell, Devon; Beechwood House, Sparkwell, Devon; Valletta House, Torquay, Devon
Died: Torquay 17 April 1863
Sources: ANCW; ARLI; BRFM; CHAL; DALT; DICB; DINB; ODNB; WEOF

578. *Sir Edward GIBBS (1813–1820)*
Born: London 1778
Relations: Son of Colonel Samuel Gibbs of Horsley Park and Arabella (Rowley); grandson of Admiral Sir William Rowley RN; brother of Major General Samuel Gibbs
Entry to Army: Ensign in 59th Foot 14 Nov 1798
Regimental Field Officer Promotions: Major in 52nd Foot 4 Feb 1808 (vice Ross) by purchase; Lieutenant Colonel in 52nd Foot 8 Apr 1813 (vice Arbuthnott); to half-pay of 52nd Foot 25 Jul 1816
Brevets: Brevet Lieutenant Colonel 6 Feb 1812; Brevet Colonel 27 May 1825; Major General 10 Jan 1837; Lieutenant General 9 Nov 1846
Colonelcies: 52nd Foot 7 Dec 1844 (vice Arbuthnot)
Service: Served in Ferrol 1800; served in Sicily 1806–1807; served in Peninsula with 2/52nd Aug 1808 to Jan 1809; served in Peninsula with 1/52nd Mar 1811 to Jan 1812; temporarily commanded brigade in Light Division Jan to Apr 1812, lost eye at Badajoz and invalided home; commanded 1/52nd in Peninsula May to Aug 1813; commanded 2/52nd in Netherlands 1814
Later Service: Lieutenant Governor of the Island of Jersey 14 Sep 1838 to 9 Jan 1847
Awards and Honours: AGM (CR Bad Vitt); CB 4 Jun 1815; KCB 19 Jul 1838
Residence: Grainville House, St Saviour, Jersey
Died: Jersey 9 Jan 1847
Sources: ANCB; ANCD; ANCW; ARLI; CHAL; HALL; PHIL; WEOF; WOST; WO 25/745

Majors

579. *Hon. William MONSON (1795–1798)*
Born: London 1760
Relations: Son of John Monson, 2nd Baron Monson, and Theodosia (Maddison); brother of John Monson, 3rd Baron Monson; and Lieutenant General Charles Monson; father of William John Monson, 6th Baron Monson
Education: Eton College; Harrow School
Entry to Army: Ensign in 12th Foot 22 May 1777 by purchase
Regimental Field Officer Promotions: Major in 52nd Foot 2 Sep 1795 (vice Brodie); Lieutenant Colonel in 76th Foot 21 Dec 1797 (vice Ross)
Brevets: Brevet Major 1 Mar 1794; Brevet Colonel 1 Jan 1805
Early Service: Served in East Indies 1780–1793
Service 1793–1815: Served in East Indies 1793–1806; wounded at Aliguhr 1803; commander of 'Monson's retreat' Apr to Aug 1804; second-in-command at Deig 1805; ADC to King George III 1 Jan 1805
Political Career: MP (Lincoln) 1806–1807
Residences: Ham Common, Surrey; Bath, Somerset
Died: Bath 16 Dec 1807
Sources: ANCB; ANCD; ARLI; HPON; WEOF

580. *Harcourt MASTER (1799–1800)*
Born: Kent 1766
Relations: Son of Captain Harcourt Master of Greenwich RN, and Charlotte (Teissier); father of Lieutenant Colonel Harcourt Master, 4th Light Dragoons
Entry to Army: Ensign in 52nd Foot 15 Aug 1782 by purchase
Regimental Field Officer Promotions: Major in 52nd Foot 6 Jun 1799 (vice Dirom)
Brevets: Brevet Major 26 Jan 1797
Service 1793–1815: Inspecting Field Officer of Yeomanry May 1807
Retired: 23 Dec 1800
Residence: Catton, Norfolk
Died: Catton Feb 1836
Sources: ANCB; ANCD; ARLI; WEOF; The Family of Master of Henhurst

581. *William Molesworth Hatch MADDEN (1799–1801)*
Born: Dublin c.1756
Relations: Son of Wyndham Madden, clerk of commissioners of the revenue in Dublin, and Maria (Cushin); father of Lieutenant Edward Marcell Madden, 95th Rifles; Lieutenant Monsoon Molesworth Madden, 43rd Foot; Lieutenant William Sterling Madden, 52nd Foot; and Lieutenant Wyndham Carlyon Madden, 43rd Foot; step-father of Lieutenant Colonel Henry Ridewood, 45th Foot
Entry to Army: Ensign in 52nd Foot 20 Oct 1779
Regimental Field Officer Promotions: Major in 52nd Foot 25 Nov 1799 (vice Conran)
Brevets: Brevet Major 6 May 1795

Retired: 19 Mar 1801
Residence: Ashford, Kent
Died: Huddersfield, Yorkshire 20 Mar 1820
Sources: ANCW; ARLI; FMPW; GHLG; WEOF

582. *William George Philip Henry BECKWITH (1799–1803)*

Born: Yorkshire 1765
Relations: Son of Major General John Beckwith of Bluerly and Janet (Wishart); brother of Captain John Beckwith, 23rd Light Dragoons; General Sir George Beckwith; Brigadier General Ferdinand Amelia Fairfax Beckwith; and Lieutenant General Sir Thomas Sydney Beckwith; father of Lieutenant John Ferdinand Beckwith, Rifle Brigade; uncle of Major General John Charles Beckwith; Lieutenant Colonel Sydney Beckwith, Rifle Brigade; Lieutenant Colonel Henry Ferdinand Beckwith, Rifle Brigade
Entry to Army: Ensign in 28th Foot 19 Oct 1778 by purchase
Regimental Field Officer Promotions: Major in 52nd Foot 26 Nov 1799; Lieutenant Colonel in 1st Battalion of Reserve 17 Sep 1803; to half-pay of 27th Foot 14 Nov 1804; to half-pay unattached 1815
Brevets: Brevet Colonel 1 Jan 1812; Major General 4 Jun 1814
Early Service: Served in West Indies 1780–1782
Service 1793–1815: Served in West Indies 1794–1798; served in Helder 1799; served in Ferrol 1800; Assistant Adjutant General in Ireland 1804–1814
Retired: 9 Jun 1825
Residence: Chester, Cheshire
Died: Chester Mar 1844
Sources: ANCB; ANCD; ANCW; ARLI; PHIL; WEOF; WO 25/744; The Beckwiths

583. *William WARDROBE (1800–1803)*

See 446.
Major in 52nd Foot 23 Sep 1800 (vice Master) by purchase

584. *Robert SMYTHE (1801–1802)*

Born: Perthshire 1778
Relations: Son of David Smythe, Lord Methven, and Elizabeth (Murray); brother-in-law of General Sir John Oswald; and Lieutenant Colonel Robert Oswald, Greek Light Infantry
Entry to Army: Ensign in 3rd Foot Guards 12 Nov 1794 by purchase
Regimental Field Officer Promotions: Major in 52nd Foot 4 Apr 1801 (vice Madden) by purchase; Lieutenant Colonel in 68th Foot 26 Apr 1802 (vice Mannoch) by purchase; to half-pay of 68th Foot 25 Jul 1802; Lieutenant Colonel in 5th Garrison Battalion 21 May 1807 (vice Ainslie); Lieutenant Colonel in 90th Foot 1808 (vice Macdonald) by exchange
Retired: 29 Mar 1810
Residence: Methven Castle, Methven, Fifeshire
Died: Methven 5 Oct 1847
Sources: ANCB; ANCD; ARLI; PHIL; WEOF

585. *James ORDE (1802)*

Born: Northumberland 1774
Relations: Son of Commodore John Orde of Weetwood and Rosamund (Daglish); son-in-law of Henry Charles Somerset, 6th Duke of Beaufort and Lady Charlotte Sophia Leveson-Gower
Education: St John's, Cambridge
Entry to Army: Ensign in 22nd Foot 4 Dec 1794 by purchase
Regimental Field Officer Promotions: Major in 52nd Foot 22 Apr 1802 (vice Smyth) by purchase; Lieutenant Colonel in 4th Foot 13 Aug 1802 (vice Twysden) by purchase; to half-pay of 4th Foot 25 Nov 1802; Lieutenant Colonel in 99th Foot 17 Oct 1805 (vice Taylor) by exchange
Brevets: Brevet Colonel 4 Jun 1811; Major General 4 Jun 1814; Lieutenant General 22 Jul 1830; General 9 Nov 1846
Service 1793–1815: Served in Bermuda; court-martialled in Bermuda in Aug 1812 on various charges; sentenced to be cashiered but verdict overturned by Prince Regent
Residence: Avon Cottage, Ringwood, Hampshire
Died: Teddington, Middlesex 21 May 1850
Sources: ANCW; ARLI; WEOF

586. *William COAST (1802–1803)*

Born: Kent 1777
Relations: Son of William Stacey Coast of Chartham and Hester (Lade); brother of Major Michael Coast, 21st Foot; father of Captain Michael William Lade Coast, Rifle Brigade
Entry to Army: Ensign in West Kent Militia; Ensign in 20th Foot 29 Jul 1796
Regimental Field Officer Promotions: Major in 52nd Foot 13 Aug 1802 (vice Orde) by purchase; Major in 96th Foot 13 Aug 1802
Retired: 10 Mar 1804
Residence: Lawrence Weston, near Henbury, Gloucestershire
Died: Lawrence Weston 10 Nov 1846
Sources: ANCB; ANCD; ARLI; WEOF

587. *William WADE (1803–1808)*

Born: County Cavan c.1778
Entry to Army: Ensign in 52nd Foot 8 Feb 1792 by purchase
Regimental Field Officer Promotions: Major in 52nd Foot 13 Dec 1803 (vice Stewart) by purchase; Lieutenant Colonel in 8th Garrison Battalion 8 Sep 1808 (vice Gubbins); Lieutenant Colonel in 6th Foot 14 Dec 1808
Service 1793–1815: Served in British East Indies 1793–1795; served in capture of Ceylon 1795–1796; served in British East Indies 1796–1799; served in Portugal 1800–1801; served in Sicily 1806–1807; served in Peninsula with 52nd Foot Aug to Oct 1808; commanded 1/6th Foot in Peninsula Nov 1812 to Feb 1813
Died: Lisbon 26 Feb 1813
Sources: ANCW; ARLI; CHAL; HALL; WEOF; WO 25/748

588. *Sir Bagnall William BURDETT, 3rd Bt (1804–1805)*

See 26.
Major in 52nd Foot 21 Aug 1804

589. *Henry Richard RIDEWOOD (1806–1811)*

See 387.
Major in 52nd Foot 29 May 1806 (vice Barclay)

590. *John Philip HUNT (1808–1813)*

Born: Middlesex 1781
Relations: Son of Richard Hunt of Tottenham and Mary (Parrell); father of Lieutenant John Philip Hunt, 56th Foot
Entry to Army: Ensign in West Suffolk Militia; Ensign in 52nd Foot 14 Feb 1799
Regimental Field Officer Promotions: Major in 52nd Foot 8 Sep 1808 (vice Wade); Lieutenant Colonel in 8/60th Foot 11 Nov 1813; to half-pay of 60th Foot 25 Mar 1817; Lieutenant Colonel in 11th Foot 19 Nov 1818 (vice Cuyler)
Brevets: Brevet Lieutenant Colonel 27 Apr 1812
Service 1793–1815: Served in Ferrol and Cadiz 1800; ADC to Sir John Moore in Sicily 1806; ADC to Sir John Moore in Peninsula Aug to Oct 1808; served in Peninsula with 2/52nd Oct 1808 to Jan 1809; served in Walcheren with 2/52nd 1809; served in Peninsula with 2/52nd Mar to Oct 1811; served in Peninsula with 1/52nd Mar 1812 to Sep 1813, commanded 1/52nd at Badajoz; badly wounded at San Sebastian Aug 1813; Inspecting Field Officer of a Recruiting District 26 May 1814
Retired: 4 Apr 1824
Awards and Honours: AGM (Bad Sal SS); CB 4 Jun 1815; MGSM (FDO Pyr)
Residence: Castle Street, Walmer, Kent
Died: Walmer 26 Nov 1858
Sources: ANCB; ANCD; ARLI; CHAL; GEMA (1859); HALL; WEOF; Records of Walmer

591. *Charles ROWAN (1811–1822)*

Born: County Antrim 1782
Relations: Sons of Robert Rowan of Mullans and Eliza (Wilson); brother of Captain Robert Rowan, 52nd Foot; Lieutenant Colonel John Rowan, Antrim Militia; Captain Edward Rowan RN; and Field Marshal Sir William Rowan
Entry to Army: Ensign in 80th Foot 15 May 1797
Regimental Field Officer Promotions: Major in 52nd Foot 9 May 1811 (vice Arbuthnott)
Brevets: Brevet Lieutenant Colonel 27 Apr 1812
Service 1793–1815: Served in Sicily 1806; served in Copenhagen 1807; served in Peninsula with 1/52nd Aug 1808 to Jan 1809; Brigade Major in Peninsula Jul 1809 to Mar 1811; Assistant Adjutant General to Light Division in Peninsula Mar 1811 to May 1813, also Apr 1814; wounded at Waterloo 1815
Retired: 25 Apr 1822
Later Service: Recommended by Duke of Wellington to the post of first Senior Commissioner of London Metropolitan Police 7 Jul 1829; devised police beats on the basis of light infantry garrison patrols used by 52nd Foot at Shorncliffe
Awards and Honours: CB 4 Jun 1815; WatM 23 Apr 1816; KCB 6 Mar 1848
Residence: Norfolk Street, Park Lane, London
Died: London 8 May 1852
Sources: ANCD; ARLI; CHAL; DALT; GHHI; ODNB; WEOF

592. *Sir George Thomas NAPIER (1811–1814)*

Born: London 1784
Relations: Son of Colonel George Napier and Lady Sarah (Lennox); grandson of Charles Lennox, 2nd Duke of Richmond; brother of General Sir Charles James Napier; General Sir William Francis Patrick Napier; Captain Henry Edward Napier RN; father of Lieutenant General George Thomas Conolly Napier; Captain John Moore Napier, 62nd Foot; Colonel William Craig Emilius Napier, 25th Foot; father-in-law of Colonel Henry William St Pierre Bunbury, 21st Foot
Entry to Army: Cornet in 24th Light Dragoons 25 Jan 1800 by purchase
Regimental Field Officer Promotions: Major in 52nd Foot 27 Jun 1811 (vice Ridewood); Lieutenant Colonel in 71st Foot 24 Mar 1814 (vice Peacocke);

Captain and Lieutenant Colonel in 3rd Foot Guards 25 Jul 1814; Lieutenant Colonel in 44th Foot 22 Feb 1821 (vice Berkeley) by exchange; to half-pay of Sicilian Regiment 19 Apr 1821 (vice Morrison) by exchange
Brevets: Brevet Lieutenant Colonel 6 Feb 1812; Brevet Colonel 27 May 1825; Major General 10 Jan 1837; Lieutenant General 9 Nov 1846; General 28 Nov 1854
Colonelcies: 1st West India Regiment 29 Feb 1844 (vice Nicolay)
Service 1793–1815: Served in Sicily 1806; served in Baltic 1808; served in Peninsula Aug 1808 to Jan 1809; ADC to Sir John Moore in Peninsula Nov 1808 to Jan 1809; served in Peninsula with 1/52nd Jul 1809 to Apr 1812, wounded at Busaco and Casal Nova; commanded Light Division stormers at Ciudad Rodrigo 1812, lost right arm; served in Peninsula with 1/52nd Jan to Feb 1814
Later Service: Governor and Commander in Chief Cape Colony 22 Jan 1838 to 18 Mar 1844
Awards and Honours: AGM (CR); MGSM (Cor Bus Ort Toul); KCB 19 Jul 1838
Residence: Nice, Alpes-Maritimes, France
Died: Geneva, Switzerland 16 Sep 1855
Sources: ANCB; ANCD; ARLI; CHAL; DINB; GEMA (1855); ODNB; PHIL; WEMR; WEOF

593. *Sir James Henry REYNETT, Kt (1813–1820)*

Born: County Waterford c.1784
Relations: Son of Rev. Henry James Reynett and Henrietta (Johnson); cousin of Captain James Henry Reynett, 45th Foot
Entry to Army: Ensign in 52nd Foot 25 Nov 1799
Regimental Field Officer Promotions: Major in 52nd Foot 8 Apr 1813 (vice Gibbs); to half-pay of 52nd Foot 20 Mar 1817 (vice Mein) by exchange
Brevets: Brevet Lieutenant Colonel 1 Jun 1814; Brevet Colonel 22 Jul 1830; Major General 23 Nov 1841; Lieutenant General 11 Nov 1851; General 5 May 1860
Colonelcies: 48th Foot 25 Nov 1850 (vice Middlemore)
Service 1793–1815: Served in Ferrol 1800; served in Peninsula with 1/52nd Aug to Nov 1808; Deputy Assistant Quartermaster General in Peninsula Nov 1808 to Jan 1809; served in Peninsula with 1/52nd Jul 1809 to Sep 1811; Assistant Quartermaster General in Germany 1813 to 1814
Later Service: Military secretary to HRH Duke of Cambridge 1820; Inspector of Foreign outpatients at Chelsea Hospital 1820; Groom of the Bedchamber to King William IV 1831–1837; Lieutenant Governor of Guernsey
Awards and Honours: KCH 12 Aug 1824; Knight Bachelor 4 Dec 1824; KCB 9 Nov 1862
Residences: Brunswick Terrace, Brighton, Sussex; Eaton Square, Westminster, London
Died: Hampton Court Palace 9 Aug 1864
Sources: ANCD; ANCW; ARLI; CHAL; GEMA (1864); PHIL; WEOF; <https://archive.waterford-council.ie/ Historical%20Newspapers,%20Books%20 and%20Journals/ Decies/Decies%20XLVIII%20-%20 1993.pdf>

594. *William MEIN (1813–1818)*

Born: Midlothian 1779
Relations: Son of Andrew Mein of Canonbie and Elizabeth (Dalzell); brother of Lieutenant Colonel Nichol Alexander Mein, 43rd Foot; and Surgeon Pulteney Mein, 73rd Foot; cousin of Colonel John Alexander Mein, 74th Foot
Entry to Army: Ensign in 74th Foot 20 Sep 1797 by purchase
Regimental Field Officer Promotions: Major in 52nd Foot 11 Nov 1813 (vice Hunt); to half-pay of 52nd Foot Mar 25 Jul 1816; Major in 52nd Foot 20 Mar 1817 (vice Reynett) by exchange; to half-pay of 3rd Foot 16 Jul 1818 (vice Tylden) by exchange; rank stationary thereafter
Brevets: Brevet Major 6 Feb 1812; Brevet Lieutenant Colonel 7 Oct 1813
Service 1793–1815: served in Ferrol 1800; served in Sicily 1806–1807; served in Peninsula with 1/52nd Aug 1808 to Jan 1809; served in Peninsula with 1/52nd Jul 1809 to Dec 1813, wounded at Casal Nova, Ciudad Rodrigo, Badajoz, Bidassoa and Nive; invalided home Nov 1813; missed Waterloo due to ill health
Later Service: Served in Allied Army of Occupation in France 1817–1818
Awards and Honours: AGM (Niv); CB 4 Jun 1815
Residence: Marsh House, Canonbie, Dumfriesshire
Died: Canonbie 20 Apr 1836
Sources: ANCB; ANCD; ARLI; CHAL; HALL; PHIL; WEOF

595. *Sir Thomas Trayton FULLER-ELIOTT-DRAKE, 1st Bt (1814–1815)*

Born: Thomas Fuller in Sussex 1785
Relations: Son of John Trayton Fuller of Brightling and Anne Pollexfen (Elliott); grandson of George Augustus Elliott, 1st Baron Heathfield; brother of Captain Rose Henry Fuller RN; and Captain William Stephen Fuller RN; took Elliott and Drake surnames upon inheritance in 1813
Entry to Army: Ensign in 21st Foot 21 Jan 1804
Regimental Field Officer Promotions: Major in

52nd Foot 26 May 1814 (by purchase) vice Napier; to half-pay of 52nd Foot 25 May 1815
Service 1793–1815: Served in Baltic 1808; served in Peninsula with 1/52nd Aug to Nov 1808; served in Peninsula with 2/52nd Dec 1808 to Jan 1809; served in Walcheren with 2/52nd 1809; served in Peninsula with 2/52nd Mar 1811 to Mar 1812; served in Peninsula with 1/52nd Mar to Dec 1812, wounded at San Muñoz
Retired: 1825
Creations and Dignities: 1st Baronet Fuller-Drake-Eliott of Nutwell Court 22 Aug 1821
Awards and Honours: MGSM (FDO CR)
Residences: Upper Brook Street, Mayfair, London; Nutwell Court, Lympstone, Devon; Buckland Abbey, Devon
Died: Nutwell Court 6 Jun 1870
Sources: ANCB; ANCD; ANCW; ARLI; CHAL; WEOF

596. *Sir Octavius CAREY, Kt (1815–1816)*
Born: Guernsey 1785
Relations: Son of Jean Carey, jurat of the Royal Court of Guernsey, and Marie (Le Ray); brother of Lieutenant General Peter Evelyn Carey; son-in-law of Major General John Le Marchant; father of Major General Robert Carey, Deputy Adjutant General to the Forces in Australian colonies
Entry to Army: Ensign in 85th Foot Mar 1801 by purchase
Regimental Field Officer Promotions: Major in 10th Foot 2 Nov 1809 (vice Short) by purchase; Major in 52nd Foot 25 May 1815 (vice Drake); to half-pay of 52nd Foot 31 Mar 1816; Major in 62nd Foot 13 Jun 1816 (vice Blommart); to half-pay of 62nd Foot 1817; Major in 57th Foot 2 Jul 1818 (vice McGibbon) by exchange; Lieutenant Colonel in 57th Foot 30 Sep 1819 (vice Spring) by purchase
Brevets: Brevet Lieutenant Colonel 27 May 1813; Brevet Colonel 27 May 1825; Major General Jan 10 Jan 1837
Service 1793–1815: Served in Sicily; commanded Calabrian Free Corps in Peninsula Aug 1812 to Apr 1814
Later Service: Inspecting Field Officer of Militia in Ionian Islands 24 Jan 1828
Awards and Honours: CB 4 Jun 1815; Knight Bachelor 4 Aug 1830; KCH 12 Aug 1835
Residence: Castel, Guernsey; Thayer Street, Manchester Square, London
Died: London 13 Mar 1844
Sources: ANCB; ANCD; ARLI; PHIL; PHIL; WEOF; Annals of Some of the British Norman Isles Constituting the Bailiwick of Guernsey

Selected Regimental Histories

Leeke, William, *The History of Lord Seaton's Regiment: (the 52nd Light Infantry) at the Battle of Waterloo; Together with Various Incidents Connected with that Regiment* (London: Hatchard and Company, 1866)
Moorsom, William, *Historical Record of the Fifty-second Regiment (Oxfordshire Light Infantry) from the Year 1755 to the Year 1858* (London: Richard Bentley, 1860)

Regimental Museum

Soldiers of Oxfordshire Museum, Park Street, Woodstock, Oxfordshire

---

53rd Regiment of Foot

Secondary Title:	Shropshire
Nicknames:	The Brickdusts
	The Old Five and Threepennies
Jacket:	Red
Facings:	Red

Regimental Lineage, 53rd Regiment of Foot

1755:	Raised in Shropshire by Colonel William Whitmore as 55th Regiment of Foot
1756:	53rd Regiment of Foot
1782:	53rd (Shropshire) Regiment of Foot
1803:	Oct – 2nd Battalion formed in Sunderland
1817:	Oct – 2nd Battalion disbanded in Canterbury
1881:	1st Battalion, King's Shropshire Light Infantry (on amalgamation with 85th (King's Light Infantry) Regiment of Foot)

1968: 3rd Battalion, The Light Infantry (on amalgamation with the Somerset and Cornwall Light Infantry, King's Own Yorkshire Light Infantry, and Durham Light Infantry)
1993: The Light Infantry (reduced to two battalions)
2007: 3rd or 5th Battalion, The Rifles (on amalgamation with 1st Battalion, The Light Infantry, 1st Battalion, Devonshire and Dorset Light Infantry, 1st Battalion Royal Gloucestershire, Berkshire and Wiltshire Light Infantry, and Royal Green Jackets)

Service History, 1st Battalion 53rd Regiment of Foot

1793: Ayr and Beith; Mar – Leith; Yarmouth; to Holland; Apr – flank companies to Marquain; May – Famars; Jul – Valenciennes; Sep – Dunkirk; Oct – NIEUPORT [Nieuwpoort]; Nov – Oudenaarde
1794: Wevelgem; Apr – Cateau; Premont; Landrecies; May – Tourcoing; TOURNAY; Antwerp; Oct – Nijmegen; Dec – line of River Waal
1795: Geldermalsen; retreat to Bremen; Mar – Bremenlee; to England; May – Harwich; Jun – Norwich; Jul – Framlingham and Saxmundham; Aug – Tilbury; Sep – Southampton; Nov – to West Indies; dispersed by storms in the Channel
1796: Mar – four companies in Barbados; Apr – seven companies in ST LUCIA; Morné Chabot; Jun – capture of St Vincent
1797: St Vincent; Feb – capture of Trinidad; Apr – Martinique; Puerto Rico; May – St Vincent
1798–1799: St Vincent
1800: St Vincent; May – St Lucia
1801: St Lucia
1802: St Lucia; Oct – to England; Dec – Portsmouth
1803: Hilsea; Feb – Shrewsbury; Mar – Bridgnorth; Jun – Ipswich; Jul – Bramwell Heath; Oct – Sunderland
1804: Sunderland; Mar – Morpeth; Jul – Cheriton; Sep – Barham Downs; Nov – Canterbury
1805: Canterbury; Mar – Riding Street; Apr – Portsmouth; to East Indies; Sep – Kolkata [Calcutta]; Fort William; Dec – Dinapore [Dinapur]
1806: Dinapore; Jul – Berhampore [Berhampur]
1807: Berhampore; Nov – Cawnpore [Kanpur]
1808: Cawnpore
1809: Cawnpore; Feb – three companies to Bundelcund [Bundelkhand] and Adjighion [Badagaon]; Mar – battalion reunited; Nov – Calpee [Kalpi]; Dec – Chattapore [Jatapur]
1810: Bandery [Banderi]; Mar – Dowleetpore [Dulhepur]; Apr – Cawnpore
1811: Cawnpore
1812: Five companies to Callinger [Kalinjar]; Feb – capture of Callinger; Mahakarah; Mar – Cawnpore; Nov – Oonchasheer [Unchasia]; Dec – Meerut
1813: Meerut
1814: Meerut; Oct – to Nepal; Jesmore [Jasmour]; Nov – Fort Kalunga [Khalanga]; Dec – Nahan
1815: Nahan; Mar – Jeytuck [Jaithak]; Jun – Ghurmukleshire [Garh Mukteshwar]; Ganges River; Aug – Berhampore; Nov – Fort William; Dec – to Madras [Chennai]
1823: To England (after 18 years away)

Service History, 2nd Battalion 53rd Regiment of Foot

1803: Oct – formed in Sunderland from Army of Reserve recruits; Dec – Hexham
1804: Carlisle; Feb – Whitehaven; to Ireland; Mar – Dublin; Aug – Curragh of Kildare; Oct – Dublin
1805: Dublin; Jul – Galway; Nov – Loughrea; Dec – Limerick
1806: Limerick; Mar – Rathkeale; Nov – Limerick
1807: Limerick; Dublin; to England; Liverpool; Feb – Shrewsbury; Mar – Bridgnorth; Apr – Shrewsbury; May – Wolverhampton; Jun – Shrewsbury; Sep – Bridgnorth; Oct – Weymouth
1808: Weymouth; Apr – Portsmouth; to Ireland; Cork; Limerick; Sep – Fermoy
1809: Fermoy; Mar – Cork; to Portugal; PENINSULA; Apr – Almada; Leiria; May – Oporto; Jun – Abrantes; Jul – TALAVERA; Aug – Lobón; Sep – Nuestra Señora de Bótoa; Oct – Olivenza; Dec – Abrantes

1810: Guarda; Mar – Lageosa; May – Faia; Jul – Guarda; Aug – Faia; Sep – Busaco; Salgueiral; Oct – Ribaldeira; Nov – Alenquer

1811: Alenquer; Mar – Moimenta de Beira; Apr – São Pedro Rio Seco; May – Fuentes d'Oñoro; Gallegos de Argañán; Jun – Arronches; Jul – Alpedrinha; Aug – Gallegos de Argañán; Sep – Espeja; Oct – Pena Verde

1812: La Albergueria de Argañán; Feb – Coria; Mar – Almendralejo; Apr – Aldea de St Margarette; May – La Roca de la Sierra; Jun – Salamanca forts; Jul – SALAMANCA; Nava de Arévalo; Aug – Olmedo; Sep – siege of Burgos; Oct – Dueñas; Nov – Martillán; Dec – Ranhados; drafted into four companies and merged with 2nd Foot in 2nd Provisional Battalion, cadre to England

1813: Four service companies at Ranhados; Mar – Almofala; May – Especiosa; Jun – VITTORIA; Pamplona; Aug – Lesaka; PYRENEES; Oct – Bera; Nov – NIVELLE; Ascain; Dec – Arrauntz
Feb – six home companies in Portsmouth; Mar – Brabourne Lees

1814: Four service companies in Ustaritz; Feb – Saint Jean de Luz; Mar – Sainte-Foy-de-Peyrolières; Apr – TOULOUSE; Valence-sur-Baïse; May – Éauze
Six home companies in Brabourne Lees; Mar – to Spain; Pasaies; Tarbes; Apr – Lourdes; Jun – battalion reunited in Bordeaux; to Ireland; Jul – Cork; Charlesfort; Cork; to England; Aug – Spithead; Hilsea

1815: Hilsea; Feb – Portsmouth; Aug – to St Helena; Oct – St Helena; Huts Gate

1817: St Helena; Jul – to England; Sep – Portsmouth; Oct – disbanded in Canterbury

Establishments, 1st Battalion 53rd Regiment of Foot

Year	Subunits	Field Off	Off/ Staff	Sjts	Mus	Corp/ Pvts	Total
Dec 1792	10co	3	32	22	12	430	499
Jan 1793	10co	3	32	32	22	600	689
Dec 1793	10co	3	32	42	22	850	949
Dec 1795	10co+2r	5	51	62	30	1,010	1,158
Dec 1797	10co	5	38	53	22	600	718
Dec 1801	10co	5	43	34	22	750	854
Dec 1802	10co	5	46	54	22	1,000	1,127
Dec 1803	10co	5	36	54	22	1,000	1,117
Dec 1805	10co	5	46	54	22	1,000	1,127
Apr 1809	10co+r	5	50	72	26	1,208	1,361
Dec 1809	10co+r	5	50	62	26	1,008	1,151
Dec 1811	10co+r	5	50	63	26	1,008	1,152
Dec 1813	10co	5	46	55	22	1,000	1,128
Dec 1815	10co+r	5	49	63	22	1,008	1,147

Establishments, 2nd Battalion 53rd Regiment of Foot

Year	Subunits	Field Off	Off/ Staff	Sjts	Mus	Corp/ Pvts	Total
Oct 1803	10co	3	35	53	22	1,000	1,113
Dec 1804	10co	3	36	43	22	800	904
Jan 1807	10co	3	35	24	22	400	484
Dec 1807	10co	3	35	43	22	800	903
Apr 1809	10co+r	3	40	52	26	808	929
Dec 1809	10co+r	3	40	51	26	808	928
Dec 1810	10co+r	3	39	42	26	608	718
Dec 1811	10co+r	3	39	43	26	608	719
Dec 1813	10co	3	36	45	22	800	906
Dec 1815	10co+r	3	39	43	22	608	715

Service Statistics, 53rd Regiment of Foot

	Lieutenant Colonels	Majors
Number of officers in period 1793–1815	9	18
Average age on appointment to substantive rank	33	31
Average time in rank in regiment (years)	9	6
Total field officers by nationality	10 S / 8 E / 7 I / 3 W / 1 F	
Demographics of other ranks 1803	93% EW / 3% I / 3% S / 1% F	
Demographics of other ranks 1808	1/53rd: 81% EW / 13% I / 5% S / 1% F	
Demographics of other ranks 1815	2/53rd: 81% EW / 15% I / 4% S	
Months of overseas service 1793–1815	1/53rd: 240 2/53rd: 67	

Significant Militia/Volunteer Intakes

1805: Nottinghamshire; Oxfordshire; East Suffolk
1807: Dorset, Shropshire, Montgomeryshire
1808: North Yorkshire; 3rd West Yorkshire; Lanarkshire; South Mayo
1811: North Gloucestershire; Shropshire
1813: South Hampshire; Forfarshire; Glamorganshire

Regimental Colonels

597. *Robert Dalrymple-Horn-ELPHINSTONE (1770–1794)*

Born: Robert Dalrymple in Edinburgh 1718
Relations: Son of Sir Hew Dalrymple of Drummore, Bt, Lord President of the Court of Session, and Ann (Horn); brother of Colonel Campbell Dalrymple, 3rd Dragoons, Governor of Guadeloupe; cousin of General Sir Hew Whiteford Dalrymple, Bt; added Horn-Elphinstone surnames on marriage 1754; father of Lieutenant Colonel Sir Robert Dalrymple-Horn-Elphinstone, 1st Bt
Entry to Army: Ensign in 1st Foot c.1736
Regimental Field Officer Promotions: Lieutenant Colonel in 2/1st Foot 20 Jun 1753
Brevets: Brevet Colonel 19 Feb 1762; Major General 30 Apr 1770; Lieutenant General 29 Aug 1777; General 12 Oct 1793
Colonelcies: 120th Foot 3 Aug 1762; 53rd Foot 5 Feb 1770 (vice Toovey)
Early Service: Served at Cartagena 1740
Residence: Restalrig, Midlothian
Died: Restalrig 20 Apr 1794
Sources: ANCB; ANCD; ARLI; The Genealogy of The Existing British Peerage, with Sketches of the Family Histories of the Nobility

598. *Rt Hon. Gerard LAKE, 1st Viscount Lake (1794–1796)*

Born: Middlesex 1744
Relations: Son of Lancelot Charles Lake of Flambards and Letitia (Gumley); father of Lieutenant General Francis Gerard Lake; and Lieutenant Colonel George Augustus Frederick Lake, 29th Foot
Entry to Army: Ensign in 1st Foot Guards 9 May 1758 by purchase
Regimental Field Officer Promotions: Captain and Lieutenant Colonel in 1st Foot Guards 19 Feb 1776; Third Major in 1st Foot Guards 20 Oct 1784; Second Major in 1st Foot Guards 12 Mar 1789; Lieutenant Colonel in 1st Foot Guards 8 Aug 1792
Brevets: Brevet Colonel 16 Feb 1782; Major General 28 Apr 1790; Lieutenant General 26 Jan 1797; General 29 Apr 1802
Colonelcies: 53rd Foot 30 Apr 1794 (vice Elphinstone); 73rd Foot 2 Nov 1796 (vice Medows); 80th Foot 14 Feb 1800 (vice St Leger)
Early Service: Served in Germany 1760–1762; served in North America 1781
Service 1793–1815: Commanded Brigade of Guards in Flanders 1793–1794; Commander in Chief in Ireland Apr to Jun 1798; Commander in Chief in East Indies Jul 1801 to Jul 1805 (vice Clarke); Commander in Chief in East Indies Oct 1805 to Oct 1807 (vice Cornwallis); Governor of Plymouth 1807–1808
Political Career: MP (Aylesbury) 1790–1802
Creations and Dignities: 1st Baron Lake of Delhi and Laswary and of Aston Clinton 1 Sep 1804; 1st Viscount Lake of Delhi and Laswary and of Aston Clinton 31 Oct 1807
Residence: Aston Clinton, near Aylesbury, Buckinghamshire
Died: London 20 Feb 1808
Viscount Lake was reputedly an inveterate gambler who lost most of his family's fortune, leaving his children with little or no inheritance on his death
Sources: ARLI; DINB; ODNB; WEOF

599. *Welbore Ellis DOYLE (1796–1797)*
Born: Dublin 1758
Relations: Son of Charles Doyle of Bramblestown and Elizabeth (Milley); brother of General Sir John Doyle; father of Major General Sir Francis Hastings Doyle, Bt; and Major General Carlo Joseph Doyle; uncle of Lieutenant General Charles William Doyle; and Lieutenant Colonel Sir John Milley Doyle, Portuguese service
Entry to Army: Ensign in 55th Foot 12 Dec 1770 by purchase
Regimental Field Officer Promotions: Lieutenant Colonel in 105th Foot 21 Mar 1783; to half-pay1783; Lieutenant Colonel in 14th Foot 13 Mar 1789 by purchase
Brevets: Brevet Colonel 12 Oct 1793; Brigadier General (Continent) Nov 1794; Major General 26 Feb 1795
Colonelcies: 53rd Foot 2 Nov 1796 (vice Lake)
Early Service: Served in North America 1775–1781; military envoy to Poland
Service 1793–1815: Commanded 14th Foot in Flanders 1793; served in Belle Isle 1795; Military Governor of Ceylon 1 Jan to 30 Jul 1797 (vice Stuart)
Died: Colombo, Ceylon 2 Jul 1797
In his will, Doyle left everything to his great friend Lord Moira 'to be applied as he shall judge for the benefit of my family'
Sources: ANCB; ANCD; ANCW; ARLI; DINB; WEOF; WOST

600. *Charles CROSBIE (1798–1807)*
Born: County Wicklow 1722
Relations: Son of Major John Crosbie, Governor of the Fort of Aberdeen, and Mary Thompson; father of General Sir John Gustavus Crosbie
Entry to Army: Captain in 86th Foot 24 Aug 1759
Regimental Field Officer Promotions: Major in 86th Foot 17 Jun 1763 by purchase; Lieutenant Colonel in 67th Foot 27 Nov 1778
Brevets: Brevet Lieutenant Colonel 25 May 1772; Brevet Colonel 17 Nov 1780; Major General 28 Sep 1787; Lieutenant General 26 Jan 1797; General 29 Apr 1802
Colonelcies: Royal Dublin Regiment 20 Oct 1794; 53rd Foot 3 Jan 1798 (vice Doyle)
Early Service: Served in Senegal 1760
Residence: Seymour Street, Marylebone, London
Died: London 18 Mar 1807
Sources: ANCB; ANCD; ARLI; Historical Record of the Fifty-Third, or the Shropshire Regiment of Foot

601. *Sir John ABERCROMBIE (1807–1817)*
Born: Clackmannanshire 1772
Relations: Son of General Sir Ralph Abercromby and Mary Ann (Menzies); brother of Colonel Hon. Alexander Abercromby, Coldstream Foot Guards; nephew of General Sir Robert Abercromby
Entry to Army: Cornet in 5th Dragoons 13 Apr 1782 by purchase
Regimental Field Officer Promotions: Major in 94th Foot 28 May 1794; Lieutenant Colonel in 112th Foot 22 Jul 1794; Lieutenant Colonel in 53rd Foot 29 Jul 1795 (vice Mathews) by exchange
Brevets: Brevet Colonel 1 Jan 1800; Major General 2 Nov 1805; Lieutenant General (Bombay) 19 Mar 1810; Lieutenant General 1 Jan 1812
Colonelcies: 53rd Foot 21 Mar 1807 (vice Crosbie)
Service 1793–1815: ADC to father in Flanders 1793–1794; served in West Indies 1796–1797; served in Irish rebellion 1798; military secretary to father in Helder 1799; Deputy Adjutant General in Egypt 1801; POW in France 1803–1808; Commander in Chief Bombay 28 Nov 1809 to 10 Oct 1812 (vice Nicolls); commanded land forces at capture of Mauritius Nov 1810; Commander of Mauritius 29 Nov 1810 to 3 Dec 1810; Commander in Chief Madras and Governor of Madras 12 Feb 1813 to 21 May 1814
Political Career: MP (Clackmannanshire) 1815–1817
Awards and Honours: KCB 2 Jan 1815; GCB 7 Apr 1815
Residence: Tullibody, Clackmannanshire; Marseilles, Provence-Alpes-Côte d'Azur, France
Died: Marseilles 14 Feb 1817
Sources: ANCB; ANCD; ARLI; DINB; HPON; ODNB; WEOF; WOST

Lieutenant Colonels

602. *Richard Mitchelbourne SYMES (1792–1794)*
Born: County Wicklow 1747
Relations: Son of Richard Mitchelbourne Symes of Ballyarthur and Eleanor (Cliffe); brother of Lieutenant Colonel Michael Symes, 76th Foot
Entry to Army: Ensign in 14th Foot 23 Jun 1762 by purchase
Regimental Field Officer Promotions: Lieutenant Colonel in 53rd Foot 26 Apr 1792 (vice Powell)
Brevets: Brevet Lieutenant Colonel 31 Dec 1782; Colonel (America) 10 Nov 1790; Brigadier General (West Indies) 1794
Early Service: Served in American War of

Independence
Service 1793–1815: Commanded brigade in West Indies 1794
Died: St Kitts 19 Jul 1794
Sources: ANCB; ARLI; By Fire and Bayonet

603. *Robert MATHEWS (1794–1796)*
Born: [spec.] Scotland c.1745
Relations: Son-in-law of Alexander Saunders Simpson, Provost Marshal of Québec
Entry to Army: Ensign in 8th Foot 28 Feb 1761
Regimental Field Officer Promotions: Major in 53rd Foot 22 Sep 1783 (vice Nairne); Lieutenant Colonel in 53rd Foot 15 Oct 1794 (vice Symes); Lieutenant Colonel in 112th Foot 29 Jul 1795 (vice Abercrombie) by exchange
Brevets: Brevet Lieutenant Colonel 13 Nov 1793
Early Service: Served in Germany 1761–1762; served in British North America 1768–1775; served in American War of Independence
Service 1793–1815: Major of Royal Hospital, Chelsea 1802–1814
Died: Chelsea 5 Jul 1814
Sources: ANCW; DICB; SCMA (1814)

604. *Sir John ABERCROMBIE (1795–1807)*
See 601.
Lieutenant Colonel in 53rd Foot 29 Jul 1795 (vice Mathews) by exchange

605. *Stafford LIGHTBURNE (1795–1814)*
Born: [spec.] County Wexford c.1757
Relations: Son of John Lightburne, Mayor of Wexford, and Mary (Tench)
Entry to Army: Ensign in 37th Foot 15 Aug 1775
Regimental Field Officer Promotions: Major in 119th Foot 22 Aug 1794; Lieutenant Colonel in Royal Dublin Regiment 3 Dec 1794; Lieutenant Colonel in 53rd Foot 1 Sep 1795; removed from the regiment as a general officer 1814
Brevets: Brevet Colonel 1 Jan 1801; Brigadier General (home staff) 1805; Major General 25 Apr 1808; Lieutenant General 4 Jun 1813
Early Service: Served in American War of Independence 1775–1781, wounded at Yorktown; served in British North America 1784–1788
Service 1793–1815: Served in Flanders 1793–1794; served in West Indies 1795–1798; and 1799–1802; commanded brigade in Peninsula Jul 1809 to Jan 1810; commanded brigade in 4th Division in Peninsula Jan and Feb 1810; commanded brigade in 3rd Division in Peninsula Feb to Oct 1810; not employed thereafter
Residence: Haymarket, St James's, London
Died: London 27 Sep 1827
'...there is General Lightburne, whose conduct is really scandalous. I am not able to bring him before a court-martial as I should wish, but he is a disgrace to the army which can have such a man as a Major General...I pray God and the Horse Guards to deliver me from General Lightburne' – Duke of Wellington, Aug 1810
Sources: ANCD; ANCW; CHAL; PHIL; WEBC; WEOF; WO 25/746

606. *Sydney Edward SCROGGS (1803–1805)*
Born: Wiltshire 1764
Relations: Son of Edward Scroggs of Chute Lodge and Mary (Pulse)
Entry to Army: Ensign in 18th Foot 5 Jul 1780 by purchase
Regimental Field Officer Promotions: Major in 4th Foot 6 Aug 1799; Lieutenant Colonel in 53rd Foot 9 Jul 1803 by purchase
Brevets: Brevet Lieutenant Colonel 1 Jan 1801
Retired: 14 Mar 1805
Residence: Standen Chute, Wiltshire
Died: Standen Chute 11 Apr 1845
Sources: ANCB; ANCD; ARLI; WEOF

607. *Sebright MAWBY (1804–1825)*
Born: British North America c.1770
Relations: Son of Major John Mawby, 18th Foot, and Sarah (Huddlestone)
Entry to Army: Volunteer in Gibraltar 1787; Ensign in 18th Foot 20 Jun 1787
Regimental Field Officer Promotions: Major in 18th Foot 1 Jun 1799 (vice Conolly) by purchase; Lieutenant Colonel in 53rd Foot 5 Oct 1804; removed from the regiment as a general officer 1825
Brevets: Brevet Colonel 4 Jun 1813; Major General 12 Aug 1819; Lieutenant General 10 Jan 1837
Early Service: Served in Gibraltar 1787–1793
Service 1793–1815: Served in siege of Toulon 1793; served in Corsica 1794; Assistant Quartermaster General in Corsica 1795; commanded 18th Foot in Minorca and Egypt 1800–1802; commanded 1/53rd Foot in British East Indies 1805–1814 and in Nepal War 1814–1815; commanded forces in Fort Kalunga after death of Major General Gillespie
Residence: Portman Square, Marylebone, London
Died: London 26 Nov 1850
Sources: ANCW; ARLI; GEMA (1851); PHIL; WEOF

608. *Sir George Ridout BINGHAM (1805–1825)*

Born: Dorset 1777
Relations: Son of Colonel Richard Bingham, Dorset militia, and Elizabeth (Ridout); brother of Commander John Bingham RN; half-brother of Colonel Charles Cox Bingham RA
Entry to Army: Ensign in 69th Foot Jun 1793 by purchase
Regimental Field Officer Promotions: Major in 82nd Foot 22 Jan 1801 (vice Griffiths) by purchase; Lieutenant Colonel in 53rd Foot 14 Mar 1805 (vice Scroggs); removed from the regiment as a general officer 1825
Brevets: Brevet Colonel 4 Jun 1813; Brigadier General (St Helena) 1819; Major General 12 Aug 1819
Colonelcies: Colonel Commandant of 2/Rifle Brigade 18 Jun 1831 (vice Beckwith)
Service 1793–1815: Served in Corsica 1793–1795; served aboard fleet as marine; served at Cape of Good Hope 1796–1798; served in Minorca 1800; commanded 2/53rd in Peninsula Apr 1809 to Dec 1813; commanded brigade in 6th Division in Peninsula Jul to Nov 1812, wounded at Salamanca
Awards and Honours: AGM (Tal Sal Vitt Pyr Nlle); KCB 2 Jan 1815
Residences: Deans Leaze, Witchampton, Dorset; Manchester Square, Marylebone, London
Died: London 3 Jan 1833
Sources: ANCW; ARLI; CHAL; DINB; WEOF; WO 25/744

609. *John BUCKLAND (1811–1817)*

Born: Hampshire 1771
Relations: Son of Christopher Buckland of Alverstoke and Anna Maria (Johns)
Entry to Army: Ensign in 53rd Foot 14 Jun 1786 by purchase
Regimental Field Officer Promotions: Major in 53rd Foot 7 Jan 1801 (vice Braban); Lieutenant Colonel in 53rd Foot 13 Jun 1811; to half-pay of 53rd Foot 25 Dec 1817
Brevets: Brevet Lieutenant Colonel 25 Apr 1808; Brevet Colonel 4 Jun 1814
Early Service: Served in British North America 1786–1789
Service 1793–1815: Served in Flanders 1793–1795; served in West Indies 1796–1797; served in East Indies 1805–1815
Residence: Poole, Dorset
Died: Poole Mar 1823
Sources: ANCB; ANCD; ANCW; ARLI; GEMA (1824); WEOF; WO 25/744

Majors

610. *John BAIRD (1794–1795)*

Born: Aberdeenshire 1754
Relations: Son of William Baird of Newbyth and Alicia (Johnston); brother of General Sir David Baird, Bt; Major General Joseph Baird; and Captain Robert Baird, 82nd Foot
Entry to Army: Ensign in 53rd Foot 22 Sep 1769 by purchase
Regimental Field Officer Promotions: Major in 53rd Foot 15 Oct 1794 (vice Mathews)
Brevets: Brevet Lieutenant Colonel 1 Mar 1794
Retired: 5 Aug 1795
Militia Career: Lieutenant Colonel in Aberdeenshire Militia 21 Oct 1803
Residence: Byth, Aberdeenshire
Died: Ferntower House, Perthshire 4 Aug 1819
Sources: ANCD; ARLI; LFBI

611. *Sir Thomas [MAKDOUGALL-] BRISBANE, 1st Bt (1795–1800)*

Born: Ayrshire 1773
Relations: Son of Thomas Brisbane of Stenhouse and Eleanora (Bruce); changed surname to Makdougall-Brisbane in 1826
Education: University of Edinburgh; DCL (Oxford); DCL (Cambridge)
Entry to Army: Ensign in 2/71st Foot 10 Jan 1782
Regimental Field Officer Promotions: Major in 53rd Foot 5 Aug 1795 (vice Baird) by purchase; Lieutenant Colonel in 69th Foot 4 Apr 1800 by purchase; to half-pay of York Rangers 21 Feb 1805; removed from the regiment as a general officer 1814
Brevets: Brevet Colonel 25 Jul 1810; Brigadier General (staff) 25 Nov 1812; Major General 4 Jun 1813; Lieutenant General 27 May 1825; General 23 Nov 1841
Colonelcies: 34th Foot 16 Dec 1826 (vice Cole)
Service 1793–1815: Served in Flanders 1793–1795; served in West Indies 1796–1797; commanded 69th Foot in Jamaica 1801–1803; commanded brigade in 3rd Division in Peninsula Mar 1813 to Apr 1814; commanded brigade in France Aug to Nov 1814; commanded brigades in Allied Army of Occupation in France Nov 1815 to Nov 1818
Later Service: Governor of New South Wales 1 Dec 1821 to 1 Dec 1825
Creations and Dignities: 1st Baronet Makdougall-Brisbane 8 Mar 1836
Awards and Honours: AGC (Vitt Pyr Nlle Ort Toul); KCB 2 Jan 1815; GCH 12 Aug 1831; GCB 6 Feb 1837; MGSM (Niv); FRS; FRSE
Residence: Brisbane House, Largs, Ayrshire
Died: Brisbane House 17 Jan 1860

Sources: ARLI; CHAL; DINB; PHIL; WEBC; WEOF; WOST; WO 25/744; Australian Dictionary of Biography, Vol.1

612. *William BRABAN (1795–1801)*
Born: [spec.] Sussex c.1762
Entry to Army: Ensign in 37th Foot 29 Jul 1779 by purchase
Regimental Field Officer Promotions: Major in 131st Foot 3 Dec 1793; Major in 53rd Foot 5 Oct 1795
Brevets: Brevet Lieutenant Colonel 3 May 1796
Service 1793–1815: Served in West Indies 1796–1801
Died: Martinique 5 Jan 1801
Sources: ANCW; ARLI

613. *Charles STEWART (1800–1805)*
See 517.
Major in 53rd Foot 4 Apr 1800 (vice Brisbane) by purchase

614. *James CONWAY (1803–1804)*
Born: County Kerry c.1768
Relations: Son of Edward Conway and Ellen (Mahony); cousin of Colonel James Henry, Count Conway; father of General Thomas Sydenham Conway
Entry to Army: Major in 6th Irish Brigade 1 Oct 1794
Regimental Field Officer Promotions: Major in 6th Irish Brigade 1 Oct 1794; to half-pay of Irish Brigade 1798; Major in 53rd Foot 9 Jul 1803
Brevets: Brevet Lieutenant Colonel 1 Jan 1800
Retired: 8 Nov 1804
Residences: Killadysert, County Clare; Acton, Middlesex
Died: Acton 5 Jan 1861
Sources: ANCD; ANCW; ARLI; Illustrations, Historical and Genealogical, of King James's Irish Army List; Selections from Old Kerry Records

615. *Sir William DOUGLAS (1803–1804)*
Born: Roxburghshire 1770
Relations: Son of Archibald Douglas of Timpendean and Bonjedward, and Helen (Bennett); father of Major George Douglas, 16th Foot
Entry to Army: Ensign in 1/1st Foot 14 Feb 1786 by purchase
Regimental Field Officer Promotions: Major in 53rd Foot 9 Jul 1803; Lieutenant Colonel in 98th Foot 22 May 1804; to half-pay of 97th (late 98th) Foot 1818
Brevets: Brevet Major 29 Apr 1802; Brevet Colonel 4 Jun 1813; Major General 12 Aug 1819
Colonelcies: 2nd Royal Veteran Battalion 1 Nov 1819
Early Service: Served in West Indies 1786
Service 1793–1815: Served in West Indies; served in Irish rebellion 1798; Assistant Quartermaster General in Ireland; commanded 98th Foot in British North America 1805–1815
Awards and Honours: KCH 12 Aug 1832
Residences: Timpendean, Roxburghshire
Died: London Apr 1834
Sources: ANCW; ARLI; UNSM (1834); WEOF

616. *Hon. Henry CADOGAN (1804–1805)*
Born: London 1780
Relations: Son of Charles Sloane Cadogan, 1st Earl Cadogan and Mary (Churchill); grandson of former PM Robert Walpole; half-brother of Captain Charles Henry Sloane Cadogan, 2nd Earl Cadogan, 61st Foot; Captain Hon. Thomas Cadogan RN; Captain Hon. Edward Cadogan, 49th Foot; brother of Admiral George Cadogan, 3rd Earl Cadogan; and Lieutenant Colonel Hon. Edward Cadogan, 8th West India Regiment
Education: Eton College
Entry to Army: Ensign in 18th Foot 9 Aug 1797 by purchase
Regimental Field Officer Promotions: Major in 53rd Foot 8 Nov 1804 (vice Conway) by purchase; Lieutenant Colonel in 18th Foot 22 Aug 1805 (vice O'Dogherty) by purchase; to half-pay of Birmingham Fencibles 5 Mar 1807; Lieutenant Colonel in 71st Foot 7 Jan 1808 (vice Blaquiere)
Brevets: Brevet Colonel 4 Jun 1813
Service 1793–1815: Served in Gibraltar 1797; ADC to Wellesley in Peninsula Jun 1809 to Sep 1810; commanded 1/71st Foot in Peninsula Sep 1810 to Nov 1812; commanded brigade in 2nd Division in Peninsula Nov 1812 to Jun 1813
Awards and Honours: AGM (FDO Vitt)
Died: Of wounds at Vittoria 21 Jun 1813
Sources: ANCB; ANCD; ARLI; CHAL; DINB; WEOF

617. *Gaspard Terence MacMAHON, Count (1805–1817)*
Born: County Limerick 1766
Relations: Son of Terence MacMahon of Newcastle and Christine (O'Rouke); cousin of Colonel Thomas St Austin MacMahon, French Consul at Cork
Entry to Army: 2nd Lieutenant in Walsh's Regiment, Irish Brigade in French service 8 Jun 1782; Captain in Walsh's Regiment, Irish Brigade in British service 1 Oct 1794

Regimental Field Officer Promotions: Major in 53rd Foot 28 Feb 1805
Brevets: Brevet Major 1 Apr 1801; Brevet Lieutenant Colonel 25 Apr 1814; Brevet Colonel 4 Jun 1814
Service 1793–1815: Served in West Indies 1797–1801, ADC to Trigge; served in France Apr 1814
Awards and Honours: Knight of the Royal and Military Order of St Louis (France)
Residence: Newcastle West, County Limerick
Died: Gers, Midi-Pyrénées, France 17 Jul 1817
This officer was actually promoted to major in 1814, but his promotion date was back-dated to Feb 1805. He was more commonly referred to as Terence MacMahon in British service
Sources: ARLI; FMPD; WEOF; <https://gw.geneanet.org/sderoux?lang=en&n=macmahon&p=gaspard+terence>

618. *John MANSELL (1805–1818)*

Born: Carmarthenshire 1778
Relations: Son of Sir William Mansell of Iscoed, 9th Bt, MP and Mary (Philipps); brother of Lieutenant General Robert Christopher Mansell; and Sir William Mansell, 10th Bt; father of Lieutenant Colonel George Pleydell Mansell, 53rd Foot
Entry to Army: Ensign in 53rd Foot Jan 1795
Regimental Field Officer Promotions: Major in 53rd Foot 22 Aug 1805 (vice Baillie) by exchange; Lieutenant Colonel in 53rd Foot 12 Feb 1818
Brevets: Brevet Lieutenant Colonel 1 Jan 1812
Service 1793–1815: Served in West Indies 1795–1800; served in East Indies 1809–1810; served in Peninsula Sep 1811 to Oct 1812, and Apr 1814
Retired: 7 Jun 1827
Awards and Honours: AGM (Sal Toul); CB 4 Jun 1815
Residence: Smedmore House, Kimmeridge, Dorset,
Died: Kimmeridge 29 Jan 1863
Sources: ANCB; ANCD; ARLI; CHAL; PHIL; WEOF; WO 24/747

619. *John JAMIESON (1805–1806)*

Born: Edinburgh 1769
Relations: Son of John Jamieson of Leith, merchant, and Christian (Cairns); father of Lieutenant Colonel Thomas Loughnan Jameson, Bombay service
Entry to Army: Lieutenant in 23rd Light Dragoons 1 Oct 1794
Regimental Field Officer Promotions: Major in 53rd Foot 28 Mar 1805 (vice Stewart) by purchase
Retired: 11 Dec 1806
Residence: Drummond Place, Edinburgh
Died: Edinburgh 16 Oct 1848
Sources: ANCB; ANCD; ANCW; ARLI

620. *Henry KNIGHT-ERSKINE (1806)*

Born: Aberdeenshire c.1780
Relations: Son of Lieutenant Colonel Henry Knight-Erskine of Pittodrie, 27th Foot, and Mary (Erskine); brother of Colonel William Howe Knight-Erskine, 27th Foot; and Lieutenant Augustus Pitt Knight, Bombay service
Entry to Army: Lieutenant in 72nd Foot 21 Aug 1794
Regimental Field Officer Promotions: Major in 53rd Foot 19 Sep 1805 (vice Cadogan) by purchase
Service 1793–1815: Served in East Indies 1805
Died: Kolkata, Bengal 3 Oct 1805
Sources: ARLI; SCMA (1806); WEOF

621. *Nigel KINGSCOTE (1806–1811)*

Born: Gloucestershire 1784
Relations: Son of Nigel Kingscote of Kingscote House and Maria (Clunes)
Entry to Army: Ensign in North Gloucestershire Militia; Ensign in 52nd Foot 14 Dec 1799
Regimental Field Officer Promotions: Major in 53rd Foot 11 Dec 1806 (vice Jamieson) by purchase; Lieutenant Colonel in 56th Foot 17 Oct 1811 (vice Prevost) by purchase; to half-pay of 56th Foot 25 Dec 1818
Service 1793–1815: Served in Peninsula Apr to Sep 1809, wounded at Talavera
Residence: Kingscote House, near Tetbury, Gloucestershire
Died: Kingscote House May 1825
Sources: ANCB; ANCD; ANCW; ARLI; CHAL; WEOF

622. *William Spencer THURSBY (1806–1813)*

Born: Northamptonshire 1769
Relations: Son of John Harvey Thursby of Abington MP and Ann (Hanbury); brother of Lieutenant John Harvey Thursby, 14th Light Dragoons
Education: Lincoln College, Oxford
Entry to Army: Ensign in 66th Foot 21 Jun 1789
Regimental Field Officer Promotions: Major in 53rd Foot 14 Aug 1806 (vice Erskine) by purchase
Brevets: Brevet Lieutenant Colonel 4 Jun 1813
Early Service: Served in West Indies 1789–1791
Service 1793–1815: Served East Indies 1805–1808; served in Peninsula Apr 1809 to Sep 1811
Retired: 26 Aug 1813

Residence: Northampton, Northamptonshire
Died: Northampton Dec 1827
Sources: ARLI; CHAL; GHLG; WO 25/748; Alumni Oxoniensis

623. *Jeffery PIERCY (1811–1817)*
Born: County Cork c.1784
Relations: Son of Jeffrey Piercy of Cork, merchant
Entry to Army: Ensign in 20th Foot Jun 1800
Regimental Field Officer Promotions: Major in 53rd Foot 13 Jun 1811 (vice Buckland)
Service 1793–1815: Served in East Indies 1805–1817
Died: Batavia 4 Jul 1817
Sources: ANCW; ARLI; FMPD; WEOF

624. *William INGLEBY (1810–1824)*
Born: Flintshire 1763
Relations: Son of Hugh Ingleby of Flint and Ann (Davies)
Entry to Army: Ensign in 58th Foot 4 Oct 1797 by purchase
Regimental Field Officer Promotions: Major in 53rd Foot 24 Oct 1811 (vice Kingscote) by purchase
Brevets: Brevet Lieutenant Colonel 12 Aug 1819
Service 1793–1815: Served in Minorca 1798; served in Egypt 1801; served in East Indies 1805–1814; served in Nepal 1814
Retired: 11 Mar 1824
Residences: Springfield, Flintshire; Chelsea, London
Died: Hammersmith, London 13 Nov 1843
Sources: ANCW; ARLI; GEMA (1844); WEOF

625. *Oliver George FEHRZEN (1813–1820)*
Born: Olaf Godlieb Fehrzen in Cape Colony 1784
Relations: Son of Hendrick Fehrzen of Cape Town, Commissioner of the Court of Civil and Petty Cases, and Anna Catharina (Blanckenburg); brother of Lieutenant James Fehrszen, 21st Light Dragoons
Entry to Army: Ensign in 39th Foot 17 Mar 1803 by purchase
Regimental Field Officer Promotions: Major in 53rd Foot 24 Dec 1813 (vice Thursby) by purchase; to half-pay of 53rd Foot 25 Dec 1817; Major in 53rd Foot 12 Feb 1818 (vice Mansell)
Brevets: Brevet Major 26 Aug 1813; Brevet Lieutenant Colonel 25 Dec 1817
Service 1793–1815: Served in Mediterranean 1805; served in Peninsula Apr 1809 to Apr 1814, wounded and POW at Salamanca, wounded at Nivelle; served in St Helena 1814–1817
Later Service: Served in East Indies 1818–1820
Died: Namakkai, Tamil Nadu, India 19 Jan 1820
Sources: ARLI; CHAL; WEOF; https://peek-01.livejournal.com/27727.html

Selected Regimental Histories
Moulsdale, J.R.B., *The King's Shropshire Light Infantry (The 53rd/85th Regiment of Foot)* (London: Leo Cooper, 1972)
Rogerson, William, *Historical Records of the 53rd, Shropshire, Regiment, now the 1st Battalion the King's, Shropshire Light Infantry* (Devonport: Simpkin, Marshall, Hamilton Kent & Co., 1890)

Regimental Museum
Soldiers of Shropshire Museum, Castle Court, Castle Street, Shrewsbury

---

54th Regiment of Foot

Secondary Title:	West Norfolk
Nicknames:	The Popinjays The Flamers
Jacket:	Red
Facings:	Popinjay green
Badge:	The Sphinx superscribed Egypt

Regimental Lineage, 54th Regiment of Foot

1755:	Raised in Salisbury by John Campbell, Marquess of Lorne as 56th Regiment of Foot
1756:	54th Regiment of Foot
1782:	54th (the West Norfolk) Regiment of Foot
1800:	May – 2nd Battalion formed in Winchester

1802:	May – 2nd Battalion disbanded in Gibraltar
1881:	2nd Battalion, The Dorsetshire Regiment (on amalgamation with the 39th (Dorsetshire) Regiment of Foot)
1951:	The Dorset Regiment
1958:	2nd Battalion, The Devonshire and Dorset Regiment (on amalgamation with The Devonshire Regiment)
2005:	The Devonshire and Dorset Light Infantry
2007:	1st Battalion, The Rifles (on amalgamation with 1st Battalion, Royal Gloucestershire, Berkshire and Wiltshire Light Infantry)

Service History, 1st Battalion 54th Regiment of Foot

1793:	Dover Castle and Purfleet; Apr – Guernsey; Sep – Petersfield; Oct – Southampton; Nov – to Flanders; to Guernsey due to storms
1794:	Guernsey; Netley; Southampton; May – to Flanders; Jun – Ostend; Jul – Alost; Malines; Sep – Boxtel; Dec – line of River Waal
1795:	Waal; retreat to Bremen; Apr – to England; Southampton; Jun – Lymington; Jul – to West Indies; Sep – St Vincent
1796:	St Vincent; Mt William; Aug – to England; Oct – Chelmsford
1797:	Chelmsford; Jun – drafted in St Vincent, cadre to England; Liverpool; to Ireland
1798:	Birr; Aug – Dublin
1799:	Nenagh; Roscrea; Limerick
1800:	Ireland; Mar – to England; Apr – Winchester; Jul – Southampton; Aug – Netley camp; to Mediterranean; Belle Isle; Ferrol; Sep – Gibraltar; Nov – Minorca; Dec – to Egypt
1801:	Bay of Marmorice [Marmaris]; Mar – EGYPT; Mandora; Lake Mareotis; Apr – siege of Alexandria; Aug – Marabout; to Minorca
1802:	Minorca; Feb – Gibraltar; put down mutiny
1803–1804:	Gibraltar
1805:	Gibraltar; Nov – to England; one ship and 129 men taken POW en route
1806:	Portsmouth; Bexhill; Feb – Colchester; Jul – Chelmsford; Aug – Faversham; Sep – Ospringe; two POW companies paroled at Cape of Good Hope; Dec – two companies to South America
1807:	To West Indies; Jun – two companies in Montevideo; Oct – other eight companies in Jamaica
1808–1810:	Jamaica (reduced to six companies)
1811:	Six service companies in Jamaica, four home companies in Yarmouth
1812:	Six service companies in Jamaica, four home companies in Ipswich; Mar – new companies raised in Ipswich; Nov – six companies in Woodbridge
1813:	Nive companies in Woodbridge; May – Colchester; Jun – Harwich; to Pomerania; Aug – Stralsund; Rostock; Oct – Jamaica service company remnants to England; Nov – Hanover companies to England, diverted to Antwerp
1814:	Feb – Merxcem; Mar – Antwerp; Dec – Jamaica companies to Belgium, battalion reunited in Nieuport [Nieuwpoort]
1815:	Nieuport; Feb – Ostend; Mar – Dixmuide; Apr – Courtrai [Kortijk]; Grammont; Jun – Hal (missed Waterloo); Jul – Paris; Allied Army of Occupation

Service History, 2nd Battalion 54th Regiment of Foot

1800:	May – formed from Irish militia recruits in Winchester; Aug – Netley camp; to Mediterranean; Belle Isle; Ferrol; Sep – Gibraltar; Nov – Minorca; Dec – to Egypt
1801:	Bay of Marmorice [Marmaris]; Mar – EGYPT; Mandora; Lake Mareotis; Apr – siege of Alexandria; Aug – Marabout; to Minorca
1802:	Minorca; Feb – Gibraltar; May – disbanded in Gibraltar

Establishments, 1st Battalion 54th Regiment of Foot

Year	Subunits	Field Off	Off/ Staff	Sjts	Mus	Corp/ Pvts	Total
Dec 1792	10co	3	32	22	12	430	499
Jan 1793	10co	3	32	32	22	600	689
Dec 1793	10co	3	32	42	22	850	949
Dec 1795	10co+2r	5	51	62	30	1,010	1,158
Jan 1798	10co	5	49	52	22	600	728
Mar 1800	10co	5	42	43	22	800	912
Dec 1800	10co	5	46	43	22	800	916
Jun 1802	10co	5	33	34	22	750	844
May 1803	10co	5	36	34	22	750	847
Dec 1804	10co	5	36	44	22	800	907
Jun 1805	10co	5	46	54	22	1,000	1,127
Dec 1806	10co	4	36	44	22	800	906
Dec 1807	10co	4	46	54	22	1,000	1,126
Dec 1808	10co	4	46	34	22	600	706
May 1809	10co+r	4	50	42	26	608	730
Dec 1809	10co	4	46	34	22	410	516
Dec 1811	10co	4	46	45	22	610	727
Dec 1812	10co	4	36	45	22	800	907
Dec 1813	10co+r	4	39	53	22	808	926
Dec 1815	10co	4	36	45	22	800	907

Establishments, 2nd Battalion 54th Regiment of Foot

Year	Subunits	Field Off	Off/ Staff	Sjts	Mus	Corp/ Pvts	Total
Dec 1800	10co	5	46	43	22	800	916

Service Statistics, 54th Regiment of Foot

	Lieutenant Colonels	Majors
Number of officers in period 1793–1815	7	18
Average age on appointment to substantive rank	34	35
Average time in rank in regiment (years)	8	3
Total field officers by nationality	15 E / 6 S / 6 I	
Demographics of other ranks 1803	92% I / 8% EW	
Demographics of other ranks 1807	82% I / 17% EW / 1% S	
Demographics of other ranks 1810	89% I / 11% EW	
Months of overseas service 1793–1815	1/54th: 197 2/54th: 21	

Significant Militia/Volunteer Intakes

1800: County Antrim, County Carlow, County Clare, County Limerick, County Louth, County Mayo, County Roscommon, County Tipperary
1805: Warwickshire, Glamorganshire, County Fermanagh, King's County
1806: County Leitrim
1808: Lanarkshire
1810: County Galway
1811: East Norfolk, West Norfolk, Stirlingshire
1812: East Norfolk, County Galway, County Leinster, County Meath
1813: County Galway, County Meath

Regimental Colonels

626. *Marescoe FREDERICK (1770–1801)*
Born: London 1725
Relations: Son of Sir Thomas Frederick, Kt, Governor of Fort St George in Madras, and Mary (Moncrieff); brother of Sir John Frederick, 4th Bt; and Sir Charles Frederick, 7th Bt; father of Lieutenant Colonel Thomas Frederick, unattached; Lieutenant Colonel Robert Frederick, 55th Foot; and Lieutenant Charles Frederick, 54th Foot
Entry to Army: Ensign in 3rd Foot Guards c.1745
Regimental Field Officer Promotions: Captain and Lieutenant Colonel in 3rd Foot Guards 11 Jun 1753 by purchase
Brevets: Brevet Colonel 15 Jan 1762; Major General 30 Apr 1770; Lieutenant General 29 Aug 1777; General 12 Oct 1793
Colonelcies: 75th Foot 15 Jan 1762; 54th Foot 30 Apr 1770 (vice Parslow)
Residence: Walcot, Somerset
Died: Walcot 24 Apr 1801
Sources: ANCB; ANCD; ARLI; <https://www.seekingmyroots.com/members/files/G002431.pdf>

627. *Rt Hon. Sir David BAIRD, 1st Bt (1801–1807)*
Born: Haddingtonshire 1757
Relations: Son of William Baird, merchant of Newbyth and Alicia (Johnston)
Entry to Army: Ensign in 2nd Foot 14 Dec 1772 by purchase
Regimental Field Officer Promotions: Major in 71st Foot 5 Jun 1787; Lieutenant Colonel in 71st Foot 8 Dec 1790
Brevets: Brevet Colonel 21 Aug 1795; Brigadier General (Cape of Good Hope) Dec 1797; Major General 18 Jun 1798; Lieutenant General 30 Oct 1805; General 4 Jun 1814
Colonelcies: 54th Foot 8 May 1801 (vice Frederick); 24th Foot 19 Jul 1807 (vice Whyte)
Early Service: Served in Gibraltar 1773–1776; served in India 1780–1787; severely wounded, POW and held in chains at Seringapatam 1780–1784; served in India 1791–1793; commanded brigade at capture of Seringapatam 1792
Service 1793–1815: Served in India 1793–1795; served at Cape of Good Hope and commanded brigade Dec 1795 to Jun 1798; commanded brigade at capture of Seringapatam 1799; commanded Anglo-Indian column in Egypt 1801; taken POW when returning to England 1803; Commander in Chief at re-capture of Cape Colony Jan 1806; Military Governor of Cape Colony 10 Jan 1806 to 17 Jan 1807; Commander in Chief at invasion of Buenos Aires 1806; commanded brigade at Copenhagen 1807; commanded Curragh camp Aug 1808; commanded division and lost left arm at Corunna 1808–1809
Later Service: Governor of Kinsale 1819; Commander in Chief in Ireland 1820–1822
Creations and Dignities: 1st Baronet of Newbyth 13 Apr 1810
Awards and Honours: Knight Bachelor 19 Jun 1804; KB 15 Oct 1808; GCB 2 Jan 1815
PC 1820; PC (Ire) 1821
Residences: Newbyth, near Whitekirk, Haddingtonshire; Whitekirk, near East Linton, Haddingtonshire; Ferntower House, Crieff, Perthshire
Died: Ferntower House 29 Aug 1829
Sources: ARLI; DINB; PHIL; WEOF; WO 25/744; WOST

628. *Oliver Anthony NICOLLS (1807–1808)*
Born: County Wexford 1742
Relations: Son of Jasper Nicolls of Duncannon Fort and Mary (Darby); brother of Colonel Gustavus Nicolls of East Farleigh, 1st Foot; father of Lieutenant Colonel George Green Nicolls, 1st Dragoon Guards; uncle of Lieutenant General Sir Jasper Nicolls
Entry to Army: Ensign in 1/1st Foot 22 Nov 1756 by purchase
Regimental Field Officer Promotions: Major in 1/1st Foot 14 Mar 1781 by purchase; Lieutenant Colonel in 1st Foot 5 Feb 1787; Lieutenant Colonel in 45th Foot 31 Mar 1787 (vice Dundas) by exchange
Brevets: Brevet Colonel 1 Mar 1794; Brigadier General (West Indies) 25 Dec 1794; Major General 3 May 1796; Lieutenant General 25 Sep 1803; General 4 Jun 1813
Colonelcies: 4th West India Regiment 20 May 1795; 54th Foot 19 Jul 1807 (vice Baird); 66th Foot 3 Aug 1808 (vice Clanricarde)
Early Service: Served at Gibraltar 1768; served in West Indies 1780–1783; commanded 45th Foot in West Indies 1787–1794
Service 1793–1815: Commanded forces in Grenada 1792–1794; Quartermaster General in West Indies 1795; Commander in Chief Bombay 22 Jan 1801 to Feb 1807 (vice Stuart)
Residence: Chichester, Sussex
Died: Chichester Dec 1829
Sources: ANCB; ANCD; ANCW; ARLI; PHIL; WEOF; WO 25/747

629. *Hon. Edward FINCH (1808–1809)*
Born: London 1756
Relations: Son of Heneage Finch, 3rd Earl of Aylesford and Lady Charlotte (Seymour); cousin of Charles, 4th Duke of Rutland
Education: Westminster School; Trinity College, Cambridge (BA 1777)
Entry to Army: Cornet in 11th Light Dragoons 27 Dec 1778 by purchase
Regimental Field Officer Promotions: Captain and Lieutenant Colonel in Coldstream Foot Guards 3 Oct 1792 (vice Fitzgerald) by purchase; Second Major in Coldstream Foot Guards 9 Nov 1800 (vice Lambart); First Major in Coldstream Foot Guards 18 Jun 1801 (vice Lambart)
Brevets: Brevet Colonel 3 May 1796; Major General 1 Jan 1801; Lieutenant General 25 Apr 1808; General 12 Aug 1819
Colonelcies: 54th Foot 3 Aug 1808 (vice Nicolls); 22nd Foot 18 Sep 1809 (vice Craig)
Early Service: Served in West Indies and North America 1780–1782
Service 1793–1815: Served in Flanders 1793–1795; served in Irish rebellion 1798; commanded 1/Coldstream Foot Guards in Netherlands 1799; commanded cavalry brigade in Egypt 1801; Groom of Bedchamber to King George III 1802; commanded Brigade of Guards in Copenhagen 1807
Political Career: MP (Cambridge) 1789–1819
Residences: Meriden, near Solihull, Warwickshire
Died: Meriden 27 Oct 1843
Sources: ANCB; ANCD; ARLI; DINB; HPON; PHIL; WEOF; WO 25/745

630. *Rt Hon. James Ochonar Forbes, 17th Baron, Lord FORBES (1809–1816)*
Born: Aberdeen 1765
Relations: Son of James Forbes, 16th Baron Forbes, and Catherine (Innes); father of Captain and Lieutenant Colonel Hon. James Forbes, Coldstream Foot Guards
Entry to Army: Ensign in Coldstream Foot Guards 13 Jun 1781 by purchase
Regimental Field Officer Promotions: Captain and Lieutenant Colonel in Coldstream Foot Guards 28 Aug 1793 (vice Eld)
Brevets: Brevet Colonel 3 May 1796; Major General 29 Apr 1802; Lieutenant General 25 Apr 1808; General 12 Aug 1819
Colonelcies: 3rd Garrison Battalion 19 Jul 1807 (vice Maitland); 94th Foot 14 Apr 1809 (vice Dundas); 54th Foot 10 Sep 1809 (vice Finch); 21st Foot 1 Jun 1816 (vice Gordon)
Service 1793–1815: Served in Flanders 1793–1795; served in Helder 1799; second in command of forces in Mediterranean Mar 1808
Creations and Dignities: 17th Baron Forbes 29 Jul 1804
Awards and Honours: Knight of the Illustrious Royal Order of Saint Januarius (Two Sicilies)
Residence: Corse Castle, near Lumphanan, Aberdeenshire
Died: Bregenz, Vorarlberg, Austria 4 May 1843
Sources: ARLI; DINB; PHIL; WEOF

Colonel Commandant

631. *Rt Hon. Sir John Francis CRADOCK [CARADOC], 1st Baron Howden (2nd Battalion) (1801–1803)*
See 316.
Colonel Commandant of 2/54th Foot 8 May 1801

Lieutenant Colonels

632. *William Goodday STRUTT (1792–1800)*
Born: Essex 1762
Relations: Son of John Strutt of Terling Place and Anne (Goodday)
Entry to Army: Ensign in 61st Foot 23 May 1778 by purchase
Field Officer Promotions: Major in 3/60th Foot 24 Sep 1787; Lieutenant Colonel in 3/60th Foot 18 Nov 1790 (vice McArthur) by purchase; Lieutenant Colonel in 54th Foot 4 Apr 1792 (vice Bruce)
Brevets: Brevet Major 9 Aug 1783; Brevet Colonel 21 Aug 1795; Brigadier General (West Indies) 9 Sep 1795; Major General 23 Jun 1798
Early Service: Served in Minorca 1778; served in West Indies 1780–1781; served in Gibraltar 1782–1783; served in West Indies 1787–1791
Service 1793–1815: Served in Flanders 1793–1795; served in West Indies 1795–1796, lost left leg on St. Vincent; Governor of Québec City Apr 1800 to Feb 1848 (mostly as a sinecure)
Residence: Tofts, Little Baddow, Essex
Died: Tofts 5 Feb 1848
Sources: ANCW; ARLI; DINB; GEMA (1848); PHIL; WEOF; WOST

633. *Christopher DARBY (1795–1814)*
Born: Buckinghamshire 1758
Relations: Son of Jonathan Darby of Leap Castle and Soulbury, and Susannah (Lovett); brother of Admiral Sir Henry D'Esterre Darby RN
Entry to Army: Ensign in 33rd Foot 26 Nov 1775 by purchase

Field Officer Promotions: Major in 54th Foot 2 May 1794 (vice Wollaston); Lieutenant Colonel in 54th Foot 1 Sep 1795
Brevets: Brevet Major 1 Mar 1794; Brevet Colonel 25 Sep 1803; Brigadier General (Jamaica) 8 Nov 1806; Major General 25 Jul 1810; Lieutenant General 4 Jun 1814
Early Service: Served in American War of Independence 1775–1783; served in British North America 1784–1791
Service 1793–1815: Served in Flanders 1794–1795; served in West Indies 1795–1796; commanded 1/54th Foot 1798–1805; served in Ferrol 1800; served in Egypt 1801; served in Jamaica 1807–1810
Later Service: Commandant of Limerick District 1814–1832
Residence: Limerick, County Limerick
Died: Limerick 10 Jan 1832
Sources: ANCB; ARLI; GEMA (1832); PHIL; WEOF; WO 25/745

634. *John Thomas LAYARD (1800–1815)*

Born: Huntingdonshire 1753
Relations: Son of Sir Daniel Pierre Reymond Layard M.D., and Suzanna Henriette (Chevalleau de Boisragon); brother of Lieutenant General Anthony Lewis Layard
Entry to Army: Ensign in 54th Foot 21 Jun 1772 by purchase
Field Officer Promotions: Major in 54th Foot 1 Sep 1795 (vice Darby); Lieutenant Colonel in 54th Foot 16 May 1800; removed from the regiment as a general officer 1815
Brevets: Brevet Major 1 Mar 1794; Brevet Lieutenant Colonel 1 Jan 1798; Brevet Colonel 25 Apr 1808; Brigadier General (West Indies) 25 Dec 1809; Major General 4 Jun 1811; Lieutenant General 19 Jul 1821
Early Service: Served in American War of Independence 1775–1779; served in West Indies 1781–1783; served in Grenada 1787–1792
Service 1793–1815: Served in St. Vincent 1795–1796; commanded 54th Foot in Egypt 1801; served in Malta and Sicily 1803–1805; served in Jamaica 1807–1808; Governor of Curaçao 20 May 1809 to 18 Jun 1811
Later Service: Acting Governor and Commander in Chief Malta 27 Jun 1815 to 18 Sep 1815; 19 Feb 1816 to 14 May 1817; 26 Jun 1817 to 26 Sep 1817; and 2 Dec 1818 to 4 Oct 1819
Residence: Walcot St Swithin, Somerset
Died: Bath, Somerset 22 May 1828
Sources: ANCB; ANCD: ARLI; GEMA (1828); PHIL; WEOF; WOST

635. *Hon. William BLIGH (1800–1802)*

Born: Kent 1775
Relations: Son of John Bligh, 3rd Earl of Darnley and Mary (Stoyte); brother of General Hon. Edward Bligh; brother-in-law of General Charles William Vane-Stewart, Marquess of Londonderry; son-in-law of John Stewart, 7th Earl of Galloway
Education: Eton College
Entry to Army: Cornet in 10th Light Dragoons 24 Feb 1793
Regimental Field Officer Promotions: Major in 26th Light Dragoons 10 May 1799 (vice Ditcher) by purchase; Lieutenant Colonel in 54th Foot 30 Jul 1800 (vice Strutt) by purchase; to half-pay25 Jul 1802; Lieutenant Colonel in 14th Foot 16 Aug 1804
Service 1793–1815: Commanded 2/14th Foot 1804–1806
Retired: 12 Jun 1806
Residence: Bryanston Square, Marylebone, London; Upper Seymour Street, Portman Square, London
Died: Brighton, Sussex 8 Aug 1845
Sources: ANCB; ANCD; ARLI; BUPE; WEOF

636. *Sir Neil CAMPBELL, Kt (1808–1811)*

See 337.
Major in 54th Foot 20 Feb 1806 (vice Pye); Lieutenant Colonel in 54th Foot 20 Jun 1808

637. *William Samuel CURREY (1809–1812)*

Born: Kent 1770
Relations: Son of Rev. John Currey of Dartford and Mary (Eliott); brother of Major John Currey, 6th Foot; and Colonel Sir Edmund Currey RA
Entry to Army: Ensign in 53rd Foot 29 Mar 1793
Field Officer Promotions: Major in 54th Foot 26 Dec 1805; Lieutenant Colonel in 54th Foot 13 Jul 1809
Brevets: Brevet Major 25 Aug 1803
Service 1793–1815: Deputy Quartermaster General in British North America 25 Aug 1803; commanded 54th Foot 1809–1811
Retired: 26 Nov 1812
Residence: Lismore Castle, Lismore, County Waterford
Died: Lismore Castle 17 Feb 1840
Sources: ANCB; ANCD; ARLI; PHIL; WEOF

638. *Rt Hon. John James, 6th Earl WALDEGRAVE (1812–1819)*

Born: Somerset 1785
Relations: Son of George Waldegrave, 4th Earl

Waldegrave and Lady Elizabeth (Waldegrave); brother of Lieutenant Edward William Waldegrave, RN; and Vice Admiral William Waldegrave RN, 8th Earl Waldegrave
Education: Eton College
Entry to Army: Ensign in 3rd Foot Guards 27 May 1802 by purchase
Regimental Field Officer Promotions: Major in 8th Garrison Battalion 9 Jun 1808 (vice Bayley) by purchase; Major in 72nd Foot 20 Mar 1808 (vice Tucker) by exchange; Major in 15th Light Dragoons 25 Jul 1809 (vice Leitch) by exchange; Major in 12th Light Dragoons 13 Mar 1812 (vice Wyndham); Lieutenant Colonel in 54th Foot 26 Nov 1812 (vice Currey) by purchase; to half-pay of 98th Foot 17 Jun 1819
Service 1793–1815: Served in Peninsula Jul to Dec 1812; commanded 54th Foot 1812–1815 and in Waterloo campaign
Creations and Dignities: 6th Earl Waldegrave 29 Jun 1794
Awards and Honours: WatM 23 Apr 1816
Residences: Navestock Hall, near Brentwood, Essex; Strawberry Hill House, Twickenham, Middlesex
Died: Strawberry Hill House 31 Jul 1835
Sources: ANCB; ANCD; ARLI; CHAL; DALT; OFBE; PHIL; WEOF

Majors

639. *John Peter ADDENBROOKE (1792–1793)*

Born: London 1754
Relations: Son of William Addenbrooke of St Clement, grocer, and Mary Lucy (de Varennes)
Entry to Army: Ensign in 57th Foot 28 Aug 1775 by purchase
Regimental Field Officer Promotions: Major in 54th Foot 30 Nov 1792 (vice Fitzgerald) by purchase
Service 1793-1815: Gentleman Usher to Queen Charlotte 1814–1817; Equerry to Princess Charlotte
Retired: 14 Nov 1793
Residence: Versailles, Yvelines, France
Died: Versailles 9 Sep 1821
Was apprenticed to a merchant tailor in London in 1768
Sources: ANCB; ANCD; ARLI; GEMA (1821)

640. *Hon. Sir Edward PAGET (1793–1794)*

Born: Staffordshire 1775
Relations: Son of Henry Bayly (Paget), 1st Earl of Uxbridge and Jane (Champagné); brother of Field Marshal Hon. Henry William Paget, Earl of Uxbridge; Major Hon. Berkeley Thomas Paget, 7th Hussars; Admiral Hon. Charles Paget RN; and Captain Hon. William Paget RN; son-in-law of William, 1st Baron Bagot; son-in-law of George Legge, 3rd Earl of Dartmouth; brother-in-law of Lieutenant General Josiah Champagné; and Lieutenant General Forbes Champagné
Education: Westminster School; Dresden University
Entry to Army: Cornet and Sub-Lieutenant in 1st Life Guards 23 Mar 1792 by purchase
Field Officer Promotions: Major in 54th Foot 14 Nov 1793 (vice Addenbrooke) by purchase; Lieutenant Colonel in 28th Foot 30 Apr 1794 (vice Kingston) by purchase
Brevets: Brevet Colonel 1 Jan 1798; Brigadier General (Ireland) Oct 1803; Major General 1 Jan 1805; Lieutenant General (Portugal) 12 Apr 1809; Lieutenant General 4 Jun 1811; General 27 May 1825
Colonelcies: 80th Foot 25 Feb 1808 (vice Lake); 28th Foot 26 Dec 1815 (vice Prescott)
Early Service: Commander in Chief in India 1822–1825; commanded forces in Burma 1824–1825; Governor of Royal Military College 1826–1837; Governor of Chelsea Hospital 1837–1849
Service 1793–1815: Served in Flanders 1793–1795; ADC to King George III 1 Jan 1798; served in Minorca 1798; served and wounded in Egypt 1801; served in Sweden 1808; served in Peninsula Sep 1808 to Jan 1809, commanded reserved division at Corunna; served in Peninsula May and Jun 1809, lost right arm at Oporto 12 May 1809; commanded 1st Division in Peninsula Oct 1812; POW 17 Nov 1812 to Apr 1814
Later Service: Groom of the Bedchamber 1816–1822; Governor of Cowes Castle 1818–1826; Governor of Ceylon 2 Feb to 6 Nov 1822; Commander in Chief in India 1822–1825; Governor of Royal Military Academy Sandhurst 1826–1837; Governor of Royal Hospital, Chelsea 1837–1849
Political Career: MP (Caernarvon Boroughs) 1796–1806; MP (Milborne Port) 1810–1820
Awards and Honours: KB 12 Jun 1812; AGM (Cor); GCB 2 Jan 1815
Residences: Cowes Castle, Isle of Wight
Died: Cowes 13 May 1849
Purchased all his promotions from cornet to lieutenant colonel in a little over two years, just before the Duke of York introduced minimum time in rank requirements
Sources: ARLI; CHAL; DINB; HALL; HPON; PHIL; WEOF; WOST; WO 25/747

641. *Frederick William WOLLASTON (1794)*

Born: Suffolk 1762
Relations: Son of Rev. Frederick Wollaston of Bury St Edmunds and Priscilla Lambert (Ottley); brother of Lieutenant Colonel George Wollaston, Suffolk Militia, and Vice Admiral Charles Wollaston RN
Entry to Army: Cornet in 7th Light Dragoons 18 Dec 1779 by purchase
Regimental Field Officer Promotions: Major in 54th Foot May 1794 (vice Paget) by purchase; Lieutenant Colonel in 22nd Light Dragoons 1 May 1794
Brevets: Brevet Colonel 1 Jan 1800
Retired: 3 Dec 1800
Awards and Honours: Deputy Lieutenant of Leicestershire; High Sheriff of Leicestershire 1806–1807
Residence: Shenton Hall, Shenton, Leicestershire
Died: London 15 Aug 1849
Sources: ANCB; ANCD; ANCW; ARLI; PEER

642. *Robert Alexander MONTGOMERY (1795–1798)*

Born: County Down c.1758
Relations: Of the Montgomerys of Grey Abbey; brother of Lieutenant Frederick Hamilton Montgomery, Marines
Entry to Army: Ensign in 54th Foot 26 Nov 1775
Regimental Field Officer Promotions: Major in 54th Foot 1 Sep 1795
Died: Limerick, County Limerick Oct 1798
Sources: ANCW; FMPW

643. *Robert GARDEN (1799–1802)*

See 360.
Maj in 54th Foot 5 Jan 1799 (vice Montgomery); to half-pay of 54th Foot 25 Jul 1802

644. *Thomas DIGBY (1800–1802)*

Born: County Kildare c.1753
Relations: Son of Rev. Benjamin Digby of Geashill and Mary (Jones); uncle of Lieutenant Colonel Dunlop Rigby, 65th Foot
Entry to Army: Ensign in 46th Foot 15 Aug 1775 by purchase
Regimental Field Officer Promotions: Major in 54th Foot 16 May 1800 (vice Layard); Major in 5th Foot 22 Oct 1802 (vice Bellew) by exchange
Brevets: Brevet Major 1 Mar 1794; Brevet Lieutenant Colonel 1 Jan 1798
Retired: 24 Oct 1802
Residences: Kensington, Middlesex; St Stephen's Green, Dublin
Died: Dublin Jun 1817
Sources: ANCB; ANCD; ANCW; ARLI

645. *Andrew ROSS (1800–1803)*

Born: Wigtownshire 1773
Relations: Son of Rev. Andrew Ross of Balsarroch and Elizabeth (Corsane); brother of polar explorer Admiral Sir John Ross RN; father of Major General James Kerr Ross
Entry to Army: Ensign in 60th Foot 26 Aug 1783 by purchase
Field Officer Promotions: Major (unattached) 12 Jun 1794; to half-pay of Reay Fencibles 1797; Major in 54th Foot 17 May 1800 (vice Garden); Lieutenant Colonel in 70th Foot 8 Oct 1803 (vice Nicoll)
Brevets: Brevet Lieutenant Colonel 1 Jan 1800; Brevet Colonel 25 Oct 1809
Service 1793–1815: Commanded 2/54th Foot in Egypt 1801; commanded on Sainte Croix 1807; acting Lieutenant Governor of Demerara-Essequibo 24 Jun 1808 to 3 Apr 1809; ADC to King George III 27 Oct 1809; commander of British forces in Cartagena 1812
Died: Of fever in Cartagena, Colombia 26 Sep 1812
Sources: ANCW; ARLI; DINB; WEOF; WOST

646. *Frederick Peter DELMÉ (1800–1802)*

Born: London 1775
Relations: Son of Peter Delmé MP and Lady Elizabeth (Howard); brother of Lieutenant William Delmé, 68th Foot; grandson of Henry Howard, 4th Earl of Carlisle; cousin of Major Hon. Frederick Howard, 10th Hussars
Entry to Army: Ensign in 2nd Foot 20 Jun 1792 by purchase
Regimental Field Officer Promotions: Major in 103rd Foot 18 Sep 1794; to half-pay of 103rd Foot 1796; Major in 54th Foot 18 May 1800
Brevets: Brevet Lieutenant Colonel 1 Jan 1800
Retired: 25 Mar 1802
Residence: Paris, Île-de-France, France
Died: Paris 4 Oct 1830
Sources: ANCB; ANCD; ARLI; WikiTree

647. *John Granby CLAY (1800–1802)*

Born: Nottinghamshire 1767
Relations: Son of William Clay of Southwell and Jemima (Pelham); brother of Major General William Waldegrave Pelham Clay
Entry to Army: Ensign in Independent Company 6 Nov 1782
Regimental Field Officer Promotions: Major in

105th Foot 16 Sep 1795; to half-pay of 105th Foot 1795; Major in 54th Foot 19 May 1800; to half-pay of 54th Foot 25 Jul 1802; Major in 3rd Foot 9 Jul 1803; to half-pay of 24th Light Dragoons 15 May 1806 (vice Monckton) by exchange
Brevets: Brevet Lieutenant Colonel 1 Jan 1801; Brevet Colonel 25 Jul 1810; Major General 4 Jun 1813; Lieutenant General 27 May 1825; General 23 Nov 1841
Early Service: Served in West Indies 1786; served in West Indies 1790–1793
Service 1793–1815: Served in Leeward Islands 1794; served in Irish Rebellion 1798; served in Egypt 1801; Assistant Inspector General of Additional Force Jun 1804; Inspecting Field Officer of Manchester recruiting district Nov 1805; commander of Norman Cross prison camp Jun 1813 to Sep 1814
Residence: Exeter, Devon
Died: Exeter 13 Dec 1846
Sources: ANCD; ANCD; ANCW; ARLI; PHIL; WEOF; WO 25/744

648. *Sir William WILLIAMS (1802–1803)*

Born: London 1776
Relations: Son of Thomas Williams of Marylebone and Mary (Rudd); father of Cornet George Bigoe Williams, 16th Lancers; and Captain Thomas Bigoe Williams, 4th Dragoon Guards; cousin of General Sir Andrew Francis Barnard
Entry to Army: Ensign in 54th Foot 1 Aug 1792 by purchase
Regimental Field Officer Promotions: Major in 54th Foot 24 Jun 1802 (vice Delmé) by purchase; Major in 16th Battalion of Reserve 9 Jul 1803; Major in 81st Foot 26 Oct 1804 (vice Sharpe) by exchange; Lieutenant Colonel in 1/60th Foot 15 Nov 1809; Lieutenant Colonel in 13th Foot 25 Jun 1812 (vice Keane) by exchange; to half-pay in Portuguese service 4 Oct 1821
Brevets: Brevet Colonel 12 Aug 1819; Major General 22 Jul 1830
Service 1793–1815: Served in Flanders 1793–1794; served in West Indies 1795–1796; served in Irish Rebellion 1798; served in Ferrol 1800; served in Egypt 1801; served in Peninsula with 81st Foot Nov 1808 to Jan 1809; commanded 5/60th Foot and composite light battalions in Peninsula Jun 1810 to Jul 1812, wounded four times; commanded 13th Foot 1812–1815; trained 13th Foot in light infantry tactics in British North America 1814–1815
Awards and Honours: KTS 11 Mar 1813; AGM (Cor FDO CR Bad Sal); KCB 4 Dec 1815
Residence: Marlborough Buildings, Bath, Somerset
Died: Bath 17 Jun 1832
Sources: ANCB; ANCW; CHAL; PHIL; WEOF; WO 25/748; The Annual Biography and Obituary for the Year 1833

649. *Patrick Edward BELLEW (1802–1804)*

Born: County Cork c.1766
Relations: Son of Major General Patrick Bellew of Ballendiness and Sarah (Pratt); brother of Lieutenant Christopher Bellew, Bengal service; Captain Francis John Bellew; and Captain Henry Walter Bellew, Bengal service
Entry to Army: Ensign in 5th Foot 23 Jan 1794 by purchase
Regimental Field Officer Promotions: Major in 5th Foot 16 Jul 1800 (vice Bunbury) by purchase; Major in 54th Foot 22 Oct 1802 (vice Digby) by exchange
Service 1793–1815: Served in Helder 1799
Died: Gibraltar 15 Apr 1804
Sources: ARLI; GHLG; WEOF

650. *Alleyne Hampden PYE (1804–1806)*

See 52.
Major in 54th Foot 23 Nov 1804 (vice Bellew)

651. *William CLUNES (1809–1811)*

Born: Sutherland 1774
Relations: Son of Colonel Gordon Clunes of Crakaig and Anne (Gordon)
Entry to Army: Ensign in 50th Foot 18 Aug 1790
Regimental Field Officer Promotions: Major in 54th Foot 20 Jul 1809 (vice Currey)
Brevets: Served in Peninsula Aug 1808 to Jan 1809, wounded at Corunna; served in Walcheren 1809
Retired: 31 Oct 1811
Residences: Torrish, Sutherland
Died: Crakaig, Sutherland 24 Nov 1830
Sources: ANCB; ARLI; BLEM (1831); CHAL; WEOF; Set Adrift Upon the World: The Sutherland Clearances

652. *Allen KELLY (1811–1829)*

Born: King's County c.1781
Relations: Son of Burrows Kelly of Portarlington and Eleanor (unk.)
Entry to Army: Ensign in 54th Foot 1 Nov 1797 by purchase
Regimental Field Officer Promotions: Major in 54th Foot 31 Oct 1811 (vice Clunes); Lieutenant Colonel unattached 8 Jun 1826; Lieutenant Colonel in 54th Foot 1 Oct 1829 (vice Grant)
Brevets: Brevet Lieutenant Colonel 12 Aug 1819
Service 1793–1815: Served in Belgium 1815
Retired: 24 Dec 1829

Awards and Honours: WatM 23 Apr 1816
Residence: Millgrove, near Bracknagh, King's County
Died: Millgrove 11 Sep 1848
Sources: ARLI; DALT; FMPD; PHIL; WEOF

Selected Regimental Histories
Anon., *Records of the 54th West Norfolk Regiment* (India: Printed at the Thomason Civil Engineering College Press, 1881)

Regimental Museum
The Keep Military Museum, Barrack Road, Dorchester, Dorset

55th Regiment of Foot

Secondary Title:	Westmoreland
Nicknames:	The Two Fives The Cattle Reavers
Jacket:	Red
Facings:	Dark green

Regimental Lineage, 55th Regiment of Foot

1755:	Dec – raised in Scotland by Colonel George Perry as 57th Regiment of Foot
1756:	55th Regiment of Foot
1782:	55th (Westmoreland) Regiment of Foot
1881:	2nd Battalion, The Border Regiment (on amalgamation with the 34th (Cumberland) Regiment of Foot)
1959:	The King's Own Royal Border Regiment (on amalgamation with the King's Own Royal Regiment (Lancaster))
2006:	3rd Battalion, Duke of Lancaster's Regiment (King's Lancashire and Border) (on amalgamation with the King's Regiment and the Queen's Lancashire Regiment)

Service History, 55th Regiment of Foot

1793:	Londonderry; Coleraine; Nov – flank companies to Belgium; Ostend; Dec – flank companies to West Indies
1794:	Mar – flank companies in Martinique; St Lucia; Jun – Guadeloupe; Oct – taken POW at Berville, ceased to exist May – battalion companies to Flanders; Linselles; Oct – Nijmegen; Dec – line of River Waal
1795:	Waal; retreat to Bremen; Mar – Bremen; Apr – to England; May – Harwich; Jun – Sunderland; Aug – Cowpens camp; Oct – Southampton; to West Indies, caught in storms
1796:	In Channel; Feb – to West Indies; Apr – St Lucia; Morne Fortunée
1797:	St Lucia; May – Martinique; to England; Aug – Horsham
1798:	Horsham; Jun – Winchester; Nov – Eling
1799:	Eling; Jul – Portsmouth; Aug – Barham Downs camp; to Helder; Groet-Keeten; Sep – Zuyper-Sluis; Bergen; Egmont-op-Zoom; Oct – Castricum; Alkmaar; Nov – to England; Yarmouth; Shorncliffe; Dec – Whitstable and Herne Bay
1800:	Canterbury; May – Brighton, Shoreham and Uckfield; Portsmouth; Jun – Hilsea; Jul – Guernsey
1801:	Guernsey; Aug – Lewes; Oct – Silverhill
1802:	Silverhill; Apr – Portsmouth; to West Indies; Jul – Jamaica; Maroon Town
1803:	Jamaica; Trelawney
1804–1807:	Jamaica
1808:	Jamaica; May – three companies put down mutiny of 2nd West India Regiment

1809: Jamaica; Jun – flank companies in expedition to St Domingue
1810: Jamaica; four companies sent home to Carlisle
1811: Six service companies in Jamaica, four home companies in Carlisle; Aug – quelled Maroon riots
1812: Six service companies in Jamaica, four home companies in Carlisle; May – additional two service companies in Carlisle; Oct – six home companies in Newcastle-upon-Tyne; North Shields; Dec – Chatham
1813: Service companies in Jamaica formed into one company, home companies in Canterbury; May – service company remnants ordered home, home companies in Colchester; Aug – Windsor; Nov – Greenwich; to Netherlands; Dec – Tholen
1814: Feb – Merxcem; Mar – Bergen-op-Zoom, battalion captured but colours saved; Jun – to England; Yarmouth
1815: Harwich; Apr – Chelmsford; Jul – Strand Bridge; Oct – Brighton

Establishments, 55th Regiment of Foot

Year	Subunits	Field Off	Off/ Staff	Sjts	Mus	Corp/ Pvts	Total
Dec 1792	10co	3	32	22	12	430	499
Jan 1793	10co	3	32	32	22	600	689
Apr 1794	12co	3	38	50	26	990	1,107
Jun 1795	10co	3	32	42	22	850	949
Dec 1795	10co+2r	5	51	62	30	1,010	1,158
Dec 1797	10co	5	38	53	22	600	718
Aug 1799	11co	5	38	58	24	660	785
Dec 1800	10co	5	46	43	22	800	916
Dec 1802	10co	5	43	34	22	750	854
May 1803	10co	5	46	34	22	750	857
Dec 1804	10co	5	46	44	22	800	917
Dec 1806	10co	4	46	44	22	800	916
Dec 1807	10co	4	46	34	22	600	706
May 1809	10co+r	4	50	42	26	608	730
Dec 1809	10co	4	46	34	22	410	516
Dec 1811	10co	4	46	45	22	610	727
Dec 1812	10co	4	35	35	22	600	696
Dec 1813	10co+r	4	38	43	22	608	715
Dec 1814	10co	4	35	35	22	600	696
Dec 1815	10co	4	36	35	22	600	697

Service Statistics, 55th Regiment of Foot

	Lieutenant Colonels	Majors
Number of officers in period 1793–1815	7	20
Average age on appointment to substantive rank	32.5	35
Average time in rank in regiment (years)	7	2.5
Total field officers by nationality	11 S / 5 E / 5 I / 3 A / 2 F	
Demographics of other ranks 1801	50% EW / 43% I / 6% S / 1% F	
Demographics of other ranks 1808	48% I / 40% EW / 10% S / 2% F	
Demographics of other ranks 1815	69% EW / 20% S / 11% I	
Months of overseas service 1793–1815	180	

Significant Militia/Volunteer Intakes

1799: Cheshire, East Essex, Herefordshire, 1st Lancashire, 4th Lancashire, Northamptonshire, East Yorkshire, County Antrim
1800: King's County, County Limerick
1806: Cambridgeshire
1811: Cumberland, Westmoreland, Berwickshire, Dumfriesshire
1812: North Cork

Regimental Colonels

653. *Anthony Loftus TOTTENHAM (1791–1811)*

Born: County Wexford c.1723
Relations: Son of Charles Tottenham of Tottenham Green, MP, and Ellinor (Cliffe); brother of Sir John Tottenham, 1st Bt
Entry to Army: Lieutenant in 33rd Foot 16 Apr 1747
Regimental Field Officer Promotions: Major in 52nd Foot 11 Mar 1760; Lieutenant Colonel in 122nd Foot 13 Feb 1762
Brevets: Brevet Colonel 29 Aug 1777; Major General 19 Oct 1781; Lieutenant General 12 Oct 1793; General 1 Jan 1798
Colonelcies: 90th Foot 25 Nov 1777; 55th Foot 9 Nov 1791 (vice Grant)
Residence: Wakefield, Yorkshire
Died: Wakefield 16 Mar 1811
Sources: ARLI; GEMA (1811); A Genealogical and Heraldic Dictionary of the British Empire

654. *Donald MacDONALD (1811–1812)*

Born: Isle of Skye c.1756
Relations: Son of Major Allan MacDonald of Knock and Sibella (MacLeod)
Entry to Army: Ensign in 55th Foot 17 Sep 1773 by purchase
Regimental Field Officer Promotions: Major in 55th Foot 26 Oct 1793 (vice Fitch); Lieutenant Colonel in 55th Foot 6 Dec 1793 (vice Cuyler)
Brevets: Colonel (West Indies) 20 Oct 1796; Brevet Colonel 26 Jan 1797; Brigadier General (Guernsey) 21 Feb 1799; Major General 25 Sep 1803
Colonelcies: Cape Regiment 9 Aug 1804
Service 1793–1815: Commanded 55th Foot 1793–1803; commanded brigade at Helder 1799; Lieutenant Governor of Fort William 1804–1812
Residence: St James's, London
Died: London 9 Oct 1812
Sources: ARLI; WEOF; The Brave Sons of Skye

655. *Colin CAMPBELL (1812–1814)*

Born: Edinburgh 1754
Relations: Son of John Campbell of the Bank and Anne Carolina (Campbell); father of Major General Sir Guy Campbell, Bt.
Entry to Army: Ensign in 71st Foot 1771 by purchase
Regimental Field Officer Promotions: Major in 35th Foot Apr 1789 by purchase; Lieutenant Colonel in 81st Foot 1 Apr 1795; Lieutenant Colonel in 6th Foot 29 Apr 1795 (vice Whyte) by purchase
Brevets: Brevet Lieutenant Colonel 1 Mar 1794; Brevet Colonel 1 Jan 1798; Brigadier General (Leeward Islands) May 1799; Major General 1 Jan 1805; Lieutenant General 4 Jun 1811
Colonelcies: 5th Garrison Battalion 25 Mar 1808 (vice Trench); 55th Foot 10 Oct 1812 (vice Macdonald)
Service 1793–1815: Served in Ireland 1798; acting Commander in Chief and Governor of Gibraltar 16 Aug 1810 to 25 Aug 1814
Residence: Marylebone, London
Died: Gibraltar 2 Apr 1814
Sources: ANCB; ARLI; DINB; ODNB; WEOF; WOST

656. *Sir William Henry CLINTON (1814–1846)*

Born: Lyon 1769
Relations: Son of General Sir Henry Clinton and Harriet (Carter); brother of Lieutenant General Sir Henry Clinton; father of Colonel Henry Clinton, 1st Foot Guards; and Colonel Frederick Clinton, 1st Foot Guards
Education: Eton College
Entry to Army: Cornet in 7th Light Dragoons 22 Dec 1784 by purchase
Regimental Field Officer Promotions: Captain and Lieutenant Colonel in 1st Foot Guards 29 Dec 1794 (vice Stanhope) by purchase; 3rd Major in 1st Foot Guards 30 Jul 1812 (vice Warde); 2nd Major in 1st Foot Guards 21 Jan 1813 (vice Warde); 1st Major in 1st Foot Guards 21 Oct 1813 (vice Leslie)
Brevets: Brevet Colonel 1 Jan 1801; Brigadier General (Madeira) 25 Sep 1801; Major General 25

Jul 1810; Lieutenant General 4 Jun 1814; General 22 Jul 1830
Colonelcies: 55th Foot 25 Apr 1814 (vice C. Campbell)
Service 1793–1815: Served in Flanders 1793–1794; ADC to Duke of York 1796–1799; served in Irish Rebellion 1798; observer to Russian forces on continent 1799; served in Helder 1799; commanded Foot Guards light battalion 1800; Inspector General of foreign troops 1801; Governor of Madeira 23 Jul 1801 to Mar 1802; Military Secretary to Duke of York 1803–1804; Quartermaster General in Ireland 1804–1812; commanded forces on east coast of Spain 1812–1814
Later Service: Lieutenant General of the Ordnance 11 Apr 1825 to Jun 1829; commanded division in Miguelist War in Portugal 1826–1828; Lieutenant Governor of Royal Hospital, Chelsea 17 Nov 1842 to 16 Feb 1846
Political Career: MP (East Retford) 1794–1796; MP (Boroughbridge) 1806–1818; MP (Newark) 1818–1829
Awards and Honours: GCB 2 Jan 1815
Residences: Audley Square, Mayfair, London; Cockenach, near Royston, Hertfordshire
Died: Cockenach 16 Feb 1846
Sources: ANCW; ARLI; CHAL; DINB; HPON; PHIL; WEOF; WO 25/744; WOST

Lieutenant Colonels

657. *Cornelius CUYLER (1777–1793)*
Born: New York State 1740
Relations: Son of Cornelius Cuyler of Albany and Catalyntie (Schuyler); uncle of Colonel George Cuyler, 11th Foot
Entry to Army: Ensign in 55th Foot 31 May 1759 by purchase
Field Officer Promotions: Major in 55th Foot 15 Jan 1776; Lieutenant Colonel in 55th Foot 16 Nov 1777
Brevets: Brevet Colonel 20 Nov 1782; Brigadier General (West Indies) Nov 1782; Major General 12 Oct 1793; Lieutenant General (West Indies) 15 Jun 1797; Lieutenant General 1 Jan 1798; General 25 Sep 1803
Colonelcies: 86th Foot 30 Oct 1793; 69th Foot 20 Jun 1794 (vice Powell)
Early Service: Served in French and Indian War 1759–1760; ADC to Howe in American War of Independence 1775–1778; Quartermaster General in West Indies Nov 1782 to Apr 1784; Quartermaster General in West Indies 1787 to Nov 1792
Service 1793–1815: Commander in Chief Leeward and Windward Islands Nov 1792 to Jun 1793; Commander in Chief Leeward and Windward Islands Jun 1797 to May 1798; Commander in Chief Portugal 9 Jan to Nov 1799; Governor of Kinsale 4 May 1806
Awards and Honours: Baronet of St. John's Lodge 29 Oct 1814
Residence: St. John Lodge, Welwyn, Hertfordshire
Died: Welwyn 8 Mar 1819
Sources: ARLI; PHIL; WEOF

658. *Donald MacDONALD (1793–1804)*
See 654.
Major in 55th Foot 26 Oct 1793 (vice Fitch); Lieutenant Colonel in 55th Foot 6 Dec 1793 (vice Cuyler)

659. *James LUMSDEN (1795–1802)*
Born: Aberdeenshire 1764
Relations: Son of John Lumsden of Cushnie and Anne (Forbes); brother of Major William Lumsden, 55th Foot; father of Captain John Lumsden, Bengal service; and Captain David Lumsden, Bengal service
Entry to Army: Volunteer in British North America; Ensign in 55th Foot 18 Aug 1778
Regimental Field Officer Promotions: Major in 55th Foot 6 Jun 1795 (vice Wiseman); Lieutenant Colonel in 55th Foot 1 Sep 1795
Service 1793–1815: Served in Flanders 1794–1795, badly wounded at Ostend
Retired: 9 Apr 1802
Residence: Clifton, Bristol
Died: Clifton 9 Feb 1816
Sources: ARLI; Memorials of the Families of Lumsdaine, Lumisden, or Lumsden

660. *John Cornelius CRAIGIE-HALKETT (1802–1803)*
Born: Fifeshire 1768
Relations: Son of Colonel Charles Halkett, Governor of Namur, and Anne (Craigie)
Entry to Army: Ensign in 71st Foot 3 Feb 1783
Regimental Field Officer Promotions: Major in 55th Foot 3 Oct 1799 (vice Lumsden); Lieutenant Colonel in 55th Foot 9 Apr 1802 (vice Lumsden); to half-pay of 55th Foot 25 May 1803
Brevets: Brevet Colonel 4 Jun 1811
Service 1793–1815: ADC and wounded at Helder 1799; Inspecting Field Officer of Inverness Recruiting District 25 May 1803
Residence: Inverness, Inverness-shire
Died: Inverness 22 May 1813
Sources: ANCW; ARLI; BUPE; WEOF; WikiTree

661. *Robert DOUGLAS (1804–1814)*

Born: Fifeshire 1766
Relations: Son of Colonel Robert Douglas of Strathenry and Cecilia (Craigie)
Entry to Army: Ensign in 65th Foot 25 Mar 1782 by purchase
Regimental Field Officer Promotions: Major in 56th Foot 10 Mar 1797 (vice Alexander) by purchase; Lieutenant Colonel in 18th Foot 9 Jul 1803; Lieutenant Colonel in 55th Foot 14 Sep 1804; removed from the regiment as a general officer 1814
Brevets: Brevet Lieutenant Colonel 29 Apr 1802; Major General 4 Jun 1814
Early Service: Served as marine at Gibraltar 1782; served in British North America 1785–1793
Service 1793–1815: Served in West Indies 1794; commanded 2/18th Foot 1803–1804; Assistant Adjutant General in Helder 1799; commanded 55th Foot in West Indies 1804–1812; Adjutant General at capture of Guadeloupe 1815; Governor of St. Martin Aug 1815 to 6 Jan 1816
Residence: Baddow Court, Great Baddow, Essex
Died: Great Baddow 20 Aug 1828
Sources: ANCD; ANCW; ARLI; GEMA (1828); WEOF; WOST

662. *John Nugent SMYTH (1813–1815)*

Born: Dublin 1773
Relations: Son of Captain John Smyth, 9th Foot, and Margaret (Nugent); father of Captain Henry Montague Smyth, 57th Foot
Entry to Army: Ensign in 9th Foot 30 Jun 1787
Regimental Field Officer Promotions: Major in 9th Foot 5 Sep 1799 (vice Arbuthnot); to half-pay of 9th Foot 24 Oct 1802; Major in 55th Foot 25 Nov 1802 (vice Morgan) by exchange; Lieutenant Colonel in 55th Foot 14 Oct 1813; Lieutenant Colonel in 8th West India Regiment 19 Oct 1815 (vice Alen) by exchange; to half-pay of 8th West India Regiment 1816
Brevets: Brevet Lieutenant Colonel 1 Jan 1805; Brevet Colonel 4 Jun 1813; Major General 12 Aug 1819
Early Service: Served in West Indies 1788–1793
Service 1793–1815: Served in Leeward Islands 1794; POW aboard a prison hulk 1794–1796; served in Helder 1799; served in Jamaica 1805–1809; Superintendent of British Honduras 15 Sep 1809 to 20 Jul 1814; served in Martinique 1815–1816
Later Service: Lieutenant Governor of Scilly Isles 1819–1838
Residence: Great Clacton, Essex
Died: Scilly Isles, Cornwall, 2 Nov 1838
Sources: ANCB; ANCD; ANCW; ARLI; PHIL; WEOF; WOST

663. *Luke John Patrick ALEN (1815–1817)*

Born: France 1775
Relations: Son of Major General Luke Alen, French service, and Marie Charlotte Adelaide (de Behague); nephew of General Comte de Behague, Governor of French West Indies; brother-in-law of Colonel Pierre Louis de Person, *Corps Impérial de l'Artillerie de la Marine*; father of Captain Luke John Henry Alen, 74th Foot
Entry to Army: Lieutenant in 6th Irish Brigade 1 Oct 1794
Regimental Field Officer Promotions: Major in 3rd West Indian Regiment 16 May 1805 (vice Walker); Lieutenant Colonel in 8th West India Regiment 11 Jul 1811 (vice Prevost); Lieutenant Colonel in 55th Foot 19 Oct 1815 (vice Smyth)
Service 1793–1815: Served in West Indies 1805–1815
Awards and Honours: AGM (Mart); CB 4 Jun 1815
Retired: 10 Dec 1817
Residence: Dublin, County Dublin
Died: Dublin 18 Mar 1841
Court-martialled in 1817 for offences related to military discipline and the quartering of troops; found guilty, he was allowed to retire from the service and sell his commission. He published a defence of his actions in 1822
Sources: ARLI; LFBI; WEOF; WO 25/744

Majors

664. *William FITCH (1792–1793)*

Born: New York State 1757
Relations: Son of Samuel Fitch of Long Island and Elizabeth (Lloyd)
Entry to Army: Ensign in 65th Foot 16 Aug 1775 by purchase
Regimental Field Officer Promotions: Major in 51st Foot 30 Nov 1791 (vice Knollis); Major in 55th Foot 25 Apr 1792 (vice Fisher) by exchange; Lieutenant Colonel-Commandant of 83rd Foot 28 Sep 1793
Service 1793–1815: Served in West Indies 1795
Died: Killed in action in Jamaica 18 Sep 1795
Sources: ANCB; ARLI; Annals of the Wars of the Eighteenth Century, Vol.4

665. *William GOMM (1793–1794)*

Born: Russia 1754
Relations: Son of William Gomm, merchant of St Petersburg and Bath, and Jeanne Marie (Poggenpohl); father of Ensign Richard Gomm, 65th Foot; Lieutenant Colonel Henry Gomm, 6th Foot; and Field Marshal Sir William Maynard

Gomm
Education: Harrow School; Sidney College, Cambridge
Entry to Army: Ensign in 46th Foot 3 Jul 1772 by purchase
Regimental Field Officer Promotions: Lieutenant Colonel Commandant of French émigré corps 20 Jun 1793; Major in 55th Foot 6 Dec 1793 (vice MacDonald)
Brevets: Brevet Major 25 Jun 1788
Early Service: Served in American War of Independence; served in West Indies 1779–1782
Service 1793–1815: Served in West Indies 1794
Died: Killed in action at Pointe-a-Pitre, Guadeloupe 2 Jul 1794
Sources: ANCB; ANCW; ARLI; DINB; WEOF; Letters and Journals of Field-Marshal Sir William Maynard Gomm

666. *James WISEMAN (1794–1795)*
Born: Banffshire 1747
Relations: Son of George Wiseman of Rathven and Jean (Taylor)
Entry to Army: Ensign in 53rd Foot 15 Nov 1765 by purchase
Regimental Field Officer Promotions: Major in 55th Foot 15 Jul 1794 (vice Gomm); Lieutenant Colonel in 91st Foot 6 Jun 1795
Brevets: Brevet Major 18 Nov 1790; Brevet Lieutenant Colonel 1 Mar 1794
Retired: 1 Sep 1795
Residence: Banff, Banffshire
Died: Banff 25 Jul 1800
Sources: ANCB; ANCD; ANCW; ARLI

667. *John LINDSEY (1795–1799)*
Born: Hampshire c.1772
Entry to Army: Ensign in 55th Foot 12 Feb 1780 by purchase
Regimental Field Officer Promotions: Major in 55th Foot 1 Sep 1795 (vice Wiseman); Lieutenant Colonel in 5th Foot 6 Aug 1799; to half-pay of 46th Foot 8 Oct 1802
Brevets: Brevet Lieutenant Colonel 6 Aug 1799; Brevet Colonel 25 Oct 1809; Major General 1 Jan 1812
Service 1793–1815: Served on staff in Dominica; Governor of Martinique Jul to Sep 1814 (vice Wale)
Residence: Brighton, Sussex
Died: Brighton 16 Feb 1820
Sources: ANCD; ANCW; ARLI; PHIL; WEOF; WOST

668. *George CLEGHORN (1795–1798)*
Born: Edinburgh 1756
Relations: Son of John Cleghorn and Barbara (Pullan)
Entry to Army: Ensign in 108th Foot May 1794
Regimental Field Officer Promotions: Major in 55th Foot 2 Sep 1795
Service: High Sheriff of County Meath 11 Feb 1793
Retired: 21 Feb 1798
Militia Career: Lieutenant Colonel in Royal Meath Militia 1798
Residence: Kilcarty, County Meath
Died: Committed suicide at Cork 20 May 1799
Sources: ARLI; FMPW; GEMA (1799)

669. *James Eyre CAULFIELD (1798–1800)*
Born: County Armagh 1765
Relations: Son of Hon. Francis Caulfield MP and Hon. Mary (Eyre); grandson of James Caulfield, 3rd Viscount Charlemont, and John Eyre, 1st Baron Eyre; brother-in-law of William Howard, 3rd Earl of Wicklow
Entry to Army: Ensign in 11th Foot 1783 by purchase
Regimental Field Officer Promotions: Major in 55th Foot 21 Feb 1798 (vice Cleghorn)
Brevets: Brevet Major 1 Jan 1798
Retired: 16 Jul 1800
Residence: Blessington Street, Dublin, County Dublin
Died: Dublin 8 Jan 1837
Sources: ARLI; DEPE; FMPD

670. *William LUMSDEN (1799)*
Born: Aberdeenshire 1767
Relations: Son of John Lumsden of Cushnie and Anne (Forbes); brother of Lieutenant Colonel James Lumsden, 55th Foot
Entry to Army: Ensign in 55th Foot 6 Feb 1782 by purchase
Regimental Field Officer Promotions: Major in 55th Foot 9 Aug 1799 (vice Lindsey)
Service 1793–1815: Served in West Indies 1796–1797; served in Helder 1799
Died: Killed in action at Egmont-op-Zee 2 Oct 1799
Sources: ARLI; Memorials of the Families of Lumsdaine, Lumisden, or Lumsden

671. *Henry Green BARRY (1800–1801)*
Born: County Cork c.1770
Relations: Son of James Barry and Elizabeth

(Greene); father of Sir Redmond Barry, eminent colonial judge; Captain James Barry, 15th Foot; Captain Henry Barry, Bengal service; Captain St Leger Barry, 65th Foot; and Lieutenant John Richard Barry, 86th Foot; and Major General William Wigram Barry, RA
Entry to Army: Ensign in 15th Foot 25 Jun 1789 by purchase
Regimental Field Officer Promotions: Major in 55th Foot 6 Jul 1800 (vice Caufield) by purchase; Lieutenant Colonel in 15th Foot 4 Mar 1801 (vice Bathe) by purchase; removed from the regiment as a general officer 1814
Brevets: Brevet Colonel 25 Jul 1810; Major General 4 Jun 1813
Service 1793–1815: Served in West Indies; served in Irish rebellion 1798; commanded 1/15th Foot 1801; served in West Indies 1805 to 1806; commanded 1/15th Foot in Guadeloupe 1810
Later Service: High Sheriff of County Cork 1821
Retired: 14 Oct 1824
Residence: Ballyclough House, County Cork
Died: Ballyclough House 14 May 1838
Sources: ARLI; GHLG; LFBI; WEOF

672. *John CARRUTHERS (1800–1801)*

Born: Cumberland c.1760
Relations: Son of Cornet William Carruthers of Lanercost, 4th Dragoons, and Mary (Armstrong); brother of Captain James Carruthers, 4th Dragoons; and Captain Joseph Carruthers, 43rd Foot
Entry to Army: Lieutenant on half-pay of 11th Foot 1783
Regimental Field Officer Promotions: Major in 15th Foot 28 Nov 1799; Major in 55th Foot 2 Oct 1800 (vice Barry) by exchange
Retired: 13 Nov 1801
Later Service: Inspecting Field Officer of Yeomanry in Ireland 1802–1803
Died: Kilbeggan, County Westmeath 5 Feb 1803
Sources: ANCB; ANCD; ARLI; WEOF

673. *Rt Hon. Godfrey BOSVILLE-MACDONALD, 3rd Baron MacDonald (1801–1802)*

Born: Godfrey MacDonald in Edinburgh 1775; adopted surname Bosville-MacDonald in 1824
Relations: Son of Alexander MacDonald, 1st Baron MacDonald and Elizabeth Diana (Bosville); brother of Alexander Wentworth MacDonald, 2nd Baron MacDonald, 10th Light Dragoons; Captain Archibald MacDonald, 10th Light Dragoons; and Lieutenant Colonel Hon. James William MacDonald, 1st Foot Guards; father of Lieutenant General Hon. James William Bosville MacDonald
Education: Harrow School; Oriel College, Oxford
Entry to Army: Ensign in Loyal Kelso Regiment 28 Aug 1794
Field Officer Promotions: Major in 55th Foot 21 Nov 1801 (vice Carruthers) by purchase; Lieutenant Colonel in 24th Foot 28 Apr 1802 (vice Forster) by purchase; Captain and Lieutenant Colonel in 1st Foot Guards 11 Feb 1808 (vice Drummond) by exchange
Brevets: Brevet Colonel 4 Jun 1811; Major General 4 Jun 1814; Lieutenant General 22 Jul 1830
Service 1793–1815: Served in Ostend raid 1798; served in Helder 1799; served in West Indies 1801–1802; commanded 1/24th Foot 1802–1807; served in Cape of Good Hope 1806; served in Peninsula with 1/1st Foot Guards Sep 1812 to Apr 1814
Creations and Dignities: 11th Baronet of Sleat 19 Jun 1824; 3rd Baron Macdonald of Sleat 19 Jun 1824
Residences: Thorpe Hall, near Bridlington, Yorkshire
Died: Bridlington 13 Oct 1832
Sources: ANCB; ANCD; ANCW; ARLI; CHAL; PHIL; WEOF

674. *Charles MORGAN (1801–1802)*

Born: County Galway c.1781
Relations: Son of Charles Morgan of Monksfield and Mary (Blake)
Entry to Army: Ensign in 12th Foot 19 Apr 1796 by purchase
Regimental Field Officer Promotions: Major in 55th Foot 20 Apr 1802 (vice Halkett) by purchase; to half-pay of 9th Foot 25 Nov 1802 (vice Smyth) by exchange
Brevets: Brevet Lieutenant Colonel 25 Oct 1809
Retired: 1812
Residence: Monksfield, County Galway
Died: Monksfield 28 May 1829
Newspaper reports for this officer's death have him as being on the half-pay of the 53rd Foot; this is most likely due to corruption of passed down family information
Sources: ARLI; WEOF

675. *Alexander Jekyll CHALMERS (1802–1807)*

Born: Pennsylvania c.1774
Relations: Son of Colonel James Chalmers of Philadelphia, commander of Maryland Loyalists, and Arianna Margaretta (Jekyll); father of Lieutenant John Chalmers, 22nd Foot
Entry to Army: Volunteer in 60th Foot 1790; Ensign in 4/60th Foot 24 Mar 1794

Regimental Field Officer Promotions: Major in 20th Foot 20 Jun 1801 (vice Power) by purchase; commission rescinded 29 May 1802; Major in 55th Foot 17 Jun 1802 (vice Macdonald) by purchase
Service 1793–1815: Served in Jamaica 1802–1807
Retired: 2 Apr 1807
Residences: St Luke, Chelsea, Middlesex; Winkfield, Berkshire
Died: Of fever in Madeira 2 Apr 1811
Sources: ARLI; The Provincial Councillors of Pennsylvania, who Held Office Between 1733-1776

676. *John HEYLIGER (1807–1808)*
Born: Johannes Heyliger in St Croix, Dutch West Indies 1782
Relations: Son of Captain Martin Meyers Heyliger and Elizabeth (Markoe)
Entry to Army: Ensign in 55th Foot 12 Jun 1800 by purchase
Regimental Field Officer Promotions: Major in 55th Foot 2 Apr 1807 (vice Chalmers) by purchase
Service 1793–1815: Served in Jamaica 1802–1808
Died: Of fever in Jamaica 8 Oct 1808
Sources: ANCB; ANCD; ARLI; WEOF

677. *Robert FREDERICK (1808–1817)*
Born: London 1774
Relations: Son of General Marescoe Frederick and Sarak (Pickering); brother of Lieutenant Colonel Thomas Frederick, unattached; and Lieutenant Charles Frederick, 54th Foot
Entry to Army: Ensign in 54th Foot 25 Jan 1792
Regimental Field Officer Promotions: Major in 55th Foot 15 Dec 1808 (vice Heyliger); Lieutenant Colonel in 55th Foot 18 Dec 1817
Brevets: Brevet Lieutenant Colonel 4 Jun 1814
Service 1793–1815: Served in Flanders 1794–1795; served in Egypt 1801; served in Jamaica 1807–1810; served in Netherlands 1814
Retired: 24 Oct 1821
Residences: Corsham, Wiltshire; Dalston, Middlesex
Died: Alton, Hampshire 4 Jun 1844
Sources: ANCB; ANCD; ANCW; ARLI; PHIL; WO 25/745

678. *Alexander HOG (1813–1820)*
Born: Perthshire 1778
Relations: Son of Captain Thomas Hog of Thorngreen and Margaret (Man); brother of Dr Thomas Hog, surgeon in EIC service
Entry to Army: Ensign in 55th Foot 25 Sep 1793 by purchase
Regimental Field Officer Promotions: Major in 55th Foot 14 Oct 1813 (vice Smyth)
Brevets: Brevet Lieutenant Colonel 17 Mar 1814
Service 1793–1815: Served in Netherlands 1814
Retired: 27 Jan 1820
Residence: Wester Kinloch, Perthshire
Died: Wester Kinloch 2 Nov 1834
Court-martialled for being drunk on duty in Plymouth in 1819; was found guilty and allowed to retire by the sale of his commission
Sources: ARLI; FMPD; PHIL; WEOF; A Collection of the Charges, Opinions, and Sentences of General Courts Martial

Selected Regimental Histories
Sutherland, Douglas, *Tried and Valiant: The History of the Border Regiment (the 34th and 55th Regiments of Foot)* 1702–1959 (London: Leo Cooper, 1972)

Regimental Museum
Cumbria's Museum of Military Life, The Castle, Alma Block, Castle Way, Carlisle

---

56th Regiment of Foot

Secondary Title:	West Essex
Nicknames:	The Pompadours
Jacket:	Red
Facings:	Purple

Regimental Lineage, 56th Regiment of Foot

1755:	Raised by Major General Lord Charles Manners in Northumbria as 58th Regiment of Foot
1756:	56th Regiment of Foot
1782:	56th (West Essex) Regiment of Foot
1804:	Dec – 2nd Battalion formed in Farnham
1813:	Nov – 3rd Battalion formed in Horsham

1814: Oct – 3rd Battalion disbanded in Sheerness
1817: Jun – 2nd Battalion disbanded in Rochester
1881: 2nd Battalion, Essex Regiment (on amalgamation with the 44th (East Essex) Regiment of Foot)
1958: 3rd East Anglian Regiment (16th/44th Foot) (on amalgamation with 1st Battalion, Bedfordshire and Hertfordshire Regiment)
1964: 3rd Battalion, Royal Anglian Regiment (on amalgamation with 1st East Anglian Regiment (Royal Norfolk and Suffolk), 2nd East Anglian Regiment (Duchess of Gloucester's Own Royal Lincolnshire and Northamptonshire), and Royal Leicestershire Regiment)
1992: 3rd Battalion disbanded, lineage perpetuated by 1st and 2nd Battalions

Service History, 1st Battalion 56th Regiment of Foot

1793: Wexford; Jun – quelled local riot in Enniscorthy; Aug – Cork; Nov – to West Indies
1794: Barbados; Feb – five companies in Grenada, three companies in St Kitts, two companies in Martinique; May – five companies in Grenada, three companies in St Kitts, two companies in St Kitts; Jul – five companies in Grenada, three companies in St Kitts, two companies in Guadeloupe; Sep – seven companies in Grenada, three companies in Guadeloupe; Oct – five companies in Grenada, two companies in Martinique, three companies at Berville
1795: Drafted out to other regiments, cadre to England; Feb – Gravesend; Mar – Fareham; Apr – Chatham; Sep – Gravesend; to Ireland; Oct – Cork
1796: Cork; Feb – to West Indies; Barbados; St Domingue; Jun – Bombarde
1797: St Domingue; Apr – Port Jack Thomas; Irois; St Mary's; to Jamaica
1798: Jamaica; Nov – to England
1799: Gravesend; Chatham; May – Aylesbury; Jun – Gloucester; Jul – Barham Downs; Sep – Deal; to Helder; Bergen; Oct – Egmont-op-Zee; Nov – to England; Yarmouth; Dec – Chelmsford; Horsham
1800: Horsham; Feb – Portsmouth; to Ireland; Kilkenny; Clonmel; Kinsale
1801: Kinsale; Apr – Fermoy; Jul – Kinsale; Aug – Cork
1802: Cork; Nov – Limerick
1803: Limerick; Sep – Galway
1804: Galway; Jul – Tuam; Dec – Loughrea
1805: Charlesfort; Feb – Isle of Wight; Apr – to East Indies; Sep – Bombay [Mumbai]; Oct – Colaba
1806: Colaba
1807: Colaba
1808: Colaba
1809: Colaba; Bombay; Aug – Madras; Fort St George; Oct – Bellary [Ballari]
Feb – detachment to Bourbon [Réunion]; Sep – Saint-Paul; Oct – Rodrigues
1810: Bellary
Detachment in Rodrigues; Jul – capture of Bourbon; Nov – capture of Mauritius
1811: Bellary; Apr – Mauritius detachment returned
1812: Bellary; Sep – Cauloore [Koulur]; Oct – Mootkie [Mutkod]; Nov – Sangoolie [Sangurli]; Dec – Coodoorinhutty
1813: Yecoondy [Yekkambi]; Feb – Marihal; Mar – Ambooly [Amboli]; Apr – Raree [Rajgad fort]; May – Sankaseer [Sankasara]; Jun – Catabaugy [Kotabagi]; Oct – Boodiaul [Budihal]; Nov – Bellary; Dec – Canool [Kurnool]
1814: Gooty; Feb – Goonoonujpilly [Govindampalle?]; Mar – Fort St George
1815: Fort St George; Jul – to Mauritius; Nov – Mahebourg

Service History, 2nd Battalion 56th Regiment of Foot

1804: Dec – formed in Farnham
1805: Farnham; Jun – Hilsea; Jul – Forton; Aug – Gosport; Aug – Isle of Wight
1806: Isle of Wight; Apr – Guernsey
1807: Guernsey; Apr – Isle of Wight; Jun – to East Indies; Cape of Good Hope; Dec – Madras [Chennai]
1808: Madras; Apr – Bombay [Mumbai]
1809: Bombay; Feb – Barachi [Bharuch]; Baroda [Vadodara]; Jul – detachment at Mallia Feb – marine detachment to Travancore; Dec – battalion reunited at Barachi
1810: Barachi
1811: Barachi; Jun – Bombay
1812: Bombay; Nov – Colaba
1813: Coalaba; Mar – Surat; Apr – Domus [Dumas]; June – Surat; four companies to Oclasceer; Sep – two add companies to Oclasceer; Oct – Domus; Nov – detachment at Palampore [Palanpur]; Dec – Domus
1814: Domus; Mar – Bhimpore; Sep – Surat; Oct – Colaba; Dec – Bombay
1815: Panwell [Panvel]; Feb – Assaye; Mar – Dongergaum [Dongargaon]; Apr – Bowan [Bhawan]; May – Jalna; Aug – Seroor [Shirur]

Service History, 3rd Battalion 56th Regiment of Foot

1813: Nov – formed in Horsham; Ramsgate; Dec – to Netherlands; Willemstadt
1814: Merxcem; Feb – Antwerp; Mar – Bergen-op-Zoom; Antwerp; Sep – Ostend; to England; Oct – disbanded in Sheerness

Establishments, 1st Battalion 56th Regiment of Foot

Year	Subunits	Field Off	Off/ Staff	Sjts	Mus	Corp/ Pvts	Total
Dec 1792	10co	3	32	22	12	430	499
Feb 1793	10co	3	32	32	22	600	689
Dec 1795	10co+2r	5	51	62	30	1,010	1,158
Dec 1797	10co	5	38	53	22	600	718
Jul 1802	10co	5	33	34	22	750	844
Jan 1805	10co	5	36	44	22	800	907
May 1805	10co	5	46	54	22	1,000	1,127
Apr 1807	10co+r	5	50	62	26	1,008	1,151
Dec 1807	10co+r	5	50	72	26	1,208	1,361
Dec 1811	10co+r	5	50	73	26	1,208	1,362
Dec 1813	10co+r	5	49	73	22	1,208	1,357
Dec 1815	10co+r	5	49	63	22	1,008	1,147

Establishments, 2nd Battalion 56th Regiment of Foot

Year	Subunits	Field Off	Off/ Staff	Sjts	Mus	Corp/ Pvts	Total
Dec 1804	10co	3	35	23	22	400	483
Jul 1805	10co	3	35	33	22	600	693
Dec 1805	10co	3	36	43	22	800	904
Jun 1807	10co+r	3	40	51	26	808	928
Dec 1807	10co+r	4	50	62	26	1,008	1,150
Dec 1808	10co+r	4	50	52	26	808	940
Dec 1809	10co+r	4	50	62	26	1,008	1,150
Dec 1810	10co+r	4	50	72	26	1,208	1,360
Dec 1811	10co+r	4	50	73	26	1,208	1,361
Dec 1813	10co+r	4	49	73	22	1,208	1,356
Dec 1815	10co+r	4	49	63	22	1,008	1,146

Establishments, 3rd Battalion 56th Regiment of Foot

Year	Subunits	Field Off	Off/ Staff	Sjts	Mus	Corp/ Pvts	Total
Dec 1813	6co	2	23	35	12	600	672

Service Statistics, 56th Regiment of Foot

	Lieutenant Colonels	Majors
Number of officers in period 1793–1815	13	22
Average age on appointment to substantive rank	34.5	33.5
Average time in rank in regiment (years)	7.5	4.5
Total field officers by nationality	16 E / 7 I / 5 S / 2 W / 2 A / 2 F	
Demographics of other ranks 1799	95% EW / 3% S / 2% I	
Demographics of other ranks 1810	1/56th: 61% EW / 34% I / 4% S / 1% F 2/56th: 75% EW / 23% I / 1% S / 1% F	
Demographics of other ranks 1815	2/56th: 75% EW / 22% I / 2% S / 1% F	
Months of overseas service 1793–1815	1/56th: 182 2/56th: 102 3/56th: 10	

Significant Militia/Volunteer Intakes

1799:	West Norfolk, Northumberland, Shropshire, West Suffolk, Tarbert Fencibles
1800:	County Monaghan
1803:	County Louth
1804:	Additional Force Act men from Surrey
1806:	North Lincolnshire, Flintshire, Merionethshire, County Limerick, County Mayo
1807:	1st Surrey, 2nd Surrey, County Carlow
1809:	3rd Lancashire, 1st Surrey, 2nd Surrey, 2nd Tower Hamlets
1810:	1st Tower Hamlets, South Mayo
1811:	1st Surrey
1812:	North Gloucestershire, 1st Surrey, West Yorkshire
1813:	North Gloucestershire, 1st Surrey, North Yorkshire, Monmouth & Breconshire

Regimental Colonels

679. *Hunt WALSH (1766–1795)*

Born: Queen's County 1720
Relations: Son of John Walsh of Ballykilcavan and Abigal (Burton); uncle of General Sir Henry Johnson, 1st Bt
Regimental Field Officer Promotions: Major in 28th Foot 28 Aug 1753; Lieutenant Colonel in 28th Foot 2 Feb 1757
Brevets: Brevet Colonel 19 Feb 1762; Major General 25 May 1772; Lieutenant General 21 Aug 1777; General 12 Oct 1793
Colonelcies: 56th Foot 22 May 1766 (vice Durand)
Early Service: Served in North America during Seven Years War
Political Career: MP (Ire) 1764–1776
Residence: Ballykilcavan, near Stradbally, Queen's County
Died: Ballykilcavan 28 Feb 1795
Sources: ANCW; ARLI; Historical Record of the Fifty-Sixth, or the West Essex Regiment of Foot

680. *Rt Hon. Samuel HULSE (1795–1797)*

Born: Hampshire 1747
Relations: Son of Sir Edward Hulse, 2nd Baronet and Hannah (Vanderplank)
Education: Eton College
Entry to Army: Ensign in 1st Foot Guards 17 Dec 1761 by purchase
Regimental Field Officer Promotions: Captain and Lieutenant Colonel in 1st Foot Guards 20 Feb 1776 by purchase; Second Major in 1st Foot Guards 12 Mar 1789 (vice Lake); First Major in 1st Foot Guards 8 Aug 1792 (vice Lake); Lieutenant Colonel in 1st Foot Guards 30 Apr 1794 (vice Lake)
Brevets: Brevet Colonel 20 Nov 1782; Major General 12 Oct 1793; Lieutenant General 1 Jan 1798; General 25 Sep 1803; Field Marshal 22 Jul 1830
Colonelcies: 56th Foot 7 Mar 1795 (vice Walsh); 19th Foot 24 Jun 1797 (vice Graeme); 62nd Foot 25 Jun 1810 (vice Coote)
Early Service: Present at Gordon riots in London 1780; Treasurer and Receiver-General to the Prince of Wales Jan 1787

Service 1793–1815: Commanded 1/1st Foot Guards in Flanders 1793; commanded 1st Brigade of Guards in Flanders 1794–1795; commanded Brigade of Guards in Ireland 1798; served in Helder 1799; Lieutenant Governor of Chelsea Hospital 1806; Master of the Royal Household 1812–1827
Later Service: Governor of Chelsea Hospital 1820–1837; Vice-Chamberlain of the Royal Household 1827–1830
Awards and Honours: KCH 12 Aug 1820; PC 1827
Residences: West Heath House, Woolwich Road, Erith; Royal Hospital, Chelsea
Died: Royal Hospital, Chelsea 1 Jan 1837
Sources: ARLI; ODNB; PHIL; UNSM (1837); WEOF; WO 25/746

681. *Hon. John Chapple NORTON (1797–1818)*

Born: Yorkshire 1746
Relations: Son of Fletcher Norton, 1st Baron Grantley, attorney-general, and Grace (Chapple)
Entry to Army: Ensign in 19th Foot 2 Apr 1762 by purchase
Regimental Field Officer Promotions: Major in 1st Foot 14 Jul 1769 by purchase; Captain and Lieutenant Colonel in Coldstream Foot Guards 1 Jun 1774 by purchase; Second Major in Coldstream Foot Guards Apr 1786; First Major in Coldstream Foot Guards 26 May 1789
Brevets: Brevet Colonel 17 Nov 1780; Major General 28 Sep 1787; Lieutenant General 26 Jan 1797; General 29 Apr 1802
Colonelcies: 81st Foot 25 Mar 1795 (vice Bertie); 56th Foot 24 Jan 1797 (vice Hulse)
Early Service: Served in Gibraltar; served in American War of Independence
Political Career: MP (Guildford) 1784–1790; MP (Guildford) 1796–1806 and 1807–1812
Residence: Wonersh Park, near Shalford, Surrey
Died: Wonersh Park 19 Mar 1818
Sources: ANCB; ARLI; DINB; HPON; WEOF; Historical Record of the Fifty-Sixth, Or the West Essex Regiment of Foot

Lieutenant Colonels

682. *Peter William CRAIG (1779–1799)*

Born: London 1747
Relations: Son of Hew Craig, judge of the civil and military courts in Gibraltar, and Margaret Frances (Dumas); brother of General Sir James Henry Craig
Entry to Army: Ensign in 30th Foot 28 May 1762 by purchase
Regimental Field Officer Promotions: Major in 57th Foot 14 Dec 1774; Lieutenant Colonel in 56th Foot 9 Jan 1779; to half-pay of 62nd Foot 25 Jun 1802
Brevets: Brevet Lieutenant Colonel 30 May 1778; Brevet Colonel 20 Nov 1782; Major General 12 Oct 1793; Lieutenant General 1 Jan 1798; General 25 Sep 1803
Colonelcies: Colonel Commandant of 2/62nd Foot 25 Nov 1799; 67th Foot 9 Mar 1803 (vice D'Oyley)
Early Service: Served in Gibraltar 1779–1783
Residence: Charlotte Street, St Pancras, London
Died: London 23 Dec 1810
Sources: ANCW; ARLI; EDMA (1810); WEOF; Historical Record of the 67th, or the South Hampshire Regiment

683. *William Earle BULWER (1795)*

Born: London 1757
Relations: Son of William Wiggett Bulwer and Mary (Earle); father of Henry Bulwer, 1st Baron Dalling and Bulwer; and Edward George Earle Lytton Bulwer-Lytton, 1st Baron Lytton
Education: Pembroke College, Cambridge
Entry to Army: Ensign in 40th Foot 15 Jul 1784 by purchase
Regimental Field Officer Promotions: Major Commandant of 106th Foot 18 Sep 1794; Lieutenant Colonel Commandant of 106th Foot 18 Sep 1794; Lieutenant Colonel in 56th Foot 1 Sep 1795; to half-pay of 103rd Foot 18 Nov 1795 (vice Whitwell) by exchange
Brevets: Brevet Colonel 1 Jan 1800; Brigadier General 15 Jun 1804
Residences: Heydon Hall, Heydon, Norfolk
Died: Heydon Hall 14 Jul 1807
Sources: ANCB; ANCD; ARLI; GHHC; WEOF

684. *John WHITWELL (1795–1796)*

Born: Essex c.1774
Relations: Son of Captain Edward Whitwell of Springfield, Horse Grenadier Guards, and Mary (Milnes); nephew of Sir Robert Shore Milnes, 1st Bt, Lieutenant Governor of Lower Canada
Entry to Army: Ensign in 82nd Foot Apr 1794
Regimental Field Officer Promotions: Major in 105th Foot (vice Crewe) 21 Apr 1795; Lieutenant Colonel in 103rd Foot 18 Aug 1795; Lieutenant Colonel in 56th Foot 18 Nov 1795 (vice Bulwer) by exchange
Died: St Pierre, Martinique Apr 1796
Sources: ARLI; The Baronetage of England

685. *Sir Thomas PICTON (1796–1811)*

Born: Pembrokeshire 1758
Relations: Son of Thomas Picton of Poyston and Cecil (Powell); nephew of General Sir William Picton

Education: Lochée's Military Academy, Chelsea
Entry to Army: Ensign in 12th Foot 14 Nov 1771
Regimental Field Officer Promotions: Major in 68th Foot 19 Nov 1794; Lieutenant Colonel in 56th Foot 1 May 1796 (vice Whitwell) (antedated 22 Jun 1795)
Brevets: Brevet Major 1 Mar 1794; Brevet Lieutenant Colonel 16 Nov 1794; Brevet Colonel 1 Jan 1801; Brigadier General (West Indies) 22 Oct 1801; Major General 25 Apr 1808; Lieutenant General 1813
Colonelcies: 77th Foot 15 Oct 1811 (vice Hastings)
Early Service: Served in Gibraltar 1773–1778
Service 1793–1815: Served in West Indies 1794–1803; ADC to Vaughan in Martinique 1794; Deputy Quartermaster General in Leeward Islands Nov 1794 to 1796; ADC to Abercromby at capture of Trinidad 1797; Governor of Trinidad Mar 1797 to Jul 1802 (vice Abercromby); Civil Commissioner of Trinidad Jul 1802 to May 1803; commandant of Tobago 30 Jun 1803; commanded brigade in Walcheren 1809; commanded 3rd Division in Peninsula Feb 1810 to Jul 1812, and Apr 1813 to Apr 1814, slightly wounded at Badajoz; commanded 5th Division in Waterloo campaign, wounded at Quatre Bras
Political Career: MP (Pembroke Boroughs) 1813–1815
Awards and Honours: KB 1 Feb. 1813; AGM (Bus FDO CR Bad Vitt Pyr Ort Toul); GCB 2 Jan. 1815; WatM 23 Apr 1816
Residence: Iscoed, Carmarthenshire
Died: Killed in action at Waterloo 18 Jun 1815
Sources: ANCB; ANCD; ANCW; ARLI; CHAL; DALT; HPON; ODNB; WEOF; WOST; WO 25/747

686. *Philip Kearny SKINNER (1799–1814)*

Born: New Jersey 1758
Relations: Son of Cortland Skinner, Attorney General and Speaker of the House of Assembly in New Jersey, and Elizabeth (Kearny); brother of Midshipman William Skinner RN; Captain John Frederick Skinner RN; and Captain Cortland Skinner, 70th Foot; brother-in-law of Field Marshal Sir George Nugent, Bt
Entry to Army: Ensign in 1st New Jersey Volunteers 11 Oct 1781; Ensign in 23rd Foot 21 Dec 1782
Field Officer Promotions: Major in 23rd Foot 1 Sep 1795; Lieutenant Colonel in 56th Foot 11 Dec 1799 (vice Craig)
Brevets: Brevet Colonel 25 Oct 1809; Major General 1 Jan 1812; Lieutenant General 27 May 1825
Early Service: Served in American War of Independence 1782–1783
Service 1793–1815: Served and taken POW in Ostend raid 1798; served in British East Indies 1805–1815; Quartermaster General in East Indies 1 Aug 1811
Residence: Regent Street, Mayfair, London
Died: London 7 Apr 1826
Sources: ANCB; ANCD; ANCW; ARLI; PHIL; WEOF; WO 25/748

687. *Sir Henry Sheehy KEATING (1804–1812)*

Born: County Tipperary 1775
Relations: Son of Bryan Keating of Bansha and Anne (Sheehy); father of Lieutenant Colonel James Singer Keating, 1st Dragoons; and Lieutenant Bryan Keating, 56th Foot
Entry to Army: Ensign in 33rd Foot 31 Aug 1793 by purchase
Regimental Field Officer Promotions: Major in 56th Foot 3 Sep 1800 (vice Barrington); Lieutenant Colonel in 56th Foot 1 Aug 1804
Brevets: Brevet Colonel 4 Jun 1813; Major General 12 Aug 1819; Lieutenant General 10 Jan 1837
Colonelcies: Lieutenant Colonel Commandant of Bourbon Regiment 25 Jan 1812; 90th Foot 29 Sep 1837 (vice Darling); 54th Foot 2 Sep 1841 (vice Gascoyne); 33rd Foot 4 Apr 1845 (vice Wale)
Service 1793–1815: Served in West Indies 1794, taken POW on Guadeloupe; served and wounded at capture of Martinique Nov 1810; commanded land forces at capture of Bourbon 1810; Governor of Bourbon 7 Jul 1810 to 9 Jul 1810; 20 Dec 1810 to 26 Apr 1811; and 10 Jul 1811 to 5 Apr 1815
Awards and Honours: CB 4 Jun 1815; KCB 21 Dec 1836
Residence: Cheltenham, Gloucestershire
Died: Cheltenham 12 Sep 1847
Sources: ANCB; ANCD; ANCW; ARLI; GEMA (1847); ODNB; PHIL; WEOF; WOST

688. *John Vere Fletcher BARCLAY (1811–1831)*

Born: Cornwall 1775
Relations: Son of Lieutenant General John Barclay and Honoria (Wolrige)
Entry to Army: Ensign in 56th Foot 30 Jun 1791 by purchase
Regimental Field Officer Promotions: Major in 56th Foot 27 Aug 1804; Lieutenant Colonel in 56th Foot 27 Jun 1811
Brevets: Brevet Lieutenant Colonel 4 Jun 1811; Brevet Colonel 27 May 1825

Service 1793–1815: Served in West Indies 1794; served in Helder 1799; served in East Indies 1808–1817
Retired: 26 Apr 1831
Residence: Oxford Place, Cheltenham, Gloucestershire
Died: Bristol 29 Jan 1835
Sources: ANCW; ARLI; GEMA (1835); PHIL; WEOF

689. *John Augustus PRÉVOST (1811)*
Born: New York State 1769
Relations: Son of Major William Augustus Prévost and Susannah (Croghan); brother of Major George William Augustus Prévost, US Army; Captain James Prévost, 60th Foot; and Lieutenant Henry Prévost, 7th Foot; nephew of Lieutenant General Sir George Prévost, Bt
Entry to Army: Ensign in 3/60th Foot 15 Mar 1779 by purchase
Regimental Field Officer Promotions: Major in 7th Foot 16 Aug 1804; Lieutenant Colonel in 8th West India Regiment 27 Nov 1808 (vice Scott); Lieutenant Colonel in 56th Foot 26 Jun 1811
Early Service: Served in Gibraltar 1790; served in British North America 1791–1794
Service 1793–1815: Served in Nova Scotia 1794–1802; served in West Indies 1802–1804; served in Martinique 1808–1809
Retired: 17 Oct 1811
Died: Lost at sea aboard *Albion* wrecked off the coast of Ireland 22 Apr 1822
Sources: ANCB; ANCD; ARLI; WO 25/747

690. *Nigel KINGSCOTE (1811–1818)*
See 621.
Lieutenant Colonel in 56th Foot 17 Oct 1811 (vice Prevost) by purchase

691. *Boyle TRAVERS (1812–1814)*
Born: County Cork c.1775
Relations: Son of John Travers of Lehanagh and Elizabeth (Sampson); father of Colonel Julius Brockman Travers, 25th Foot
Entry to Army: Ensign in 40th Foot 31 Jul 1790 by purchase
Regimental Field Officer Promotions: Major in 114th Foot 19 Jul 1794; to half-pay of 114th Foot 1796; Major in 56th Foot 17 Jul 1806 (vice Knight) by exchange; Lieutenant Colonel in 56th Foot 2 Jan 1812; removed from the regiment as a general officer 1814
Brevets: Brevet Lieutenant Colonel 1 Jan 1801; Brevet Colonel 25 Jul 1810; Major General 4 Jun 1813; Lieutenant General 27 May 1825
Service 1793–1815: Inspecting Field Officer on home staff 1803–1806; served in East Indies 1807–1814
Residence: Belvedere, County Cork
Died: Belvedere 10 Aug 1841
Sources: ANCD; ARLI; PHIL; WEOF; WO 25/748

692. *John Frederick BROWNE (1812–1816)*
Born: Pembrokeshire 1768
Relations: Son of John Browne of Llawhaden and Ann (Skyrme)
Entry to Army: Ensign in 28th Foot 15 Sep 1781
Field Officer Promotions: Major in 28th Foot 9 Jul 1803; Lieutenant Colonel in 56th Foot 5 Mar 1812 (vice Keating); Lieutenant Colonel in 28th Foot 9 May 1816 (vice Belson) by exchange
Brevets: Brevet Lieutenant Colonel 25 Jul 1810; Brevet Colonel 12 Aug 1819
Service 1793–1815: Served in Flanders 1793–1795; served in West Indies 1796; served in Egypt 1801; commanded 1/28th in Hanover 1805; commanded 1/28th Foot in Peninsula Aug 1808 to Jan 1809; served in Walcheren 1809; commanded flank battalion in Barrosa Mar 1811; served in Peninsula with 1/28th Apr 1810 to Apr 1812; commanded 3/56th Foot in Netherlands 1814
Retired: Retaining rank 11 Oct 1827
Awards and Honours: AGM (Bar); CB 4 Jun 1815
Residence: Laugharne, Carmarthenshire
Died: Laugharne 25 Mar 1844
Sources: ANCW; CHAL; PHIL; WEOF; WO 25/744

693. *Henry SULLIVAN (1813–1817)*
Born: Madras, India 1782
Relations: Natural son of Sir Benjamin Sullivan, judge of the Supreme Court in Madras; brother of Captain Benjamin Sullivan, 3rd Ceylon Regiment; father of Captain Benjamin Sullivan, Madras service, cousin of Captain and Lieutenant Colonel Sir Henry Sullivan, Coldstream Foot Guards
Entry to Army: Ensign in 81st Foot 17 May 1798
Field Officer Promotions: Major in 67th Foot 28 Jun 1808; Lieutenant Colonel in 56th Foot 1 Jul 1813; to half-pay of 56th Foot 6 Sep 1817; Lieutenant Colonel in 1st Ceylon Regiment May 1821 (vice Moffatt); Lieutenant Colonel in 6th Foot 6 Jan 1825 (vice Gardiner)
Brevets: Brevet Colonel 22 Jul 1830
Service 1793–1815: Served in Cape of Good Hope; served at Maida 1806
Laster Service: Served in Pindari War; served in Ceylon [Sri Lanka] 1821
Awards and Honours: CB 19 Jul 1838
Residence: Basingstoke, Hampshire

Died: Clifton, Gloucestershire Sep 1840
Sources: ANCB; ANCD; ANCW; ANCW (father); ARLI; WEOF

694. *John William MALLET (1813–1814)*
Born: London c.1778
Relations: Son of John Mallet, Surgeon to the Forces, and Sarah (unk.); brother of Captain William Mallet, 46th Foot
Entry to Army: Ensign in 56th Foot 20 Jul 1794
Field Officer Promotions: Major in 56th Foot 29 Aug 1810 (vice Walsh); Lieutenant Colonel in 56th Foot 6 Nov 1813; to half-pay of 56th Foot Oct 1814; Lieutenant Colonel in 89th Foot 9 Aug 1821; Lieutenant Colonel in 86th Foot 31 Aug 1826 (vice McCaskill) by exchange
Brevets: Brevet Colonel 22 Jul 1830
Later Service: Commanded brigade in Madras 1825–1827; acting Governor of St Lucia 15 Sep to 14 Dec 1831
Awards and Honours: CB 26 Dec 1826
Died: St Lucia 14 Dec 1831
Sources: ANCW; GEMA (1832); PHIL; WEOF; WOST

Majors

695. *Hon. Vere POULETT (1783–1793)*
Born: Middlesex 1761
Relations: Son of Vere Poulett, 3rd Earl Poulett, and Mary (Butt); father-in-law of George Nugent-Grenville, 2nd Baron Nugent
Education: Harrow School
Entry to Army: Ensign in 62nd Foot 21 Jul 1779 by purchase
Regimental Field Officer Promotions: Major in 56th Foot 6 Aug 1783 by purchase; Lieutenant Colonel in 2/60th Foot 13 May 1793 (vice Kemble) by purchase; to half-pay of Independent Company 5 Mar 1796 (vice De Berniere) by exchange
Brevets: Brevet Colonel 3 May 1796; Major General 29 Apr 1802; Lieutenant General 25 Apr 1808
Militia Career: Lieutenant Colonel in Mid Buckinghamshire Volunteers 1803
Political Career: MP (Bridgwater) 1790–1796; MP (Bridgwater) 1806–1807
Residences: Addington House, Aylesbury Vale, Buckinghamshire; St George Hanover Square, London
Died: London 15 Mar 1812
Sources: ANCB; ANCD; ARLI; HPON; WEOF

696. *Charles VALLOTON (1793)*
Born: London c.1746
Relations: Son of Jean Francis Valloton and Margaret (Dinyon)
Entry to Army: Ensign in 56th Foot 16 Jun 1764 by purchase
Regimental Field Officer Promotions: Captain and Lieutenant in 56th Foot 3 Oct 1776
Brevets: Brevet Major 20 Nov 1782
Early Service: ADC to General Elliot in Gibraltar 1782–1783
Service 1793–1815: Served in Ireland 1793; wounded in affray with anti-taxation rioters in Wygram, County Wexford
Died: Died of wounds in Wygram 11 Jul 1793
Although not a substantive major, included as he commanded the 56th Foot in Ireland in 1793, and his death at the hands of rioters attracted considerable attention
Sources: ANCW (father); ARLI; The Sentimental and Masonic Magazine, Vol.6

697. *Patrick Duff TYTLER (1793–1794)*
Born: Edinburgh 1760
Relations: Son of William Tytler of Costerton and Anne (Craig); grandson of James Erskine, Lord Barjarg and Alva; brother of Alexander Fraser Tytler, Lord Woodhouselee
Entry to Army: Ensign in 57th Foot 24 Feb 1775 by purchase
Regimental Field Officer Promotions: Major in 56th Foot 31 Aug 1793 (vice Poulett) by purchase; Major in Earl of Elgin's Fencibles 8 Oct 1794; Lieutenant Colonel in Earl of Elgin's Fencibles 1 Sep 1797 (vice Belches); to half-pay 15 Oct 1802
Early Service: Served in American War of Independence 1776–1782
Service 1793–1815: ADC to Ralph Abercromby in Flanders 1793–1794; Assistant Quartermaster General in Scotland 1805; Fort Major of Stirling Castle 1806–1849
Awards and Honours: FRSE
Residence: Melville Street, Edinburgh
Died: Ardona, Clackmannanshire 14 Mar 1849
Sources: ANCW; ARLI; GEMA (1849); ODNB (father); WEOF

698. *John ALEXANDER (1794–1797)*
Born: Scotland c.1764
Entry to Army: Ensign in 48th Foot 13 Nov 1782
Regimental Field Officer Promotions: Major in 56th Foot 8 Oct 1794 (vice Tytler)
Retired: 10 Mar 1797
Later Service: Barrackmaster of Dumbarton Castle 1814–1833

Residence: Knoxland House, Dumbarton, Dunbartonshire
Died: [spec.] Glasgow 1843
Sources: ARLI; Glasgow Commercial Directory

699. *James BARRINGTON (1795–1800)*
Born: Ireland c.1747
Relations: Son-in-law of Captain Hew Dalrymple, Attorney General of Grenada; father of Captain Richard Barrington, 56th Foot
Entry to Army: Ensign in 56th Foot 9 Nov 1769 by purchase
Regimental Field Officer Promotions: Major in 56th Foot 1 Sep 1795
Early Service: Served in Gibraltar
Service 1793–1815: Served in West Indies 1794–1795; served in Helder 1799
Retired: 3 Sep 1800
Residence: Monmouth Place, Bath, Somerset
Died: Bath 7 Aug 1815
Sources: ANCD; ARLI; WEOF; Military Register 23 Aug 1815

700. *Robert DOUGLAS (1797–1803)*
Born: Fifeshire 1766
Relations: Son of Colonel Robert Douglas of Strathenry and Cecilia (Craigie)
Entry to Army: Ensign in 65th Foot 25 Mar 1782 by purchase
Regimental Field Officer Promotions: Major in 56th Foot 10 Mar 1797 (vice Alexander) by purchase; Lieutenant Colonel in 18th Foot 9 Jul 1803; Lieutenant Colonel in 55th Foot 14 Sep 1804
Brevets: Brevet Lieutenant Colonel 29 Apr 1802; Major General 4 Jun 1814
Early Service: Served as marine at Gibraltar 1782; served in British North America 1785–1793
Service 1793–1815: Served in West Indies 1794; commanded 2/18th Foot 1803–1804; Assistant Adjutant General in Helder 1799; commanded 55th Foot in West Indies 1804–1812; Adjutant General at capture of Guadeloupe 1815; Governor of St. Martin Aug 1815 to 6 Jan 1816
Residence: Baddow Court, Great Baddow, Essex
Died: Great Baddow 20 Aug 1828
Sources: ANCD; ANCW; ARLI; GEMA (1828); PHIL; WEOF; WOST

701. *Robert OWEN (1803–1805)*
Born: Dublin c.1764
Relations: Son of William Owen of Dublin and Elizabeth (Hutcheson); father of Major William John Owen, 90th Foot; Major Edward Barry Owen, 19th Foot; and Captain Robert Owen, 90th Foot
Entry to Army: Ensign in 16th Foot 3 Jul 1782 by purchase
Regimental Field Officer Promotions: Major in 56th Foot 27 Aug 1803 (vice Douglas); to half-pay of 5th Garrison Battalion 21 Feb 1805 (vice MacLeod) by exchange
Brevets: Brevet Lieutenant Colonel 25 Jul 1810; Brevet Colonel 12 Aug 1819; Major General 22 Jul 1830; Lieutenant General 23 Nov 1841
Early Service: Served in American War of Independence 1782; served in Jamaica 1784–1787
Service 1793–1815: Served in West Indies 1794, taken POW in Guadeloupe; Assistant Adjutant General in Irish rebellion 1798; served in Helder 1799; Assistant Quartermaster General in Ireland 1800–1820
Residence: Mountjoy Place, Dublin, County Dublin
Died: Dublin 18 Sep 1846
Sources: ANCB; ANCD; ARLI; PHIL; WEOF; WO 25/747

702. *George Andrew ARMSTRONG (1804–1805)*
Born: Middlesex 1771
Relations: Son of Captain Edmund Armstrong of Forty Hall and Frances (Armstrong)
Entry to Army: Ensign in 8th Foot 24 Sep 1787 by purchase
Regimental Field Officer Promotions: Major in Independent Company 22 Jan 1795; Major in 56th Foot 1 Aug 1804 (vice Keating); to half-pay of 96th Foot 5 Jan 1805
Brevets: Brevet Lieutenant Colonel 1 Jan 1800; Brevet Colonel 25 Jul 1810; Major General 4 Jun 1813
Service 1793–1815: Inspecting Field Officer of Yeomanry and Volunteers Jan 1805
Residence: Cheshunt, Hertfordshire
Died: Cheshunt 12 Nov 1834
Sources: ANCB; ANCD; ARLI; PHIL; WEOF

703. *Robert O'NEILL (1804–1808)*
Born: County Londonderry c.1772
Relations: Son of Mark Kerr O'Neill of Flowerfield and Elizabeth (Tobin)
Entry to Army: Ensign in 56th Foot 27 Jan 1790
Regimental Field Officer Promotions: Major in 56th Foot 2 Aug 1804; to half-pay of Queen's Rangers 23 Jun 1808 (vice Walsh); Major in 57th Foot 1 Jun 1809 (vice Shadforth) by exchange
Service 1793–1815: Served in East Indies 1805–1807
Retired: 1 Mar 1810
Residence: [spec.] Portstewart, County Londonderry

Died: Portstewart c.1810
Sources: ARLI; FMPW (father); WEOF; A Genealogical and Heraldic History of the Peerage and Baronetage; <https://www.mq.edu.au/macquarie-archive/lema/biographies/profiles/oneillrobert.html>

704. *William Joseph Eyre BROOKE (1805)*
Born: Madras, India 1770
Relations: Son of Henry Brooke, Governor of Fort St George, Madras and Mary (Allbury)
Entry to Army: Cornet in 8th Light Dragoons 29 Jun 1793 by purchase
Regimental Field Officer Promotions: Major in 96th Foot 13 Dec 1794 (vice Montgomery) by purchase; Major unattached 1795; to half-pay unattached 1 Mar 1798; Major in 56th Foot 5 Jan 1805 (vice Armstrong) by exchange; Major in 5th Dragoon Guards 25 Jul 1805 (vice Knight) by exchange
Brevets: Brevet Lieutenant Colonel 1 Jan 1800; Brevet Colonel 25 Jul 1810; Brigadier General (Spain and Portugal) 14 Jan 1813; Major General 4 Jun 1813; Lieutenant General 27 May 1825
Service 1793–1815: Served in St. Domingue Mar 1795 to 1796; served in Peninsula as officer-in-charge of courts-martial at Lisbon Sep 1812 to Apr 1814
Residence: Alfred Street, Bath, Somerset
Died: Bath 9 Sep 1843
Sources: ANCD; ANCS; ANCW; ARLI; PHIL; WEOF; WO 25/744

705. *Sir John MacLEOD, Kt (1805–1808)*
Born: Inverness-shire 1766
Relations: Son of Donald Macleod of Bernara and Margaret (Macleod); brother of Major General Donald Macleod, Bengal service; and Lieutenant General Sir Charles Macleod; father of Major Donald MacLeod, 2nd Dragoons
Entry to Army: Ensign in 78th Foot 9 Mar 1793
Regimental Field Officer Promotions: Major in 5th Garrison Battalion 22 Sep 1804 (vice Popham); Major in 56th Foot 21 Feb 1805 (vice Owen) Lieutenant Colonel in 9th Garrison Battalion 5 May 1808; Lieutenant Colonel in 78th Foot 12 May 1808 (vice Scott) by exchange
Brevets: Brevet Lieutenant Colonel 1 Jan 1805; Brevet Colonel 4 Jun 1813; Major General 12 Aug 1819; Lieutenant General 10 Jan 1837
Colonelcies: 77th Foot 17 Feb 1840 (vice Campbell)
Service 1793–1815: Served in Flanders 1794–1795; commanded 2/78th Foot 1808–1816; commanded brigade in Netherlands 1814
Awards and Honours: CB 4 Jun 1815; Knight Bachelor 4 Jul 1832; KCH 12 Aug 1832
Residence: Montagu Street, Portman Square, London
Died: London 3 Apr 1851
This officer's parents married when his father (nick-named 'The Old Trojan') was 75 and his mother aged 16 – and they had six children
Sources: ANCB; ANCD; ARLI; GEMA (1851); PHIL; WEOF

706. *Henry Raleigh KNIGHT (1805–1806)*
Born: Warwickshire 1769
Relations: Illegitimate son of Robert Knight, Earl of Catherlough and Jane Davies
Entry to Army: Ensign in 22nd Foot 18 Jan 1786 by purchase
Regimental Field Officer Promotions: Major in 81st Foot 9 Jul 1803; Major in 5th Dragoon Guards 23 Jun 1804 (vice Otway) by exchange; Major in 56th Foot 25 Jul 1805 (vice Brooke) by exchange; to half-pay in 114th Foot 17 Jul 1806; Major in 4th Garrison Battalion 25 Feb 1808 (vice Shedden) by exchange
Brevets: Brevet Lieutenant Colonel 29 Apr 1802; Brevet Colonel 4 Jun 1811; Major General 4 Jun 1814; Lieutenant General 22 Jul 1830
Service 1793–1815: Served in West Indies 1795; served at Helder 1799; served in Egypt 1801; Inspecting Field Officer of Recruits 13 Jun 1811
Residence: Portman Square, Marylebone, London
Died: London 7 Aug 1836
Sources: ANCB; ANCD; ARLI; PHIL; WEOF; WO 25/746

707. *Samuel BAYLY (1808–1810)*
Born: Lancashire c.1771
Relations: Son of Major Robert Clayton Bayly of Lancaster, 58th Foot, and Perseday (Marsden)
Entry to Army: Ensign in 2nd Foot 25 Oct 1798 by purchase
Regimental Field Officer Promotions: Major in 8th Garrison Battalion 23 Apr 1807 (vice Sullivan); Major in 56th Foot 9 Jun 1808 (vice Macleod)
Service 1793–1815: Served in East Indies 1809–1810
Residences: Lancaster, Lancashire; Bath, Somerset
Died: Bombay [Mumbai] May 1810
Sources: ANCW; ARLI; FMPW; WEOF

708. *Francis Thomas Joseph David WALSH (1808–1810)*
Born: France 1777
Relations: Son of Antoine Jean Baptiste Walsh, 2nd Earl Walsh, of St Georges-sur-Loire and Marie Josephine (de Serrant); brother of Jean Baptiste,

Count Theobald Walsh; and Colonel Etienne Walsh, French service
Entry to Army: Ensign in 3rd Irish Brigade 15 Jul 1796
Regimental Field Officer Promotions: Major in 3rd West India Regiment 15 Dec 1804 (vice Belson) by purchase; to half-pay of Queen's Rangers 22 Dec 1804 (vice Petersham) by exchange; Major in 56th Foot 23 Jun 1808 (vice O'Neill) by exchange
Brevets: Brevet Lieutenant Colonel 16 May 1805
Service 1793–1815: Served in West Indies 1796–1798; served in Helder 1799; ADC to General Coote in Egypt 1801; Deputy Adjutant General in Ireland 1804; served on staff in Jamaica 1806–1808; Assistant Adjutant General in Walcheren 1809
Residence: Farnham, Surrey
Died: In a fall from a gig in Guildford, Surrey 23 Aug 1810
Author of 'Journal of the late campaign in Egypt: including descriptions of that country, and of Gibraltar, Minorca, Malta, Marmorice and Macri' in 1803
Sources: ARLI; WEOF; WO 25/748 <https://morrisonfamilyconnections.wordpress.com/2017/08/28/thomas-walsh-1777-1810/>

709. *Sir Charles Wyndham BURDETT, 5th Bt (1810–1821)*
Born: Florida 1771
Relations: Son of Sir Charles Burdett, 4th Bt and Sarah (Halsey); brother of Major George Saville Burdett, 1st West India Regiment; and Captain Jerome Burdett, 34th Foot
Entry to Army: Ensign in 6th Foot 1 Sep 1790
Regimental Field Officer Promotions: Major in 56th Foot 24 Nov 1810 (vice Bayly)
Brevets: Brevet Major 25 Apr 1808; Brevet Lieutenant Colonel 4 Jun 1814
Service 1793–1815: Served in British North America 1790–1793; served in West Indies 1793–1794; served in Gibraltar 1796–1800; served in West Indies 1800–1802
Creations and Dignities: 5th Baronet Burdett of Burthwaite 19 Jul 1803
Residence: Burthwaite, Yorkshire
Died: Colombo, Sri Lanka 27 Nov 1839
Sources: ANCB; ANCD; ARLI; PHIL; WEOF; WO 25/744; A Genealogical and Heraldic History of the Peerage and Baronetage, the Privy Council, Knightage, and Companionage; List of Inscriptions on Tombstones and Monuments in Ceylon

710. *Robert GRANT (1811–1821)*
Born: East Lothian c.1782
Relations: Son of Alexander Grant of Tullochgriban
Entry to Army: Ensign in 71st Foot 26 Dec 1799 by purchase
Regimental Field Officer Promotions: Major in 56th Foot 27 Jun 1811; Major in 82nd Foot 12 Apr 1821 (vice Montagu) by exchange; Lieutenant Colonel unattached 20 Jul 1830
Brevets: Brevet Lieutenant Colonel 12 Aug 1819
Retired: 1830
Died: At sea c.1832
Sources: ARLI; FMPD; WEOF

711. *Joseph HANNA (1812–1816)*
Born: London 1774
Relations: Son of Alexander Hanna and Sarah [unk.]; cousin of Lieutenant Alexander Hanna, 56th Foot; father of Lieutenant Joseph Hanna, 3rd Foot
Entry to Army: Ensign in Norwich Volunteers; Lieutenant in 56th Foot 30 Apr 1795
Regimental Field Officer Promotions: Major in 56th Foot 2 Jan 1812 (vice Travers)
Service 1793–1815: Served in East Indies 1805–1816
Died: At sea en route to England 6 May 1816
Sources: ANCB; ANCW; ARLI; WEOF

712. *William Somarsall FORBES (1813–1817)*
Born: St Kitts c.1778
Relations: Son of William Forbes, planter, and Mary Anne Elizabeth (Somarsall)
Entry to Army: Lieutenant in 6th West India Regiment 16 Jul 1795
Regimental Field Officer Promotions: Major in 56th Foot 6 Nov 1813; to half-pay of 56th Foot 6 Sep 1817; Major in Cape Corps 11 Sep 1823 (vice Bathurst) by exchange; Major in 89th Foot 8 Jun 1826 (vice Clifford)
Brevets: Brevet Lieutenant Colonel 22 Jul 1830
Service 1793–1815: Served in West Indies 1795–1799; served in Helder 1799; served in East Indies 1805–1809; served in Mauritius and Bourbon 1810–1813
Retired: 4 Dec 1832
Residence: Saint Pancras, London
Died: London 29 Jan 1853
Sources: ARLI; GEMA (1853); WEOF; Annual Military Obituary 1854

Selected Regimental Histories
Cannon, Richard, *Historical Record of the Fifty-Sixth, or the West Essex Regiment of* Foot (London: Parker, Furnivall and Parker, 1844)

Regimental Museum
Essex Regiment Museum, Oaklands Park, Moulsham Street, Chelmsford, Essex

57th Regiment of Foot

Secondary Title:	West Middlesex
Nicknames:	The Die Hards The Steelbacks
Jacket:	Red
Facings:	Yellow

Regimental Lineage, 57th Regiment of Foot

1755:	Raised in Somerset and Gloucester by Colonel John Arabin as 59th Regiment of Foot
1757:	57th Regiment of Foot
1782:	57th (West Middlesex) Regiment of Foot
1803:	Oct – 2nd Battalion formed in Ashford
1815:	Dec – 2nd Battalion disbanded in Winchester
1881:	1st Battalion, Duke of Cambridge's Own (Middlesex Regiment) (on amalgamation with the 77th (East Middlesex) Regiment of Foot)
1921:	The Middlesex Regiment (Duke of Cambridge's Own)
1966:	4th Battalion (Middlesex), The Queen's Regiment
1968:	4th Battalion, The Queen's Regiment
1973:	4th Battalion disbanded; traditions perpetuated by 1st to 3rd Battalions
1992:	The Princess of Wales's Royal Regiment (Queen's and Royal Hampshires) (on amalgamation with Royal Hampshire Regiment)

Service History, 1st Battalion 57th Regiment of Foot

1793:	Tynemouth and Newcastle; Apr – Tynemouth and Sunderland; Jul – Leith; Portsmouth; to Flanders; Sep – Ostend; Menin; Oct – Ostend; ordered to West Indies, diverted to England; Nov – West Cowes
1794:	Netley; Mar – on board transports; May – to Flanders; Jun – Ostend; Jul – Alost; Malines; Aug – Breda; Oct – Nijmegen; Dec – line of River Waal
1795:	Retreat to Bremen; Mar – Bremen; Apr – to England; Portsmouth; Jun – Portsea; Jul – Quiberon; Aug – Nursling Common; Sep – Portsmouth; Oct – to West Indies; dispersed by storms; Cowes
1796:	Mar – Portsmouth; to West Indies; Mar – three companies in Barbados, seven companies in East Cowes; May – St Lucia; Morné QuaQua; Jun – battalion reunited in Grenada; Charlotte Town
1797:	Grenada; Jul – Trinidad
1798–1802:	Trinidad
1803:	Trinidad; Feb – to England; Mar – Gosport; Apr – Winchester; Jun – Silverhill; Oct – Ashford
1804:	Ashford; Apr – Ramsgate; May – Guernsey; Oct – Isle of Wight; Nov – to Gibraltar
1805–1808:	Gibraltar
1809:	Gibraltar; Jul – to Portugal; PENINSULA; Lisbon; Alcantara; Abrantes; Aug – Nisa; Sep – Puebla de la Calzada; Portalegre
1810:	Montalvão; Feb – Portalegre; Apr – Alegrete; Jun – Portalegre; Jul – Atalaya; Aug – Sarzedas; Sep – Penacova; Oct – Chamusca
1811:	Espinheiro; Mar – Campo Maior; Apr – Almendralejo; May – Fort St Christoval; ALBUERA; Jun – Torre de Mouro; Jul – Vila Viçosa; Aug – Portalegre; Sep – Aldea de Santa Margarida; Oct – Condeixa-a-Nova; Nov – Portalegre
1812:	Castelo Branco; Feb – Portalegre; Mar – Mérida; Apr – Villafranca de los Barros; May – Almendralejo; Jun – Albuera; Jul – Fuente del Maestre; Aug – Berlanga; Sep – Plasencia; Oct – Villarejo de Salvanés; Nov – Martiago; Dec – Ceclavin

1813: Ceclavin; Feb – Torrejoncillo; Apr – Plascencia; May – Montejo; Jun – VITTORIA; Huarte (Pamplona); Jul – PYRENEES; Roncesvalles; Pamplona; Nov – NIVELLE; Cambo-les-Bains; Dec – NIVE; Saint-Jean-Vieux-Mouguerre
1814: Saint-Jean-Vieux-Mouguerre; Feb – Saint-Palais; Orthez; Mar – Aire sur l'Adour; Apr – Toulouse; Castanet-Tolosan; May – Blanquefort; Jun – Bordeaux; to British North America; Aug – Québec; Montréal; Sep – Coteau de Lac; Brockville
1815: Brockville; Jun – Montréal; Jul – to England; Aug – Portsmouth; Ostend; Ghent; Sep – Paris; Allied Army of Occupation
1818: Calais; Nov – to England

Service History, 2nd Battalion 57th Regiment of Foot

1803: Oct – formed in Ashford
1804: Ashford; Feb – Horsham; Mar – Ashford; Aug – Riding Street; Sep – Ashford; Oct – Riding Street; Nov – Jersey
1805–1810: Jersey
1811: Jersey; Aug – Portsmouth; Sep – Winchester
1812: Winchester; May – Brighton; Jun – Littlehampton; Sep – Chichester
1813: Chichester; Dec – Eastbourne
1814: Jersey
1815: Jersey; Jul – Portsmouth; Aug – Winchester; Dec – disbanded in Winchester

Establishments, 1st Battalion 57th Regiment of Foot

Year	Subunits	Field Off	Off/ Staff	Sjts	Mus	Corp/ Pvts	Total
Dec 1792	10co	3	32	22	12	430	499
Feb 1793	10co	3	32	32	22	600	689
Dec 1793	10co	3	32	42	22	850	949
Dec 1795	10co+2r	5	51	62	30	1,010	1,158
Dec 1797	10co	5	38	53	22	600	718
Dec 1802	10co	5	33	34	22	750	844
Jul 1803	10co	5	36	54	22	1,000	1,117
Dec 1806	10co	4	36	44	22	800	906
Dec 1807	10co	4	46	54	22	1,000	1,126
Dec 1810	10co	4	46	64	22	1,200	1,336
Dec 1811	10co	4	46	55	22	1,000	1,127
Dec 1814	10co	4	36	45	22	800	907
Dec 1815	10co+r	4	49	53	22	808	936

Establishments, 2nd Battalion 57th Regiment of Foot

Year	Subunits	Field Off	Off/ Staff	Sjts	Mus	Corp/ Pvts	Total
Dec 1803	10co	3	35	53	22	1,000	1,113
Dec 1805	10co	3	35	23	22	400	483
Dec 1807	10co	3	35	43	22	800	903
Dec 1808	10co	3	35	23	22	400	483
Dec 1810	10co	3	35	24	22	400	484
Dec 1811	10co	3	35	25	22	400	485

Service Statistics, 57th Regiment of Foot

	Lieutenant Colonels	Majors
Number of officers in period 1793–1815	7	20
Average age on appointment to substantive rank	40.5	33
Average time in rank in regiment (years)	9.5	5
Total field officers by nationality	11 S / 8 E / 6 I / 1 W	
Demographics of other ranks 1804	1/57th: 62% EW / 31% I / 5% S / 2% F	
Demographics of other ranks 1808	2/57th: 68% EW / 28% I / 3% S / 1% F	
Demographics of other ranks 1809	1/57th: 59% EW / 35% I / 4% S / 2% F 2/57th: 71% EW / 23% I / 5% S / 1% F	
Demographics of other ranks 1815	2/57th: 73% EW / 26% I / 1% S	
Months of overseas service 1793–1815	1/57th: 225 2/57th: no overseas service	

Remarkably, the West Middlesex Regiment of Foot did not have a single English substantive lieutenant colonel in the entire period 1793–1815

Significant Militia/Volunteer Intakes

1807: West Kent, East Middlesex, West Middlesex, County Wicklow
1808: Monmouth and Breconshire
1809: West Middlesex, County Tipperary
1811: West Middlesex, County Wexford

Regimental Colonels

713. *John CAMPBELL (1780–1806)*
Born: Argyllshire 1727
Relations: Son of Admiral John Campbell of Strachur and Jane (Campbell)
Entry to Army: Ensign in Loudon's Highlanders 24 Dec 1744
Regimental Field Officer Promotions: Major in 63rd Foot 6 Jan 1757; Major in 17th Foot 11 Jul 1759; Lieutenant Colonel in 57th Foot 1 May 1773
Brevets: Brevet Lieutenant Colonel 1 Feb 1762; Brevet Colonel 1 May 1777; Brigadier General (North America) Oct 1778; Major General 19 Feb 1779; Lieutenant General 28 Sep 1787; General 26 Jan 1797
Colonelcies: 57th Foot 2 Nov 1780 (vice Irwine)
Early Service: Served in Jacobite rebellion 1745–1746, wounded at Culloden; served in Flanders 1747; served in British North America 1758; served in West Indies 1762; commanded 57th Foot in American War of Independence 1776–1778; commanded forces in Florida 1779–1783; Commander in Chief in British North America 1783–1787
Residence: Strachur House, near Inveraray, Argyllshire
Died: Strachur House 28 Aug 1806
Sources: ANCB; ANCD; ARLI; Historical Records of the Fifty-seventh or West Middlesex Regiment of Foot

714. *Rt Hon. John HELY-HUTCHINSON, 2nd Earl of Donoughmore (1806–1811)*
See 232.
Colonel of 57th Foot 8 Sep 1806 (vice Campbell)

715. *Sir Hew Whitefoord DALRYMPLE, 1st Bt (1811–1830)*
See 167.
Colonel of 57th Foot 7 Apr 1811 (vice Hutchinson)

Lieutenant Colonels

716. *Hay McDOWALL (1791–1795)*
See 147.
Lieutenant Colonel in 57th Foot 6 Apr 1791 (vice Brownlow) by purchase

717. *William BALFOUR (1795–1811)*
Born: Edinburgh 1759
Relations: Son of John Balfour of Edinburgh, publisher, and Catherine (Cant)
Entry to Army: Ensign in 57th Foot 9 Oct 1775 by purchase
Regimental Field Officer Promotions: Major in 57th Foot Nov 1794 (vice Parkyns); Lieutenant Colonel in 57th Foot 1 Sep 1795 (vice McDowall)
Brevets: Brevet Major 24 Mar 1794; Brevet Colonel 25 Sep 1803; Brigadier General (home staff) Jun 1804; Major General 25 Jul 1810

Early Service: Served in American War of Independence 1776–1781, POW at Yorktown; served in British North America 1784
Service 1793–1815: Served in Flanders 1794–1795; served in West Indies 1796–1803; served in Jamaica 1805–1809; Lieutenant Governor of New Brunswick 10 Sep to 14 Nov 1811
Died: Fredericton, New Brunswick 21 Dec 1811
Sources: ANCB; ANCD; ARLI; WEOF; WOST; WO 25/744

718. *Sir Albert GLEDSTANES, Kt (1795–1814)*

Born: Dublin 1750
Relations: Son of Albert Gledstanes of Dublin, merchant, and Susannah (Paul); uncle of Major Nathaniel Gledstanes, 68th Foot
Entry to Army: Volunteer in Gibraltar 1770–1771; Ensign in 58th Foot 22 Feb 1771
Regimental Field Officer Promotions: Major in 57th Foot 12 Nov 1794 (vice Thompson) by purchase; Lieutenant Colonel in 57th Foot 1 Sep 1795
Brevets: Brevet Major 1 Mar 1794; Brevet Colonel 25 Sep 1803; Brigadier General (West Indies) 1809; Major General 25 Jul 1810; Lieutenant General 4 Jun 1814
Colonelcies: Royal Newfoundland Fencibles 21 Aug 1813 (vice Skerrett); 102nd Foot 12 May 1814 (vice Grose)
Early Service: Served in Gibraltar 1771–1783; served in British North America 1783–1788
Service 1793–1815: Served in Flanders 1793–1795; Quartermaster General in West Indies 1798; Quartermaster General in Leeward Islands 1805–1810; Adjutant General in Leeward Islands 1813
Awards and Honours: AGM (Mart Guad); Knight Bachelor 1812
Residence: Bath, Somerset
Died: Bath 25 Apr 1818
Sources: ANCB; ANCD; ARLI; PHIL; WEOF; History of the Fifty-seventh (West Middlesex) Regiment of Foot 1755–1881

719. *Sir William INGLIS (1800–1814)*

Born: Edinburgh 1764
Relations: Son of Dr William Inglis of Edinburgh and Margaret (Spens); father of Lieutenant General William Inglis
Entry to Army: Ensign in 57th Foot 11 Oct 1779 by purchase
Regimental Field Officer Promotions: Major in 57th Foot 1 Sep 1795 (vice Parkyns); Lieutenant Colonel in 57th Foot 16 Aug 1804; removed from the regiment as a general officer 1814
Brevets: Brevet Major 6 May 1795; Brevet Lieutenant Colonel 1 Jan 1800; Brevet Colonel 25 Jul 1810; Brigadier General (Spain and Portugal) 21 Jan 1813; Major General 4 Jun 1813; Lieutenant General 27 May 1825
Colonelcies: 57th Foot 16 Apr 1830 (vice Dalrymple)
Early Service: Served in British North America 1781–1791
Service 1793–1815: Served in Flanders 1793–1795; served in West Indies 1795–1802; commanded 1/57th in Peninsula Jul 1809 to Jun 1811, wounded at Albuera; temporarily commanded brigade in 2nd Division in Peninsula Aug to Oct 1810; commanded 1/57th in Peninsula Jan 1812 to May 1813; commanded brigade in 7th Division in Peninsula May 1813 to Apr 1814
Later Service: Lieutenant Governor of Kinsale; Governor of Cork
Awards and Honours: AGC (Alb Pyr Nlle Ort); KCB 7 Apr 1815
Residence: Ramsgate, Kent
Died: Ramsgate 29 Nov 1835
Supposedly the originator of the regiment's nickname 'The Die Hards' by exhorting the 1/57th at Albuera; there is however no direct evidence that he ever said it
Sources: ANCW; CHAL; HALL: PHIL; WEBC; WO 25/746; Historical Records of the Fifty-seventh or West Middlesex Regiment of Foot

720. *Duncan MacDONALD (1804–1814)*

Born: Argyllshire c.1764
Relations: Son of James MacDonald of Dalness and unk. (MacLachlan)
Entry to Army: Ensign in 76th Foot Apr 1779
Regimental Field Officer Promotions: Major in 15th Foot 26 Nov 1799 (vice Sinclair); Lieutenant Colonel in 15th Foot 16 Mar 1802 (vice Sinclair); to half-pay of 15th Foot 25 Jun 1802; Lieutenant Colonel in 3rd Battalion of Reserve 9 Jul 1803; Lieutenant Colonel in 57th Foot 28 Aug 1804; removed from the service 29 Mar 1814
Brevets: Brevet Major 1 Jan 1798; Brevet Colonel 4 Jun 1811
Service 1793–1815: Commanded 2/15th Foot 1802; commanded 2/57th Foot 1804–1811; served in capture of Martinique 1809; commanded 1/57th Foot in Peninsula Jan 1812 to Mar 1814, severely wounded at Nivelle
Awards and Honours: AGM (Vit Pyr Nlle)
Residence: Castle Street, Edinburgh
Died: Committed suicide in Edinburgh 27 Nov 1814
Received shabby treatment for his 25 years of continuous service in 1814. Wellington had asked the Duke of York that MacDonald be removed from command of the 57th

due to incapacity, mainly from wounds and failing health; the Duke of York over-reacted by dismissing him from the army
Sources: ARLI; WEOF; Sickness, Suffering, and the Sword; Historical Records of the Fifty-seventh or West Middlesex Regiment of Foot

721. *William Collis SPRING (1813–1819)*

Born: County Kerry 1769
Relations: Son of Captain John Spring, 12th Foot, and Mary Blennerhassett (Collis); father of Lieutenant Colonel William Collis Spring, 44th Foot; Major Robert Spring, Kerry Militia; Major Thomas Spring, 83rd Foot; and Captain Francis Spring, 24th Foot
Entry to Army: Ensign in 48th Foot 30 Apr 1789 by purchase
Regimental Field Officer Promotions: Major in 57th Foot 1 Sep 1804 (vice Inglis); Lieutenant Colonel in 57th Foot 4 Jun 1813
Brevets: Brevet Lieutenant Colonel 30 May 1811
Early Service: Served in West Indies 1789–1793
Service 1793–1815: Served in West Indies 1793–1803; served in Peninsula Apr to Sep 1811, wounded at Albuera; commanded 2/57th 1811–1814; commanded 1/57th in Allied Army of Occupation in France 1815
Retired: 30 Sep 1819
Later Service: Deputy Lieutenant of Kerry
Awards and Honours: AGM (Alb)
Residence: Tralee, County Kerry
Died: Tralee 14 Aug 1825
Sources: ANCB; ANCD; CHAL; PHIL; WEOF; Historical Records of the Fifty-seventh or West Middlesex Regiment of Foot

722. *Sir Thomas ARBUTHNOT (1814–1815)*

Born: County Mayo 1776
Relations: Son of John Arbuthnot of Rockfleet Castle, Inspector General of Irish Linen Board, and Anne (Stone); brother of General Sir Robert Arbuthnot
Entry to Army: Ensign in 29th Foot 23 Nov 1795
Regimental Field Officer Promotions: Major in 5th West India Regiment 7 Apr 1808; Lieutenant Colonel in 57th Foot Mar 1814 (vice MacDonald); to half-pay of 57th Foot 25 Feb 1816
Brevets: Brevet Lieutenant Colonel 24 May 1810; Brevet Colonel 4 Jun 1814; Major General 27 May 1825; Lieutenant General 28 Jun 1838
Colonelcies: 99th Foot 15 Aug 1836 (vice Campbell); 52nd Foot 23 Dec 1839 (vice Walker); 9th Foot 7 Dec 1844 (vice Cameron); 71st Foot 18 Feb 1848 (vice Reynell)
Service 1793–1815: Assistant Adjutant General in Peninsula Aug 1808 to Jan 1809; Quartermaster General in Cape of Good Hope 1810; Assistant Quartermaster General in Peninsula Jul 1813 to Apr 1814, wounded at Tarbes; commanded 1/57th in British North America 1814; commanded 2/57th 1814–1815
Later Service: Commanded brigade in Portugal 1826
Awards and Honours: AGM (Rol Vim Cor Pyr Nlle Ort); KCB 2 Jan 1815
Residence: The Crescent, Salford, Lancashire
Died: Salford 26 Jan 1849
Sources: ANCD; ARLI; CHAL; PHIL; WEOF; Historical Records of the Fifty-seventh or West Middlesex Regiment of Foot

Majors

723. *Thomas THOMPSON (1783–1794)*

Born: [spec.] Norfolk c.1750
Relations: [spec.] Son of Lieutenant Augustus Cæsar Thompson of Thetford, Marines; brother of Lieutenant William Augustus Thompson, 57th Foot
Entry to Army: Ensign in 57th Foot 18 Apr 1769 by purchase
Regimental Field Officer Promotions: Major in 57th Foot 22 Sep 1783 by purchase
Early Service: Served in American War of Independence; served in British North America 1783–1791
Retired: 7 Jun 1794
Sources: ARLI; <https://freepages.rootsweb.com/~bldr/history/1783.html>

724. *Thomas Boothby PARKYNS, 1st Baron Rancliffe (1794)*

Born: Nottinghamshire 1755
Relations: Son of Sir Thomas Parkyns, 3rd Baronet of Bunny Hall, and Jane (Parkyns)
Education: Queen's College, Cambridge
Entry to Army: Captain in 82nd Foot 7 Apr 1794
Regimental Field Officer Promotions: Major in 57th Foot 7 Jun 1794 (vice Thompson) by purchase; Lieutenant Colonel in Leicester (Prince of Wales's) Fencibles 15 Nov 1794
Early Service: Equerry to Prince Henry, Duke of Cumberland and Strathearn 1783–1790
Political Career: MP (Stockbridge) 1784–1790; MP (Leicester) 1790–1800
Creations and Dignities: 1st Baron Rancliffe (Ire) 3 Oct 1795
Awards and Honours: FRS
Residence: Rookley Manor, Up Somborne, Hampshire
Died: Rookley Manor 17 Nov 1800
Sources: ARLI; COPE; HPON

725. *Frederick William BULLER (1795–1796)*
Born: Cornwall 1773
Relations: Son of John Buller of East Looe, MP and Elizabeth Caroline (Hunter); half-brother of Vice Admiral Edward Buller RN; father of Major General Sir George Buller
Entry to Army: Ensign in 37th Foot 20 Jan 1790
Regimental Field Officer Promotions: Major in 57th Foot 1 Sep 1795; Major in 88th Foot 27 Jun 1796 (vice Houstoun) by exchange; Lieutenant Colonel in 88th Foot 28 Aug 1804; to half-pay of 11th Garrison Battalion 6 Feb 1805; Lieutenant Colonel in 1st Foot 27 Feb 1806 (vice Burnet) by exchange; Captain and Lieutenant Colonel in Coldstream Foot Guards 1 Dec 1808 by purchase; removed from the regiment as a general officer 25 Jul 1814
Brevets: Brevet Lieutenant Colonel 1 Jan 1801; Brevet Colonel 25 Jul 1810; Major General 4 Jun 1813; Lieutenant General 27 May 1825; rank stationery thereafter
Service 1793–1815: Served in Flanders 1793–1794; Deputy Quartermaster General on Continent 1794; served in West Indies 1796–1797; ADC to King George III 1810–1813
Residences: Pelynt Lanreath, Cornwall; Bury Street, St James's, London
Died: London 8 Nov 1855
Sources: ANCB; ANCD; ANCW; DINB; HPON; PHIL; WEOF; WO 25/744

726. *Alexander HOUSTON (1796–1799)*
Born: Lanarkshire 1773
Relations: Son of Colonel Alexander Houstoun of Renfrew and Margaret (Wallace); brother of Lieutenant Colonel Hugh John Houstoun, Bengal service; and Midshipman William Adam Houstoun, RN
Entry to Army: Ensign in 57th Foot 20 Mar 1788 by purchase
Regimental Field Officer Promotions: Major in 88th Foot 15 Jul 1795; Major in 57th Foot 27 Jun 1796 (vice Buller) by exchange; to Lieutenant Colonel on half-pay of Lochaber Fencibles 13 Jan 1799; Lieutenant Colonel in 9th Foot 29 Apr 1800 (vice Crewe) by exchange; Lieutenant Colonel in Experimental Corps of Riflemen 26 Aug 1800
Service 1793–1815: Served in West Indies
Died: Gibraltar 29 Nov 1800
Sources: ANCB; ANCD; ARLI; WEOF; The First British Rifle Corps

727. *Charles ROBERTS (1799)*
Born: Hertfordshire 1754
Relations: Son of John Roberts of Cheshunt and Margaret (unk.); uncle of Captain Charles Roberts, 57th Foot
Entry to Army: Ensign in 40th Foot 23 Nov 1775 by purchase
Regimental Field Officer Promotions: Major in 57th Foot 13 Jan 1799 (vice Houston)
Early Service: Served in British North America 1783–1791
Retired: 7 Jun 1799
Residence: High Willows, Cheshunt, Hertfordshire
Died: Scarborough, Yorkshire 3 Feb 1823
Sources: ARLI; DICB (son); The Yorkshire Observer (1822)

728. *Ralph BRUCE (1800–1810)*
Born: Clackmannanshire 1768
Relations: Son of Robert Bruce of Kennet, lord of justiciary, and Helen (Abercromby)
Entry to Army: Ensign in 57th Foot 12 May 1784 by purchase
Regimental Field Officer Promotions: Major in 57th Foot 7 Mar 1800 (vice Roberts) by purchase
Brevets: Brevet Lieutenant Colonel 25 Apr 1808
Early Service: Served in British North America 1785–1791
Retired: 13 Dec 1810
Residence: Moray Place, Edinburgh, Midlothian
Died: Edinburgh 7 Oct 1854
Sources: ARLI; WEOF; WO 25/744; The Peerage, Baronetage, Knightage & Companionage of the British Empire for 1907

729. *Sir Charles SMITH[-DODSWORTH], 3rd Bt (1803–1804)*
Born: Charles Smith in Yorkshire 1775
Relations: Son of Sir John Silvester Smith, 1st Bt, and Henrietta Maria (Dodsworth); assumed -Dodsworth surname by Royal License 12 Mar 1846
Entry to Army: Cornet in 16th Light Dragoons 9 Feb 1791
Regimental Field Officer Promotions: Major in 22nd Light Dragoons 25 Feb 1795 (vice Lyster); to half-pay 23 Jun 1802; Major in 57th Foot 9 Jul 1803
Brevets: Brevet Lieutenant Colonel 1 Jan 1800
Retired: 25 Feb 1804
Creations and Dignities: 3rd Baronet of Newland Park and Thornton Watlass 31 Dec 1845
Residences: Newland Park, near Normanton, Yorkshire; Thornton Hall, Thornton Watlass,

Yorkshire
Died: Thornton Hall 28 Jul 1857
Sources; ANCB; ANCD; ARLI; Complete Baronetage

730. *David ROSS (1803–1809)*
Born: Inverness-shire c.1763
Entry to Army: Lieutenant in 78th Foot 1 Jan 1776
Regimental Field Officer Promotions: Major in 62nd Foot 13 Oct 1800; to half-pay of 62nd Foot 25 Jun 1802; Major in 57th Foot 9 Jul 1803
Brevets: Brevet Major 26 Jan 1797; Brevet Lieutenant Colonel 29 Apr 1802
Service 1793–1815: Served in Peninsula Jul to Dec 1809
Died: Elvas, Portugal 24 Dec 1809
Sources: ARLI; CHAL; WEOF

731. *Henry SHADFORTH (1804–1809)*
Born: Newcastle-upon-Tyne 1778
Relations: Son of Thomas Shadforth of Newcastle and Elizabeth (Orde); cousin of Lieutenant Colonel Thomas Shadforth, 57th Foot
Entry to Army: Ensign in 19th Foot 23 May 1797 by purchase
Regimental Field Officer Promotions: Major in 57th Foot 25 Feb 1804 by purchase; to half-pay of Queen's Rangers 1 Jun 1809; Major in 10th Foot 25 May 1815 (vice Carey); to half-pay of 10th Foot 25 Feb 1816
Brevets: Brevet Lieutenant Colonel 4 Jun 1811; Brevet Colonel 27 May 1825; Major General 10 Jan 1837; Lieutenant General 9 Nov 1846; General 20 Jun 1854
Service 1793–1815: Served in Ceylon 1798–1801; Assistant Adjutant General on home staff 1806–1814; served in Malta 1815
Residence: North Bailey, Durham, County Durham
Died: Newcastle-upon-Tyne 30 Mar 1866
Sources: ANCB; ANCD; ANCW (father); ARLI; PHIL; WEOF

732. *Robert O'NEILL (1809–1810)*
See 703.
Major in 57th Foot 1 Jun 1809 (vice Shadforth) by exchange

733. *John McKenzie SCOTT (1810–1811)*
Born: Inverness-shire 1775
Relations: son of William Scott of Seabank and Anna McKenzie
Entry to Army: Ensign in 78th Foot 10 Mar 1793
Regimental Field Officer Promotions: Major in 57th Foot 15 Feb 1810 (vice Ross)
Brevets: Brevet Major 25 Apr 1808
Service 1793–1815: Served in Flanders 1794–1795; served in West Indies 1795–1802; served in Peninsula Jul 1809 to May 1811
Died: Killed in action at Albuera 16 May 1811
Sources: ARLI; CHAL; WEOF; WO 25/748; Inverness Journal & Northern Advertiser 8 May 1812

734. *Robert SHELTON (1810–1816)*
Born: County Limerick c.1768
Relations: Son of Robert Shelton of Rossmore House and Margaret (Powell); uncle of Captain John Willington Shelton, 28th Foot
Entry to Army: Volunteer; Ensign in 57th Foot 9 Oct 1794
Regimental Field Officer Promotions: Major in 57th Foot 1 Mar 1810 (vice O'Neill) by purchase
Service 1793–1815: Served in Allied Army of Occupation in France 1815–1817
Died: Valenciennes, France 3 Feb 1816
Sources: ANCW; ARLI; WEOF; Belfast Commercial Chronicle 21 Feb 1816

735. *Dudley ACKLAND (1810–1813)*
Born: Pembrokeshire 1785
Relations: Son of Dudley Ackland of Dublin and Haverfordwest, and Jane (James)
Entry to Army: Ensign in 57th Foot 11 Aug 1802
Regimental Field Officer Promotions: Major in 57th Foot 13 Dec 1810 (vice Bruce) by purchase
Service 1793–1815: Served in Peninsula Jul 1809 to Feb 1811; served in Peninsula Jun 1812 to Nov 1813
Awards and Honours: AGM (Nlle)
Residence: Boulston, Pembrokeshire
Died: Killed in action at Nivelle 10 Nov 1813
Sources: ANCB; ANCW; ARLI; CHAL; HALL; WEOF

736. *Thomas SHADFORTH (1811–1830)*
Born: Newcastle-upon-Tyne 1772
Relations: Son of Henry Shadforth of Newcastle and Esther (Giles); cousin of General Henry Shadforth; father of Lieutenant Henry John Tudor Shadforth, 57th Foot; and Lieutenant Colonel Thomas Shadforth, 57th Foot
Entry to Army: Ensign in 87th Foot 31 May 1798 by purchase
Regimental Field Officer Promotions: Major in 57th Foot 20 Jun 1811 (vice Scott); Lieutenant Colonel in 57th Foot 28 Sep 1830
Brevets: Brevet Lieutenant Colonel 12 Aug 1819
Service 1793–1815: Served in Peninsula Jul 1809 to Mar 1812
Later Service: Commanded 57th Foot in New

South Wales 1826–1831; director of Bank of Australia 1826–1843
Retired: 1831
Awards and Honours: MGSM (Bus Alb)
Residences: Ravenswood, near Mulgoa, New South Wales; Eveleigh House, Redfern, Sydney, New South Wales
Died: Eveleigh House 4 Aug 1862
Sources: ANCB; ARLI; CHAL; WEOF; Australian Dictionary of Biography

737. *Walter McGIBBON (1813–1818)*
Born: Argyllshire 1781
Relations: Son of Neil McGibbon of Inveraray and Mary (Campbell)
Entry to Army: Ensign in 46th Foot 19 May 1798 by purchase
Regimental Field Officer Promotions: Major in 57th Foot 4 Jun 1813; to half-pay of 62nd Foot 2 Jul 1818 (vice Carey)
Service 1793–1815: Served in Peninsula Jul 1809 to Sep 1811, wounded at Albuera
Died: Edinburgh Jul 1823
Sources: ARLI; CHAL; FMPD; WEOF

738. *John BURROWS (1813–1816)*
Born: Essex 1769
Relations: Son of John Burrows of Bradwell juxta Coggleshall
Entry to Army: Lieutenant in 4th West India Regiment 1 Sep 1795
Regimental Field Officer Promotions: Major in 57th Foot 19 Nov 1813 (vice Ackland); to half-pay of 57th Foot 25 Feb 1816
Brevets: Brevet Major 26 Aug 1813
Service 1793–1815: Served in Peninsula Jul 1809 to Feb 1814, wounded at Pyrenees and Nivelle
Awards and Honours: MGSM (Vitt Pyr Nlle)
Residences: Hastings, Sussex; Hamilton Terrace, St Marylebone, London
Died: Hastings 20 Aug 1853
Sources: ANCD; ANCW; ARLI; CHAL; WEOF

Selected Regimental Histories
Kingsford, Charles Lethbridge, *The Story of the Duke of Cambridge's Own (Middlesex Regiment)* (London: Offices of Country Life, 1916)
Warre, Henry James, *Historical Records of the Fifty-seventh, or, West Middlesex Regiment of Foot* (London: W. Mitchell and Company, 1878)

Regimental Museum
Princess of Wales's Royal Regiment and Queens Regiment Museum, 5 Keep Yard, Dover Castle, Dover

---

58th Regiment of Foot

Secondary Title:	Rutlandshire
Nicknames:	The Steelbacks
	The Honeysuckers
Jacket:	Red
Facings:	Black

Regimental Lineage, 58th Regiment of Foot

1755:	Raised by Colonel Robert Anstruther as 60th Regiment of Foot
1757:	58th Regiment of Foot
1782:	58th (Rutlandshire) Regiment of Foot
1803:	Aug – 2nd Battalion formed in Kinsale
1815:	Dec – 2nd Battalion disbanded in Hull
1881:	2nd Battalion, The Northamptonshire Regiment (on amalgamation with the 48th (Northamptonshire) Regiment of Foot)
1960:	2nd East Anglian Regiment (Duchess of Gloucester's Own Royal Lincolnshire and Northamptonshire) (on amalgamation with 1st Battalion, Royal Lincolnshire Regiment)
1964:	2nd Battalion, Royal Anglian Regiment (Duchess of Gloucester's Own Royal Lincolnshire and Northamptonshire) (on amalgamation with 1st East Anglian Regiment (Royal Norfolk and Suffolk Regiment), 3rd East Anglian Regiment (16th/44th Foot) and the Royal Leicestershire Regiment)

Service History, 1st Battalion 58th Regiment of Foot

1793:	Cork; Jul – to England; Aug – Plymouth; Nov – to West Indies
1794:	Jan – Barbados; Mar – capture of MARTINIQUE; Apr – St Lucia; Jul – eight companies in Martinique, two companies in Guadeloupe; Sep – Martinique
1795:	Grenada; May – Grenada and Martinique; drafted out to other regiments, cadre to England; Jul – Hull; Aug – Halton; Sep – Beverley; Nov – Chatham
1796:	Chatham; Feb – Bristol; Mar – Cirencester; Jun – Fareham; Jul – West Cowes; Aug – Gosport; Sep – Cowes; Nov – Poole
1797:	Poole; Mar – Barnstaple; Jun – Jersey
1798:	Jersey; Sep – Portsmouth; to Gibraltar; Nov – capture of Minorca
1799:	Minorca; Port Mahon; Genoa
1800:	Genoa; Sep – capture of Malta; Oct – to Egypt
1801:	Bay of Marmorice [Marmaris]; Mar – EGYPT; Aboukir; Lake Mareotis; Alexandria; Jun – siege of Cairo; Oct – to Malta; Nov – Malta; to Ireland
1802:	Feb – Waterford; Mar – Kinsale; Apr – Charlesfort; May – Waterford
1803:	Waterford; Oct – Kinsale; received Irish Army of Reserve men; Nov – to Jersey
1804:	Jersey; Dec – Portsmouth
1805:	Winchester; Mar – Portsmouth; to Mediterranean; May – Gibraltar; Jul – Malta; Nov – Bay of Naples; Castellamare; Dec – Capua
1806:	Malta; Sicily; Jun – Messina; to Calabria; Jul – MAIDA; Gaeta; St Euphemia; Aug – Sicily; Messina
1807–1808:	Messina
1809:	Messina; Jun – Ischia; Aug – Messina
1810–1811:	Messina
1812:	Messina; Jun – to east coast of Spain; Aug – Alicante
1813:	Alicante; Valencia; Apr – Castalla; Jun – Tarragona; Valencia; Vinares; Sep – Ordal; Tarragona
1814:	Tarragona; Barcelona; May – to France; Bordeaux; to British North America; Jul – Montréal; Fort Henry
1815:	Fort Henry; Jun – Québec; Jul – to Belgium; Aug – Ostend; Paris; Allied Army of Occupation; St Denis; Oct – to Ireland; Birr

Service History, 2nd Battalion 58th Regiment of Foot

1803:	Aug – formed in Kinsale from Irish Army of Reserve men; Oct – Charlesfort
1804:	Charlesfort; Mar – Kinsale; Apr – to Jersey; St Helier
1805–1808:	Jersey
1809:	Jersey; Jun – to Portugal; PENINSULA; Jul – Lisbon garrison
1810:	Trancoso; Jun – Portalegre; Jul – Porto de Vide; Aug – Penalva do Castelo; Sep – Busaco; Vila Franca de Xira; Oct – Torres Vedras
1811:	Torres Vedras; Apr – Lisbon
1812:	Lisbon and Belem; Mar – Gáfete; May – Castelo de Vide; Jun – Salamanca forts; Jul – SALAMANCA; Peñaranda de Bracamonte; Aug – El Escorial; Sep – siege of Burgos; Oct – Valladolid; Nov – Naves; Dec – Vila Nova de Foz Côa; amalgamated with 2/24th Foot in 3rd Provisional Battalion (as four companies)
1813:	Four service companies at Vila Nova de Foz Côa; Feb – Torrejoncillos; Mar – Vila Nova de Foz Côa; May – Malhadas; Jun – VITTORIA; Echarri; Jul – PYRENEES; Maya; Sorauren; Aug – Echelar; Nov – NIVELLE; Saint-Pée-sur-Nivelle; Dec – Ustaritz Feb – six companies ordered home; Portsmouth; Battle; May – Hastings
1814:	Four service companies in Hasparren; Feb – ORTHEZ; Hastingues; Mar – Bordeaux; Camarsac; Apr – Lormont; May – Pauillac; Jun – to England; joined rest of battalion at Hastings Six home companies in Hastings
1815:	Hastings; May – Gravesend; Jun – Hull; Dec – disbanded in Hull

Establishments, 1st Battalion 58th Regiment of Foot

Year	Subunits	Field Off	Off/ Staff	Sjts	Mus	Corp/ Pvts	Total
Dec 1792	10co	3	32	22	12	430	499
Feb 1793	10co	3	32	32	22	600	689
Dec 1793	10co	3	32	42	22	850	949
Dec 1795	10co+2r	5	51	62	30	1,010	1,158
Dec 1797	10co	5	38	53	22	600	718
Feb 1802	10co	5	32	53	22	600	712
Oct 1803	10co	5	36	54	22	1,000	1,117
Dec 1806	10co	4	36	54	22	1,000	1,116
Dec 1807	10co	4	46	54	22	1,000	1,126
Jun 1809	10co+r	4	50	62	26	1,008	1,150
Dec 1811	10co+r	4	50	63	26	1,008	1,151
Dec 1813	10co	4	46	55	22	1,000	1,127

Establishments, 2nd Battalion 58th Regiment of Foot

Year	Subunits	Field Off	Off/ Staff	Sjts	Mus	Corp/ Pvts	Total
Mar 1804	10co	3	35	53	22	1,000	1,113
Dec 1805	10co	3	36	43	22	800	904
Dec 1806	10co	3	35	33	22	600	693
Dec 1807	10co	3	36	43	22	800	904
Jun 1809	10co+r	3	39	41	26	608	717
Dec 1811	10co+r	3	39	42	26	608	718
Dec 1813	10co	3	35	34	22	600	694
Dec 1814	10co	3	35	25	22	400	485

Service Statistics, 58th Regiment of Foot

	Lieutenant Colonels	Majors
Number of officers in period 1793–1815	11	16
Average age on appointment to substantive rank	45.5	33.5
Average time in rank in regiment (years)	6	5
Total field officers by nationality	10 S / 7 E / 7 I / 1 A / 1 F	
Demographics of other ranks 1797	46% EW / 46% I / 7% S / 1% F	
Demographics of other ranks 1804	1/58th: 79% I / 17% EW / 3% S / 1% F	
Demographics of other ranks 1808	2/58th: 85% I / 14% EW / 1% S	
Demographics of other ranks 1815	1/58th: 74% I / 23% EW / 3% S	
Months of overseas service 1793–1815	1/58th: 185 2/85th: 61	

Significant Militia/Volunteer Intakes:

1803: Irish Army of Reserve men
1804: Additional Force Act men from Cork City, Cork County and County Kerry
1806: Dublin County, County Kerry, County Louth, Queen's County
1807: County Donegal, Dublin County, County Louth
1808: County Kerry, County Louth
1811: North Mayo, South Mayo

Regimental Colonels

739. *George SCOTT (1787–1811)*
Born: England c.1734
Relations: Natural son of Francis Scott, 2nd Duke of Buccleuch
Entry to Army: Ensign in Coldstream Foot Guards 21 Dec 1749 by purchase
Regimental Field Officer Promotions: Major in 89th Foot 13 Oct 1759; to half-pay of 89th Foot 1765; Lieutenant Colonel in 61st Foot 26 Feb 1773
Brevets: Brevet Lieutenant Colonel 9 Feb 1762; Brevet Colonel 19 Aug 1777; Major General 19 Oct 1781; Lieutenant General 12 Oct 1793; General 1 Jan 1798
Colonelcies: 83rd Foot 16 Dec 1777; 58th Foot 18 Apr 1787 (vice Baugh)
Early Service: Served in East Indies; Lieutenant Governor of Windsor Castle 1782
Service 1793–1815: On staff in North Eastern District 1793
Residence: Wolston, Warwickshire
Died: Wolston 26 Jun 1811
Sources: ANCD; ANCW; ARLI; WEOF

740. *Rt Hon. Richard Ford William Lambart, 7th Earl of CAVAN (1811–1823)*
Born: London 1763
Relations: Son of Lieutenant General Richard Lambart, 6th Earl of Cavan and Elizabeth (Davies)
Entry to Army: Ensign in Coldstream Foot Guards 2 Apr 1779 by purchase
Regimental Field Officer Promotions: Captain and Lieutenant Colonel in Coldstream Foot Guards 23 Aug 1793 (vice Bosville); Second Major in Coldstream Foot Guards 9 May 1800 (vice Cowell); First Major in Coldstream Foot Guards 19 Nov 1800 (vice Cowell)
Brevets: Brevet Colonel 21 Aug 1795; Major General 18 Jun 1798; Lieutenant General 1 Jul 1811; General 4 Jun 1814
Colonelcies: Colonel Commandant of 2/68th Foot 18 Jun 1801; 2nd West India Regiment 27 Sep 1805 (vice Myers); 77th Foot 25 Mar 1808 (vice Bertie); 58th Foot 1 Jul 1811 (vice Scott); 45th Foot 10 Feb 1823 (vice Lister)
Service 1793–1815: Served in Flanders 1793, wounded at Valenciennes; served in Irish Rebellion 1798; served in Ferrol 1800; commanded Brigade of Guards in Egypt 1801, and later the army after departure of Hely-Hutchinson
Creations and Dignities: 7th Viscount Kilcoursie 1772; 7th Earl of Cavan 2 Nov 1778; 8th Baron Lambart 2 Nov 1778
Awards and Honours: KCt (Ottoman) 19 Apr 1803
Residences: Stanhope Place, Hyde Park, London
Died: London 21 Nov 1837
Sources: ANCB; ANCD; ARLI; DINB; PHIL; WEOF

Lieutenant Colonels

741. *Robert STEWART (1792–1795)*
Born: Ireland c.1747
Relations: [spec.] Son of William Stewart of Killymoon Castle, County Tyrone MP, and Elinor (King)
Entry to Army: Cornet in 2nd Horse 31 Dec 1769
Regimental Field Officer Promotions: Major in 4th Dragoon Guards 31 Oct 1790 (vice Loftus); Lieutenant Colonel in 58th Foot 30 Nov 1792 (vice Brereton)
Service 1793–1815: Commanded grenadier battalion in West Indies 1794
Died: Of fever in Martinique 5 Aug 1794
Sources: ANCB; ARLI; WikiTree

742. *William CUNNINGHAME (1794–1795)*
Born: Stirlingshire 1753
Relations: Son of Colonel George Cunninghame of Bandalloch and Esther (Jollie); brother of Major General John Cunninghame
Entry to Army: Ensign in 58th Foot 26 Dec 1770
Regimental Field Officer Promotions: Major in 58th Foot 31 Jan 1793 (vice McMyne); Lieutenant Colonel in 58th Foot 25 Oct 1794
Retired: 9 Jun 1795
Militia Career: Major in Royal Manx Fencibles Nov 1798
Residence: Ballanorris, Isle of Man
Died: Ballanorris 30 Aug 1825
Sources: ANCB; ANCD; ARLI; <http://www.isle-of-man.com/manxnotebook/history/gtaubman/jt_1791.htm>

743. *John HALLOWES (1795)*
Born: Derbyshire 1729
Relations: Son of Thomas Hallowes of Glapwell Hall and Catherine (Brabazon); grandson of Chambré Brabazon, 5th Earl of Meath; brother of Lieutenant Chambré Hallowes, 58th Foot
Entry to Army: Ensign in 29th Foot 10 Mar 1753 by purchase
Regimental Field Officer Promotions: Lieutenant Colonel 58th Foot 16 Apr 1795 (vice Stewart)
Brevets: Brevet Major 29 Aug 1777; Brevet Lieutenant Colonel 19 Feb 1783; Brevet Colonel 1 Mar 1794

Early Service: Served in Gibraltar 1774–1783
Retired: 21 Oct 1794
Service 1793–1815: Barrackmaster in Ashford 1797–1817
Residence: Ashford, Kent
Died: Ashford 24 May 1817
Sources: ARLI; <http://www.hallowesgenealogy.co.uk/halgen00.htm>

744. *Alexander BAILLIE (1795)*
Born: Inverness-shire 1731
Relations: Son of Hugh Baillie of Dochfour and Emilia (Fraser)
Entry to Army: Ensign in 62nd (later 60th) Foot 9 Dec 1756
Regimental Field Officer Promotions: Major in 9th Foot 17 Feb 1794 (vice Ritchie); Lieutenant Colonel in 58th Foot 16 Apr 1795 (vice Hallowes)
Brevets: Brevet Major 18 Nov 1790; Brevet Lieutenant Colonel 1 Mar 1794
Early Service: Served in North America 1756, wounded at Ticonderoga; served in American Revolution
Service 1793–1815: Served in capture of Tobago 1793; served in St Lucia 1794
Retired: 2 Jun 1795
Residence: Duchour, Inverness-shire; Bath, Somerset
Died: Bath 23 Feb 1799
Sources: ANCD; ANCW; ARLI; GHLG; Hadden's Journal and Orderly Books; A History and Genealogy of the Family of Baillie of Dunain, Dochfour and Lamington

745. *Sir William HOUSTOUN, 1st Bt (1795–1811)*
Born: Wigtownshire 1766
Relations: Son of Andrew Houstoun of Calderhaugh and Helen (Waddell); son-in-law of James Maitland, 7th Earl of Lauderdale; father of Colonel Sir George Augustus Frederick Houston-Boswall, Bt; and Captain William Houstoun, 10th Hussars
Entry to Army: Ensign in 31st Foot 18 Jul 1781 by purchase
Regimental Field Officer Promotions: Major in 19th Foot 30 Mar 1794 (vice Onslow) by purchase; Lieutenant Colonel in 84th Foot 21 Mar 1795 by purchase; Lieutenant Colonel in 58th Foot 10 Jun 1795 (vice Cuninghame)
Brevets: Brevet Major 1 Mar 1794; Brevet Colonel 29 Apr 1802; Brigadier General (Mediterranean) 1804; Major General 25 Oct 1809; Lieutenant General 4 Jun 1814; General 10 Jan 1837
Colonelcies: 4th Garrison Battalion 1 Jul 1811 (vice Hastings); 20th Foot 5 Apr 1815 (vice Stuart)
Early Service: Served in Jamaica 1785–1789
Service 1793–1815: Commanded 19th Foot in Flanders 1794–1795; commanded 58th Foot in capture of Minorca 1798; commanded brigade in Egypt 1801; commanded brigades in Malta and at home 1802–1803; commanded brigade in Walcheren 1809; commanded brigade in 4th Division in Peninsula Jan to Mar 1811; commanded 7th Division in Peninsula Mar to Aug 1811; commanded South West District 1814
Later Service: Groom of the Bedchamber to King George IV and King William IV 1825–1837; acting Governor of Gibraltar 8 Apr 1831 to 28 Feb 1835
Creations and Dignities: 1st Baronet 19 Jul 1836
Awards and Honours: KCt (Ottoman) 1802; AGM (FDO); KCB 2 Jan 1815; GCH 12 Aug 1827; GCB 24 Feb 1831
Residence: Bromley Hill, Kent; Arlington Street, Piccadilly, London
Died: Bromley Hill 8 Apr 1842
Sources: ANCB; ANCD; ANCW; ARLI; CHAL; DINB; ODNB; PHIL; WEMR; WEOF; WOST; WO 25/746; Wellington's Peninsular War Generals

746. *Stephen BROMFIELD (1795–1796)*
See 234.
Lieutenant Colonel in 58th Foot 2 Jul 1795 (vice Cunninghame)

747. *Robert DOUGLAS (1796–1802)*
Born: Fifeshire 1760
Relations: Son of Colonel Robert Douglas of Strathendry and Cecilia (Craigie); brother of David Douglas, Lord Reston
Entry to Army: Ensign in 58th Foot 13 May 1776 by purchase
Regimental Field Officer Promotions: Major in 58th Foot 25 Oct 1794 (vice Cunninghame); Lieutenant Colonel in 58th Foot 4 Jun 1796 (vice Bromfield) by purchase
Service 1793–1815: Served in West Indies
Retired: 27 Nov 1802
Later Service: Inspecting Field Officer of Yeomanry and Volunteers Oct 1803
Residence: Portobello, Midlothian
Died: Portobello 10 Mar 1832
Sources: ANCD; ARLI; WEOF; <https://www.douglashistory.co.uk/history/robert_douglas32.htm>

748. *George JOHNSTONE (1802–1806)*
See 368.
Lieutenant Colonel in 58th Foot 27 Nov 1802 (vice Douglas) by purchase

749. *Thomas FITZGERALD (1804–1810)*
Born: County Kilkenny c.1757
Relations: Son of Nicholas Fitzgerald of Greensborough and Margaret (Stevenson)
Entry to Army: Ensign in 3rd Foot 5 Oct 1776 by purchase
Regimental Field Officer Promotions: Major in 58th Foot 5 Apr 1801 (vice Ogle); Lieutenant Colonel in 58th Foot 28 Aug 1804
Brevets: Brevet Lieutenant Colonel 1 Jan 1798
Retired: 8 Nov 1810
Residence: Epsom, Surrey; Kilkar, County Roscommon
Died: Epsom 1 Sep 1837
Sources: ANCW; GHHI; WEOF; Dublin Mercantile Adviser 4 Sep 1837

750. *David WALKER (1809–1825)*
Born: Roxburghshire 1767
Relations: Son of Adam Walker of Kelso and Agnes (McDougall)
Entry to Army: Ensign in 20th Foot 30 Jun 1787
Regimental Field Officer Promotions: Major in 20th Foot 7 Feb 1800 (vice Grey) by purchase; Lieutenant Colonel in Royal Corsican Rangers 16 Apr 1807; Lieutenant Colonel in 58th Foot 16 Nov 1809; Lieutenant Colonel unattached 1825
Brevets: Brevet Colonel 4 Jun 1814; Major General 19 Jul 1821
Service 1793–1815: Served in West Indies 1794–1795; served in Helder 1799; served in Egypt 1801; served in Maida 1806; served in Ischia 1809; commanded 1/58th Foot in Peninsula Aug 1812 to Oct 1813; commanded brigade on east coast of Spain Oct 1813 to Feb 1814; commanded brigade in Allied Army of Occupation in France 1815
Retired: 18 Dec 1827
Residence: Riddleton Hill, Roxburghshire
Died: Holland Lodge, Edinburgh 28 Mar 1842
Sources: ANCB; ANCD; ARLI; CHAL; PHIL; WEOF

751. *Richard BUCKBY (1810–1813)*
See 429.
Major in 58th Foot 9 Jul 1803; Lieutenant Colonel in 58th Foot 8 Nov 1810 (vice Fitzgerald)

Majors

752. *William McMYNE (1791–1793)*
Born: Ayrshire 1736
Relations: Son of Surgeon William McMyne, 58th Foot
Entry to Army: Surgeon's Mate in 58th Foot 30 Apr 1760; Ensign in 58th Foot 5 Jun 1762
Regimental Field Officer Promotions: Major in 58th Foot 30 Jun 1791 (vice Bromhead)
Brevets: Brevet Major 19 Feb 1783
Early Service: Served in British North America; served in Gibraltar
Service 1793–1815: Commanded 58th Foot in Ireland early 1793 (made an honorary Freeman of the City of Cork)
Retired: 30 Jan 1793
Died: Ayrshire 1801
This officer's promotion to major created a vacancy for a new company commander in the 58th, which was filled by a certain Honourable Arthur Wesley
Sources: ANCW; ARLI

753. *John CROWGEY (1795–1803)*
Born: Cornwall 1767
Relations: Son of William Crowgey of St Gluvias and Phillippa (Richards); brother of Lieutenant Beauford Crowgey, 4th Royal Veteran Battalion
Entry to Army: Ensign in 58th Foot 9 Jun 1786 by purchase
Regimental Field Officer Promotions: Major in 58th Foot 1 Sep 1795; Lieutenant Colonel in 13th Battalion of Reserve 9 Jul 1803; Lieutenant Colonel in 1st Garrison Battalion 25 Feb 1805; Lieutenant Colonel in 72nd Foot 22 Jun 1809 (vice Seymour) by exchange; removed from the regiment as a general officer 1814
Brevets: Brevet Lieutenant Colonel 1 Jan 1801; Brevet Colonel 25 Jul 1810; Major General 4 Jun 1813
Service 1793–1815: Served in West Indies 1794–1795; served in Minorca 1798; served in Egypt 1801; commanded 2/72nd Foot 1809–1813
Residence: St Marylebone, London
Died: London 4 Jul 1815
Sources: ANCB; ANCD; ARLI; PHIL; WEOF; WO 25/744

754. *George HORSFORD (1796–1799)*
Antigua 1766
Relations: Son of John Horsford of Antigua and Christian (Jenkins); father of General Sir Alfred Hastings Horsford
Entry to Army: Ensign in 67th Foot 15 Aug 1787 by purchase
Regimental Field Officer Promotions: Major in 58th Foot 4 Jun 1796 (vice Douglas); Major in 59th Foot 30 Aug 1799 (vice Vassall) by exchange; Lieutenant Colonel in 4th West India Regiment 28 Aug 1801 (vice Cranston) by purchase; Lieutenant Colonel in 18th Foot 26 Jan 1809; removed from the Regiment as a general officer 1814

Brevets: Brevet Colonel 25 Jul 1810; Major General 4 Jun 1813; Lieutenant General 27 May 1825
Early Service: Served in West Indies 1787–1794
Service 1793–1815: Served at capture of Minorca 1798; commanded 59th Foot in West Indies 1799–1801; Deputy Adjutant General in Jamaica; commanded 1/18th Foot 1809–1812; Lieutenant Governor of Bermuda 14 Sep 1812 to 8 Jul 1816
Residence: Paris, Île-de-France, France
Died: Paris 28 Apr 1840
Sources: ANCW; ARLI; GEMA (1840); WEOF; WO 25/746; WOST

755. *Spencer Thomas VASSALL (1799–1800)*

See 194.
Major in 58th Foot 30 Aug 1799 (vice Horsford) by exchange

756. *Thomas OGLE (1800–1801)*

Born: Hampshire 1776
Relations: Son of Admiral Sir Chaloner Ogle of Worthy, 1st Bt, and Hester (Thomas); brother of Admiral Sir Charles Ogle
Entry to Army: Ensign in 7th Foot 20 Nov 1793 by purchase
Regimental Field Officer Promotions: Maj in 58th Foot 3 Apr 1800 (vice Vassall) by purchase
Service 1793–1815: Served in Minorca 1798; served in Egypt 1801
Died: Killed in action at Aboukir 8 Mar 1801
Sources: ANCB; ANCD; ARLI; WEOF

757. *John George BRADFORD (1803–1810)*

Born: Devon 1764
Relations: Son of John Bradford of Wolborough, clerk, and Elizabeth (Cooke)
Entry to Army: Ensign in 99th Foot 17 Sep 1784
Regimental Field Officer Promotions: Major in 58th Foot 9 Jul 1803 (vice Crowgey)
Service 1793–1815: Served in West Indies 1794–1796; served in Ostend raid 1798; served in Helder 1799; served in Egypt 1801; served in Mediterranean 1805–1810; served at Maida 1806
Retired: 29 Mar 1810
Residence: Bishopsteignton, Devon
Died: Bideford, Devon 13 Mar 1818
Sources: FMPB; ANCD; ANCW; ARLI; WEOF; WO 25/744

758. *Brook Henry YOUNG (1804–1812)*

Born: London 1780
Relations: Son of Sir William Young, 2nd Bt, MP and Governor of Tobago, and Sarah (Lawrence); brother of Sir William Lawrence Young, 3rd Bt
Entry to Army: Ensign in 85th Foot 18 Nov 1793
Regimental Field Officer Promotions: Major in 58th Foot 1 Sep 1804 (vice Fitzgerald)
Brevets: Brevet Lieutenant Colonel 4 Jun 1811
Service 1793–1815: Served in Gibraltar 1796; served in Egypt 1801; served in Peninsula with 2/58th Jul 1809 to Jul 1810
Retired: 5 Nov 1812
Residence: Brompton, Middlesex
Died: Brompton 21 Sep 1813
Was baptised as Brook-Harry Young
Sources: ANCB; ANCD; ARLI; CHAL; WEOF; WO 25/748

759. *Sir John Alexander Dunlop Agnew WALLACE, 7th Bt (1803–1804)*

Born: Ayrshire 1774
Relations: Son of General Sir Thomas Dunlop Wallace of Craigie, 6th Bt, and Eglantine (Maxwell); father of Sir William Thomas Francis Dunlop-Agnew-Wallace, 8th Bt
Entry to Army: Ensign in 75th Foot 28 Dec 1787 by purchase
Regimental Field Officer Promotions: Major in 58th Foot 9 Jul 1803; Lieutenant Colonel in 11th Garrison Battalion 28 Aug 1804 (vice Marriott); Lieutenant Colonel in 88th Foot 6 Feb 1805 (vice Buller); removed from the regiment as a general officer 1825
Brevets: Brevet Colonel 4 Jun 1813; Major General 12 Aug 1819; Lieutenant General 10 Aug 1837; General 11 Nov 1851
Colonelcies: 88th Foot 20 Oct 1831 (vice Campbell)
Early Service: Served in East Indies 1788–1796
Service 1793–1815: Served in Minorca 1798; served in Egypt 1801; served in Peninsula with 1/88th Foot Aug 1809 to Jul 1811; temporarily commanded brigade in 3rd Division in Peninsula May to Nov 1812; commanded 1/88th in Peninsula Nov 1812 to Jan 1813, commanded brigade in Allied Army of Occupation in France 1815
Creations and Dignities: 7th Baronet of Craigie 4 Oct 1835
Awards and Honours: AGM (Bus FDO Sal); CB 4 Jun 1815; KCB 18 Sep 1833; MGSM (Egt)
Residence: Lochryan House, Stranraer, Wigtownshire
Died: Lochryan House 10 Feb 1857
Sources: ANCB; ANCD; ARLI; CHAL; DINB; PHIL; WEOF; WO 25/748

760. *Alexander HENRY (1804–1813)*
Born: Scotland c.1769
Entry to Army: Ensign in 8th Foot Jun 1794
Regimental Field Officer Promotions: Major in 58th Foot 28 Sep 1804 (vice Wallace)
Brevets: Brevet Lieutenant Colonel 4 Jun 1811
Service 1793–1815: Served in Minorca 1800; served in Peninsula with 2/58th Jul to Dec 1809; served in east coast of Spain with 1/58th Aug 1812 to Mar 1813
Retired: 15 Jul 1813
Residence: Windsor House, Kingsbridge, Devon
Died: Kingsbridge 25 Nov 1834
Sources: ANCD; ANCW; ARLI; UNSM (1835)

761. *Francis Browne CAMPBELL (1810–1826)*
Born: Sussex c.1781
Relations: Son of John Campbell of Chichester and Sarah (unk.)
Entry to Army: Lieutenant 28 Aug 1794
Regimental Field Officer Promotions: Major in 58th Foot 29 Mar 1810 (vice Bradford) by purchase; to Lieutenant Colonel unattached on half-pay 25 Apr 1826
Brevets: Brevet Lieutenant Colonel 26 Aug 1813
Service 1793–1815: Served in Peninsula with 1/58th Aug to Dec 1812; served in Peninsula with 2/58th Apr 1813 to Apr 1814, wounded in Pyrenees; commanded 3rd Provisional Battalion at Orthez
Awards and Honours: AGM (Ort)
Residences: College Street, Westminster, London; Millbrook, Jersey, Channel Islands
Died: Jersey 1 Jun 1827
Sources: ANCD; ANCW; ANCW; WEOF

762. *Sir Frederick ASHWORTH, Kt (1810–1817)*
Born: Dublin 1783
Relations: Son of Robert Ashworth of Dublin and Elizabeth (Woodward); brother of Major General Charles Ashworth
Entry to Army: Ensign in 68th Foot 6 Jul 1799 by purchase
Regimental Field Officer Promotions: Major in 58th Foot 22 Nov 1810 (vice Buckby) by purchase; to half-pay of 58th Foot 20 Feb 1817
Brevets: Brevet Colonel 10 Jan 1837; Major General 9 Nov 1846; Lieutenant General 20 Jun 1854
Colonelcies: 44th Foot 8 Feb 1855 (vice Stuart)
Service 1793–1815: Served in Calabria 1806; served in Sicily 1809; served in Peninsula with 2/58th Feb 1812 to Jan 1813; served in Peninsula with 1/58th Nov 1813 to Apr 1814; served in British North America 1814; served in Allied Army of Occupation in France 1815
Awards and Honours: MGSM (Maid Sal); Knight Bachelor 1850
Residences: Grafton Street, Mayfair, London; Kemp Town, Brighton, Sussex
Died: London 1 Aug 1858
Sources: ANCD; ANCW; ARLI; CHAL; PBKN; PHIL; WEOF

763. *Sir Thomas KENAH (1812–1817)*
Born: County Cork 1782
Relations: Son of Thomas Kenah of Bridgefield and Alice (Pratt)
Entry to Army: Ensign in West Suffolk Militia; Ensign in 5th Foot 14 Aug 1799
Regimental Field Officer Promotions: Major in 58th Foot 5 Nov 1812 (vice Young) by purchase; to half-pay of 58th Foot 25 Feb 1816; Major in 58th Foot 20 Feb 1817; to half-pay of 58th Foot 3 Apr 1817
Brevets: Brevet Lieutenant Colonel 27 Dec 1813; Brevet Colonel 22 Jul 1830; Major General 23 Nov 1841; Lieutenant General 11 Nov 1851; General 26 Dec 1859
Colonelcies: 63rd Foot 25 Nov 1850 (vice Watson)
Service 1793–1815: Served in Helder 1799; served in Egypt 1801; served in Peninsula Jul 1812 to Sep 1813; Assistant Adjutant General in East Spain 1813; served in Genoa 1814
Awards and Honours: CB 24 Oct 1818; MGSM (Egt); KCB 28 Mar 1865
Residence: Albemarle Street, Mayfair, London
Died: London 26 Mar 1868
Sources: ANCD; ARLI; CHAL; GEMA (1868); PHIL; WEOF

764. *George DRUITT (1813–1816)*
Born: Dublin c.1775
Relations: Son of Edward Druitt of Dublin and Jane (Cottingham)
Entry to Army: Ensign in 121st Foot 11 Oct 1794 by purchase
Regimental Field Officer Promotions: Major in 58th Foot 4 Apr 1813 (vice Henry) by purchase; to half-pay of 58th Foot 25 Feb 1816; Major in 48th Foot 3 Oct 1816 (vice Marston)
Service 1793–1815: Served in Minorca 1798; served in Mediterranean 1805–1812; served in British North America 1814–1815
Later Service: Served as civil engineer in New South Wales 1817–1822
Retired: 26 Jul 1822

Residence: Mount Druitt, New South Wales
Died: Sydney, New South Wales 8 Jun 1842
Sources: ARLI; PHIL; WEOF; Australian Dictionary of Biography, Vol.1

Selected Regimental Histories
Gurney, Russell, *History of the Northamptonshire Regiment: 1742–1934* (Aldershot: Gale & Polden, 1935)

Regimental Museum
Abington Park Museum, Park Avenue South, Northampton, Northamptonshire

---

59th Regiment of Foot

Secondary Title:	2nd Nottinghamshire
Nicknames:	The Lilywhites
Jacket:	Red
Facings:	White

Regimental Lineage, 59th Regiment of Foot

1755:	Raised in Leicestershire and Northamptonshire by Sir Charles Montagu as 61st Regiment of Foot
1756:	59th Regiment of Foot
1782:	59th (2nd Nottinghamshire) Regiment of Foot
1804:	Aug – 2nd Battalion formed in Chesterfield
1816:	Mar – 2nd Battalion disbanded in Gosport
1881:	1st Battalion, The West Lancashire Regiment (on amalgamation with the 30th (Cambridgeshire) Regiment of Foot)
1881:	1st Battalion, The East Lancashire Regiment
1958:	The Lancashire Regiment (Prince of Wales's Volunteers) (on amalgamation with the South Lancashire Regiment (Prince of Wales's Volunteers))
1970:	The Queen's Lancashire Regiment (on amalgamation with The Loyal Regiment (North Lancashire))
2006:	1st Battalion, The Duke of Lancaster's Regiment (on amalgamation with 1st Battalion, King's Regiment, and 1st Battalion, King's Own Royal Border Regiment)

Service History, 1st Battalion 59th Regiment of Foot

1793:	Hilsea; Apr – Jersey; Oct – on transports ordered to Flanders; Ostend; Nov – to England
1794:	On board transports; May – to Flanders; Jun – Ostend; Jul – Alost; Oct – Nijmegen; Dec – line of River Waal
1795:	Lent; retreat to Bremen; Mar – Bremen; Apr – to England; May – Gosport; Jun – Eling; Jul – Southampton; to West Indies; Sep – St Vincent; Kingstown; Oct – La Vigie
1796:	St Vincent; Mount William; Millar's Ridge; Jun – New Vigie; Jul – St Kitts and Antigua
1797:	St Kitts and Antigua; Oct – Antigua
1798–1801:	Antigua
1802:	St Vincent; Jun – to England; Sep – Hilsea; Oct – Trowbridge and Bradford
1803:	Trowbridge and Bradford; Jun – Dungeness; Aug – Shorncliffe; Dec – Hythe
1804:	Shorncliffe; Jul – Hythe; Nov – Dover
1805:	Dover; Jun – Riding Street; Jul – Hilsea; Aug – to Cape of Good Hope
1806:	Capture of CAPE OF GOOD HOPE; Feb – to East Indies; Apr – Madras [Chennai]; May – Poonamallee; Aug – Vellore
1807:	Vellore; Mar – Bangalore [Bengaluru]
1808:	Bangalore

1809:	Bangalore; Feb – Mysore [Mysuru]; Mar – Travancore [Thiruvithamkoor]; Apr – Lackeny Cottah [Lakkenahalli]; May – Bangalore; Aug – Seringapatam [Srirangapatna]; Nov – Bangalore
1810:	Bangalore; Sep – Madras; to Mauritius; Nov – capture of Mauritius; Dec – to Madras
1811:	At sea; Feb – Madras; St Thomas Mount; Apr – to JAVA; Aug – capture of Batavia; Fort Cornelis; Weltevreden; Sep – Jattoo
1812	Batavia; Apr – five companies to Sumatra; May – Banca; Jun – Batavia; grenadier company to Jogjakarta
1813–1814:	Batavia
1815:	Batavia; Jul – to India; Sep – Diamond Harbour; Oct – Calcutta [Kolkata]; Fort William

Service History, 2nd Battalion 59th Regiment of Foot

1804:	Aug – formed in Chesterfield
1805:	Chesterfield
1806:	Ashbourne; Dec – Newark
1807:	Newark; Aug – Peterborough; Sep – Colchester
1808:	Colchester; Mar – Weeley; Sep – Harwich; Falmouth; Oct – to Spain; Nov – Corunna; Nov – Astorga; Dec – Mayorga; Astorga
1809:	Retreat to Corunna; CORUNNA: to England; Feb – Weeley; Aug – to Walcheren; Oct – to England; Weeley
1810:	Weeley; Feb – to Ireland; Fermoy; Apr – Dublin; Jul – Drogheda; Aug – Newry
1811:	Newry; Apr – Fermoy; Jul – to England; Aug – Chichester; Sep – Jersey
1812:	Chichester; Sep – to Portugal; PENINSULA; Lisbon; Cadiz
1813:	Cadiz; Mar – to Portugal; Apr – Santarem; May – Outeiro; Jun – VITTORIA; Salvatierra; siege of San Sebastian; Aug – SAN SEBASTIAN; Oct – St Jean de Luz; Nov – Nivelle; Bidart; Dec – NIVE; Bidart
1814:	Arbonne; Feb – Bayonne; Mar – Arcangues; Apr – Bayonne; Jul – Bordeaux; Aug – to Ireland; Sep – Cork; Nov – Carlow; Dec – Dublin
1815:	Dublin; Feb – to England; Apr – Deal; May – Dover; to Belgium; Jun – Hal (missed Waterloo); Jul – Paris; Allied Army of Occupation
1816:	To Ireland; 278 men lost when transport *Seahorse* lost in Tramore Bay; Feb – Cork; Mar – to England; disbanded in Gosport

Establishments, 1st Battalion 59th Regiment of Foot

Year	Subunits	Field Off	Off/ Staff	Sjts	Mus	Corp/ Pvts	Total
Dec 1792	10co	3	32	22	12	430	499
Feb 1793	10co	3	32	32	22	600	689
Dec 1793	10co	3	32	42	22	850	949
Dec 1795	10co+2r	5	51	62	30	1,010	1,158
Dec 1797	10co	5	38	53	22	600	718
Dec 1802	10co	5	33	34	22	750	844
Dec 1803	10co	5	36	34	22	750	847
Dec 1804	10co	5	46	54	22	1,000	1,127
Dec 1807	10co	5	46	64	22	1,200	1,337
Dec 1808	10co+r	5	50	72	26	1,208	1,361
Dec 1809	10co	5	46	54	22	1,000	1,127
Dec 1810	10co	5	46	64	22	1,200	1,337
Dec 1811	10co	5	46	65	22	1,200	1,338
Dec 1812	10co+r	5	50	73	26	1,208	1,362
Dec 1813	10co+r	5	49	73	22	1,208	1,357
Dec 1814	10co	5	46	55	22	1,000	1,128
Dec 1815	10co	5	46	45	22	800	918

Establishments, 2nd Battalion 59th Regiment of Foot

Year	Subunits	Field Off	Off/ Staff	Sjts	Mus	Corp/ Pvts	Total
Dec 1804	10co	3	35	23	22	400	483
Dec 1807	10co	3	35	33	22	600	693
Aug 1808	10co+r	3	39	51	26	808	927
May 1809	10co	3	46	53	22	1,000	1,124
Jan 1810	10co	4	46	54	22	1,000	1,126
Dec 1811	10co	3	46	55	22	1,000	1,126
Dec 1812	10co+r	3	50	63	26	1,008	1,150
Dec 1813	10co+r	3	49	63	22	1,008	1,145

Service Statistics, 59th Regiment of Foot

	Lieutenant Colonels	Majors
Number of officers in period 1793–1815	10	21
Average age on appointment to substantive rank	35	33.5
Average time in rank in regiment (years)	9.5	4
Total field officers by nationality	11 S / 9 E / 7 I / 2 A / 1 F	
Demographics of other ranks 1803	64% EW / 22% I / 12% S / 2% F	
Demographics of other ranks 1808	2/59th: 61% EW / 35% I / 4% S	
Demographics of other ranks 1815	1/59th: 58% EW / 28% I / 12% S / 2% F	
Months of overseas service 1793–1815	1/59th: 219 2/59th: 36	

Significant Militia/Volunteer Intakes

1806: County Tyrone
1807: Ross-shire, County Kildare, County Tipperary
1808: Cumberland, South Cork
1809: North Lincolnshire, 1st Somerset, Aberdeenshire, County Kildare, County Tipperary
1810: County Kildare, County Louth
1811: South Cork, County Kildare, County Westmeath
1812: County Antrim, South Cork
1813: County Louth

Regimental Colonels

765. *Sir David LINDSAY, 4th Bt (1776–1797)*
Born: Sutherlandshire c.1732
Relations: Son of Sir Alexander Lindsay, 3rd Bt, and Amelia (Murray); brother of Admiral Sir John Lindsay; nephew of William Murray, 1st Earl of Mansfield; father of William Lindsay, Governor of Tobago; and Captain Charles Lindsay RN
Entry to Army: Major in 1/1st Foot 27 May 1758 by purchase
Field Officer Promotions: Captain and Lieutenant Colonel in 1st Foot Guards 12 Oct 1758 by purchase
Brevets: Brevet Colonel 7 Aug 1771; Major General 6 Sep 1777; Lieutenant General 27 Feb 1779; General 14 May 1796
Colonelcies: 59th Foot 30 Jan 1776 (vice Owen)
Early Service: *Custos Brevium* of the Court of King's Bench 1758–1776; ADC to King George III 1771–1776; no active service after 1779
Dignities and Creations; 4th Baronet of Evelick 6 May 1762
Residences: Evelick, Sutherlandshire; Cavendish Square, Marylebone, London
Died: London 6 Mar 1797
This officer has not been found in any army list or the Gazette prior to 1758
Sources: ANCB; ANCD; ANCW; A Genealogical and Heraldic History of the Extinct and Dormant Baronetcies of England, Ireland, and Scotland

766. *Andrew GORDON (1797–1801)*
Born: Aberdeenshire c.1739
Relations: Son of James Gordon of Ellon and Elizabeth (Glen); brother of Lieutenant Colonel James Gordon, 80th Foot
Entry to Army: Ensign in 56th Foot 8 Sep 1759 by purchase
Field Officer Promotions: Major in 26th Foot 18 Jan 1777; Lieutenant Colonel in 101st Foot 13 Nov 1781; Lieutenant Colonel in 26th Foot 29 Jul 1784 (vice Stuart) by exchange
Brevets: Lieutenant Colonel (East Indies) 23 May 1781; Brevet Lieutenant Colonel 13 Jun 1782; Colonel (East Indies) 13 Jun 1782; Brevet Colonel 18 Nov 1790; Major General 3 Oct 1794; Lieutenant General (Jersey) 10 Nov 1799
Colonelcies: 89th Foot 23 Dec 1795; 59th Foot 2 Mar 1797 (vice Lindsay); 26th Foot 28 Mar 1801 (vice Stuart)
Early Service: Served in East Indies 1781–1784
Service 1793–1815: Lieutenant Governor of Jersey 1797–1806
Residence: St Helier, Jersey
Died: Jersey 17 Apr 1806
Sources: ANCD; ARLI; WEOF; Gordons Under Arms

767. *Alexander ROSS (1801–1827)*
Born: Aberdeenshire 1742
Relations: Son of James Ross of Midmar and Agnes (Dun)
Entry to Army: Ensign in 50th Foot 4 Feb 1760 by purchase
Field Officer Promotions: Major in 76th Foot 25 Oct 1787; Lieutenant Colonel in 76th Foot 1 Sep 1795
Brevets: Brevet Major 25 Oct 1780; Brevet Lieutenant Colonel 19 Feb 1783; Brevet Colonel 12 Oct 1793; Major General 26 Feb 1795; Lieutenant General 29 Apr 1802; General 1 Jan 1812
Colonelcies: 89th Foot 22 Dec 1797 (vice Bowyer); 59th Foot 28 Mar 1801 (vice Gordon)
Early Service: Served in Seven Years War; ADC to Cornwallis in American War of Independence 1775–1781; Deputy Adjutant General in East Indies 1791–1792
Service 1793–1815: Surveyor General of the Ordnance 1795–1804; Governor of Fort George and Fort Augustus 1804–1827
Residence: Portland Place, Marylebone, London
Died: London 20 Nov 1827
Sources: ANCB; ANCD; ANCW; DINB; PHIL; WEOF; WO 25/748

Lieutenant Colonels

768. *Sir George DON (1789–1799)*
Born: Edinburgh 1756
Relations: Son of John Don of Edinburgh, wine merchant, and Anna (Seton)
Entry to Army: Ensign in 51st Foot 26 Nov 1770 by purchase
Regimental Field Officer Promotions: Major in 71st Foot 25 Nov 1783 by purchase; Major in 59th Foot 21 Apr 1784 by exchange; Lieutenant Colonel in 59th Foot 9 Apr 1789
Brevets: Brevet Colonel 26 Feb 1795; Major General 1 Jan 1797; Lieutenant General 1 Jan 1803; General 4 Jun 1814
Colonelcies: 7th West India Regiment 22 Nov 1799 (vice Moore); 96th Foot 10 Oct 1805 (vice Ludlow); 36th Foot 4 Apr 1818 (vice St. John)
Early Service: Served on Minorca 1774–1782; served in Gibraltar 1782–1792; served in Jersey 1792–1793
Service 1793–1815: Deputy Adjutant General in Flanders 1793; commanded brigade at Helder 1799; commanded brigade at Hanover 1805; Lieutenant Governor of Jersey 21 Jun 1806 to 23 Jul 1814; acting Commander in Chief and Governor of Gibraltar 25 Aug 1814 to 15 Nov 1821 (vice Campbell)
Awards and Honours: GCB 20 May 1820; GCH 12 Aug 1820
Died: Gibraltar 17 Jan 1832
Sources: ARLI; ODNB; PHIL; WEOF; WOST

769. *Francis FULLER (1794–1815)*
Born: London 1763
Relations: Son of John Fuller of Beaconsfield and Anne (Ludbey); father of Lieutenant Colonel Francis Fuller, 59th Foot
Entry to Army: Ensign in 36th Foot 26 Feb 1778 by purchase
Regimental Field Officer Promotions: Major in 101st Foot 21 Dec 1785 by purchase; to half-pay 1785; Lieutenant Colonel in 59th Foot 30 Jun 1794; removed from the regiment as a general officer 1815
Brevets: Brevet Lieutenant Colonel 1 Mar 1794; Brevet Colonel 1 Jan 1798; Major General 1 Jan 1805; Lieutenant General 4 Jun 1811; General 27 May 1825
Colonelcies: 2nd West India Regiment 23 Jan 1828 (vice Byng)
Early Service: Served in British East Indies 1781–1785
Service 1793–1815: Served in Flanders 1794–1795; commanded 59th Foot in West Indies 1795–1801; commanded brigade at capture of The Saints 1801;

Governor of St Croix 1 Apr 1801 to 16 Feb 1802; served in East Indies and commanded division 1806–1810; Lieutenant Governor and Commander in Chief in Jamaica 1815
Residences: Salisbury, Wiltshire; Bath, Somerset; Versailles, Île-de-France, France
Died: Versailles 26 May 1841
Sources: ANCB; ANCW; ARLI; PHIL; WEOF; WO 25/745; WOST

770. *William MacLEOD (1799–1805)*
Born: British North America c.1759
Relations: Son of Major William MacLeod RA and Hannah (Waldon); brother of Colonel Alexander MacLeod, 59th Foot; cousin of Major General William MacLeod, Madras service
Entry to Army: Ensign in 59th Foot 29 Mar 1775 by purchase
Field Officer Promotions: Major in 59th Foot 1 Sep 1795 (vice Woodward); Lieutenant Colonel in 59th Foot 25 Nov 1799 (vice Don)
Brevets: Brevet Major 1 Mar 1794; Brevet Lieutenant Colonel 1 Jan 1798
Early Service: Served in Gibraltar 1789–1791
Service 1793–1815: Served in Flanders 1793; served in Corsica 1794–1796; served in West Indies
Retired: 1 Oct 1803
Died: New York USA after 1803
Sources: ARLI; WEOF; The Macleods of Arnisdale

771. *Bryan PHILPOT (1803–1804)*
Born: London 1766
Relations: Son of Thomas Philpot of St Olave and Esher, merchant, and Mary (Gomm); brother of Lieutenant Colonel Philip Philpot, 24th Light Dragoons
Entry to Army: Ensign in 2nd Foot 13 Feb 1782 by purchase
Field Officer Promotions: Major in 59th Foot 28 Aug 1801 (vice Horsford); Lieutenant Colonel in 59th Foot 1 Oct 1803 (vice MacLeod); Lieutenant Colonel in 77th Foot 31 Mar 1804 (vice Dunlop) by exchange; Lieutenant Colonel in 65th Foot 21 Nov 1806 (vice Maddison) by exchange
Service 1793–1815: Served in East Indies 1804–1807
Died: Surat, India 1 May 1807
Sources: ANCB; ARLI; FMPD

772. *James DUNLOP (1804–1814)*
Born: Ayrshire 1759
Relations: Son of John Dunlop of Dunlop and Frances Anne (Wallace); brother of Sir Thomas Dunlop-Wallace, 6th Bt; Brigadier General Sir Andrew Wallace Dunlop; Lieutenant John Dunlop, 89th Foot; father of Captain and Lieutenant Colonel Sir John Dunlop, Bt, Grenadier Foot Guards; and Vice Admiral Sir Hugh Dunlop RN
Entry to Army: Lieutenant in 82nd Foot 11 Jan 1778
Field Officer Promotions: Major in 77th Foot 1 Sep 1795 (vice Stirling); Lieutenant Colonel in 77th Foot 13 Nov 1795; Lieutenant Colonel in 59th Foot 31 Mar 1804; removed from the regiment as a general officer 1814
Brevets: Brevet Major 1 Mar 1794; Brevet Colonel 25 Sep 1803; Brigadier General (home staff) 1804; Major General 25 Jul 1810; Lieutenant General 4 Jun 1814
Colonelcies: 75th Foot 10 Nov 1827 (vice Abercromby)
Early Service: Served in British North America 1779–1783; served in East Indies 1788–1800
Service 1793–1815: Deputy Paymaster in Bombay 1794; Military secretary to Governor of Bombay 1796; commanded brigade in 5th Division in Peninsula Nov 1810 to Mar 11; temporarily commanded 5th Division in Peninsula Apr to Oct 1811
Political Career: MP (Kirkcudbright Stewartry) 1812–1826
Residences: Dunlop, Ayrshire; Southwick, Kirkcudbrightshire
Died: Southwick 30 Mar 1832
Sources: ANCW; ARLI; CHAL; DINB; HPON; PHIL; WEBC; WEOF

773. *Sir Samuel GIBBS (1804–1814)*
Born: London 1770
Relations: Son of Colonel Samuel Gibbs of Horsley Park and Arabella (Rowley); brother of Lieutenant General Sir Edward Gibbs
Entry to Army: Ensign in East Suffolk Militia; Ensign in 102nd Foot 8 Oct 1783 by purchase
Regimental Field Officer Promotions: Major in 11th Foot 5 Aug 1799 (vice Armstrong) by purchase; Lieutenant Colonel in 10th West India Regiment 25 Dec 1801 (vice De Soter) by purchase; Lieutenant Colonel in 12th Battalion of Reserve 9 Jul 1803; Lieutenant Colonel in 59th Foot 1 Aug 1804; removed from the regiment as a general officer 1814
Brevets: Brevet Colonel 25 Jul 1810; Brigadier General (Java) 1811; Major General 4 Jun 1813
Early Service: Served in British North America 1788–1792; served in Gibraltar 1792
Service 1793–1815: ADC to James Grant 1793–1795; served in Corsica 1794–1795; taken POW at Ostend Raid 1798; commanded 11th Foot in attack

on St Martin 1800; served in Cape of Good Hope 1805–1806; served in British East Indies 1806; served in capture of Mauritius 1810; served in Java 1811; served in Stralsund 1813; commanded brigade in Netherlands 1814; second in command in New Orleans 1815
Awards and Honours: KCB 2 Jan 1815
Died: Of wounds received in New Orleans 9 Jan 1815
Sources: ARLI; DINB; ODNB; WEOF; WO 25/745

774. *Charles FANE (1805–1813)*
Born: London 1781
Relations: Son of Hon. Henry Fane of Little Panton Hall and Anne (Batson); brother of General Sir Henry Fane; and General Mildmay Fane
Entry to Army: Captain in 13th Light Dragoons 22 Aug 1795 by purchase
Regimental Field Officer Promotions: Major in 8th Foot 18 Apr 1805 (vice Fortye); Lieutenant Colonel in 59th Foot 20 Jun 1805 (vice Strickland) by purchase
Service 1793–1815: Served in Egypt 1801; served in Peninsula with 1/59th Foot Sep 1808 to Jan 1809, wounded at Corunna; commanded 2/59th Foot in Peninsula Feb to Jun 1813, wounded at Vittoria
Residence: Fulbeck, Lincolnshire
Died: Died of wounds at Vittoria 27 Jun 1813
Sources: ARLI; CHAL; HALL; WEOF

775. *Alexander MacLEOD (1811–1821)*
Born: Scotland c.1770
Relations: Son of Major William MacLeod RA and Hannah (Waldon); brother of Lieutenant Colonel William MacLeod, 59th Foot; cousin of Major General William MacLeod, Madras service
Entry to Army: Ensign in 59th Foot 23 Sep 1793
Field Officer Promotions: Major in 59th Foot 1 Oct 1803 (vice Philpot) by purchase; Lieutenant Colonel in 59th Foot 13 Jun 1811
Brevets: Brevet Lieutenant Colonel 25 Jul 1810; Brevet Colonel 12 Aug 1819
Service 1793–1815: Served in Flanders 1794–1795; served in West Indies 1795–1800; served in capture of Cape of Good Hope 1806; served in East Indies 1806–1811; served in Batavia 1811–1815
Later Service: Served in East Indies 1815–1821
Awards and Honours: CB 4 Jun 1815
Residence: Cheltenham, Gloucestershire
Died: Pattna, East Indies 29 Mar 1821
Sources: ANCW; ARLI; WEOF; WO 25/747; The Macleods of Arnisdale; History of the Organization, Equipment, and War Services of the Regiment of Bengal Artillery

776. *George MacGREGOR (1813–1828)*
Born: Morayshire 1780
Relations: Son of James MacGregor of Dalbuiack and Elizabeth (Grant); brother of Captain James MacGregor, 59th Foot; brother-in-law of Major General William MacLeod, Madras service; father of Lieutenant John Campbell MacGregor, 59th Foot; and Captain Robert MacGregor, 15th Foot
Entry to Army: Ensign in 78th Foot 12 Feb 1794 by purchase
Field Officer Promotions: Major in 59th Foot 30 May 1805 (vice Browne); Lieutenant Colonel in 59th Foot 4 Jun 1813
Brevets: Brevet Lieutenant Colonel 1 Jan 1812
Service 1793–1815: Served at capture of Cape of Good Hope 1795; served in East Indies 1797–1799; served in West Indies 1800–1802; served in Peninsula Oct 1808 to Jan 1809; commanded 2/59th in Walcheren 1809; served in Batavia 1812–1815
Later Service: Served in East Indies 1816–1828
Awards and Honours: CB 26 Dec 1826
Died: Portsmouth, Hampshire 7 Aug 1828
Sources: ANCB; ANCD: ANCW; ARLI; CHAL; PHIL; WEOF; WO 25/747

777. *Henry AUSTEN (1813–1816)*
Born: Kent 1779
Relations: Son of Francis Motley Austen of Wilmington and Elizabeth (Wilson); brother of Colonel Thomas Austen, 60th Foot; second cousin of novelist Jane Austen
Entry to Army: Ensign in 60th Foot 8 Aug 1795
Field Officer Promotions: Major in 59th Foot 3 Jul 1806 (vice Ogilvie) by purchase; Lieutenant Colonel in 59th Foot 23 Sep 1813 (vice Fane); to half-pay of 59th Foot 25 May 1816; Lieutenant Colonel in 90th Foot 12 Aug 1819
Brevets: Brevet Lieutenant Colonel 25 Jan 1812
Service 1793–1815: Served in West Indies 1796; served in Irish rebellion 1798; served in East Indies; commanded 2/59th in Netherlands 1814 and during Waterloo campaign 1815
Later Service: Commanded 90th Foot in Malta 1820–1821
Retired: 12 Jul 1821
Awards and Honours: WatM 23 Apr 1816
Residence: Belle Vue, Sevenoaks, Kent
Died: Sevenoaks 1850
Sources: ANCB; ANCD; ANCW; PHIL; WEOF; WO 25/744

Majors

778. *Walter HAYNES (1789–1794)*
Born: Staffordshire 1744
Relations: [spec.] Son of John Haynes of Wolverhampton
Entry to Army: Ensign in 59th Foot 5 May 1769 by purchase
Field Officer Promotions: Major in 59th Foot 9 Apr 1789 (vice Don)
Retired: 28 Apr 1794
Militia Career: Major in Staffordshire Provisional Cavalry 16 Apr 1798
Residence: Shutt End, Staffordshire
Died: Shutt End Jun 1806
Sources: ANCD; ARLI; Aris's Birmingham Gazette 16 Apr 1798

779. *Rt Hon. Stapleton COTTON, 1st Viscount Combermere (1794)*
Born: Denbighshire 1773
Relations: Son of Sir Robert Salusbury Cotton, 5th Bt, and Frances (Stapleton); brother of Major Lynch Cotton, 15th Light Dragoons; son-in-law of Thomas Pelham-Clinton, 3rd Duke of Newcastle
Education: Westminster School; Norwood House Military Academy
Entry to Army: 2nd Lieutenant in 23rd Foot 26 Feb 1790 by purchase
Regimental Field Officer Promotions: Major in 59th Foot 28 Apr 1794 (vice Haynes) by purchase; Lieutenant Colonel in 25th Light Dragoons 9 Mar 1794 (backdated); Lieutenant Colonel in 16th Light Dragoons 14 Feb 1800 (vice Lee) by exchange
Brevets: Brevet Colonel 1 Jan 1800; Major General 30 Oct 1805; Lieutenant General (Spain and Portugal) 31 Aug 1809; Lieutenant General 1 Jan 1812; General 27 May 1825; Field Marshal 2 Oct 1855
Colonelcies: 20th Light Dragoons 27 Jan 1813 (vice Bentinck); 3rd Light Dragoons 25 Jan 1821 (vice Cartwright); 1st Life Guards 16 Sep 1829 (vice Harrington)
Service 1793–1815: Served in Flanders 1793–1794; served at Cape of Good Hope and India 1796–1800; commanded cavalry in Peninsula Jan to Jun 1809; commanded cavalry brigade in Peninsula Jun to Dec 1809; commanded cavalry in Peninsula May 1810 to Jan 1811; commanded cavalry in Peninsula Apr to Jun 1811; commanded cavalry division in Peninsula Jun 1811 to Dec 1812, severely wounded at Salamanca; commanded cavalry in Peninsula Jun 1813 to Apr 1814; commanded cavalry in Army of Occupation 1816
Later Service: Commander in Chief in Leeward Islands 1817; Governor of Sheerness 1821; Commander in Chief in Ireland 1821; Commander in Chief in India 1825–1830; Constable of the Tower and Lord Lieutenant of the Tower Hamlets Oct 1852
Political Career: MP (Newark) 1806–1814
Creations and Dignities: 1st Baron Combermere 3 May 1814; 1st Viscount Combermere 8 Feb 1827
Retired: 1830
Awards and Honours: AGC (Tal FDO Sal Ort Toul); GCB 4 Jan 1815; GCH 12 Aug 1817; PC (Ire) 5 Dec 1822; Gold Stick 1829–1865; PC 16 Dec 1834; MGSM (Bus CR Pyr); KSI 19 Aug 1861
Residence: Combermere Abbey, near Burleydam, Cheshire
Died: Clifton, Gloucestershire 21 Feb 1865
Sources: ANCB; ANCD; ANCW; ARLI; CHAL; HALL; PHIL; WEOF; WO 25/744

780. *Dennett Milton WOODWARD (1794–1795)*
See 87.
Major in 59th Foot 12 Nov 1794 (vice Haynes)

781. *Lewis Evans BRUCE (1795–1796)*
Born: County Cork c.1762
Relations: Son of George Bruce of Cork and Mary (Evans); nephew of Chaplain Lewis Bruce, 35th Foot
Education: Trinity College, Dublin
Entry to Army: Ensign in 27th Foot 5 Aug 1785
Field Officer Promotions: Major in 59th Foot 2 Sep 1795
Brevets: Brevet Major 22 Aug 1794
Retired: 1 Sep 1796
Residence: Norton Cottage, Tenby, Pembrokeshire
Died: Tenby 30 Dec 1834
Sources: ANCD; ARLI; FMPB; UNSM (1835); Alumni Dublinenses; Church book of St. Mary the Virgin, Tenby

782. *Spencer Thomas VASSALL (1796–1799)*
See 194.
Major in 59th Foot 1 Sep 1796 (vice Bruce) by purchase

783. *George HORSFORD (1799–1801)*
See 754.
Major in 59th Foot 30 Aug 1799 (vice Vassall) by exchange

784. *Sir Thomas BROWNE, Kt (1799–1805)*
Born: Gibraltar 1771
Relations: Son of Colonel Arthur Browne, Lieutenant Governor of Kinsale, and Catherine (Kitson); half-brother of Colonel St John Thomas Browne RA
Entry to Army: Ensign in 59th Foot 24 Sep 1787 by purchase
Field Officer Promotions: Major in 59th Foot 25 Nov 1799 (vice MacLeod); Lieutenant Colonel in 69th Foot 30 May 1805
Brevets: Brevet Major 23 Aug 1799; Brevet Colonel 25 July 1810; Major General 4 Jun 1813; Lieutenant General 27 May 1825; General 23 Nov 1841
Early Service: Served in Gibraltar 1789–1791
Service 1793–1815: Served in Flanders 1793; served in Corsica 1794–1796; served in West Indies 1799–1801; commanded 2/69th Foot 1805–1811; commanded auxiliary force in Goa 1812–1813
Later Service: On staff in Madras 1815–1822
Awards and Honours: KCH 12 Aug 1832; Knight Bachelor 6 Nov 1832
Residence: Knockduffe House, near Kinsale, County Cork
Died: Kinsale 27 Sep 1843
Sources: ANCB; ANCW; ARLI; FMPD; PHIL; UNSM (1843); WEOF; WO 25/744; <https://iar.ie/archive/arthur-browne-ms/>

785. *James OGILVY (1804–1806)*
Born: Edinburgh c.1762
Entry to Army: Ensign in 50th Foot 31 Aug 1779 by purchase
Field Officer Promotions: Major in 59th Foot 7 Sep 1804
Service 1793–1815: Served at Cape of Good Hope 1806; served in East Indies 1806
Retired: 3 Jul 1806
Residence: Fitzroy Square, St Pancras, London
Died: London Nov 1807
Sources: ANCD; ANCW; ARLI; WEOF

786. *William Morton PLEYDELL (1804–1808)*
Born: Dorset 1770
Relations: Son of Edmund Morton Pleydell of Milborne St. Andrew and Ann (Luttrell)
Entry to Army: Cornet in 1st Dragoon Guards 26 Oct 1787
Regimental Field Officer Promotions: Major in 21st Light Dragoons 24 Feb 1794 by purchase; to half-pay 1 Mar 1795; Major in 6th Battalion of Reserve 9 Jul 1803; Major in 59th Foot 14 Sep 1804
Brevets: Brevet Lieutenant Colonel 1 Jan 1805
Retired: 19 May 1808
Residence: Crick Manor, Crick, Monmouthshire
Died: Crick Manor 13 Jan 1824
Sources: ANCB; ANCD; ANCW; ARLI; WEOF

787. *John LAING-WEIR (1808–1813)*
Born: John Laing in Orkney 1777
Relations: Son of Robert Laing of Strynzie, provost, and Barbara (Blaw); added -Weir surname in 1801
Entry to Army: Volunteer; Ensign in 65th Foot 11 Jul 1794
Field Officer Promotions: Major in 59th Foot 19 May 1808 (vice Pleydell) by purchase
Brevets: Brevet Lieutenant Colonel 15 May 1806
Service 1793–1815: Served in Peninsula, Sep 1812 to Jul 1813, badly wounded at Vittoria
Died: Died of wounds 4 Jul 1813
Sources: ARLI; CHAL; HALL; WEOF

788. *William OLPHERTS (1811)*
Born: County Armagh c.1775
Relations: Son of Richard Olpherts of Armagh and Barbara (Blacker)
Entry to Army: Ensign in 59th Foot 3 Sep 1795
Field Officer Promotions: Major in 59th Foot 13 Jun 1811 (vice MacLeod)
Service 1793–1815: Served in East Indies 1806–1811; served in Batavia 1811
Died: Killed in action in Batavia 26 Aug 1811
Sources: ANCB; ARLI; WEOF; The Wolfes of Forenaghts, Blackhall, Baronrath, &c

789. *Alexander MacPHERSON (1811–1820)*
Born: Inverness-shire 1774
Relations: Son of MacPherson of Strathdearn; brother of Lieutenant Æneas MacPherson, 59th Foot; Captain Evan MacPherson, 59th Foot; and Lieutenant Duncan MacPherson, 79th Foot
Entry to Army: Ensign in 1/82nd Foot 23 Oct 1794
Field Officer Promotions: Major in 59th Foot 26 Aug 1811 (vice Olpherts); Lieutenant Colonel as Inspecting Field Officer of a Recruiting District 17 Jun 1813; to half-pay of 59th Foot 25 Mar 1816; Major in 60th Foot 5 Apr 1831
Brevets: Brevet Major 4 Jun 1811; Brevet Lieutenant Colonel 12 Aug 1819
Service 1793–1815: Served in Peninsula Sep 1808 to Jan 1809; served in Walcheren 1809; served in Peninsula Sep 1812 to Mar 1813; Inspecting Field Officer of a recruiting district 1813–1815

Retired: 12 Apr 1831
Residence: Kerrow, Kingussie, Inverness-shire
Died: Kerrow 23 Nov 1856
Sources: ANCD; ARLI; CHAL; HALL; PHIL; WEOF

790. *Matthew SHAWE (1813–1817)*
Born: County Galway 1780
Relations: Son of Colonel Robert Shawe, 74th Foot; cousin of Lieutenant Colonel Meyrick Shawe, 76th Foot; Lieutenant Henry Shawe, 74th Foot; and Captain Charles Fielding Shawe, 6th Foot
Entry to Army: Ensign in 12th Foot 7 May 1799
Field Officer Promotions: Major in 59th Foot 4 Jun 1813 (vice MacGregor); Lieutenant Colonel in 84th Foot 15 Apr 1817 (vice Campbell); Lieutenant Colonel in 87th Foot 30 Apr 1818 (vice Doyle) by exchange
Brevets: Brevet Major 30 May 1811; Brevet Lieutenant Colonel 27 Apr 1812
Service 1793–1815: Served in East Indies 1801–1805, wounded at Assaye; served in Peninsula Feb 1810 to Oct 1812, severely wounded at Badajoz
Later Service: Commanded 87th Foot in East Indies 1819–1825
Awards and Honours: AGM (Bad); CB
Died: At sea off Kolkata, India 11 Apr 1826
Sources: ANCW; ARLI; PHIL; WEMR; WEOF

791. *Frederick William HOYSTED (1813–1817)*
Born: County Kildare 1759
Relations: Son of James Hoysted of Foxhill and Temperance (Bagot)
Entry to Army: Ensign in 64th Foot 12 Sep 1777 by purchase
Field Officer Promotions: Major in 59th Foot 17 Jun 1813 (vice MacPherson)
Brevets: Brevet Lieutenant Colonel 26 Dec 1813
Early Service: Served in American War of Independence
Service 1793–1815: Served in Peninsula Aug 1813 to Jan 1814, badly wounded at Nive and Bayonne; served in Waterloo campaign 1815
Retired: 17 Jul 1817
Awards and Honours: AGM (Niv); WatM 23 Apr 1816
Residence: Kilboggan, County Kildare
Died: Kilboggan 23 Feb 1818
Sources: ANCB; ANCD; ARLI; CHAL; HALL; WEOF; Journal of the Co. Kildare Archaeological Society and Surrounding Districts

792. *Joseph CREIGHTON (1813–1819)*
Born: Nova Scotia 1781
Relations: Son of Lieutenant Colonel John Creighton of Lunenburg and Lucy (Clapp); brother of Lieutenant John Creighton, 19th Foot; and Lieutenant Charles Creighton, Lunenburg Militia
Entry to Army: Ensign in 59th Foot 1 Jan 1801
Field Officer Promotions: Major in 59th Foot 23 Sep 1813 (vice Austen); to half-pay of 59th Foot 20 Sep 1819
Brevets: Brevet Lieutenant Colonel 22 Jul 1830; Brevet Colonel 10 Nov 1846
Service 1793–1815: Served in East Indies 1809–1819
Residence: Halifax, Nova Scotia
Died: Halifax 1854
Sources: ANCW; ARLI; PHIL; WEOF; History of the County of Lunenburg

793. *John Thomas HORSLEY (1813–1815)*
Born: Kent 1783
Relations: Son of John Horsley of Faversham and Sarah (Tolly)
Entry to Army: Cornet in 7th Light Dragoons 28 Feb 1798 by purchase
Field Officer Promotions: Major in 59th Foot 1813 (vice Weir)
Service 1793–1815: Served in Peninsula Sep 1808 to Jan 1809; served in Walcheren 1809; served in Peninsula Sep 1812 to Apr 1813, and Mar to Apr 1814
Died: Llanbedrog, Caernarvonshire 8 Apr 1815
Sources: ANCB; ANCD; ARLI; CHAL; WEOF

794. *Charles Robert DOUGLAS (1815–1816)*
Born: County Kildare 1787
Relations: Son of Captain Charles Douglas, 11th Foot, and Harriott (Nicholson)
Entry to Army: Ensign in 59th Foot 6 Aug 1803 by purchase
Field Officer Promotions: Major in 59th Foot 20 Apr 1815 (vice Horsley)
Service 1793–1815: Served in Peninsula Dec 1813 to Apr 1814; served in Waterloo campaign 1815
Awards and Honours: WatM 23 Apr 1816
Died: Lost at sea in wreck of *Seahorse* transport off Ireland 30 Jan 1816
Sources: ARLI; CHAL; WEOF; <https://www.douglashistory.co.uk/history/ships/ wreck_sea_horse.htm>

Selected Regimental Histories
James, F.M., *Annals of the Five and Nine; being the history of HM 59th (2nd Nottinghamshire) Regiment of Foot, now the Second Battalion, the East Lancashire Regiment* (Poona: S. Shalom and Brothers, 1906)

Regimental Museum
Lancashire Infantry Museum, Fulwood Barracks, Preston, Lancashire

60th Regiment of Foot

Secondary Title:	Royal American
Nicknames:	The Jaggers
Jacket:	1st-4th Battalions: Red (to Dec 1815, green thereafter) 5th-8th Battalions: Green
Facings:	1st-4th Battalions: Dark blue (to Dec 1815, red thereafter) 5th-8th Battalions: Red
Motto:	*Celer et Audax* (swift and bold); whilst conferred in 1759, was not used until formally granted in 1824
Badges:	1st-4th Battalions: The Royal Cypher with the Garter 5th Battalion: A Maltese Cross 6th-8th Battalions: The bugle with strings

Regimental Lineage, 60th Regiment of Foot

1755:	Raised as 62nd (Royal American) Regiment of Foot in North America (four battalions)
1756:	60th (Royal American) Regiment of Foot
1763:	4th Battalion disbanded
1764:	3rd Battalion disbanded
1787:	Sep – 3rd and 4th Battalions re-formed in Chatham
1797:	Dec – 5th Battalion formed in Barbados
1799:	Jul – 6th Battalion formed in Cowes
1813:	Sep – 7th Battalion formed in Gibraltar
1813:	Nov – 8th Battalion formed in Lisbon
1815:	Dec – 1st to 4th Battalions redesignated as light infantry
1816:	May – 8th Battalion disbanded in Gibraltar
1817:	Jun – 7th Battalion disbanded in Halifax, Nova Scotia
1818:	Feb – 6th Battalion disbanded in Portsmouth
1818:	May – 5th Battalion disbanded in Cowes
1819:	Apr – 1st Battalion disbanded in Portsmouth
1819:	May – 2nd and 3rd Battalions re-designated 1st (Rifle) and 2nd (Light Infantry)
1819:	Jul – 4th Battalion disbanded in Portsmouth
1824:	60th (The Duke of York's Own Rifle Corps and Light Infantry)
1824:	60th (The Duke of York's Own Rifle Corps)
1830:	60th (King's Royal Rifle Corps)
1958:	2nd Green Jackets, the King's Royal Rifle Corps (on amalgamation with the Oxfordshire and Buckinghamshire Light Infantry and the Rifle Brigade)
1966:	2nd Battalion, The Royal Green Jackets
1992:	1st Battalion disbanded, lineage perpetuated by 2nd Battalion, which became 1st Battalion
2007:	2nd Battalion, The Rifles (on amalgamation with the Devonshire and Dorset Light Infantry, Royal Gloucestershire, Berkshire and Wiltshire Light Infantry, and the Light Infantry)

Note: Locations shown are for the battalion headquarters only; companies were often dispersed

Service History, 1st Battalion 60th Regiment of Foot

1793:	Montréal
1794:	Montréal; Oct – Québec
1795–1796:	Montréal
1797:	Montréal; May – Québec; Jun – men drafted into 2nd Battalion at Québec, cadre to England; Nov – battalion re-formed in Guernsey from French and Dutch personnel; Dec – Jersey
1798:	Guernsey; Feb – Portsmouth; to West Indies; Mar – Barbados
1799:	Barbados; May – Jamaica

1800–1809:	Jamaica
1810:	Jamaica; Guadeloupe; Apr – to England; Aug – Cowes; Nov – Jersey
1811:	Jersey; Apr – Cowes; May – Hilsea; Jun – to Cape of Good Hope; Aug – Cape Town
1812–1815:	Cape Town
1819:	Apr – disbanded in Portsmouth, fit men into 2nd Battalion in Québec

Service History, 2nd Battalion 60th Regiment of Foot

1793:	Québec; Fort Ontario, Oswego
1794:	Fort Ontario, Oswego; Aug – Québec
1795:	Fort Ontario, Oswego
1796:	Québec
1797:	Québec
1798:	Québec; Mar – absorbed men from Hompesch Chasseurs in Antigua
1799:	Québec; Montréal; May – four companies to West Indies; Jun – eight companies in Barbados
1800:	Barbados
1801:	Barbados
1802:	Barbados; Tobago
1803:	Barbados; Tobago; Jul – St Vincent
1804:	St Vincent; Apr – rifle company at capture of Surinam
1805:	St Vincent; Jun – Grenada
1806:	Grenada; received drafts from 3rd Battalion
1807:	Grenada; May – to England; Jul – Cowes; Oct – Jersey
1808:	Jersey; Sep – Plymouth; Oct – to Spain; Nov – Corunna
1809:	Corunna; Feb – Cowes; Jul – Guernsey; Nov – to West Indies; Dec – Barbados
1810:	Barbados; Feb – grenadier company at capture of Guadeloupe
1811:	Barbados; Nov – detachment to Demerara
1812:	Barbados; May – seven companies to Demerara, three companies to Berbice and Tobago
1813–1815:	Barbados
1819:	Québec; May – re-designated 1st (Rifle) Battalion

Service History, 3rd Battalion 60th Regiment of Foot

1793:	Nine companies in Antigua, one company in Montserrat; Jun – seven companies in Antigua, two companies in Dominica and one company in Montserrat
1794:	Seven companies in Antigua, two companies in Dominica and one company in Montserrat; Feb to Apr – drafted out to 4/60th, cadre to Guernsey; Mar – detachment at capture of Martinique; Apr – detachment at capture of St Lucia; detachment at capture of Guadeloupe; Guernsey
1795:	Guernsey; May – to West Indies; Jul – St Vincent
1796:	St Vincent; Jul – Tobago
1797:	Tobago; Feb – four companies to Trinidad; May – four companies in Puerto Rico; Jun – Tobago and Grenada; Oct – Tobago; Dec – received draft of York Rangers
1798–1800:	Tobago
1801:	Grenada
1802:	Grenada; drafted temporarily into 2nd Battalion
1803:	Grenada; to England
1804:	Cowes
1805:	Cowes
1806:	Cowes; Mar – Guernsey; Jul – men drafted into 2nd Battalion; battalion re-formed at Portsmouth
1807:	Spithead; to West Indies; Mar – Barbados; Dec – The Saints
1808:	Barbados; Feb – detachment at capture of Fort Dessaix, Martinique; Apr – rifle company at capture of Les Saintes; May – Antigua
1809:	Antigua; Feb – capture of MARTINIQUE; The Saints; Antigua

1810: Martinique and Antigua
1811: Martinique; May – one company quelled rebellion in St Pierre; Oct – three companies to Dominica
1812: Martinique; May – Dominica companies returned
1813–1814: Martinique and Guadeloupe
1815: Martinique; Guadeloupe; Dominica; St Lucia
1819: May – re-designated 2nd (Light Infantry) Battalion

Service History, 4th Battalion 60th Regiment of Foot

1793: Barbados; Apr – nine companies at capture of Tobago; Jun – seven companies in Tobago, two companies in Barbados, one company in Dominica
1794: Seven companies in Tobago, two companies in Barbados, one company in Dominica; Mar – detachment at capture of Martinique; May – detachment at capture of Guadeloupe; six companies in Tobago, four companies in St Vincent; Nov – six companies in Tobago, two companies in St Vincent, two companies in Guadeloupe
1795: Eight companies in Tobago, two companies in St Vincent; Feb – Tobago; Sep – eight companies in Tobago, two companies in Dominica
1796: Eight companies in Tobago, two companies in Dominica; Jul – drafted out to other regiments, cadre to England; Oct – Guernsey
1797: Guernsey
1798: Mar – absorbed Waldstein's Chasseurs in Martinique; detachment in St Domingue
1799: Four companies in Martinique; May – Jamaica
1800–1804: Jamaica
1805: Jamaica; Sep – to England; Nov – Cowes
1806: Cowes; Apr – Lymington; Jun – to Cape of Good Hope; Aug – Cape Town
1807: Cape Town
1808: Cape Town; Mar – to West Indies; Apr – rifle company at capture of Les Saintes; Jul – Antigua
1809: Barbados; Feb – capture of MARTINIQUE; The Saints; Antigua
1810: Martinique; Feb – grenadier company at capture of Guadeloupe; Dominica
1811: Dominica; Jul – to England; Sep – Cowes
1812: Cowes; May – to West Indies; Jun – Barbados; Dominica
1813–1815: Dominica
1819: Jul – disbanded in Portsmouth, fit men into 2nd Battalion in Québec

Service History, 5th Battalion 60th Regiment of Foot

1797: Formed in Barbados from Lowenstein's Chasseurs and Fusiliers; entire battalion armed with rifles
1798: Service companies in Barbados; May – service companies in Grenada
Mar – three home companies formed in Cowes from Hompesch's Chasseurs; Apr – three home companies to Ireland; Bandon; Jun – Lacken Hill; Goff's Bridge; Vinegar Hill; Aug – Carrick-on-Shannon; Cork
1799: Seven service companies in Grenada, three home companies in Cork; Feb – three home companies to West Indies; May – battalion reunited in Martinique; Aug – capture of Surinam
1800–1802: Fort New Amsterdam, Surinam
1803: Surinam; Oct – to Nova Scotia; Halifax
1804: Halifax
1805: Halifax; Nov – to England; Portsmouth
1806: Cowes; Feb – Hilsea; Apr – Haslar
1807: Haslar; May – Brabourne Lees; Aug – to Ireland; Oct – Cork

1808:	Cork; Jul – to PENINSULA; Aug – Portugal; ROLICA; VIMIERO; Sep – five companies in Lisbon, five companies in Elvas; Oct – advance into Spain; Nov – Salamanca; Dec – ordered to Lisbon
1809:	Five companies in Lamego, five companies in Cascais; Mar – battalion reunited in Belem; Apr – Pombal; May – Coimbra; five companies attached to infantry brigades; Oporto; Jun – Castelo Branco; Jul – TALAVERA; Aug – Arroyo del Puerco; Oct – Campo Maior; Dec – Montemore-o-Novo
1810:	Montemore-o-Novo; Feb – Vila Nova; all companies attached to infantry brigades; Mar – Trancoso; Apr – Pombal; May – Pinhel; Sep – Palheiros; BUSACO; Oct – Cardosas; Nov – Torres Vedras; Dec – Alcoentre
1811:	Alcoentre; Feb – Penheira; Mar – Pombal; Casal Nova; Pinhanços; Apr – Sabugal; Poço Velha; May – six companies at FUENTES DE ONORO; four companies at ALBUERA: Campo Maior; Jul – Castelo Branco; Aug – Albergaria; Sep – Pastores; El Bodon; Aldea de Ponte; Oct – Arroyomolinos; Albergaria; Nov – Villa Encina; Dec – La Alberguería de Argañán
1812:	CIUDAD RODRIGO; Feb – La Alberguería de Argañán; Mar – Badajoz; Apr – BADAJOZ; May – Almaraz; Jun – Salamanca forts; Jul – SALAMANCA; Nava de Arévalo; Aug – Madrid; Oct – Valdemoro; Nov – Fuenteguinaldo; Dec – Paredes da Beira
1813:	Paredes da Beira; Apr – Vermosa; May – Huerta; Jun – VITTORIA; Jul – Maya; PYRENEES; Sorauren; Aug – Arizuen; Oct – Zugarramurdi; Nov – NIVELLE; Arrauntz; Dec – NIVE; Urcuray
1814:	Hasparren; Feb – passage of the Adour; Sauveterre-de-Béarn; ORTHEZ; Mar – Anan; Apr – TOULOUSE; Grenade; May – Capitieux; Jun – Blanquefort; Jul – Pauillac; to Ireland; Cork; Aug – Youghal
1815:	Youghal; Oct – Buttevant
1818:	May – disbanded in Cowes, fit men into 2nd Battalion in Québec

Service History, 6th Battalion 60th Regiment of Foot

1799:	Jul – formed in Cowes from German recruits; flank company armed with rifles; Aug – rifle company to Helder; Oct – rifle company at Bergen-op-Zoom
1800:	Cowes; Nov – to West Indies; Jamaica
1801–1815:	Jamaica; detachment in Curaçao
1818:	Feb – disbanded in Portsmouth, fit men into 3rd Battalion in Halifax NS

Service History, 7th Battalion 60th Regiment of Foot

1813:	Sep – formed in Cowes from German and Swiss POWs; Nov – Guernsey
1814:	Guernsey; Mar – to Nova Scotia; Halifax; Aug – two companies in expedition to Penobscot River
1815:	Halifax; Annapolis
1817:	Jun – disbanded in Halifax, fit men into 2nd and 3rd Battalions

Service History, 8th Battalion 60th Regiment of Foot

1813:	Nov – formed in Lisbon from battalion of Foreign Recruits (ex-Cadiz)
1814:	Cadiz; Aug – Gibraltar
1815:	Gibraltar
1816:	May – disbanded in Portsmouth; fit men into 5th Battalion in Gibraltar

Establishments, 1st Battalion 60th Regiment of Foot

Year	Subunits	Field Off	Off/ Staff	Sjts	Mus	Corp/ Pvts	Total
Dec 1792	10co	4	32	22	12	430	500
Jan 1793	10co	4	32	32	22	600	690
Dec 1795	10co+2r	6	51	62	30	1,010	1,159
Dec 1797	10co	6	51	53	22	1,000	1,132
Jun 1802	10co	6	43	34	22	750	855

May 1803	10co	6	46	34	22	750	858
Dec 1804	10co	6	46	44	22	800	918
Dec 1806	10co	5	46	44	22	800	917
Dec 1808	10co	5	46	34	22	600	707
Dec 1809	10co	5	46	24	22	400	497
Dec 1810	10co	5	46	54	22	1,000	1,127
Dec 1811	10co	5	46	55	22	1,000	1,128
Dec 1814	10co	6	46	55	22	1,000	1,129

Establishments, 2nd Battalion 60th Regiment of Foot

Year	Subunits	Field Off	Off/ Staff	Sjts	Mus	Corp/ Pvts	Total
Dec 1792	10co	3	32	22	12	430	499
Jan 1793	10co	3	32	32	22	600	689
Dec 1795	10co+2r	5	51	62	30	1,010	1,158
Dec 1798	10co	5	51	53	22	1,000	1,131
Dec 1802	10co	5	43	34	22	750	854
Dec 1803	10co	5	46	34	22	750	857
Dec 1804	10co	5	46	44	22	800	917
Dec 1806	10co	4	46	44	22	800	916
Dec 1807	10co	4	35	24	22	400	485
Apr 1809	10co	4	35	34	22	600	695
Sep 1809	10co	4	46	64	22	1,200	1,336
Dec 1810	10co	4	46	44	22	800	916
Dec 1809	10co	4	46	64	22	1,200	1,336
Dec 1811	10co	4	46	65	22	1,200	1,337
Dec 1815	10co	4	46	55	22	1,000	1,127

Establishments, 3rd Battalion 60th Regiment of Foot

Year	Subunits	Field Off	Off/ Staff	Sjts	Mus	Corp/ Pvts	Total
Dec 1792	10co	3	32	22	12	430	499
Jan 1793	10co	3	32	32	22	600	689
Apr 1794	12co	3	38	50	26	990	1,107
Dec 1794	10co	3	32	32	22	600	689
Dec 1795	10co+2r	5	51	62	30	1,010	1,158
Dec 1798	10co	5	51	53	22	1,000	1,131
Dec 1802	10co	5	43	34	22	750	854
Dec 1803	10co	5	46	34	22	750	857
Dec 1804	10co	5	46	44	22	800	917
Dec 1806	10co	5	46	54	22	1,000	1,127
Aug 1807	10co	4	46	64	22	1,200	1,336
Dec 1807	10co	4	46	74	22	1,400	1,546
Dec 1808	10co	4	46	54	22	1,000	1,126
Dec 1810	10co	4	46	44	22	800	916
Dec 1811	10co	4	46	55	22	1,000	1,127
Dec 1812	10co	4	46	65	22	1,200	1,337
Dec 1814	10co	4	46	55	22	1,000	1,127
Dec 1815	10co	4	46	45	22	800	917

Establishments, 4th Battalion 60th Regiment of Foot

Year	Subunits	Field Off	Off/ Staff	Sjts	Mus	Corp/ Pvts	Total
Dec 1792	10co	3	32	22	12	430	499
Jan 1793	10co	3	32	32	22	600	689

Year	Subunits	Field Off	Off/ Staff	Sjts	Mus	Corp/ Pvts	Total
Dec 1795	10co+2r	5	51	62	30	1,010	1,158
Dec 1798	10co	5	51	53	22	1,000	1,131
Dec 1802	10co	5	43	34	22	750	854
Dec 1803	10co	5	46	34	22	750	857
Dec 1804	10co	5	46	44	22	800	917
Dec 1805	10co	5	36	44	22	800	907
Dec 1806	10co	4	36	44	22	800	906
Dec 1807	10co	4	46	44	22	800	916
Dec 1810	10co	4	46	54	22	1,000	1,126
Dec 1811	10co	4	46	55	22	1,000	1,127
Dec 1812	10co	4	46	65	22	1,200	1,337
Dec 1814	10co	4	46	55	22	1,000	1,127
Dec 1815	10co	4	46	45	22	800	917

Establishments, 5th Battalion 60th Regiment of Foot

Year	Subunits	Field Off	Off/ Staff	Sjts	Mus	Corp/ Pvts	Total
Dec 1797	10co+2r	5	51	63	30	1,010	1,159
Dec 1802	10co	5	33	34	22	750	844
Dec 1803	10co	5	36	34	22	750	847
Dec 1804	10co	5	36	44	22	800	907
Dec 1805	10co	5	46	44	22	800	917
Jul 1807	10co	4	46	54	22	1,000	1,126
Dec 1808	10co	4	36	44	22	800	906
Dec 1809	10co	4	45	44	22	610	726
Dec 1810	10co	4	46	44	22	610	726
Dec 1811	10co	4	46	55	22	810	937
Dec 1812	10co	4	46	65	22	1,010	1,147
Jul 1814	10co	5	46	65	22	1,010	1,148

Establishments, 6th Battalion 60th Regiment of Foot

Year	Subunits	Field Off	Off/ Staff	Sjts	Mus	Corp/ Pvts	Total
Dec 1799	10co+2r	5	51	63	30	1,010	1,159
Jun 1802	10co	5	43	34	22	750	854
Dec 1803	10co	5	46	34	22	750	857
Dec 1804	10co	5	46	44	22	800	917
Dec 1806	10co	4	46	44	22	800	916
Dec 1809	10co	4	46	54	22	1,000	1,126
Dec 1811	10co	4	46	55	22	1,000	1,127
Dec 1812	10co	4	46	65	22	1,200	1,337
Dec 1814	10co	4	46	55	22	1,000	1,127
Dec 1815	10co	4	46	45	22	800	917

Establishments, 7th Battalion 60th Regiment of Foot

Year	Subunits	Field Off	Off/ Staff	Sjts	Mus	Corp/ Pvts	Total
Dec 1813	10co	4	46	45	22	800	917
Dec 1814	10co	4	36	45	22	800	907
Dec 1815	10co	4	46	45	22	800	917

Establishments, 8th Battalion 60th Regiment of Foot

Year	Subunits	Field Off	Off/ Staff	Sjts	Mus	Corp/ Pvts	Total
Dec 1813	10co	4	36	34	22	600	696
Dec 1814	10co	4	36	45	22	800	907
Dec 1815	10co	4	36	35	22	600	697

Service Statistics, 60th Regiment of Foot

	Lieutenant Colonels	Majors
Number of officers in period 1793–1815	51	83
Average age on appointment to substantive rank	37.5	34
Average time in rank in regiment (years)	5.5	3.5
Total field officers by nationality	53 EW / 29 S / 26 F / 16 I / 10 A	
Demographics of other ranks 1794	1/60th: 50% EW / 25% I / 13% F / 12% S	
	2/60th: 52% EW / 22% F / 19% I / 7% S	
Demographics of other ranks 1797	1/60th: 44% EW / 22% F / 22% I / 12% S	
	2/60th: 48% EW / 28% F / 18% I / 6% S	
Demographics of other ranks 1804	5/60th: 100% F	
Demographics of other ranks 1807	5/60th: 100% F	
Demographics of other ranks 1808	1/60th: 82% F / 10% I / 7% EW / 1% S	
	2/60th: 90% F / 5% EW / 3% I / 2% S	
	3/60th: 79% F / 10% EW / 9% I / 2% S	
	4/60th: 98% F / 1% EW / 1% I	
Demographics of other ranks 1810	6/60th: 99% F / 1% E,S+I	
Demographics of other ranks 1813	3/60th: 97% F / 2% EW / 1% I	
	5/60th: 100% F	
Demographics of other ranks 1814	7/60th: 99% F / 1% E,S+I	
Months of overseas service 1793–1815	1/60th: 252	
	2/60th: 251	
	3/60th: 216	
	4/60th: 250	
	5/60th: 154	
	6/60th: 185	
	7/60th: 21	
	8/60th: 26	

Significant Militia/Volunteer and Foreign Intakes

1797: Nottinghamshire Fencibles, 2nd Caithness Fencibles, Reay Fencibles, Hompesch's Light Infantry, Loewenstein's Chasseurs, Loewenstein's Fusileers, Royal Foreigners, Waldstein's Light Infantry
1799: West Lowland Fencibles
1800: County Durham
1801: County Durham

Regimental Colonels

795. *Rt Hon. Jeffrey Amherst, 1st Baron, Lord AMHERST (1758–1797)*

Born: Kent 1717
Relations: Son of Jeffrey Amherst of Sevenoaks and Elizabeth (Kerrill); brother of Admiral John Amherst, RN; and Lieutenant General William Amherst
Entry to Army: Ensign in 1st Foot Guards 1735 by purchase
Regimental Field Officer Promotions: Captain and Lieutenant Colonel in 1st Foot Guards 25 Dec 1745 by purchase
Brevets: Major General in North America 23 Jan 1758; Major General 25 Jun 1759; Lieutenant General 19 Jan 1761; General 19 Mar 1778; Field Marshal 30 Jul 1796
Colonelcies: 15th Foot 22 May 1756 (vice Jordea); 60th Foot 20 Sep 1758 (vice Abercrombie); 3rd Foot 7 Nov 1768 (vice Burton); 2nd Troop Horse Grenadier Guards 21 Apr 1779 (vice Harrington); 2nd Life Guards 25 Jun 1788
Early Service: Served in Seven Years War; Commander in Chief North America 1758–1763; Lieutenant Governor and Commander in Chief of the Colony and Dominion of Virginia 4 Mar 1760 to 12 Aug 1768 (never actually visited); Governor of Guernsey Oct 1770 to 3 Aug 1797
Service 1793–1815: Commander in Chief of the British Army Jan 1793 to 3 Apr 1795
Creations and Dignities: 1st Baron Amherst of Holmesdale 20 May 1776; 1st Baron Amherst of

Montréal 9 Sep 1788
Awards and Honours: KB 11 Apr 1761
Residences: Lower Grosvenor Street, London; Montréal Park, near Sevenoaks, Kent
Died: Montréal Park 3 Aug 1797
Sources: ARLI; MENA; ODNB; WEOF; WOST

796. *H.R.H. Prince Frederick Augustus, DUKE OF YORK and ALBANY (1797–*

Born: London 1763
Relations: Second son of King George III and Princess Charlotte (of Mecklenburg-Strelitz); nephew of Field Marshal HRH William Henry, Duke of Gloucester and Edinburgh; brother of Colonel HRH Prince George Augustus Frederick, Prince of Wales; Admiral HRH Prince William Henry, Duke of Clarence, RN; Field Marshal HRH Prince Edward, Duke of Kent and Strathern; Field Marshal HRH Prince Ernest Augustus, Duke of Cumberland; Colonel HRH Prince Augustus Frederick, Duke of Sussex; Field Marshal HRH Prince Adolphus Frederick, Duke of Cambridge; and Field Marshal HRH Prince William Frederick, Duke of Gloucester
Education: University of Göttingen, Hanover
Entry to Army: Brevet Colonel 4 Nov 1780
Brevets: Major General 20 Nov 1782; Lieutenant General 27 Oct 1784; General 12 Apr 1793; Field Marshal 18 Feb 1795
Colonelcies: 2nd Troop Horse Grenadier Guards 26 Mar 1782 (vice Amherst); 60th Foot 23 Aug 1797 (vice Amherst); 1st Foot Guards 5 Sep 1805 (vice Duke of Gloucester)
Service 1793–1815: Commanded allied forces in Flanders 1793–1794; Field Marshal on the Staff (de facto Commander in Chief) 3 Apr 1795 (vice Amherst); Commander in Chief of HM Land Forces 4 Apr 1798; Commanded allied forces at Helder 1799; resigned as Commander in Chief after Mary Anne Clarke affair 25 Mar 1809; Commander in Chief of the British Army 29 May 1811 to 5 Jan 1827
Creations and Dignities: Duke of York and Albany 27 Nov 1784; Earl of Ulster 27 Nov 1784
Awards and Honours: KB 30 Dec 1767; KG 19 Jun 1771; KOSA (Prussia) 11 Apr 1814; KOSE (France) 21 Apr 1814; KSAA (Russia) 9 Jun 1814; GCAN (Russia) 9 Jun 1814; GCCT (Spain) 21 Aug 1814; GCMT (Habsburg) 1814; GCB 2 Jan 1815; GCH 12 Aug 1815
Residences: Stable Yard, St James's, London; Oatlands Park, near Weybridge, Surrey
Died: London 5 Jan 1827
Sources: ARLI; MENA; ODNB; PHIL; WEOF; The Noble Duke of York

Colonels Commandant

797. *Sir Alured CLARKE (1st Battalion) (1791–1794)*

Born: London 1744
Relations: Son of Charles Clarke of Godmanchester, Baron of the Exchequer, and Jane (Mullins); half-brother of General Thomas Clarke
Education: Eton College
Entry to Army: Ensign in 50th Foot 20 Mar 1759 by purchase
Regimental Field Officer Promotions: Major in 54th Foot 28 Nov 1771 (vice Powell); Lieutenant Colonel in 7th Foot 10 Mar 1777 (vice Prescott)
Brevets: Brevet Colonel 16 May 1782; Major General 1 May 1790; Lieutenant General (East Indies) 3 May 1796; Lieutenant General 4 Feb 1797; General 11 May 1802; Field Marshal 22 Jul 1830
Colonelcies: Colonel Commandant of 1/60th Foot 8 Jul 1791 (vice Haldimand); 68th Foot 6 Aug 1794 (vice Dundas); 5th Foot 25 Oct 1794 (vice Stopford); 7th Foot 21 Aug 1801 (vice Duke of Kent)
Early Service: Served in Germany 1759; served in North America 1776–1782; Lieutenant Governor of Jamaica 1782–1784; Captain General and Governor in Chief Jamaica 7 Jul 1784 to 17 Mar 1790; acting Governor of Québec 19 Aug 1791 to 24 Sep 1793
Service 1793–1815: Commanded forces in capture of Cape of Good Hope 1795; acting Governor General of British East Indies 25 Mar 1798 to 18 May 1798; Commander in Chief in British East Indies 1798–1801
Awards and Honours: KB 14 Jan 1797; GCB 4 Jan 1815
Residence: Mansfield Street, Marylebone, London
Died: Llangollen, 16 Sep 1832
Sources: ARLI; DICB; PHIL; ODNB; PHIL; WEOF; WOST

798. *Gabriel CHRISTIE (2nd/1st Battalion) (1786–1799)*

Born: Stirlingshire 1722
Relations: Son of James Christie, merchant and manufacturer, and Catherine (Napier); nephew of Lieutenant General Robert Napier; father of General Napier Christie-Burton
Entry to Army: Lieutenant in 27th Foot 1745
Field Officer Promotions: Lieutenant Colonel in 60th Foot 23 Dec 1768; Lieutenant Colonel in 2/60th Foot 14 Aug 1773
Brevets: Brevet Major 7 Apr 1759; Brevet Lieutenant Colonel 27 Jan 1762; Brevet Colonel 29

Aug 1777; Major General 19 Oct 1781; Lieutenant General 12 Oct 1793; General 1 Jan 1798
Colonelcies: Colonel Commandant of 2/60th Foot 14 May 1778 (vice Robertson); Colonel Commandant of 1/60th Foot 6 Aug 1794 (vice Clarke)
Early Service: Served at Culloden 1746; Assistant Deputy Quartermaster General in British North America 1756–1769; Deputy Quartermaster General in British North America 1769–1773; served in West Indies 1773–1781; Commander in Chief Leeward Islands 1781
Residence: Rue Saint-Paul, Montréal, Québec
Died: Montréal 20 Jan 1799
Sources: ANCB; ANCD; ANCW; ARLI; DICB

799. *William Neville GARDINER (1st Battalion) (1798–1806)*

Born: Dublin 1748
Relations: Son of Charles Gardiner and Florinda (Norman); brother of Colonel Luke Gardiner, 1st Viscount Mountjoy, Dublin County Militia
Entry to Army: Cornet in 18th Light Dragoons 31 Dec 1767 by purchase
Field Officer Promotions: Major in 10th Foot 30 Oct 1777; Lieutenant Colonel in 45th Foot 29 Jun 1778; Lieutenant Colonel in 88th Foot 9 Jan 1782; to half-pay3 Sep 1783
Brevets: Brevet Major 4 Mar 1777; Brevet Colonel 28 Feb 1783; Major General 20 Dec 1793; Lieutenant General 26 Jun 1799
Colonelcies: 99th Foot 28 Mar 1795; Colonel Commandant of 1/60th Foot 11 Mar 1799 (vice Christie)
Early Service: Served in American War of Independence 1775–1778, ADC to Sir William Howe; ADC of Lord Lieutenant of Ireland 1783; Special Envoy to the Austrian Netherlands 1789–1792
Service 1793–1815: Governor of Kinsale 1 Jan 1802; Commander in Chief Nova Scotia and New Brunswick 1805 to 7 Feb 1806
Political Career: Minister Plenipotentiary to Poland 1792–1795; MP (Ire) 1800
Died: Halifax, Nova Scotia 7 Feb 1806
Sources: ARLI; DINB; GEMA (1806); WEOF

800. *Rt Hon. Sir William KEPPEL, Kt (1st Battalion) (1806–1811)*

Born: London 1756
Relations: [spec.] Illegitimate son of one of the Keppels, Earls of Albemarle
Entry to Army: Ensign in 25th Foot 19 Jan 1775 by purchase
Regimental Field Officer Promotions: Major in 82nd Foot 29 Apr 1782 (vice Craig); Lieutenant Colonel in 93rd Foot 20 Feb 1783; to half-pay24 Apr 1783
Brevets: Brevet Colonel 1 Mar 1794; Major General 3 May 1796; Lieutenant General 25 Sep 1803; General 4 Jun 1813
Colonelcies: 3rd West India Regiment 20 May 1795; Colonel Commandant of 1/60th Foot 24 Apr 1806 (vice Gardiner); 67th Foot 7 Feb 1811 (vice Craig); 2nd Foot 25 Aug 1828 (vice Torrens)
Early Service: Served in American War of Independence 1775–1778; served in West Indies
Service 1793–1815: Governor of Martinique 16 Apr 1796 to 13 Sep 1802 (vice Milnes)
Later Service: Groom of the Bedchamber and Equerry to King George IV 1812–1830; Governor of Portsmouth Dec 1826; Governor of Guernsey 3 Nov 1827 to 11 Dec 1834
Awards and Honours: Knight Bachelor 1 Feb 1813; GCB 2 Jan 1815; PC 16 Nov 1827
Residence: Scethrog, Breconshire
Died: Paris, Île-de-France, France 11 Dec 1834
Parentage details seem unconfirmable (he was baptised in a foundling hospital), but he left property to William Charles Keppel, Earl of Albemarle in his will, as well as money for the sons of the late Frederick Keppel
Sources: ANCB; ANCD; ANCW; ARLI; GEMA (1835); PHIL; WEOF; WOST

801. *Arthur WHETHAM (1st Battalion) (1811–1813)*

Born: London 1753
Relations: Son of Thomas Whetham and Anne (Barnardiston); brother of Lieutenant John Whetham, 12th Foot; nephew of General Thomas Whetham, 12th Foot; cousin of Major General John Whetham
Entry to Army: Ensign in 58th Foot 28 Feb 1772 by purchase
Regimental Field Officer Promotions: Captain and Lieutenant Colonel in 1st Foot Guards 30 Apr 1794 (vice Campbell) by purchase; Third Major in 1st Foot Guards 15 Sep 1808 (vice Thornton)
Brevets: Brevet Colonel 1 Jan 1798; Brigadier General (Leeward Islands) 18 Feb 1801; Major General 1 Jan 1805; Lieutenant General 4 Jun 1811
Colonelcies: Colonel Commandant of 1/60th Foot 7 Feb 1811 (vice Keppel)
Early Service: Served in Gibraltar 1772–1773, and 1776–1783
Service 1793–1815: ADC to King George III 1 Jan 1798; Lieutenant Governor of Portsmouth 1808–1813; First Gentleman of the Bedchamber to HRH Duke of Cumberland

Residences: Eaton Socon, Bedfordshire; Fort Monckton, Gosport, Hampshire
Died: Gosport 18 May 1813
Sources: ANCB; ANCD; ARLI; WEOF; WO 25/748

802. *Sir Henry CLINTON (1st Battalion) (1813–1815)*
Born: Surrey 1771
Relations: Son of General Sir Henry Clinton of Weybridge and Harriett (Carter); grandson of Francis Wemyss Charteris, Lord Elcho; brother of General Sir William Henry Clinton
Education: Eton College
Entry to Army: Midshipman on *HMS Salisbury* 1786; Ensign in 18th Foot 10 Oct 1787 by purchase; Ensign in 1st Foot Guards 12 Mar 1789 by purchase
Regimental Field Officer Promotions: Major in 30th Foot 28 Sep 1795; Lieutenant Colonel in 66th Foot 30 Sep 1795; Captain and Lieutenant Colonel in 1st Foot Guards 20 Oct 1796 (vice Dalrymple) by exchange
Brevets: Brevet Major 22 May 1794; Brevet Colonel 25 Sep 1803; Brigadier General (Baltic) 25 Jan 1808; Major General 25 Jul 1810; Lieutenant General (Spain and Portugal) 8 Apr 1813; Lieutenant General 4 Jun 1814
Colonelcies: Colonel Commandant of 1/60th Foot 20 May 1813 (vice Whetham); 3rd Foot 9 Aug 1815 (vice Leigh)
Early Service: Served in Netherlands with Brunswick forces 1788–1789
Service 1793–1815: ADC to Duke of York in Flanders 1793–1795, wounded at Camphin; served in West Indies 1795–1796; ADC to Cornwallis in Ireland 1798; Adjutant General in British East Indies Oct 1803 to Mar 1805; British military attaché to Russian army Nov 1805; commanded garrison of Syracuse, Sicily May 1806 to Nov 1807; Adjutant General in Peninsula Aug 1808 to Jan 1809; commanded 6th Division in Peninsula Feb 1812 to Jun 1813; Inspector General of Infantry 1814; commanded 2nd Division in Waterloo Campaign
Political Career: MP (Boroughbridge) 1808–1818
Awards and Honours: KB 29 Jun 1813; AGM (Sal Nlle Niv Ort Toul); GCB 2 Jan 1815; WatM 23 Apr 1816; KMT (Habsburg) 1816; KStG (Russia) 1816; KMWO (Netherlands) 1816; GCH 12 Aug 1816
Residence: York Street, Portman Square, Marylebone, London; Ashley, Hampshire
Died: Ashley 11 Dec 1829
Sources: ANCB; ARLI; CHAL; DALT; DINB; HPON; PHIL; WEOF; WO 25/744

803. *Sir Wroth Palmer ACLAND (1st Battalion) (1815–1816)*
Born: Somerset 1770
Relations: Son of Arthur Palmer Acland of Fairfield House and Elizabeth (Oxenham)
Entry to Army: Ensign in 17th Foot 25 Apr 1787 by purchase
Regimental Field Officer Promotions: Major in 19th Foot 21 Mar 1795 by purchase; Lieutenant Colonel in 19th Foot 1 Sep 1795; Captain and Lieutenant Colonel in Coldstream Foot Guards 10 May 1800 (vice Hewgill) by exchange; removed from the regiment as a general officer 25 Jul 1814
Brevets: Brevet Colonel 25 Sep 1803; Brigadier General (Mediterranean) 25 Mar 1805; Brigadier General (home staff) 25 Dec 1808; Major General 25 Jul 1810; Lieutenant General 4 Jun 1814
Colonelcies: Colonel Commandant of 1/60th Foot 9 Aug 1815
Service 1793–1815: Served in Flanders 1793; served in Leeward Islands 1794; served in West Indies 1795; served in British East Indies and Ceylon 1796–1799; served on staff in Mediterranean 1805; served in Maida 1806; served in Montevideo 1807; commanded brigade in Portugal Aug to Nov 1808; served in Walcheren 1809
Awards and Honours: KCB 2 Jan 1815
Residence: Bath, Somerset
Died: Bath 8 Mar 1816
Sources: ANCB; ANCD; ARLI; DINB; PHIL; WO 25/744

804. *Thomas CARLETON (2nd Battalion) (1794–1817)*
Born: County Tyrone 1735
Relations: Son of Christopher Carleton of Newry and Catherine (Ball); brother of General Guy Carleton, Lord Dorchester; uncle of Lieutenant Colonel Christopher Carleton, 29th Foot
Entry to Army: Ensign in 20th Foot 12 Feb 1753 by purchase
Regimental Field Officer Promotions: Lieutenant Colonel in 29th Foot 2 Aug 1776 (vice Gordon); Lieutenant Colonel in 5th Foot 26 Sep 1788 (vice Fitz-Gerald) by exchange
Brevets: Brevet Major 23 Jul 1772; Brevet Lieutenant Colonel 31 Jul 1776; Brevet Colonel 20 Nov 1782; Major General 12 Oct 1793; Lieutenant General 1 Jan 1798; General 25 Sep 1803
Colonelcies: 93rd Foot 2 Jul 1794 (vice Balfour); Colonel Commandant of 2/60th Foot 6 Aug 1794 (vice Christie)
Early Service: Served in Seven Years' War 1757–1762; observer during Russo-Turkish War 1774–1775; Quartermaster General in British

North America 1776–1782; Lieutenant Governor of New Brunswick 1784 to 28 Aug 1802
Residence: Ramsgate, Kent
Died: Ramsgate 2 Feb 1817
Was appointed as the first Lieutenant Governor of New Brunswick, where he helped to re-settle the Loyalists leaving the United States
Sources: ANCB; ANCD; ARLI; DICB; WEOF; WO 25/785

805. *William ROWLEY (3rd Battalion) (1787–1807)*

Born: County Londonderry 1733
Relations: Son of Admiral Sir William Rowley and Arabella (Dawson); brother of Rear Admiral Josiah Rowley
Entry to Army: 1st Lieutenant in Marines 5 Apr 1755
Regimental Field Officer Promotions: Major in 68th Foot 12 Jun 1760; Lieutenant Colonel in 120th Foot 13 Feb 1762; to half-pay of 120th Foot 1762
Brevets: Brevet Colonel 29 Aug 1777; Major General 19 Oct 1781; Lieutenant General 12 Oct 1793; General 1 Jan 1798
Colonelcies: Colonel Commandant of 3/60th Foot 3 Oct 1787
Residence: Binfield Place, Berkshire
Died: Binfield Place 23 Aug 1807
Sources: ANCB; ANCD; ANCW; ARLI; WEOF

806. *Hon. Edmund PHIPPS (3rd Battalion) (1807–1837)*

Born: London 1760
Relations: Son of Constantine Phipps, 1st Baron Mulgrave, and Hon. Levell (Hervey); brother of Hon. Henry Phipps, 1st Earl of Mulgrave
Education: Eton College; St John's, Cambridge
Entry to Army: Ensign in 85th Foot 17 Mar 1780 by purchase
Regimental Field Officer Promotions: Captain and Lieutenant Colonel in 1st Foot Guards 9 Oct 1793 (vice Talbot) by purchase
Brevets: Brevet Colonel 3 May 1796; Major General 29 Apr 1802; Lieutenant General 25 Apr 1808; General 1819
Colonelcies: Colonel Commandant of 3/60th Foot 25 Aug 1807 (vice Rowley)
Early Service: Served in Jamaica 1780–1781; served at siege of Gibraltar 1782–1783; ADC to Lord Lieutenant of Ireland 1784–1787
Service 1793–1815: Served in Flanders 1793; Member of the Clothing Board 1805–1809; Under Secretary to the Master General of Ordnance 1809–1810; Paymaster of Marines 1810–1812; Clerk of deliveries at the Ordnance 1812–1830
Political Career: MP (Scarborough) 1794–1818; MP (Queenborough) 1818–1820; MP (Scarborough) 1820–1832
Residence: Mulgrave Castle, Lythe, Yorkshire
Died: Venice, Veneto, Italy 14 Sep 1837
Nicknamed 'The Governor of Finland' due to his incapacitated right arm, which 'hung down like the fin of a turtle', caused by drinking sherry infused by lead
Sources: ANCB; ANCD; ARLI; HPON; PBKN; PHIL; WEOF; WO 25/747

807. *James ROOKE (4th Battalion) (1788–1796)*

See 188.
Colonel Commandant of 4/60th Foot 20 Oct 1788 (vice Gordon)

808. *Peter HUNTER (4th Battalion) (1796–1804)*

Born: Perthshire 1746
Relations: Son of John Hunter, Laird of Knapp and Euphemia (Jack)
Entry to Army: Ensign in 1st Foot 1767 by purchase
Regimental Field Officer Promotions: Major in 92nd Foot 28 Dec 1779; Major in 1/60th Foot 20 Oct 1781; Lieutenant Colonel in 4/60th Foot 24 Sep 1787
Brevets: Brevet Lieutenant Colonel 23 Nov 1782; Brevet Colonel 12 Oct 1793; Major General 26 Feb 1795; Lieutenant General 29 Apr 1802
Colonelcies: Colonel Commandant of 4/60th Foot 2 Aug 1796 (vice Rooke); 9th Foot 15 Jun 1804 (vice Bertie)
Early Service: Served on Minorca 1771–1775; served in West Indies 1779–1786; served in Nova Scotia 1787–1789; Acting Superintendent of British Honduras 1790–1791
Service 1793–1815: Lieutenant Governor of Upper Canada 10 Apr 1799 to Mar 1802; acting Commander in Chief in British North America Aug 1800 to Mar 1802; Commander in Chief in British North America Mar 1802 to 21 Aug 1805
Residence: Suffolk Street, Charing Cross, London
Died: Québec 21 Aug 1805
Sources: ARLI; DICB; WEOF; WOST

809. *Charles, Lord FITZROY (4th Battalion) (1804–1805)*

See 465.
Colonel Commandant of 4/60th Foot 15 Jun 1804 (vice Hunter)

810. *Edward MORRISON (4th Battalion) (1805–1813)*
Born: London 1760
Relations: Son of General George Morrison RA, Quartermaster General to the Forces, and Mary (Becher)
Entry to Army: Ensign in Coldstream Foot Guards 20 Jan 1777 by purchase
Regimental Field Officer Promotions: Captain and Lieutenant Colonel in Coldstream Foot Guards 13 Jan 1790 by purchase; Second Major in Coldstream Foot Guards 2 Dec 1795 (vice Morshead); First Major in Coldstream Foot Guards 30 Dec 1797 (vice Morshead); Lieutenant Colonel in Coldstream Foot Guards 9 May 1800 (vice Stanwix)
Brevets: Brevet Colonel 26 Feb 1795; Major General 1 Jan 1797; Lieutenant General 1 Jan 1805; General 15 Feb 1813
Colonelcies: Prince of Wales's Loyal Leicester Fencibles 19 Nov 1800 (vice Parkyns); Colonel Commandant of 4/60th Foot 1 Jan 1805 (vice Fitzroy); 13th Foot 15 Feb 1813 (vice Campbell)
Early Service: Assistant Quartermaster General in North America 1777–1781; ADC to Archibald Campbell in Jamaica 1781–1783
Service 1793–1815: Served in Flanders 1793–1794; served on staff in Ireland 1798; served on staff at home 1803–1808; Lieutenant Governor and Commander in Chief in Jamaica May 1809 to 1812 (vice Coote)
Residence: Devonshire Place, Marylebone, London
Died: London 3 Dec 1843
Sources: ARLI; PHIL; WEOF; WO 25/747

811. *Hon. Charles HOPE (4th Battalion) (1813–1818)*
See 171.
Colonel Commandant of 4/60th Foot 15 Feb 1813 (vice Morrison)

812. *William MORSHEAD (5th Battalion) (1797–1800)*
See 538.
Colonel Commandant of 5/60th Foot 30 Dec 1797

813. *Thomas Slaughter STANWIX (5th Battalion) (1800–1806)*
Born: London 1749
Relations: Son of Captain Robert Slaughter of Hampstead and Jane (Stanwix); added Stanwix surname at marriage 1790
Entry to Army: Ensign in Coldstream Foot Guards 26 Sep 1766 by purchase
Regimental Field Officer Promotions: Captain and Lieutenant Colonel in Coldstream Foot Guards 22 Feb 1779 by purchase; Second Major in Coldstream Foot Guards 1 Apr 1795 (vice Pennington); First Major in Coldstream Foot Guards 23 Jun 1795 (vice Pennington); Lieutenant Colonel in Coldstream Foot Guards 2 Dec 1795 (vice Martin)
Brevets: Brevet Colonel 9 Apr 1789; Major General 20 Dec 1793; Lieutenant General 26 Jun 1799; General 25 Apr 1808
Colonelcies: Colonel Commandant of 5/60th Foot 9 May 1800 (vice Morshead); 97th Foot 8 Sep 1806 (vice Stuart); 85th Foot 25 Feb 1807 (vice Asgill)
Early Service: ADC to King George III 9 Apr 1789
Service 1793–1815: Served in Flanders 1793–1794; commanded Brigade of Guards in Irish Rebellion 1798
Residences: Shanbally Castle, County Tipperary; Sunbury-on-Thames, Middlesex
Died: Sunbury-on-Thames 25 Nov 1815
Sources: ANCB; ANCW; ARLI; WEOF; WO 25/748; An Alphabetical List of the Officers of the Eighty-Fifth, Bucks Volunteers

814. *Sir George PRÉVOST, 1st Bt (5th Battalion) (1806–1814)*
Born: New Jersey 1767
Relations: Son of Major General Augustine Prévost of Bergen and Annette Francoise Marguerite (Grand); brother of Major Augustine Prévost, 60th Foot; and Major General William Augustine Prévost, 67th Foot; uncle of Captain James Prévost, 60th Foot; and Lieutenant Henry Prévost, 7th Foot, both of whom died of wounds in the Peninsula in 1811
Education: Locke's Military Academy, Chelsea
Entry to Army: Ensign in 60th Foot 3 May 1779
Regimental Field Officer Promotions: Major in 3/60th Foot 18 Nov 1790 by purchase; Lieutenant Colonel in 3/60th Foot 6 Aug 1794
Brevets: Brevet Colonel 1 Jan 1798; Brigadier General (West Indies) Jan 1798; Major General 1 Jan 1805; Lieutenant General (Nova Scotia) Jan 1808; Lieutenant General 4 Jun 1811
Colonelcies: Colonel Commandant of 5/60th Foot 8 Sep 1806 (vice Stanwyx); 76th Foot 2 Jan 1813 (vice Musgrave); 16th Foot 17 Feb 1814 (vice Green)
Early Service: Served in Gibraltar; commanded 3/60th Foot in West Indies 1791–1793
Service 1793–1815: Served in Demerara and in St. Vincent and Dominica 1795; commanded 3/60th Foot in West Indies 1796; Inspecting Field Officer in England 1797; Lieutenant Governor and Commander in Chief St. Lucia Jul 1798 to Mar

1802; Commanding General and Governor of Dominica 25 Dec 1802 to 24 Jun 1805; commanded troops at defence of Dominica Feb 1804; Lieutenant Governor of Portsmouth Nov 1805; Lieutenant Governor and Commander in Chief Nova Scotia 13 Apr 1808 to 25 Aug 1811; second in command in Martinique expedition 1809; Governor of Lower Canada and Commander in Chief British North America 13 Sep 1811 to 3 Apr 1815; summoned home to face enquiry in late 1815 but died a week before convening
Creations and Dignities: 1st Baronet of Belmont 6 Dec 1805
Residences: Baker Street, Portman Square, London; Belmont House, Bedhampton, Hampshire
Died: London 5 Jan 1816
Sources: ARLI; CHAL; DICB; HALL; WEOF; WO 25/747; WOST

815. *John ROBINSON (5th Battalion) (1813–1818)*

Born: Suffolk c.1757
Relations: Son of Lieutenant Colonel John Robinson of Denston Hall and Elizabeth (Coates); son-in-law of Robert Clive, 1st Baron Clive
Entry to Army: Adjutant and Sub-Lieutenant in 1st Horse Grenadier Guards 1 Sep 1773 by purchase
Regimental Field Officer Promotions: Major in 1st Troop Horse Grenadier Guards 16 Apr 1788 (vice Haynes) by purchase; to half-pay of Horse Grenadier Guards 25 Jun 1788; Colonel in Suffolk Fencibles 30 Oct 1794
Brevets: Brevet Colonel 1 Jan 1798; Major General 1 Jan 1805; Lieutenant General 4 Jun 1811
Colonelcies: 2nd Garrison Battalion 25 Feb 1805; Colonel Commandant of 5/60th Foot 2 Jan 1813 (vice Prevost)
Service 1793–1815: Served in Irish rebellion 1798
Political Career: MP (Bishop's Castle) 1802–1819
Residence: Denston Hall, Denston, Suffolk
Died: Paris, France 23 May 1819
Sources: ARLI; HPON; WEOF; WO 25/748

816. *Sir Robert William Colebrooke BROWNRIGG, 1st Bt (6th Battalion) (1799–1805)*

Born: County Wicklow 1759
Relations: Son of Captain Henry Brownrigg of Rockingham and Martha (Alcock); brother of Major General Thomas Brownrigg and Lieutenant Colonel Henry Quin Brownrigg; father of Lieutenant Colonel Robert James Brownrigg, 2nd Ceylon Regiment; father-in-law of Major General Sir John Ross
Education: Royal Military Academy, Woolwich
Entry to Army: Ensign in 14th Foot 22 Nov 1775
Regimental Field Officer Promotions: Lieutenant Colonel in 88th Foot 25 Sep 1793; Captain and Lieutenant Colonel in Coldstream Foot Guards 21 Jun 1795 by exchange
Brevets: Brevet Major 19 May 1790; Brevet Colonel 3 May 1796; Major General 29 Apr 1802; Lieutenant General 25 Apr 1808; General 12 Aug 1819
Colonelcies: Colonel Commandant of 6/60th Foot 25 Jul 1799; 9th Foot 3 Oct 1805 (vice Hunter)
Early Service: Served in Nova Scotia 1776; served on board fleet as adjutant of marines 1780; served in Jamaica 1782–1784; Deputy Adjutant General in Jamaica 1790
Service 1793–1815: ADC to Duke of Richmond 1793; Deputy Quartermaster General in Flanders 27 Nov 1793; Military Secretary to Duke of York Feb 1795 to 11 Mar 1803; Quartermaster General to the Forces 12 Mar 1803 to 9 Aug 1811 (vice Dundas); served at Walcheren 1809; Governor and General Officer Commanding Ceylon 11 Mar 1812 to 1 Feb 1820 (vice Wilson); commanded forces in Kandian War 1815
Creations and Dignities: 1st Baronet of London Mar 1816
Awards and Honours: KCB 2 Jan 1815; GCB 23 Feb 1821
Residences: Eton, Buckinghamshire; Hilston Park, near Newcastle, Monmouthshire
Died: Hilston Park 27 May 1833
Sources: ARLI; ODNB; PHIL; WEOF; WO 25/744; WOST

817. *Rt Hon. Sir John HOPE, 4th Earl of Hopetoun (6th Battalion) (1805–1806)*

Born: West Lothian 1765
Relations: Son of John, 2nd Earl of Hopetoun and Jean (Oliphant); half-brother of General Alexander Hope; brother-in-law of Henry Dundas, Viscount Melville
Entry to Army: Cornet in 10th Light Dragoons 28 May 1784 by purchase
Regimental Field Officer Promotions: Major in 1st Foot 25 Apr 1792 by purchase; Major in 25th Foot 2 Apr 1793 (vice Sayer) by exchange; Lieutenant Colonel in 25th Foot 26 Apr 1793 (vice Rigby); to half-pay of North Lowland Fencibles 6 Aug 1802
Brevets: Brevet Colonel 3 May 1796; Brigadier General (West Indies) 26 Oct 1796; Brigadier General (Mediterranean) 9 May 1800; Major General 29 Apr 1802; Lieutenant General 25 Apr 1808; General 12 Aug 1819

Colonelcies: North Lowland Fencibles 27 Aug 1799; Colonel Commandant of 6/60th Foot 3 Oct 1805 (vice Brownrigg); 92nd Foot 3 Jan 1806 (vice Gordon); 42nd Foot 29 Jan 1820 (vice Gordon)
Service 1793–1815: Adjutant General in Leeward Islands 1795–1797; served in Helder 1799; Assistant Adjutant General in Egypt 1801; served in Hanover 1805; served in Peninsula Sep 1808 to Jan 1809, commanded evacuation force from Corunna after Moore's death; commanded reserve in Walcheren 1809; Commander of the forces in Ireland 24 Jan 1812 to Aug 1813 (vice Stanhope); commanded 1st Division in Peninsula Oct 1813 to Apr 1814; POW in Bayonne Apr 1814
Later Service: Lord Lieutenant of Linlithgowshire 1816–1823
Political Career: MP (Linlithgowshire) 1790–1800
Creations and Dignities: 1st Baron Niddry of Niddry Castle 17 May 1814; 4th Earl of Hopetoun 29 May 1816
Awards and Honours: KB 21 Apr 1809; PC (Ire) 10 Apr 1812; AGM (Cor Nive) 1814; GCB 2 Jan 1815; FRSE
Residence: Craighall Castle, Linlithgowshire
Died: Paris, France 27 Aug 1823
Sources: ARLI; HPON; ODNB; PHIL; WEOF

818. *Napier CHRISTIE-BURTON (6th Battalion) (1806–1819)*

Born: Napier Christie in New York State 1758; took -Burton surname by Royal License 16 Nov 1784
Relations: Son of General Gabriel Christie of Montréal and Sarah (Stevenson)
Entry to Army: Ensign in 22nd Foot 15 Aug 1775 by purchase
Regimental Field Officer Promotions: Captain and Lieutenant Colonel in 3rd Foot Guards 13 Oct 1789 by purchase; Second Major in 3rd Foot Guards 5 Aug 1799 (vice Manners); First Major in 3rd Foot Guards 21 May 1801 (vice Watson); Lieutenant Colonel in 3rd Foot Guards 22 Apr 1802 (vice Lister)
Brevets: Brevet Colonel 26 Feb 1795; Brigadier General (Guernsey) 1796; Major General 1 Jan 1798; Lieutenant General 1 Jan 1805; General 4 Jun 1814
Colonelcies: Colonel Commandant of 6/60th Foot 3 Jan 1806 (vice Hope); Colonel Commandant of 1/60th Foot 27 Apr 1819
Early Service: Served in American War of Independence 1779–1782, POW at Yorktown
Service 1793–1815: Served in Flanders 1793–1795; served on staff at home 1796–1799; Lieutenant Governor of Upper Canada 1799–1802; served on staff at home 1803–1806
Political Career: MP (Beverley) 1796–1806
Residences: Hull Bank, near Beverley, Yorkshire; New Street, Dorset Square, Marylebone, London; Grove End Road, St John's Wood, London
Died: London 2 Jan 1835
Burton was imprisoned for debt at Maidstone in 1809
Sources: ANCD; ARLI; HPON; PHIL; WEOF; WO 25/744

819. *Rt Hon. Sir George MURRAY (7th Battalion) (1813–1817)*

Born: Perthshire 1772
Relations: Son of Sir William Murray of Ochtertyre Bt, and Lady Augusta (Mackenzie); grandson of George Mackenzie, 3rd Earl of Cromarty; brother-in-law of Field Marshal Henry William Paget, Earl of Uxbridge; General Sir Edward Paget; and Vice Admiral Sir Charles Paget
Education: Edinburgh University
Entry to Army: Ensign in 71st Foot 12 Mar 1789 by purchase
Regimental Field Officer Promotions: Captain and Lieutenant Colonel in 3rd Foot Guards 5 Aug 1799
Brevets: Brevet Colonel 9 Mar 1809; Major General (Spain and Portugal) 26 Oct 1811; Major General 1 Jan 1812; Lieutenant General 27 May 1825; General 23 Nov 1841
Colonelcies: Colonel Commandant of 7/60th Foot 9 Aug 1813; 72nd Foot 24 Feb 1817 (vice Hill); 42nd Foot 6 Sep 1823 (vice Hope); 1st Foot 29 Dec 1843 (vice Graham)
Service 1793–1815: Served in Flanders 1793–1795; Assistant Quartermaster General in Helder 1799, wounded at Texel; Assistant Quartermaster General in Egypt 1801; Adjutant General in West Indies 1802; Assistant Quartermaster General at Horse Guards 1804–1804; Deputy Quartermaster General in Ireland 1804–1812; Deputy Quartermaster General in Hanover 1805; Quartermaster General in Copenhagen 1807; Quartermaster General in Portugal Aug 1808 to Jan 1809; Quartermaster General in Peninsula May 1809 to Dec 1811; Quartermaster General in Peninsula Mar 1813 to Apr 1814; Adjutant General in Ireland 1814; Provisional Lieutenant Governor and Commander of Upper Canada 25 Apr 1815 to 10 Jun 1815 (vice Drummond); Chief of Staff of Allied Armies and Quartermaster General of British forces in France 1815–1818
Later Service: Governor of Edinburgh Castle 1818–1819; Governor of Royal Military College Sandhurst 18 Aug 1819 to Mar 1824; Commander in Chief Ireland Feb 1825 to May 1828; Governor of Fort George 7 Sep 1829; President of the Royal

Geographical Society 1833–1835
Political Career: MP (Perthshire) 1824–1832, and 1834; Lieutenant General of the Ordnance Mar 1824 to Feb 1825; Secretary of State for War and the Colonies Mar 1828 to Nov 1830; Master General of the Ordnance Dec 1834 to May 1835, and Sep 1841 to Jul 1846
Awards and Honours: AGM (Cor Tal Bus FDO Vit Nlle Niv Ort Toul); KB 11 Sep 1813; GCB 2 Jan 1815; GCH 12 Aug 1816; FRS 19 Jun 1823; PC 30 May 1828
Residences: Bleaton, Perthshire; Belgrave Square, Westminster, London
Died: London 28 Jul 1846
Sources: ARLI; CHAL; DICB; HPON; PHIL; WEOF; WOST

820. *Rt Hon. Sir James KEMPT (8th Battalion) (1813–1816)*

Born: Edinburgh 1775
Relations: Son of Gavin Kempt of Botley Hill and Sarah (Walker)
Entry to Army: Ensign in 8th Grenadier Regiment of Bombay Sepoys (later 101st Grenadiers in Bombay service) 31 Mar 1783
Regimental Field Officer Promotions: Major in 113th Foot 18 Sep 1794; to half-pay of 113rd Foot 1 Mar 1798; Major in 66th Foot 9 Jul 1803; Lieutenant Colonel in 81st Foot 23 Jul 1803 (vice McKenzie)
Brevets: Brevet Lieutenant Colonel 28 Aug 1799; Brevet Colonel 9 Mar 1809; Major General 1 Jan 1812; Lieutenant General 27 May 1825; General 23 Nov 1841
Colonelcies: Colonel Commandant of 8/60th Foot 4 Nov 1813; 3rd West India Regiment 31 Mar 1815 (vice Murray); 81st Foot 12 Jul 1819 (vice Johnson); 40th Foot 8 Jan 1829 (vice Spencer); 2nd Foot 23 Dec 1834 (vice Keppel); 1st Foot 7 Aug 1846 (vice Murray)
Service 1793–1815: Inspecting Field Officer of Recruiting Service in Scotland 1796–1799; served in Helder 1799, ADC to Abercromby; served on staff in Egypt 1801; commanded light infantry at Maida 1806; Quartermaster General in Canada 24 Aug 1807; ADC to King George III 9 Mar 1809; commanded brigade in 3rd Division in Peninsula Jan to Jul 1812, wounded at Badajoz; commanded brigade in Light Division in Peninsula Jan 1813 to Apr 1814, wounded at Nivelle; commanded brigade in Waterloo campaign 1815, wounded at Waterloo; commanded 5th Division in advance on Paris 1815
Later Service: Governor of Nova Scotia 1 Jun 1820 to 23 Aug 1828; acting Governor of Québec 8 Sep 1828 to 20 Oct 1830; Master General of the Ordnance 30 Nov 1830 to 18 Dec 1834 (vice Beresford)
Awards and Honours: AGC (Mai Bad Vit Nlle Niv Ort Toul); KCB 2 Jan 1815; GCB 22 Jun 1815; WatM 23 Apr 1816; GCH 12 Aug 1816; KMWO (Netherlands) 1816; KMT (Habsburg) 1816; KStG (Russia); PC 8 Dec 1830; MGSM (Egt)
Residence: South Street, Grosvenor Square, London
Died: London 20 Dec 1854
Many sources give his birth date as 1765, whereas in fact his baptismal record is from 26 Jan 1775; further confirmed by his age in the 1841 and 1851 censuses, as well as his burial record, all of which point to a birth year of 1775
Sources: ARLI; CHAL; DINB; ODNB; PHIL; WEOF; WOST; WO 25/746

Lieutenant Colonels

821. *Stephen KEMBLE (1778–1793)*

Born: New Jersey 1740
Relations: Son of Peter Kemble of New Brunswick and Gertrude (Bayard)
Entry to Army: Ensign in 44th Foot 8 Jan 1756 by purchase
Regimental Field Officer Promotions: Major in 60th Foot 20 Sep 1775; Lieutenant Colonel in 1/60th Foot 14 May 1778 (vice Christie)
Brevets: Brevet Major 7 Aug 1772; Brevet Colonel 20 Nov 1782
Early Service: Deputy Adjutant General in British North America 1772–1776; Assistant Deputy Adjutant General in British North America 1776–1780; Brigadier General in expedition to Nicaragua 1780–1781; served in West Indies 1782–1786; served in British North America 1786–1788
Service 1793–1815: Deputy Judge Advocate in British North America 1793
Retired: 13 May 1793
Residence: New Brunswick, New Jersey
Died: New Brunswick 20 Dec 1822
Sources: ARLI; <https://findingaids.lib.umich.edu/catalog/umich-wcl-M-1735kem>

822. *John Adolphus HARRIS (1788–1814)*

Born: Essex 1743
Relations: Son of John Harris of Greensted and Catherine (Meetkerke)
Education: Charterhouse School
Entry to Army: Ensign in 34th Foot 11 Jan 1760 by purchase
Regimental Field Officer Promotions: Major in 84th Foot 22 Oct 1779 by purchase; to half-pay of 84th Foot Jun 1784; Major in 60th Foot 20 Oct

1787 (vice Hunter); Lieutenant Colonel in 1/60th Foot 16 Jan 1788; removed from the regiment as a general officer 1814
Brevets: Brevet Colonel 26 Feb 1795; Major General 1 Jan 1798; Lieutenant General 1 Jan 1805; General 4 Jun 1814
Early Service: Served in West Indies 1762; served in American War of Independence 1775–1781; served in British North America 1781–1784; commanded 1/60th Foot 1788–1797
Residence: Hoddesdon, Hertfordshire
Died: Hoddesden 21 Jan 1827
Sources: ANCB; ANCW; ARLI; GEMA (1827); PHIL; WEOF; Alumni Carthusiani

823. *Gerrit FISHER (1792–1794)*
Born: Dublin c.1741
Entry to Army: Ensign in 55th Foot 8 Sep 1761 by purchase
Regimental Field Officer Promotions: Major in 55th Foot 26 Sep 1787 (vice Lamont); Major in 51st Foot 25 Apr 1792 (vice Fitch); Lieutenant Colonel in 3/60th Foot 25 Apr 1792 (vice Strutt); Lieutenant Colonel in 9th Foot 17 Feb 1794 (vice Campbell)
Brevets: Brevet Colonel 2 May 1796; Major General (Southern District) 1796; Major General 1 Jan 1801; Lieutenant General 25 Apr 1808
Colonelcies: Colonel Commandant of 3/9th Foot 23 Aug 1799
Service 1793–1815: Adjutant General and Military Secretary in Leeward Islands 1794
Died: Hounslow, London 1 Mar 1810
Sources: ANCD; ARLI; WEOF

824. *Hon. Vere POULETT (1793–1796)*
See 695.
Lieutenant Colonel in 2/60th Foot 13 May 1793 (vice Kemble) by purchase

825. *John RITCHIE (1794–1795)*
Born: Scotland c.1760
Entry to Army: Ensign in 44th Foot 5 Oct 1778 by purchase
Regimental Field Officer Promotions: Major in 91st Foot 25 Feb 25 Feb 1783 by purchase; Major in 9th Foot 7 Jul 1784 (vice Money) by exchange; Lieutenant Colonel in 3/60th Foot 17 Feb 1794 (vice Fisher)
Service 1793–1815: Served in West Indies 1794–1795
Died: Of wounds in St Vincent 11 Oct 1795
Sources: ARLI; GEMA (1795); Officers of the Black Watch 1725 to 1937

826. *John, Lord ELPHINSTONE (1794–1797)*
Born: Dunbartonshire 1764
Relations: Son of Captain John Elphinstone, 11th Lord Elphinstone and Hon. Lady Anne (Ruthven); brother of Admiral Hon. Charles Elphinstone Fleeming RN; nephew of Admiral Lord Keith RN; father of Captain John Elphinstone, Royal Horse Guards, 13rd Lord Elphinstone
Entry to Army: Ensign in 60th Foot 6 Sep 1779 by purchase
Field Officer Promotions: Major in 1/60th Foot 14 Sep 1792 (vice Benson); Lieutenant Colonel in 1/60th Foot 20 Jul 1794; Lieutenant Colonel in 61st Foot 18 Jan 1798 (vice Taylor); Lieutenant Colonel in 26th Foot 11 Jul 1798 (vice Duke) by exchange
Brevets: Brevet Colonel 1 Jan 1800; Major General 30 Oct 1805; Lieutenant General 1 Jan 1812
Colonelcies: 26th Foot 24 Apr 1806 (vice Gordon)
Service 1793–1815: Served in British North America 1794–1795; ADC to Duke of York 1795; served in Egypt 1801
Political Career: House of Lords 1803–1807
Creations and Dignities: 12th Lord Elphinstone 19 Aug 1794
Residence: Bath, Somerset
Died: Bath 20 May 1813
Sources: ARLI; COPE; WEOF; The Elphinstone Family Book of the Lords Elphinstone, Balmerino and Coupar

827. *Duncan McINTOSH (1795–1805)*
Born: Scotland c.1757
Entry to Army: Ensign in 1/60th Foot 4 Jan 1782
Regimental Field Officer Promotions: Major in 2/60th Foot 20 Apr 1793 (vice Murray); Lieutenant Colonel in 2/60th Foot 1 Sep 1795
Brevets: Brevet Colonel 25 Sep 1803
Service 1793–1815: Commanded 2/60th Foot in British North America and West Indies 1796–1805
Retired: 20 Jun 1805
Residence: Québec, Canada
Died: Québec 1815
Sources: ARLI; More Scottish Settlers, 1667–1827

828. *Johann Freidrich Bernard GOTTSCHED (1795–1797)*
Born: Hessen-Kassel 1756
Relations: Son of Johann Heinrich Gottsched of Kassel and Katharine Friderike (Scipio)
Entry to Army: Ensign in 2/60th Foot 29 Feb 1776
Regimental Field Officer Promotions: Major in 4/60th Foot 15 Jul 1793 (vice Gordon); Lieutenant Colonel in 4/60th Foot 2 Sep 1795

Service 1793–1815: Paymaster of 1st Line Infantry Battalion, Dutch Brigade 1802; Inspector of Dutch troops in British service
Retired: 13 Oct 1797
Residence: Pimlico, Middlesex
Died: Pimlico Sep 1805
Sources: ANCD; ARLI; <https://www.lagis-hessen.de/pnd/102532842>

829. *Sir Martin HUNTER (1796–1797)*

See 469.
Lieutenant Colonel in 3/60th Foot 12 Jan 1796

830. *John Anthony de BERNIERE (1796–1798)*

Born: County Antrim 1744
Relations: Son of Captain Louis Crommelin de Berniere of Lisburn and Elinor (Dunlevy); brother of Lieutenant Colonel Henry Abraham Crommelin de de Berniere, 9th Foot
Entry to Army: Lieutenant 9 Aug 1760 by purchase
Regimental Field Officer Promotions: Lieutenant Colonel unattached 1795; Lieutenant Colonel in 2/60th Foot 5 Mar 1796 (vice Poulett) by exchange
Brevets: Brevet Lieutenant Colonel 17 Feb 1795
Early Service: Served in American War of Independence
Service 1793–1815: Commanded 2/60 Foot 1796–1798
Retired: 5 Apr 1798
Residence: Charleston, South Carolina, USA
Died: Charleston 10 May 1812
Sources: ARLI; WEOF; <https://www.findagrave.com/memorial/91948269/john-anthony-de_berniere>

831. *John Robert Milliken-NAPIER (1796–1800)*

Born: Robert John Napier in Stirlingshire 1765
Relations: Son of William Napier of Culcreuch and Jane (Milliken); added Milliken- surname in 1776
Entry to Army: Lieutenant in 98th Foot 27 Dec 1780
Regimental Field Officer Promotions: Major in 63rd Foot 1 Mar 1794 (vice Stewart); Lieutenant Colonel in 4/60th Foot 10 Aug 1796 (vice Hunter); Lieutenant Colonel in 68th Foot 8 Feb 1800 (vice Cunynghame) by exchange; to half-pay of (late) 95th Foot 10 Apr 1801 (vice Vansittart) by exchange
Brevets: Brevet Colonel 1 Jan 1805
Early Service: Served in East Indies 1781–1783
Service 1793–1815: Served in West Indies 1796–1800
Residence: Cartside House, Johnstone, Renfrewshire
Died: Cartside House 13 Feb 1808
This officer is usually shown as John Robert Napier in Army Lists, but as Robert John (Milliken) Napier in genealogical records
Sources: ALRI; FMPB; FMPD; WEOF; <https://johnstonehistory.org/1265653336.html>

832. *George William RAMSAY (1797–1815)*

Born: Kent 1761
Relations: Son of George Ramsay of Cheltenham and Ann (Clement); son-in-law of Baron de Salve de Bruneton en Geldre; father of Major George Antoine Deliverance Ramsay, 77th Foot; and Lieutenant William Edward Ramsay RN
Entry to Army: Ensign in 36th Foot 13 Jan 1777 by purchase
Regimental Field Officer Promotions: Major Commandant of Ramsay's York Chasseurs (later York Rangers) 29 Jun 1793; Lieutenant Colonel Commandant of York Rangers 25 May 1795; to half-pay; Lieutenant Colonel in 3/60th Foot 30 Dec 1797 (vice Hunter); removed from the regiment as a general officer 1815
Brevets: Brevet Colonel 30 Oct 1805; Brigadier General (West Indies) 11 Nov 1806; Major General 4 Jun 1811; Lieutenant General 12 Aug 1819
Early Service: Served in American War of Independence 1778–1783
Service 1793–1815: Commanded Ramsay's York Chasseurs in Flanders 1793–1795; commanded 3/60th Foot 1805–1809; Adjutant General to the Forces in Leeward and Windward Islands 11 Nov 1806; Governor of St. Croix 1 May 1813 to 15 Apr 1815
Later Service: Governor of Antigua and Montserrat 13 Feb 1816 to 1 Nov 1819
Awards and Honours: AGM (Mart Guad)
Residence: Cheltenham, Gloucestershire
Died: Antigua 1 Nov 1819
Sources: ANCB; ANCD; ANCW; ARLI; WEOF; WOST; https://www.biddr.com/auctions/mortonand-eden/ browse?a=1403&l=1509346 (medal)

833. *Friedrich, Baron von ROTTENBURG, Kt (1797–1813)*

Born: Danzig 1757
Relations: Son of Franz Gottfried Rottenburg, merchant and Anne-Marie (Brunatti); father of Captain George Frederick de Rottenburg, 81st Foot
Entry to Army: 2nd Lieutenant in French *Régiment de La Marck* 1 Mar 1782
Regimental Field Officer Promotions: Major in Hompesch Hussars 25 Dec 1795; Lieutenant

Colonel in Hompesch Chasseurs 25 Jun 1796; Lieutenant Colonel in 5/60th Foot 30 Dec 1797
Brevets: Brevet Colonel 1 Jan 1805; Brigadier General (North America) Apr 1808; Major General 25 Jul 1810; Lieutenant General 12 Aug 1819
Early Service: Served in French army 1782–1791; commanded battalion in Polish army 1791–1794
Service 1793–1815: Served in Irish rebellion 1798; served in Surinam 1799; commanded light troops in Walcheren 1809; served in British North America 1810–1815; acting Lieutenant Governor and Commander of Upper Canada 19 Jun 1813 to 13 Dec 1813 (vice Sheaffe)
Awards and Honours: KCH 12 Aug 1817; Knight Bachelor 12 Feb 1818
Residence: Portsmouth, Hampshire
Died: Portsmouth 25 Apr 1832
Author of 'Regulations for the Exercise of Riflemen and Light Infantry and Instruction for Their Conduct in the Field' in 1798
Sources: ARLI; DICB; FMPW; WEOF; WO 25/748; WOST

834. *Robert CRAUFURD (1797–1802)*

Born: Essex 1764
Relations: Son of Sir Alexander Craufurd, 1st Bt, and Jane (Crokatt); brother of Sir James Gregan-Craufurd, 2nd Bt; and Lieutenant General Sir Charles Gregan Craufurd
Education: Harrow School; Göttingen University
Entry to Army: Ensign in 13th Foot 21 Apr 1779 by purchase
Regimental Field Officer Promotions: Lieutenant Colonel in Hompesch's Fusiliers Dec 1797; Lieutenant Colonel in 4/60th Foot 30 Dec 1797; Lieutenant Colonel in 86th Foot 11 Feb 1802 (vice Bell); to half-pay of 60th Foot 24 Feb 1803
Brevets: Brevet Lieutenant Colonel 26 Jan 1797; Brevet Colonel 30 Oct 1805; Major General 4 Jun 1811
Early Service: Served in East Indies 1790–1792
Service 1793–1815: Attached to Austrian staff 1793–1797; commanded 4/60th Foot 1797–1799; liaison officer with Russo-Austrian forces in Switzerland and in Helder 1799; commanded brigade in South America 1807; commanded Light Brigade in Peninsula Oct 1808 to Jan 1809; commanded Light Brigade in Peninsula Jul 1809 to Jan 1810; commanded Light Division in Peninsula Jan 1810 to Jan 1811; and again Apr 1811 to Jan 1812
Political Career: MP (East Retford) 1802–1806; Under Secretary of State for War and the Colonies 1806
Awards and Honours: AGM (Bus CR)
Residence: Blyth Hall, near Bawtree, Yorkshire
Died: Died of wounds after Ciudad Rodrigo 24 Jan 1812
Sources: ANCW; DINB; HPON; WEOF

835. *John BONAMY (1797–1798)*

Born: Guernsey c.1769
Relations: Father of Lieutenant Colonel John Henry Folkes Bonamy, 6th Foot
Entry to Army: Lieutenant in 53rd Foot 13 Dec 1786
Regimental Field Officer Promotions: Major in 4/60th Foot 27 Aug 1794; Lieutenant Colonel in 4/60th Foot 13 Oct 1797 (vice Gottsched) by purchase
Service 1793–1815: Commanded 4/60th Foot 1797–1803
Residence: Clifton, Gloucestershire
Died: Jamaica 21 Oct 1798
Sources: ARLI; FMPM; GHLG (wife)

836. *Henry COUPER (1797–1801)*

Born: [spec.] Scotland c.1765
Entry to Army: Captain in York Hussars 25 Jun 1795
Regimental Field Officer Promotions: Major in Hompesch's Fusileers 4 Jul 1796; Lieutenant Colonel in 5/60th Foot 30 Dec 1797
Service 1793–1815: Deputy Inspector of Foreign Troops on Isle of Wight 1797
Retired: 15 Jan 1801
Residence: Standen House, near Newport, Isle of Wight
Died: Standen House 7 Jun 1802
Sources: ANCD; ANCW; ARLI

837. *Friedrich August Ludewig VON SCHLAMMERSDORF (1797–1798)*

Born: Hessen-Kassel c.1735
Entry to Army: *Fähnrich* in Brandenburg-Ansbach service; later *Hauptmann* in *Regiment von Schmettau*
Regimental Field Officer Promotions: Lieutenant Colonel in Hessen Kassel Guards; Lieutenant Colonel in Loewenstein's Chasseurs 24 Apr 1795; Lieutenant Colonel in 5/60th Foot 30 Dec 1797
Early Service: In Hessian service until 1795
Service 1793–1815: Served in West Indies 1798
Died: Of fever in Grenada Aug 1798
Sources: ARLI; Riflemen

838. *William DOWDESWELL (1798–1803, 1808–1814)*

Born: London 1761
Relations: Son of William Dowdeswell, Chancellor

of the Exchequer, and Bridget (Codrington)
Education: Westminster School
Entry to Army: Ensign in 1st Foot Guards 6 May 1780 by purchase
Regimental Field Officer Promotions: Captain and Lieutenant Colonel in 1st Foot Guards 2 May 1794 (vice Prince William) by purchase; Lieutenant Colonel in 12th Foot 30 Dec 1797 (vice Wortley) by exchange; Lieutenant Colonel in 60th Foot 18 Jan 1798 (vice Elphinstone); Lieutenant Colonel in 86th Foot 26 Feb 1803 (vice Craufurd); Lieutenant Colonel in 6/60th Foot 2 Jun 1808 (vice Drummond) by exchange; removed from the regiment as a general officer 1814
Brevets: Brevet Colonel 26 Jan 1797; Major General 25 Sep 1803; Lieutenant General 25 Jul 1810; General 19 Jul 1821
Early Service: ADC to Duke of Portland in Ireland 1782
Service 1793–1815: Served in Flanders 1793; Governor and Commander in Chief Bahamas 13 Mar 1798 to 2 Apr 1801; on staff of Bengal army Dec 1804; commanded division under Lake in British East Indies 1805; temporary Commander in Chief in British East Indies Feb 1807
Political Career: MP (Tewkesbury) 1792–1797
Residence: Stratton Street, Piccadilly, London; Pull Court, Bushley, Worcestershire
Died: Bushley 1 Dec 1828
Sources: ANCB; ANCD; ANCW; ARLI; DINB; HPON; WEOF

839. *John HUGHES (1798–1799)*
Born: Ayrshire 1763
Relations: Son of John Hughes of Mount Charles
Entry to Army: Ensign in 33rd Foot 1 Sep 1779 by purchase
Regimental Field Officer Promotions: Major in 2nd Life Guards 10 Jun 1794 (vice Mawhood) by purchase; Major in 60th Foot 16 Feb 1797 (vice Rebow) by exchange; Lieutenant Colonel in 2/60th Foot 5 Nov 1798 (vice de Berniere) by purchase; to half-pay of Independent Company 25 Apr 1799
Early Service: Served in British East Indies and wounded 1787
Service 1793–1815: Served in North America 1797–1801; on half-pay for health reasons 1801–1820
Brevets: Brevet Colonel 25 Apr 1808; Major General 4 Jun 1811; Lieutenant General 19 Jul 1821
Residences: Mount Charles, near Alloway, Ayrshire; Balkissock, near Ballantrae, Ayrshire
Died: Mount Charles 3 Apr 1832
Sources: ARLI; PEER; WEOF; History of the County of Ayr

840. *Sir Charles MARSH, Kt (1799)*
Born: Berkshire 1735
Relations: Son of John Marsh of Hawkesbury
Entry to Army: Lieutenant in 84th Foot 3 Jan 1759
Regimental Field Officer Promotions: Lieutenant Colonel unattached 10 Feb 1795; Lieutenant Colonel in 2/60th Foot 25 Apr 1799 (vice Hughes) by exchange
Brevets: Brevet Major 6 Aug 1783; Brevet Lieutenant Colonel 1 Mar 1794; Brevet Colonel 1 Jan 1798
Early Service: Served in East Indies 1759–1764
Retired: 20 Jun 1799
Awards and Honours: Knight Bachelor 23 Aug 1786
Residences: Salisbury, Wiltshire; Reading, Berkshire
Died: Salisbury 20 Aug 1805
Sources: ANCB; ANCD; ARLI; Oracle and Daily Advertiser 4 Sep 1805

841. *Thomas Philip AINSLIE (1799–1802)*
Born: Roxburghshire 1766
Relations: Son of Thomas Ainslie, collector of Customs in Québec, and Mary Potts
Entry to Army: Ensign in 31st Foot 26 Sep 1782 by purchase
Regimental Field Officer Promotions: Major in 4/60th Foot 17 Aug 1797 (vice de Chambault); Lieutenant Colonel in 2/60th Foot 20 Jun 1799 (vice Marsh) by purchase
Service 1793–1815: Commanded 2/60th Foot 1799–1802
Retired: 9 Mar 1802
Residence: Over Wells, Jedburgh, Roxburghshire
Died: Newcastle upon Tyne, Northumberland 18 May 1837
Sources: ANCB; ANCD; ARLI; History of the Berwickshire Naturalists' Club

842. *Lauchlan McLEAN (1799–1804)*
Born: Mull, Argyllshire 1754
Relations: Son of Rev. Alexander McLean of Torloisk and Christian (McLean); brother of Lieutenant John McLean, 84th Foot
Entry to Army: Lieutenant in 84th Foot 14 Jun 1775
Regimental Field Officer Promotions: Major in 1/60th Foot 5 Aug 1794 (vice Elphinstone); Lieutenant Colonel in 6/60th Foot 25 Jul 1799; to half-pay of 60th Foot 25 Mar 1804
Brevets: Brevet Major 1 Mar 1794; Brevet Lieutenant Colonel 1 Jan 1798; Brevet Colonel 25 Apr 1808; Major General 4 Jun 1811; Lieutenant General 19 Jul 1821

Early Service: Served in American War of Independence
Service 1793–1815: Commanded 6/60th Foot 1799–1804; Quartermaster General in West Indies 1811–1815
Later Service: Lieutenant Governor of Québec 5 May 1825 to 12 Dec 1826
Retired: 12 Dec 1826
Residence: Livorno, Toscana, Italy
Died: Livorno 8 Sep 1829
Sources: *ANCB; ANCD; ANCW; ARLI; PHIL; WEOF; The Second Battalion, formerly the Royal Highland Emigrants*

843. *George Burgess MORDEN (1799–1803)*

Born: Surrey 1766
Relations: Son of James Morden, storekeeper of ordnance in Halifax, Nova Scotia, and Elizabeth (Burges)
Entry to Army: Ensign in 70th Foot 13 Oct 1778
Regimental Field Officer Promotions: Major in 20th Foot 1 Sep 1795 (vice Clephane); Major in 87th Foot 3 Aug 1796 (vice Wood) by exchange; Lieutenant Colonel in 6/60th Foot 26 Jul 1799
Brevets: Brevet Major 1 Mar 1794; Brevet Lieutenant Colonel 1 Jan 1798
Service 1793–1815: Deputy Adjutant General in Leeward Islands Aug 1802
Died: Jamaica 8 Jul 1803
Sources: ANCB; ANCW (father); ARLI; WEOF

844. *Sir David CUNYNGHAME, 5th Bt (1800–1801)*

Born: West Lothian 1769
Relations: Son of Sir William Augustus Cunynghame of Livingstone, 4th Baronet of Milncraig, and Frances (Myrton); brother of Captain and Lieutenant Colonel Francis Cunynghame, Coldstream Foot Guards; father of Sir Francis Thurlow Cunynghame, 8th Bt; and Major General Sir Arthur Thurlow Cunynghame
Entry to Army: Ensign in 92nd Foot 14 Nov 1781 by purchase
Regimental Field Officer Promotions: Captain and Lieutenant Colonel 3rd Foot Guards 15 Jan 1794 (vice Stead) by purchase; Lieutenant Colonel in 68th Foot 16 Aug 1799 (vice Anstruther) by exchange; Lieutenant Colonel in 60th Foot 8 Feb 1800 (vice Napier) by exchange; to half-pay of 82nd Foot 5 Feb 1801; rank stationary thereafter
Brevets: Brevet Colonel 26 Jan 1797; Brigadier General (West Indies) 22 Jan 1801
Service 1793–1815: POW in Ostend raid 1798, paroled 1799; served in West Indies 1800–1801
Creations and Dignities: 5th Baronet of Milncraig 17 Jan 1828
Residence: Plaisance Terrace, St Saviour, Jersey
Died: Jersey 19 May 1854
Sources: ANCB; ANCD; ARLI; PHIL; WEOF

845. *Friedrich VON VOSS (VOß) (1801–1802)*

Born: c.1771
Entry to Army: Lieutenant in 1/60th Foot 26 Sep 1787
Regimental Field Officer Promotions: Major in 1/60th Foot 22 May 1797 (vice Porter) by purchase; Lieutenant Colonel in 5/60th Foot 16 Jan 1801 (vice Couper) by purchase
Service 1793–1815: Served in British North America
Retired: 8 Mar 1802
Sources: ARLI; Riflemen

846. *Sir Fitzroy Jefferies Grafton McLEAN, 8th Bt (1801–1804)*

See 174.
Lieutenant Colonel in 2/60th Foot 5 Feb 1801 (vice Cunynghame) by exchange

847. *Robert LETHBRIDGE (1802–1804)*

Born: Cornwall 1760
Relations: Son of John Lethbridge of Launceston and Sybilla (Luxmoore)
Entry to Army: Ensign in 4/60th Foot 12 Feb 1776 by purchase
Regimental Field Officer Promotions: Major in 3/60th Foot 25 Nov 1795; Lieutenant Colonel in 4/60th Foot 10 Feb 1802 (vice Craufurd); to half-pay of 60th Foot 25 Oct 1804
Brevets: Brevet Major 6 May 1795; Brevet Lieutenant Colonel 1 Jan 1800; Brevet Colonel 25 Jul 1810; Major General 4 Jun 1813; Lieutenant General 27 May 1825
Early Service: Served in American War of Independence 1776–1779; served in Jamaica 1780–1786; served in British North America 1787–1788; served in West Indies 1789; served in British North America 1790–1793
Service 1793–1815: Served in West Indies 1795–1799; commanded 4/60th Foot in West Indies 1802–1804; Inspecting Field Officer of recruiting district in Ireland 1804–1812; Inspecting Field Officer in British North America 1812
Retired: 21 Nov 1828
Residence: Launceston, Cornwall
Died: Launceston 5 Jan 1831

Sources: ANCB; ANCD: ANCW; ARLI; PHIL; WEOF; WO 25/746

848. *John CAMPBELL (1802–1803)*
Born: Stirlingshire c.1773
Relations: Father of Lieutenant Arthur Campbell, Bengal artillery
Entry to Army: Ensign on half-pay of 93rd Foot 24 Sep 1787; Ensign in 2/60th Foot 28 Aug 1789
Regimental Field Officer Promotions: Major in 3/60th Foot 20 Dec 1798 (vice Robertson) by purchase; Lieutenant Colonel in 1/60th Foot 8 Mar 1802 (vice von Voss) by purchase
Service 1793–1815: Commanded 1/60th Foot 1802–1803
Retired: 20 Apr 1803
Later Service: Acting Captain General and Governor-in-Chief of Tobago 13 Nov 1816 to 1819
Residence: Underhills, Bletchingley, Surrey
Died: Bletchingley 23 Dec 1837
Sources: ANCD; ANCW; ARLI; UNSM (1838); WOST; Records of Clan Campbell in the Military Service of the Honourable East India Company

849. *Gabriel GORDON (1802–1804)*
Born: Lanarkshire 1763
Relations: Son of William Gordon of Glasgow and Elizabeth (Christie); nephew of General Gabriel Christie
Entry to Army: Ensign in 2/60th Foot 8 Jan 1781 by purchase
Field Officer Promotions: Major in 6/60th Foot 16 May 1800 (vice Schoedde); Lieutenant Colonel in 4/60th Foot 9 Mar 1802 (vice Ainslie) by purchase; Lieutenant Colonel on half-pay of 4th Foot 14 Jan 1808
Brevets: Brevet Colonel 4 Jun 1811; Major General 4 Jun 1814; Lieutenant General 22 Jul 1830; General 9 Nov 1846
Colonelcies: 91st Foot Apr 1837 (vice Campbell)
Early Service: Served in West Indies and British North America 1781–1794
Service 1793–1815: Served in West Indies 1794–1803; Superintendent of British Honduras 14 Sep 1805 to 26 Apr 1806 (vice Barrow); Deputy Quartermaster General in West Indies 1808; served at the capture of Martinique and Guadeloupe 1809–1810
Awards and Honours: AGM (Mart Guad)
Residence: Higher Ardwick Lodge, near Manchester, Lancashire
Died: Manchester 7 Aug 1855
Sources: ANCB; ANCD; ARLI; WEOF; WO 25/745; The Military Obituary 1854

850. *Charles Louis Theodore SCHOËDDE (1802–1804)*
Born: Hanover c.1758
Relations: Brother of Major Johan Schoëdde, 60th Foot; father of Lieutenant General Sir James Holmes Schoëdde
Entry to Army: Ensign in 2/60th Foot 18 May 1776 by purchase
Regimental Field Officer Promotions: Major in Loewenstein's Levy 20 Jun 1799; Lieutenant Colonel in 5/60th Foot 25 Apr 1802
Brevets: Brevet Lieutenant Colonel 16 May 1800
Service 1793–1815: Served in Egypt 1801; commanded 5/60th Foot 1802–1804
Retired: 29 Dec 1804
Residence: Suffolk Street, St Martin-in-the-Fields, London
Died: London Jan 1805
Sources: ANCD; ANCW; ARLI; <https://www.findagrave.com/memorial/250237073/capt_carl_lewis-theodore-schoedde>

851. *Gervaise RAINEY (1803–1808)*
Born: Lincolnshire 1759
Relations: Son of Edward Rainey of Partney and Mary (Carver)
Entry to Army: Ensign in 18th Foot 24 Aug 1781 by purchase
Regimental Field Officer Promotions: Major in 3/60th Foot 8 Mar 1798 (vice Bonamy) by purchase; Lieutenant Colonel in 1/60th Foot 20 Apr 1803 (vice Campbell) by purchase
Brevets: Brevet Lieutenant Colonel 16 May 1800
Service 1793–1815: Commanded 1/60th Foot 1804–1808
Retired: Court-martialled and dismissed 22 Jul 1808
Residence: St Saviour, Guernsey
Died: Guernsey 12 Sep 1815
Sources: ANCB; ANCD; ARLI; WEOF

852. *Lewis VON MOSHEIM (1804–1810)*
Born: Hessen-Kassel c.1765
Entry to Army: Served with Württemberg *Garde-Regiment zu Fuß* 1789; Captain in Loewenstein's Chasseurs 1794
Regimental Field Officer Promotions: Major in Loewenstein's Chasseurs 25 Oct 1796; Major in 5/60th Foot 30 Dec 1797; Lieutenant Colonel in 6/60th Foot 14 Sep 1804
Brevets: Brevet Lieutenant Colonel 29 Apr 1802; Brevet Colonel 4 Jun 1811; Major General 4 Jun 1814; Lieutenant General 22 Jul 1830
Service 1793–1815: Served in Flanders 1794–1796; served in West Indies 1795–1800, taken POW;

commanded 6/60th Foot 1804–1806 and 1808–1810; served on staff positions 1806–1808; Assistant Adjutant General in Walcheren 1809; commander of depot for foreign troops in Britain 16 Aug 1810
Residence: Darmstadt, Hesse, Germany
Died: Darmstadt Sep 1839
Sources: ARLI; PHIL; WEOF; WO 24/747

853. *Edward CODD (1804–1825)*

Born: Devon 1770
Relations: Son of John Edward Codd of Dean Prior and Joan (Gidley)
Entry to Army: Ensign in 60th Foot 10 Dec 1789 by purchase
Regimental Field Officer Promotions: Major in 5/60th Foot 25 Dec 1800 (vice Dörsner) by purchase; Lieutenant Colonel in 5/60th Foot 26 Oct 1804; removed from the regiment as a general officer 1825
Brevets: Brevet Colonel 4 Jun 1813; Major General 12 Aug 1819
Early Service: Served in British North America 1789–1794
Service 1793–1815: Served in British North America 1795–1800; served in West Indies 1800–1804; commanded 2/60th Foot 1804–1813; served in Peninsula Oct 1808 to Jan 1809; commanded 2/60th Foot in West Indies 1810–1816; Lieutenant Governor of Demerara 12–17 May 1813, 24 Aug to 9 Dec 1813, and 25 Jul to 3 Oct 1815
Residence: Queen's Buildings, Brompton, Middlesex
Died: Brompton 22 Dec 1829
Sources: ANCB; ANCD; ANCW; CHAL; PHIL; WEOF; WEMR; WOST; WO 25/744

854. *Edward DRUMMOND (1804–1808)*

Born: London 1775
Relations: Son of Robert Drummond of Westminster and Winifred Mary (Thomson)
Entry to Army: Ensign in 19th Foot 24 Jan 1795 by purchase
Regimental Field Officer Promotions: Major in 5/60th Foot 11 Jun 1801 (vice de Vos) by purchase; Lieutenant Colonel in 60th Foot 29 Dec 1804 (vice Schoedde) by purchase; Lieutenant Colonel in 86th Foot 2 Jun 1808 (vice Dowdeswell) by exchange
Brevets: Brevet Colonel 4 Jun 1813
Service 1793–1815: Commanded 6/60th Foot 1806–1808; commanded brigade at taking of Bourbon 1810; Acting Lieutenant Governor of Mauritius 9 Apr to 12 Jul 1811
Retired: 18 Nov 1813
Residence: Grand Parade, Brighton, Sussex
Died: Brighton 4 May 1859
Sources: ANCB; ANCD; ARLI; PHIL; WEOF; WOST; WO 25/745

855. *Thomas AUSTEN (1805–1817)*

Born: Kent 1775
Relations: Son of Francis Motley Austen of Wilmington and Elizabeth (Wilson); brother of Lieutenant Colonel Henry Austen, 59th Foot; second cousin of novelist Jane Austen
Education: St John's College, Cambridge
Entry to Army: Cornet in 22nd Light Dragoons 26 Aug 1794 by purchase
Field Officer Promotions: Major in 60th Foot 3 Jul 1801 (vice von Verna) by purchase; Lieutenant Colonel in 2/60th Foot 20 Jun 1805 (vice McIntosh) by purchase
Brevets: Brevet Colonel 4 Jun 1813
Service 1793–1815: Commanded 4/60th Foot 1805–1811 commanded 1/60th Foot 1812–1813
Later Service: High Sheriff of Kent 1823–1824
Political Career: MP (West Kent) 1845–1847
Retired: 24 Feb 1817
Residence: Kippington, near Sevenaoks, Kent
Died: Kippington 23 Jul 1859
Sources: ANCB; ANCD; ANCW; ARLI; WEOF; Alumni Cantabrigienses

856. *Paul ANDERSON (1808–1817)*

See 254.
Lieutenant Colonel in 4/60th Foot 14 Jan 1808 (vice Gordon); to half-pay of 60th Foot 25 Feb 1817

857. *Edward Amherst Saunders SEBRIGHT (1808)*

Born: Hertfordshire 1771
Relations: Son of General Sir John Sebright, Bt of Beechwood and Sarah (Knight)
Education: Christ Church, Oxford (BA 1793)
Entry to Army: Lieutenant in 88th Foot 8 Jul 1794 by purchase
Regimental Field Officer Promotions: Major in 5th West India Regiment 7 Apr 1808 (vice McDonald) by purchase; Lieutenant Colonel in 3/60th Foot 24 Apr 1808 by purchase; Captain and Lieutenant Colonel in 1st Foot Guards 10 May 1808 (vice Lake) by exchange
Service 1793–1815: Commanded 2/1st Foot Guards in Peninsula Mar 1810 to Apr 1811, severely wounded at Barrosa; served with 1/1st Foot Guards in Peninsula Sep to Nov 1812
Awards and Honours: AGM (Bar)
Retired: 20 Dec 1812
Residence: Upper George Street, Portman Square, London
Died: London Jul 1842
Sources: ANCB; ANCW; ARLI; CHAL; WEOF

858. *Rt Hon. Francis Gerard, 2nd Viscount LAKE (1808–1815)*

Born: London 1772
Relations: Son of General Gerard Lake, 1st Viscount Lake and Elizabeth (Barker); brother of Lieutenant Colonel George Augustus Frederick Lake, 29th Foot
Entry to Army: Ensign in Coldstream Foot Guards 30 Nov 1790 by purchase
Regimental Field Officer Promotions: Captain and Lieutenant Colonel in 1st Foot Guards 22 Aug 1798 (vice Boone) by purchase; Lieutenant Colonel in 3/60th Foot 10 May 1808 (vice Sebright) by exchange; removed from the regiment as a general officer 1815
Brevets: Brevet Colonel 25 Apr 1808; Major General 4 Jun 1811; Lieutenant General 19 Jul 1821
Service 1793–1815: Commanded 1/1st Foot Guards 1805
Creations and Dignities: 2nd Viscount Lake of Delhi and Laswary and Aston Clinton 20 Feb 1808
Residence: Aston Clinton, near Aylesbury, Buckinghamshire
Died: London 12 May 1836
Sources: ANCB; ANCW; ARLI; PHIL; PEER; WEOF

859. *George MACKIE (1808–1825)*

Born: Caithness 1776
Relations: Son of James Mackie of Thurso and Janet (Sinclair)
Entry to Army: Ensign in Rothesay & Caithness Fencibles 19 Dec 1794
Regimental Field Officer Promotions: Major in 2/60th Foot 8 Mar 1802 (vice Campbell) by purchase; Lieutenant Colonel in 3/60th Foot 22 Dec 1808 (vice Rainey); Lieutenant Colonel unattached 18 Jun 1825
Brevets: Brevet Colonel 4 Jun 1814; Major General 27 May 1825
Service 1793–1815: Served in West Indies 1795–1804; served in West Indies 1805–1807; commanded 3/60th Foot in West Indies 1808–1813
Later Service: Governor and Commander in Chief of St Lucia 10 Jan to 8 Mar 1831
Awards and Honours: AGM (Mart); CB 4 Jun 1815
Residence: Bath, Somerset
Died: St Lucia 8 Mar 1831
Sources: ANCW; ARLI; PHIL; UNSM (1832); WEOF; WOST; WO 25/747

860. *Sir William WILLIAMS (1809–1812)*

Born: London 1776
Relations: Son of Thomas Williams of Marylebone and Mary (Rudd); father of Cornet George Bigoe Williams, 16th Lancers; and Captain Thomas Bigoe Williams, 4th Dragoon Guards; cousin of General Sir Andrew Francis Barnard
Entry to Army: Ensign in 54th Foot 1 Aug 1792 by purchase
Regimental Field Officer Promotions: Major in 54th Foot 24 Jun 1802 (vice Delmé) by purchase; Major in 16th Battalion of Reserve 9 Jul 1803; Major in 81st Foot 26 Oct 1804 (vice Sharpe) by exchange; Lieutenant Colonel in 1/60th Foot 15 Nov 1809; Lieutenant Colonel in 13th Foot 25 Jun 1812 (vice Keane) by exchange; to half-pay in Portuguese service 4 Oct 1821
Brevets: Brevet Colonel 12 Aug 1819; Major General 22 Jul 1830
Service 1793–1815: Served in Flanders 1793–1794; served in West Indies 1795–1796; served in Irish Rebellion 1798; served in Ferrol 1800; served in Egypt 1801; served in Peninsula with 81st Foot Nov 1808 to Jan 1809; commanded 5/60th Foot and composite light battalions in Peninsula Jun 1810 to Jul 1812, wounded four times; commanded 13th Foot 1812–1815; trained 13th Foot in light infantry tactics in British North America 1814–1815
Awards and Honours: KTS 11 Mar 1813; AGM (Cor FDO CR Bad Sal); KCB 4 Dec 1815
Residence: Marlborough Buildings, Bath, Somerset
Died: Bath 17 Jun 1832
Sources: ANCB; ANCW; CHAL; PHIL; WEOF; WO 25/748; The Annual Biography and Obituary for the Year 1833

861. *James LOMAX (1809–1818)*

Born: Lancashire 1773
Relations: Son of Marsden Lomax of Manchester and Ann (Gilchrist)
Entry to Army: Acting Ensign in 19th Foot 1 Sep 1789; Lieutenant in 62nd Foot 2 Jul 1796
Regimental Field Officer Promotions: Major in 3/60th Foot 20 Apr 1803 (vice Rainey) by purchase; Lieutenant Colonel in 6/60th Foot 16 Nov 1809; to half-pay of 60th Foot 25 Dec 1818
Brevets: Brevet Colonel 12 Aug 1819; Major General 22 Jul 1830; Lieutenant General 23 Nov 1841
Early Service: Served in West Indies 1789–1791
Service 1793–1815: Served in West Indies 1796–1805; commanded 4/60th Foot in Cape of Good Hope 1806–1808 and West Indies 1808–1815
Residence: Park Street, Bristol, Gloucestershire
Died: Bristol 14 Nov 1848
Sources: ANCW; ARLI; GEMA (1832); WEOF; WO 25/746

862. *Anthony WHARTON (1810–1814)*

Born: British North America c.1769
Entry to Army: Sub-Brigadier and Cornet in 2nd Troop of Horse Guards 26 Apr 1785 by purchase; Cornet in 2nd Life Guards 25 Jun 1788
Regimental Field Officer Promotions: Major in 6/60th Foot 26 Jul 1804 (vice Campbell); Lieutenant Colonel in 60th Foot 16 Aug 1810 (vice Mosheim)
Service 1793–1815: Commanded 6/60th Foot 1810–1814
Retired: 1 Jun 1814
Later Service: Fort Major at New Geneva
Residences: Alverstoke, Hampshire; Swinton Street, St Pancras, London
Died: London 24 Nov 1858
Sources: ANCD; ANCW; ARLI; WEOF; WO 25/748

863. *Rt Hon. Sir John KEANE, 1st Baron Keane (1812–1814)*

Born: County Waterford 1781
Relations: Son of Sir John Keane of Belmont and Sarah (Kelley); brother of Lieutenant Colonel Sir Richard Keane, Waterford Militia; and Colonel Edward Keane, Grenadier Foot Guards
Entry to Army: Ensign in Ward's Regiment 11 Oct 1793 by purchase
Regimental Field Officer Promotions: Major in 60th Foot 27 May 1802 (vice Ciesielsky) by purchase; Lieutenant Colonel in 13th Foot 20 Aug 1803 (vice Tyndale) by purchase; Lieutenant Colonel in 5/60th Foot 25 Jun 1812 (vice Williams) by exchange; removed from the regiment as a general officer 1814
Brevets: Brevet Colonel 1 Jan 1812; Major General 4 Jun 1814; Lieutenant General 22 Jul 1830
Colonelcies: 94th Foot 18 Apr 1829 (vice Bradford); 68th Foot 13 Apr 1831 (vice Warde); 46th Foot 6 Apr 1838 (vice Wynyard); 43rd Foot 1 Aug 1839 (vice Lord Howden)
Service 1793–1815: Served in Egypt 1801; served in Malta 1802–1803; served in Gibraltar 1804–1805; commanded 13th Foot in West Indies 1808–1812; served in Martinique 1809; commanded 5/60th Foot in Peninsula Apr to Aug 1813; commanded brigade in Peninsula Aug 1813 to Apr 1814; commanded brigade in British North America 1814; commanded brigade and wounded at New Orleans Jan 1815
Later Service: Commanded brigade in Army of Occupation in France 1815–1817; Governor of St Lucia 25 Jun 1818 to Jun 1821, and Feb 1823 to 23 Apr 1823; Commander in Chief Jamaica 1823–1829; acting Captain General and Governor in Chief Jamaica 3 Jul 1827 to 19 Feb 1829; Commander in Chief Bombay 1833–1839; commanded Army of Indus in 1st Afghan War 1839
Creations and Dignities: 1st Baron Keane of Ghuznee and Cappoquin 12 Aug 1839
Awards and Honours: KCB 8 Jun 1815; GCH 12 Aug 1831; GCB 12 Aug 1839
Residence: Burton Lodge, Hampshire
Died: Burton Lodge 26 Aug 1844
Sources: ARLI; CHAL; ODNB; PHIL; WEBC; WEOF; WOST; WO 25/746

864. *Henry JOHN [FREKE] (1813–1815)*

Born: Cornwall 1777
Relations: Son of Henry John of Truro and Bridget (Spencer); changed surname to Freke in Aug 1835
Entry to Army: Ensign in Independent Company 3 Dec 1793
Regimental Field Officer Promotions: Major in 93rd Foot 17 Aug 1809 (vice Brown) by purchase; Major in 95th Foot 11 Oct 1810 (vice Creagh) by exchange; Lieutenant Colonel in 7/60th Foot 9 Aug 1813; to half-pay of 18th Foot 9 Feb 1815 (vice Walker) by exchange; Lieutenant Colonel in 58th Foot 9 Aug 1821; to half-pay unattached 29 Nov 1827 (vice Clifford) by exchange
Brevets: Brevet Colonel 22 Jul 1830
Service 1793–1815: Commanded 7/60th Foot 1813–1815; commanded Penobscot expedition (Maine) 1814
Awards and Honours: CB 8 Feb 1817
Residence: Hannington Hall, Hannington, Wiltshire
Died: Hannington Hall 20 Aug 1848
Sources: ANCB; ANCD; ARLI; PHIL; WEOF

865. *John Philip HUNT (1813–1817)*

See 590.
Lieutenant Colonel in 8/60th Foot 11 Nov 1813; to half-pay of 60th Foot 25 Mar 1817

866. *Francis William MARLTON (1814–1815)*

Born: [spec.] Jamaica 1767
Relations: Son of Thomas Marlton of Jamaica and Mary (Lee); father of Captain Francis William Marlton, 60th Foot; and Colonel Edward Henry Francis Marlton, 76th Foot
Entry to Army: Ensign in 60th Foot 1 Jan 1794 by purchase
Regimental Field Officer Promotions: Major in 5/60th Foot 25 Jul 1805 (vice Austen) by purchase; Lieutenant Colonel in 1/60th Foot 26 May 1814 (vice Hunt)

Brevets: Brevet Lieutenant Colonel 1 Jan 1812
Service 1793–1815: Served in West Indies 1794–1799 and 1800–1810; commanded 1/60th Foot in Cape of Good Hope 1811–1814
Died: Cheltenham, Gloucestershire 30 Nov 1815
Sources: ANCD; ANCW; ARLI; WEOF; WO 25/747

867. *Sir Adolphus John DALRYMPLE, 2nd Bt (1814)*

Born: London 1784
Relations: Son of General Sir Hew Whitefoord Dalrymple and Frances (Leighton); brother of Lieutenant Colonel Leighton Cathcart Dalrymple, 15th Light Dragoons
Education: Harrow School
Entry to Army: Ensign in 55th Foot 25 Oct 1799
Regimental Field Officer Promotions: Major in 3rd Foot 15 Sep 1808 (vice Portarlington) by purchase; Major in 19th Light Dragoons 17 Nov 1808 (vice Roberts) by exchange; Lieutenant Colonel in 6/60th Foot 1 Jun 1814 (vice Wharton) by purchase; to half-pay of 2nd Garrison Battalion 24 Dec 1814
Brevets: Brevet Colonel 22 Jul 1830; Major General 23 Nov 1841; Lieutenant General 11 Nov 1851; General 11 Apr 1860
Service 1793–1815: ADC to Sir Hew Dalrymple 1799–1801; ADC to Sir James Craig 1802; Military secretary to Sir Hew Dalrymple 1806–1808; Deputy Assistant Quartermaster General in Peninsula Aug to Oct 1808
Political Career: MP (Weybridge and Melcombe Regis) 1817–1818; MP (Appleby) 1819–1826; MP (Haddington Burghs) 1826–1831; MP (Brighton) 1837–1841
Creations and Dignities: 2nd Baronet of High Mark 9 Apr 1830
Residences: Park Street, Grosvenor Square, London; Delrow House, near Aldenham, Hertfordshire
Died: Delrow House 3 Mar 1866
Dalrymple was given limited opportunities after August 1808, due to reflected prejudices against him due to his father's signing of the unpopular Convention of Cintra in Portugal
Sources: ANCB; ANCD; ANCW; ARLI; CHAL; ODNB; PHIL; WEOF; WO 25/745

868. *William WOODGATE (1814–1817)*

Born: London 1778
Relations: Son of Robert Woodgate of Dedham, solicitor, and Martha (Watford)
Entry to Army: Ensign in 6th Foot 21 Mar 1800 by purchase
Regimental Field Officer Promotions: Major in 2/60th Foot 13 Aug 1807 (vice Robertson) by purchase; Lieutenant Colonel in 5/60th Foot 16 Jun 1814; to half-pay of 60th Foot 24 Aug 1817
Brevets: Brevet Lieutenant Colonel 30 May 1811; Brevet Colonel 19 Jul 1821; rank stationary thereafter
Service 1793–1815: Served in British North America 1800–1802 and 1803–1805; served in West Indies 1805–1807; served in Peninsula Aug 1808 to Mar 1812, wounded at Fuentes d'Oñoro
Later Service: Commanded troops in Berbice 1815–1816
Awards and Honours: AGM (FDO); CB 8 Dec 1815; MGSM (Rol Vim Tal Bus CR)
Residences: Dedham, Essex; Paris, Île-de-France, France
Died: Paris 12 Jan 1861
Sources: ANCB; ANCD; ANCW; ARLI; CHAL; GEMA (1861); PHIL; WEOF; WO 25/748

869. *Edward WALKER (1815–1816)*

Born: London c.1775
Entry to Army: Ensign in 59th Foot 26 Nov 1796 by purchase
Regimental Field Officer Promotions: Major in 18th Foot 4 Dec 1806 (vice Gubbins); Lieutenant Colonel in 18th Foot 1 Oct 1812; to half-pay of 18th Foot 25 Dec 1814; Lieutenant Colonel in 7/60th Foot 9 Feb 1815 (vice John) by exchange; to half-pay of 60th Foot 25 Mar 1816
Brevets: Brevet Colonel 22 Jul 1830; Major General 28 Jun 1838
Service 1793–1815: Served in Gibraltar 1797–1800; served in Egypt 1801; served in West Indies 1805–1809; commanded 2/18th Foot 1812–1814
Awards and Honours: KH 12 Aug 1835
Residence: Great Québec Street, Marylebone, London
Died: London 3 Jul 1848
Sources: ANCD; ANCW; PHIL; UNSM (1848); WEOF; WO 25/748

870. *James STOPFORD (1815–1818)*

Born: Dublin 1785
Relations: Son of Lieutenant General Hon. Edward Stopford and Letitia (Blacker); brother of Captain Edward Stopford RN; Colonel William Henry Stopford-Blair RA; and Commander Thomas Stopford RN; cousin of Lieutenant General Hon. Sir Edward Stopford
Entry to Army: Cornet in 4th Dragoons May 1801 by purchase
Regimental Field Officer Promotions: Major in 7/60th Foot 10 Feb 1814 (vice Wyndham) by purchase; Lieutenant Colonel in 60th Foot 9 Mar 1815 (vice Wyndham) by purchase; to half-pay of

60th Foot 25 Mar 1818
Service 1793–1815: Served in Peninsula Oct 1812 to Feb 1814, badly wounded at Nivelle
Residence: Pisa, Tuscany, Italy
Died: Pisa 13 May 1823
Sources: ANCB; ANCD; ARLI; GHLG; WEMR; WEOF; The Inscriptions in the Old British Cemetery of Leghorn

871. *Alexander ANDREWS (1815–1818, 1819–1823)*
Born: Scotland c.1777
Relations: Father of Lieutenant Colonel Robert Alexander Andrews, 30th Foot
Entry to Army: Ensign in 95th Foot 26 Sep 1795
Regimental Field Officer Promotions: Major in 1/60th Foot 17 Jan 1811 (vice Forneret) by purchase; Lieutenant Colonel in 1/60th Foot 14 Dec 1815 (vice Marlton) by purchase; to half-pay of 60th Foot 25 Mar 1818; Lieutenant Colonel in 60th Foot 12 Aug 1819
Service 1793–1815: Served in Peninsula Aug 1808 to Dec 1810, wounded at Talavera and Busaco; acting Provost Marshal in Lisbon Dec 1810 to Apr 1814
Awards and Honours: AGM (Tal)
Residence: Kingston, Ontario, Canada
Died: Kingston 24 Oct 1823
Sources: ANCD; ANCW; ARLI; CHAL; WEOF

Majors

872. *Patrick MURRAY (1784–1793)*
Born: Scotland c.1749
Relations: Natural son of Rear Admiral George Murray, 6th Lord Elibank; nephew of General James Murray; father of Captain James Murray RN
Entry to Army: Lieutenant in 60th Foot 26 Dec 1770
Regimental Field Officer Promotions: Major in 2/60th Foot 6 Oct 1784 (vice Thompson) by purchase
Early Service: Served in American War of Independence; served in British North America, commandant at Detroit 1789–1790
Retired: 20 Apr 1793
Militia Career: Colonel of Montréal Militia 1812
Service 1793–1815: Commanded 5th Battalion of Embodied Militia in Québec during War of 1812
Residence: Montréal, Québec, Canada
Died: Montréal 14 Jul 1823
Sources: ANCD; ARLI; A Scion of Heroes

873. *William GORDON (1791–1793)*
Born: Aberdeenshire c.1764
Relations: Son of Charles Gordon, 12th of Abergeldie and Alison (Hunter); brother of Captain Peter Gordon, 81st Foot; Captain Alexander Sinclair Gordon, London and Westminster Volunteers; and Lieutenant Colonel Sir Charles Gordon, 41st Foot
Entry to Army: Ensign in 26th Foot 15 Feb 1780
Regimental Field Officer Promotions: Major in 4/60th Foot 30 Mar 1791 (vice Whitelocke) by purchase
Service 1793–1815: Served in West Indies 1793
Died: Of fever in Dominica 6 Jul 1793
Sources: ANCD; ARLI; WEOF

874. *George Townsend WALKER (1794–1798)*
See 515.
Major in 1/60th Foot 28 Aug 1794

875. *Christopher Coates (Richard) PORTER (1795–1797)*
Born: Sussex 1753
Relations: Son of Rev. Thomas Porter, rector of East Hoathley, and Mary (Coates); father of Edward Porter, consul to Brazil
Entry to Army: Ensign in 22nd Foot 24 Jun 1775 by purchase
Regimental Field Officer Promotions: Major in 2/60th Foot 1 Sep 1795 (vice McIntosh)
Brevets: Brevet Major 6 May 1795
Early Service: Served in British North America 1790–1797
Retired: 22 May 1797
Militia Career: Major in West London Militia 11 May 1803
Residence: East Hoathley, Sussex
Died: London Feb 1811
Sources: ARLI; London Chronicle 26 Aug 1822; A Royal Descent [of the Family of Sharpe]

876. *John James ECUYER (1795)*
Born: British North America c.1762
Relations: [spec.] Son of Captain Simeon Ecuyer, 60th Foot, and Therese (Voyer); brother of Captain Benjamin Ecuyer, Canadian Voltigeurs
Entry to Army: Lieutenant in 1/60th Foot 20 Oct 1781
Regimental Field Officer Promotions: Major in 3/60th Foot 2 Sep 1795
Brevets: Brevet Major 1 Mar 1794
Early Service: Served in West Indies

Service 1793–1815: Served in West Indies 1793–1795
Died: West Indies Nov 1795
Parentage highly likely as Simeon describes two existing but un-named children in his will (1762), plus location and regimental connection
Sources: ANCW (father); ARLI; <https://www.collectionscanada.gc.ca/obj/s4/f2/dsk2/ftp01/MQ29505.pdf>

877. *Wilhelm LACHENWITZ (1795–1796)*

Born: Germany c.1750
Entry to Army: Lieutenant in 4/60th Foot 4 Oct 1775
Regimental Field Officer Promotions: Major in 4/60th Foot 3 Sep 1795
Brevets: Brevet Major 6 May 1795
Early Service: Served in Jamaica
Service 1793–1815: Served in West Indies 1793–1796
Died: Tobago Aug 1796
Sources: ARLI; De Bernardy's Index Register for Next of Kin

878. *Charles INGRAM (1795–1796)*

Born: Dorset c.1766
Entry to Army: Ensign in 56th Foot 4 Jul 1781
Regimental Field Officer Promotions: Major in 2/60th Foot 4 Sep 1795
Brevets: Brevet Major 6 May 1795
Early Service: Served in British North America 1790–1796
Retired: 20 Feb 1796
Militia Career: Captain in Regiment of Fencible Infantry May 1799
Died: London Mar 1800
Allegedly fell out of an open window of a tavern in King's Bench Prison whilst intoxicated
Sources: ARLI; The Monthly Magazine (1800); Tracing Your Insolvent Ancestors

879. *William MARTIN (1795–1797)*

Born: Antigua c.1757
Relations: Son of Josiah Martin, collector of customs in Antigua, and Mary (Yeamans); nephew of Admiral Sir Thomas Byam-Martin RN
Entry to Army: Ensign in 37th Foot 7 Oct 1777
Regimental Field Officer Promotions: Major in 4/60th Foot 5 Sep 1795
Brevets: Brevet Major 6 May 1795
Retired: 25 Oct 1797
Residence: Bryanston Square, Marylebone, London
Died: London 19 Apr 1824
Sources: ANCD; ANCW; ARLI; DEBA; <https://www.ucl.ac.uk/lbs/person/view/2146640299>

880. *Francis Slater REBOW (1796–1797)*

Born: Francis Slater in Derbyshire 1770
Relations: Son of Richard Slater, attorney-at-law of Chesterfield and Katherine (Heaton); added Rebow surname by Royal License at marriage in 1796; son-in-law of Colonel Isaac Martin Rebow
Entry to Army: Ensign in 4/60th Foot 14 Nov 1787 by purchase
Regimental Field Officer Promotions: Major in 2/60th Foot 20 Feb 1796 (vice Ingram) by purchase; Major in 2nd Life Guards 16 Feb 1797 (vice Hughes) by exchange; Second Major in 2nd Life Guards 25 Sep 1799; Major and Lieutenant Colonel in 2nd Life Guards 25 Sep 1802; Lieutenant Colonel in 1st Life Guards 20 Aug 1807 (vice Poyntz) by purchase
Brevets: Brevet Colonel 25 Oct 1809; Major General 1 Jan 1812; Lieutenant General 27 May 1825; General 23 Nov 1841
Early Service: Served in West Indies 1788–1793
Service 1793–1815: Served in Leeward Island 1794, wounded in Guadeloupe; commanded Household Cavalry brigade in Peninsula Jan to Mar 1813
Retired: 25 Dec 1818
Residence: Wivenhoe House, near Colchester, Essex
Died: Wivenhoe House 7 Oct 1845
Rebow grew cork oaks in the grounds of Wivenhoe Park from cuttings he brought home from the Peninsula
Sources: ARLI; PHIL; WEBC; WEOF; WO 25/748

881. *Louis Joseph Fleury DESCHAMBAULT (1796–1797)*

Born: Québec c.1755
Relations: Son of Joseph Fleury Deschambault of Montréal, merchant, and Catherine (Veron)
Entry to Army: Volunteer in British North America; Ensign in 24th Foot 8 Oct 1777
Regimental Field Officer Promotions: Major in 4/60th Foot 3 Aug 1796 (vice Lachenwitz); to half-pay of 109th Foot 17 Aug 1797
Brevets: Brevet Major 6 May 1795; Brevet Lieutenant Colonel 1 Jan 1800
Residence: Montréal, Québec
Died: Montréal 24 Jul 1824
Sources: ARLI; DICB (father); Dublin Correspondent 4 Jan 1825

882. *Georg Ludwig von VERNA (1797–1801)*
Born: Hessen-Kassel 1743
Relations: Son of Carl Wilhelm von Verna of Kassel and Johanna Maria Elonora (Van der Velde); father of Lieutenant Wilhelm Ludwig von Verna, 60th Foot; and Lieutenant Friedrich Ludwig von Verna, 60th Foot
Entry to Army: Hessen-Kassel service c.1760
Regimental Field Officer Promotions: Major in Hompesch's Light Infantry; Major in 5/60th Foot 30 Dec 1797
Service 1793–1815: Served at capture of Surinam 1799
Retired: 3 Jul 1801
Residence: Münden, Hessen-Kassel, Germany
Died: Münden 1804
Sources: ANCB; ANCD; ANCW; ARLI; Riflemen

883. *Wilhelm [Adam] DÖRSNER (1797–1800)*
Born: Hessen-Darmstadt c.1765
Regimental Field Officer Promotions: Major in Loewenstein's Chasseurs 24 Apr 1795; Major in 5/60th Foot 30 Dec 1797
Service 1793–1815: Served in West Indies; served at capture of Surinam 1799
Retired: 25 Dec 1800
This officer is shown variously as William or Adam in English language sources
Sources: ARLI; The Annals of the King's Royal Rifle Corps

884. *Wilhelm von CIESIELSKI (1797–1802)*
Born: East Prussia c.1768
Regimental Field Officer Promotions: Major in Loewenstein's Fusileers 25 Dec 1796; Major in 5/60th Foot 30 Dec 1797
Service 1793–1815: Served in West Indies
Retired: 27 May 1802
Later Service: Major in *1.Magdeburgischen Infanterie-Regiment* and *2.Garde-Grenadiere-Landwehr-Regiment* in Prussian service 1803–1816
Sources: ARLI; Geschichte des 1.Magdeburgischen Infanterie-Regiments Nr.26

885. *François Ignace STREICHER (1797–1804)*
Born: Alsace c.1756
Relations: Son of François-Joseph Streicher of Molsheim and Marie Cunégonde (Berrmann)
Entry to Army: In French (Bourbon) service
Regimental Field Officer Promotions: Major in Royal Foreigners 25 May 1796; Major in 3/60th Foot 30 Dec 1797; Lieutenant Colonel in York Light Infantry Volunteers 16 Jan 1804
Brevets: Brevet Lieutenant Colonel 20 Apr 1802; Brevet Colonel 4 Jun 1811; Major General 4 Jun 1814
Service 1793–1815: Served in West Indies
Residences: Molsheim, Bas-Rhin, France
Died: Molsheim 8 May 1828
Sources: ARLI; FMPW; WEOF

886. *Julines HERING (1797–1798)*
Born: Barbados 1767
Relations: Son of Julines Hering of Jamaica and Mary (Inglis)
Entry to Army: Lieutenant on half-pay of 42nd Foot 12 Feb 1783
Regimental Field Officer Promotions: Major in 4/60th Foot 25 Oct 1797 (vice Martin) by purchase
Service 1793–1815: Served in West Indies 1793–1798
Retired: 19 Mar 1798
Militia Career: Colonel of Westmoreland Militia (Jamaica)
Residences: Linton, Westmoreland, Jamaica
Died: Linton 23 Mar 1813
Sources: ARLI; <http://www.jamaicanfamilysearch.com/Members/ bcarib20.htm>

887. *Daniel ROBERTSON (1798)*
Born: Perthshire c.1735
Relations: Son of (unk.) Robertson of Dunkeld; father of Major John Robertson, 60th Foot
Entry to Army: Surgeon's mate in 42nd Foot Apr 1754; Ensign in 42nd Foot 26 Jul 1760
Regimental Field Officer Promotions: Major in 60th Foot 6 Sep 1798 (vice Walker)
Brevets: Brevet Major 18 Nov 1790; Brevet Lieutenant Colonel 1 Mar 1794; Brevet Colonel 1 Jan 1798
Early Service: Served in British North America 1756–1762; served in West Indies 1762; served in British North America 1763–1775; served in American War of Independence 1775–1782, POW at Fort St John; to half-pay 1784
Retired: 20 Dec 1798
Militia Career: Major in Montréal Militia 1775; Colonel of Argenteuil Militia 1808
Residence: Montréal, Québec
Died: Montréal 5 Apr 1810
Sources: ARLI; DICB

888. *Edmund BURKE (1798–1799)*

Born: County Limerick c.1763
Entry to Army: Ensign in 52nd Foot 31 Mar 1783
Regimental Field Officer Promotions: Major in 4/60th Foot 19 Mar 1798 (vice Hering) by purchase
Service 1793–1815: Served in West Indies
Retired: 19 Dec 1799
Died: [spec.] County Limerick 1815
Sources: ARLI; FMPD

889. *Warren JOHNSON (1798–1801)*

Born: Québec 1777
Relations: Son of Brigadier General Sir John Johnson, 2nd Baronet, and Mary Nicoll (Watts); brother of Lieutenant Colonel William Johnson, 28th Foot; Lieutenant Colonel Adam Gordon Johnson, New York Militia; Colonel John Johnson, New York Militia; Captain James Stephen Johnson, 28th Foot; Captain Robert Thomas Johnson, 100th Foot; Lieutenant Colonel Charles Christopher Johnson, 9th Lancers; brother-in-law of Major General Barnard Foord Bowes
Entry to Army: Ensign in 24th Foot 4 Jul 1792 by purchase
Regimental Field Officer Promotions: Major in 2/60th Foot 6 Sep 1798 (vice Hughes) by purchase
Service 1793–1815: Served in West Indies 1800–1802
Residence: Montréal, Québec
Died: At sea 5 Aug 1802
Sources: ANCB; ANCD; ARLI; BPBK; DICB (father)

890. *John BYNG, 1st Earl of Strafford (1799–1800)*

Born: Middlesex 1772
Relations: Son of George Byng of Wrotham Park and Anne (Conolly)
Education: Westminster School
Entry to Army: Ensign in 33rd Foot 30 Sep 1793
Regimental Field Officer Promotions: Major in 4/60th Foot 28 Dec 1799 (vice Burke) by purchase; Lieutenant Colonel in 29th Foot 14 Mar 1800 (vice Enys) by purchase; Captain and Lieutenant Colonel in 3rd Foot Guards 4 Aug 1804 (vice Cole); removed from the regiment as a general officer 25 Jul 1814
Brevets: Brevet Colonel 25 Jul 1810; Brigadier General (Spain and Portugal) 25 Nov 1812; Major General 4 Jun 1813; Lieutenant General 27 May 1825; General 23 Nov 1841; Field Marshal 2 Oct 1855
Colonelcies: York Light Infantry Volunteers 26 Dec 1815 (vice Campbell); 4th West India Regiment 12 Dec 1816 (vice Leith); 2nd West India Regiment 26 Jul 1822 (vice Torrens); 29th Foot 23 Jan 1828 (vice Forbes); Coldstream Foot Guards 15 Aug 1850 (vice Duke of Cambridge)
Service 1793–1815: Served in Flanders 1794–1795; served in Ireland 1798; served in Hanover 1805; served in Copenhagen 1807; served in Walcheren 1809; commanded brigade in 2nd Division in Peninsula Sep 1811 to Apr 1814, wounded at Nivelle; commanded Brigade of Guards in Waterloo campaign 1815
Political Career: MP (Poole) 1831–1835
Creations and Dignities: 1st Baron Strafford 12 May 1835; 1st Earl of Strafford 18 Sep 1847
Awards and Honours: AGM (Vit Pyr Nlle Niv Ort); KCB 2 Jan 1815; WatM 23 Apr 1816; KMT (Habsburg) 1816; KStG (Russia) 1816; GCB 6 Jun 1831; GCH 12 Aug 1826; MGSM (Toul)
Residences: Portman Square, Marylebone, London; Bellaghy, County Londonderry
Died: London 3 Jun 1860
Sources: ANCD; ARLI; CHAL; DALT; ODNB; WEBC; WEOF; WO 25/744

891. *Robert FORSYTH (1800–1802)*

Born: Aberdeenshire 1766
Relations: Son of William Forsyth of Huntly, silk manufacturer, and Jean (Phyn)
Entry to Army: Ensign in 72nd Foot 6 Apr 1785
Regimental Field Officer Promotions: Major in 4/60th Foot 28 Mar 1800 (vice Byng) by purchase
Service 1793–1815: Served in West Indies
Retired: 5 Mar 1802
Residence: Huntly, Aberdeenshire
Died: Huntly 7 Oct 1825
Sources: ARLI; SCMA (1825); <https://househistree.com/people/william-forsyth>

892. *John LENNOX (1801–1802)*

Born: England c.1760
Relations: Son of Alexander Lennox and Charlotte (Ramsay); brother-in-law of Lieutenant Colonel John Campbell, Superintendent of Indian Affairs in Canada
Entry to Army: Ensign in 1/60th Foot 28 Apr 1784
Regimental Field Officer Promotions: Major in 2/60th Foot 25 Sep 1801 (vice Johnson)
Service 1793–1815: Served in West Indies 1800–1802
Residence: Montréal, Québec
Died: Jamaica 29 Mar 1802
Sources: ANCD; ANCW; ARLI; La Corne St. Luc – His Flame

893. *James MAITLAND (1802–1803)*

Born: New York State 1772
Relations: Natural son of Colonel Hon. Richard Maitland of Lauderdale and Mary (McAdam); brother of Captain Richard Maitland RN; Patrick Maitland RN; and Admiral John Maitland RN; nephew of Rear Admiral Frederick Lewis Maitland RN; Captain Hon. Patrick Maitland, EIC naval service; and Lieutenant Colonel Hon. John Maitland, 71st Foot; cousin of Lieutenant General Rt Hon. Sir Thomas Maitland
Entry to Army: Ensign in 62nd Foot 14 Sep 1797
Regimental Field Officer Promotions: Major in 60th Foot 5 Mar 1802 (vice Forsyth) by purchase; Lieutenant Colonel in 1st West India Regiment 23 Apr 1803 (vice Rutherford) by purchase; Lieutenant Colonel in 75th Foot 18 Feb 1804 (vice Cumine) by exchange
Service 1793–1815: Commanded 75th Foot 1804–1805
Died: Killed in action at Bhurtpore, East Indies 4 Jan 1805
Sources: ANCB; ANCD; ARLI; 3 Papers relating to Claims to the Earldom of Lauderdale

894. *Sir John Pringle DALRYMPLE, 5th Bt (1802–1804)*

Born: East Lothian 1778
Relations: Son of Sir John Dalrymple, 2nd Bt, Lord Provost of Edinburgh, and Anne-Young (Pringle); brother of Sir James Dalrymple, 4th Bt
Entry to Army: Lieutenant in 90th Foot 5 Apr 1796 by purchase
Regimental Field Officer Promotions: Major in 2/60th Foot 13 Mar 1802 (vice Lethbridge) by purchase; Lieutenant Colonel in Royal Regiment of Malta 29 Dec 1804; to half-pay of Royal Regiment of Malta 26 Apr 1811
Brevets: Brevet Colonel 4 Jun 1813; Major General 12 Aug 1819
Service 1793–1815: Served in Gibraltar 1798–1800; Assistant Adjutant General in Mediterranean 1801; served in West Indies 1803; commanded Royal Regiment of Malta 1804–1807; Inspector of foreign troops in Calabria 1808–1809
Retired: 11 Aug 1829
Creations and Dignities: 5th Baronet Dalrymple of Hailes Dec 1800
Awards and Honours: KB 28 Dec 1807
Residence: Woodside, Lymington, Hampshire
Died: Bath, Somerset 18 Oct 1829
Sources: ANCB; ANCD; ANCW; PHIL; WEOF; WO 25/745; A Genealogical and Heraldic History of the Extinct and Dormant Baronetcies of England, Ireland, and Scotland

895. *William FORSTER (1802–1803)*

Born: Northumberland 1776
Relations: Son of Ralph Forster of Berwick-upon-Tweed and Mary (Grieve)
Entry to Army: Ensign in New South Wales Corps 13 Apr 1791
Regimental Field Officer Promotions: Major in 6/60th Foot 15 Apr 1802 (vice Gordon) by purchase
Retired: 16 Jun 1803
Residence: Downham, Northumberland
Died: Downham 25 Jun 1803
Sources: ANCB; ARLI; The European Magazine, and London Review (1803)

896. *Thomas CLARKE (1802–1807)*

Born: [spec.] British North America c.1765
Entry to Army: Ensign in Georgia Loyalists; Ensign in 4/60th Foot 5 Sep 1779
Regimental Field Officer Promotions: Major in 4/60th Foot 24 Jun 1802 (vice Lennox)
Residence: Chelsea, London
Died: Chelsea 2 Feb 1807
Sources: ARLI; FMPD

897. *James William Edward Wheeler UNWIN (1803–1807)*

Born: Essex 1763
Relations: Son of James Unwin of Wootton Lodge and Frances (Stephenson)
Entry to Army: Lieutenant in 102nd Foot 28 Sep 1781
Regimental Field Officer Promotions: Major in 1/60th Foot 21 Apr 1803 (vice Maitland) by purchase
Brevets: Brevet Major 6 May 1795; Brevet Lieutenant Colonel 29 Apr 1802
Retired: 12 Mar 1807
Residence: Wootton Lodge, near Ellastone, Staffordshire
Died: Marseille, Bouches-du-Rhône, France 13 Dec 1818
Sources: ANCB; ANCD; ANCW; ARLI; WEOF

898. *Robert SEWELL (1803)*

See 486.
Major in 6/60th Foot 16 Jun 1803 (Vice Forster) by purchase

899. *Sir James BATHURST (1803–1810)*

Born: Oxfordshire 1782
Relations: Son of Henry Bathurst, Bishop of Norwich, and Grace (Coote); brother of Henry Bathurst, Archdeacon of Norwich; nephew of Lieutenant General Sir Eyre Coote

Entry to Army: Volunteer; Ensign in 70th Foot 10 May 1794
Regimental Field Officer Promotions: Major in 4/60th Foot 1 Oct 1803 (vice Keane) by purchase; Major on Quartermaster General staff 31 May 1810 (vice Blaquiere) by exchange; Major in 5th Foot 7 Feb 1811; to half-pay of Argyllshire Fencibles 13 Jun 1811
Brevets: Brevet Lieutenant Colonel 10 Oct 1805; Brevet Colonel 4 Jun 1813; Major General 12 Aug 1819; Lieutenant General 10 Jan 1837
Service 1793–1815: Served in Gibraltar 1798; served in West Indies 1799; served in Egypt 1801; served in West Indies; served at capture of Surinam 1804; served in Hanover 1805; observer with Russian army 1807; served in Copenhagen 1807; Assistant Quartermaster General in Peninsula Aug 1808 to Jan 1809; Assistant Quartermaster General and Military Secretary to Wellington in Peninsula May 1809 to Mar 1810, and Jul to Dec 1810
Later Service: Lieutenant Governor of British Virgin Islands 1816; Governor of Berwick-upon-Tweed 1833
Awards and Honours: AGM (Rol&Vim, Cor Tal Bus); CB 11 Jun 1815; KCB 28 Sep 1831
Residence: Kibworth Rectory, Kibworth Beauchamp, Leicestershire
Died: Kibworth Rectory 20 Apr 1850
Sources: ANCB; ANCD; ARLI; CHAL; GEMA (1850); PHIL; WEOF; WO 25/744

900. *Robert CAMPBELL (1803–1804)*

Born: Argyllshire c.1762
Relations: Son of Dugald Campbell of Kintarbert and Isabella (Campbell); brother of Lieutenant Colonel Archibald Campbell, Bengal service
Entry to Army: Ensign in 14th Foot 29 Jun 1785
Regimental Field Officer Promotions: Major in 6/60th Foot 24 Nov 1803 (vice Sewell); to half-pay of Prince of Wales's Fencibles 26 Jul 1804
Brevets: Brevet Lieutenant Colonel 1 Jan 1800; Brevet Colonel 25 Jul 1810; Major General 4 Jun 1814; Lieutenant General 22 Jul 1830
Residence: Kintarbert, Argyllshire
Died: Gartnagrenoch, Argyllshire 13 May 1837
Sources: ANCW; WEOF; A Memorial History of the Campbells of Melfort; Records of Clan Campbell in the Military Service of the Honourable East India Company

901. *John ROBERTSON (1804–1807)*

Born: Québec c.1766
Relations: Son of Colonel Daniel Robertson of Montréal, 60th Foot; son-in-law of General Gabriel Christie
Entry to Army: Ensign in 44th Foot 1 Aug 1782
Regimental Field Officer Promotions: Major in 2/60th Foot 14 Sep 1804 (vice Mosheim)
Early Service: Served in British North America 1790
Service 1793–1815: Deputy Adjutant General at capture of Surinam 1804
Retired: 13 Aug 1807
Later Service: Secretary and registrar in Curaçao; served in Wars of Liberation in Venezuela 1810–1811
Died: Jamaica 1815
Sources: ARLI; DICB; Genealogical Memoirs of the Scottish House of Christie

902. *Marie François Xavier de SAINT-MART, Baron (1805–1814)*

Born: Eure-et-Loir, France c.1774
Entry to Army: Lieutenant in Royal Foreigners May 1795
Regimental Field Officer Promotions: Major in 3/60th Foot 5 Jan 1805 (vice Drummond) by purchase
Brevets: Brevet Lieutenant Colonel 1 Jan 1812
Service 1793–1815: Served in Flanders with *Armée de Condé* (Austrian service) 1793–1794; served in Hanover 1795; served in West Indies 1796; served in West Indies, commanded 3/60th Foot at capture of The Saints 1807
Retired: 20 Apr 1814
Awards and Honours: Royal and Military Order of Saint Louis (Bourbon)
Died: After 1830
Sources: ARLI; WEOF; WO 25/748; Liste Générale Par Ordre Alphabétique, Des Émigrés De Toute La République

903. *Sir William Gabriel DAVY, Kt (1807–1809)*

Born: Gloucestershire 1779
Relations: Son of Major William Davy, Bengal service, and Harriett (Preston)
Education: Eton College
Entry to Army: Ensign in 61st Foot 21 Mar 1797 by purchase
Regimental Field Officer Promotions: Major in 4/60th Foot 5 Feb 1807 (vice Clarke) by purchase; Lieutenant Colonel in 7th Garrison Battalion 28 Dec 1809 (vice Powlett); to half-pay of 7th Garrison Battalion 1814
Brevets: Brevet Colonel 12 Aug 1819; Major General 22 Jul 1830; Lieutenant General 23 Nov 1841; General 28 Nov 1854
Colonelcies: Colonel Commandant of 1/60th Foot

2 Nov 1842 (vice Maclean)
Service 1793–1815: Served in Cape of Good Hope 1799; served in British North America 1802; served in West Indies 1803–1805; commanded 5/60th in Peninsula Aug 1808 to Dec 1809
Awards and Honours: AGM (Rol&Vim Tal); CB 4 Jun 1815; Knight Bachelor 23 Mar 1836; KCH 12 Aug 1836
Residence: Tracy Park, near Wick, Gloucestershire
Died: Tracy Park 25 Jan 1856
Sources: ANCB; ANCD; ARLI; CHAL; GEMA (1856); PHIL; WEOF; WO 25/744

904. *William DRUMMOND (1807–1809)*

Born: Perthshire 1778
Relations: Son of John Drummond of Keltie, surgeon in EIC, and Euphemia (Aytoun); brother of James Drummond, Dutch service; and Lieutenant Mark Howard Drummond, 27th Foot; nephew of Major General Robert Aytoun
Entry to Army: Ensign in Breadalbane Fencibles 1793; Lieutenant in 2nd West India Regiment 1 Jul 1795
Regimental Field Officer Promotions: Major in 1/60th Foot 12 Mar 1807 (vice Unwin) by purchase; Major in New Brunswick Fencibles 9 Nov 1809 (vice Fitzgerald) by exchange; Lieutenant Colonel in 104th Foot (late New Brunswick Fencibles) 4 Jun 1813
Brevets: Brevet Major 12 Mar 1807
Service 1793–1815: Served in West Indies 1795–1801; served in West Indies 1803; ADC to Charles Green in Surinam 1804; served in British North America 1809–1814
Retired: 27 Oct 1814
Residence: Madderty, Perthshire
Died: Madderty 28 Jan 1838
Sources: ARLI; WO 25/745; Genealogical Memoir of the most Noble and Ancient House of Drummond

905. *George Louis Victor FORNERET (1809–1811)*

Born: Switzerland 1765
Relations: Son of Albert Forneret, member of the Council of Sixty of Lausanne, and Marie Anne Sophie (Grobéty); father of Captain Cuthbert Augustus Forneret, 60th Foot; and Lieutenant Colonel Charles Alexander Forneret, Lower Canada Sedentary Militia
Entry to Army: Ensign in 2/60th Foot 1 Oct 1787
Regimental Field Officer Promotions: Major in 3/60th Foot 3 Feb 1809 (vice Mackie)
Brevets: Brevet Major 25 Apr 1808
Early Service: Served in British North America 1788–1796
Service 1793–1815: Served in West Indies 1796–1797, POW in Tobago; served in British North America 1798–1806
Retired: 17 Jan 1811
Residence: Berthier, Québec, Canada
Died: Berthier 1821
Sources: ARLI; WO 25/745; Revue d'Histoire de l'Amérique Française

906. *James GRANT (1809–1815)*

Born: West Lothian 1775
Relations: Son of John Grant of Abercorn and Mary (Johnson)
Entry to Army: Lieutenant in 97th Foot 8 Feb 1794
Regimental Field Officer Promotions: Major in 2/60th Foot 8 Nov 1809
Brevets: Brevet Major 25 Apr 1808; Brevet Lieutenant Colonel 4 Jun 1814
Service 1793–1815: Served in West Indies 1797–1800; served in British North America 1800–1805
Residence: Auchindoun, Nairnshire
Died: Auchindoun 6 May 1815
Upon joining the 97th Foot in 1797, 16 out of 31 officers had the surname Grant
Sources: ANCB; ANCD; ARLI; WEOF; WO 25/745

907. *Sir John FORSTER FITZGERALD (1809–1824)*

Born: County Clare 1784
Relations: Son of Edward FitzGerald of Carrigoran and Anne Catherine (Burton); brother of Sir William FitzGerald, 2nd Bt; brother-in-law of Major Robert Hazen, 60th Foot; father of Captain John Forster FitzGerald, 14th Light Dragoons
Entry to Army: Ensign in Independent Company 29 Oct 1793
Regimental Field Officer Promotions: Major in New Brunswick Fencibles 27 Jul 1809; Major in 4/60th Foot 9 Nov 1809 (vice Drummond) by exchange; Lieutenant Colonel in 60th Foot 9 Oct 1823 (vice Andrews); Lieutenant Colonel in 20th Foot 5 Feb 1824 (vice Bunbury) by exchange; removed from the regiment as a general officer 22 Jul 1830
Brevets: Brevet Major 25 Sep 1803; Brevet Lieutenant Colonel 25 Jul 1810; Brevet Colonel 12 Aug 1819; Major General 22 Jul 1830; Lieutenant General 23 Nov 1841; General 20 Jun 1854; Field Marshal 29 May 1875
Colonelcies: 85th Foot 4 Apr 1840 (vice Thornton); 62nd Foot 21 Nov 1843 (vice Campbell); 18th Foot 9 Mar 1850 (vice Aylmer)
Service 1793–1815: Served in British North

America 1803–1809; served in Peninsula with 5/60th Mar 1812 to Apr 1814, slightly wounded at Badajoz; commanded brigade in 2nd Division in Peninsula Jul 1813
Later Service: Commandant of Québec 1818; Commandant of Montreal 1819; commanded division in Madras 1838; commanded division in Bombay 1840
Political Career: MP (County Clare) 1852–1857
Awards and Honours: AGM (Bad Sal Vitt Pyr); CB 2 Jan 1815; KCB 13 Sep 1831; GCB 19 Nov 1862
Residence: Tours, Centre-Val de Loire, France
Died: Tours 24 Mar 1877
Upon his death in France, was given the same form of state funeral as awarded to French marshals
Sources: ARLI; BRFM; DINB; CHAL; ODNB; WEOF; WO 25/745

908. *Jean Pierre GALIFFE (1810–1825)*

Born: Switzerland 1767
Relations: Son of Barthélémy Galiffe of St Pierre and Marie (Naville); brother of Lieutenant Colonel Jeanne-Louise Andrienne Galiffe, Sardinian service; and Captain Charles-Francois de Galiffe, Prussian and later French service; father of Major John-Frederic Galiffe, 60th Foot
Entry to Army: 1st Lieutenant in *Régiment de Chateauvieux* (Swiss service) 1785; Lieutenant in 2nd West India Regiment 20 Sep 1795
Regimental Field Officer Promotions: Major in 5/60th Foot 15 Mar 1810 (vice Davy); Lieutenant Colonel in 60th Foot 18 Jun 1825
Brevets: Brevet Major 25 Apr 1808; Brevet Lieutenant Colonel 3 Mar 1814
Early Service: In Swiss service 1785–1792
Service 1793–1815: In Dutch service in Flanders 1794–1795; served in West Indies 1796 and 1799–1803; served in British North America 1803–1805; served in Peninsula Aug 1808 to Apr 1814, wounded at Talavera and Salamanca
Later Service: Served in British North America; Commandant in Halifax NS; Commandant in Bermuda 1821–1824; Commandant in Berbice 1824–1825
Retired: 25 Dec 1825
Awards and Honours: AGM (Vitt Nlle Ort Toul); CB; MGSM (Rol Vim Tal Bus FDO Alb CR Bad Sal Pyr Niv)
Residence: Geneva, Switzerland
Died: Geneva 21 Nov 1847
Sources: ARLI; CHAL; HALL; PHIL; WEOF; WO 25/745 <https://galiffe.net/line%20of%20descent.htm>

909. *Hon. George BLAQUIERE (1810)*

Born: London 1782
Relations: Son of John, 1st Baron de Blaquiere, and Elinor (Dobson); brother of Major Hon. John Blaquiere, 2nd Baron de Blaquiere of Ardkill, 83rd Foot; and Lieutenant General William de Blaquiere, 3rd Baron de Blaquiere of Ardkill
Entry to Army: Cornet in 24th Light Dragoons 13 Oct 1800 by purchase
Regimental Field Officer Promotions: Major on Quartermaster General staff 5 Nov 1807; Major in 2/60th Foot 31 May 1810 (vice Bathurst) by exchange
Service 1793–1815: Served with Austrian army on continent 1799; Assistant Quartermaster General in Hanover 1805; Assistant Quartermaster General to KGL in Copenhagen 1807; Assistant Quartermaster General in Baltic 1808; Assistant Quartermaster General in Peninsula Aug 1808 to Jan 1809, and Apr to Sep 1809; served on staff in Walcheren 1809
Retired: 14 Jun 1810
Awards and Honours: AGM (Cor)
Residence: Regent Street, Marylebone, London
Died: London 22 Mar 1826
Sources: ANCB; ANCD; ARLI; CHAL; WEOF; WO 25/745; <https://www.findagrave.com/memorial/259248068/george-blaquiere>

910. *Robert HAZEN (1810–1813)*

Born: New Brunswick 1773
Relations: Son of Hon. William Hazen of St John, and Sarah Leonard (Le Baron); brother of Paymaster William Hazen, 60th Foot; brother-in-law of Field Marshal Sir John Forster Fitzgerald
Entry to Army: Lieutenant in New Brunswick Regiment 25 Jun 1793
Regimental Field Officer Promotions: Major in 2/60th Foot 14 Jun 1810 (vice Blaquiere) by purchase
Service 1793–1815: Served in West Indies 1803–1807; served in British North America
Residence: St John, New Brunswick, Canada
Died: St John 17 Jul 1813
Sources: ANCW; ARLI; Collections of the New Brunswick Historical Society

911. *François Antoine RUMPLER (1810–1826)*

Born: Alsace 1760
Relations: Son of Johann Michael Rumpler of Obernai and Ottilia (Richert)
Entry to Army: Captain in Royal Foreigners 25 Dec 1795; Captain in 60th Foot 30 Dec 1797

Regimental Field Officer Promotions: Major in 6/60th Foot 16 Aug 1810 (vice Wharton); Lieutenant Colonel on half-pay unattached Oct 1826; Lieutenant Colonel in 17th Light Dragoons 18 Oct 1826 (vice Stanhope) by exchange
Brevets: Brevet Major Jul 1810; Brevet Lieutenant Colonel 12 Aug 1819; Lieutenant Colonel (continent) 11 Dec 1826
Service 1793–1815: Served in Jamaica 1810–1817
Retired: 9 Nov 1826
Residence: St James's, Jamaica
Died: Jamaica c.1827
Sources: ARLI; PHIL; WEOF; <https://www.ucl.ac.uk/lbs/person/view/2146653131/>

912. *Charles Claude Nicolas de La HOUSSAYE BOUVERIE (1811–1819)*
Born: Normandy 1763
Relations: Son of Bon Jean Nicolas de La Houssaye and Catherine Geneviève (de Serrouer)
Entry to Army: Lieutenant in Royal Foreigners 25 Mar 1796; Captain in 60th Foot 30 Dec 1797
Regimental Field Officer Promotions: Major in 3/60th Foot 2 Oct 1811
Brevets: Brevet Major 25 Jul 1810; Brevet Lieutenant Colonel 14 Jul 1814
Service 1793–1815: Served in Cape of Good Hope
Retired: 15 Apr 1819
Residence: Mont Plaisir, near St Servan, Brittany, France
Died: Mont Plaisir 28 Dec 1826
Sources: ARLI; WEOF; <https://man8rove.com/fr/blason/drzamf9-la-houssaye>

913. *Gustav Heinrich Gottlieb BRAUN (1811–1815)*
Born: Saxony 1775
Relations: Son of Johanna Christiana Großmann of Arneburg
Entry to Army: Kadett in *Kadettenkorps Sachsen* 1786; Ensign in Loewenstein's Chasseurs 1 Nov 1794
Regimental Field Officer Promotions: Major in 2nd *Caçadores* in Portuese service 21 Apr 1810; Lieutenant Colonel in 7th Portuguese Line 3 Nov 1810; Lieutenant Colonel in 9th *Caçadores* 6 Jun 1811; Major in 6/60th Foot 3 Oct 1811; Lieutenant Colonel in Portuguese service 9 Aug 1815; to half-pay in Portuguese service 25 Dec 1816; Marechal de Campo in Portuguese service 6 Sep 1823; Lieutenant Colonel in 95th Foot 1 Dec 1823
Brevets: Brevet Major 25 Jul 1810; Brevet Lieutenant Colonel 17 Aug 1812
Service 1793–1815: Served in Flanders 1794; served in West Indies 1797; served in Surinam 1799; served in Peninsula with Portuguese army Apr 1810 to Jan 1814, badly wounded at Nive
Retired: 7 Jul 1825
Later Service: Marechal de Campo in Brazilian army 1826–1831
Awards and Honours: AGM (Sal Pyr Nlle Niv); CB 16 Sep 1815; CTS (Portugal); Military Order of St Bento D'Aviz (Portugal); Imperial Ordem do Cruzeiro (Brazil); Ordem Nacional do Cruzeiro do Sul (Brazil)
Residence: Dresden, Saxony, Germany
Died: Dresden 8 May 1865
Sources: ARLI; CHAL; PHIL; WEOF; <https://www.napoleon-series.org/research/biographies/GreatBritain/Brown/GustavusBrown.pdf>

914. *Sir Henry WYNDHAM (1813–1814)*
Born: Henry Wyndham-Ilive in Sussex 1790
Relations: Natural son of George Wyndham, 3rd Earl of Egremont, and Elizabeth (Ilive); brother of Colonel George Wyndham, 1st Baron Leconfield, 20th Light Dragoons; and Colonel Charles Wyndham, 36th Foot; received approval to drop -Ilive surname in 1830
Entry to Army: Ensign in 31st Foot 27 Mar 1806
Regimental Field Officer Promotions: Major in 8th Portuguese cavalry 7 Apr 1811; Major in 60th Foot 9 Aug 1813; Lieutenant Colonel in Dillon's Regiment 20 Jan 1814 (vice Watson) by purchase; Captain and Lieutenant Colonel in Coldstream Foot Guards 25 Jul 1814; Lieutenant Colonel in 19th Light Dragoons 11 Jul 1816 (vice O'Neill); to half-pay of 19th Light Dragoons (Lancers) 10 Sep 1821; Lieutenant Colonel in 10th Light Dragoons (Hussars) 18 Mar 1824 (vice Quentin); to half-pay of 9th Light Dragoons 22 Mar 1833 (vice Gore) by exchange
Brevets: Brevet Colonel 27 May 1825; Major General 10 Jan 1837; Lieutenant General 10 Nov 1846; General 28 Nov 1854
Colonelcies: 11th Hussars 19 Nov 1847 (vice Cathcart)
Service 1793–1815: Served in Peninsula with Portuguese cavalry Apr 1811 to May 1812; severely injured at Waterloo 1815
Later Service: ADC to King William IV 7 Jun 1825
Political Career: MP (Cockermouth) 1852–1857; MP (West Cumberland) 1857–1860
Awards and Honours: WatM 23 Apr 1816; MGSM (Rol Vim Alb Vitt); KCB 21 Jun 1859
Residences: Cockermouth Castle, Cumberland; Mount Street, Grosvenor Square, London
Died: Cockermouth Castle 2 Aug 1860

Sources: ANCB; ANCD; ARLI; CHAL; DALT; PHIL; WEOF

915. *Otto Ernst Gelder TRIP von Zoudtlandt, Baron (1813–1816)*

Born: Netherlands 1776
Relations: Son of Johan Louis Trip of Groningen and Anna Wilhelmina (van Limburg-Stirum); brother of Lieutenant General Albert Dominicus Trip van Zoudtlandt, Netherlands service
Entry to Army: Cornet in 10th Light Dragoons 3 May 1800
Regimental Field Officer Promotions: Major in Royal Africa Corps 1 Apr 1813 (vice Kinsley); Major in 8/60th Foot 10 Nov 1813
Brevets: Brevet Lieutenant Colonel 20 Apr 1815
Service 1793–1815: Served in Helder 1799; ADC to Wellington in Peninsula Aug 1808 to Jan 1809; Deputy Assistant Adjutant General in Peninsula Mar 1810 to Apr 1811; Deputy Assistant Adjutant General in Peninsula Sep 1813 to Jan 1814; ADC to Prince of Orange in Waterloo campaign 1815
Awards and Honours: CB 27 Jan 1816; WatM 23 Apr 1816
Residence: Florence, Tuscany, Italy
Died: Committed suicide in Florence 2 Nov 1816
Sources: ANCB; ANCD; ARLI; CHAL; DALT; WEOF; Jaarboek van den Nederlandschen Adel, Vol.3

916. *Henry FITZGERALD (1813–1825)*

Born: Dublin c.1785
Relations: Son of Rev. Gerald Fitzgerald, vice Provost of Trinity College, and Elizabeth (Preston)
Entry to Army: Lieutenant in 46th Foot 26 Feb 1801
Regimental Field Officer Promotions: Major in 8/60th Foot 11 Nov 1813; to half-pay of 60th Foot 1818; returned to full pay 15 Apr 1819 (vice Bouverie); Lieutenant Colonel in 60th Foot 25 Dec 1825 (vice Galiffe)
Service 1793–1815: Served in Peninsula Oct 1810 to Nov 1813, and Dec 1813 to Apr 1814
Retired: 18 Dec 1828
Residence: Tours, Centre-Val de Loire, France
Died: Tours 24 Feb 1830
Sources: ARLI; CHAL; PHIL; WEOF; Kerry Evening Post 13 Mar 1830

917. *Charles-Michel d'Irumberry de SALABERRY (1813–1822)*

Born: Québec 1778
Relations: Son of Ignace-Michel-Louis-Antoine d'Irumberry de Salaberry and Françoise-Catherine Hertel (de Saint-François); father of Lieutenant Colonel Charles-René-Lĕonidas d'Irumberry de Salaberry, Québec Voltigeurs; and Lieutenant Colonel Melchior-Alphonse de Salaberry, Lower Canada Militia
Entry to Army: Ensign in 44th Foot 1792
Regimental Field Officer Promotions: Major in 2/60th Foot 18 Nov 1813 (vice Hazen); to half-pay of Canadian Voltiguers 1822
Brevets: Brevet Lieutenant Colonel 24 Sep 1812
Service 1793–1815: Inspecting Field Officer of Voltigeurs in Canada 4 Jun 1814
Retired: 1825
Awards and Honours: AGM (Chat); CB 6 Nov 1817
Residence: Chambly, Québec, Canada
Died: Chambly 27 Feb 1829
Sources: ARLI; DICB; WEOF; <https://www.findagrave.com/memorial/84311815/charles-michel-d'irumberry_de_salaberry>

918. *William HART (1814)*

Born: Gloucestershire 1773
Relations: Son of George Hart of Westbury-on-Trim and Elizabeth (Williams); father of Lieutenant General Henry George Hart
Entry to Army: Cornet in 8th Light Dragoons 30 Jul 1796
Regimental Field Officer Promotions: Major in 60th Foot 14 Apr 1814
Brevets: Brevet Lieutenant Colonel 1 Jan 1812
Service 1793–1815: Served in Cape of Good Hope 1796
Retired: 21 Apr 1814
Residence: Wynberg, Cape Colony, South Africa
Died: Wynberg 1 Sep 1848
Sources: ARLI; WikiTree

919. *Sir Emmanuel Felix AGAR, Kt (1814)*

Born: London 1781
Relations: (poss. illegitimate) Son of Welbore Ellis Agar, commissioner of customs and Mary Ann (unk.)
Entry to Army: Cornet and Sub-Lieutenant in in 1st Life Guards 2 Feb 1803 by purchase
Regimental Field Officer Promotions: Major in 3/60th Foot Apr 1814 (vice St Mart) by purchase; Major in 2nd Life Guards 28 Apr 1814 (vice Barton) by exchange
Brevets: Brevet Major 20 Apr 1814
Political Career: MP (Sudbury) 1807–1812
Awards and Honours: Knight Bachelor 18 Jul 1812
Retired: 27 Apr 1815
Residence: New Norfolk Street, Grosvenor Square, London
Died: London 28 Aug 1866

Sources: ANCB; ANCD; ARLI; CHAL; HPON

920. *Henry TARLETON (1814–1817)*
Born: Cheshire 1787
Relations: Son of Thomas Tarleton of Bolesworth and Mary (Robinson); nephew of General Sir Banastre Tarleton
Entry to Army: Cornet in 1st Dragoon Guards 25 Feb 1804 by purchase
Regimental Field Officer Promotions: Major in 7/60th Foot 12 Apr 1814 (vice Hart) by purchase; Lieutenant Colonel in 2/60th Foot 24 Feb 1817 (vice Austen) by purchase; to half-pay of 60th Foot 25 Mar 1817
Brevets: Brevet Lieutenant Colonel 24 Feb 1817
Service 1793–1815: Served in Peninsula with 2/7th Foot Sep 1810 to Jul 1811, wounded at Albuera; served in Peninsula with 1/7th Foot Oct 1812 to Apr 1814, POW in Pyrenees; served in British North America
Residence: Penley, near Ellesmere, Shropshire
Died: Ellesmere 24 Feb 1829
Sources: ANCB; ANCD; ARLI; CHAL; PHIL; WEOF

921. *Sir Robert Johnstone BARTON (1814–1816)*
Born: County Tipperary 1770
Relations: Son of William Barton of Fethard and Grace (Massy); brother of Lieutenant General Charles Barton
Entry to Army: Cornet in 11th Light Dragoons 21 May 1794
Regimental Field Officer Promotions: Major in 11th Light Dragoons 17 Feb 1803 (vice Cumming) by purchase; Major and Lieutenant Colonel in 2nd Life Guards 14 Jun 1805 (vice C. Barton) by purchase; Major in 3/60th Foot 28 Apr 1814 (vice Agar) by exchange; to half-pay of 60th Foot 25 Mar 1816
Brevets: Brevet Colonel 4 Jun 1813; Major General 12 Aug 1819; Lieutenant General 10 Jan 1837; General 11 Nov 1851
Early Service: Served in Garde Nationale in France 1790
Service 1793–1815: Served in Flanders 1794–1795; served at Helder 1799; commanded 2nd Life Guards in Peninsula Oct to Dec 1812
Awards and Honours: KCH Apr 1837
Residence: Montague Place, Marylebone, London
Died: London 17 Mar 1853
Sources: ARLI; CHAL; WEOF; WO 25/744; Barton Historical and Genealogical Society

922. *John Williams ALDRED (1814–1818)*
Born: West Indies c.1781
Entry to Army: Lieutenant in 6th West India Regiment 17 Aug 1797
Regimental Field Officer Promotions: Major in 6/60th Foot 26 May 1814 (vice Marlton); to half-pay of 60th Foot 25 Dec 1818
Brevets: Brevet Major 1 Jan 1812; Brevet Lieutenant Colonel 19 Jul 1821; Brevet Colonel 10 Jan 1837; Major General 9 Nov 1846; Lieutenant General 20 Jun 1854
Service 1793–1815: Commanded 6/60th Foot in West Indies 1817–1818
Residence: Eaton Place, Belgravia, London
Died: London 12 Mar 1858
Sources: ANCB; ANCD; ANCW; ARLI

923. *William BATTLEY (1814–1817)*
Born: County Clare c.1771
Relations: Son of John Battley of Willbrook, solicitor, and Hannah (Watson)
Entry to Army: Volunteer Apr 1788; Ensign in 69th Foot 30 Sep 1788
Regimental Field Officer Promotions: Major in 1/60th Foot 11 Aug 1814 (vice Woodgate)
Brevets: Brevet Major 25 Apr 1808; Brevet Lieutenant Colonel 4 Jun 1814
Service 1793–1815: Served in West Indies; served in Cape of Good Hope 1812–1817
Retired: 7 Aug 1817
Died: Killed in accident at Gibraltar c.Oct 1817
Sources: ANCW; ARLI; LFBI; GHLG; <https://www.latrobesociety.org.au/LaTrobeana/LaTrobeanaV19n2.pdf>

924. *Edward NORTON (1814)*
Born: Ireland c.1771
Entry to Army: Ensign in 60th Foot Dec 1794
Regimental Field Officer Promotions: Major in 2/60th Foot 11 Aug 1814 (vice de Salaberry)
Brevets: Brevet Major 4 Jun 1814
Service 1793–1815: Served in West Indies
Died: Barbados Dec 1814
Sources: ARLI; WEOF

925. *Louis Charles de MANGON (1814–1816)*
Born: Normandy c.1777
Entry to Army: Volunteer 1794; 2nd Ensign in British Legion (Montalembert's) 9 Dec 1795; 1st Lieutenant in 4/60th Foot 14 May 1797
Regimental Field Officer Promotions: Major in 2/60th Foot 8 Dec 1814 (vice Norton)
Brevets: Brevet Major 4 Jun 1814

Service 1793–1815: Served in Demerara
Retired: 11 Jul 1816
Later Service: Major in *58e Régiment de Ligne* in French service 9 Jul 1817
Awards and Honours: Chevalier of Military Royal Order of St Louis (France, Bourbon)
Died: After 1821
Sources: ARLI; WEOF; Annuaire de l'etat Militaire de France 1821

926. *Carl HINCKELDEY (1815–1818)*
Born: Baden c.1785
Relations: Son of Major Christian Reinhardt Hinckeldey, *Régiment Royal Deux-Ponts* in French (Bourbon) service
Entry to Army: Ensign in Loewenstein's Chasseurs 13 Oct 1796; Ensign in 60th Foot 21 Apr 1797
Regimental Field Officer Promotions: Major in 60th Foot 9 Mar 1815 (vice Stopford) by purchase; to half-pay of 60th Foot 20 Nov 1819
Service 1793–1815: Served in West Indies
Died: Guadeloupe 28 Dec 1820
Sources: ARLI; FMPW; PHIL; Historisches und genealogisches Adelsbuch des Grossherzogthums Baden

927. *Christophe Philippe Bérard de MAURIAGE (1815–1818)*
Born: France c.1759
Entry to Army: 2nd Lieutenant in *Régiment d'Agénois* in French (Bourbon) service 4 Nov 1779; Lieutenant in Royal Foreigners 25 Mar 1796
Regimental Field Officer Promotions: Major in 6/60th Foot 9 Aug 1815 (vice Braun); to half-pay of 60th Foot 25 Dec 1818
Brevets: Brevet Major 4 Jun 1814
Early Service: Served in American War of Independence (French service), wounded and POW at Savannah 1780
Residence: Maubeuge, Hauts-de-France, France
Died: Maubeuge 13 Jun 1823
Sources: ANCW; ARLI; Historical Register of Officers of the Continental Army

928. *John McMAHON (1815–1818)*
Born: County Clare c.1773
Entry to Army: Lieutenant in Clare Militia 1798; Ensign in 27th Foot 25 Mar 1800
Regimental Field Officer Promotions: Major in 2/60th Foot 10 Aug 1815 (vice Grant); to half-pay of 60th Foot 25 Sep 1818; Major in 59th Foot 18 Dec 1827 (vice Fuller); Major in 2nd Foot 12 Nov 1829 (vice Waring) by exchange; to half-pay unattached 29 Mar 1833 (vice Powell) by exchange
Brevets: Brevet Major 4 Jun 1814; Brevet Lieutenant Colonel 22 Jul 1830
Service 1793–1815: Served in Irish rebellion 1798; served at Ferrol 1800; served in Peninsula Nov 1808 to Feb 1813
Awards and Honours: MGSM (Bus Alb Bad)
Residence: Madeira
Died: Madeira 25 May 1850
Sources: ARLI; CHAL; Atlas, 22 Jun 1850

929. *Charles GARDINER (1815–1818)*
Born: Ayrshire 1780
Relations: Son of Lieutenant General William Neville Gardiner and Harriett (Wrottesley)
Entry to Army: Ensign in 89th Foot 9 Apr 1806
Regimental Field Officer Promotions: Major in 60th Foot 14 Dec 1815 (vice Andrews) by purchase; to half-pay of 60th Foot 25 Jun 1819
Brevets: Brevet Lieutenant Colonel 10 Jan 1837
Residence: Bath, Somerset
Died: Cheltenham, Gloucestershire 22 Oct 1838
Sources: ANCD; ANCW; ARLI; DEPE; PHIL

Selected Regimental Histories
Butler, Lewis, *The Annals of the King's Royal Rifle Corps, Vol. I* (London: Smith, Elder & Co., 1913)
Butler, Lewis, *The Annals of the King's Royal Rifle Corps, Vol. II* (London: John Murray, 1923)
Wallace, Nesbit Willoughby, *A Regimental Chronicle and List of Officers of the 60th, Or the King's Royal Rifle Corps, Formerly the 62nd, Or the Royal American Regiment of Foot* (London: Harrison, 1879)
Griffith, Robert, *Riflemen: The History of the 5th Battalion, 60th (Royal American) Regiment 1797–1818* (Warwick: Helion, 2021)

Regimental Museum
The Royal Green Jackets (Rifles) Museum, Peninsula Barracks, Romsey Road, Winchester, Hampshire

Appendices

Abstract 1: Miscellaneous Statistics for the British Army

Number of Officers serving in British Army at the close of the Peninsular War[1]

Ranks	Officers on full pay	Percentage of officer corps	Officers on half pay
General officers	344	2.5%	120
Field officers	1,330	9.7%	181
Captains	2,876	21%	462
Lieutenants, cornets and ensigns	6,630	48.3%	1,268
Adjutants, paymasters, quartermasters, recruiting service	986	7.2%	515
Medical	1,176	8.6%	188
Chaplains, commissariat and provosts marshal	378	2.7%	235
TOTAL	13,720	100%	2,969

Estimate of Recruits and Losses 1793–1815[2]

	Total number	Percentage
Recruits raised for British regiments	519,040	69.4%
Recruits raised for foreign regiments	198,630	26.6%
Recruits raised for foreign regiments temporarily employed	30,000	4%
TOTAL – RECRUITING	747,670	100%
Deaths	219,040	37.7%
Discharges	229,141	39.4%
Desertions	113,273	19.5%
Prisoners of war	20,000	3.4%
TOTAL – LOSSES	581,454	100%

The death rate represents approximately 1.15% of the population of Great Britain and Ireland in 1815, compared with approximately 1.9% in World War 1, and approximately 0.94% in World War 2. This is a loose approximation due to the inclusion of foreigners in the 1793–1815 totals and the changed status of Ireland in the WW2 figures.

1 On the Mortality, p.224.
2 On the Mortality, p.232.

Resources available in selected years[3]

UNIT TYPE	1793	1795	1801	1808	1812	1815
Life Guard regiments	2	2	2	2	2	2
Horse Guard regiments	1	1	1	1	1	1
Dragoon Guard regiments	7	7	7	7	7	7
Dragoon regiments	6	6	5	5	5	5
Light Dragoon regiments	14	27	25	22	19	19
Foot Guard regiments	3	3	3	3	3	3
Line Infantry regiments	76	135	94	94	96	96
Light Infantry regiments	0	0	2	8	8	8
Artillery companies	59	59	77	124	134	138
Engineer officers	76	77	89	142	191	215
Sapper and miner companies	6	8	10	15	35	35
West Indies regiments	0	7	12	8	8	8
Colonial and foreign regiments	0	7	17	22	35	46
Veteran and Garrison regiments	0	0	1	20	18	12
Fencible infantry battalions	0	45	52	7	4	5
Fencible cavalry regiments	0	28	2	0	0	0
General officers on Army List	185	244	389	526	692	751
Colonels on Army List	122	170	408	293	271	363
Lieutenant colonels on Army List	242	451	904	862	767	950
Majors on Army List	292	571	516	734	851	1,286

Includes officers holding local rank. Does not include regimental colonels. Only includes units on Army List; not short-lived and ephemeral foreign corps in Europe and West Indies.

3 Based upon Army Lists, TNA WO 65 series.

Abstract 2: Battle Honours

Number of Battle Honours Awarded 1793–1815[4]

Regiment	No. Actions 1793–1815	No. Battle Honours to 1793	No. Battle Honours 1793–1815
95th Foot (Rifles) / Rifle Corps	65	Not formed	16
60th Foot / Rifles	56	2	17
1st Foot (Royal Scots)	46	1	12
27th Foot (Inniskillings)	39	1	11
40th Foot (1st Somerset)	39	1	13
52nd Light Infantry (Oxfordshire)	37	2	14
23rd Foot (Welsh Fuzileers)	34	6	14
43rd Light Infantry (Monmouthshire)	33	1	13
3rd Foot Guards	31	1	6
5th Foot (Northumberland)	31	1	12
Coldstream Foot Guards	30	3	6
42nd Foot (Black Watch)	30	0	10
71st Light Infantry (Highland)	30	3	13
92nd Foot (Gordon Highlanders)	30	Not formed	12
88th Foot (Connaught Rangers)	28	Not formed	11
1st Light Dragoons / Hussars KGL	27	Not formed	3
28th Foot (North Gloucestershire)	27	3	12
7th Foot (Royal Fusiliers)	26	0	10
45th Foot (1st Nottinghamshire)	26	1	14
11th Light Dragoons	24	0	4
16th Light Dragoons	24	0	7
14th Light Dragoons	23	0	6
9th Foot (East Norfolk)	23	0	9
1st Foot Guards	21	5	5
		31	250

4 Based upon author's private research: see also Baker, *Battle Honours of the British and Commonwealth Armies* (London: Ian Allen Ltd, 1986).

Battle Honours Awarded up to 1815[5]

Regiment	No.	Battle Honours to 1815
23rd Foot (Welsh Fuzileers)	20	Ble Ram Oud Mal Det Min Egt Pen Cor Mar Alb Bad Sal Vit Pyr Nvl Niv Ort Tou Wat
60th Foot / Rifles	19	Lou Que Pen Rol Vim Mar Tal Bus FDO Alb CR Bad Sal Vit Pyr Nvl Niv Ort Tou
52nd Light Infantry (Oxfordshire)	16	Mys Hin Pen Vim Cor Bus FDO CR Bad Sal Vit Nvl Niv Ort Tou Wat
71st Light Infantry (Highland)	16	Min Car Sho Mys CGH Pen Rol Vim Cor FDO Alm Vit Pyr Niv Ort Wat
95th Foot (Rifles) / Rifle Corps	16	Cop MV Pen Rol Vim Cor Bus FDO CR Bad Sal Vit Nvl Niv Tou Wat
28th Foot (North Gloucestershire)	15	Ram Lou Que Egt Pen Cor Bar Alb Vit Pyr Nvl Niv Ort Tou Wat
45th Foot (1st Nottinghamshire)	15	Lou Pen Rol Vim Tal Bus FDO VR Bad Sal Vit Pyr Nvl Ort Tou
40th Foot (1st Somerset)	14	StL MV Pen Rol Vim Tal Bad Sal Vit Pyr Nvl Ort Tou Wat
43rd Light Infantry (Monmouthshire)	14	Que Pen Vim Cor Bus FDO CR Bad Sal Vit Nvl Niv Ort Tou
1st Foot (Royal Scots)	13	Lou EOZ Egt StL2 Pen Cor Bus Sal Vit SS Niv Nia Wat
5th Foot (Northumberland)	13	Wil Pen Rol Vim Cor Bus CR Bad Sal Vit Nvl Ort Tou
27th Foot (Inniskillings)	12	StL1 Egt Mai Pen Bad Sal Vit Pyr Nvl Ort Tou Wat
92nd Foot (Gordon Highlanders)	12	EOZ Man Egt Pen Cor FDO Alm Vit Pyr Niv Ort Wat
88th Foot (Connaught Rangers)	11	Egt Pen Tal Bus FDO CR Bad Sal Vit Nvl Ort
1st Foot Guards	10	Ble Ram Oud Mal Det Lin Pen Cor Bar Wat
7th Foot (Royal Fusiliers)	10	Pen Tal Mar Alb Bad Sal Vit Pyr Ort Tou
42nd Foot (Black Watch)	10	Egt Pen Cor FDO Pyr Nvl Niv Ort Tou Wat
Coldstream Foot Guards	9	Oud Mal Det Lin Egt Pen Tal Bar Wat
9th Foot (East Norfolk)	9	Pen Rol Vim Cor Bus Sal Vit SS Niv
16th Light Dragoons	7	Pen Tal FDO Sal Vit Niv Wat
3rd Foot Guards	7	Det Lin Egt Pen Tal Bar Wat
14th Light Dragoons	6	Pen Dou Tal FDO Vit Ort
11th Light Dragoons	4	Egt Pen Sal Wat
1st Light Dragoons / Hussars KGL	3	Pen ElB Wat

5 Based upon author's private research, with the data set limited to those regiments with the highest number of honours; many other regiments had them also, although a smaller quantity.

Bibliography

The National Archives, Kew (TNA)

WO 3	Commander in Chief Correspondence (volumes /330 to /370, and /592 to /623)
WO 5	Marching and Militia Orders (volumes /69 to /75)
WO 8	Muster Master General of Ireland: Out-letters (volumes /8 to /11)
WO 17/783	Returns for Great Britain and Ireland, 1 February 1793
WO 17	Monthly Returns to the Adjutant General, Ireland (volumes /1071 to /1090)
WO 17	Monthly Returns to the Adjutant General, British East Indies (volumes /1742 to /1756)
WO 17	Monthly Returns to the Adjutant General, Spain and Portugal (volumes /2465 to /2474)
WO 17	Monthly Returns to the Adjutant General, Windward and Leeward Islands (volumes /2482 to /2492)
WO 17	Monthly Returns of the Quarters of HM Forces (volumes /2782 to 2786)
WO 24	Papers Concerning Establishments (volumes /574 to /607)
WO 25	Commission Books (volumes /61 to /116)
WO 25/120	Staff Appointments 1801 to 1812
WO 25	Returns of Officer's Services (volumes /744 to /807)
WO 25	Services of Retired Officers (volumes /808 to /821)
WO 25/3998	General and Field Officer's Service Book
WO 25/3999	General and Field Officer's Service Book
WO 27	Inspection Returns (volumes /79 to /145)
WO 42	Officer's Wills (volumes /1 to /74)
WO 65	List of the Officers of the Army and Royal Marines (volumes /1 to /122)
WO 89/4	General Courts Martial
WO 90/1	General Courts Martial – Abroad
WO 92/1	General Courts Martial Confirmed at Home – Registers
WO 100	Campaign Medal and Award Rolls (volumes /1 to /13, /16)
WO 379/1	Adjutant General's Office: Reliefs (1793–1800), Dispositions 1793–1794
WO 379/2	Adjutant General's Office: Disposition and Movement of Regiments (1803–1815)

Referenced Biographical Sources – Printed

ALBE Anon., *Alphabetical List of the Officers of the Bengal Army: With the Dates of Their Respective Promotion, Retirement, Resignation, Or Death, Whether in India Or in Europe, from the Year 1760 to the Year 1834 Inclusive, Corrected to September 30, 1837* (London: Longman, Orme, Brown, and Company, 1838)

ALBO Dodwell, Edward, *Alphabetical List of the Officers of the Indian Army: With the Dates of Their Respective Promotion, Retirement, Resignation, Or Death, Whether in India Or in Europe, from the Year 1760 to the Year 1834 Inclusive, Corrected to September 30, 1837* (London: Longman, Orme, Brown, 1838)

ALMA Dodwell, Edward, *Alphabetical List of the Officers of the Madras Army: With the Dates of Their Respective Promotion, Retirement, Resignation, Or Death, Whether in India Or in Europe; From the Year 1760, to the Year 1834 Inclusive, Corrected to September 30, 1837* (London: Longman, Orme Brown & Co., 1838)

ANRE *The Annual Register* (London: J.G. & F. Rivington, various years)

ARLI War Office, *A List of the Officers of the Army and Marines, with an Index, a Succession of Colonels, and a list of the Officers of the Army and Marines on Half-Pay* (London: War Office, 1754 to 1862); WO 65/1 to WO 65/138

BEAL *The Bengal Almanack: With a Companion and Appendix Containing Celestial & Terrestrial Phenomena; Chronological Information; Extracts from Acts of Parliament Relating to India; Bengal Military and Commercial Regulations; Regulations of the Public Institutions* (Calcutta: Bengal Hurkaru and Chronicle Press, various years)

BLEM *Blackwood's Edinburgh Magazine* (Edinburgh: William Blackwood, various years)

BRBM Birch, Diana., Hayward, John B., Bishop, Richard J., *British Battles and Medals* (United Kingdom: Spink, 2006)

BRFM Heathcote, T.A., *The British Field Marshals, 1736–1997: A Biographical Dictionary* (Barnsley: Pen & Sword Books, 2012)

BUPB Burke, John, *A General and Heraldic Dictionary of the Peerage and Baronetage of the British Empire* (London: H. Colburn and R. Bentley, 1832)

COPE Cokayne, George Edward, Clarenceux King of Arms, *The Complete Peerage of England, Scotland, Ireland, Great Britain, and the United Kingdom Extant, Extinct, or Dormant* (London: George Bell and Sons, 1887 to 1898) (8 vols.)

DALT Dalton, Charles, *The Waterloo Roll Call* (London: Eyre & Spottiswoode, 1904)

DEBA Debrett, John, *Debrett's Baronetage of England: With Alphabetical Lists of Such Baronetcies as Have Merged in the Peerage, Or Have Become Extinct, and Also of the Existing Baronets of Nova Scotia and Ireland* (London: J.G. & F. Rivington, 1835)

DEPE Debrett, John, *Debrett's Peerage of England, Scotland, and Ireland. revised, corrected and continued by G.W. Collen* (London: William Pickering, 1840)

DINB Stephen, Leslie, and Lee, Sidney (ed)., *The Dictionary of National Biography* (Oxford: Oxford University Press, 1908) (63 volumes)

EDAR *The Edinburgh Annual Register* (Edinburgh: John Ballantyne and Company, various years)

EIMC Philippart, John, *The East India Military Calendar: Containing the Services of General and Field Officers of the Indian Army* (London: Kingsbury, Parbury and Allen, 1823)

EMLM *The Edinburgh Magazine, Or Literary Miscellany* (Edinburgh: J. Sibbald, various years)

GEMA *Gentleman's Magazine and Historical Review* (London: E. Cave, various years)

GHHC Burke, John, *A Genealogical and Heraldic History of the Commoners of Great Britain and Ireland, Enjoying Territorial Possessions or High Official Rank: But Uninvested with Heritable Honours* (London: Henry Colburn, 1833)

GHHI Burke, Bernard, Burke, Ashworth Peter, *A Genealogical and Heraldic History of the Landed Gentry of Ireland* (London: Harrison & Sons, 1899)

GHLG Burke, Bernard, *A Genealogical and Heraldic Dictionary of the Landed Gentry of Great Britain & Ireland* (London: Colburn and Company, 1852)

GHPB Burke, John, *A Genealogical and Heraldic Dictionary of the Peerage and Baronetage of the British Empire* (London: Henry Colburn, 1839)

HALL Hall, John Alexander, Oman, Charles William Chadwick, *A History of the Peninsular War: The Biographical Dictionary of British Officers Killed and Wounded, 1808–1814* (London: Clarendon Press, 1998)

HOKN Nicolas, Nicholas Harris, *History of the Orders of Knighthood of the British Empire; of the Order of the Guelphs of Hanover; and of the Medals, Clasps, and Crosses, Conferred for Naval and Military Services* (London: J. Hunter, 1842)

MENA Anon., *State Calendar, or, Memorandums and Narratives, Parliamentary, Civil, Military, Naval, and Ecclesiastical* (London: R. Scholey, 1810)

NALI *The Navy List* (London: H.M. Stationery Office, various years)

PBBE Lodge, Edmund, *The Peerage of the British Empire as at Present Existing: Arranged and Printed from the Personal Communications of the Nobility* (London: Saunders and Otley, 1843)

PBKN Dod, Charles, *The Peerage, Baronetage and Knightage, of Great Britain and Ireland, Including All the Titled Classes* (London: S. Low, Marston & Company, 1855)

PHIL Phillipart, John, *Royal Military Calendar: Army Service and Commission Book Containing the Services and Progress of Promotion of the Generals, Lieutenant Generals, Major Generals, Colonels and Majors of the Army* (Naval & Military Press, 2007), 5 volumes

SCMA Anon., *The Scots Magazine and Edinburgh Literary Miscellany* (Edinburgh: Archibald Constable and Company, various years)

UNSM *The United Service Journal and the Naval and Military Magazine* (London: various years).

WEBC Burnham, Robert, McGuigan, Ron, *Wellington's Brigade Commanders: Peninsula and Waterloo* (Barnsley: Pen & Sword Books, 2017)

WEMR Bromley, Janet, Bromley, David, *Wellington's Men Remembered* (Barnsley: Praetorian Press, 2012–2015), 2 volumes

WEOF Reid, Stuart, *Wellington's Officers* (Leigh-On-Sea: Partizan Press, 2008–2011), 3 volumes

WLHB Treasure, G.R.R., *Who's Who in British History: Late Hanoverian Britain, 1789–1837* (Mechanicsburg: Stackpole Books, 2002)

WPWG Heathcote, T.A., *Wellington's Peninsular War Generals and Their Battles: A Biographical and Historical Dictionary* (Barnsley: Pen and Sword Books, 2010)

Referenced Biographical Sources – Online

ADIB Australian Dictionary of Biography – https://adb.anu.edu.au/

ANCB Baptismal records on Ancestry – https://www.ancestry.com/

ANCM Marriage records on Ancestry – https://www.ancestry.com/

ANCD Burial records on Ancestry – https://www.ancestry.com/

ANCS Soldier records on Ancestry – https://www.ancestry.com/

ANCW Wills and probate records on Ancestry – https://www.ancestry.com/

BGNW McGuigan, Ron, 'British Generals of the Napoleonic Wars' – *The Napoleon Series*, https://www.napoleon-series.org/research/biographies/BritishGenerals/c_Britishgenerals1.html

CADB Cambridge Alumni – database https://venn.lib.cam.ac.uk/

CHAL Lionel S. Challis's 'Peninsula Roll Call', *The Napoleon Series* – https://www.napoleon-series.org/biographies/lionel-s-challiss-peninsula-roll-call/

CRAC Heraldic Media Limited, *Cracroft's Peerage* – http://www.cracroftspeerage.co.uk/

DICB *Dictionary of Canadian Biography* – http://www.biographi.ca/en/

DIIB *Dictionary of Irish Biography* – https://www.dib.ie/

FFBI	The Royal Society of Edinburgh, *Former Fellows of the Royal Society of Edinburgh Biographical Index* – https://rse.org.uk/resources/biographical-index-former-rse-fellows-1783–2002–part-1-j/
FMPB	Baptismal records on Find My Past – https://www.findmypast.co.uk/
FMPM	Marriage records on Find My Past – https://www.findmypast.co.uk/
FMPD	Burial records on Find My Past – https://www.findmypast.co.uk/
FMPS	Soldier records on Find My Past – https://www.findmypast.co.uk/
FMPW	Wills and probate records on Find My Past – https://www.findmypast.co.uk/
GENE	Geneanet – https://en.geneanet.org/
HPON	*History of Parliament Online* – https://www.historyofparliamentonline.org/research/members
LFBI	*Landed Families of Britain and Ireland* – https://landedfamilies.blogspot.com/
ODNB	*Oxford Dictionary of National Biography* – https://www.oxforddnb.com/
PEER	*The Peerage* – https://www.thepeerage.com/
UATS	*Under A Tropical Sun* – https://www.mq.edu.au/macquarie-archive/under/research/biographies.html
WOST	*World Statesmen* – https://www.worldstatesmen.org/

Selected Printed Secondary Sources

Agnew, David C.A., *Protestant Exiles from France in the Reign of Louis XIV: or, The Huguenot Refugees and Their Descendants in Great Britain and Ireland* (London: Reeves & Turner, 1866)

Anon., *A Compendious Abstract of the Public General Acts of the United Kingdom of Great Britain and Ireland* (London: E.B. Ince, 1836)

Anon., *An Historical Description of Westminster Abbey, its Monuments and Curiosities* (London: J. Newbery, 1764)

Anon., *Mauriceguide 1971* (Mauritius: Standard Print. Establishment, 1971)

Anon., *The New Annual Register, or, General Repository of History, Politics, and Literature for the Year…* (London: G.G.J. and J. Robinson, various years)

Anon., *Notes and Queries, Eleventh Series, Volume VIII* (London: John C. Francis and J. Edward Francis, 1913)

Anon., *Records of the 54th West Norfolk Regiment* (India: Printed at the Thomason Civil Engineering College Press, 1881)

Anon., *Reports from Committees of the House of Commons: Reprinted by Order of the House* (London: House of Commons, 1803)

Anon., *Transactions of the Leicestershire Architectural and Archaeological Society* (Leicester: The Society, 1866)

Aspinall, Arthur (ed.), *The Later Correspondence of George III* (Cambridge: University Press, 1962), 5 vols.

Axon, William E.A. (ed)., *The Annals of Manchester: A Chronological Record from the Earliest Times to the End of 1885* (London: J. Heywood, Deansgate and Ridgefield, 1886)

Baker, Anthony, *Battle Honours of the British and Commonwealth Armies* (London: Ian Allen Ltd, 1986)

Berry, William, *County Genealogies: Pedigrees of the Families in the County of Sussex* (London: Sherwood, Gilbert and Piper, 1830)

Brereton, John Maurice, Savory, A. C. S., *The History of the Duke of Wellington's Regiment (West Riding) 1702-1992* (Halifax: Duke of Wellington's Regiment (West Riding), 1993)

Brock, Isaac, *The Life and Correspondence of Major-General Sir Isaac Brock, K. B.* (London: Simpkin, Marshall & Company, 1847)

Brown, Steve, *Wellington's Redjackets: The 45th (Nottinghamshire) Regiment on Campaign in South America and the Peninsula, 1805–14* (Barnsley: Pen & Sword Books, 2015)

Buckland, C. E., *Dictionary of Indian Biography* (New York: Haskell House, 1906)

Burke, Bernard, *A Selection of Arms Authorized by the Laws of Heraldry* (London: Harrison, 1860)

Burke, Bernard, *A Visitation of the Seats and Arms of the Noblemen and Gentlemen of Great Britain* (London: Colburn, 1852), 2 vols.

Burke, John, Burke, Bernard, *A Genealogical and Heraldic History of the Extinct and Dormant Baronetcies of England, Ireland and Scotland* (London: J. R. Smith, 1844)

Butler, Lewis, *The Annals of the King's Royal Rifle Corps, Vol. I* (London: Smith, Elder & Co., 1913)

Butler, Lewis, *The Annals of the King's Royal Rifle Corps, Vol. II* (London: John Murray, 1923)

Cannon, Richard, *Historical Record of the...* series of regimental history books, namely:

Historical record of the Fifty-Sixth, or the West Essex Regiment of Foot: containing an account of the formation of the regiment in 1755, and of its subsequent services to 1844 (London, Parker, Furnivall, and Parker, 1844)

Historical record of the Fifty-Third, or the Shropshire Regiment of Foot : containing an account of the formation of the regiment in 1755 and of its subsequent services to 1848 (London: Parker, Furnivall, and Parker, 1849)

Historical record of the Forty-second, or, the Royal Highland Regiment of Foot: containing an account of the formation of six companies of Highlanders in 1729 ... and were regimented in 1739 and of the subsequent services of the regiment to 1844 (London: Parker, Furnivall, & Parker, 1845)

Historical record of the Forty-Sixth, or the South Devonshire Regiment of Foot: containing an account of the formation of the regiment in 1741 and of its subsequent services to 1851 (London: Parker, Furnivall, & Parker, 1851)

Historical record of the Thirty-first, or, The Huntingdonshire Regiment of Foot [electronic resource] : containing an account of the formation of the regiment in 1702, and of its subsequent services to 1850 (London: Parker, Furnivall, & Parker, 1850)

Historical record of The Thirty-Fourth, or, The Cumberland Regiment of Foot: containing in account of the formation of the regiment in 1702, and its subsequent services to 1844 (London: Parker, Furnivall, and Parker, 1844)

Historical record of The Thirty-ninth, or, The Dorsetshire Regiment of Foot: containing an account of the regiment in 1702 and of its subsequent services to 1853 (London: G.E. Eyre and W. Spottiswoode, Parker, Furnivall and Parker, 1853)

Historical record of the Thirty-sixth, or the Herefordshire Regiment of Foot: containing an account of the formation of the regiment in 1701, and of its subsequent services to 1852 (London: Parker, Furnivall, and Parker, 1853)

Carter, Thomas, *Historical Record of the Forty-Fourth: Or the East Essex Regiment* (Chatham: Gale & Polden, 1887)

Clode, Charles Mathew, *The Military Forces of the Crown: Their Administration and Government* (London: John Murray, 1869), 2 volumes

Cokayne, George E., *Complete Baronetage, List of printed baronetages, previous to 1900* (Exeter: William Pollard & Co. Ltd, 1900)

Douglas, Robert, Wood, John Philip, *The Scots Peerage: Founded on Wood's Edition of Sir Robert Douglas's Peerage of Scotland; Containing an Historical and Genealogical Account of the Nobility of that Kingdom* (Edinburgh: David Douglas, 1904), 9 volumes

Foster, Joseph, *Alumni Oxonienses: the Members of the University of Oxford, 1715–1886: Their Parentage, Birthplace, and Year of Birth, with a Record of Their Degrees: Being the Matriculation Register of the University, Alphabetically Arranged, Revised and Annotated* (Oxford: Parker and Company, 1887)

Fortescue, Hon. J.W., *A History of the British Army* (Uckfield: The Naval and Military Press Ltd, 2004). Five volumes

Fortescue, Hon. J.W., *The British Army 1783 To 1802* (London: Macmillan and Co, 1905)

Fortescue, John William, *A History of the 17th Lancers (Duke of Cambridge's Own)* (London: Macmillan and Company, 1895)

Fyler, Arthur Evelyn, *The History of the 50th Or (the Queen's Own) Regiment from the Earliest Date to the Year 1881* (London: Chapman and Hall, 1895)

Gaudêncio, Moisés, Burnham, Robert, *In the Words of Wellington's Fighting Cocks: The After-action Reports of the Portuguese Army During the Peninsular War 1812–1814* (Barnsley: Pen & Sword Books, 2021)

Glover, Gareth, *Fighting Napoleon: The Recollections of Lieutenant John Hildebrand 35th Foot in the Mediterranean and Waterloo Campaigns* (Barnsley: Pen & Sword Books, 2017)

Glover, Gareth; Burnham, Robert, *The Men of Wellington's Light Division: Unpublished Memoirs from the 43rd Light Infantry in the Peninsular War* (Barnsley: Pen & Sword Books, 2022)

Grehan, John., Mace, Martin., *British Battles of the Napoleonic Wars 1793–1806* (Barnsley: Pen and Sword Military, 2013)

Grehan, John., Mace, Martin., *British Battles of the Napoleonic Wars 1807–1815* (Barnsley: Pen and Sword Military, 2013)

Griffith, Robert, *Riflemen: The History of the 5th Battalion, 60th (Royal American) Regiment 1797–1818* (Warwick: Helion, 2021)

Groves, John Percy, *History of the 42nd Royal Highlanders: The Black Watch, now the First Battalion The Black Watch (Royal Highlanders) 1729–1893* (Edinburgh: W. & A.K. Johnston, 1893)

Gurney, Russell, *History of the Northamptonshire Regiment: 1742–1934* (Aldershot: Gale & Polden, 1935)

Hadden, James Murray, *Hadden's Journal and Orderly Books: A Journal Kept in Canada and Upon Burgoyne's Campaign in 1776 and 1777* (Albany: J. Munsell's Sons, 1884)

Haythornthwaite, Philip J., *The Armies of Wellington* (London: Arms and Armour, 1994)

Haythornthwaite, Philip J., *Redcoats: The British Soldiers of the Napoleonic Wars* (Barnsley: Pen and Sword Books, 2012)

Howard, Joseph Jackson, and Crisp, Frederick Arthur, *Visitation of England and Wales Notes: Volume 5 1903* (Privately printed, 1903)

Hunter, Joseph, *Familiae Minorum Gentium* (London: Harleian Society, various years), 4 vols.

James, Charles, *A Collection of the Charges, Opinions, and Sentences of General Courts Martial: As Published by Authority; from the Year 1795 to the Present Time* (London: T. Egerton, 1820)

James, F.M., *Annals of the Five and Nine; being the history of HM 59th (2nd Nottinghamshire) Regiment of Foot, now the Second Battalion, the East Lancashire Regiment* (Poona: S. Shalom and Brothers, 1906)

Joass, James Maxwell., Bulloch, John Malcolm., Ree, Stephen., Wimberley, Douglas, *The House of Gordon: Bibliography of Gordon Genealogy* (Aberdeen: New Spalding Club, 1907)

Johnston-Liik, E.M., *MPs in Dublin: Companion to History of the Irish Parliament, 1692–1800* (Dublin: Ulster Historical Foundation, 2006)

Kingsford, Charles Lethbridge, *The Story of the Duke of Cambridge's Own (Middlesex Regiment)* (London: Offices of Country Life, 1916)

Knight, Roger, *Britain Against Napoleon: The Organisation of Victory, 1793–1815* (London: Penguin Books Limited, 2013)

Leeke, William, *The History of Lord Seaton's Regiment: (the 52nd Light Infantry) at the Battle of Waterloo; Together with Various Incidents Connected with that Regiment* (London: Hatchard and Company, 1866)

L'Estrange, George B., *Bravo, Young Buffs! – The Recollections of an Officer of the 31st (Huntingdonshire) Regiment of Foot During the Peninsular War* (United Kingdom: Leonaur, 2016)

Levinge, R. G. A., *Historical Records of the 43rd Regiment, Monmouthshire Light Infantry* (London: W. Clowes, 1868).

Lewis, John Penry, *List of Inscriptions on Tombstones and Monuments in Ceylon, of Historical or Local Interest, with an Obituary of Persons Uncommemorated* (Sri Lanka: Dalcassian Publishing Company, 1913)

Lomax, David Alexander Napier, *A History of the Services of the 41st (the Welch) Regiment, (now 1st Battalion the Welch Regiment) from Its Formation, in 1719, to 1895* (Devonport: Hiorns & Miller, 1899)

Malcolm, David, *A Genealogical Memoir of the Most Noble and Ancient House of Drummond, and of the Several Branches that Have Sprung from It, from Its First Founder Maurice, to the Present Family of Perth* (Edinburgh: Mr. Graham Maxwell, and Archibald Constable & Company Edinburgh, 1808)

McKenna, Michael G., *The British Army – And Its Regiments and Battalions* (West Chester: The Nafziger Collection. 2004)

Moorsom, William, *Historical Record of the Fifty-second Regiment (Oxfordshire Light Infantry) from the Year 1755 to the Year 1858* (London: Richard Bentley, 1860)

Moulsdale, J.R.B., *The King's Shropshire Light Infantry (The 53rd/85th Regiment of Foot)* (London: Leo Cooper, 1972)

Muir, Howie, McGuigan, Ron, Burnham, Robert, Muir, Rory, *Inside Wellington's Peninsular Army: 1808–1814* (Barnsley: Pen and Sword Books Limited, 2014)

Myatt, Frederick, *The Royal Berkshire Regiment (the 49th/66th Regiment of Foot)* (London: Hamish Hamilton, 1968)

Nelson, Paul David, *Sir Charles Grey, First Earl Grey: Royal Soldier, Family Patriarch* (Cranberry N.J.: Fairleigh Dickinson University Press, 1996)

Norman, C.B., *Battle Honours of the British Army* (London: David and Charles Reprints, 1971)

Oman, Sir Charles, *History of the Peninsular War* (Uckfield: Naval and Military Press, 2017), seven volumes

Oman, Sir Charles, *Wellington's Army 1809–1814* (London: Greenhill Books, 1986)

Park, S.J. and Nafziger, G.F., *The British Military – Its System and Organization 1803–1815* (Cambridge: Rafm Co. Inc. 1983)

Paterson, James, *History of the County of Ayr: With a Genealogical Account of the Families of Ayrshire* (Ayr: J. Dick, 1847)

Paul, James Balfour, *The Scots Peerage: Founded on Wood's Edition of Sir Robert Douglas's Peerage of Scotland; Containing an Historical and Genealogical Account of the Nobility of that Kingdom* (Edinburgh: D. Douglas, 1904), 9 vols.

Purdon, Henry, *An Historical Sketch of the 47th (Lancashire) Regiment: and of the Campaigns through which they Passed* (Preston: Guardian Printing Works, 1907)

Rogerson, William, *Historical Records of the 53rd, Shropshire, Regiment, now the 1st Battalion the King's, Shropshire Light Infantry* (Devonport: Simpkin, Marshall, Hamilton Kent & Co., 1890)

Seaver, Jesse Montgomery, *Gordon Family Records* (Charlottesville: American Historical-Genealogical Society, 1929)

Sheardown, William, *Records and Family Notices of Military and Naval Officers connected with Doncaster and its Neighbourhood* (Doncaster: Gazette Office, 1873)

Six, Georges, *Dictionnaire Biographique des Généraux & Amiraux Français de la Révolution et de l'Empire (1792–1814)* (Paris: G. Saffroy, 1934)

Smith, Digby, *The Greenhill Napoleonic Wars Data Book* (London: Greenhill Books, 1998)

Smith, Henry Stooks, *An Alphabetical List of the Officers of the Eighty-Fifth, Bucks Volunteers, the King's Light Infantry Regiment, from 1800 to 1850* (London: Simpkin, Marshall, 1851)

Smythies, Raymond Henry Raymond, *Historical Records of the 40th (2nd Somersetshire) Regiment* (Devonport, A.H. Swiss, 1894)

Summerville, Christopher, *Who Was Who at Waterloo: A Biography of the Battle* (Abingdon: Taylor & Francis, 2014)

Sutherland, Douglas, *Tried and Valiant: The History of the Border Regiment (the 34th and 55th Regiments of Foot) 1702–1959* (London: Leo Cooper, 1972)

Swiney, George Clayton, *Historical Records of the 32nd, Cornwall, Light Infantry, Now the 1st Battalion Duke of Cornwall's L. I.: From the Formation of the Regiment in 1702 Down to 1892* (London: Simpkin, Marshall, Hamilton, Kent & Co., 1893)

Taylor, James, *The Great Historic Families of Scotland* (Dumfries: James Macveigh, 1888), 2 vols.

Trimen, Richard (ed.), *An Historical Memoir of the 35th Royal Sussex Regiment of Foot* (Southampton: Southampton Times Newspaper and Printing and Publishing Company (Limited), 1873)

Vale, Walter Leonard, *History of the South Staffordshire Regiment* (Aldershot: Gale & Polden, 1969)

Venn, John (ed.) *Alumni Cantabrigienses: A Biographical List of All Known Students, Graduates and Holders of Office at the University of Cambridge, from the Earliest Times to 1900* (Cambridge: Cambridge University Press, 2011)

Wallace, Nesbit Willoughby, *A Regimental Chronicle and List of Officers of the 60th, Or the King's Royal Rifle Corps, Formerly the 62nd, Or the Royal American Regiment of Foot* (London: Harrison, 1879)

Warre, Henry James, *Historical Records of the Fifty-seventh, or, West Middlesex Regiment of Foot* (London: W. Mitchell and Company, 1878)

Wheater, William, *A Record of the Services of the Fifty-first (Second West York), the King's Own Light Infantry Regiment. With a list of Officers from 1755 to 1870 (reprinted from The United Service Magazine for 1869)* (London: Longmans, Green & Company, 1870)

Whitting, Captain John Everard, *Annals of the Thirty-Seventh North Hampshire Regiment* (Warren & Son, 1878)

Wright, Christine, *Wellington's Men in Australia: Peninsular War Veterans and the Making of Empire c.1820–40* (Basingstoke: Palgrave Macmillan UK, 2011)

Wyllie, H.C., *History of the 1st and 2nd Battalions, The Sherwood Foresters, Nottinghamshire and Derbyshire Regiment 1740-1914* (Frome: Butler & Tanner, 1929)

Wylly, H.C., *Loyal North Lancashire Regiment 1741–1914* (Uckfield: Naval & Military Press, 2014)

Theses

Linch, Kevin Barry, *The Recruitment of the British Army 1807*–1815 (University of Leeds (School of History, 2001).

Pimlott, J. L., *The Administration of the British Army, 1783–1793* (University of Leicester, 1975).

Journal Articles

Greenwood, Major, 'British Loss of Life in the Wars of 1794–1815 and in 1914–1918,' *Journal of the Royal Statistical Society*, Vol.105, No.1 (1942), pp.1–16.

MacArthur, Roderick, 'British Army Establishments During the Napoleonic Wars', *Journal of the Society for Army Historical Research,* Vol.87, No.350 (Summer 2009), pp. 150–172.

Unpublished Sources

British Army Establishments for all years 1802–1816. Provided by Roderick MacArthur.

Newspapers, Lists and Periodicals

Davies, J., *The Royal Military Chronicle or British Officers' Monthly Registers and Mentor* (London: various years)

A Collection of State Papers Relative to the War Against France Now Carrying on by Great Britain and the Several Other European Powers (London: J. Debrett, various years)

Annual Military Obituary (London: Parker, Furnivall and Parker, various years)

The Annual Biography and Obituary for the Year…. (London: Longman, Hurst, Rees, Orme, and Brown, various years)

The New Monthly (London: H. Colburn, various years)

Websites and Online Resources

Australian Dictionary of Biography, https://adb.anu.edu.au/

Bamford, Andrew, Napoleon Series: British Army Theatre Returns: 1808–1815, Northern Europe, https://www.napoleon-series.org/military-info/organization/Britain/Strength/Bamford/c_BritishArmyStrengthStudyNorthernEurope.html

de Brito, Pedro: British officers in the Portuguese service 1809–1820, https://www.academia.edu/34780108/British_officers_in_the_Portuguese_service
Burnham, Robert, Napoleon Series: The British Battalions of Detachment in 1809, https://www.napoleon-series.org/military-info/organization/Britain/Infantry/Detachments/c_detach.html
The Douglas Archives; Heraldry Online (blog), https://www.douglashistory.co.uk/history/heraldry/index.htm
Find a Grave, https://www.findagrave.com/
Freedom's mercenaries: British Volunteers in the Wars of Independence of Latin America https://uelac.ca/loyalist-trails/loyalist-trails-2015–27/
Library Ireland, Irish Pedigrees, https://www.libraryireland.com/Pedigrees1/title.php
Lord Belmont in Northern Ireland, http://lordbelmontinnorthernireland.blogspot.com/
More Than Nelson: The Royal Navy 1776-1815, A Biographical History And Chronicle, https://morethan-nelson.com/
Nafziger, George. Collection of Orders of Battle,
http://www.cgsc.edu/carl/nafziger.htm
National Library of Australia: 17th-18th Century Burney Collection Newspapers, https://www.nla.gov.au/app/eresources/item/3304
National Library of Australia: 18th Century British Newspapers Online, https://www.nla.gov.au/app/eresources/item/4314
National Library of Australia: The House of Commons Parliamentary Papers (HCPP) online, http://www.nla.gov.au/app/eresources/item/1642
The Centre for the Study of the Legacies of British Slavery, UCL, https://www.ucl.ac.uk/lbs/
The Times Digital Archive:
http://gale.cengage.co.uk/times-digital-archive/times-digital-archive-17852006.aspx
Waterloo 200 Descendants Book, https://ageofrevolution.org/waterloo-200-descendants-book/

From Reason to Revolution – Warfare 1721-1815

http://www.helion.co.uk/series/from-reason-to-revolution-1721-1815.php

The 'From Reason to Revolution' series covers the period of military history 1721–1815, an era in which fortress-based strategy and linear battles gave way to the nation-in-arms and the beginnings of total war.

This era saw the evolution and growth of light troops of all arms, and of increasingly flexible command systems to cope with the growing armies fielded by nations able to mobilise far greater proportions of their manpower than ever before. Many of these developments were fired by the great political upheavals of the era, with revolutions in America and France bringing about social change which in turn fed back into the military sphere as whole nations readied themselves for war. Only in the closing years of the period, as the reactionary powers began to regain the upper hand, did a military synthesis of the best of the old and the new become possible.

The series examines the military and naval history of the period in a greater degree of detail than has hitherto been attempted, and has a very wide brief, with the intention of covering all aspects from the battles, campaigns, logistics, and tactics, to the personalities, armies, uniforms, and equipment.

Submissions

The publishers would be pleased to receive submissions for this series. Please email reasontorevolution@helion.co.uk, or write to Helion & Company Limited, Unit 8 Amherst Business Centre, Budbrooke Road, Warwick, CV34 5WE

You may also be interested in:

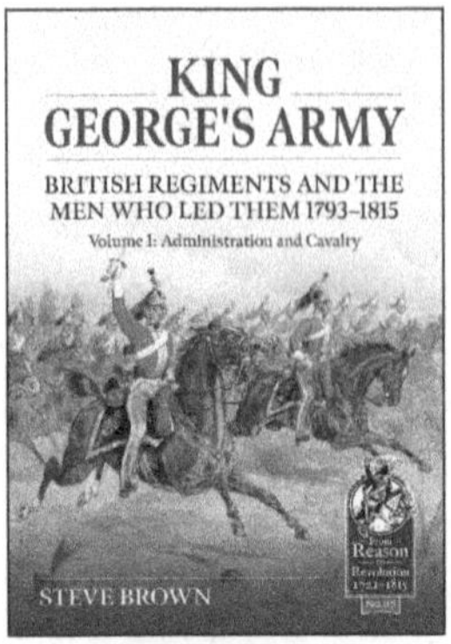

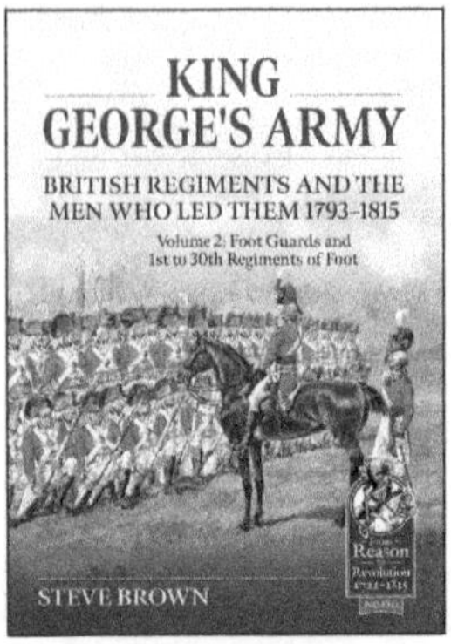

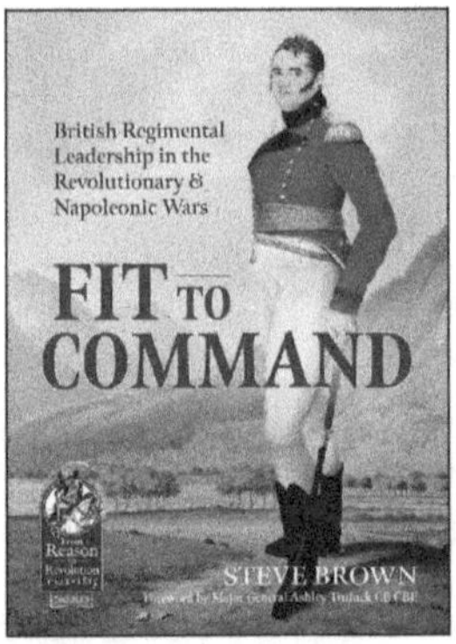